Chris bestselling
roma Heart Lane
series by *Canal Boat*
Dream. She lives in a ramshackle cottage in a quaint village
in the heart of Staffordshire with her four children and two
dogs.

Her writing career came as a lovely surprise when she
decided to write a book to teach her children a valuable life
lesson and show them that they are capable of achieving
their dreams. Christie's dream was to become a writer and
the book she wrote to prove a point went on to become a #1
bestseller in the UK, USA, Canada, and Australia.

When Christie isn't writing she enjoys playing the piano, is
a keen gardener, and loves to paint and upcycle furniture.

Christie loves to hear from her readers and you can get in
touch via Twitter, Facebook, and Instagram.

facebook.com/ChristieJBarlow
twitter.com/ChristieJBarlow
bookbub.com/authors/christie-barlow
instagram.com/christie_barlow

Also by Christie Barlow

HEARTCROSS CASTLE

CHRISTIE BARLOW

One More Chapter
a division of HarperCollins*Publishers* Ltd
1 London Bridge Street
London SE1 9GF
www.harpercollins.co.uk
HarperCollins*Publishers*
1st Floor, Watermarque Building, Ringsend Road
Dublin 4, Ireland

This paperback edition 2022
1
First published in Great Britain in ebook format
by HarperCollins*Publishers* 2021
Copyright © Christie Barlow 2021
Christie Barlow asserts the moral right to
be identified as the author of this work
A catalogue record of this book is available from the British Library

ISBN: 978-0-00-841313-2

Printed and bound in the UK using 100% Renewable Electricity
by CPI Group (UK) Ltd

For Colin and Jacqui Fletcher
Chance made us neighbours, how lucky was I?
Thank you for being just the best!

Loveheart L

Primrose Park

The Lake House

CLOVER COTTAGE ESTATE

The Old Bakehouse

The B

Bumblebee Cottage

Starcross Manor

THE GREEN

HIGH STREET

Scott's Veterinary Practice

Primary School

Post Office

H

Peony Practice

Callie's apartment

Dolores' apartment

Solicitors Office

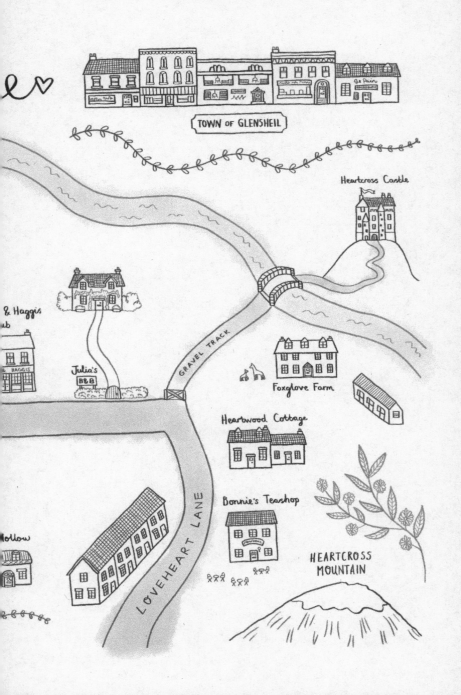

Prologue

'Wait there! Don't move a muscle and cover up your eyes!' Cole ordered mysteriously, as he abandoned Grace on the edge of the sand.

Grace had no idea what was going on except that it was their second anniversary of the day they'd first met, and forty-eight hours earlier Cole had whisked her back to the town where they'd had their very first date. He'd booked a tiny cottage on top of the cliff overlooking the steely-blue sea, with a row of pastel-coloured cottages that huddled together on the opposite hillside.

That morning, Cole had woken up like the cat who'd got the cream, which surprised Grace after the argument they'd had last night. But she'd woken to hear him busying himself in the kitchen for at least an hour and her only instruction was to wrap up warm as they left the cottage and headed down the familiar coastal path towards the sand.

'Don't leave me here, I look like an idiot!' Grace shouted.

She was standing on the edge of the cove with her scarf wrapped around her eyes. All she could hear was the crash of the waves and the fizz of the foam; the gulls were crying up above and wind whistled around the top of the cliffs. Further up the beach she could hear the chatter of the local fishermen and children's laughter as their kite streamers rattled in the wind.

Grace pulled her hat down over her ears as she drew in the salty air. Whatever Cole was up to, he was excited, and Grace stood and waited patiently.

'Two minutes. Just stand still, my absolute favourite,' bellowed Cole.

Freezing cold, Grace shivered and shuffled her feet, trying to keep warm. It was the beginning of November and the temperature had dropped dramatically, but despite the cold, this was Grace's favourite time of year. As she stood there, she thought about Cole's words. He'd called her his absolute favourite from the second they started dating, and it had indeed been a whirlwind romance that had swept her off her feet. Now, he only used those words when he needed to smooth things over, and Grace knew this was one of those times.

She'd ended up in Devon on a whim, estranged from her Scottish family at the age of sixteen. She'd arrived at Sandy Cove with nothing more than the rucksack on her back and a handful of cash. After checking into the local public house that provided B&B, Grace had sweet-talked the landlord into giving her a job and the very next week she'd served up the most hearty roast dinner to the most gorgeous man she had ever set eyes on… Cole.

'I'm back!' Cole lifted Grace off her feet, causing her to squeal and slap him playfully on his shoulder.

'Put me down, you loon! Can I take off this blindfold yet?'

'Not yet!' replied Cole, twisting her towards him and carefully guiding her across the sand.

'Okay,' he said finally, 'Now you can take it off.'

Grace lowered the scarf from her eyes.

'Ta-dah!' Cole was grinning broadly as he gestured towards the romantic picnic laid out on the beach next to the roaring fire.

Grace was suitably impressed, the scenery the perfect backdrop. 'Wow! Look at this! And I'm loving the fire. And what's this in aid of?' She held her hands out towards the burning logs, then rubbed them together.

Cole gave her a sexy grin. 'Because you are you, and this is the day we met.' Looking adoringly into her eyes, he took her hands in his. 'The day I met you, my life changed. If you remember, this was the very spot we had our first kiss, opposite the lighthouse.'

Of course Grace could remember. Her whole body had trembled with anticipation waiting for that very moment.

The first time she'd seen Cole in the pub, Grace had thought he was good-looking and spoke with a posh accent, so different from her Scottish twang, which she'd toned down until it had completely disappeared. He had been with a group from work, and Grace couldn't help thinking he was a lovable rogue with dirt smeared over his T-shirt, tattoos inked all over his arms, and a pint in his hand after a hard day's work. While the rest of the boys drank more and more, Cole had hung around at the end of the bar, chatting to her. Surprised by the attention, she'd quite liked it.

The next day they'd met for a coffee at the little cafe next to the bay and Grace allowed herself to be swept away by his charm. That weekend they were inseparable; they dined at the seafood restaurant, ambled along the coastal trails and cupped their cold hands around hot chocolate from the pub. It was the Sunday evening they'd kissed at this very spot. They enjoyed a roast dinner at the pub, then walked down to the cove. The moon was full and a handful of stars sparkled in the darkening sky as they stood on the beach overlooking the lighthouse. Cole had persuaded Grace to take off her socks and shoes and turn up the bottom of her jeans and they paddled barefoot, squealing at the cold ocean. Cole had that look in his eye when he gazed at her, and Grace's pulse had raced in anticipation. She knew he was going to kiss her, and he did. With her heart already melting, Grace had taken the plunge and they'd spent the night together. It was only the next morning that Cole had revealed his job in the town had come to an end and he'd be moving on. Then he uttered the words, 'Come with me. Let's go on an adventure.'

Grace had only taken a split second to think about it, and her answer was 'Yes!' What exactly did she have to lose? What was the worst that could happen? It had only taken a matter of minutes to pack her belongings in her rucksack before they hopped on the train to their next destination.

In the past two years they had moved around so much with Cole's job that Grace had lost count of the number of places she'd called home. He had to go where the work was and at first that suited Grace; she felt like a free spirit with no ties and had seen so many places she would have never visited before, but now she was beginning to tire of it. She wasn't quite sure where she belonged and at times felt lonely, with no real friends she could count on. Often she would be left alone in rented accommodation that had seen better days whilst Cole went out drinking with the lads from the building site. It wasn't the adventure she was anticipating. He'd roll in in the early hours steaming drunk and, more often than not, he'd squandered his weekly wage on beer and gambling.

Last night's argument had reached another level. Cole wanted to move on again but Grace wanted to settle in one place, put down roots and make a proper future. He'd lashed out, telling her that wasn't an option and his temper had escalated.

After every argument Cole would always remind her she was his absolute favourite, and all they had in the world was each other. He'd apologise, tell her that he loved her and he wouldn't lose his temper again … but that promise was wearing thin. But Grace still lived in hope. Today, he'd excelled himself and had gone that extra mile. The picnic was perfect. Maybe he really was trying to change and this time he meant it. She knew she had the news that could hopefully make that change happen.

With a smile, Grace wrapped her arms around his waist as she stared out over the sea.

'What are you thinking?' asked Cole, pulling her in tighter towards his chest.

For the first time in a long time, Grace was thinking about her past life in Scotland. Recently, she'd began to miss it more and more, especially now with the news she had to share. 'I'm thinking I'm the luckiest girl in the world,' she replied, knowing that's exactly what Cole wanted to hear. With the morning starting off on a good note, she didn't want a repeat performance of last night.

'Champagne?' He leant over and held up the bottle and passed Grace a flute from the basket.

Her heart went into overdrive. This was the nice Cole, and despite his flaws he was right: all they had was each other and deep down she knew he loved her. Cole was trying to put everything right like he'd promised ... like he always promised after a row.

'Thank you,' she said and beamed, taking the glass from him.

Cole popped the cork and poured the fizz into both glasses, then clinked his against hers.

'Here's to us, our future ... together.' He paused. 'I know you don't want to keep travelling around and I promise I will try and find a stable job. '

Grace was amazed. These were the words that she wanted to hear.

He looked deep into her eyes. She watched him take a breath and he stood up. 'I can't imagine my life without you... I don't want to imagine my life without you.' He walked around the blanket towards her and she gasped as he went down on one knee at her side. After reaching into his pocket, he was now clutching a small burgundy box. Her heart was racing as Cole opened the lid.

'Grace, would you marry me?'

Feeling herself trembling, Grace looked at the diamond ring nestled inside the red velvet lining of the box. Never in a million years had she expected Cole to propose.

Cole didn't take his eyes off her.

She hesitated. 'You've taken me completely by surprise.' Her heart was pounding as she looked down at the simple yet stunning diamond ring that took her breath away.

'Please tell me that's a yes. I kind of can't feel my knee with the cold.'

Swept up in the moment, Grace finally replied. 'Sorry! Of course it's a yes!'

His eyes lit up as he swept Grace up in his arms. 'Thank God for that!' He laughed nervously, slipping the ring onto her finger before kissing her. 'You have made me the happiest man alive. Me and my absolute favourite together for ever.'

But Grace didn't feel the happiest woman alive. She felt apprehension. Cole was asking her to commit for a lifetime. Wasn't this every girl's dream? And her heart should be dancing like it had never danced before, and their love for each other should be soaring higher than the gulls flying above them, because that's what happened in the movies . . . but there was a huge worry at the back of Grace's mind. Because Grace was pregnant with Cole's baby.

Did she really want to bring a baby into this relationship with Cole's temper escalating? But Grace had no choice; she was already three months' pregnant with nowhere else to go and no one else to turn to. If she turned down Cole's proposal, where was that going to leave her? Out in the cold with a baby in tow. Maybe, when Cole heard the news, he was going to be a dad that would change everything; maybe this was what they needed, a fresh start, solid roots and a baby to make their family complete. All Grace could do was hope.

Chapter One

Eight years later

G race was staring at her reflection in the mirror, the bathroom door safely locked behind her. Her eye was blackened. Again. Gently dabbing antiseptic on to the sliced cut just above her cheekbone, she winced. Things were on a fast downward spiral and knowing her three young boys were on the other side of the door in the tiny living room of their high-rise flat, she fought back the tears. This was not the life she'd ever envisaged for her or her children. Times had changed dramatically in the last few years and life with Cole was now becoming unbearable. Grace couldn't physically or mentally take any more. She was at the end of her tether.

His promises were empty, and he'd let her and the boys down time after time. In the last eighteen months Grace had refused to keep uprooting the boys for Cole's short-term jobs that he chased all around the country, which had resulted in Cole being out of their lives for long periods of time. The upside to this was it gave her and the boys breathing space from the toxic relationship, but it often left her with no money. Their relationship had been over for a very long time, and the only connection between them now was when his fist pounded her body.

This time he'd been gone for eight weeks. Last night he'd walked through the door with no prior warning, stinking of beer and body odour. His clothes were dirty, his face unshaved and, once again, he'd returned with no money; no doubt he'd pissed it all up the wall. He knew of a job in Ireland and he wanted to take the boys, make yet another fresh start. He was delusional. Grace had said no. Immediately his temper flared and, quickly, Grace had ushered the boys to their bedroom to shield them from the argument that was about to erupt. The result once more was physical: he struck her. For the first time ever, Grace hit back. She slapped him so hard across his face he stumbled backwards. 'Get out,' she said, her voice surprisingly calm and controlled. 'Get out now.' She'd stunned him, taking him and herself by surprise. 'Go back to wherever you've come from and stay there.'

His eyes were wide, his pupils dilated, his words slurred. 'You'll regret this.'

Grace wasn't sure where she'd got her inner strength from; she'd never tackled him before or stood up to him, afraid it would just fuel the fire, but she was prepared to take the consequences. 'You turn up again after weeks on end without any word, making empty promises to the boys. You've not provided for this family for as long as I can remember. I've had enough. In fact I'd had enough a long time ago. This relationship was dead and buried years ago. I'm so over it. The only thing I regret is staying around you for so long. Now go before I phone the police.'

He smirked, which made her whole body erupt in goosebumps for all the wrong reasons. She walked past him and flinched, not knowing if he would grab her again, but this time he didn't. Trembling, Grace continued to walk towards the front door and opened it wide. 'Just go.' She didn't make eye contact as he walked past her and out through the door. She hadn't anticipated he'd leave so easily but as soon as he stepped outside she double-locked the door. Squeezing her eyes shut for a second, she brought her hand up to her face. Feeling the trickle of blood, she vowed that was the last time he would ever lay a finger on her. She had no clue when he would be back, if ever, but she was past caring. She had no feelings for him. She was numb. She needed to keep herself and her boys safe. She went into the bathroom, closed the door, sat down on the toilet and wept … with relief.

'Mum! Are you there? I need the toilet.' Freddie banged on the door, causing Grace to jump out of her skin.

'I'm just coming,' she replied, standing up and quickly patting foundation around her eye to hide the blackness before opening the door.

'You've been ages.' Freddie pushed past her and flung the toilet seat up.

'Sorry, Freddie,' she said, walking back into the living room and staring around the dingy apartment. The murky daylight wasn't enough to penetrate the grimy window that Grace couldn't remember ever being cleaned.

Joey, Freddie's twin, was sitting on the carpet pushing Billy's train around the track whilst Billy, the youngest, was sitting on the edge of the settee swinging his feet in their bright-yellow wellies, waiting patiently for her to come out of the bathroom.

Grace gathered herself together. 'Come here, you little ragamuffin!' She reached out her tickling hands and Joey squealed in delight and quickly ran around the settee.

Up above came the sound of a broom being banged on the floor, 'They just don't know how to have to have fun, do they?' Grace whispered, then she rolled her eyes at the ceiling and put her finger to her lips. Then, with a playful look in her eye and still holding out her arms, she waggled her fingers towards Joey again.

'Mum! Stop!'

'Okay, just this once.' She smiled, looking towards Billy, 'Do you want to play with the trains?'

Billy shook his head, then ran towards her and wrapped his arms around her legs.

'Come here,' she said, lifting him clean off the floor and cuddling him tight.

Billy traced the cut on Grace's cheek with his finger, then nestled his head into her shoulder.

'Come on, let's put the TV on and watch your favourite programme. Would you like that?'

Billy nodded, but didn't speak. Billy hadn't spoken for nearly eight weeks, ever since he'd witnessed Cole strike her the last time he was home.

Hearing the letterbox clang, Grace jumped out of her skin but quickly calmed herself when she realised it was only the postman. Placing Billy down on the sofa, she picked up the post from the mat. Usually it was a bill or junk mail, but this time there was an envelope with her name on the front in bold type. She wasn't sure why, but she immediately felt guilty, wondering what she had done wrong to warrant such official-looking post. With her heart hammering against her chest and her hands visibly shaking, Grace tore open the envelope and quickly scanned the letter. Immediately, the words 'Heartcross Castle' jumped out from the page.

'Oh my God,' she murmured. She read and reread the letter. They'd actually managed to track her down. Taking a deep breath, Grace stood up and, clutching the letter, walked into the bathroom and shut the door behind her again. Cupping cold water in her hands, she splashed it on her face and then gave herself a hard stare in the mirror.

'What the hell am I going to do?' she repeated over and over again in her mind.

Ignoring the letter was not an option. Pulling her phone out of her pocket, she stared at the screen. Trying to calm her beating heart, she looked down at the telephone number in the letter – an area code Grace immediately recognised, but a number she hadn't seen in a very long time. What did she have to lose by dialling the number? All she had to do was ring the number and confirm she was indeed Grace Power.

With a shaky hand she punched in the digits and after three rings the call was answered.

'Heartcross Solicitors, how may I help you?'

For a second Grace froze, and the voice on the other end of the line spoke again.

'Hello, how may I help you?'

'Hello, may I speak with Jaydon Fairbrother, please?' said Grace politely.

'Who may I say is calling?' came the receptionist's firm but polite response.

'Grace Power… It's in connection with Heartcross—'

'Castle.' The receptionist finished her sentence. 'I will put you through immediately.'

Hearing the call being connected, Grace waited.

'Jaydon Fairbrother, how may I help you?'

As soon as Grace heard the strong Scottish accent, she felt a little homesick. How was that even possible after all this time? As she listened to Jaydon Fairbrother, she stared into space. She'd known this day would eventually come, but now she didn't feel prepared. Her grandfather Marley, the owner of Heartcross Castle, had finally passed away and she was his only living relative. Immediately, tears sprang from her eyes as the guilt from the past consumed her. Managing to thank the solicitor, Grace hung up the call, slumped at the side of the bath, pulled her knees up to her chest and hugged them tight. The feeling of devastation hit her like a high-speed train, taking her breath away. It was now too late; she could never make amends with her grandfather.

When she was a teenager, Grace's life had spiralled out of control. She'd always had a loving relationship with her grandfather until her mother had passed away when Grace was fifteen, leaving her shaken to her core. With no father on the scene, Grace was thrown into life under the strict supervision of her grandfather, which neither of them had been prepared for. At the time Grace had been rebellious and out of control. She'd backchat him, refuse to help out around the Castle, but she had been hurting, grieving for her mother, and, looking back, it had been one of the hardest times of her life. Then she'd run away in the dead of the night after an argument and had never looked back. Once she'd met Cole, life had just got in the way and it had been harder to get in touch. And now it was all too late.

As she remembered the last time she'd set eyes on her grandfather, the memories were so vivid that she exhaled. Marley Power had been one of the richest men in Scotland. Heartcross Castle was a tourist attraction everyone wanted to visit. Hundreds of thousands of people wandered around the Castle and the gardens, providing a lucrative business for Marley.

The night Grace ran away, her friend Felicity Simons had turned eighteen and her mother Rona had organised a party in the local pub, The Grouse and Haggis. Grace was still only sixteen and underage in Marley's eyes and he'd put his foot down: she wasn't allowed to go. Undeterred, Grace went against his wishes; she wasn't going to miss her friend's birthday party at any cost. After sneaking out of the Castle and returning just after midnight, she discovered Marley pacing the floor of her bedroom, crossing in and out of the shaft of moonlight that fell between the gap in the drawn curtains. The dark look of anger on his face because she had dared to defy him didn't leave her in any doubt that she was in severe trouble. Thinking back, Grace's chest tightened. It was simple: if she didn't follow her grandfather's rules she was out. After a blazing row, she'd left Heartcross Castle, and hadn't looked back – until now.

Feeling a heaviness in her chest and limbs, Grace pushed herself up off the bathroom floor. She folded the letter and stuffed it into her pocket. Even though in the past she had been stubborn and hot-headed, she'd written a letter to her grandfather four weeks after she ran away, to let him know she was okay, but she hadn't divulged any more details. Now she was wishing she could turn back time, but of course she couldn't. How must he have felt, spending the rest of his life never setting eyes on her again? And now, after all this time, her grandfather might have just thrown her destiny into a brand-new direction.

Dazed by the phone call, Grace joined the boys back in the living room. With the twins playing with the train track and Billy distracted by the TV, Grace began to think, her thoughts tumbling over each other, her mind still spinning with the news she had just received.

Of course she had regrets, huge regrets, and she choked with tears that after everything, her grandfather was throwing her a get-out-of-jail-free card, the lifeline that she needed to get her and her boys to safety and make a fresh start. How she wished she'd made amends with him in the years she'd been away.

Glancing at the clock on the wall, Grace had no idea whether Cole would turn up again. She prayed he was on his way to Ireland and she would never have to lay eyes on him again. But just in case he did reappear, she needed to act quickly. 'Boys, we need to go into town. Quickly, go and put your shoes on. Hurry!'

All three boys looked up at her with astonishment, since it was raining outside, but they instantly recognised that tone in Grace's voice ... the same tone she used when telling them to run to their room, close their eyes and pretend to be asleep.

With the boys wearing their raincoats and wellies, they set off on the one-mile walk into town. Knowing she'd left Heartcross under a dark cloud, Grace never in her life anticipated returning to the picturesque village in the Scottish Highlands, but maybe destiny was calling. Her emotions were a mixture of excitement and trepidation, her mind spinning with endless possibilities. Excitement that they could leave this godforsaken place, the dingy flat, and eradicate Cole from their lives, but also trepidation about how the villagers would react when they discovered she was back in town. She had left that night without saying goodbye to her best friends, Felicity, Isla and Allie, and she had no clue whether they still lived in the village or even how they'd felt about her disappearance. If they did still live there, Grace had an awful lot of apologising to do.

It was quite ironic when she thought about it. The fresh start that she thought she craved back then as a teenager had become her worst nightmare – and now she was heading back to where she belonged. Grace did wonder what her mother would have thought about the way she'd behaved as a teenager. Feeling ashamed, she didn't need to question that further. She swallowed a lump in her throat. The bond she'd shared with her mother was one she strived for with her own children, an unbreakable bond of kindness, love and protection. Grace knew her mum would be devastated to learn of the unhappiness of her relationship, the abuse she endured from Cole. She was disappointed with herself for not seeking help and leaving sooner. But she'd been isolated in a hellish situation, and all she could ever do was find the strength to get through one day at a time.

When talking with the solicitor, Grace had agreed to attend the office in Heartcross to collect the keys to the Castle. Already she was wondering what the hell was she going to do with it. Grace knew if she sold it, she'd have no more financial worries. She and the boys would be set up for life; they could buy a house and live off the profits and begin a brand-new life. And that new life started right here, right now, standing on the pavement outside the pawnshop. Grace looked at the tinted windows and took a huge breath. She really was going to do this. As she pushed open the door and stepped inside the shop, an old-fashioned bell rang above her head. A wizened-looking man behind the counter looked up as he was blasted with cold air from outside. The boys fell into the shop, grateful to be out of the rain, and Grace instructed them to stand still and not to touch anything. The shop was crammed with possessions from people's lives, every item telling a story. All their hopes and dreams, now sold to make a few quid. Grace was no different. She stared at the long, narrow aisles holding various merchandise. A glass case in front of the shop-owner, which served as a counter, housed swords and tactical knives alongside jewellery of all kinds. With his spectacles balanced on the bridge of his nose, the man looked at Grace and pushed a bowl of complimentary peppermints across the counter towards her. She politely refused.

'How can I help you?' he asked, looking between her and the boys.

Grace looked down at the ring on her finger. When Cole had proposed, the cracks were already beginning to show in their relationship but she'd told herself it would be all right. Their life together promised hope, the tone of his voice full of love, but now it was over. She'd agreed to a lifetime commitment to him, through the good and the bad times, but all the good times were long gone and the bad times she no longer wanted. She slid the ring from her finger. She had to stay strong; she was doing this for her and the boys.

'How much would you give me for this?' replied Grace, placing the ring in the palm of his hand.

'Is it a real diamond?'

Her skin prickled with unease, her stomach churned. Grace had always assumed the diamond was real and was now hoping with all her might that it was, because this was the only way she could get the money together for the train tickets to return to Heartcross. She gave a little intake of breath.

'I think so.'

For an uncomfortable two minutes Grace watched as the man scrutinised the ring through a magnifying glass. Why was it taking so long? Her heart was thumping nineteen to the dozen as she expected him to look up and tell her it was a fake diamond, worth absolutely nothing. He placed the ring back on a silver plate in front of him and Grace watched him turn and walk over to the oversized, old-fashioned brown cash register behind him that looked like it had been through the war. He punched in some numbers, pulled down the handle and the drawer shot open like a bullet from a gun.

The man began to count out twenty-pound notes, then turned back towards Grace. 'This is what I can offer you. Four hundred pounds.'

Grace exhaled with relief, and did everything in her power not to lean across the counter and give the man a kiss.

'Thank you, I'll take it,' she replied, watching him fill out a ticket. Within seconds her ring was inside the glass case with a price double what he'd just given her.

Grace stared at him and shook her head in despair. 'That seems a little unfair. Cashing in on other's misfortunes.'

The man shrugged. 'It's the name of the game. I have to make a living somehow.'

Folding the notes, Grace stuffed the money in her purse and prayed. All she had to do now was get through the night without Cole returning and noticing the lack of a ring on her finger. It seemed unlikely, but he was unpredictable. Tomorrow, she was going to take her chance. She was finally making a fresh start with her boys. Grace was returning to the old life she had once left behind, but wasn't sure whether she would be welcomed back with open arms.

Chapter Two

The next morning the sky was grey, but, thankfully, the rain had eased a little. This was British summer time at its best. Thankfully Cole hadn't returned last night and Grace was relieved. Once the boys had gone to bed, she'd bundled some essentials together, packing them each a rucksack, which she'd hidden under the bed. She'd barely slept a wink in case Cole turned up and rumbled her. But now all they had to get through was the morning. They were leaving late afternoon and travelling on the overnight train to Glensheil, followed by a short bus ride to Heartcross, so they would arrive the following morning. With such a long journey ahead of them, Grace let the boys sleep in. Quietly, she wandered into the kitchen and switched on the kettle followed by the radio to drown out the row that was still going on in the flat above. She couldn't wait to escape from this squalor.

The morning passed slowly. Grace was clock-watching

and on edge; every car door she heard bang, she was up looking out of the window on to the car park below, praying it wasn't Cole returning. But thankfully, with no sign of him, they were ready to make their move after lunch. She zipped up Billy's coat and put his boots on. This was it, the end of her life with Cole.

She looked at the mobile phone in her hand. She'd erased everything from it. She left it on the kitchen table alongside her house keys. Her stomach was in knots as she placed a small rucksack on each of the boys' backs whilst she took the large one and wheeled the holdall to the door. She stopped and looked in the mirror on the wall, staring at the blackness around her eye. She was actually going to do this. Her grandfather Marley had provided her with an escape plan and Grace never thought in a million years she would be grateful to him. Heartcross was giving her a second chance when she needed it most.

'Come on, boys!' She rallied them all around her and bent down in front of them. She held out her hand and each of them placed a hand on top of hers. 'Our gang is very special and we look after each other. Are we ready? Just one last thing – I've got you a little something for your rucksack.' Grace pulled out three chocolate bars. The boys' eyes widened. They weren't used to treats as such, with money being tight, but the smiles on their faces said it all.

'Thank you,' said Joey and Freddie in unison, while Billy wrapped his arms around Grace and kissed her on the cheek.

'But where's yours?' asked Joey, looking up at Grace.

'Don't you worry about me,' she replied, knowing she had to watch the pennies because she had no clue how she was going to survive with not much money to her name. But she would worry about that when she got to Heartcross. At least they would have a roof over their heads until she could sell the Castle.

The three boys looked at each other, Joey broke his bar in half then Freddie and Billy followed suit, sharing their chocolate with Grace. Her eyes welled up with tears, feeling emotional she pulled them all in for a hug. 'My boys are the best boys.' She was so proud of them. 'Thank you,' she said, popping the chocolate in her bag. 'Okay, are we ready?'

Pulling the door shut, Grace didn't look back. As she hurried the boys to the gloom of the stairwell, voices drifted from a nearby flat which once again escalated into shouts. Alongside the sound of dripping water, the walls were full of graffiti and the pungent smell of urine hit her every time. In the distance the rattle and roar of the passing trains could be heard and Grace knew the anxious swirl in her stomach wouldn't go away until she and the boys were sitting safely on that train.

Thankfully, within seconds, they were out in the fresh air and the train station was in sight. There were two tracks, one going in each direction and Grace was buffeted by the wind from a passing high-speed train. She purchased their tickets and stored them safely in her purse, then led the boys to the warmth of the waiting room. Billy pointed to a pigeon that was pecking crumbs in between the benches outside while Joey sat down and looked up at the bright-coloured posters on the wall. Grace felt a sense of relief as she pulled Billy, who was clutching his teddy bear, on to her knee. The train was due in five minutes and then they would be safely on their way. Acknowledging the woman sitting opposite them, Grace guessed she was in her mid-sixties.

'Does your teddy bear have a name?' the woman asked, smiling warmly at Billy, who held his bear up but didn't speak.

'He's a little shy,' replied Grace, squeezing Billy, 'but the teddy bear is called Ralph.'

'And are you and Ralph going anywhere nice today? A day trip out?'

Before Grace could answer again, Freddie piped up, 'We are off to live in a castle in Scotland.' His face beamed as he shared the information.

The woman gave a little chuckle. 'Scotland! That is a long way to go, and to live in a castle, you say?'

'There may be a moat with crocodiles and dragons.' Freddie joked. 'Who knows? We will just have to wait and see.'

Grace couldn't help but smile at Freddie's enthusiasm, which was immediately shot down by Joey. 'There aren't any crocodiles in Scotland.'

The woman was smiling at the boys, then she looked at Grace, 'Don't you just love children with the best imaginations, they will go far. You should be proud of them.'

'Oh, I am,' replied Grace instantly, listening to the

announcement coming over the Tannoy. 'That's us, boys, are we ready?'

The train could be heard rumbling towards them, followed by the sound of the brakes squealing as it slowed down. 'Here we go, make sure you've got everything.'

'Have fun in your castle,' said the woman, smiling and giving the boys a wave as they walked towards the door of the waiting room.

'We will and thank you,' replied Freddie, hauling his rucksack up on to his back. Once they were outside, 'I don't think she believes us,' said Freddie with a giggle.

'But we know it's the truth,' said Grace, giving all the boys a look of adoration.

Grace knew she wouldn't be returning to Devon. She'd arrived a naive sixteen year old and had fallen in love with a man she thought would protect her against all odds – and hadn't. That life was gone and the second she stepped on the train, she felt relief. After all these years, Grace Power was on her way home.

The ticket inspector tipped his hat at the boys as they ran on to the train. Grace was grateful they were in good spirits. They settled down at a table and the boys took off their rucksacks whilst she stored the holdall safely in the overhead compartment.

'Anything you want from your bags put on the table now,' instructed Grace, looking up at the rosy-cheeked ticket inspector who'd appeared in the aisle at the side of their table wearing a huge hearty smile.

'Tickets, please.'

Immediately, Grace reached for her purse.

'Please, can I hand the tickets over?' urged Joey and Freddie both holding out their hands.

Grace placed two tickets in each of their hands.

'Where to, boys?' asked the ticket inspector.

'Heartcross,' chattered Joey and Freddie excitedly.

'It's in Scotland,' added Freddie, with a pleased smile on his face.

'It is too,' replied the ticket inspector, checking the ticket, 'and it's a very long way.'

'Men wear skirts in Scotland,' claimed Joey, causing the ticket inspector to laugh.

'That they do,' he replied.

'But we won't be wearing skirts.' Freddie screwed his face up. 'Eww! That's for girls!'

Grace laughed and shook her head at the ticket inspector, who was chuckling away.

'And here's a ticket for your teddy, young man, we can't be leaving him behind now, can we?'

Billy looked up, took the pretend ticket from the ticket inspector, and gave him a smile.

'And if you need anything on the journey, just give me a shout.' He looked towards Grace, who nodded her appreciation. 'As soon as the whistle is blown, we will be off!' he declared, walking over to the next travellers.

Freddie and Joey had taken the window seats and were chatting happily away whilst looking at the rest of the late passengers clambering on board. Billy looked up and waggled teddy's ticket.

'You are the cutest four year old I know,' confirmed Grace, knowing that the love she had for her children was the best love in the world.

Numerous doors slammed and the whistle blew, followed by a shout, and the train began to chug slowly out of the station. This was it. Grace watched the trees and houses whizz pass the window and they were on their way to Scotland. This journey was the ride back to her future. Her grandfather might just have saved her life.

Billy, holding his teddy bear, cuddled up with Grace, his eyes already closing with the motion of the train.

As night began to fall, the boys spread out across the vacant seats and Grace covered them up with their coats. They soon fell asleep and her thoughts turned towards her old friends she had left behind … Isla, Felicity and Allie. Had they woken up to the news that she'd gone or had it taken a few days to filter through the grapevine? Back then all four of them went to the same school and were thick as thieves, even though Grace was a couple of years younger than the others. During school holidays, most days were spent together grabbing a milkshake from Bonnie's teashop and spending time in the hide-away on the edge of the mountain. Grace wondered if the tree-house in the grounds of the Castle was still there. The four of them belonged to a made-up club that Allie had named the 'Friends For Ever' club. They'd sit in the tree-house at weekends and talk about their favourite bands and boys they fancied and eat their penny chews from the local village shop. But it was Grace who'd broken their pact to stay loyal to each other.

Her old friends had every right to be mad with her; she'd let them down. Grace hadn't reached out to any of them; she knew they would have enticed her back and, at the time, Grace had wanted to go it alone. Now, on her return, she had so many bridges to build. In all the years that had passed, she had never come close to finding good loyal friends like those three. Grace's chest heaved just thinking about it and now she wished she'd made more of an effort to stay in touch. She did have happy memories of the place and she was beginning to question why she'd been so eager to leave it all behind. Had it really been that bad?

Feeling glum, Grace dug her hands deep in the pockets of her coat as she leant her head against the window and fought back the tears of sadness as a pang of guilt hit her hard. Memories of the small, bustling village suddenly enveloped her and gave her an overwhelming feeling of comfort and belonging. She'd been swept away on the tide of her argument with her grandfather and should have just let things lie until morning, but, being sixteen and hotheaded, Grace thought she knew best; she didn't need anyone. Over the years she tried to block out her past, but Heartcross had always been there at the back of her mind.

She remembered sadly how her grandfather held her hand at her mother's funeral. She remembered how his cheeks were rosy; he went to bed wearing his flat cap and he always had a crossword on the go. Guilt ricocheted through her body as she dabbed her eyes with a tissue and tried to compose herself. Why hadn't she got in touch? Grace knew arriving back in Heartcross wouldn't be easy.

Facing the music would be one of the hardest things she'd ever done.

For a couple of hours she watched the boys sleep and marvelled at the night sky. It didn't matter that she was exhausted, Grace just couldn't sleep. Thoughts of the past were still very much on her mind. She wondered what Heartcross Castle was like now. She remembered it as a place of elegance; rooms of splendour and expensive artworks. The crystal chandelier that hung in the main entrance hall was insured for thousands of pounds and wouldn't look out of place in a royal palace. Grace had often watched the glittering reflections of the jewels spin around the room on sunny days, which reminded her of a kaleidoscope that her mum had bought her as a child. Each room was filled with Chesterfields, dressers and wingback chairs, and the guest bedrooms each had a four-poster bed.

On Saturdays, Grace had a job in the Castle shop, which sold all things touristy, and of course on hot days ice cream, but her favourite place were the Castle gardens – in all weathers. She loved the outdoors and spent a lot of time in the greenhouses that were situated in parts of the grounds that were not open to the public. Her grandfather's trusted friend Hector was also the Castle gardener and lived in a tiny cottage on the estate. He'd shown her how to sow seeds and grow vegetables and different types of fruits and he'd given her an old radio which she kept in one of the sheds. Grace loved spending time in his company.

After a few more hours the sun began to rise and Grace knew it wouldn't be long before the train rumbled into the station at Glensheil. She was still feeling a little anxious. The sight that was whizzing past the window was becoming all so familiar: towering mountains, dense woodlands, glittering lochs. The train continued to trundle past magnificent bays and rolling hills. The boys began to stir and Grace opened her arms wide just like she did every morning. 'I wouldn't miss my early morning cuddles with my boys for anything.' She hugged them tight. 'The first day of the rest of our lives,' murmured Grace, resting her head on top of the boys as they all huddled together. Noticing Billy had dropped his bear, she reached down, picked it up and handed it back to him. He cuddled it tight.

'Where are we?' asked Freddie, the early morning chill causing him to shiver as he slipped his arms inside his coat.

Joey was already standing up, both hands pressed against the window. 'Woah! Look at that mountain,' he said, his eyes wide. 'It's huge.'

Grace lifted her head to look at the mountain in the distance; it was getting closer by the second. 'That is Heartcross Mountain. It's beautiful, people travel from far and wide to hike to the top, and right at the foot of the mountain is a teashop...' As the words left her mouth, Grace realised she had no idea if the teashop was still there. 'Bonnie's teashop,' she continued. 'A place my mum used to take me for a cooked breakfast every first Saturday of the month. It was our special treat. And I went there for milkshakes with my friends. It was owned by Bonnie and my friend's mum, Rona, worked there too.'

'And what was your friend's name?' asked Joey.

'Felicity,' replied Grace.

Freddie was rubbing his tummy, 'Sausages ... bacon...' He wafted his nose in the air, causing Billy to giggle.

'My tummy is hungry,' announced Joey.

'You don't say. Listening to that growl, there must be a huge monster living inside there,' joked Grace, taking the chocolate from her bag that the boys had shared with her at the start of the journey. 'And don't think chocolate is the new breakfast,' she said, handing it out. 'Our first stop is the solicitor's office to pick up the keys to the Castle.'

'And then can we go to Bonnie's teashop for a cooked breakfast?' asked Freddie, staring at Grace as he popped the last block of chocolate into his mouth.

By Grace's reckoning she had just over fifty pounds left in her purse. Inside, she was panicking. How exactly was she going to feed the boys? She hadn't worked out how the hell she was going to survive, but she knew she needed a job, preferably one that somehow fitted in around the boys. All three boys were looking hopefully at her. She nodded, knowing if they filled up on a breakfast mid-morning then that would possibly keep them going until much later on. 'We still have to go to the solicitor's first. Boys, the teashop may not be there but we can go and have a look.'

The boys clapped their hands. Grace was so proud of them; it had been an extremely long journey and they had been very well behaved.

'You might see your friend,' added Joey, still staring up at the mountainous terrain.

Grace smiled briefly. 'Yes I might,' she replied, feeling a

slight knot in her stomach. How was she going to face Felicity? What did she say? It was only a matter of time before she knew the answers to those questions.

Through the window of the train, Grace recognised the station as the train began to slow. In all this time nothing seemed to have changed. She glimpsed the sign 'Welcome to Glensheil' and glanced at her watch. It was ten minutes until 9 a.m., which hopefully meant there was a bus due very soon.

'Boys, make sure we have everything.'

'Is this it? Are we nearly there?' asked Joey, grabbing hold of Freddie's arm.

'This is it,' replied Grace, blinking slowly, her eyelids heavy. She was exhausted after watching over the boys all night. What she wouldn't do to lay her head on a soft pillow and fall fast asleep.

Despite the long journey, the twins were excited. They stood up, pulled on their rucksacks, then moved back towards the window. Billy was as curious as his older brothers. He was standing next to them watching the hustle and bustle of the commuters strolling along the platform.

'This is like a proper adventure!' exclaimed Joey.

'Can we see the Castle yet?' asked Freddie. 'I can't wait, this is going to be brilliant!'

The boys' enthusiasm gave Grace renewed strength to be positive, but somehow she was going to have to sell the idea to the boys that the Castle was a stop-gap, just the start of their adventure. Grace knew the easiest option would be to sell the Castle as soon as possible. The quicker it was sold, the sooner Grace would be financially secure and could begin to plan where to move next. There were endless possibilities.

'Are we ready, boys?' she asked, smiling at them.

They saluted, making Grace laugh. Grabbing the holdall, she was the first to step down from the train. The moment was full of optimism, hope, the world was their oyster and that old life was gone. The last time she'd been standing on this platform was when she was sixteen and thinking she knew best, vowing she would never return to this life. It was funny how things could change in a blink of an eye.

Grace lingered for a second and took in the view before turning back towards Billy and swinging him down from the train. He giggled, then slipped his hand firmly into hers. Grace gave it a squeeze. With Freddie and Joey by her side, she followed the crowd towards the exit of the station. If she remembered correctly, there was a bus stop located directly outside.

'There's the bus,' said Grace, observing the sign on the front of the bus that displayed the destination 'Heartcross'. 'Come on, boys, not long now.'

There were already a number of passengers sitting on the bus and after helping the boys on board, Grace paid for the tickets and settled next to them on the very front seats. They didn't have to wait long before the bus started its engine and navigated its way along the road towards the centre of Glensheil. As soon as they'd travelled down the high street, everything became instantly recognisable. The bus stopped at the traffic lights right outside the coffeehouse, an old favourite place of Grace's. The long counter was stacked with chrome espresso and frothing machines, jars filled with aromatic coffee blends, bottles of coffee flavourings and toppings. Grace took in the aroma through the small open window. Already it was doing a roaring trade, people queuing outside wanting a coffee on their way to work. They travelled past the flower shop and the bookshop and, of course, the boys immediately noticed the old-fashioned sweetshop situated on a corner of the street. Nothing much had changed except for a couple of new bistros that Grace didn't recognise.

'That's the River Heart,' said Grace, pointing to the left. Grace knew in the summer months the river was a firm favourite with the tourists. There were shallow spots for children to paddle and places to picnic along the coastal path.

'Woah, look at that boat,' said Freddie, pointing towards the water taxi on the river.

'That's Flynn's water taxis, taking the diners over to The Lake House for breakfast,' answered the bus driver, looking over his shoulder towards Grace.

'The Lake House?' questioned Grace.

'A restaurant that attracts the rich and famous, owned by millionaire tycoon Flynn Carter. Are you staying at Starcross Manor?' he asked.

'Starcross Manor?' Grace was perplexed, she'd never heard of Starcross Manor.

'The multi-award-winning hotel on the edge of the village, also owned by Flynn Carter.'

'No, we are off to live in the Castle,' chipped in Freddie, watching the town fly past through the window.

'Of course you are,' replied the driver, tipping Freddie a wink. 'And do make sure you give The Lake House a try. Those water taxis take you on lots of excursions, they even sail you past Heartcross Castle.'

Although everywhere seemed the same since Grace had left, an awful lot had changed too. She was still looking out of the window. 'The bridge – what happened to the bridge? It looks different,' Grace asked the driver.

'So you're not a newcomer to the village,' he observed. 'The bridge collapsed in a storm. Horrendous it was. The villagers stranded for weeks. A local girl, Felicity Simons, set up a fundraising page and before you know it raised thousands to have this bridge erected.'

The second Grace heard Felicity's name, she sat up straight, 'Felicity, so she's still around these parts?'

'You know her?' quizzed the driver, 'She's still at the teashop. Tourism has doubled since Heartcross was catapulted all over the news. I'm surprised you didn't see any of the reports. It's become a very famous little village.'

Grace was listening to the driver, but she knew the second they turned the next corner that she would have her first glimpse of Heartcross Castle. Feeling her heart begin to beat a little faster, her eyes widened and there it was, the magnificent pinkish harled Castle was standing tall right before her very eyes. It took her breath away and it looked exactly the same, a building she never thought she would see again. The elegant tower was spellbindingly beautiful, set amongst the rolling hills. Grace was feeling excited; maybe only now did she appreciate the beauty of where she once lived. The Castle grounds were equally bewitching, with woodland trails, glen gardens and a meadow floor that glowed with bluebells. She couldn't wait to discover if the old greenhouses were still standing and maybe she would discover the old radio too.

Grace nudged the boys and nodded towards the Castle. They all gasped at the same time. Excitedly, Freddie grabbed hold of Joey who grabbed hold of Billy.

The driver rang her bell as they travelled over the bridge. 'First stop, Love Heart Lane.'

Passengers behind them began to gather their things and walk to the front of the bus, holding on to the leather loops that dangled above their heads. They held on tight as the bus bounced along the gravel trail on the other side of the bridge and pulled up in the small shingled layby at the bottom of the lane.

Freddie began to giggle and pointed out of the window towards the field. 'Look at those, Mummy, they look funny.'

'Alpacas,' confirmed the bus driver.

The comical-looking creatures were grazing on the grass not far from the river that ran through the bottom of the farmland.

'Foxglove Farm,' read Grace out loud, looking at the sign through the window. 'Who lives there?' she asked, remembering Drew Allaway lived there with his family when they were growing up.

'Drew and Isla own the farm. There's vintage

campervans too and a campsite. The alpacas are a huge attraction. You can take an alpaca for a walk,' said the driver, smiling at the boys, who were now bouncing up and down on their seats.

'Can we, Mum, please?' pleaded Joey.

But Grace didn't answer. Her mouth had fallen open. 'Isla married Drew,' she murmured to herself. She knew they were childhood sweethearts, so maybe she shouldn't be surprised. Grace really did have a lot of catching up to do.

As the passengers got off the bus in single file, Grace glanced up the lane and laid eyes on the teashop, which was open for business, then noticed the line of hikers already on the trail passing between the sheer rock faces. The trail seemed to disappear through overgrown sections, but one thing that Grace noticed was that the purple heather was still as striking as ever.

Once the folding doors of the bus had closed, the driver set off again. 'The next stop is the Grouse and Haggis pub, centre of the village.'

Grace rummaged inside her bag and pulled out the crumpled piece of paper on which she'd written down the solicitor's address. If they got off at the next stop they could walk up the high street and, if she remembered correctly, if they turned left at the end of the road the solicitor's was located in that direction.

'That's us, boys,' she said, noticing they passed a sign for a B&B on the right which she didn't remember at all. But when the Grouse and Haggis came into sight, the high street was all too familiar.

The bus pulled in next to Hamish's village shop, which looked exactly the same, the colourful striped awning still shielding the front from the sun. A carousel of postcards whirled next to wooden crates of fresh fruit and veg while fishing nets stood to attention looking like a line of soldiers. Taking a trip down memory lane, Grace remembered the penny chew section at the back of the shop, which she and her friends loved to raid. The boys were going to love that if it was still there.

'Here you go,' said the driver, pressing the button that opened the doors. He turned and spoke to the boys. 'I hope you have fun in your Castle,' he said and winked.

Full of energy, the twins fist-bumped the driver then jumped down on to the pavement and began looking through the postcards outside Hamish's shop before Grace had a chance to grab the holdall from the luggage rack.

'You have your hands full there,' observed the driver, tipping his cap at Grace.

'That I have, but I wouldn't change it for the world,' she confirmed, looking at her boys with admiration. She took Billy's hand. 'Have a lovely day,' she said, smiling at the driver.

Taking her first steps back in Heartcross, of course Grace felt nervous. It was hard not to, knowing how people would react to her return. She might be confronted with hostility, for running like that from Heartcross and never returning in all these years. Would they think it was unforgivable, her deserting her grandfather as well as Heartcross? Would people actually recognise her?

She swallowed and told herself everything was going to be okay because she was going to make it okay. This new life was about the new Grace and her boys, and she was going to do everything to make that a smooth ride. If that meant apologising, showing everyone that she really was truly sorry, then that's what she would have to do. One thing Grace had already learned on the train journey here was how much she had missed her friends and having a good support network around her. That wasn't something she was going to jeopardise again in a hurry.

On the pavement outside the pub, Grace noticed a couple of women stood chatting, then she swung a glance towards the woman cleaning the tables outside the pub and immediately recognised Meredith. Meredith looked over in her direction and shouted, 'Good morning,' but she hadn't seemed to recognise her. Maybe that was because she'd grown her hair out, so it was now long and rusty red, a huge difference from the short blond bob she used to wear. Grace wondered if Allie still lived at the pub.

'Boys, put those back.' Grace had turned round to see the twins hitting each other over the head with fishing nets.

'Take that,' declared Joey, taking a step towards Freddie and pretending to stab him in the stomach.

'Boys!'

They both stood still.

'We are jousting. We need to practise. After all, we are about to live in a Castle,' announced Freddie, handing the

41

fishing nets over to Grace who propped them back up outside the shop. Grace couldn't help but smile at the twins. Sometimes she wished she was that age again without a single care in the world.

'Okay, come on… First stop the solicitor's…'

'Then breakfast,' chipped in Joey, 'at the teashop, because we know it's still there. We've seen it.'

Grace was feeling hungry and would have liked more time to prepare for her first trip back to the teashop – mentally and physically. Not only did she feel grimy after the long journey and exhausted, but also a little teary. She was trying to keep jolly for the boys' sake – after all, this was their brand-new adventure. 'Then breakfast,' confirmed Grace. She might as well let the villagers know she was back sooner rather than later.

'I need the toilet,' announced Joey, squirming from side to side.

'There will be one at the solicitor's office. By my reckoning it's just at the top of this road. Let's hurry.'

Holding Billy's hand and pulling the holdall behind her, Grace walked to the top of the high street. According to the directions the solicitor's office was next to Peony Practice, opposite the school. At the top of the road Grace noticed that Scott's veterinary surgery had been changed back to the cottage and wondered if Stuart and Meredith still lived there and what had become of Rory. She didn't have to wonder for long when the front door opened and Stuart stepped outside to retrieve the newspaper that was sticking out of his mail box. He hadn't changed much, just a little older and a little less hair.

'Here we are,' said Grace, looking up at the sign. 'Boys, I need you to be on your best behaviour for just a little longer.' She pushed open the door and immediately the receptionist sitting at the desk in front of them looked up from the uncluttered desk.

'Hi, can I help you?' asked the receptionist.

'Hi, Grace Power to see Jaydon Fairbrother,' replied Grace, suddenly feeling nervous. 'But please, have you got a bathroom my son can use? We've had a long journey and he's bursting for the toilet.'

The receptionist pointed to the door off the waiting room and Grace showed him the way. Jules, according to her name badge, tapped on the keyboard in front of her then looked up at Grace. 'Take a seat. Mr Fairbrother will be with you in a minute.' She smiled towards Billy and Freddie, but Billy took a step behind Grace, still clutching her hand. Grace sat Billy on her knee in the waiting room, which resembled that of a dental surgery. Everything was clean and clinical. There were numerous chairs with a table in the centre of the room piled with well-thumbed magazines.

Grace had no clue what to expect from this visit. She'd even tried to calculate how old her grandfather was when he passed away, but she simply had no clue, only an educated guess. Had he left anything else for her apart from the keys to the Castle, a message maybe? She wouldn't have long to find out. Looking around the room at the framed pictures on the wall, Grace soon realised she was looking at old photographs of Heartcross, from maybe around the 1900s. Moving Billy to the chair next to her she stood up to take a closer look. The first black and white photo was of the high street. It was a snowy day with one old car travelling past the Grouse and Haggis, which stood in prime position opposite the old village shop. Grace wondered who owned them back in those times. She moved along the wall and stood and stared at Heartcross Castle in all its glory. Joey was now standing by her side. 'Look, back in the olden days,' she said.

'Who lived there, then?' he asked.

'I'm not sure,' Grace replied, knowing there was an awful lot to discover about her new home. She thought about her grandfather, knowing she had no clue about his background or family. She was becoming intrigued about her family's past and how exactly Heartcross Castle had come to be in their possession. She'd never asked the question, growing up.

Taking a seat, she waited another five minutes before Jules appeared in the doorway. 'Mr Fairbrother will see you now.'

'Thank you,' replied Grace, standing up and reaching for Billy's hand. They followed Jules down a small narrow corridor then she gestured towards the door at the bottom on the right.

'We are going to live in a castle,' announced Freddie, looking proud as punch.

'I know, and what an adventure for you!' replied the

receptionist, smiling at the boys before hurrying back to answer the telephone that was ringing from behind the reception desk.

'Mum, she believed us!' said Freddie, looking pleased.

Grace ruffled his head. 'She did. Now remember, best behaviour, and then we can go and get some breakfast.'

Knocking on the door, they waited outside. Jaydon Fairbrother's name was displayed on a brass plaque on the door. The door swung open and Grace was met by a very tall, slim man. She looked up and felt Billy's grip on her hand become tighter.

'Do come in, Ms Power. Who have we here?' Mr Fairbrother looked towards the three boys.

'Freddie, Joey and Billy, my boys,' replied Grace.

She watched his eyes narrow as he squinted at her blackened eye. Grace knew he'd noticed immediately. After such a long, tiring journey her make-up would have slid off hours ago, but there was nothing she could do about it now.

Mr Fairbrother's office was another minimalist room. It was drab with beige walls, the window was tiny and the only colour in the room was from a green-leafed potted plant fighting for survival on the window sill. The desk was bare, no computer, only a file of papers and a stained coffee cup. He gestured for Grace to sit on the chair whilst the boys stood by her side. Reaching for his spectacles, Mr Fairbrother balanced them on the bridge of his nose and picked up the file in front of him.

'Are you Grace Power, grand-daughter of Marley Power?'

'I am,' replied Grace, sliding over a passport that was very much out of date which she'd kept hidden in a zipped compartment of her bag for many years. She was unrecognisable from the photograph. 'Sorry, that's all I have.'

'Driver's licence?' he prompted.

Grace shook her head. 'I've never learned to drive.'

'Okay, bills? Have you any bills in your name?' asked Mr Fairbrother, looking straight at her through his spectacles.

'I haven't, no. But that is me,' Grace gestured towards the passport. 'I just haven't any need for a new one.'

Mr Fairbrother took another look at the passport and scrutinised Grace, then repeated his actions. 'Mmm, the hair is very different,' he mumbled. He slid his chair back over the black ridged carpet and walked over to the locked cabinet at the back of the room. He rummaged in the pocket of his brown corduroy trousers and pulled out a key and promptly unlocked the cabinet. There were numerous labelled keys hanging inside on hooks. He unhooked the bunch of keys on the far right and double-checked the white tag hanging on the string, then closed the door.

Mr Fairbrother turned back around. 'Marley Power was ninety-six years of age when he passed away – on his birthday.' He looked up and gave a grim smile.

Grace blew out a breath. Ninety-six was a good age, but to die on his birthday... She was hit by another wave of sadness.

'Marley passed peacefully in his sleep, he didn't suffer.'

Grace nodded her appreciation for the added information. What were the last years of her grandfather's life like? Had he rattled about in the Castle all by himself? Grace swallowed a lump and blinked back the tears. She was consumed by guilt that he passed on his own with no family around. She was his only living relative. Mr Fairbrother passed her a tissue.

'How was he discovered?' she asked.

Mr Fairbrother referred to the notes in the file in front of him. 'I'm not sure. I'm sorry I do not have that information.' He shuffled the papers in front of him, 'Your grandfather has already been cremated,' he added.

Grace nodded.

Mr Fairbrother continued, 'There are just a few signatures I require, and then I can hand over the keys.'

Grace was presented with numerous legal documents laid out on the desk in front of her. Mr Fairbrother drew crosses in various places, then tapped his pen on the desk. 'Your signature is required next to all the crosses.' He handed her the pen.

After Grace had signed the documents in all the right places, Mr Fairbrother perused them then took the pen from her hand. 'That all seems in order,' he said, banging the papers on the desk to get them straight before replacing them in a pile and closing the file.

He held up a huge bunch of keys and then pushed a separate key over the desk. 'This one is for the door at the main entrance that takes you into the living quarters.'

'Thank you,' said Grace, turning the key over in her hand.

'Congratulations! You are the proud owner of a ... castle, a very stunning castle. It's not every day I say that.'

'I bet,' replied Grace. This was a bitter-sweet moment: the loss of her grandfather, with whom she had never made amends, and yet security, a safe haven for her and the boys until it was sold and they became financially secure.

'Here are the rest of the keys. Trial and error, I'm afraid – there are many keys which means there are many locks.'

Grace already knew there were more locks and bolts in the Castle than in the local hardware shop. 'We'll figure it out,' she said, storing the keys safely in her bag. 'Thank you,' she said once again, before turning towards the boys. 'Are we ready?'

'Do you need directions to the Castle?' asked Mr Fairbrother.

Grace smiled and shook her head. 'I think we'll be just fine.'

'Of course you don't, no one can miss the magnificent Castle on the hill. Oh, and before you go, a Mr Andrew Glossop rents the servants' quarters, he's been there six months now.'

'Andrew Glossop?' queried Grace, recognising the name. She racked her brains but couldn't place who he was. 'I feel like I've heard the name before and should know who he is.'

'Global superstar, celebrity chef. Apparently his new cooking show is to be televised from the Castle or so I've heard... Usually the rumours that circulate are true, and my wife should know as she's very smitten with him – follows him on all his social media. Do you know, she makes me frequent the pub numerous times a week in hope of a glimpse of seeing him.' He gave a little chuckle. 'Is there anything else I can help you with today?'

'And does the Castle still generate any revenue? Is it still open to the public?' asked Grace.

'Afraid not, the Castle gardens have been closed for many years now.'

'Thank you, Mr Fairbrother. I have your number if I think of anything else.'

He stood up and showed them to the door.

Grace looked down towards the boys. 'Who's ready for breakfast?'

All three boys thrust a hand up in the air. 'ME!' chorused Joey and Freddie whilst Billy gave a thumbs-up.

Within seconds, Grace and the boys were walking back along the high street and continuing towards Love Heart Lane. With her own stomach rumbling away, she knew the boys must be famished and she was in need of a decent cup of tea. As they turned into Love Heart Lane they ambled past Foxglove Farm and the boys stood on the fence pointing and laughing at the alpacas. Grace smiled; they did look comical with their bouncing mops of hair.

Whilst the boys were watching the animals, Grace took a moment and inhaled the fresh Highland air and took in the view of the lane. The whitewashed terraced houses on the right looked exactly the same. Heartwood Cottage, just before Bonnie's teashop, looked untouched by time too and the teashop was already busy with customers, mainly hikers heading up the mountain pass. Grace felt jittery. It was more than likely in a couple of minutes' time she was about to come face to face with her old friend Felicity. Would she even recognise her? Grace knew people didn't change that much, but with her long red hair she looked somewhat different these days. Then there was the dilemma: what if Felicity didn't recognise her? Grace told herself to stop overthinking it.

There was only one way to find out.

'Come on, boys,' hollered Grace, walking up the lane, pulling the holdall behind her. She pointed towards the teashop. 'Breakfast!'

They ran in front of her, their rucksacks bouncing up and down on their backs, and jumped sideways to let the hikers pass who were heading down the lane. As soon as Grace read the sign 'Bonnie's Teashop', it reminded her how much family mattered. This teashop was a family business that spanned three generations. Taking a deep breath, Grace walked nervously towards the door. All she could do was focus on the here and now, and that meant facing up to her old friend Felicity. It was now or never.

Chapter Three

The vintage teashop with its china teapots and cups and floral triangular bunting draping the walls provided warmth and familiarity. The aroma was one Grace remembered well: coffee, toasted bread, savoury spices and a full Scottish breakfast all mixed into one. The boys' eyes widened as they spotted the glass counter filled with glazed doughnuts drizzled with frosting and sprinkles. There were paper-wrapped muffins ready for takeaway and a section of savouries including sausage rolls and cheese and onion pasties. There was an open doorway to the kitchen, with flour-dusted counters and berry pies cooling, their juices oozing through decorative slits in the crust.

There was nobody behind the counter and Grace noticed a vacant table just near the window. 'Boys, let's grab that table and I'll go and get us some menus. What would you like to drink? Orange juice?'

They nodded before racing over to the table. After

51

shuffling the rucksacks off their backs, they pulled out the chairs. Grace nervously stood at the counter and glanced up at the daily specials written on the chalkboard hanging on the wall behind the counter. As she did so, she recognised Felicity's voice filtering from the kitchen. 'Breakfasts for table seven are ready, I'll take them out now.'

Felicity appeared in the doorway, juggling two Scottish breakfasts which not only looked amazing but smelled divine. Their eyes met and Grace held Felicity's gaze. Her heart was hammering against her ribcage. This was the first time she'd seen her friend since Felicity's eighteenth birthday. A wave of nervousness cascaded over her, leaving flutters in the pit of her stomach. She reminded herself to breathe, not knowing how Felicity was going to react.

'Good morning,' sang Felicity with a huge smile. 'I'll be with you in a second.'

Grace nodded. Felicity hadn't immediately recognised her. She watched as Felicity placed the plates in front of a couple on the far side of the teashop. She handed over the cutlery and a couple of serviettes before placing a number of condiments on the table. After a quick chat with the customers, Felicity made her way back to the counter.

'Good morning, and what a lovely morning it is,' said Felicity, smoothing down her apron and picking up the nearby tea-towel. 'Not as sunny as we would like for this time of year, but apparently the sun is on its way and at least it's not raining. What can I get for you? Is it takeaway or eating in?'

Grace had frozen on the spot; all she could do was stare

at her old friend. She knew if she spoke her voice would crack, and all of a sudden she was overcome by emotion and felt like she was going to burst into tears. Grace would never have predicted that she would feel this way, but standing there, looking at her old friend, it suddenly hit her how much she'd missed her – which was daft in a way because they hadn't been in each other's lives all these years, and over time Grace had parked Heartcross in the very back of her mind.

Felicity was staring at her, still smiling.

Grace couldn't let the moment pass. 'Flick, it's me.' She waited for the penny to drop.

Felicity narrowed her eyes. Grace watched the look of puzzlement change to one of recognition. Felicity's eyes widened and her mouth dropped open.

'It's just I don't have short blonde hair anymore and maybe I've put on a few extra pounds.' Grace twizzled her hair then looked down to her feet. Her hands were shaking and she stuffed them in her pockets.

'Holy Mother of God,' exclaimed Felicity. 'Holy Mother of God,' she repeated louder. She dropped the tea-towel and turned towards the door behind her. 'Mum! she hollered, 'Get out here now. Mum!'

After shouting through the open doorway Felicity hurried around the counter towards her old friend. Without hesitation, she flung her arms around Grace and hugged her tight, much to Grace's relief. The floodgates opened, and a tsunami of tears rolled down Grace's cheeks. She couldn't remember the last time she'd been hugged that way. The warmth of Felicity's hug had felt good.

Still amazed, Felicity took a step back. 'Where the hell have you been? What the hell happened to you? It's been years... I never ever expected to see you again...' Felicity's words were tripping over each other as she hugged her friend again.

Grace felt wretched and genuinely remorseful. 'I am so sorry, I'm so sorry,' she said shakily. She was relieved that Felicity had welcomed her back without judgement, and there was no awkwardness between them.

'Wait until I tell Isla and Allie, they won't believe me. Gosh, I really can't believe this.'

Grace wasn't as nervous about coming face to face with Isla, who had always been the sensible, placid friend, whereas she knew it might not be as easy to build bridges with Allie. Allie had always been the feisty one of the group; if she had something to say, you knew about it. Her schoolteachers used to describe her as a girl with lots of character. Grace hoped she'd mellowed, because in the past Allie could hold a grudge until the cows came home.

'We have a lot of catching up to do,' agreed Grace.

Felicity was close to tears, 'So many blooming questions, I know... What the hell has happened to your eye?' Felicity studied it closely then held Grace's hands in hers.

'It's a long story.'

'But please tell me you aren't rushing off. Are you staying for a while?'

'I'm staying for a wee while.'

Rona suddenly appeared in the doorway looking flustered. 'Where's the fire?' she asked. 'Honestly, can I not go to the bathroom in peace?'

'Mum!' Felicity was fizzing with excitement and gestured towards Grace. 'Look who's come home.'

The word 'home' hung in the air. It was quite strange but that's exactly how Grace felt, even after all this time: she'd come home.

Rona looked more closely at Grace.

'The last time you saw me, I was maybe a little skinnier, short bob, not so sweet sixteen and maybe cheeky, a little bit of a handful.' Grace shrugged with a smile.

Rona didn't need to be told twice, 'Christ on a bike, Grace! Is that really you?'

'It is,' replied Grace.

'God love you, girl, you look like you've just come home from battle.'

'Mother!' exclaimed Felicity, knowing that her mother was stating the obvious without thinking.

'Sorry, sorry, I didn't mean... But my gosh, we never thought we'd ever see you again. I'm so glad we were wrong.' Immediately Rona smothered her in a hug. 'I cannot believe this. We are sorry to hear about—' Rona gave Felicity a swift glance, then asked tentatively, 'You do know your grandfather has passed away?'

Grace nodded. 'Yes, that's why I'm back and I'm not alone.' She turned towards her boys, who were pushing the salt and pepper shakers around the table as if they were on a racing track.

'Three boys! Wow! Just look at them… And the father?' asked Felicity, 'is he with you too?'

Grace shook her head. 'That's a story for another day. We've…' She flapped a hand in front of her face. 'Don't make me cry, I'm trying to hold it all together as it is.' Her voice cracked a little.

Felicity gave Grace's arm a squeeze. 'Say no more, a chat for another time.'

Grace managed a smile and swiftly changed the subject. 'We've only just arrived, after travelling for a day, and haven't really eaten since yesterday teatime. We are all absolutely starving.'

'Four full Scottish breakfasts coming up with juice, toast and a pot of tea for you, and it's on the house… No arguing,' announced Rona. 'It's absolutely lovely to see you. Welcome home!' Her voice carried as he hurried towards the kitchen.

Felicity was still smiling at Grace, shaking her head in disbelief that she was actually standing in front of her. 'When I woke up this morning I never thought to myself, Grace Power is going to walk back into the teashop.' She placed a jug of orange juice on a tray along with four glasses.

'Forty-eight hours ago, I didn't think so either. Everything has been a whirlwind and now it seems I'm an owner of a castle.'

'Wow! No way! How amazing is that? The whole village was wondering what was going to happen to that place.'

'I'm not sure exactly what is going to happen to it. It's

too big for me and the boys. I was thinking maybe of selling up and buying a smaller property that is more manageable, but I don't have to make a decision about that today.'

'Were you in contact with your grandfather at all before his passing?'

Grace only trusted herself to shake her head.

'Oh, Grace, I'm so sorry.'

'I can't change that now.' Grace swallowed. 'Did he venture down to the village much?' she asked, composing herself.

'From time to time, but not so much in recent years.' Felicity pointed out of the window. 'That's your new neighbour. Andrew resides in the servants' quarters.'

Grace swung around, flitting her eyes towards the window of the teashop. She couldn't help but stare in Andrew Glossop's direction. Even though she wasn't an avid watcher of his TV programme, she recognised him instantly as he stepped from his parked car on to the pavement. Even from a distance Grace was impressed with his physique and good looks. His striking deep-ocean eyes and his prominent jawline didn't go unnoticed. Wearing a bomber jacket, skinny jeans and expensive-looking shoes, he raked his hand through his tousled blond hair. For a second it seemed he was going to cross the lane towards the teashop, but after glancing at his phone he headed down Love Heart Lane, and from out of nowhere a swarm of giggling girls followed him, waving their cameras in the air and taking as many photographs of him as they possibly could.

'What it's like to be famous,' observed Grace.

'Every day it's the same. The poor man can't venture out without being harassed. I'm sure the tourists just frequent the village to get a glimpse of him. Hamish loves it when he's on the front of any magazine because it's an instant sell-out at the village shop. His Instagram likes and followers are off the scale, his fame is growing day by day and it seems Heartcross is getting more like Hollywood – but Andrew takes it all in his stride.'

Grace's eyes were still fixed on the window. She could understand why the general public were obsessed with his every move; she'd only set eyes on him for a moment and she wanted to know more about Andrew Glossop. He was mesmerising – gorgeous, in fact.

'And where has Andrew come from? He's not originally from around these parts.'

'London. He was head-hunted by Flynn Carter, the owner of Starcross Manor, to work in the restaurant. You have so much catching up to do. Andrew had every intention of moving on after six months but once Heartcross gets its claws into you, you don't go anywhere. Even you're back, but you took your blooming time about it,' teased Felicity. 'In fact, Fergus said he's living the life of luxury up at the Castle. He's renovated the servants' quarters. Apparently it's decked out with the latest technology, TV screens bigger than the size of Mum's living room ... allegedly.'

'Oooh, the boys are going to love it.' Grace thought of the dull dismal squalor they had just left behind. She couldn't wait to show them the inside of their new home. They were going to be so excited.

And although Grace wanted to know all about Andrew Glossop, Felicity had just mentioned another name she hadn't heard in a very long time.

'Fergus?' said Grace. 'Fergus Campbell? Is he still around these parts?'

'Yes, Fergus,' replied Felicity, 'My Fergus!'

'No way! You and Fergus? I've got so much catching up to do.'

'You have and everyone is going to be so pleased to see you. I can't wait to tell the girls you're home.'

'Home,' repeated Grace under her breath, the word resonating with her. The second she had stepped back into the village it had felt strange, like she'd never been away. Everywhere was instantly familiar and the welcome that Felicity and Rona had given her was truly unexpected, especially in the circumstances. 'I can't wait to see everyone. Come and meet the boys,' said Grace, smiling, but then she whispered, 'The youngest, Billy, doesn't talk. When I say he doesn't talk, he does talk but is struggling.' Grace pointed to her eye.

'Say no more, you're back now and we all will look after you. Just promise me one thing...' Grace looked at Felicity. 'No matter how hard things get, do not disappear like that ever again. We went through hell and back until your letter arrived to say you were okay. I know your grandfather was strict and it felt tough for you without your mum, but that doesn't mean any of us ever stopped caring.'

Grace waved her hand in front of her face. 'Don't, you'll make me cry, you're being so kind. I was so nervous walking back in here. I didn't know how you'd react.'

'I'm just glad you're back.' Felicity hugged Grace again. 'I want to know all about the forgotten years but let's get the drinks to the boys and food in their stomachs.'

'Thank you, Flick, you've made me feel...' Grace's voice faltered, and she swallowed a lump. 'Very welcome.'

Felicity gave Grace a look that told her she was no longer on her own, she had a friend for life, and that had never changed.

'Billy ... Freddie ... Joey ... I want you to meet one of my oldest best friends, Felicity! Felicity owns the teashop with her mum Rona.'

Three pairs of eyes looked up at Felicity. 'Look at you, all so adorable!' she gushed.

Freddie bypassed the compliment and pointed over to the glass counter where one of the trays was laden with gingerbread men. 'So are all those gingerbread men actually yours?' he asked.

Felicity laughed. 'They sure are, would you like one?'

Freddie looked fit to burst. 'Yes, please!' he replied, sitting up straight in his chair and looking towards the glass counter.

'After your breakfast, which happens to be here!' Grace pulled out a chair and seated herself next to Billy. 'Look at this, boys, this feast is fit for a king!'

'Well, that's good,' declared Joey, 'because we are just about to become kings of the Castle.'

Grace smiled at her three boys. 'And you are all just the best kings.'

Rona placed the tray on the table next to them then handed out four full Scottish breakfasts. 'The toast is just coming. We have sausages and bacon from Foxglove Farm, fried eggs from the chickens at the farm too, baked beans, haggis, fried tomatoes and mushrooms.'

'What's haggis?' asked Joey, looking at the mountain of food on his plate.

'Something you will be eating a lot of now you live in Scotland,' replied Grace.

With no further questions and a mouth-watering breakfast waiting to be demolished, the boys picked up their knives and forks and began to eat.

'And, boys, every time you find yourself near Love Heart Lane you be sure to pop in for a free gingerbread man.' Felicity gave Grace's shoulder a small squeeze. 'They were always your mum's favourite too.'

'FREE! That'll be every day!' declared Freddie.

'Thank you,' replied Grace.

She looked proudly at her three boys.

'I think I'm going to like this place,' shared Joey. 'Everyone smiles.'

'Is a very colourful place,' added Freddie, looking around the teashop. 'And it smells so good.' He wrinkled his nose and took a big sniff, making Grace laugh.

'What about you, Billy, do you think you are going to like this place?'

Billy gave a beatific smile that lit up his whole face and waggled a sausage in the air on the end of his fork.

'I take it that's a yes.'

Yesterday, after leaving the cold and dingy high-rise flat on the council estate, and with a long journey ahead, Grace had questioned whether she was doing the right thing running back to Heartcross. For a very long time she had thought of it as a place of unhappiness, a place where she would never be happy again, yet within an hour of arriving her boys looked more relaxed than she had seen them for a long time.

Rona had popped four gingerbread men into white paper bags and balanced them on the edge of the table. 'One for you too,' she said, touching Grace's shoulder before heading back into the kitchen. 'It's so good to have you back.'

'It's good to be back,' replied Grace, meaning every word.

The moment Felicity had thrown her arms around her, she had felt the familiar warmth of her friendship flooding back. She'd missed her and had never known how much until now. It was funny: last week she would never have predicted she would be back sitting in the teashop in Heartcross alongside her three boys. It was true, you never know what is around the corner. The old life they'd left behind only a little over twenty-four hours earlier was already becoming a distant memory.

Chapter Four

'**W**ow!' exclaimed Joey. 'It's huge!'

Heartcross Castle was built around 1660 and was situated on the bend of the River Heart, dominating the skyline of Heartcross. Grace couldn't help admiring the perfect backdrop of the cobalt sky and mountainous terrain as she walked across the bridge with the boys.

'How are we ever going to find our way around inside?' asked Freddie. 'It's going to be the best game of hide and seek.'

'Let's just not go getting lost as soon as we step inside,' suggested Grace, noticing Billy was lagging behind. Even with a full breakfast inside his tummy, he looked tired – it had been an exhausting twenty-four hours. She walked back towards him and hoisted him up on to her back. 'Hold on tight, not long to go.'

With his arms cradling Grace's neck Billy rested his head

63

on her shoulder, looking up at the gigantic Castle in front of him.

'Keep walking, Joey, not far to go,' encouraged Grace, wheeling the holdall behind her whilst navigating the tourists standing on the bridge taking photographs of the River Heart.

But Joey had stopped dead in his tracks. He pointed towards the Castle steps.

'There are one hundred and fifty steps in total. Fact,' shared Grace.

'That's going to take for ever. It'll be midnight before we get to the top,' protested Joey.

'Not if you know a secret passage that leads from the gatehouse at the bottom to the Castle entrance.' She winked. 'One last spurt, boys, and we can explore our new home. Thankfully we don't need to go out again today for anything else.'

When they left the teashop Rona had slipped them a bottle of juice, teabags and milk and suggested that they put a box of food together for Grace and drop it off after the dinner-time rush, so they could settle in and didn't need to worry about food for tonight. Grace was extremely grateful for their kindness; this would definitely make things a little easier today.

Within five minutes they were standing at the gates of the Castle. Grace lowered Billy to the ground. She felt emotional. All those years ago she'd flounced from the Castle late at night, not taking the easy route through the passage but stomping down all of the one hundred and fifty steps. Her grandfather had never followed her. He'd probably thought she would be back the following day with her tail between her legs. What he hadn't realised was how stubborn and resilient Grace actually was.

The Castle towered over them, and she listened to Joey and Freddie having a playful debate about whether the turrets actually touched the sky. While they decided they most probably did, Grace wondered how her grandfather had come to live in a place like this. She wasn't sure how he'd accumulated enough wealth to own one of the most stunning castles in the Scottish Highlands.

Grace noticed the security guards standing at the main entrance to the Castle and assumed they were positioned there to stop Andrew's fans wandering into the grounds. Thankfully, Grace knew of a separate entrance. With the impressive stone gatehouse standing boldly in front of them, she found the correct key and pushed open the creaky door.

'It's a bit creepy,' observed Freddie, who was usually the bolder of the twins. 'Do you think people have died in here?'

Grace didn't think this was the time to point out that the holes on the battlements were called murder holes and were where boiling tar and human waste were poured to kill invaders. 'Don't be daft,' she jollied. 'It's not so bad in the daylight. Come on, wait until you see this. You are going to love it.'

None of the boys looked convinced, and they let Grace go first. She turned around and smiled at them. 'It's still here. Honestly, boys, you are going to love this. Remember the magic elevator in *Charlie and the Chocolate Factory*? This is the Castle's magic elevator and not many people know it exists. Look.'

Attached to the stone wall of the gatehouse were four metal seats attached to rails. There was an operation panel on the wall with buttons including an emergency stop button. One button was marked 'Castle Entrance'.

'Jump on to a seat.'

The boys stayed standing still.

'Come on, it's either this or we have to climb up all the stone steps… The choice is yours.'

All three boys weighed up their options and the prehistoric contraption in front of them won hands down. They climbed on to the metal seats, then, balancing the holdall across her knee, Grace reached over and pressed the button. 'Let's hope this still works. Are we ready?'

Looking petrified, the boys clutched at the cold metal handrails either side of them. The sound of metal rubbing against metal, squeaks and more squeaks echoed all around, then the metallic hum of the machinery sounded as the metal seats began to move slowly upwards.

The boys' enthusiasm immediately rocketed.

'Wow!' Joey exclaimed, 'this is so cool.'

'Isn't it just,' replied Grace, giving Billy's knee a squeeze.

As the lift continued its jerky shuddering ascent towards

the Castle, the darkness of the gloomy gatehouse disappeared and they were now riding in the fresh air alongside the steps leading up to the Castle entrance.

The boys began squealing with delight. 'This is magic,' said Joey with a grin, 'Look at the Castle.'

Everyone's eyes turned towards the impressive Castle, towering over the village and town in all its glory.

'It's like Cinderella's Castle,' hollered Freddie over the sound of the clanging machinery. 'We are actually going to live in a proper Castle!'

'Boys, I need you to promise me one thing. We all need to look after each from now on. Deal?'

'Deal!' they all chorused, not questioning Grace in the slightest.

'And look at the river,' Joey pointed.

The view was impressive, they could see for miles around. They stared out at the sterling blue river lapping against the rocky shoreline of colourful stones. The water taxi was heading back towards the boathouse. 'Can you see that small sandy bay, boys?' Grace pointed further down the river. 'It's the perfect spot for a picnic and paddling,' she said, remembering a fantastic Sunday she'd spent with her grandfather when she was a small child. Grace was beginning to realise that past times weren't always as tainted as she'd wanted to believe.

'Can we go soon?' asked Freddie.

'Absolutely, and we can take a picnic just like I did when I went with my grandfather all those years back. And there's lots of small fish in those shallow parts you can try and catch.'

'Can we buy some fishing nets from the village shop?' asked Joey.

'I'm sure we can.'

Hearing a loud creak, Grace looked in front of her. The moving seats levelled with the ground then halted.

They all jumped down to the ground. 'What did you think to that?' asked Grace, taking Billy's hand.

'Amazing!' said Freddie, 'It was like flying in the sky.'

Grace smiled. 'It saved us traipsing up those steps but we won't be taking the lazy route every time,' she said, standing at the foot of the Castle. This was the first time she actually appreciated how beautiful it was up close and how spectacular the setting. In fact everything about the Castle had been designed to make a statement and impress everyone that set eyes upon it, and it didn't disappoint. As a teenager Grace just hadn't appreciated the beauty of the place but now it was simply stunning. For the time being, until she decided their next plan of action, this was her sanctuary, a safe haven for her and the boys, and she couldn't wait to show them inside.

'Do you think it's haunted?' asked Joey, looking at Grace then back towards the Castle.

'No, don't be daft,' she replied, knowing there were always rumours that the Castle was haunted but she would not be repeating that to the boys any time soon. She remembered there was a suit of armour just hanging around in the hallway and it used to scare her silly. Then there were the old paintings of aristocracy that hung in the Grand Hall, their eyes following her around the room. She always felt like she was being watched. The Hall was vast, with windows from floor to ceiling, and with a view over the Castle gardens. Grace remembered the long oak table that seated over forty guests and huge floral displays in each corner of the room. The chandelier that hung in the centre of the ceiling, bigger than a small car. That room was kept for best and was only used for special occasions. Then there was the secret passageway that led from the library and linked the main Castle to the servants' quarters.

'How do we get up there?' asked Joey, pointing up at the tower. 'I bet you can touch the aeroplanes from up there.'

Freddie pushed Joey playfully. 'Don't be an idiot, as if you can reach the aeroplanes.'

'I bet you can,' protested Joey.

Grace could still remember how to get to the tower, though it was somewhere she hadn't been more than twice. She wasn't keen on heights or the steep spiral steps that led to the very top of the tower.

'Boys, don't start bickering now, let's get inside and we can explore. How exciting is this?'

Grace dropped the holdall outside the sturdy double oak doors. 'Home sweet home,' she murmured.

Taking a deep breath, she turned the key and stepped on to the worn red carpet that stretched out in front of her. It wasn't quite what she was expecting. Once it resembled a carpet that film stars would walk down on the night of their film premiere, but now the flea-bitten thing was threadbare and had seen better days. Even though it was July, the instant coldness of the place reminded Grace of winter. She remembered the heat was mainly generated by open fires in every room. There was a log store outside the main kitchen at the back of the Castle, which housed logs that the lumberjack chopped down from the trees in the Castle grounds each year. It had been a mammoth task lugging the logs in each morning to keep the fires burning inside the Castle in the winter months, and if that was still the case, Grace didn't look forward to that task each day.

The entrance hall was bigger than the flat that they had just left behind. Once this had been filled with extravagant furniture and watercolour landscapes hanging on the wall that wouldn't have looked out of place in a royal palace, but all there was now was a tattered throne-like velvet chair and a dusty dresser which Grace remembered used to have pride of place, filled with framed photographs of people she never knew. Off the entrance hall was a cloakroom and directly above the once-stunning staircase was a regally arching balcony, but now the paint was chipped and looked drab. The once-immaculate wallpaper was torn, damp and flapping in the draft of a broken window. Grace shivered; it seemed to be warmer outside than in.

'I'm not sure Cinderella would live in a Castle like this,' remarked Joey, straining his neck and looking up at the high ceilings that swirled with yellow-coated aertex stained by the sun shining through the window. The chandelier was swamped with cobwebs. Grace reached and switched the lights on. Nothing.

She couldn't agree more: everything looked in a state and not how she remembered it. 'Shall we have a look downstairs first?' she asked, looking at the three unimpressed boys in front of her.

Freddie shrugged.

Grace knew they were expecting to walk into rooms bursting with colour, lush carpet underneath their feet, extravagant drapes hanging from the windows, and oversized comfy furniture. She'd thought this wasn't going to be the case, but she hadn't anticipated this kind of welcome. From the outside the Castle seemed like a stunning piece of architecture that one could only dream of living in, yet inside it was a different story, one of sadness and a love that had been extinguished a long time ago.

The boys followed Grace along the grand hallway, where once a plush carpet lined the way but now they were walking on a dusty wooden floor. The pictures that lined the walls were long gone, leaving visible outlines on the faded wallpaper where they once hung.

'The living room is just down here.' Grace swung open a door and peered inside. 'Okay, maybe not what I was expecting.' The room was vast with an impressive inglenook, logs stacked up at the side. There was one leather wingback chair with a crimson cushion and a small coffee table. Noticing the items on the coffee table, Grace felt a flurry of goosebumps. Abandoned was a pair of spectacles and a newspaper. She walked across and picked up the newspaper; it was dated the 20th of June, two days before her grandfather had passed away. Folding up the newspaper and resting the spectacles on top, she felt a wave of sadness at the way her grandfather had been living. His final days in this place must have been excruciatingly lonely.

'Where's the TV, settee?' asked Joey, standing in the middle of the vast open space with his hands on his hips.

'I'm not quite sure,' answered Grace, a little perplexed as to where all the furniture had disappeared. Everything had gone. She walked over to the window and gasped. 'But, boys, come and look at this.'

The boys ran over to her with new enthusiasm and stood by her side. 'What are we looking at?' asked Freddie.

'That view, look at the view! It's amazing … out of this world.'

The boys looked up at her like she'd gone completely mad.

'You can see everything from this window – look, you can even make out the alpaca farm and there's the river and the boats,' said Grace, trying to muster up a little interest from the boys. But if the truth be known she felt as deflated as they did; they might have a roof over their heads but it really wasn't what she was expecting at all. The dream of walking into a showroom was quenched the second she'd opened the Castle door. How exactly were they going to live like this, with nowhere to sit?

'Just think, this is an adventure, we can paint these walls any colour we want, make it our own,' she said, trying to stir up more enthusiasm.

'And buy a huge TV,' chipped in Joey, looking hopeful.

Grace knew the cost of furnishing this place to even a basic standard would be astronomical, and with no job at present, how the hell was she going to afford that? But she wasn't a quitter, she was a believer, and had to focus on the positives. She and the boys were safe and that was her first priority; and she was hopeful that the rent from Andrew Glossop would at least see her through each week until a rich tycoon snapped up this historical place.

'We will see,' replied Grace. 'It's our first day here and things can only get better. Let's keep exploring. Are we ready for the next room, explorers Billy, Freddie and Joey?' She saluted, trying to rally the children around, and with a half-hearted salute in return they followed Grace back down the hallway.

'There's more stairs,' Freddie said, pointing in front of them.

'There are quite a few staircases and even a secret spiral one from the upstairs bedroom! But look at this room – the Grand Hall. The place where the lords and ladies, the kings and queens would dine and dance.' Grace pushed open the door. She felt like time had stood still; the room was exactly the same as twenty years ago. The long oak table that stood in the centre of the room, a table that accommodated approximately forty diners. Grace stretched out her arms and began to waltz around the room, making the boys giggle. Then the twins dropped their rucksacks onto the floor and began to chase each other around the table, Billy following his brothers. There was another impressive fireplace and windows from the floor to the ceiling.

Grace looked out over the private garden. This part had never been open to the general public in the past. Bizarrely, the gardens were immaculate, unlike the inside of the Castle. She looked over to the walled patio and beyond a lawn with pruned and shaped hedging. The edges of the lawn were flanked with trees and, if Grace remembered rightly, there were possibly plum trees at the end of the garden. The path through the lawned area led to the best part of the garden, where the greenhouses were, the place Grace most loved and escaped to when she living here. Beyond that was a small courtyard behind the kitchen, and across the way the servants' quarters. Beyond again was the Castle shop and the grounds that were open to the public. There had always been a specular display of colourful blooms, trees and a water fountain. She smiled as she remembered the maze. The boys were going to love the maze, if it was still there, of course.

With the boys still chasing each other around the table, Grace stood in front of yet another open fireplace and looked up. There he was, Marley Power, her grandfather, staring back at her. He looked regal in his army uniform with a long row of medals pinned to his jacket. Grace was aware he'd served in the war, but didn't know any other details. He looked distinguished and handsome and seemed to be staring back at her. That painting had hung there for as long as Grace could remember. A proud soldier who served his country. Standing there, Grace realised she knew nothing about her grandfather's military life. This made her feel a little sad as she wished she'd taken the time to get know him when he was alive, hear stories about his life that she could pass on to the boys.

'Mum, please can we have a drink?' asked Joey, trying to catch his breath after tearing around the table umpteen times.

'Of course, come on, let's go to the kitchen,' she replied, taking one last look at the painting before scooping up the rucksacks from the floor. 'This way.'

She led the boys back down the hallway to the kitchen at the bottom on the right. Every room in the Castle was huge and the kitchen was no exception.

'There you go, boys, a settee!'

Immediately the boys bounded over to it and jumped straight on to it.

'And a TV!' noticed Joey, scrambling for the remote control.

Granted, it wasn't a state-of-the-art TV but it was still a TV. Looking around the kitchen, Grace realised this must have been where her grandfather spent most of his time. It made sense; living in one room where you had everything close by.

She walked around the huge island in the middle of the kitchen. The cupboards were still the same from years ago. Herb pots soaked up the sunlight on the window sills and there were shelves of dusty cookbooks that had probably never been read. The greasy hood towered over the cooker, and a pungent smell came from the kitchen bin in the corner. The Belfast sink was full of dirty dishes and cereal floating in dishwater. Grace was in need of a pair of

Marigolds, and this kitchen needed a good dose of disinfectant. There were shopping lists stuck to the front of the fridge in what, after all this time, she still recognised as her grandfather's writing. The flowery ceramic tea, coffee and sugar jars standing by the kettle were the same jars. A dried-out teabag lay on a teaspoon next to the kettle with a bottle of milk that hadn't been returned to the fridge.

The TV came on, proving that there was power in this part of the Castle. There was also a small open fire with a pile of logs in a worn-out wicker basket to the side. Stools stood under the island and wooden chairs were tucked under the old oak table – the same table where Grace used to eat her meals. She walked to the far end of the table, lifted up the old round placemat and ran her finger over the carved words in the wood. 'I love you.' She remembered at every mealtime always sitting in the same place. When she was a young girl she'd carved the words in the table with her knife. At first her grandfather wasn't too impressed with her graffiti until Grace explained that whenever she wasn't there he could look at the words and they would make him smile. Her grandfather liked her explanation but now Grace was downhearted – how many times had he looked at those words since she left? Back in the Castle, she was remembering more of the good times that had completely slipped her mind.

Hearing the roar of an engine outside the kitchen window, Grace walked over and looked out. Parked in the courtyard to the right was a car that wouldn't look out of place in a James Bond movie, and there was Andrew

Glossop striding towards it with a huge smile on his face. Grace gawped at him – she couldn't help it. She knew a gorgeous man when she saw one. Andrew was now wearing a black dinner suit which was exquisitely cut, sharp-looking and well fitted. Even though he was a complete stranger to her, he also seemed very familiar. For a moment Grace lost herself in watching him. He opened the door of the car and another man climbed out and shook his hand heartily before slapping him lightly on the back; he was similarly dressed. They stood chatting for a moment before Grace noticed a man and a woman walking towards them. The man was balancing a camera on his shoulder whilst the woman was holding a long fluffy microphone, just like ones that Grace had seen many times on TV when she'd been watching the news. They were being filmed.

'Wow! Look at that car.' Freddie was standing on tiptoes peering over the herb pots in the window.

'You only have of those if you are a millionaire,' exclaimed Joey, standing next to his brother.

'Billionaire!' replied Freddie. 'Can we go and have a look?'

The moment was broken by the sound of the doorbell ringing.

Everyone stood still.

'Who's that?' asked Freddie.

Joey threw up his hands. 'How do we know until we answer it?'

'You boys stay here whilst I go and see who it is,' Grace ordered as she hurried out of the kitchen, hearing the bell sound again. It seemed a little surreal wandering down the hallway towards the giant double doors. On the other side stood Felicity and Rona, smiling and holding two large cardboard boxes packed with food and household necessities.

'We have a box of food and other bits and bobs you may need,' said Felicity, juggling a heavy-looking box.

'Step inside. This is amazing. Thank you so much,' exclaimed Grace, astonished by their generosity. 'I wasn't expecting all this.'

'You nearly didn't have it. We had to get through security at the Castle gates,' replied Rona, placing the box on the dusty dresser in the entrance hall before staring up at the ceiling and taking a good look around the room.

'I suppose I should have a chat with them to let them know I'm back.'

'Or fly a flag from the tower,' joked Felicity, 'let everyone know you are back in residence!'

'Those security men have become a regular feature,' added Rona. 'Since Andrew has been in residence, hordes of fans hang around those gates.'

'Every girl swooning on their Instagram hoping they are going to become Mrs Glossop – and look at you, living right next door.' Felicity gave a chuckle. 'Heartcross Castle has thousands of posts every day, it's become very famous. Tourists hang out at those gates all day and sometimes block the road. Check it out on your phone.'

'Just to get a glimpse of Andrew?' questioned Grace.

'Exactly that,' replied Felicity. 'Honestly, check out his social media.'

Grace could see why Andrew Glossop was popular. His looks were striking, and in his dinner suit he looked more like a catwalk model than a chef.

'I would but I don't have a phone,' admitted Grace. 'I left it behind,' she confessed. 'And I'll have to do without one until I work out my financial situation. I've literally arrived home with fewer belongings than I ran away with and I wasn't expecting the state of this place to be so—'

'In need of so much love,' cut in Rona. 'It's a little depressing,' she said, taking a look around the hallway.

'You haven't seen anything yet. I'm just beginning to question whether I should have brought the boys here without checking it out first – but I really didn't have any choice.'

'The Castle gardens were shut to the public soon after you left. I suppose without the revenue it was difficult to maintain the upkeep of this place,' added Rona.

'I'll need a miracle to help modernise this place.' Grace was feeling guilty at Rona's words. Was she the reason that the place was left to rack and ruin?

'Why did my grandfather close the Castle to the public, do you know?' asked Grace.

The look between Felicity and Rona didn't go unnoticed.

'The rumour is retirement and heartbreak,' replied Felicity, placing a hand on Grace's arm.

'We know you butted heads with your grandfather and

he was a little strict as you got older. Believe me, we've had our moments, haven't we?' Rona looked towards Felicity, who looked a little sheepish. 'And with the loss of your mother, you must have been consumed with grief. It's such a difficult thing to cope with at my age, never mind yours. You mustn't have known whether you were coming or going.'

Grace knew that Rona must have experienced the same sense of loss when her own mother passed away. 'It was difficult ... still is difficult. I try not to think about it,' admitted Grace. 'I just wish I could change—'

'Now don't dwell,' cut in Rona. 'It won't change anything. Concentrate on you and those boys. I've popped some cream in the box for that cut on your face. If nothing else, you are safe now.'

'Thank you, I am. Fresh start. If I'm honest with you both, my relationship was over years ago and I'm not sure why I didn't come back then.'

'You are here now and that's all that matters,' reassured Rona.

'I am and thank you for all this.' Grace was touched by their kindness.

'I hope you don't mind, but I've let Isla and Allie know you're back and they are excited to catch up with you,' chipped in Felicity. 'It took them a while to believe me.'

'I bet, and I don't mind at all, it'll be good to see them,' replied Grace.

'We will leave you to settle in. You must be exhausted. But please just shout if you need anything,' encouraged Rona.

'I will.' Grace watched as they climbed into their car and drove slowly down the long sloping driveway towards the gates. The security men stepped aside as the gates opened.

One of the boxes that they'd left behind was filled with household cleaning products, toilet rolls and bin bags and a pair of Marigolds – it was like they'd read Grace's mind. In the second box there was everything from cereal, milk, teabags and pastries to a homemade lasagne, which only needed to be popped into the oven. Grace was close to tears. She hadn't seen these people for over ten years and here they were, going out of their way to help her, their kindness taking her completely by surprise.

Lifting up the first box she headed back towards the kitchen and instantly felt a breeze. The door leading to the courtyard was wide open. Quickly, Grace placed the box on the island and hurried to the door. She looked over towards the posh car, but the boys weren't anywhere to be seen.

Feeling a little panicky, Grace called out, 'Boys.' She walked out into the middle of the courtyard and looked all around, but still there was no sign of them. With her heart thumping nineteen to the dozen, she took off across the courtyard shouting out their names. Out of the corner of her eye she spotted movement at the side of the servants' quarters. All three boys were standing on overturned wooden barrels peeping through a window.

'Boys, what do you think you're doing? Get down at once.'

Joey flapped his hand, 'Come and take a look,' he whispered.

'We can't go peeping through windows,' said Grace. 'That's being nosey.' But curiosity got the better of her and she stood on tiptoes to take a peep.

Inside was a hive of activity. 'Look at that place.' Through the window the present told a different story from the past. The servants' quarters no longer looked like the dark, dreary rooms that no one had frequented for years, but were now a vibrant, colourful setting for what looked like an intimate dinner. Andrew Glossop and the man that Grace had seen in the car park were sitting at a table that looked as if it belonged in a fancy restaurant. Alongside them were two beautiful woman dressing in the most stunning of outfits and sipping from crystal champagne flutes. They were being filmed by a TV crew. It looked like some sort of promotional video. Grace and the boys watched in silence.

'What's that?' whispered Joey as a waiter appeared balancing four plates of food on his arm. 'Why are they eating shells?'

Grace watched as he placed the food down on the table, then poured more champagne. She chuckled. 'They're eating oysters,' she said, keeping her voice low. 'Come on, let's leave them to it. And don't you three go disappearing on me again without telling me – you nearly gave me a heart attack.'

Joey turned round on top of the barrel, which began to wobble.

'Joey, keep still.'

But it was too late, the barrel overturned and came

crashing down with a loud clatter as it hit an old wheelbarrow. Joey screamed but, much to Grace's surprise, landed on his feet. She quickly looked back through the window, hoping that the chaos outside had gone unnoticed, but that hope disappeared when she locked eyes with Andrew. Instantly, she was hit with a sinking feeling. He'd caught them watching. For a second he held her gaze and Grace forced a sorry-for-making-a-noise smile on her face, but Andrew's look didn't soften. He was up out of his chair and heading towards the door.

'Quick, boys, run back to the kitchen,' ordered Grace, swinging Billy to his feet. 'GO!'

The boys took off faster than Usain Bolt. She grinned. Those ragamuffins – always up to mischief. But then she turned back to face Andrew Glossop, who was tapping his extravagant-looking watch. Grace found herself staring at him with a fluttering of nervousness in her stomach. This was Andrew Glossop, international superstar and a vison of total gorgeousness. The expensive waft of his aftershave made her body tingle in a way she hadn't felt for years. At first Grace had wondered what all the fuss was about, why there was security at the Castle gates, why girls were swooning at his feet and hanging around the Castle gates for a glimpse of him . . . he was just a normal person like everyone else. But now, coming face to face with him, Grace knew exactly why: he was captivating.

'Good afternoon,' she chirped with a smile, wishing to God she didn't look like she'd just rolled off a train after a twenty-four-hour journey with no sleep or shower, but that's exactly what she did look like and there was nothing she could do about it now.

But Andrew frowned. 'You are late, you should have been here one hour ago, and where is your uniform?' His tone was firm.

'Uniform?' queried Grace, not having a clue what he was talking about.

'Yes, your uniform,' replied Andrew. 'I'm assuming you have a bag with you to change?'

'Change?' asked Grace, looking down at her bobbled baggy jumper and scuffed worn-out boots that hadn't been polished in a lifetime. She noticed some sort of stain on her jeans and licked her finger to try and rub it off.

'And what is that smell?' continued Andrew, sniffing in the air like one of those police dogs in documentaries on TV.

'Possibly me … eau de natural,' said Grace with a French accent. She lifted up her arm and smelled her armpit, making Andrew's eyes widen. There was no question about it, she was in definite need of a shower. While Grace tried to stifle her laughter, a look of horror spread across his face. She knew she was winding him up, but couldn't quite help herself. 'Who do you think I am?' she asked.

'My new housekeeper… Are you my new housekeeper?' asked Andrew slowly, now watching her closely.

Grace shook her head. 'Afraid not.'

'Then who are you? And how have you got through the

security?' He tilted his head to one side and watched Grace closely.

'To be honest, those security men are a waste of time. I'm sure they were napping when I sneaked past them.'

Andrew's jaw fell wide open. He reached inside his pocket and pulled out his phone and began frantically scrolling.

'You need to remove yourself from these premises. This is private property.'

Grace extended her hand and gave him the warmest of smiles. 'Grace Power, pleased to meet you.'

Instantly, Andrew's eyebrows rose. 'Power?'

'Yes, Power,' she repeated.

Grace could see panic ricocheting through Andrew's body as he suddenly realised the mistake he had just made.

'And I'm sorry I don't smell the best, I've been travelling for the past day and literally have just arrived.' Grace held out her hand. 'Grand-daughter of Marley Power, and the new owner of Heartcross Castle.'

Andrew held her gaze as he shook her hand. 'I'm so sorry, I really am,' he apologised. 'I thought you were the new housekeeper. I'm absolutely mortified.'

'There's no need to apologise, but it looks like you still don't have a housekeeper, I'm afraid.'

'But it seems like I have a new landlady,' he said, smiling broadly, 'and I still can't believe—'

'Don't worry about it,' she cut in. 'And I think it's probably best I go and have a shower,' she said, sniffing again. 'Yep, that's exactly what I need to do. You get back to what you were doing. No doubt we will be seeing a lot of each other,' she added with a smile before she turned and walked back across the courtyard towards the kitchen door. She didn't look back over her shoulder but she knew Andrew was watching her every step of the way.

Chapter Five

G race was standing over the double bed watching the three boys sleeping. She couldn't quite believe that out of seven bedrooms, this was the only one in the Castle with a bed in it. The upstairs of the Castle was just as shabby as the downstairs, vast rooms abandoned with the odd rug or wooden chair scattered about. The boys had flopped just a little after 7 p.m., exhausted from the travelling but content, stomachs full of Rona's homemade lasagne.

After kissing them lightly on their heads, she watched them sleep for a moment longer. They all looked so peaceful. Even though they were a joy they could be a handful at times. The twins weren't identical and each had his own distinct personality: Freddie was the one who would always instigate mischief whilst Joey was a little more sensitive and took things a little more seriously. He was a deep thinker and sometimes asked questions that

Grace found difficult to answer. Billy was Billy, lovable, adorable Billy, who gave the best cuddles, but Grace was worried about him. He hadn't spoken since he'd witnessed Cole strike her; he was traumatised, and Grace was hoping that in the security of their new home he would feel settled and loved once more. Today, all three of them had been brilliant; they had just got on with everything, and even though the Castle wasn't quite what everyone was expecting, they'd taken it in their stride and treated it like one huge adventure.

Tonight, Grace had no option but to make herself comfy on the settee in the kitchen for the night. It wasn't where she was expecting to sleep, but she didn't mind. Knowing she could finally breathe again, this was the first night for as long as Grace could remember when she wasn't consumed with anxiety. There wasn't the fear of hearing Cole's key in the door, there weren't the arguments in the flat above and she certainly wasn't walking on eggshells. Despite the Castle being in a state, Grace felt like a huge weight had been lifted off her shoulders.

Quietly, she padded down the spiral staircase that led to the kitchen. Even though she felt shattered, Grace's first job of the evening was to give the kitchen a good scrub down. She picked up the boys' shoes which had been kicked off and lined them up near the back door, and plumped up the well-worn cushions on the settee that had seen better days. Then, pulling on the bright-yellow Marigolds, Grace switched on the radio that was standing on a small wooden table at the side on the settee. It sprang into life and she smiled at the upbeat song that played and danced her way over to the Belfast sink, which she filled with hot water and squirted in a lovely zesty lemon-smelling disinfectant that Felicity had packed in the box. Grace inhaled the fresh smell, which thankfully was overpowering the musty smell of the kitchen. Finding a floral rag in one of the drawers, she tied it around her head to keep her hair off her face, then set to work.

After disinfecting all the worktops, bleaching the Belfast sink and wiping down the cooker hood, Grace disposed of the rancid bin outside, then sprayed air freshener. She boiled the kettle then filled up the mop bucket. It didn't take long before the whole room was beginning to gleam and feel a little more homely. Hearing one of her favourite songs on the radio, she turned up the volume and jigged in front of the mirror, posing and singing her heart out. Grace couldn't remember the last time she'd felt so free and relaxed, and dancing around the kitchen she made a promise to herself to do it more often. She stepped onto the coffee table and played air guitar before leaping off. When her feet were on the ground, a movement caught her eye in the mirror. Startled, she spun round and locked eyes with an amused-looking Andrew, who was staring back at her through the glass in the back door. Bringing her hand up to her beating heart she blew out a breath, then grinned.

With her sleeves rolled up her arms and her bright-yellow Marigolds on show, Grace walked towards the door, casually propped the mop against the worktop, and stepped outside. She had already noticed he'd changed from his earlier attire and was now wearing a navy-blue T-shirt with a designer logo. It clung to his torso, which she admired. And there it was again, that tingle – goosebumps and flutters in her stomach. He actually made her nervous, but in a good way. There was just something about him.

'Busted!' She grinned. 'You can't beat a little bit of lip-syncing to Whitney Houston whilst cleaning, can you?'

'I quite agree, she's my go-to after a hard day at work too,' replied Andrew with a twinkle in his eye.

'Really?' questioned Grace, taken by surprise.

Andrew shook his head. 'Er, no!' he replied, laughing. 'But do you do requests?'

'Maybe … maybe not,' she joked. For a second they held each other's gaze, then Grace shook her head and laughed. 'What brings you over to this side of the courtyard?'

'I'm here to grovel, apologise again.'

'Sorry for—'

'Sorry for mistaking you for the hired help, who wasn't hired and didn't actually turn up. You kind of took me by surprise so I thought I'd pop over and introduce myself properly. I'm Andrew,' he said, holding out his hand, and Grace shook it. 'But it is a shame about the requests,' he said with a smile, looking down at the bright-yellow Marigold.

'Believe me, you've been saved. I'm actually tone deaf, but my lip-syncing isn't bad. Apology accepted.'

'That's a relief,' he replied. He stepped forward and lightly kissed Grace on each cheek, taking her completely by surprise. She supposed that's what the rich and famous did. She noted the aroma of his divine spicy masculine aftershave.

'And by way of an apology, I've brought you this. Call it a grovelling-cum-moving-into-the-Castle house-warming present.' He handed Grace a bottle of expensive wine which she stared at. 'Even though I'm sure your wine cellar is full to the brim, please accept this.'

Grace knew there was no wine in the cellar at all, as she'd already explored that area of the Castle. It was now just an empty room full of wooden racks that housed a million spiders. She also knew the price of the wine she was now holding in her hand, not because she'd ever been in the fortunate position of being able to purchase a bottle – she could never have afforded such extravagance – but because in the past she'd worked in a pub. She remembered a case of this wine in the cellar, hidden away under lock and key. The landlord claimed it was there just in case royalty ever dropped in. And here was Andrew casually giving it away.

'I can't accept this.' Grace was cradling the bottle in her hands like she'd just been given the crown jewels to hold.

'Why not?' Asked Andrew. 'It's just a bottle of wine.'

'A bottle of Lambrini is just a bottle of wine.'

Andrew looked puzzled. 'I have to admit that's one I've not heard of. I'll have to look it up.'

'You do that, you'll love it,' she replied, knowing full well that Andrew didn't look like he'd ever sipped wine that cost less than five pounds. 'But this is still too much.'

'I insist. And these are for you from Delia and Nigella.' He held up a carrier bag.

'Delia Smith and Nigella Lawson?' Grace was taken by surprise, 'Are they neighbours?' she asked, thinking this town was becoming more like the glitz and glamour of Hollywood.

'You could say that. They live just down through the walled garden, left of the greenhouses, and you'll find them mainly scratching about under the hedgerows or taking dust baths in the soil, but they do live in a mighty fine coop.'

Grace laughed. 'Chickens!'

'They are indeed,' he said, handing her the bag. 'Enjoy!'

'I'll have these for breakfast. Would you like to come in and share a glass of wine?'

Andrew shook his head. 'Unfortunately, I have a prior engagement,' he said, looking up at the sky, and Grace followed his gaze.

Suddenly, she became aware of a whirling noise above and was amazed to witness a royal-blue helicopter hovering above the Castle gardens. 'That's for you?' she exclaimed. 'It's like something for the rich and famous.' As soon as the words left her mouth – 'You are the rich and famous,' she added, grinning.

He touched her elbow. 'Another time. I'll hold you to that and you can treat me to a bottle of Lambr—'

'Lambrini,' Grace finished off his sentence. 'Deal!'

'How are you settling in? It must be exciting. I've never actually been inside,' he said, looking at Grace. 'I can see your grandfather had begun to renovate the kitchen.'

Grace looked over her shoulder. She could see it possibly looked that way.

'I have the best kitchen designers. If you need any ideas, I can put you in touch with the best people. Mine was good value for money, just short of two hundred.'

'Two hundre...'

'Thousand,' said Andrew.

Grace gulped. 'Absolute bargain, I'll bear that in mind.'

'Oh, before I go – Rose used to deal with this.'

'Rose?'

'My cleaner, admin assistant and a complete godsend. A good all-rounder, technically a personal assistant.' Andrew took out a small red book bound by an elastic band with what seemed like a wad of cash folded up inside, and handed it to Grace.

'My rent money. Your grandfather liked things the simple way. My rent paid on the tenth of the month by cash and he'd tick off my book. He wasn't one for technology or bank transfers. So if you could just initial in the received column, I'm assuming this method works for you?'

Grace was astounded. She couldn't take her eyes off the money. The instant relief at seeing the cash washed over her. She had to do everything in her power not to punch the air or lean across and place a huge whopper of a kiss on Andrew's lips. He'd just taken away her biggest worry of the month and he had no clue. But somehow Grace managed to stay calm. 'Absolutely, works for me,' she replied.

'Good, good, and please pop it back to Rose at some point.'

'Of course.'

'And what are you doing?' Andrew looked down at her yellow Marigolds. 'Why don't you get your people to do the cleaning?'

'People?' Grace was mystified.

'Yes, assistants. I suppose "servants" is an old-fashioned term these days. Oh, and just for the record, I'm loving the designer headband,' he added with a grin. 'Suits you.'

'Only the best designer headgear for me,' she said with a grin, swiping the rag from her head.

'I have to go.' He glanced at his watch. 'Dinner in Glasgow.'

'Enjoy!'

Andrew went to walk away and hovered, 'And what is it you do, Grace?'

'Me?' she said. 'I'm a good all-rounder.'

Andrew looked puzzled, but smiled as he walked away.

Grace stood in the doorway and watched him hurry across the courtyard. Within a few minutes the helicopter began to rise slowly. The blades spun round and the machine lifted effortlessly off the ground and in seconds took to the sky. Her eyes stayed glued to the helicopter until it had disappeared behind the clouds.

Grace couldn't wait to get back inside the kitchen. She placed the eggs and the wine on the side and opened up the old-fashioned rent book. She squealed as the wad of money fell on to her lap.

'Holy shit,' she exclaimed, her hands shaking as she began to count the money, then placed it on the coffee table. Immediately, she recognised her grandfather's initials and stared at the entries in the book before fanning out the money in her hand. She had had not a penny to her name, and it had all changed in an instant. Her relief was overwhelming. She wiped a happy tear from her cheek. After counting the money again, she noticed Billy standing in the doorway clutching his teddy bear.

She stretched out her arms. 'Come here. It's okay, Billy, these are happy tears. I promise.'

He ran towards her and flung his arms around her while Grace kissed the top of his head. 'I think we are going to be okay. Your great-grandfather may have just thrown us the best lifeline.'

As she cuddled Billy, Grace began to think. She knew she needed to manage this money carefully and of course she needed to get advice.

Tomorrow, she was going to take a trip into town. There were a number of charity shops in Glensheil and hopefully she would be able to pick up a few items of clothing for the boys, and maybe other bargains to make them feel like they were at home.

'Who needs planes, expensive wines and designer clothes, when we have each other?' she murmured.

Billy looked up with huge, tired, adorable eyes.

'Come on, let me tuck you back into bed. Tomorrow is our first proper day at the Castle.'

She picked Billy up and he flung his arms around her

and nestled into her neck. By the time she'd climbed to the top of the stairs and tucked him back into bed, he was already fast asleep.

Soon afterwards, Grace was back in the kitchen finishing off the cleaning. 'Why don't you get your people to clean,' she said out loud, chuckling. There was one thing she'd already learned about Andrew Glossop: he didn't appear to live in the real world and probably didn't have a clue about real people's struggles. She thought back to Cole and looked in the mirror. Her black eye was thankfully now a little less obvious. Things were changing for the better. She'd never thought she'd think that about being back here, especially after discovering how run-down the place was, but she felt a glimmer of hope and was excited by what the future would hold for her and the boys.

Picking up the bottle of wine, 'Why not?' she said, searching for a corkscrew and taking out a cracked mug from the cupboard.

Grace switched on the TV and couldn't believe her eyes when the news reporter switched to a live scene of Andrew Glossop arriving by helicopter. 'Multi-millionaire Andrew Glossop will be presenting the Pride of Scotland Award tonight and here he is arriving now. These awards are nominated by the public, and the winners are from all walks of life, of all ages and from all over the country. Their awe-inspiring achievements will be celebrated in this star-studded event tonight.'

Grace watched as Andrew slowly walked along the red carpet signing autographs and having his photograph taken with the frenzy of fans outside. She chuckled as she uncorked the wine. The irony of pouring an expensive wine into an old cracked mug.

'Cheers!'

After such a long journey to their new life, the day had begun on a high and ended on a high. From rekindling her friendship with Felicity to looking at the cash inside the rent book, it had been a good first day. She'd wondered for a moment if she had done the right thing, finding the Castle in such a run-down state, but, as in her past, all she could do was take one day at a time. Taking a sip of the wine, she pulled a face.

'You might be expensive, but that doesn't mean to say you taste better than a chilled glass of Lambrini,' she said with a chuckle, though of course she was appreciative of Andrew's lovely gesture.

'Cheers!' Grace raised a glass to herself. 'Here's to my grandfather, Heartcross and the future.'

Chapter Six

The next morning, when Grace opened her eyes, for a second she wondered where she was. The sun was shining through the kitchen blinds and it was surprisingly pleasantly warm. Last night, after a couple of glasses of wine, Grace had fallen asleep on the settee with her head on a cushion and her coat thrown over her. She hadn't noticed how uncomfortable the settee was to sleep on until now and was paying the price as she stood up, stretched her arms and rolled her head from side to side.

Awake before the boys, she switched on the kettle. The Castle was silent except for the sound of the ticking clock on the wall that showed it was a little after 8 a.m.

Knock … knock … knock …

'A visitor at this time?' murmured Grace.

Whoever it was, was persistent. As Grace pulled the cord of the blind that covered the back door it sprang up, releasing a cloud of dust. Standing on the other side of the door, grinning back at Grace, was her old friend Isla.

With a trembling hand, she turned the key in the lock and as soon as the door was open she was greeted by Isla's outstretched arms, which immediately pulled her in for a hug.

'How are you?' they said in unison, then burst out laughing.

Isla took a step back. 'It's true, you are home, and look at you. Your hair … it suits you.'

There was no awkwardness, no animosity, just true friendship. It was like nothing had changed. Their friendship was still the same from the day Grace had left, but just a little bit older and in Grace's case a little bit wiser.

'I think I'm actually going to cry,' declared Isla. 'We had no clue what happened to you. We all thought we would never see you again but look at you, you are here and real.'

'I am very much real,' replied Grace.

'I didn't quite believe it when Felicity told me you were back but thank God you've got rid of that awful black eyeliner and the back-combed hair.'

'My back-combed hair was cool,' protested Grace.

Isla placed her bag on the worktop and looked around the kitchen. 'And you've inherited the Castle, which is amazing, but I am sorry to hear about your grandfather.'

'Thank you,' replied Grace. 'It's all a little surreal if I'm honest, and sad in a way. It wasn't quite what I was expecting or how I remembered it.'

Isla looked all around her. 'I see what you mean – a little tired?'

'You haven't seen anything yet.'

'That bad?'

'No beds.' Grace gestured towards the settee.

'Please tell me you haven't slept on there?'

'Afraid so.' Grace put her hands on her hips and stretched her back again.

'Surely there's enough bedrooms in this place?'

'Oh, yes, there are enough bedrooms, all lacking furniture, and only one double bed, which has three little people fast asleep in.'

'Flick told me… Three boys, you have been busy! We have so much catching up to do. I have two boys, Finn and Angus.'

'And married to Drew Allaway. You were always smitten with him. Cup of tea?'

'I wouldn't say no.'

Grace grabbed a mug from the cupboard and gave it a quick rinse. 'I think my grandfather must have just used the same mug all the time, as they all seem a little dusty.'

'How are you feeling about your grandfather?'

Grace turned around and took a deep breath. 'Numb, full of regrets and wishing I could turn back time.' She moved her coat from the settee to let Isla sit down.

'Since arriving back there have been so many memories. Good and bad, but actually not so bad. My childhood was great, a fabulous relationship with my mum and grandfather, and now I've come to realise I was probably at a difficult age and still grieving for my mum and how exactly was my elderly grandfather meant to keep control of a teenager who thought she knew everything about the world? I let him down so badly...' Grace could barely finish her sentence and brought her hand up to her mouth. Feeling her lips begin to quiver, Isla enveloped Grace in the biggest hug and held her tight.

'And look what he's done for me – given me a roof over my head when I needed it the most. I should have brought the boys back to see him when he was still alive, but as time went on it just got more and more difficult. I'm sorry, I didn't mean to cry on you. I'm all over the place.'

Isla took both of Grace's hands in hers and they sat down on the settee together. 'And you have every right to feel all over the place. He really did care about you. Maybe he was a little over-protective at times, but we know what it's like as a parent now – it's not easy, is it? He was doing the job of your mother and not one he'd anticipated.'

Isla's words resonated with Grace. She appreciated that now, but of course didn't at the time.

'When you didn't come home, your grandfather organised a search party. At first he thought you'd be back the next day, but when you didn't come back he began to think the worst. He even had all the boats out on the river looking for you and the mountain was searched.'

Subdued, Grace swallowed a lump. All this was heartbreaking to hear. She'd never thought how her actions would have affected anyone else at the time.

'It was only when your letter arrived that we knew you

were safe. But, honestly, everyone thought you would turn up again sooner.'

'I messed up and, if the truth be known, I didn't run to a happier place.' She pointed to her eye. 'It's been no walk in the park, believe me.'

'You're on a roller coaster ride at the minute.'

'I'm strapped in but there are so many twists and turns. What happened to the tours of this place, the gift shop?'

'Your grandfather wasn't getting younger and once you'd gone, who was he keeping the business going for? He didn't have any other family to pass it on to. He found it difficult to see people and locked himself away from the rest of the world. He just gave up hope ... maybe.'

Grace took a breath. The business that her grandfather had worked so hard for lay in ruins. She never thought the Castle grounds would close to the general public. Heartcross Castle had been at the heart of the tourist industry for many years. She swallowed hard and felt shaken by it all. The comforting and familiar life her grandfather knew had shut down. She knew she was responsible for the demise of his empire, leaving him destitute, and yet, after everything she put him through, he still left her all he had.

For a moment they both sat in silence. The jovial atmosphere had somewhat plummeted. Grace reflected again on the pain she'd caused.

'It's been a tough few years, hasn't it?'

'It doesn't look like it's been plain sailing for you either.' Isla nodded towards the bruised eye.

'Maybe it's karma,' replied Grace. 'And at times I feel like a failure.'

'Don't be daft.' Isla reached over and touched her friend's knee. 'You are an incredible mother with a big heart. Flick told me how adorable your boys are. And you have all your friends when you need them most. Unless you are thinking of doing a runner again?' Isla tipped her head to the side and waited for an answer.

'Not a runner as such…'

'But?'

'I think my plan is to sell this place as quickly as possible.'

Isla sat up straight. 'Why would you sell this place?' She looked mystified.

'So I can buy a manageable house and live off the profits and have no more financial worries.'

Isla was listening. 'You don't have to make any rash decisions today, just settle in, take a breather.'

'I know you're right, but I need to make a decision soon – short of winning the lottery. The electricity doesn't work in the entrance of the Castle, the carpets are worn, the windows in need of repair, there's barely any furniture and it took me nearly forty minutes to run the bath for the boys last night because the water kept running cold and I had to keep boiling the kettle.'

'If there's anyone who can turn this place around, it's you. You were always headstrong, coming up with money-making ideas… Remember when you used to buy penny chews from Hamish's shop then sell them on the bridge to tourists for three times the price? Genius,' said Isla laughing. 'Good times!'

'Until Hamish clocked what I was doing and wasn't impressed.' Grace smiled at the memory. 'I've missed you,' she declared, again realising how lucky she was to have such good friends.

'And we've missed you. But it looks like you're doing okay,' observed Isla, picking up the bottle of wine which was half empty on the table. 'Very nice bottle.' She raised her eyebrows.

'A house-warming present, I couldn't even afford the cork and I'm still a Lambrini girl through and through,' Grace said with a smile.

'Ha, I'm glad to see nothing changes. So what's the plan now?'

. 'I've no idea, look for a job that'll fit in around the boys. It's quite nice it's school holidays at the minute so the routine is relaxed. I have Andrew's rent which is helpful, but that's not nearly enough money to restore this place. I need to go into town today and pick up a few bits, but I'm on a tight budget. I'm just waiting for the boys to wake.'

'How about I take the boys today, give you time to get yourself sorted? Finn and Angus would love it. They can walk the alpacas, mess about on the hay bales, and I'm sure Drew will give them a ride around the field on the back of the trailer. What do you say?'

Grace wanted to say yes, but she hesitated. 'I'm not sure that is possible.'

'Why? What is it?' asked Isla, sitting up straight and moving to the edge of the settee.

Grace looked towards the door then back towards Isla. 'It's Billy. He's given up on speaking and I'm not sure how he'd cope.'

'What do you mean?' asked Isla tentatively.

'He's witnessed some things he shouldn't have and overheard arguments.' Grace pointed to her eye. 'And I really don't know what to do except keep reassuring him it's all going to be okay and give him all the cuddles he needs.'

'Oh, Grace, I don't know what to say. Kids are resilient. Maybe have a chat to Dr Sanders at Peony Practice for some advice.'

'Yes, I will. So you see, I don't know how he would feel about it.'

'Why don't you ask the boys? He'll have his brothers with him and the weather today is going to be sunny. Maybe just for a couple of hours. I can pick them up, give them some lunch and drop them back. It saves dragging them around town.'

It was very tempting and it would make her life easier. 'Okay, but promise you'll ring me if they are unsettled… What am I saying? I don't even have a phone. I left it behind.'

'Felicity mentioned that and it just so happens …' Isla leant across, grabbed her bag from the island and balanced it on her knee. She reached inside and handed Grace a phone. 'It's an old one, the battery isn't brilliant, but it works. I've charged it up and put some contact details in for you. There's mine, Felicity's, Allie's ...' Isla handed the phone towards Grace. 'It's pay as you go and there's credit on it, too.'

Grace had brought her hands up to her chest. She was overwhelmed. 'Isla, I don't know what to say, except thank you.'

'You are very welcome and, whatever you need, don't hesitate to ask. Shall I pop back in a couple of hours and pick up the boys? If they really don't fancy it, you can text me?'

'Let me give you something for the phone,' offered Grace, thinking of the rent money that Andrew had given her.

'I won't hear of it.' Isla stood up. 'I've got to get back to the farm, but I'll see you later and come here.' Isla gave Grace one last hug before saying goodbye.

Placing the two empty mugs in the sink and with the phone in her hand, Grace wandered outside. She sat down on the rickety old bench just outside the back door and took in the view across the garden before tilting her face upwards to the sun that was breaking through the clouds. It was a different view from the concrete jungle that Grace was used to waking up to, and a welcome change. The mountain air was fresh and the sporadic clouds rising over the mountain top gave the whole place a dreamy feel. Grace had never appreciated the view or the beauty of the place before. 'Oh, Grandfather, I am sorry,' she murmured to herself.

Her quiet moment was interrupted by the sound of an engine followed by a door slamming. She watched as a laundry van pulled up in the courtyard and a harassed-looking woman hurried towards the van. Grace assumed she must be Rose, Andrew's personal assistant. At a guess, Rose was mid-fifties. Her auburn curls bounced just above her shoulder, she had a curvy figure and was a little over five foot, yet she looked important carrying a clipboard. Grace watched as a metal clothes rail was lifted from the back of the van and the driver hooked on numerous suit carriers. Grace counted fifteen suits altogether and was amazed anyone could actually own that many.

She looked down at the clothes she'd travelled in, which also happened to be the ones she'd slept in. Her wardrobe had never been extensive or expensive. Grace didn't even own a pair of heels or a decent handbag. She couldn't remember the last time she'd got dressed up or been out on a date night.

Rose was looking flustered, checking through the garments, sliding them up and down the rail frantically. Grace wondered what it was like to work for a global superstar, because, from where she was sitting, Rose was looking a little stressed.

'Where is Mr Glossop's favourite suit?' she asked the driver whilst looking down at the clipboard then checking the labels. The driver simply shrugged.

'Rose, Rose,' Andrew's voice bellowed across the courtyard. 'Have you seen my pinny?'

Grace chuckled to herself. They weren't words she'd

ever expected to hear shouted across a courtyard by a grown man.

Frantically, Rose slid the items on the clothes rail back and unhooked a garment.

Practically running across the courtyard, Rose quickly unzipped the bag. Grace watched in amusement as Rose fussed round Andrew, then popped a pristine white apron over his head and tied it around his waist before he disappeared back inside. Rose hurried back to the abandoned driver, who was still standing by the clothes rail.

'Rose … ROSE!' Andrew's voice bellowed again. 'There's a chicken in the house. Delia has messed everywhere!'

Rose was at Andrew's beck and call, and Grace could see the poor woman was run off her feet.

'Rose… Rose… Get the bloody chicken out of here!'

This was comedy gold, and Grace was desperately trying to get her face under control. She was wholeheartedly enjoying the entertainment that was going on all around her. It made a change from all the rows that had gone on in the upstairs flat for the last six months. Rose was now running back over the gravel courtyard like her life depended on it. She stepped inside the doorway and quickly reappeared, followed by a loud squawk. A mass of white feathers flew up into the air followed by a chicken. Delia's wings flapped furiously as she landed on the ground. The strange fur-like feathering gave the chicken an unusual and somewhat comical appearance. It had feathered legs and a powder-puff-like crest resembling a pompom on top of its head. Grace remembered her grandfather had kept chickens in the past and she knew this type was called a silkie.

'Billy is going to absolutely love you,' she said, out loud.

After a great deal of commotion inside the building, the chicken was safely minding its own business doing what chickens did best, scratching amongst the soil in the flower bed at the side of the courtyard.

'It's okay, Mr Glossop, Delia is safely outside,' announced Rose triumphantly, swiping her hands.

'Rose! I need my suit too!'

Grace couldn't help but think that Andrew was a little high maintenance, but she supposed that was the world he lived in. Always surrounded by people, being waited on hand and foot, when all she had to rely on was herself.

'Coming, Mr Glossop!'

For the next five minutes all was peaceful again and Grace thought about her day ahead. If she headed down to the town and the boys agreed to go over to Foxglove Farm, they could explore the Castle grounds this afternoon and then they could prepare dinner together and maybe she could ask Isla if she had some old board games that they could all play tonight. The peace and quiet were short-lived, interrupted by numerous transit vans arriving in the courtyard.

Grace spotted straightaway it was a film crew and they seemed to be here for the duration. She'd never seen so much recording equipment being unloaded from the van.

'You'd think the Castle was just about to have a visit

from the royal family,' she muttered, not taking her eyes off the commotion over the courtyard.

Dougie, whose name was in big bold letters on the back of his T-shirt, alongside the word 'producer', was standing with a clipboard. He was slim and had a Roman nose and thick wavy hair. He looked friendly as he asked everyone to gather round. Andrew appeared and from a distance Grace admired him. He was handsome, mesmerising, and had the whole sexy chef thing going on with his sleeves rolled up revealing his tanned forearms, but Grace couldn't help thinking that what she'd seen of his life so far resembled life in a movie. She watched as Andrew made time for each of the crew with a handshake. They didn't seem to be fazed at all by Andrew's superstardom. After a quick chat whilst huddled in their group, Andrew's laughter wafted over the courtyard and then the crew dispersed indoors.

Grace turned her attention to the phone that Isla had given her. It took a couple of minutes to fire up and then there was a continuous beeping. There were texts from Allie, Rory, Fergus and Drew, the old gang saying hello. After scrolling and reading through them all, Grace couldn't believe how everyone was going out of their way to welcome her back.

'Good morning. You seem popular,' said Andrew, looking at the phone in her hand.

'Not as popular as you, it seems. Was that a TV crew?' asked Grace.

'There are no flies on you,' he said with a grin. 'How was your first night?'

'Out like a light,' she replied.

Andrew's name was called by Dougie and he waved his arm in the air. 'I need to go. We're running through the filming of the TV show this morning, then it's the actual filming this afternoon... Catch up later if you are around.'

'I'm around,' replied Grace. She watched Andrew stride across the courtyard, then called out his name. 'Oh, and have an eggscellent time,' she joked, giving Andrew a lopsided grin. 'And a cracking day,' she continued, laughing to herself.

Fortunately, Andrew took the teasing in the spirit intended and waved his hand as he shook his head. Even though he didn't look back in her direction, she knew he was smiling.

As soon as he was out of sight, she Googled him on the phone... Andrew Glossop was a Michelin Star chef with numerous awards under his belt. Grace spent the next couple of minutes scrolling through images of Andrew and then saw him with his arms around Magdalene Glossop. 'No way,' she murmured, putting two and two together. Andrew Glossop came from one of the richest families in Britain, his mother a multi-millionaire born into money from her father's wealth and now the owner and creator of the world-famous fashion brand 'M.V. Glossop', a label Grace would never ever be able to afford. Grace carried on reading an article about her; she had mansions in Beverly Hills as well as a yacht that graced the waters of St Tropez. Andrew was her only child and had had the best education at a prestigious private boarding school. One of the most eligible bachelors in the world, it was rumoured he'd dated some of the world's most beautiful women.

Grace looked down at her dowdy clothes. She couldn't remember the last time she'd worn a dress, or anything in colour, and she had never owned a pair of designer sunglasses in her life. Bringing up three boys, her T-shirts were always stained with spaghetti sauce or dirt from playing in the sandpit at the park, but she could never imagine sending her boys off to boarding school. She wanted to be there when they got home from school, she wanted to read them bedtime stories and wash their dirty play clothes – to her that's what being a mother was all about. It didn't matter how much money you had, her boys were the only people that called her Mum and that meant the world to her.

Andrew's Instagram was flooded with likes and comments and there were numerous photos of the Castle too. Most of the photos pictured food, award ceremonies or numerous famous people that Grace instantly recognised. Her scrolling was interrupted by Andrew's shouts echoing through the door again: 'Will someone get rid of that chicken!'

In a repeat performance there was another squawk and Delia was relegated from the servants' quarters a second time, but this time the door was firmly shut behind her.

Grace was chuckling away to herself and was just going to have another five minutes before waking up the boys when she heard footsteps approaching. A short, slim man with a beard that hung down to the top of his chest appeared from around the corner. He was dressed in a black suit and Grace couldn't help thinking he looked too solemn to be part of the glitz and glamour of the TV show.

'Andrew Glossop is that way, through those doors,' said Grace with a smile and pointed to the pile of feathers that were flapping about in the breeze. 'Follow the feathers.'

'I'm looking for Grace Power, owner of Heartcross Castle, I believe.'

'That's me, how can I help you?' she asked.

The man handed over a brown envelope. 'Burns Funeral Crematory Services.'

Grace cocked an eyebrow. She knew she was now in Scotland and Burns was a popular surname around these parts, but she wasn't sure that was the best name to use for a crematory service, though it definitely did what it said on the tin – or the urn. The man's face was deadpan but he waited patiently while Grace ripped open the envelope to reveal an outstanding bill of over nine hundred pounds. She swallowed.

'Your grandfather's funeral costs. It will be another seventy-five pounds if you would like your grandfather's ashes returned,' he stated. 'You are the only living relative, therefore responsible for this amount.'

Grace assumed this would have already been settled, 'And when does this need to be paid by?'

'It's already overdue,' he replied. 'Interest will accrue by the day.'

Eye contact was not lost between them as Grace stood up. 'Can you excuse me a moment?' she said. With the bill

114

in her hand, she left Mr Burns standing outside and walked into the kitchen, where she took out Andrew's rent book, still stuffed with the cash. The money had been in her hands less than twenty-four hours but she had no choice but to pay the bill. She sighed, knowing there would be barely any cash left to live on for the rest of the month, which wasn't what she anticipated – but what could she do?

Mr Burns hadn't moved a muscle when Grace returned. 'There you go, it's all there,' she said, handing over the cash.

'And your grandfather's ashes? What would you like me to do with them?' he asked, marking the money off in a little black book he'd whipped out from his suit pocket.

'Please return the ashes,' she replied, counting out and handing over another seventy-five pounds.

The man nodded his understanding and tore off Grace a receipt from his book.

With the money safely tucked away in his inside pocket, 'I'm sorry for your loss,' he said before turning and walking away.

Grace didn't know whether he actually meant the loss of her grandfather or the thousand pounds that she'd just parted with. She counted the two hundred and fifty pounds left in her hand and wondered how the hell she was going to get through the month on that. But in the past Grace had managed on a shoestring before and she could do it again. She would have to budget carefully, bulk up the meals and stretch them out, wash the clothes by hand, save on electricity until she could find some work and make a decision about the sale of the Castle.

She felt a tug at her T-shirt. Billy was standing next to her.

'Good morning! Did you sleep well?' she asked, pulling him in for a cuddle and sitting him on her knee on the bench.

Billy nodded.

'You'll never guess what we have for breakfast,' said Grace, pointing over to Delia, who was scratching about in the soil. 'Scrambled eggs, courtesy of Delia.'

Billy's eyes grew wide and a huge beam spread across his face.

'Go and say hello.' Grace slowly lowered him to the ground and watched as Billy walked towards Delia, then sat crossed-legged on the grass verge and began pulling up tufts of grass, catching Delia's eye. Curious, Delia cocked her head to one side and made a clucking sound that gave Billy the giggles.

'I think you have a new friend there,' claimed Grace, smiling at him.

Watching Billy interact with Delia, Grace's heart swelled with happiness. She might not have any money to her name but the sun was shining, the mountain air fresh and Grace could only see the positives. Today was the first day of the rest of their lives. Hearing the twins race into the kitchen, she beckoned them to come outside. She ruffled Joey's bed hair, which looked wild. 'Mum,' he protested, smoothing down his hair, 'get off!'

'Boys, remember when we first arrived and you noticed the alpacas in the field at the farm?'

They all nodded.

'My friend Isla owns the farm and has two boys, Finn and Angus, and if you all wanted, you could go over this morning and have a ride on the tractor, meet the animals and maybe have some lunch... But only if you want to,' she quickly added.

Immediately, the twins began to jump up and down. 'Yes, please!' they chorused excitedly.

Grace looked over to Billy, who was still occupied with Delia. 'How about you, Billy, would you like that?'

Billy nodded and smiled then pointed to Delia.

'You can't take Delia, but she'll be waiting for you when you get back. There's another chicken somewhere, I believe ... Nigella. We'll have to look out for her too. Come on, you boys can help with breakfast, but wash your hands first.'

As the boys raced inside, Grace quickly pinged a text to Isla. 'The boys would be delighted to come over, thank you.'

With their hands washed, Freddie and Joey were standing by the cooker playfully fighting over the frying pan whilst Billy was placing the knives and forks on the table. Grace looked at the three of them, all mucking in, and felt a pang of sadness.

They could have been standing here with her grandfather, sharing simple precious moments like these with him. On the verge of tears again and with her emotions high, Grace managed to hide it from the boys and poured them a glass of juice each. The twins were chattering away, talking about their morning at the farm and meeting the alpacas.

'This is the best place we have ever lived,' shared Freddie, handing the box of eggs to Grace then swiping his hands in a triumphant way. 'And it's going to be our home for ever.'

'This is the best place in the world,' added Joey. Their excitement was about to bubble over as they carried on their conversation.

The twins didn't care there were no smart TVs or technology, and the lack of furniture didn't seem to bother them at all. The wide smiles on their faces said it all as they took the plates out of the cupboard and placed them on the table.

'And what's so good about it?' asked Grace.

'What's not good about it?' replied Freddie.

'Home,' added Joey.

Suddenly Grace knew she needed to plant the seed that there was the possibility that this might not be their for ever home. She didn't want them getting attached and upset when it came to selling the Castle. 'Boys, I need to tell you that this place might just be a stop-gap. I might need to sell the Castle so we can buy a house and, in the words of every fairy tale, live happily ever after.'

The twins stopped dead in their tracks.

'Why would we need a house when we have got a Castle?' asked Freddie, holding his hands up and looking all around.

'I know it's difficult to understand, but this place costs an awful lot of money to run and isn't in the best state. It's going to take a lot of money to get a lot of new stuff for it.'

'But we don't need new stuff, we are happy with what we have,' challenged Freddie.

Grace looked at them all adoringly. It was wonderful to see them so happy and settled so quickly. She knew it was imperative to plant the seed and keep them in the loop, yet manage their expectations in a sensitive manner, but the reality was there was a possibility that they couldn't stay here. Grace had to come up with a Plan B, but she knew they would be better off with the money in the bank from the sale of the property. They could afford the kind of adorable house that Grace had fantasised about when flicking through *Country Life* magazine in the dentist's surgery, with an oak beam porch, cosy furnishings and a small manageable garden that maybe overlooked a valley.

'Please, Mum, we've only just arrived,' protested Joey.

Grace glanced at them. 'Come here. I have just the best boys.'

Freddie was reluctant to walk towards her.

'Wouldn't you like to live abroad, by the seaside in a hot country?' queried Grace.

'We have the river and the boats, mountains that reach the sky, and this is the best place to play hide and seek,' declared Freddie.

Grace had never imagined that in such a short time the twins would settle so quickly. But staying? Grace couldn't see it as a viable option. This place would cost way too much to run, and short of a lottery win or a genius plan it was going to prove difficult to modernise the Castle without any cash flow, let alone keep it running.

'And don't forget friends,' added Joey. 'Even though we haven't met Finn and Angus yet. We've never really had proper friends, have we?' He looked towards Freddie and Billy.

These words caused a pang in Grace's heart. The twins were right, they had moved around so much and time after time had had to fit into a new place, which couldn't have been easy. 'Friends are good to have,' she admitted, instantly thinking of Isla, Felicity and Allie.

Freddie gave her the widest of smiles and put his hands together in a prayer-like stance. Grace realised with a jolt that the boys had never expressed an interest in staying at any of their previous dwellings. She really hadn't seen that coming. She felt her stomach sink a little and she swallowed. It wasn't financially practical for her to keep hold of the Castle.

After giving the boys a tight squeeze, 'Poached, scrambled or fried?' she asked, holding up the egg box.

'Scrambled,' declared the twins, with a thumbs-up from Billy. Grace cracked the eggs into a bowl and gave them a good beat. She exhaled and looked around the room. The boys were just too little to understand. It was complicated. If she made a snap decision to stay, this soon after they arrived, it would be insane if she then had to sell because she couldn't afford to stay. The boys would be even more heartbroken. But Grace knew she wasn't opposed to a challenge or hard work and she didn't want to let her boys down. It was time to get her thinking hat on. Would it actually be that bad staying on at the Castle? She watched the boys as they sat down on the settee and switched on the TV. They were chatting enthusiastically about their morning ahead at the farm. Freddie looked over his shoulder and dazzled Grace with a beatific smile that melted her heart.

'We could wash cars to make more money,' suggested Freddie.

'Sell eggs if we get more chickens,' added Joey. 'Any odd jobs to make money.'

No one could appreciate this kind of enthusiasm to make money more than Grace. She was used to coming up with hairbrained schemes to put a few quid in her pocket, but this time they would need a lot more than a few quid. Their camaraderie was admirable.

'You boys are too smart for your own good.' Grace admired their solidarity. She knew that if it meant the boys were happy and settled, she needed to find a way to make money to keep the roof over their heads that the boys wanted. It made her feel good to see them excited about their future and how they were all in it together. She, of course, was the captain of the ship and they all needed to be steered in the right direction. She looked around the kitchen. Was staying in the Castle actually doable? Grace started to think, and suddenly the idea excited her rather than scared her.

Chapter Seven

The short walk into the town of Glensheil was busy. Grace weaved her way through the pedestrians on the high street past all the fancy boutiques towards the less-affluent part of the town. She passed the once-familiar deli, and the coffeehouse, and took in the aroma of the beautiful blooms outside the florist. The tree-lined pavements looked picturesque in the mid-morning sunshine and the hanging baskets bursting with colour swayed from the lampposts in the light breeze. Grace needed food for the rest of the week, but her budget was minimal, which meant rummaging through the reduced aisle in the supermarket to pick up a bargain. Following the road, she remembered a row of charity shops on Claret Row, a place she used to frequent often in her teenage years, looking for vintage clothes. She navigated the streets like it was only yesterday she'd walked down them and took a turn down an alley, stepping amongst stacks of water-stained crates, crumpled litter and empty liquor bottles thrown on the ground. She walked past graffitied brick walls, grimy barred windows and doorways, and heard the clink of bottles and bin lids slamming from the night club's back entrance.

As she stepped from the alley's debris on to Claret Row, the row of charity shops was right in front of her. Outside was a long trestle table strewn with children's clothes, and boxes of shoes underneath, and Grace began to rummage through the pile. Within five minutes, she'd rooted out numerous boys' T-shirts which amounted to no more than three pounds. Pleased with her findings, she stepped inside the shop and immediately the volunteers behind the counter greeted her like she was a long lost friend. With the mid-morning sun shining through the window, lighting up this place of chance, Grace browsed the rows of items from settees to second-hand fridges, lamps to cutlery. She hovered at the side of a single bed and turned over the price tag, which, after paying her grandfather's funeral bill, was now one she couldn't afford. She turned towards the woman behind the counter who stood tall and slim, her grey hair neatly flicked out and likely styled with old-fashioned rollers, her make-up far from discreet with bright-blue eyeshadow and cherry-red lips.

'Is it possible to reserve an item?' Grace asked politely, hoping the woman was going to say yes but knowing it was most unlikely.

'Which item were you thinking?' she replied, walking towards Grace.

'The bed. I could leave a deposit and pay it off over a

couple of months.' The second-hand bed would be perfect for one of the boys.

The woman scanned the price tag then raised an eyebrow. 'It's forty pounds. A couple of months? We don't usually hold on to items that long.'

'I understand,' replied Grace, suddenly feeling close to tears. She thought about the money she had to last her the rest of the month. Could she actually part with forty pounds right now?

The assistant must have noticed the tears well up in Grace's eyes. 'How much could you afford?' she asked softly.

'Twenty,' replied Grace, knowing that was still a push, but she could skip a few meals at the end of the month as long as the children didn't go hungry.

Grace watched as the assistant took the tag from the bed and marked it as sold. 'And how are you going to transport the bed?' the woman asked.

That thought hadn't even crossed Grace's mind.

'It's ten pounds for delivery to the local area and unfortunately I have no control over that cost.'

'Can you bear with me a moment?' asked Grace, taking her mobile phone out of her bag and punching a text over to Isla.

Within seconds Isla had replied and was sending Drew with the trailer to pick up the bed as he was out delivering goods to the farmers' market nearby. After paying for the bed and thanking the kind woman profusely, Grace stepped outside and made her way over to the market hall, back through the high street, her next stop the supermarket. After picking up a bag of potatoes and a block of cheese she ambled past the clock on the stone tower that linked the two walkways across the high street. The clock struck midday as Grace crossed the road.

Immediately, she spotted Andrew sitting at a table under the burgundy-and-gold-striped awning of an affluent-looking bistro with a group of friends, maybe part of the film crew. Their voices were loud as they laughed, and they were enjoying what looked like champagne. Grace couldn't begin to imagine affording such an extravagance at lunchtime, but she didn't begrudge anyone who could. Andrew and his friends reminded her of a painting that she'd seen on a TV arts programme; they wouldn't look out of place sitting outside one of the bistros of Paris. Goodness, he was attractive, his crisp white short-sleeved shirt complementing his tan perfectly, and his mass of curly hair falling over his eyes. Seeing Andrew had been an unexpected pleasure and Grace allowed herself a discreet smile as she slowly wandered past him.

It wasn't Grace's intention to listen into the conversation as she walked by, but she guessed it was some sort of business deal that Andrew was negotiating.

'Of course it's my objective to buy the place at any cost. It will be perfect,' he said.

'But what if she doesn't want to sell?' asked his friend.

'Who would ever refuse such an offer? Only a fool,' Andrew replied and the group laughed. That place will be good for the brand and it's my intention to get it at a knock-down price. I've every intention of making a global brand at whatever cost. I'll keep you posted.'

All four of them raised their glasses and chinked them together before tucking into their food that the waiter had just brought out.

Grace had bent her head low as she scuttled past. She hoped Andrew wouldn't spot her; she didn't want to be introduced to anyone looking the way she did. It was safe to say she was feeling slightly underdressed, wearing a stretched grey T-shirt, a pair of baggy washed-out jeans and trainers that were well worn and were getting on for four years old. But unfortunately she heard her name called and her heart sank.

'Grace!'

She turned her head to see Andrew looking directly at her. 'How's your morning?'

Grace was conscious of the other three people sitting around the table looking at her.

'It's been lovely, thank you, but please don't let me distract you from your lunch.'

She noticed one of the woman holding up the empty bottle of champagne and beckoning the waiter over to order another.

'We are just having a well-earned lunch. Are you going shopping? Treating yourself, I hope. There's a couple of new designer shops over on old Barton Road.' Andrew gestured towards the numerous designer bags stacked up under his table.

'I may just take a look,' Grace replied, knowing that she could never afford those prices.

'You must! Would you like to join us for some lunch?' asked Andrew.

Of course Grace wasn't going to accept. She already felt out of her depth hovering by the edge of the table with everyone's eyes on her. What would she ever be able to contribute to the conversation of the rich and famous, with everyone dressed up to the nines, their hair just so and day clothes that wouldn't look out of place at a wedding. She wasn't sure, but she thought she saw a look pass between the two woman sitting at the table, leaving Grace blushing slightly.

'Thank you, but I've got a busy schedule today,' she replied, kicking herself as she noticed her own accent sounding a little posher than normal.

Luckily, Grace was saved by the waiter arriving with more food, which looked and smelled divine.

'Enjoy your food,' she said.

As Grace turned, she noticed a photographer standing on the edge of the pavement taking a snap of Andrew, but he was promptly removed by what Grace thought was Andrew's bodyguard. She couldn't ever imagine just sitting and trying to eat lunch with her every move photographed by the paparazzi. Only a few steps further, Grace could hear laughter from the table and a comment that stopped her in her tracks.

'And who was that? She's a funny little thing, isn't she, I'm assuming new staff? You really do need to keep your work life and personal life separate, think of the image. Did you really just offer for her to join us?'

Grace couldn't quite believe what she'd just heard. Were they actually talking about her? Feeling out of sorts at the cruel comment, Grace turned and was just about to march over to the table and extend her hand, introducing herself as the owner of Heartcross Castle, but took a deep breath and quickly counted to ten. This was a coping mechanism she'd practised with Cole when it was better not to aggravate the situation. Thankfully on this occasion she realised that she really didn't need to explain herself to anyone or prove her worth. She might not be sitting at their table, dressed to the nines, sipping champagne and eating mouth-watering food, but, quite frankly, she didn't want to. How dare anyone judge her? Grace's opinion of Andrew was fading fast: he hadn't corrected the people at the table and she couldn't help but wonder why. He looked up from the conversation and locked eyes with her. She turned away. It was none of her business what other people thought of her and even though she felt a tiny bit crushed by their judgement, she walked away with an air of dignity. Grace knew she might be penniless, but since she'd arrived back at Heartcross her boys were smiling and happy, and now she had an afternoon with them to look forward to and the Castle grounds to explore. She was winning at life in ways that those people sitting at the table would probably never understand... You didn't need wealth to be happy and kind.

Chapter Eight

G race brushed off the conversation; she wasn't going to let her spirits take a nosedive. She walked up the steps towards the Castle and took in the view. The scenery was simply stunning, the mountains that rose steadily in the background towering over the town and the gardens of the Castle, and down below the River Heart tumbling over the rocks underneath the bridge. Her initial exuberance wavered as she stopped halfway up the steps for a breather and her eyes roamed the Castle. It looked so grand and Grace wondered again how exactly such a famous landmark in Scotland came to belong to her family. From the stories her mother had told her as a child, her grandfather's family were farmers and he himself was in the military for a number of years. How long had it been in her family? Had it spanned generations? Grace was curious. Maybe there were answers in one of the history books in the

Castle's library. She really wished she'd asked more questions growing up.

'Grace!' It was Andrew, shouting from the bottom of the stone steps. 'Wait.'

She was surprised to see him racing up the steps towards her, his hands laden with the umpteen carrier bags.

Grace braced herself and flashed him a cool stare while she waited for him to catch his breath.

'Grace, I'm so sorry for what happened back there.' This was the second time in twenty-four hours that Grace had seen Andrew looking genuinely mortified. 'I'm horrified, I really am, that you overheard that conversation.'

'Sorry that I heard it?'

'No, I'm sorry it was even said.' He touched her arm. 'I'm really sorry.'

Grace shrugged good-naturedly. She was impressed that Andrew had abandoned his champagne lunch to come and apologise. 'You thought I was the new housekeeper and your friends think I'm staff,' she replied, and, seeing the funny side, her face broke into a wide grin. 'Honestly, don't worry about it. There's more things to worry about in life than what my occupation is,' she said, taking a look up at the Castle again.

Andrew beamed. 'Thanks, Grace, are we good? I really don't want to go upsetting my landlady the day after she arrives.'

'We're good,' she said, giving him a reassuring smile, not wanting any sort of ill-feeling between them.

'I did put them straight,' he admitted. 'I said you were a

good all-rounder.' He gave a lopsided grin. 'And of course the owner of this beautiful piece of architecture.' He took a bottle of water out of one of the bags and took a swig. 'You really do have a lovely place here. I'd give my right arm for a spot like this.'

Grace looked at Andrew. 'I know I'm very lucky,' she admitted, following his gaze. He was right: she really did. This place was actually hers.

'And that view gets me every time.' He gave Grace a sideward glance.

'Yes, it's very impressive,' she replied, holding his gaze for a moment longer than necessary before she turned and pointed towards the Castle gates, which had swung open for three BBC Scotland vans travelling up the sloping driveway towards the Castle. 'For you,' she said.

'Yes, we're filming the first episode of the new show this afternoon, which is going to be aired at the beginning of next week.'

Suddenly, hearing Andrew's name being chanted, they noticed a gathering of fans at the gates. Andrew turned and waved, and they were engulfed by the cheers. 'You *are* in demand,' she said, wondering how anyone coped with the constant attention. 'I best let you get on with your day.'

He put his hand on the small of her back as they took the last few steps towards the top.

'I've still got a little time before I start filming. Do you fancy a drink? Over at mine?'

Now there was an offer Grace wasn't going to refuse. She had to admit she was itching to see what it was like in the servants' quarters and this was the perfect opportunity. It had been a long time since she'd set foot in there and she was curious to see how much it had changed.

'That'll be lovely,' she replied, 'I'll nip and get your rent book, that'll give you time to put away your shopping.'

They walked across the courtyard in a comfortable silence. Grace kept flicking her eyes in his direction and as she looked at him, he looked at her. She smiled, and her heart beat a little faster.

'Have you taken a walk around the Castle grounds yet?' asked Andrew, saluting the film crew, who were unloading their equipment from their vans.

Grace shook her head. 'It's on my to-do list this afternoon.'

'Well, if you need a tour guide…'

Grace gave a little chuckle. 'That would be lovely but I did use to live here.'

'Actually live here?' He looked up at the Castle and paused. 'I didn't know that. How long is it since you've been home?'

'A fair few years,' she replied.

'Is it good to be back?' asked Andrew, then quickly added, 'Maybe not under the current circumstances.'

'Maybe not under the current circumstances,' she repeated, 'but on the whole it's good to be back. I'll follow you over in a moment, I'll just put my bag away and pick up your rent book.'

She watched Andrew walk past the TV production vans, to be met at the door by Rose, who immediately took his bags from him. As she opened the back door Grace peeped inside her carrier bag; there were no expensive designer clothes from newly opened boutiques staring back at her, only charity clothes for the boys alongside potatoes and a block of cheese. She and Andrew were leading completely different lives. He was a TV superstar and she was a down-to-earth, frazzled mother of three trying to make ends meet. Even though they lived in the same castle building, they were worlds apart.

Hearing the buzz of her phone in her bag Grace checked out the short video Isla had pinged across. With her hand on her heart, she smiled. The boys were having the best time, laughing and splashing in the stream and swinging across the water on the old tyre swing.

'Just the perfect day,' Grace replied, placing the phone back on the worktop. Then she noticed a pool of water of the floor.

'Oh God,' she murmured. 'What now?'

She sighed as she opened the freezer, which was fully defrosted, and saw there was no light inside the refrigerator. How the hell was she going to afford a brand-new fridge right now? Mopping up the water, Grace knew she had bitten off more than she could chew.

The upkeep of the Castle was playing on her mind, and she knew she didn't want to be lying awake night after night worrying about it. Her head was confused; this place was beginning to feel like home, but without an injection of money she and the boys could be living in this state for a long time.

'It's no fun being an adult,' she said, wiping away a tear and picking up her phone. With a heavy heart, she Googled an estate agent, then dialled their number. She wasn't thrilled about upsetting the boys; it was incredibly exciting for them living in a castle, and they had their heart set on staying here, but Grace knew she needed to look at all options. If the place was valued, surely it would give her a clearer picture.

She cleared her throat as the estate agent picked up the phone and Grace arranged a valuation. The appointment was something she was going to keep to herself for the time being.

Taking a breather, Grace wandered through to the Grand Hall and looked up at her grandfather's portrait hanging on the wall above the inglenook, before stepping outside into the private gardens through the door at the back of the room. It was a gorgeous day and for a little while she watched the butterflies that hovered around the lavender and the rose bushes that lined the stone wall, while her thoughts swirled in her mind.

Grace was torn; this place had history and memories. She'd sat out in this garden with her mother on a picnic blanket reading books and in winter built a snowman on this very spot. What Grace couldn't understand was that if her grandfather was one of the richest men in Scotland, what happened to his fortune?

Grace followed the neatly mown path that had been recently strimmed and looked around. The gardens were immaculate – how was that even possible after all this time?

The borders were seeded with long grasses and meadow flowers. She ambled down the path and headed towards the servants' quarters. Passing the broad oak tree with its wide branches she stopped and traced her grandfather's initials carved alongside her very own. Those initials must have been there years. Grace closed her eyes for a moment and put her hand on her chest, then continued to walk along the path lined with ox-eye daisies and blue forget-me-nots, then pushed open the wooden gate and crossed the courtyard towards the servants' quarters.

A couple of moments later, Grace was standing on an impressive doormat embossed with Andrew Glossop's logo. She pressed the brass doorbell and the bell rang out and Grace waited.

She was greeted by Rose. 'Hello, how may I help you?'

'Grace Power to see Andrew Glossop,' proclaimed Grace, wondering why she'd just announced herself like she was about to see royalty.

Rose checked and double-checked the notepad that she was holding. 'Are you with the production crew?'

Grace shook her head. 'No,' she replied.

'Unfortunately, no unauthorised people can be on the premises this afternoon.'

'Andrew is expecting me,' confirmed Grace. 'If you would just let him know I'm here.'

'I'm sorry, if your name isn't on this list, Mr Glossop is not to be disturbed. It's more than my job's worth—'

But Rose didn't finish her sentence as Andrew appeared in the hallway behind her. 'It'll be more than your job's worth if you don't let Grace in. She's the owner of Heartcross Castle.'

Immediately, Rose looked flustered and began to apologise. 'I'm sorry, so sorry, Mr Glossop. I should have recognised the name.' Rose sidestepped and gave Grace a welcoming smile then bowed, taking Grace completely by surprise.

'No harm done,' said Andrew with a smile.

'The lobsters have also arrived. What would you like me to do with them, Mr Glossop?'

'Can you put them in the tank for me? And, Rose, I need my chef's apron ironed. Can I leave that with you?'

'Yes, Mr Glossop, and don't forget your mother will be arriving in a few days' time. Shall I make up the room overlooking the mountain?'

'Perfect. That'll be all. Thanks, Rose,' said Andrew, dismissing Rose, who once again bowed, then hurried down the hallway. 'I'm sorry about that. Let me show you around.'

'Wow! Your staff just bowed,' observed Grace, amused.

'Rose has been working in my family for a very long time. Line of respect... boundaries. Mother's input. She sets out the terms and conditions of the contract.'

Grace didn't question it any further, but it all seemed a little pretentious to her.

'This way,' said Andrew. 'Come on, this way.'

He walked in front of her and Grace couldn't help but observe his broad back in his tight white shirt, his slim waist and, she had to admit, a very nice bum in his faded jeans. He looked over his shoulder and she felt herself blush and hoped he hadn't caught her looking.

'It's a little different in here, isn't it?' Andrew opened his arms wide while Grace took in her surroundings. She couldn't quite believe it. This place was no longer the run-down servants' quarters that she remembered, but looked like the lobby of the poshest of hotels, leaving her living quarters across the courtyard resembling a squat. She felt like the poor relative, which wasn't actually far from the truth. The long hallway with its high ceiling was lined with columns, and the bright lighting lit up the royal blue walls and a long line of gold-framed pictures, which at a glance looked like photographs of Andrew.

'It's all so different,' she exclaimed, gazing at objects standing on raised platforms and pedestals with placards of information by their side, reminding Grace of a museum. As a young teenager Grace had used the abandoned servants' quarters as her own playground, especially in the winter months when she couldn't escape outside. This had been the ideal place to race her second-hand yellow bike around the empty rooms and rollerskate along the long hallway. The place was now unrecognisable; the once-dowdy walls and scuffed floor tiles had been replaced with great extravagance.

'And these would be…' said Grace, staring into the glass cabinets on the raised platforms.

'My awards,' finished off Andrew, proudly.

'Wow, not just a pretty face,' she joked, taking a closer look at one in the cabinet straight in front of her.

'Am I noting a hint of sarcasm?' replied Andrew with a grin

'Absolutely not, but I was just wondering, should I whip out my duster and dust these down for you? Especially in my new role of housekeeper.'

'I think you are teasing me now, Miss Power,' he replied, his eyes playfully glinting at her, 'but don't you worry – hopefully my new housekeeper will be starting very soon.' He left Grace wondering how many staff one man needed.

She studied a trophy in a box. 'Is this alarmed?' she asked, noticing the small device attached to the red box. 'Is that actually gold?' She raised an eyebrow.

'Yes and yes, it's an award I won in Paris,' Andrew confirmed.

'This place has changed since I was last running wild in here. You must have a spent a small fortune.' Grace was looking up at the high ceilings with their long line of glass chandeliers. 'It's gorgeous, isn't it?'

'I think so,' replied Andrew, catching her eye and leaving Grace wondering if he was talking about chandelier – or her.

As they continued to head down the hallway, Grace rummaged in her bag and pulled out the rent book.

'Here, before I forget,' she said, tapping the rent book on his chest. 'And just for the record, if you are late paying, you will be immediately evicted with no grounds for appeal.'

Andrew smiled. 'So harsh.'

They continued to walk, Grace glancing at every framed

picture that she passed. The celebrities featured with Andrew were mainly Hollywood superstars whom Grace recognised from films or magazines. He'd already led such an amazing life.

'These are mainly from my early career, my restaurant in London.' Andrew gestured to the line of photographs hanging on the wall.

'How did you end up here?' asked Grace, intrigued. 'From the bright lights of the city to a small town in the Scottish Highlands.'

'I landed a TV series and the TV company filmed my road trips around Italy and France, which catapulted me on to a bigger platform, and then Flynn Carter, owner of Starcross Manor, turned up at my Michelin-starred restaurant and convinced me Heartcross was my next adventure. I have to admit I was sceptical because I'd always been in the bright lights of the city. At the time my mother was trying to entice me to New York, but I quite fancied the quiet life for a while.'

What with the private helicopters, fast cars and TV shows, Grace didn't know what was actually quiet about his life. 'Multi-millionaire Flynn Carter,' she said out loud, thinking: was everyone in Heartcross and nearby a millionaire? Technically, she owned a castle and on paper she was rich, but in the real world Grace didn't have a penny to her name.

'I was only staying for six months, but as the saying goes, and the villagers kept reminding me all the time, once you arrive in Heartcross there's no escaping, which must be true because you've returned.'

'Yes, it must be true,' she replied, her feelings for Heartcross becoming fonder by the day.

'Well, I'm glad to hear it, because I'm very intrigued by the woman in the Castle.'

'Believe me, my life is boring in comparison to yours. There really isn't much to tell,' she protested.

'Mmm, time will tell,' he replied.

As she followed Andrew she admired the large crystal vases of pink roses that were placed at intervals down the hallway, and took in their aroma. Then she spotted Andrew in a family photograph. She hovered in front of it.

'My younger days, with my parents.'

'You haven't changed a bit… Cuteness overload in those short pants and long socks – and look at that hair.'

'Did you just say I was cute?' quizzed Andrew, his eyes dancing at Grace.

'Back in the day,' she confirmed. 'Not so sure about now,' she joked.

Andrew brought his hands up to his chest, 'Stick the knife in,' he replied, pretending to look hurt.

'You must have been what age there?' asked Grace.

'I'm not entirely sure, maybe seven years old.'

She moved onto the next photograph, a young man in his army uniform, which reminded Grace of the portrait of her grandfather hanging in the Grand Hall. 'And who's this?'

'My grandfather. He was killed in battle in the war.'

'Oh, I'm sorry to hear that.'

'That's okay,' he replied, as they stood looking at the photograph.

Grace could see the family resemblance. Andrew was the spitting image of his grandfather, both strikingly handsome men.

'Did you know your grandfather?'

Andrew shook his head. 'No, unfortunately not, and sadly this is the only photograph I have of him.'

Gazing at the photograph for a second longer, Grace turned and walked straight into a display table beside her. To her horror, the table wobbled and the glass crystal award standing in pride of place rocked from side to side and then began to fall, heading straight for the wooden floor.

Time slowed.

Grace froze as Andrew reacted quickly. With an outstretched arm he miraculously caught the award centimetres from being smashed to smithereens. He blew out a breath, then placed the award carefully back on the table before giving Grace a lopsided grin.

'Oh my God, I'm so sorry. I should have been looking where I was going,' she said, wide-eyed, both hands on her chest. 'I feel an utter idiot.'

He looked at her and raised his eyebrow, 'No harm done. Thank God, I used to play tennis back in the day at boarding school. I've still got the reach.'

'Is there anything you don't do? A chef, TV, play tennis...'

'And catcher of awards that are about to smash on the floor,' he joked, with a glint in his eye.

Embarrassed, Grace covered her face with her hands. 'Honestly, you can't take me anywhere.'

'Well, maybe I should give that a try sometime,' he said, grinning and leaving Grace wondering whether he was actually flirting a little.

The moment was interrupted by Rose appearing in the doorway. Once more she bowed, much to Grace's amusement.

'I'm sorry to bother you, Mr Glossop, but your apron is ironed, your shoes polished and the rest of your clothes are laid out on your bed. Is there anything else I can do for you before I take my lunch?'

'We are all good here, thank you, Rose. Enjoy your lunch.'

'That I will, Mr Glossop, and don't forget to look over that business proposal. A decision needs to be made – the deadline is looming,' she reminded him.

'I will, thank you, Rose.'

Once more Rose bowed before she left the room.

'Business proposal? What else is on the horizon for Mr Glossop – or is it okay if I call you Andrew?' asked Grace with a hint of hilarity in her voice before she took a bow. She knew she was teasing, but it was all so very much over the top to her.

'Maybe it's me who should be calling you Miss Power. After all, you are my landlady. Or would that be Mrs Power?'

'Miss Power to you,' replied Grace.

Catching her eye, he said, 'That's good to know.' He paused for a second. 'In fact, this business proposal is something I probably do need to talk to you about, as technically you do own the Castle.'

'Me? What would it have to do with me? Go on, I'm all ears.'

'Let's walk and talk and we can get a drink from the holding room.'

Grace followed Andrew towards the room she remembered as the living room in the servants' quarters.

'My mother thinks it's a good idea to get involved in a reality TV show. The real life of Andrew Glossop – which means it does exactly what it says on the tin. They'll literally follow my every move all day every day. Apparently this type of programme is all the rage these days, but that means there will be a film crew at the Castle most days.'

Grace had felt a little twinge of guilt, knowing that she'd made an appointment to have the Castle valued, and as she walked through the servants' quarters that guilt had been growing. Andrew must have spent a fortune renovating this part of the Castle. If she did decide to sell, what would happen to all this? That was something else Grace would have to work out.

'Did you have a contract with my grandfather regarding this place?' Grace asked curiously.

'A gentleman's handshake,' replied Andrew. 'Initially, twelve months to see if it worked out for the both of us, but

I couldn't be happier here.' He held open the door to what he called the holding room.

Twelve months... Grace mulled that little bit of information over in her mind. What exactly would happen to Andrew and all the money he'd put into this place if the Castle was sold? And now he was saying there was another six months on his contract, even though there wasn't a legally binding document. Grace had a lot of thinking to do, but she knew the bottom line was she had to do right by her and her boys.

'Look at this place! It's changed so much,' she enthused, stepping inside the room.

The holding room – once a dull living room with brown patterned curtains and a green carpet – was now bright with appealing décor. The small window had been replaced with large bi-fold doors that were folded back to reveal a gorgeous decking area with a tranquil water feature and an outdoor seating area with a canopy. Grace took a look around. Inside there were comfortable chairs and sofas with vibrant, plush cushions to lounge on, and a bar stocked with bottled waters and staple liquors. There was fresh fruit in glass bowls dotted around the room, buckets of ice and platters of food lining a small buffet table. On the walls were even more portraits and posters of celebrities posing alongside Andrew.

'What would you like to drink? A glass of champagne?'

Grace shook her head, 'Just water for me, thank you.'

Grace watched in amazement as Andrew rang a bell that was placed at the end of the bar. Within seconds a butler appeared holding a silver tray. 'What can I get for you, Mr Glossop?' he asked.

The unexpected extravagance of a butler left Grace open-mouthed. She watched him retrieve a bottle of water from the fridge behind the bar and serve it to her with ice and a slice of lemon. She couldn't quite believe how Andrew was waited on hand and foot.

'No drink for me, otherwise it'll be non-stop trips to the bathroom during filming and that would play havoc with the schedule. Thank you, Giles.'

Once more Andrew didn't bat an eyelid as the butler bowed and left the room. He was also oblivious to the fact that Grace's jaw had dropped somewhere below her knees as he continued to talk. 'The make-up room is through there, and, as I'm sure you remember, the kitchen is through *there*, and this is where my friends and the production team or guests can chill and watch the show,' he said.

'And you need five TVs for that because…'

'Each one shows a different angle of the kitchen so you can see what is going on at all times. Have a seat.'

Sitting down, Grace gawped at the multiple TV screens that were tuned into the kitchen. She spotted Dougie, the producer, reviewing the cue cards and another member of the production team setting up lighting.

'I feel like I'm in the cinema,' she said, sinking into the comfiest settee she'd ever sat on.

'The cinema room is behind the living room.'

'No way!' exclaimed Grace, thinking how the boys would love that. 'I don't even recognise this place anymore, it's been transformed,' she went on. 'But what I want to know is how exactly you ended up here, at the Castle?'

Andrew perched on the edge of the settee. 'It was when I was working up at Starcross Manor and the cookery road trips were aired on TV. They had tremendous viewing figures and that's when I negotiated this TV deal, but unfortunately Flynn declined the offer of it being filmed up at Starcross Manor – which was understandable because once word got out I was working there, hordes of followers from social media used to hang about outside the reception.'

'Nice problem to have in your line of work.'

'But very off-putting to the hotel guests that were paying customers. The cost of security would have been way too much, so we racked our brains for an alternative place to film, and that's when I wrote your grandfather a letter to put the suggestion forward and was quite surprised when he agreed. I fell in love with this place straightaway. It had huge potential and it's perfect away from the public.'

'You have turned it into something special,' admitted Grace.

Hearing the door open, Grace looked up to see Dougie walk in. 'We need you in Make-up very soon,' he said to Andrew.

'No problem. Dougie, meet Grace Power, owner of Heartcross Castle. Dougie is the producer on this show and my good friend. We've worked together on a lot of projects.'

'Power, the same name as Marley?'

'Grand-daughter,' replied Grace, immediately taking

Dougie's outstretched hand and shaking it. 'Pleased to meet you.'

'I hope Andrew is looking after you.'

'Absolutely, it's been a long time since I've been in here and it looks fabulous.'

'Sit back and watch the filming, if you like. It's the first episode of the new show,' offered Dougie. 'I'm so sorry, I have to shoot, but lovely to meet you.'

Dougie wandered back through the door, where Grace could hear the buzz from the film crew. Andrew stood up. 'I'm sorry, I need to go and quickly get changed and get myself into Make-up, but sit back and relax. Try not to knock over any tables or trophies.'

Watching Andrew walk out of the door, Grace took a sip of her drink then stood up. She wandered around the room perusing the artwork, then stumbled across a couple of old photos of the Castle and the grounds. There was a photo of her grandfather standing outside the Castle shop and in the next photo there was Hector, whom Grace instantly recognised as her grandfather's oldest friend and right-hand man at the Castle. 'Hector,' Grace gasped. 'What happened to you?' Hector had been the chief gardener at Heartcross Castle and she'd loved spending time with him. He had been a jolly man and always had time for her. You would find him up at the greenhouses where Grace loved to hang out, and in the school holidays she would often work alongside him, planting and pruning. She smiled at her memories. Hector had given her a packet of seeds and joked that they were magic and would grow into a high beanstalk and help her reach the sky. The magic seeds he gave her grew into the tallest sunflower she had ever seen and they planted it together in her own special garden at the side of the greenhouse.

Sitting back down on the settee, Grace looked at the clocks on the far wall, telling the time in different cities all over the world. Sipping her water, she watched the TV screens in front of her. Everything was calm in the kitchen. She decided to watch the filming for fifteen minutes before she walked over to Foxglove Farm to collect the boys. Isla had texted constantly throughout the morning giving her updates and the boys were having so much fun. She couldn't wait to hear all about it.

There was movement on the TV screen. Dougie and the camera crew were huddled in conversation and a couple of moments later Andrew appeared on the TV screen, taking Grace completely by surprise. His presence lit up the screen. She knew she was staring at him but couldn't help it, she couldn't take her eyes off him. She already knew he was drop-dead gorgeous, but now she could stare at him without him knowing it. He was mesmerising. The TV cameras began to follow him around a kitchen she no longer recognised. It wasn't just a kitchen and certainly it was nothing like the open space of the servants' quarters she once knew that housed a cracked Belfast sink and a long wooden table for preparing food in the middle of the room. Now there were approximately eight workstations, each with decorative triangular bunting that hung from the corners and draped across the front. Each workstation was equipped with baking trays, utensils, bowls and a mixer. At the back of the kitchen, huge letters hanging from the ceiling spelled out the words 'Andrew's Kitchen', and his logo was painted on the wall. There was a line of American-type fridges, ovens and pans hanging from the ceiling, giving it all a rustic feel, and jars of spices in a wooden rack attached to the wall. Grace admired the fresh fruit scattered in bowls around the room and noticed a tank of fresh lobsters.

As she watched Andrew walk towards the camera, Grace's heart beat faster and she sat up straight. He was staring into the camera at her, causing her stomach to flip. 'Hi, Grace!' he said, giving her a wolfish grin before he took his place behind a workstation.

Even though Grace knew he couldn't see her, there was a flush to her cheeks and she suddenly felt shy. Dougie's voice could be heard in the background counting down and the cameras began to roll.

The theme tune sounded and the cameras panned round the kitchen. 'Welcome, welcome to Andrew's kitchen,' he gushed. 'Today is the first of our brand-new shows live from Heartcross Castle and it's all about cooking up delicious family meals. Today it's all about the lobster.' Andrew gestured towards the tank of fresh lobsters.

In mid-sentence Grace's phone pinged with a text message from Isla. The boys were on the back of Drew's trailer, making their way home towards the Castle. Although Andrew was charismatic on the screen and Grace wanted to watch some more of the show, she was up on her feet walking towards the door.

'Lobster.' She shook her head in amusement. She might not have Andrew's culinary knowledge, but she knew the average family didn't have a tank of fresh lobsters in their kitchen. She herself was lucky to even have electricity and – at the moment – a working fridge. 'You need to try cooking on a budget,' she murmured, heading back down the hallway, thinking that Andrew had no concept of how an average family gets by, day to day. He simply had no clue about the struggles of real life.

Chapter Nine

Grace burst out laughing. Her three boys, looking like ragamuffins, were sitting on hay bales and waving madly at her. With their rosy cheeks and dirty knees, they beamed with happiness. The tractor bounced along towards her and Grace waved back. This was what life was about: having fun and the best time out in the fresh air.

'Mum, we walked the alpacas, and paddled in the stream. There's cows and chickens too,' shouted Freddie, the excitement carrying in his voice.

'And we've baked bread!' exclaimed Joey, pointing enthusiastically to a wrapped loaf in Billy's hands. 'We've had the best time!'

'You have been busy!' exclaimed Grace, happy to see the boys' faces lit up with excitement. Immediately, her thoughts turned back to her own mum. A staple memory of Grace's childhood was her mum's floral-patterned apron tied around her waist. They baked most weekends together, and the aroma of fresh bread came back to her, flooding her brain.

The tractor pulled up in the courtyard and as soon as Drew cut the engine Grace swung the boys down, then took a step back. 'Have you boys had a good time?'

'Yes!' the twins chorused, 'Can we go again? Please!'

'And there was a tyre swinging from the huge oak tree over the stream and we made new friends ... Finn and Angus,' shared Joey. 'The manure pile was a bit smelly though.' He frantically wafted his hand in front of his nose.

'And breathe,' encouraged Grace with a chuckle.

It felt good to see the boys being boys with dirt on their knees and straw in their hair. This was exactly what childhood should be about. Grace knew their lives had been far from fun, and even worse in the last year. Cole hadn't been one for spending any time with the children, and whenever he *did* remember where he lived, his idea of fun was usually to dump the kids in front of the TV and tell them to be quiet.

Grace hadn't seen the children fizzing with excitement like this for a long time and her heart swelled with happiness.

'We've picked some strawberries too!' added Freddie. 'And we've eaten a fair few!'

'You don't say. I think the juice stains on your T-shirt give a lot away. I can't wait to hear all about it. And what about you, Billy?' Grace took the bread from his hands and inhaled the aroma. 'Did you help to make this?'

With a sparkle in his eye Billy gave an emphatic nod,

then wrapped his arms around Grace, giving her the biggest of hugs.

Hearing the cab door of the tractor slam shut, Grace swung round. Standing in front of her was Drew Allaway with his arms open wide and a friendly beam on his face. The last time she'd seen Drew he had been a lanky seventeen year old, wearing khaki overalls, and here he was with the same lopsided grin, looking exactly the same.

'Welcome home, Grace Power! Long time no see! You are the talk of the village.' Drew hugged her tight.

'Again!' she joked, as Drew released her from his hug and took hold of both of her hands.

'Isla couldn't believe it when she heard you were back. You've kept us waiting a long time.'

'I know, I'm sorry … but I'm here now.' Grace was still smiling at her very old friend.

'Last night Isla and I were chatting all about old times and we were telling the boys about the time we attempted to make that raft and it sank, leaving us in the middle of the river. Do you remember? Good times!'

Grace chuckled. 'I do remember.' In the past, whenever Grace had thought about Heartcross her memories had seemed dark, but since she'd arrived back the happy memories were outweighing the bad. 'And it's good to see you, Drew Allaway! You haven't changed a bit – maybe expanded around the waist a little, so I'm assuming they aren't still the same overalls that you use to wear twenty-four-seven.'

'Oi, cheeky, there's nothing wrong with my overalls,' he

replied, letting go of her hands and leaning over the side of the trailer. He picked up a wicker basket and handed it to her. 'The boys have had a whale of a time; they've made bread and picked strawberries. And we've packed you Foxglove Farm sausages, burgers, cheese and milk – and before you say anything, it's on the house. It's good to have you home.'

Grace took a peep inside the basket. Immediately, her eyes brimmed with tears, overwhelmed by the kindness. 'That's a feast fit for a king.'

'Well, you do live in a castle! And I've picked the bed up for you.'

'Thank you, this is amazing. I can't thank you enough.' She turned towards the boys. 'Boys, go and put these in the kitchen for me and get yourself some juice.' Grace handed the basket to the twins and they carried it towards the kitchen whilst Billy stayed by her side.

Drew looked down at him. 'And this one will make a farmer one day, if he's not king of the Castle of course. He helped me with the animal feeds and he's taken a liking to the chickens.'

'Talking of chickens, there's Delia.' Grace pointed over to the bushes.

Billy took a couple of steps forward then stopped, turned, gave Drew a smile and held up his hand. Grace watched in amazement as he high-fived Drew before clomping over to Delia in his bright-yellow wellington boots.

'Don't go far, Billy,' shouted Grace.

Billy gave Grace a cheeky thumbs-up before sprawling on to the grass next to Delia.

'High-fives! You are honoured,' said Grace, still looking at Billy. 'How's he been?'

'At first a little quiet, just watching everything, but as soon as he saw the animals he joined in with everything.'

'Did he speak?' asked Grace hopefully, but already knowing the answer.

Drew shook his head. 'He didn't, but there were lots of smiles and laughter. Isla told me... I hope you are all right?' Drew touched her arm lightly before he began to take the bed out of the back of the trailer.

'It's been a difficult few years.' Grace composed herself. 'But we are here now and the fresh air, change of scenery and getting my old friends back will do us all the world of good.'

'It will. We are always here. Oh, and Isla sent up these too, she thought they may come in handy.' Drew handed over a folded-up duvet and cover, and pillowcases decorated with brightly coloured dinosaurs. 'Now let's get this bed inside. I've brought my tools, I'll put it up for you.'

Grace put her hand on her chest as it heaved a little. Isla had thought of everything – it hadn't even crossed her mind that she would need a duvet and cover. 'Thank you, this is so kind.'

Drew began to lower the bed frame from the trailer and they carried it between them across the cobbled courtyard.

'How is it, living in such an incredible space? I bet you're giving Andrew a run for his money in the luxury stakes, living in the main part of the Castle. Everyone was surprised when Marley turned down Andrew's offer to buy the Castle,' said Drew, admiring the magnificent building in front of him.

Grace was a little taken back by what Drew had revealed. She'd no idea that Andrew was interested in buying the Castle; he'd never mentioned it – but then, why would he? She'd only just arrived. Maybe her grandfather didn't want to sell it because he had nowhere to live? But surely Andrew wouldn't have evicted him in his old age. Or maybe he just didn't want the hassle.

'I could stand here and tell you how blooming marvellous it is and I can't believe my luck... That sounds so ungrateful, doesn't it? I don't mean it to sound like that. My grandfather has given me a roof – a very tall roof,' she joked, making light of the situation. 'And it's given me a fresh start.' Her voice faltered. 'I do wish it was under better circumstances.' Guilt was rising inside her again.

Drew cut in, 'It's an incredible space and undeniably impressive – just a little...' He stopped in his tracks as Grace swung open the back door.

'Run-down and dated,' Grace finished off his sentence. 'Not so luxurious.'

Drew was looking around in wonderment. 'I never thought it would look like this. I reckoned it would probably resemble a royal palace or one of those affluent manor houses tucked away in the countryside.'

'It's exactly the same as the day I left, in terms of decor, but everything else seems to be at breaking point.

The shower trickles, there's no heating as such, only the logs... I can't wait for winter.' She rolled her eyes. 'The windows are single-glazed, there are high ceilings and even a few of the windows are cracked. We've moved into this room as we have everything in here. That is the only settee in the Castle, and upstairs each and every bedroom is stripped bare. It's not what I was expecting. And I'm not sure where I'm going to store the meat you've brought me because the fridge and freezer packed up this morning.'

'Look at it as character-building,' replied Drew, trying to inject enthusiasm into his voice.

'I'm not sure I need my character building this much.'

'I'll take a look at the fridge.' Drew gave it a glance. 'It looks like it's been standing there since the war.' He blew out a breath. 'And just across the courtyard it's a different story.'

'Oh, I know, designer clothes, posh cars, lobsters and more staff than I own mugs.'

'Lobsters?' Drew raised an eyebrow.

'Ha, don't worry about it. Let me show you where the bed is going.'

Drew followed Grace through the kitchen along the dowdy hallway. Grace didn't need to point out the peeling wallpaper, windows with cloudy corners or the ceiling, discoloured from a past leak. Or the outdated lighting fixtures that didn't work, a warped, foggy mirror and doors that didn't open smoothly. The smell was unpleasant, an aroma of mould, mildew and a lack of ventilation.

'I'd think about opening those windows,' said Drew, taking in his surroundings.

'I will, but I'm just hoping the windows don't actually fall out of their frames, as they look a little rotten and that's the last thing I need.'

'Grace, how are you going to live like this? There's a hell of a lot of work that needs doing here. The cost of putting all this right, I wouldn't like to estimate.'

'I know and the Castle was my only inheritance. I've no idea how I'm going to generate such an income to put any of this right...' She felt her voice crack. 'But thankfully the boys don't seem to mind. They think it's amazing,' she added, climbing up the once-handsome staircase. She pushed open a creaking door to reveal a run-down bathroom. There was a dripping faucet, a rust-stained wash-basin, exposed plumbing, cracked tiles with dirty grout lines... It was a room lacking any kind of love and had been neglected over the years.

'Wow!' was all Drew could say. 'New bathrooms aren't cheap either.'

'And of course it's not the only bathroom in the Castle. And along this hallway there are seven bedrooms, all in need of love and attention.'

Drew went to open the door next to the bathroom, but Grace stopped him in his tracks. 'No, not that room,' she said firmly, making Drew withdraw his hand from the wooden knob. 'This way.'

Ever since she'd arrived back at the Castle, that door had stayed firmly shut. It led to her old bedroom and Grace wasn't ready to take a look at what was behind it just yet. Was it as empty and as drab as all the other rooms? Had her grandfather removed all her teenage possessions, the posters from the walls, or was the room exactly the same as the night she'd left the Castle all those years ago? That room was full of so many memories, good and bad, but the argument with her grandfather had taken place in there, and that was the last time she'd ever seen him. She wasn't quite ready to face her demons yet.

'This bedroom is in the best state of them all. The window seems to be intact,' remarked Grace, pushing open the creaky door.

Drew's eyes were wide. 'The best state?'

'At least there isn't that horrible musty smell in here, and the carpet has a little more thread on it than some of the others.'

Drew walked into the middle of the room and swung a glance around, 'It's not exactly...'

'An inviting, warm, cosy room, or one that looks anything like a boy's bedroom. No, but it won't look that bad when we have the bed up and the duvet covers on. It'll look a little less gloomy,' said Grace, trying to put a positive spin on it.

'And what about curtains?' asked Drew.

Grace walked over to the window. 'I'll wait until next month and see how much money I have. Unfortunately, the second I turned up I had to hand over the little I had to pay my grandfather's funeral bill so it's going to be rather a tight month.'

'I'm sure Martha can whip you up some curtains, no problem.'

'Isla's grandmother? Is she living around here?'

'With us up at the farm. She made Isla's curtains for all the vintage caravans on the campsite. I'll ask Isla what material we have and I'll check the shed for paint that will cover up this dark burgundy wallpaper, even though it may need a few coats.'

'Thank you, Drew.'

'I'll go and bring up the bed.' He disappeared out of the room and once more Grace felt overwhelmed by the kindness that radiated from her friends that she abandoned for many years and hadn't even given a second thought. Yet here they were offering her help. It filled her heart with joy.

Opening the window, Grace breathed in a lungful of the summer air. She stared out across the beautiful gardens. Once the bed was up she was going to explore the grounds with the boys. The servants' quarters were in full view from this room, though their old name no longer reflected the reality. It felt like *she* was living on the poorer side of the Castle.

She spotted Andrew as he stepped outside into the small garden at the back of the holding room to take a breather. He was leaning against the wall with his leg bent, looking up at the mountain view, when the butler appeared with a bottle of water on a tray. Grace quietly observed Andrew as he pushed his hair out of his eyes and tilted his face towards the sky. She knew she was staring at him, but she couldn't take her eyes off him. He'd gotten her full

attention with that sultry, damn-right sexy look he had
going on.

Dougie appeared with a clipboard, and then the make-
up artist was by Andrew's side powdering his face. After a
few seconds everyone disappeared back inside, leaving
Andrew swiping a few grapes from the fruit bowl on the
table. He must have sensed he was being watched. He
swung a glance in her direction then looked away, but
immediately looked back towards the window where she
was standing.

Damn, he'd caught her watching him. His gaze
intensified as their eyes locked. She momentarily froze and
didn't look away. Neither did he. It was a bizarre feeling:
they were both staring at each other and neither of them
faltered.

'Penny for them,' said Drew, causing Grace to jump out
of her skin. 'I see you've got the window open.' He propped
the bed frame up against the wall.

'Yes,' she replied, still holding Andrew's gaze, before he
gave a slight smile and followed the others inside. Through
the window Grace had felt some sort of moment between
them, and she was certain he'd felt it too.

'Andrew Glossop – what do you know about him?'
asked Grace, turning around and helping Drew with the
slats from the bed frame.

'Rich, a famous mother, passionate about cooking,
always talking about fancy food I've never heard of. I just
like a good pie and homemade chips with lashings of
vinegar and brown sauce ... good pub grub.' He gave a

small chuckle as he set to work. 'I'm not interested in food on a plate that looks pretty and the small portions in those fancy restaurants.'

They set to work putting the bed up together, which didn't take long. Drew went downstairs and fetched the mattress, and they made up the bed with a sheet and the dinosaur duvet. 'All done, let's grab a drink,' she said triumphantly, her head turning towards the open window as he heard some sort of commotion outside. She looked out into the courtyard and witnessed Andrew ushering the twins out of the door of the servants' quarters.

'What the ...' Before she could finish her sentence she hot-footed across the landing and down the staircase with Drew fast on her heels. Racing across the courtyard, she found the twins standing next to Andrew looking very sheepish.

Grace's heart was pounding. Annoyance began to rise inside her when she heard Andrew's raised voice through the window, and she couldn't help but make mental comparisons to her past. How dare he raise his voice at her boys? Grace had moved here to protect her sons, not to have history repeating itself. After everything they'd been through, she wasn't standing for that.

'What's going on here?' Her tone was far from friendly. She wanted immediate answers.

'Their mother needs to be found. These kids have caused havoc in my kitchen. Filming has stopped. How have they even sneaked past the security on the gates?' Andrew was looking towards Dougie for answers, but none were forthcoming.

'They haven't sneaked in anywhere, they live here,' Grace said, and immediately got Andrew's attention. She opened her arms and the boys came and stood close to her.

'What do you mean, they live here?'

'Exactly what I said, the boys live here. They are my children. What gives you the right to shout at them? I'll tell you now, if you ever shout at my boys again you will have to find another place to film. I don't care what arrangement you had with my grandfather. This is our home.' She glared at him.

A look passed between Andrew and Dougie and Dougie stepped in, 'Okay, let's all calm down here,' he said softly, trying to defuse the situation.

Grace's words had finally registered with Andrew. 'These are your children?'

'Yes, they are, and shouting at them isn't something I'll tolerate. We have been through enough.' Moments earlier Grace had endured the same feeling of dread that Cole used to instil in her when he raised his voice. This place was their safe haven and no one was going to make her feel that way again, not even Andrew. She was sure of that.

Andrew looked flustered. 'I didn't mean to upset you,' he offered, touching Grace's arm, but she pulled away.

She tried to betray no emotion on her face, yet deep down her heart was hammering against her chest. They stared at each other for a second.

Andrew's voice softened. 'Grace, I'm so sorry, you never said you had children.'

'You never asked,' came her curt reply.

'We didn't mean to do anything wrong, we just followed the secret tunnel,' admitted Freddie.

Grace knew exactly which tunnel they were talking about – the secret passageway that led from behind a bookcase in the library all the way to the servant quarters. In the past it would have been used by the servants to travel between the two buildings, cutting out the courtyard.

'That's right, the secret tunnel,' confirmed Joey. 'We took a book from the shelf and wham bam, the bookcase swung back. It was magic.'

Andrew was looking between the twins. 'I feel like I'm in the middle of a TV show but the wrong TV show.'

Grace turned towards Drew. 'Would you take the boys to the Castle, please, get them a drink?'

'Of course. Come on, boys.' The twins followed Drew. Grace was still fuming.

'We've just had to halt filming. Time is money, Grace,' exclaimed Andrew.

With her eyes cartoon wide and shaking her head in disbelief, Grace stood rooted to the spot. 'Time is money,' she repeated, in a stern voice. 'Not everything in life is about money but I don't suppose you understand that, do you? What exactly have they done that's so disastrous?' She watched Andrew's expression as he raised a perfectly arched eyebrow. The tension between them could be cut with a knife. She noticed his cheeks colouring fast as they stared at each other.

Grace was wary of most men, and most of the time she was level-headed, but when it came to her children that was another matter entirely. She didn't feel an ounce of guilt at the way she reacted. All she was doing was sticking up for her own.

He gave a short, strangled laugh. 'I'll show you exactly what they've done. Come and take a look.'

Grace followed Andrew in silence with Dougie following closely behind. All three of them stood in the holding room in front of the TV.

Andrew pressed a few buttons on the remote control and suddenly the recorded show played out on the screen. Grace looked over towards Dougie whose mouth was beginning to lift at the corners. Andrew was pointing at the screen, 'See, look … you can see them creeping behind that workstation... Look,' he repeated. The twins' heads bobbed up and down as they crouched and crawled behind the workstations, the cameras recording their every move. They looked comical and Grace bit her lip to hide her smile. The boys were just being boys. They were having fun. They could be seen whispering to each other as they bunny-hopped towards Andrew's workstation while he was talking to the camera, preparing a lobster paste. He turned his back from the camera for a second and Freddie could be seen running towards the bowl and sticking in his finger before popping it into his mouth.

'Oh my!' exclaimed Grace, pressing her lips together to stop the laughter escaping. 'Is that it?'

Andrew stared at her.

By the look on Freddie's face he'd never tasted anything so foul in his life, and unfortunately at his age politeness didn't prevent him from spitting it out.

'Ew, that's horrible. Don't eat that, Joey, it will kill you.'

Grace couldn't help herself, but laughed out loud.

On screen Andrew spun round, a look of horror on his face mixed with astonishment, 'Who are you? Where have these children come from? Someone call Security... NOW.' Andrew's voice was raised.

'Spit it out,' encouraged Joey, now in full view as he stood up. Which was exactly what Freddie did – all over the floor.

'Oh my God, the kid is feral,' exclaimed Andrew. 'Get them out of my kitchen.'

'Mister, that's not good cooking, not even tomato ketchup would make that taste better,' Freddie said, wiping his mouth with the back of his hand.

Dougie could be heard laughing in the background before he shouted 'cut', but Andrew was not seeing the funny side. 'That lobster is the best money can buy... Dougie, they've just spat it out. Where have these children come from?'

The filming came to a halt and Andrew pressed Stop on the remote control. Grace turned towards him and he stared at her, waiting for some sort of explanation.

'And that's all they've done, criticised your cooking?

Guess what, Andrew, kids usually tell the truth. Maybe the lobster wasn't all that. There's no point feeling crabby about it.' Grace already surmised that Andrew was a perfectionist, and maybe under pressure, but his reaction was a little over the top by any standard.

'And did you just call my kids feral? FERAL.'

The word hung in the air.

Had Grace actually heard him right? She didn't take her eyes off him. 'Honestly, the cheek of you. I think you need to remember your own childhood and think about what you got up to. Feral...' Grace was fuming and she knew she needed to remove herself before she said something she regretted. 'You know where I am when you want to apologise. Now I'm going to make sure my boys are okay.' Grace knew she was giving him a dressing-down.

Still fuming, she nodded at Dougie before turning and heading towards the door. Then she stopped in her tracks, swamped by a sudden anxious feeling. 'Billy, where's Billy?'

Andrew and Dougie looked at each other. 'Billy?' repeated Andrew. 'Who's Billy?'

Grace hadn't passed Billy in the courtyard and now she was beginning to panic. If Billy heard the twins being shouted at, how was he going to react? She couldn't help the fear rising inside her and felt close to tears as that all-too-familiar anguish engulfed her.

'My younger son... You don't understand...' Grace's voice was getting higher and higher. 'He doesn't like shouting...' Grace put on a spurt and took off outside with

Andrew and Dougie close behind. Billy was nowhere to be seen.

'Billy!' Grace shouted.

Andrew attempted to take control of the situation. 'He can't have gone far,' he reassured her.

Grace couldn't help herself. 'You have no clue. This is your fault,' she said looking Andrew straight in the eye before running towards the back door of the Castle.

As she flung open the back door, Drew had the fridge pulled out from the wall and was looking at the wires. He met Grace's worried stare. 'You okay?'

Grace's eyes spanned the room but Billy wasn't there. 'Where's Billy? He's not here or in the courtyard. Did he go down the passageway to the kitchens with you?' Grace was staring straight at the twins who both immediately shook their heads.

'We need to look for him.'

Drew was up on his feet. 'Don't panic, he won't have gone far. Boys, you stay there and don't move,' he said, following Grace out into the courtyard and shutting the back door behind him.

'All this isn't familiar to him. What if ...' Grace's initial thought was that somehow Cole had tracked them down. She knew that was unlikely, but that didn't take away the feeling in the pit of her stomach that she wouldn't wish on her worst enemy. 'He can't even ask for help.' Grace could feel herself shaking.

Just then, Andrew appeared. 'Is he home?' he asked.

Her eyes pricking with tears, Grace shook her head. She

felt her whole body begin to tremble Andrew must have noticed it too, because he stepped forward and clutched her elbows. 'You're shaking,' he said softly, taking her hands and looking directly into her eyes. 'Don't worry, we'll find him.'

Grace didn't have the energy to fight with him. All she wanted was to find Billy and she needed all the help she could get. The Castle grounds were vast, there was a lot to search. Not trusting herself to speak, Grace managed a nod. Andrew gently let go of her hands. 'I'll ring the front gate to make sure no one has got through Security.' He walked to the edge of the courtyard and within seconds hung up. 'The good news is no one has been in or out of the gates. The last person they let through was Drew. So Billy couldn't have gone too far.'

'We will find him,' soothed Drew. 'Try not to panic.'

But Grace was panicking – she knew that if Billy had heard shouting it would have triggered him. She'd been doing everything to make sure his life had stayed as calm as possible since leaving Devon. Full of mixed emotions, she turned towards Andrew. 'This is a little boy that is in turmoil.'

Andrew nodded his understanding. 'Where would you like us to start searching?'

'I'll take the maze area,' suggested Drew, 'I know it like the back of my hand. It could be possible he's lost his way in the middle.'

'I'll cover the grounds near the fountain and the path to the gatehouse,' put forward Dougie, who had joined them.

'We'll take the outhouses, the walled gardens, the orchards and the old greenhouse area.' Grace looked at Andrew.

The unknown was stabbing in the pit of Grace's stomach as they split up and went in different directions. Grace and Andrew hurried towards the outhouses calling out Billy's name, checking every inch of the old sheds, but Grace realised it didn't matter how loud she shouted, Billy was never going to answer – he hadn't spoken for weeks, since being traumatised by the life they used to live. This morning had been a huge step in the right direction. Grace remembered his genuine smile after spending time at the farm and his joy at making friends with Delia.

'There's the old toolshed too,' observed Grace, pointing towards it. Within seconds she was pushing open the ramshackle door. A shaft of light was filtering through the dirty windows and clouds of dust motes floated in the air. In front of her was a large work table, a rusty old lawnmower, and paint tins stacked in the corner. The shed housed hundreds of spiders with cobwebs clinging on to every roof beam, and there were dead flies on the windowsill and mouse droppings on the floor. Grace shuddered and couldn't wait to close the door behind her. 'Nothing,' she said grimly.

'Has he ever wandered off before?' asked Andrew, looking up in the trees to see if Billy had climbed up there.

Grace shook her head. 'Never,' she replied. 'Andrew, I'm beginning to worry. There's things you don't know... Billy hasn't spoken for a while. This was our fresh start...' She gestured to her eye.

'It's okay, you don't need to explain, and for what it's worth I'm sorry, truly sorry.' Andrew looked stricken.

Grace's legs were still trembling as they darted towards the wall gardens that led to the orchard and the place where the old greenhouses were situated. Even though Grace hadn't been here for years it was all so familiar to her. She'd spent most of her childhood in this part of the garden, pottering about. Looking around now, she was amazed to see how well maintained the gardens were. This wasn't what she was expecting. She'd imagined it to be wild, overgrown and out of control, but the grass was mowed to within an inch of its life and the flower beds pruned to perfection, exactly like the gardens outside the Grand Hall. They raced through the orderly rows of trees, past the bench where she used to sit and read books, scanning every bush as they went. Frantic, her chest heaved as they both continued to call out Billy's name.

Then Grace stopped dead in her tracks and grabbed Andrew.

'What is it?' he asked.

Grace could feel herself shaking as she spotted a familiar figure pottering away in the greenhouse. It felt like time had stood still. Everything looked exactly the same. Seedling trays on wire racks with new shoots poking out, shelving units holding a variety of pots, a watering can hanging near the door, baskets full of strawberries and cherry tomatoes – nothing seemed to have changed in all these years.

'Oh my gosh, is that you?' Grace couldn't believe her eyes as she sprinted towards the glass building and stopped outside the door. The man inside spun round and she locked eyes with a wizened face that was staring straight back at her. His face was a map of wrinkles, his hazel eyes framed by thick white bushy brows, and his spectacles were perched on the tip of his nose. He was dressed in a blue checked shirt with his sleeves rolled, his trousers held up by braces.

The man squinted and took a step forward. Grace saw his chest heave and tears spring to his eyes. 'Lady Grace, is that you?' He immediately dropped the fork and pulled off his gloves, placing them on the table in front of him.

'Hector, it is you, isn't it?'

'It sure is,' he replied, the tears freely flowing down his old man's cheeks as he quickly retrieved a handkerchief from his pocket and dabbed his eyes. 'Oh, Lady Grace, I never thought I'd see you again.' Hector was shaking and Grace steadied him before hugging him tight.

'It's really you, isn't it?'

'It's really me,' replied Grace.

It was a long time since she'd heard Hector call her Lady Grace and the words instantly melted her heart. It was his special name for her. 'I'm so sorry, Hector, I really am,' were the only words she could muster up as she took a step back and looked at one of her grandfather's oldest friends, the Castle gardener she had known for years.

'Where have you been? There are so many questions.'

Grace put her hands on his elbows. 'I'm here now but,

Hector, my little boy is missing. He's about this high—' But before Grace could finish her sentence, Hector pointed to just past the vegetable patch. 'Would that be him? I've just rung Andrew's mobile to ask did he know who the boy belonged to. I left a message. I didn't want to approach him in case I frightened him.'

Andrew quickly pulled the phone out of his pocket as it pinged.

With relief, Grace grabbed Andrew's arm, the tears now free-flowing down her cheeks. With her hand on her heart, 'Thank God,' she murmured. 'I'm sorry for crying ... actually not sorry,' she smiled through her tears, 'I was just worried sick.'

'You don't need to apologise.' Andrew soothed, 'I'm just happy he's here and safe.'

Billy was bent down inside a weathered wood frame bound with chicken wire creating a yard enclosure. Inside was a board rising on a slant, leading to an old chicken coop that had seen better days. The coop door was open, and Billy was stuffing in hay from a nearby bale. Grace spotted Delia and Nigella pecking for bugs in the beaten earth.

'He's very taken with those chickens,' observed Hector. 'Here,' he said, handing Grace a tissue.

Grace was just about to approach Billy when she heard footsteps. Drew and Dougie came racing up through the orchard, a little breathless.

'He's safe,' confirmed Andrew. 'He's at the coop.'

'Thank God,' replied Drew, looking towards Billy, who was oblivious to everything going on around him. Grace watched Billy smiling to himself as he pulled at the hay. It was a smile that had resurfaced since arriving at the Castle and Grace noticed how relaxed and happy he looked. 'This place is doing him the world of good,' she said, looking at Drew, who nodded.

Once Billy had put fresh hay in the coop he began filling up the water dispenser from the nearby stream.

Grace turned towards Drew. 'Drew, could you do me a favour, go back to the Castle and make sure the twins are okay?'

'Twins?' quizzed Hector, a huge beam spread across his face. 'There are more of you?'

'Yes, I have three boys,' answered Grace with pride. She turned back towards Drew. 'And put the kettle on. I'll bring Billy back in a moment. Would you like to come back with us, Hector?'

'Very much so, Lady Grace.'

Hector, Drew and Dougie began to walk back towards the Castle but Andrew stayed behind for a moment, 'I am sorry, Grace. I didn't mean to...'

'There's no harm done, I'm just relieved he's here and safe. Thank you for helping me to search for him.'

'I don't know what you guys have been through, but if there is anything I can do...'

'Thank you,' she replied, looking back towards Billy.

'I'll see you back at the Castle.' Andrew looked over towards Billy. 'He looks a lot like you,' he said, before touching Grace's arm and heading back to the Castle.

Grace fixed her gaze back on Billy, who spun round with

a big smile. He waved his hand at her to come quickly. Excitement was written all over his face. 'What is it, Billy?' she asked, walking over towards him. Smiling, he pointed inside the coop and Grace bent down next to him to take a look. There were two white eggs resting on the hay.

'Wow, just look at them. We can ask Andrew if you can have them for supper tonight.'

Billy's eyes sparkled.

'But first, I need a cuddle,' she insisted, opening out her arms.

Grace's heart soared with love for her little boy. He'd given her the fright of her life disappearing like that. She pressed her lips against his cheek and hugged him so tight he could barely breathe. 'And, Billy, you must promise me never to wander off without telling me where you are going.' Grace swallowed and quickly brushed away a lone tear that rolled down her face. The boys were her world. 'You had me worried for a moment,' she said, cupping her hands around his face and kissing him on the forehead. 'You like it here, don't you?'

The look on Billy's face answered Grace's question. 'Now let me get those eggs.' Grace slowly and carefully reached inside the coop and Billy's face beamed as he cradled the eggs. 'And don't squeeze them too tight or they will break.'

Together, they ambled back towards the Castle and Grace's thoughts turned back towards Hector. She'd been floored seeing him again and couldn't quite believe he was still at the Castle. She'd imagined he'd retired a long time ago, but it seemed he was far from retired, judging by all the hard work he'd put in. The Castle gardens were immaculate, not a blade of grass out of place or a weed lurking in the flowerbeds. Grace's thoughts were in overdrive. How difficult would it be to open up the Castle gardens to the public again? Surely that would put Heartcross Castle on the map and generate more income. Maybe it was something she could talk to Hector about. Then another thought flashed through her mind. Who was paying Hector to maintain the Castle gardens? Was he still living in the cottage on the edge of the estate? She had so many questions she wanted to ask him.

With Billy carrying the eggs like his life depended on it, Grace gently ruffled his hair. 'And wait till I tell you what your brothers have been up to.' She gave a little chuckle. 'They've discovered the secret passageway in the Castle and sneaked into the servants' quarters.'

Billy's eyes were wide.

'They've been upsetting the neighbour, but here's a question: would you like to eat lobster for your tea?'

Billy scrunched up his face, causing Grace to laugh, then held up the eggs.

'I thought not,' she replied, 'but maybe that's something we shouldn't go telling Andrew today.'

Chapter Ten

The boys were asleep by 8 p.m. Sitting in the kitchen Grace could hear the welcome hum of the fridge once more. Thankfully, it had been something Drew could fix, but Grace knew it was only a temporary repair – the fridge was really on its last legs. With her feet up and a mug of tea in her hand Grace began to mull over her financial position. The Castle gardens were very much on her mind. She googled Heartcross Castle. There were hundreds of images and articles in tourist magazines and newspapers featuring the Castle, some claiming the gardens were the best kept in Scotland. She stumbled across an old photograph of her grandfather and Hector, standing proudly in front of the fountain, in the *Sunday Times* magazine. The caption stated that Heartcross Castle was the tourist attraction of the summer. As she began to scroll, one article stood out in particular with its bold headline 'Heartcross Castle Gardens to close'.

It didn't give away much more information except that Marley Power had closed the Castle to the public. The next bold headline read, 'Financial ruin for Heartcross Castle'. On the screen was a photograph of a line of burly men removing the furniture from the Castle. Grace looked at the date of the article: it was one year to the day after she had left Heartcross. Her heart sank as she placed her phone on the table; she couldn't bear to read any more. After making herself another cup of tea she sat back down on the settee and picked up the outstanding electricity bill, which needed to be paid promptly. It made her think: did this bill include the electricity for the servants' quarters too? It seemed a little extortionate for the small living space that her grandfather had occupied. Grace made a mental note to talk to Andrew about what his rent actually included.

Hearing a rap on the door, Grace looked over her shoulder to see Hector smiling through the glass. He pulled his flat cap from his head and waited for Grace to open the door.

'Come on in,' she gestured. 'Don't stand outside.' Before Hector had even stepped into the kitchen Grace was tearful; she already knew that the next hour would be somewhat emotional.

'This is so strange, Lady Grace, I just never envisaged you being back here ... where you belong. Home.'

'Home,' she repeated, giving Hector a warm smile. 'What can I get you? Tea, coffee?'

'Do you mind?' asked Hector, pointing to the small oak cupboard at the side of the armchair.

Grace was puzzled, but shook her head. 'Be my guest.' She watched Hector open the cupboard door and take out two glasses and a whisky bottle.

'Your grandfather and I had our own secret stash. I'm not sure why it was a secret or why we had to hide it in a cupboard though,' he chuckled, sitting down in the armchair. 'Since Marley's passing, I haven't been back in here.' He took a moment.

'I understand, it must have been difficult for you,' replied Grace. 'You had been the best of friends for so many years.'

'A lifetime,' Hector cut in. 'We met at primary school and the rest is history, as they say.'

'You've been through so much together,' said Grace.

'More than you will ever know,' replied Hector, through bleary eyes. For a second he was lost in thought, then it looked like he was about to say something but changed his mind.

'Are you still in the cottage on the estate?'

Hector nodded. 'I am.' He offered Grace a glass and she took it from him. Hector poured the amber liquid into both glasses, then clinked his against hers. 'Here's to Marley.'

'Marley,' repeated Grace, swirling the liquid around in her glass before taking a sip. She scrunched up her face as the whisky burnt the back of her throat, but, within seconds, the instant warmth of the liquor rushed through her body.

For a moment, they sat in silence. There were so many

questions Grace wanted to ask but she didn't know where to begin.

'I bet you can't believe the state of this place, can you?' said Hector. 'It's not as grand as it used to be.'

Grace looked around the room, 'It was a bit of a shock, to be fair. Not what I was expecting. Everything seems to be run into the ground.'

'What happened, Lady Grace? Where have you been for all this time?' asked Hector cautiously. 'We've missed you so much.'

This was such a hard conversation for Grace but it was one that needed to be had.

'Running from life,' she admitted, taking a breath. 'I'm not sure what you know about the night I left but now I'm feeling deeply ashamed.' Grace explained about the argument with her grandfather the night she left and how she ended up in Devon and met Cole. As the words left her mouth her reason for running away seemed so lame, it was just a teenage argument that got out of hand, and as time went on it became harder to make amends. 'I was angry, grieving about Mum. The pain of losing her was so overwhelming, and the challenge was to stop that pain from crushing me, but I failed deeply at that. It hurt so much that she'd gone and at times I felt I could barely breathe. It's no excuse, I know. I just wanted her back.'

'We all did, Lady Grace, It was a heartbreaking time for all of us. We all tried to cope in our own way, including your grandfather.'

Grace nodded, 'And I know I didn't help, I was difficult ...'

'That you were, Lady Grace, a little rebellious.' Hector was smiling, trying to lighten the situation, but Grace knew there was some truth in what he was saying.

'My relationship with my grandfather seemed to change. One minute I was a little girl and we enjoyed fishing on the river and walks along the cliffs, and the next, everything was so strict. I just don't know what changed. It's only when you have your own kids and life becomes so difficult that...'

Grace noticed the tears welling up in Hector's eyes. 'I don't have children. I used to think of you and your mum as my family.' Hector's voice faltered. 'Your grandfather missed you every day. He was thrown into a situation that was difficult, especially at his age. He was a military man, his life was regimented, it followed routine. He was in control of most situations except you, and all I know is he didn't want history repeating itself. He wanted what was best for you.'

'History?' asked Grace, a little confused.

'Your mum was sixteen when she went to a party and fell pregnant with you.'

Grace was only fifteen when her mum passed away and it had never crossed her mind how old her mother was when she gave birth to her.

'The scandal of a schoolgirl having a baby at the age of sixteen with no father on the scene. But your grandfather supported her when it all came to light. He stood by her and protected your mum at all costs just like any good parent would do. He didn't care that they were being talked about or the constant speculation about who your father was. He made sure your mum and you were cared for the best he could.' Hector's eyes were tearful as he shared the past and it was clear to Grace that she'd had the most supportive family and hadn't realised it. What she would do to turn back time...

With her heart in a spin, Grace felt like a selfish fool. 'Why didn't my grandfather talk to me about his fears?' she asked, trying to keep her emotions under control as the full enormity of what Hector was sharing hit her.

'You were a teenage girl and hurting yourself. It was difficult. Marley wasn't getting any younger and maybe it's a generation thing – these days it's good to talk but back then...'

Knowing she'd rebelled and hit the self-destruct button when she hadn't got her own way, Grace felt Hector's words whirling in her mind. She had to live with so many regrets... And now she knew that she wasn't much older than her mother when she gave birth to the twins, she knew exactly how difficult life could be, and that her grandfather only wanted the best for her.

'I must have been a crushing disappointment to my grandfather,' she said.

For a brief moment her throat became tight and Grace forced herself to breathe calmly. She stared at the empty whisky glass and bit down on her bottom lip to stop the tears cascading down her face again. She remained silent for a moment before looking back up at Hector.

'I know for a fact, as much as your grandfather had all those fears, he loved you… And look at you and your three boys. He would have been so proud,' shared Hector, placing his hand on Grace's knee. 'We did try and look for you.'

Grace knew how difficult it would have been to find her with the constant moving around. The solicitor had only tracked her down from the electoral register, after she refused to move with Cole and settled at the flat.

'My mum was lucky to have my grandfather,' stated Grace, thinking what it would have been like for her to admit she was pregnant and being the centre of local gossip. Grace thought back to the time when her mum was alive. They were so close and always spent time together. Not once had Grace thought that she was missing out on family life by not having a father. It was only when Grace had the boys and Cole was never home that Grace began to wonder about who her father actually was. Of course she was curious – who was he? What life was he living? Did he have any other family?

'We were all lucky to have both of you,' replied Hector, and Grace could see he meant every word.

'Hector, do you know who my father is?' Grace asked the question that was burning inside.

Her chest pounded as she waited for him to answer.

Reluctantly, Hector shook his head. 'No one knew, but if it's something you wish to find out there are ways and means these days.'

'Maybe it's a journey to think about for another day. I've managed this long.' She gave a smile. 'The last few years have been difficult. The boys' father … by the end it wasn't the healthiest of relationships and looking back I should have the strength to leave a long time ago. Most days I existed to get us through…' Grace swallowed.

Hector was listening. 'I'm so sorry you've suffered, Lady Grace, you didn't deserve to be treated in that way.'

'I know I've hurt a lot of people and you've got to believe me, Hector, when I say I'm truly sorry.'

'I do. We were relieved when you sent your letter – at least we knew you were okay. We just hoped each day you would come back home.'

'Me and you both now,' admitted Grace.

Hector poured them both another drink whilst they sat in silence for a moment lost in their own thoughts.

'Since I've been home I've seen some newspaper articles about the Castle. The closure of the gardens.'

Hector nodded. 'They were closed to the public because of a combination of things. With everything that was going on, your grandfather didn't have the strength to keep going – we were both due for retirement. The constant flow of people traipsing through the grounds and the business side of it all became too much and less important to him. I think your grandfather was hoping one day you might have taken over the business, but once you'd gone he just shut it down. The only problem being most of the furniture and artwork had been loaned by prestige businesses, and when the Castle shut, most of the stuff was taken back.

'Your grandfather used his small amount of savings to keep this place going as long as he could, but over time everything fell to rack and ruin. It was only in the last six months that Andrew's rent helped to keep your grandfather afloat more than usual.'

Grace was taking everything in. 'And you're still in the cottage? I was amazed you were still here. I couldn't believe it when I saw you standing in the greenhouse like no time had passed at all.'

'I thought I was hallucinating when I saw you too, Lady Grace, and I couldn't believe it when I saw your boys. They look just like you.'

'They are quite amazing, aren't they?' she replied. 'But I thought maybe your life would take you away from the Castle once it shut down?'

'Never. This place has been my life, is my life, your grandfather is my oldest friend, we've stayed together through thick and thin and although it's a little difficult now drinking whisky on my own, I could never leave. This has been my home for all these years. Where would I go?' Hector dabbed his eyes with his handkerchief.

'You've had one hell of a friendship, haven't you?'

'We have,' replied Hector.

Smiling warmly at each other, they took a sip of their drinks. There was still so much to talk about. 'I have to say the gardens look incredible. Is all that down to you?'

'It is. Those gardens give me a purpose and come rain or shine I can't wait to get out there each day.'

'How do you get paid?' asked Grace, and noticed a look of puzzlement creep across Hector's face.

'Paid? Lady Grace, I don't get paid. I have savings and my pension to keep me going. I do it for the love of this place. It keeps my mind and body active and I don't know what I'd do without pottering around the grounds all day every day. All those years ago when I lost my Kate I knew I'd never find or want another love in my life. Those plants out there became my love. This is my home and the only way I'm leaving is in—'

'Don't say that, Hector.'

'I'm so glad you're home, Lady Grace, I know if anyone can turn this place around, it's you.' He gave her the warmest of smiles and held his glass up to her. 'Welcome home,' he toasted.

'Thank you, Hector.'

Listening to Hector, she understood the love he had for the Castle. She thought about what he had just shared with her. His loyalty to her grandfather and the Castle grounds should be commended. People like Hector were a rare breed and he'd given up his days to keep the Castle grounds looking the best they could.

'It's good to be back,' she replied.

But with the Castle valuation preying heavily on her mind, Grace couldn't imagine taking all this away from Hector. He'd genuinely looked pleased to see her – how could she possibly sell up when all he'd ever known was Castle life?

Chapter Eleven

I t was 9 a.m. and the sun was streaming through the window. Most of the night Grace had tossed and turned and stared at the ceiling. She wasn't thrilled by the idea of living in financial ruin for the rest of her life whilst there was the perfect solution of selling the Castle and purchasing a modest detached with a manageable garden, but all Grace could think about was Hector and how happy the boys were. It just wasn't an easy decision to make, but what she couldn't do was lose all sense of perspective. If the Castle had to be sold it was something she would have to talk to Hector about, but for the time being she was going to keep the valuation to herself.

Still with the future of the Castle very much on her mind, Grace opened the blinds and looked out over the courtyard, where Delia and Nigella were already scratching under the bushes. Grace smiled at the comical way that they waggled their bums, their plumage sticking up in the air like they didn't have a care in world whilst they pecked for rich pickings. All looked quiet over at the servants' quarters. Dougie's car, a shining dark-green Aston Martin, was parked in the courtyard next to a food van that was making a delivery.

Last night, after Hector had left, Grace had placed the whisky bottle back in the cupboard and begun to think about surviving on the little money she had left. After discovering a large piece of white cardboard propped up behind the dresser and a black felt-tip pen her grandfather had used for his daily crossword, Grace had set to work devising a chart like she'd done many a time when trying to make ends meet with the money that Cole had brought home. The chart was divided into columns, and a budget allocated for everyday essentials. The little money she had left she divided up and placed in the columns. Without a doubt, the next few weeks were going to be a struggle until Andrew paid his rent again. Grace had it on her to-do list to talk to Hector about the possibility of opening up the grounds again to the public, but she wasn't sure if she would be biting off more than she could chew, knowing that in the past hundreds of people could pass through the gates in one day alone –how many staff would she need to pay for an operation on that scale? Grace wasn't opposed to hard work, and she had fire in her belly to save the Castle, but already knowing that replacing the windows would run into thousands of pounds, she wasn't going to find it an easy task.

Opening up the back door to let the warmth of the

sunshine in, Grace looked down at the step. She was amazed to discover a box of fresh fruit and vegetables: potatoes, asparagus, tomatoes and strawberries. Hector must have left them there. She felt thankful – this and the food that Drew had given her from the farm would make her and the boys a few more meals.

'What do you have there?' asked Joey, appearing at the door and stretching up his arms.

'Did you sleep well?' asked Grace, carrying the box of vegetables and fruit into the kitchen and tilting it towards him. 'Come and look.'

Joey was up on the stool and began taking the food from the box and laying them on the worktop. His eyes lit up when he saw the bright purple plums and he sank his teeth straight into one. The juice ran down his chin.

He scrunched up his face causing Grace to laugh. 'A little sour?'she asked. 'Take another bite, you'll get used to the taste.'

Joey did exactly that.

'The Castle vegetable garden must be full of rich pickings. We could take a basket up when everyone is up. Drew was going to look to see if he had any paint left in his sheds so we can try and spruce up this room a little if we are living mainly in here. What do you think?'

'Can we help paint?' asked Joey.

'Of course you can!'

Within seconds Billy and Freddie appeared in the doorway and Grace beckoned them over for hugs before popping some bread under the grill for toast.

'The sun is out so we need to enjoy that fresh mountain air. Then we are going to take a look in the vegetable gardens, and at some point I need to check out the state of the old Castle shop. Does that sound like a plan?'

There was no answer. Grace spun round to see the back door wide open and all three boys out in the courtyard with their feet stuffed into their wellington boots. Freddie was chasing them with the old hosepipe that was attached to the tap on the outside wall. Billy was giggling and running in circles whilst he was being chased and Joey was trying to turn the outside tap on with both hands. Grace heard a squeal as water rushed from the hose up in the air. After quickly removing the toast from the grill she cupped her hands around her mug of tea and watched the boys having fun. She gave a huge grin. They were so carefree, smiles on their faces, without a worry in the world – unlike the financial mess that was weighing heavy on her own shoulders. Within seconds their pyjamas were soaked, water dripping from the ends of their noses, and they splashed happily about in the puddles they'd made on the ground. How things were changing for them in such a short time. Her heart gave a little leap as she carried on watching their entertainment. Out in the fresh air, squealing with fun, the boys were being boys, exactly how it should be.

She glanced up to see Andrew watching the boys from the top window of the servants' quarters. Their eyes met for a brief moment and he gave a small wave before moving away from the window. Yesterday they'd butted heads but Andrew had apologised and Grace had accepted.

With the boys enjoying the outdoors, Grace was sitting at the table and tucking into the hot buttery toast when all of a sudden a gush of water sprayed into the kitchen from the hose. 'Boys, be careful, I don't want to spend my day cleaning up!'

'Sorry, Mum!' shouted Freddie, giggling as the water then sprayed up the windows.

Grace let them run off steam for another ten minutes before making a fresh batch of toast. She popped her head out of the door and noticed Andrew standing in his doorway, on the phone. He was looking up at the tower of the Castle and seemed deep in conversation. He looked dashing in a crisp white shirt with a sage-green chequered waistcoat with matching trousers and a flat cap. Very distinguished, in fact downright handsome, thought Grace. He had a pair of wellington boots on the doormat but before putting them on he disappeared back inside.

After placing her plate in the sink, she called out to the boys. 'Turn off that hose and come and get your breakfast. In fact, you are not coming inside, you are soaking! I'll bring the toast outside.'

She did so and found the boys sitting cross-legged in a row leaning back on their hands with their legs stretched out in front of them.

'He won't know it's us,' whispered Freddie to Joey, and Billy brought his finger up to his lips to shush them.

'Who won't know it's you?' asked Grace immediately, looking between all three of them.

'Nothing,' replied the twins in unison with Billy

shrugging his shoulders and looking incredibly adorable as he silently denied all knowledge of any wrongdoing.

'Please tell me you haven't been up to any sort of mischief.' Grace looked between the boys and across the courtyard. 'Mmm,' she said, narrowing her eyes at the boys. But everywhere was calm and there wasn't a soul around. 'I still think you're up to something.'

Once the boys had finished their breakfast they were up and messing around with the hose again.

'Stop there!' Grace ordered. 'Let's go and have a wander up to the vegetable gardens and say good morning to Hector. But strip off those wet PJs before you go inside and I can hang them on the line to dry.'

Hearing voices, they all looked across the courtyard to see Andrew talking to Rose on the doorstep. Grace noticed a sheepish look pass between Freddie and Joey. All three boys raced towards the door, where they kicked off their wellies then wriggled out of their wet PJs, leaving them in a pile. Grace chuckled as she witnessed three bare bums disappearing inside. Leaning back on her hands she took a moment and tilted her face up to the early morning sun. Then she heard whispering coming from the open bedroom window. Looking up, she saw all three boys peeping over the window sill, looking across the courtyard at Andrew.

Grace swung a glace over the courtyard to see Andrew hopping on one leg whilst trying to get his balance. For a second she wondered what the hell was going on, then the penny dropped. Grace brought her hand up to her mouth and tried to stifle her laughter as Andrew picked up both wellington boots and tipped them upside down. The water gushed on to the ground.

'Oh my God, you little monkeys,' uttered Grace under her breath.

Andrew swung a look over to Grace and their eyes locked. He was now striding over the courtyard in his sodden argyle-patterned socks whilst holding his wellington boots in the air. The peal of laughter from the open upstairs window didn't go unnoticed by Grace.

Grace was up on her feet and mouthing 'sorry' to Andrew. Feeling like a naughty schoolgirl, she hot-footed it to the back door, which she firmly shut behind her before throwing her head back and laughing. She couldn't help it.

'Grace!' Andrew shouted, but the kitchen door was firmly shut.

Peeping out of the window, she saw Andrew half-hopping back to the servants' quarters. Grace just prayed once he calmed down a little he'd see the funny side.

After taking a moment to compose herself, she walked to the bottom of the stairs.

'Boys, get yourselves down here now.'

Within seconds, all three boys appeared at the bottom of the stairs.

'Which one of you filled the wellington boots with water?' she managed to say in quite a firm, stern tone, but as soon as Freddie caught her eye she cracked a smile.

'See, you think it's funny,' pointed out Freddie. 'It was just a bit of fun.'

'No, I don't,' Grace replied, biting her lip.

'Yes you do!' claimed Joey, backing up his brother, whilst Billy too was grinning.

All four of them burst out laughing.

'Boys, you are going to get me in serious trouble if you carry on. We can't go falling out with the neighbour.'

'But he's so stuck-up, la-de-dah,' exclaimed Joey. 'And don't forget he tried to poison us with some lobster paste.'

'He didn't force-feed you that paste. You sneaked into his kitchen. Which we will not be doing again.'

The boys looked at each other.

'Oh my God, what have you done now?'

'Nothing,' protested Freddie, which was backed up by Joey.

'Good, because if I find out you've continued to terrorise our neighbour, you boys will be in serious trouble.'

As much as Grace thought it was rather amusing, she knew she needed to nip any further pranks in the bud because, after all, she was relying on Andrew's rent money to get by.

'And it was only water,' protested Freddie.

'And you three know the difference between right and wrong.'

'It was just a bit of fun,' chipped in Joey.

'That might be so but you have to do the right thing and apologise to him.'

Suddenly, all three boys looked horrified.

'Do we really?' asked Joey.

'Yes, you do, but luckily for you, he's just gone out.' Grace heard the roar of a car engine and looked out of the window to see Andrew sitting in the passenger seat of a car as it travelled towards the Castle gates. 'But as soon as he is back...'

Reluctantly, all three boys nodded.

'Once I've hung your PJs on the line we'll have a wander down to the orchard and say hello to Hector and maybe collect the eggs from the coop.'

Billy clenched his fists with excitement.

'And whilst I'm hanging the clothes on the line do not go getting into any more trouble.'

Grace scooped up the wet clothes from the ground and quickly rinsed them under the outside tap before squeezing them dry and throwing them over a nearby line that ran between two trees. Hearing her phone beep from inside the kitchen, she hurried to quickly read the message from Isla.

'What are you doing at the weekend? Martha can come and measure your windows for curtains and Drew has found some paint that could be good to paint the boys' room. What do you think? I can bring the boys over too?'

'You are like my fairy godmother!' replied Grace, hugging the phone. 'Thank you, that will be perfect.'

Almost immediately a text pinged back. 'The weather will be scorching too! I'll bring the boys swimsuits, it'll be a great day for a water fight.'

Grace chuckled. 'As long as they stay out of Andrew Glossop's way that will be perfect!'

Thirty minutes later, after everyone was washed and changed, Grace pushed Billy in the wheelbarrow as they walked through the gardens. She admired the wall garden that was full of bright-coloured gladioli, standing tall over the crimson geraniums and blue delphiniums. There was a little metal patio set, two chairs and a table under the canopy of wisteria that had clung to the brick archway, with a view beyond of the mountains.

Bouncing in the barrow, Billy laughed and Grace was filled with happiness. She'd noticed that since arriving at the Castle Billy was spending more time with his brothers than clinging to her, but she wasn't sure that was a good thing if the twins were going to get up to so much mischief.

'Come on, you two, you're lagging behind,' she teased, looking over her shoulder at the twins.

Each of them was carrying a large wicker basket which Grace had found in the utility room, stacked up at the side of the washing machine. They were perfect for collecting any vegetables from the gardens. Hector saw them coming and waved from the greenhouse. 'Good morning, Lady Grace,' he said, tipping his cap.

'Good morning, Hector! We've come to thank you for our food parcel. Then I remembered the vegetable patch and fruit gardens. Would it be okay to see what you have?'

'Maybe we could sell tubs of fruit at the Castle gate?' suggested Freddie.

'Now that is an enterprising idea, young man,' encouraged Hector. 'We have all the berries on this side, blackberries, gooseberries, strawberries – and look at those peaches and plums.'

'Pie! Can we make pie?' Joey rubbed his tummy, making a 'yum' sound.

'If you have any spare pie to sample, do let me know.' Hector patted his belly. 'I love a good pie. And over here we have lettuce, radish, spring onions and tomatoes. And, Billy, I think you'll find two eggs waiting for you in the coop.'

Billy launched himself from the barrow and raced towards the coop at top speed. Within seconds he was waving the eggs madly in the air.

'This mountain air is certainly good for these boys,' said Grace, watching Hector hand him an egg box. 'Now put that box in the barrow safely.' Grace paused for a second before turning back towards Hector. 'Hector, what state is the Castle shop in?'

Hector raised an eyebrow. 'The Castle shop... Why, are you thinking of opening it up again?'

'It was something I was going to talk to you about. My financial situation isn't great and I don't have a job. I'm thinking if it's doable it'll fit in perfectly with the boys' starting their new school.'

Hector looked up at the magnificent Castle. 'It's a beautiful building. The inside doesn't reflect the outside, but the tourists don't know that. You can only try, Lady Grace. The gardens are in a wonderful state and the fountain is still running. It's operated from that lever over there.' Hector walked across to a panel attached to the side of the outhouse.

In the distance the sound of water droplets could be heard pattering against the shale at the bottom of the pool. Immediately the boys raced down the path and clambered over the edge of the walled fountain and held out their hands trying to catch the water.

'I'll switch it off because the bottom of the pool needs cleaning; it's full of leaves and moss. I can get that cleaned out for you, but as far as the shop goes I have no idea – you'll have to take a look.'

As Hector switched off the water, the boys let out a groan. 'It needs cleaning first, boys, but it'll be up and running soon,' shouted Grace.

'How much would the fountain cost to run? Any idea?' asked Grace.

'Not too much. Once it's filled the pump uses the same water – it just goes round on a cycle. So it'll be just the cost of the electricity, but the revenue from the tourists would cover that if you reopened the Castle gardens.'

Grace acknowledged what Hector was saying – one thing will pay for the other – but she needed to work out how to initially get back on track. 'Right, boys, let get this fruit picked and see how much we can sell.'

'Here, take these.' Hector disappeared back inside the greenhouse and returned with a stack of clear plastic punnets. 'Fill these up, perfect for selling at the Castle gate, and I'll get on to cleaning that fountain.'

'Thank you, Hector, you are so kind and these are brilliant. Come on, boys!'

Billy climbed back in the barrow and with the boys swinging the baskets and the sun beating down Grace began to hum a tune as they made their way through the orderly row of trees.

'Right, let's get to work. All the fallen plums, put in a pile over here,' ordered Grace, 'and the rest of the fruit and veg, let's fill those punnets… On your marks, get set, go!'

Immediately Freddie was up a ladder leaning against the tree trunk and throwing plums to Joey. Billy dashed in front and began scooping up the crop of windfalls whilst Grace picked the tomatoes and strawberries from inside the greenhouses. They all danced and the twins sang as they set to work. Within thirty minutes the punnets were brimming with brightly coloured fresh fruit, and with their bellies full and juice-stained mouths the boys had devoured as much fruit as they possibly could.

'I think we are done now, boys. Shall we see how much fruit we can sell at the Castle gates?'

All three of the boys jumped for joy. After loading the punnets on to the barrow they headed back past Hector who was scooping up leaves out of the fountain.

'Hector, look how much we have,' shouted Freddie.

Hector pushed up the peak of his cap. 'You have been busy. How much for a punnet of plums?' he asked.

Freddie and Joey looked at each other then at Grace and shrugged.

'One pound,' she suggested.

Immediately, Hector rummaged in the pocket of his trousers and handed the loose change to Freddie. 'Your first sale!'

Taking Grace by surprise, Freddie flung his arms around Hector and hugged him. 'Thank you,' he said.

'You are very welcome, young man.'

Freddie's affection brought tears to Grace's eyes. She hadn't seen the boys openly hug anyone for a long time except herself. They'd always been wary of showing their affection with the tense environment they used to live in.

'Look, Mum.' Freddie held out the shiny coins, which Billy took off him and placed inside his small purse.

Everyone laughed. 'It looks like Billy is taking charge of the finances,' observed Hector. 'Oh and, Lady Grace, there's a small picnic table outside the greenhouse with a red-checked gingham cloth. It's a perfect size to sell the fruit from.'

'Thank you, Hector!'

After a glass of juice and a quick wash of the boys' faces to remove the juice from their mouths, all of them ambled in the sunshine down the swooping drive of the Castle. There was a small group of girls hovering around the Castle gates, no doubt hoping for a glimpse of Andrew but potential customers of their fruit baskets. As she pushed the barrow of fruit with the table perched on top they heard the creak of the Castle gates opening wide. Grace noticed Dougie driving towards them. They stepped to the side as Dougie's car slowed down and he wound down his window.

'Good morning!' he chirped. 'You look like you're up to something interesting.'

'We are,' replied Grace. 'I'm teaching the boys the value of money and how to earn it. We have picked the fresh fruit and veg from the grounds and are going to sell it at the gates and then make pies with the leftovers.'

'Very impressive, entrepreneurs in the making. Could I

possibly have a punnet of strawberries? And those plums look divine.'

'You certainly can,' replied Grace.

'That'll be two pounds, thank you,' said Freddie, gathering the fruit together.

'A mathematician and politeness, you will go a long way! Thank you.' Dougie placed the fruit on the passenger seat. 'Oh and before I forget, Andrew's show is being aired in a couple of days, but I assure you we've edited out the best bit of the show.'

Grace laughed. 'I am sorry they stormed the kitchen.'

'There's no need to apologise on my account. I thought it would make for very amusing TV but Andrew was having none of it.' He tipped Grace a wink before waving at the boys and driving back towards the servants' quarters.

'Yes!' said Freddie, punching the air. 'This making money is so easy.'

If only, thought Grace.

Within seconds they set up the small table outside the Castle gates. There was a bustling ambience due to the glorious weather. The bridge between Glenshiel and Heartcross was busy with hikers and tourists, and the banks of the River Heart were packed with children.

'I don't think it will take long to sell out,' declared Grace, opening up the table and throwing the red gingham cloth over the top. The boys helped pile the fruit on it, then Billy stood up in the barrow ready and waiting to take the money.

'Teamwork!' exclaimed Grace as they all high-fived each other.

First in line were the security guards, who bought a couple of punnets, and within seconds tourists were crossing the road to see what they were selling and, much to the boys' delight, began forming an orderly queue. As the twins dished out punnet after punnet, Billy carefully placed all of the money in the purse for safekeeping.

'This is brilliant!' exclaimed Freddie. 'I can't wait to count all the money. We are selling out fast,' he continued, but Grace noticed the smile slide from his face.

There was Andrew, about to climb out of a car that had just pulled up outside the Castle gates.

'That's a Ferrari,' said Freddie. 'I know that.'

Immediately, the huddle of girls waiting patiently for Andrew to appear began screaming and ran towards the car waving their phones in the air. Grace watched the mayhem as the security guards attempted to usher them backwards. Finally Andrew stepped from the car and was greeted by a loud cheer. Straightaway he began signing autographs and posing for photos. He attire had changed; he was now dressed in a kilt, accompanied by a dirk and a sporran, and his three-buttoned waistcoat, white shirt and black bow tie left Grace once more staring in his direction. She continued to watch him as the car roared off. Other tourists, curious about the sudden commotion surrounding Andrew, crossed over the road to take a look and joined in the frenzy when they soon realised it was the famous chef off the TV. Andrew was finding it difficult to put one foot in front of the other as the crowd surged towards him, and again the security guards took control.

'Please move back. Mr Glossop will not be signing any more autographs,' ordered one of the guards with authority.

Finally, Andrew began making headway towards the gates and locked eyes with Grace. He must have wondered what the hell they were up.

'Mum, we've only got four punnets of plums left and the purse is bulging – we can't fit any more money in it,' said Joey, pointing to the purse Billy was holding.

'Isn't that a lovely problem to have?'

Grace looked up to see Andrew standing in front of her. 'What exactly are you up to?' he asked looking between Grace and the boys.

'We are selling fruit and veg from the orchards in the glorious sunshine. Don't you go thinking this crowd was here just for you, you know. We caused the frenzy before you even stepped onto the pavement from that red Ferrari.'

Andrew looked at Grace amused. 'And here was me thinking—'

'Thinking is so overrated,' she interrupted. 'It's the doing that matters – isn't that right, boys?'

'Only four punnets left… How much would two be?' asked Andrew.

'That will be four pounds,' answered Joey.

'Well, I better see what all the fuss is about then, hadn't I?'

'A little overdressed for the glorious sunshine,' remarked Grace, giving Andrew the once-over.

'It's nice of you to notice what I am wearing.' Andrew never took his eyes off her except for the moment he opened his wallet and placed his bank card in Grace's hand. She felt her cheeks colour fast, and her heart thumped as their eyes locked.

'Do you take cards?' he asked.

Grace cocked an eyebrow. 'Do we look like we take cards?' she replied, handing the card back and looking towards the twins who were frantically whispering.

They stopped as soon as they realised Grace was staring at them. Freddie stepped forward. 'I'm sorry, Mr Glossop, we only deal in proper money, not plastic money.'

'Proper money,' repeated Andrew.

'Yes, proper coins, because we don't know how to spend plastic money, do we, Joey?'

Joey was shaking his head.

'But you can take two punnets for free because we are sorry for putting water in your wellies. Really sorry, aren't we?' Freddie looked towards Joey and Billy who were both nodding.

Billy pushed the punnets across the table.

'Take them,' said Freddie.

'Apology accepted. Thank you, boys,' said Andrew, looking impressed. 'And if this produce is top notch, maybe we could do future deals. Because, boys, I've been thinking.'

All three boys were staring at Andrew.

'I think being neighbours we need to get on, what do you think? Can we be friends?'

Andrew's softness towards the boys floored Grace.

'I think that will be possible,' replied Freddie with a nod.

Andrew held out his hand and each of the boys shook it. 'I'm really glad about that because I really didn't like having wet feet this morning – and I'm not sure what you'll be capable of next.'

Freddie giggled.

'So how about to cement our new friendship, I take you all out this afternoon?'

The boys all looked towards Grace. 'You really don't need to do that,' she replied.

'I insist. Meet me in the far meadow just behind the maze in say … an hour?' Andrew wasn't giving any more away. 'Oh, and bring a swimsuit and a towel.'

And with that they watched Andrew walk through the gates. He turned back towards the crowd of people and waved. Once more the crowd let out a cheer.

Grace beamed at her boys and pulled them in for a hug. 'I am so proud of you.' She popped a kiss on each of their heads. They'd apologised to Andrew without being prompted and as much as they could be little buggers at times they were her little buggers.

'But, Mum, I think someone needs to tell him, he's wearing a skirt, it doesn't look good on boys,' shared Freddie. 'He looks funny.'

Grace chuckled but wholeheartedly disagreed; she thought Andrew looked like a true gorgeous Scotsman and she could understand why girls flocked to the gates just for the small chance of seeing him.

She glanced over her shoulder and he looked back and caught her eye. A smile hitched on Andrew's face as held the punnets up in the air then carried on walking up the Castle steps.

'Will there be any more fruit tomorrow?' shouted a woman from the back of the queue when she realised Joey had just sold the last two punnets.

Grace looked between the boys, who were nodding. 'Same time tomorrow,' she confirmed before high-fiving the boys. 'Job well done!'

Chapter Twelve

'How much did we make?' asked Grace, placing three glasses of cold juice in front of the boys.

They were kneeling on the floor with the money spread out on the table in front of them in piles.

Grace knew there had been forty punnets of fruit and they'd sold them all, but she let the boys count the money.

'Thirty-eight pounds!' exclaimed Freddie, 'But really forty because we gave two away. Does that mean we can buy an ice cream?'

'It certainly does,' replied Grace, 'with a double flake, sprinkles and chocolate sauce!' She couldn't quite believe they'd managed to sell the lot. After giving the boys enough for their ice creams, she scooped up the rest of the change.

'What are you doing?' asked Joey, watching Grace separate the money and place it in different columns on the white cardboard budget card.

'This is the money we have to live on. Things aren't free

and we need to be careful that we don't waste a single penny. Come and have a look.'

All three boys climbed on the stool next to her.

'Food, electricity, water, et cetera. Every penny is spoken for. So if we make any extra, that can be for treats.'

'It looks very complicated being an adult,' observed Freddie.

'And boring!' added Joey.

'It is but it can also be very rewarding, especially when we work hard as a team. Now, have you all got your swimming costumes and a towel?'

The boys nodded enthusiastically as Grace locked the door behind them and they headed towards the far meadow. Grace had no clue what Andrew had in store for them. She wasn't aware of any water on that side of the Castle grounds, so she had no idea why they needed to bring their swimming costumes. The boys ran ahead while Grace carried their towels slung across her arm. As soon as they reached the meadow, the twins let out an enormous 'WOAH!'

The five-seat Cessna was parked on the landing strip. The white plane looked grand with its racing-red stripes along the side and Andrew's logo on the tail.

'He's got his own plane.' Freddie clutched Joey's arm as they began to pogo up and down excitedly. 'Are we really going up in a plane?'

Grace had no idea what Andrew had planned. 'It looks like you are about to find out.' Andrew stepped from behind the plane holding three pilot caps.

'Calling Captain Freddie, Captain Joey and Captain Billy,' announced Andrew with a grin.

The twins ran straight towards him and immediately claimed their caps. Billy looked towards Grace. 'Go on, Captain Billy.' She saluted him. 'Go and get your cap.'

Billy ran towards Andrew, who placed the cap on Billy's head. He turned round towards Grace with a huge beam on his face.

'Well, I never expected this,' remarked Grace, catching the boys up. She looked at the plane rather than at Andrew.

'Is this your plane?' asked Freddie, looking up at the logo on the tail.

'It is,' replied Andrew.

'And are you taking us on a trip?' asked Joey.

'I am if that's okay with your mum.'

All eyes were on Grace. She couldn't work out if she was feeling nervous or it was excitement. She'd never been on a plane before.

'It's okay with me, boys, if it's okay with you.'

All three boys jumped excitedly and Andrew opened the door. 'Boys, if you would like to sit in the seats at the back, we can get you strapped in.'

'Look at all those dials. How cool is this?' exclaimed Freddie, jumping in his seat and already trying to work out how to operate the seatbelt.

Andrew gestured for Grace to take a seat in the front of the plane and she hesitated.

'Andrew, I have never been on a plane before.'

Andrew looked at her like she was speaking a different language. 'Never?'

'Never,' she repeated. 'I've never even been on holiday.'

'Just relax and sit back. You will love it,' he reassured her, holding out his hand and helping her into the seat. 'I've just got to do some pre-flight checks, then we are ready to go.'

With Grace sitting in the front of the plane and the boys in the back, Andrew walked around checking the body of the plane and the flaps before climbing into his seat.

'It all looks so complicated,' observed Grace.

'It's not that complicated when you know how.' Andrew smiled across at her.

'Boys, this control here is called the yoke, and works just like a steering wheel in a car. It controls the pitch of the nose, which means up or down, and your wings too. You push to go down, pull to go up, and you can move it left and right. It doesn't need much force.'

Grace was impressed with the way Andrew was explaining everything and involving the boys. They looked like they were having the time of their life and they hadn't even left the ground yet.

'I want to be a pilot when I grow up,' Freddie suddenly announced.

'You can be whatever you wish,' confirmed Grace. She had never seen the boys so excited about anything. 'You okay, Billy?'

Billy gave Grace a huge smile and a thumbs-up.

'Sit back, boys, and enjoy the view. Are we ready?'

Andrew looked over his shoulder and smiled at the boys then at Grace. 'Are *you* ready?' he asked in a professionally calm manner with a smile that was to die for.

'I'm ready,' Grace replied, but she couldn't help feeling a little jittery.

'Don't worry, you are in capable hands,' reassured Andrew.

'Maybe,' she replied, holding his gaze. He really did have lovely eyes.

Andrew started the engine and put on his headphones.

'Andrew, where is the runway?' Grace was looking all around.

'There isn't one.'

'But at the end of this field is a mountain.'

'Don't worry, I know what I'm doing.'

'This is so surreal,' Grace murmured. This time last week she would never have imagined that she'd be in a private plane flying to goodness knows where with a global superstar as the pilot.

'Let's go,' announced Andrew. The boys were at ease as the tiny plane travelled slowly along the bumpy strip, whereas Grace let out a tiny squeal and grabbed on to the sides of her seat.

Andrew looked in her direction. 'It's okay, just relax. I'd hold your hand, but...' He leant across and touched her hand. Her whole body tingled at his touch as she felt her pulse quicken and goose bumps rise.

'You keep your hands on those controls,' joked Grace

nervously, causing a wide grin to spread across Andrew's face.

'The world is our oyster!' he announced. 'And we have good weather, which is a bonus, so it shouldn't feel too rocky.'

Grace noticed that Andrew was completely at ease. As he operated the controls the plane began to pick up speed.

'How do you know what you are doing?'

'It's simple really.'

Grace was mesmerised. It didn't look simple to her at all.

The plane was now travelling faster and faster. Grace felt a tiny surge of excitement and trepidation as she squeezed her eyes shut, knowing that the edge of the field was about to disappear.

'Open your eyes, you don't want to miss this,' encouraged Andrew as he pulled back on the yoke. As they left the meadow the plane soared into the sky.

'WOAH!' exclaimed the twins, enjoying every minute of it.

As they climbed higher in the sky the boys were watching the world go by. With her eyes now wide Grace watched the town below getting smaller and smaller. Everything looked picture perfect. They flew over the River Heart with its sweeping bays and sand dunes. Heartcross Mountain was getting smaller too, and everything was beginning to look like a model village.

'How do you know where you are going?' asked Freddie. 'There are no signs in the sky.'

'Good question,' replied Andrew. 'I learned how to fly in Air Cadets. It is quite simple when you know how.

'Air Cadets,' repeated Grace. 'There's so much to find out about you, isn't there?'

'We are going to touch the clouds!' announced Freddie.

'The Castle looks so tiny!' exclaimed Joey.

The plane levelled out in the sky and Grace couldn't believe the view. Everywhere looked so peaceful. She could see for miles around. She kept snagging a glance towards Andrew's tanned forearms holding the controls. He caught her watching and smiled at her.

'How's your first trip in a plane?' he asked.

'I'm absolutely loving it,' she replied. 'I actually feel in very safe hands.'

'Glad to hear it,' he replied, giving her a sideways glance. 'Sit back and enjoy the view. Not long until we arrive at our destination.'

Andrew continued to fly the plane over the open water. The town of Glensheil and Heartcross Mountain looked like tiny dots in the distance. They flew over glorious bays, cliffs and coastal paths. The houses were minuscule and the moving cars looked like ants scurrying on the ground.

The plane gave a little bounce in the sky, 'Eek, my stomach literally flipped then,' exclaimed Grace.

'You okay? You have gone a little pale.' He stared at her with such warmth.

Grace knew her stomach was churning. 'Nerves, excitement, all mixed together,' she replied, not admitting she felt a little queasy.

'Sometimes it helps to have a go at flying. Takes your mind off the woozy feeling.'

'You can't put me in control of the plane.'

'I have every faith, you can be my wingman any day.' He gave her a cheeky wink as he quoted a line from one of his favourite movies. 'Just put your hands on the yoke in front of you. We are at a good height so you don't need to pull back, just turn it to the left … like this. We are heading for that small island over there.'

Grace looked to the left and noticed the small island approaching. She could already see a sandy beach with the waves lapping against the shore.

Grace gripped the control and Andrew took his hand off, his causing Grace to give a tiny squeal.

'Look at you, you are flying!'

'Oh my God. Boys! I'm flying!' Grace couldn't quite believe it. She felt the happiest she'd been in a long time. 'I'm on top of the world,' she announced. 'This is amazing. It's actually so much fun!' She kept her eyes firmly fixed on the sky in front and flew the plane towards the tiny island. The queasiness in her stomach had subsided and she was enjoying every minute of it. She continued to fly the plane herself for the next five minutes.

'I'll need to take over again now,' said Andrew. 'We are nearly there and it's the tricky part coming up now … landing.'

He took over the controls. The boys were sat up straight looking out of the windows.

'Wow, look at that sandy beach, those coves.' Grace

pointed out of the window to show the boys. 'This is like something out of a movie. Romantic hideaway on an island in the middle of nowhere.' Grace was in awe.

'There's lots of stories about these tiny islands, and apparently pirates used to hide their treasure here.'

'No way!' exclaimed Freddie. 'Can we look for treasure?'

'You can do whatever you want.'

'It's absolutely breathtaking,' murmured Grace and caught Andrew's eye.

'I know,' he replied. He was looking directly at her and her heart gave a little flutter.

'I never imagined when I got up this morning I'd be flying in a plane or seeing such stunning views.'

'This morning when I got up I never thought I'd have my wellingtons filled up with water.'

Everyone laughed.

'Okay, getting ready for the descent.' The plane began to lose height as it headed towards the island.

'What is this place?' asked Grace, staring out of the window.

'This is Glossop Island.'

Grace turned her head and stared at him. 'You have your own private island?'

'It sounds more extravagant than it is. There's nothing here, except trees, a beach, a waterfall and an old rickety rowing boat.'

'It sounds like paradise to me.'

'This might be a little bumpy, boys, hold on.'

The power of the plane had reduced and Grace noticed

the flaps on the wings had been lowered. Andrew's eyes were firmly fixed in front of him. He lowered the nose of the plane as they were getting closer to the tarmac strip in front of them. Grace watched as Andrew reduced the throttle to idle then the nose of the plane began to rise again as Andrew slowly pulled back on the yoke until the two main wheels kissed the ground with small, joyous bounces. As Andrew continued to hold the nose wheel off the ground, the other wheels settled on the ground and the plane began to slow down.

The boys let out a cheer and began to clap.

'That was amazing,' announced Freddie.

'Just the best,' agreed Joey.

Billy was still wearing his captain's hat and looked as proud as punch.

'I can't thank you enough for this,' said Grace. 'The boys will be talking about this for ever.'

'We will,' chipped in Freddie, listening in on the conversation.

Grace laughed. 'I can't believe you own your own private island and a plane.'

'When we don't even have a car,' added Joey.

Andrew raised an eyebrow. 'You don't have a car?'

'I can't even drive,' confirmed Grace. 'I never learned.'

'You could have told me that before I handed over the controls of my plane,' he teased. 'Right, boys, who is ready to explore and who is hungry?'

'Me!' chorused the twins and Billy pushed his arm straight in the air.

'Come on then, let's show you around.' Andrew opened the door and jumped down. Grace watched him as he walked around the front of the plane and opened her door. He held out his hand and helped her to the ground before swinging the boys out too.

Grace brought her hands up to her heart. 'What an absolute stunning location. The whole place has a magical feel about it. It's just so...'

'Beautiful,' replied Andrew, staring straight at Grace, who gave a smile. His eyes twinkled and Grace felt her heart pound.

She pointed to the boys, who were running towards a woodland area that they could see in the distance.

'My day has definitely improved from this morning,' shared Andrew, not taking his eyes off Grace.

'Mine too,' she confirmed. 'I feel like I'm living the life of someone rich and famous.' Realising what she'd just said, Grace laughed heartily. 'Which you would know all about.'

'That might be so but today I'm just Andrew ... me.'

'Well, I'll look forward to getting to know just Andrew.' She gave him a cheeky grin.

'And I'll look forward to getting to know just Grace.'

'Thank you for this, the boys are having just the best time.'

'And I am too.' Andrew held out his arm and Grace linked her arm through his. 'Let's explore.'

'Yes, let's.'

Chapter Thirteen

Andrew led them on a short walk through a small woodland area to what looked like a private driveway on water. Up in front there was a rowing boat tied to a small jetty.

'Look at this place. It's impressive,' remarked Grace.

'It's pretty special, isn't it?' Andrew gave her a sideward glance.

The way he stared at her made the whole of Grace's body tingle.

'Boys, we are getting in the boat and at the other end is lunch.'

Grace raised her eyebrows. 'How is there lunch at the other end?' she asked, puzzled, knowing all Andrew had with him was a small bag which she assumed was a towel and swimsuit.

'Just you wait and see,' he replied, not giving any more away.

As the boys stepped into the boat it began to rock gently on the calm water and when all four of them were sitting on the wooden seat Andrew retrieved the oars, which were leaning against the tree, and then began to row. They ducked under numerous weeping willows as Andrew rowed the boat, everyone taking in the view.

'I feel like I'm on the French Riviera,' breathed Grace, focusing on the beauty all around her.

Carefully, Andrew guided the boat around the next corner and Grace gasped, 'Beautiful!' as the tiny stream joined a large stretch of water.

'Look at that!' exclaimed Freddie.

Grace focused on the view in front of her and watched the water cascading down the rocks and running into a large bay.

'Can we swim in there?' Joey pointed.

'We certainly can,' confirmed Andrew.

There wasn't another soul in sight. 'Are we actually on a desert island?'

'There is no one else here but us. Welcome to Glossop Bay.'

Grace couldn't quite believe Andrew Glossop actually owned his own private island.

'It's been in the family for years. My family did think about building a small hotel here but I prefer a place to escape to when life becomes very busy.'

'It's utterly breathtaking,' said Grace.

Andrew rowed as close to the sparkling beige sand as he could. 'I'm afraid you will have to take off your shoes and socks and paddle to the sand.' The boys didn't need telling twice as already they were swinging their legs over the side of the boat. Grace followed suit, her feet finding the sandy bay bottom as she paddled to the edge of the shallow water.

Then she burst out laughing and pointed to the boys, who were wriggling out of their clothes and pulling on their swimming trunks. Within seconds all three of them had splashed into the water whilst Andrew pulled the rowing boat onto the sand and placed the oars safely inside the boat.

'This place is certainly something special, Andrew. You are very lucky.'

'If you want to get changed into your swimsuit there's a couple of small huts just over there – and there should be some fishing nets too.'

Grace nodded and headed towards a hut to get changed. When she returned, she walked to the water's edge, the fine grains of sand underfoot feeling warm from the sun beating down. She sat near the water's edge, brought her knees up to her chest and for a second tilted her face towards the sun, before watching Andrew who was standing at the water's edge. He began to peel his T-shirt from his broad shoulders, then folded it up and threw it behind him on the sand. She watched as he climbed on top of a small rock then jumped straight in the glittering water.

Splash.

The boys giggled as the water rippled all around. Just watching Andrew took her breath away. She couldn't take her eyes off him. He ducked under the water, then, when he surfaced, he stood tall in the water, bare-chested, skin glistening. Grace could see he worked out. Without a doubt there would be a personal gym within the servants' quarters.

Next minute Andrew was gently lifting the twins one by one in the air and pretending to throw them in the water. Their giggles were infectious and they were having so much fun together. Andrew turned towards Billy with his arms open wide and Grace was surprised to see he allowed Andrew to pick him up. Billy threw his head back with laughter as Andrew swung him in the air before gently placing him back down in the water.

Andrew spotted Grace by the water's edge. 'Are you coming in to join us or would you like lunch first?'

'Lunch!' the twins chorused as they ran towards Grace, who chuckled as Andrew got splashed.

With everyone out of the water, Andrew touched Grace's arm affectionately, making her feel a flush of warmth in her body again. 'The food is this way.'

That feeling wasn't one she'd felt in a long time. Being in Andrew's company seemed so easy and natural.

Andrew led them past the wooden huts into a clearing and everyone stopped dead in their tracks. Andrew's jaw fell open and Grace couldn't believe her eyes.

'Oh my God,' were the only words she could muster up. Laid out on the ground was an oversized tartan blanket and a wicker picnic basket with an open lid, with what looked like hundreds of birds pecking away at their lunch.

Quickly Andrew ran towards them, frantically clapping

his hands. The birds began to flap in the air but were still circling the picnic basket with stolen food in their beaks. He slapped the basket lid shut and continued to shoo the birds away. As soon as it was safe to open the lid again, everyone looked inside in horror.

'The pesky birds have eaten the picnic.' Andrew blew out a breath. 'We've got no food left.'

The boys were staring into the basket of carnage. Everything looked pecked to death and half eaten.

'I can't believe it. I prepared all this myself. It's an absolute disaster.'

'I'm starving,' said Freddie, who received a stern look from Grace.

'What are were going to eat now? We can't spend the afternoon here with no food.' Andrew was now looking far from relaxed.

Grace peered into the basket. 'It looks like you went all out.'

'I had, we had chorizo, quails' eggs, smoked salmon...'

'That doesn't sound like proper food to me,' interrupted Joey, pulling a face.

Grace flicked her eyes up and down at Joey and was telepathically trying to tell him not to sound ungrateful. 'Okay, it's not the end of the world, it looks like there's still some tinfoil that's not pecked to death,' she said, trying to lighten the mood. 'I have to say it's a first for me, a picnic on a private island with no picnic.'

'I'm so sorry, Grace, I had this food flown in by a private

plane. I didn't expect the birds to be able to open the basket.'

'At least the champagne hasn't been touched... Every cloud! And, boys ... lemonade for you!' Grace handed out drinks to the boys. 'It's not all doomed,' she said reassuringly.

'How is it not doomed? The boys will be starving.'

'Because as a mother we make the best out of every situation.' Grace took another glimpse inside the picnic basket. 'Okay, we have butter, we have foil and what was on these skewers?'

'Rainbow fruit, melons, grapes, et cetera,' replied Andrew, watching Grace lay the items on the red tartan picnic basket.

'Okay, boys, do you see those huts there?' Grace pointed. 'Run over there and bring me what's inside the one on the left.'

Without further questioning, the boys took off.

'And what's in those huts?' asked Andrew puzzled, watching Freddie pull open the door and the boys disappear inside.

'Call yourself a chef? Just you wait and see. There's always good in any situation. You just have to look for it.' She gave Andrew as a wink as the boys ran full pelt back towards them waving fishing nets in the air. 'We are going to catch our dinner!'

The boys jumped up and down with joy whilst Andrew was looking at Grace with admiration, 'You really are something special.'

'Ready, boys? Follow me. Do you see that shallow bay just over there?' Andrew pointed. 'That's where we will find fish.'

The sun felt glorious on Grace's skin as she followed Andrew and the boys to the edge of the water. They felt the sand between their toes as they waded through the water. 'Are we all okay?' Andrew shouted over his shoulder, striding though the water like he was some sort of superhero.

'Yes, Chef!' echoed the twins cheekily, causing Andrew to glance over his shoulder and give them a huge smile.

Grace stumbled on a rock underneath the water which toppled her off balance and before she knew it was sitting on her bum on the seabed with the water up to her chest. The boys burst out laughing and as Grace cast her eyes upwards Andrew was standing above her.

He tilted his head to the side. 'What are you doing down there?' Before she knew it, his two big strapping arms were yanking her to her feet. Every inch of her tingled with desire. The intensity between them felt hotter than the afternoon sun. They stared at each other for a second before Freddie shouted at the top of his voice, 'FISH!'

Andrew kept hold of Grace's hand as they made their way towards the boys.

Freddie was the first one to make it to the shallow part and Grace noticed the water was a lot warmer here.

'Look!' said Joey.

All three boys were staring down into the water.

Andrew sat down and encouraged the boys to stand in a

circle. He cupped his hands under the water and brought them to the surface.

'Wow!' exclaimed Freddie, as Andrew released tiny fish from his hands.

'There's thousands of them. I don't think we will be going hungry tonight, boys.' Grace was amazed, she'd never seen so many fish in one place.

'They are tickling my toes,' squealed Freddie.

'Okay, Billy, scoop your net under the water and let's see what happens,' suggested Andrew.

Billy didn't need telling twice as he scooped his net along the seabed. His face lit up with excitement when he saw the fish squirming around in his net.

'Look at those,' said Grace, kissing him on top of his head.

The boys followed suit and before they knew it their nets were full.

'It's absolutely gorgeous here,' remarked Grace, standing in the water and looking all around.

'It's one of my favourite places in the world.'

Grace had been blown away by the whole afternoon and it wasn't over yet. Next they had to collect sticks, make a fire and cook the fish.

The boys marched back to the shore like proud fishermen with their nets full of fish. Once they were back near the picnic blanket, Andrew took over the preparing of the fish whilst the boys ran towards the trees and began collecting sticks.

'And how are we going to light the fire?' asked Grace,

wrapping the fish in tin foil and adding a little bit of butter on top.

'That's easy, we need dried moss for our tinder and rub two sticks together. I was in the Scouts once, you know.' Andrew looked up and grinned.

'And why did I ever doubt it?' replied Grace, shaking her head in jest. 'Is there anything Andrew Glossop hasn't done before?' Grace noticed that Andrew looked serious for a moment. He met her gaze.

'Actually, yes ... this. I'm having the best day,' he replied, looking straight in Grace's eye. The look he gave her made her stomach flip over multiple times.

Within thirty minutes the fire was burning and a row of fish were cooking on top of the makeshift grill. The boys were sat around the camp fire right next to the water's edge watching the fish cook. As soon as Andrew declared it was ready, they all tucked in. The champagne was open and Grace sipped a glass as she stared in silence across the water. This had been the most fun-packed day she'd enjoyed in a long, long time and judging by the look on the boys' faces as they scraped the fish from the tinfoil with their fingers, that went for them too.

Chapter Fourteen

The plane touched down back in the meadow just after 7 p.m. As Andrew switched off the engine, he and Grace looked over their shoulders to see all three boys fast asleep.

'I think we've tired them out,' whispered Andrew, looking towards Grace.

'They've had the best day, and that goes for me too,' shared Grace.

After they had filled their stomachs, they spent the late afternoon swimming and jumping off rocks, and the boys rowed the boat. It had just been the perfect day.

Grace began to shake the boys gently. 'Boys, wake up! We are home.'

Sleepily, the twins opened their eyes. 'I'm so tired,' said Freddie.

'I know, but as soon as you walk across the field, you can climb into bed.'

Andrew helped Freddie and Joey down from the plane then they both looked at Billy. He looked adorable with his eyes still shut tight as he clutched Ralph, his teddy bear.

'Don't wake him, I'll carry him,' said Andrew, leaning over and unclipping his seatbelt. He carefully picked Billy up and placed him over his shoulder whilst Grace shut the door. Billy stretched a little and wrapped his arms around Andrew as he snuggled into his neck. 'He's light as a feather,' whispered Andrew. 'Shall I just put him straight into bed?'

'Sounds like a plan,' replied Grace, then suddenly an anguished feeling engulfed her. Andrew was about to see the real state of the Castle and how she'd been living – but there was nothing she could do about that now as the back door swung open.

'Boys, do you want anything else to eat?'

Freddie and Joey shook their heads and Grace bent down and hugged the twins goodnight. 'Don't forget to clean your teeth. I'll be up in a minute to tuck you in. Will you show Andrew where Billy's room is?'

They both nodded.

'And I'll put the kettle on,' she said, looking at Andrew before placing a kiss on the top of Billy's head.

Whilst Andrew followed the boys and carried Billy upstairs, Grace took the best mugs she had out of the kitchen cupboard. Both were chipped and had seen better days. Thankfully, the fridge was still working and Grace was relieved to see the light and hear the hum as she retrieved the milk from the door. She had forgotten to ask

Andrew how he took his tea but as she poured water on the teabags she became aware he was standing behind her. Instantly she could tell by the shock on his face that he had something to say.

'You aren't renovating the kitchen, are you?' Andrew blinked rapidly as his eyes scanned the room.

Grace shook her head. 'How would you like your tea?'

'Just milk,' he replied.

'Do you know you are catching flies?'

'I'm just… In fact I don't know what I am… I just never expected…'

'The Castle to be in this state.' Grace finished his sentence for him.

'Grace, how are you living like this?'

She handed him a mug. 'Sorry it's cracked, it's all I have. Have a seat. Just let me move my coat.'

Andrew was looking at the settee. 'Are you sleeping on there?'

Grace nodded, 'Yes, the twins have the double bed and I managed to pick up a second-hand bed from the charity shop for Billy.' She could see the concept of picking up a second-hand bed horrified Andrew. 'And no, I don't have people to do the cleaning, or wash the boys' clothes or any other menial tasks. It's just me and my boys managing on what little we have.'

Andrew was looking at the budget chart that was laid out on the coffee table. There were coins in each column. 'And this –' he nodded '– I don't mean to be nosey, I'm just…'

'Flabbergasted?'

Andrew blew out a breath. 'Something like that.' He perched on the edge of the settee, still looking at the chart.

'It's simple really, me and the boys don't have much. This is how we budget by dividing up the little money we have. Selling the fruit at the gates gave us a little boost today and hopefully we will do the same again tomorrow.'

Andrew was taking everything in that Grace was saying.

'I didn't expect the inside of the Castle to be so run-down, but I'm grateful the boys and I are safe and have a roof over our heads.'

'Safe?' asked Andrew tentatively.

'Yes, safe.' Grace's skin was tingling with discomfort from the memories of Cole as she shared a little of her past with Andrew. She didn't go into too much detail but just enough for him to join the dots together.

'Grace, I don't know what to say.' He reached across and touched her knee.

'And that's why Billy doesn't speak, he's been through a lot.' Grace blinked away the tears in her eyes; every time she thought about it she got emotional. 'But it's okay, we are here now and we have each other.' She took a sip of her drink. 'My plan was to sell this place and buy a modest detached house with a manageable garden and live off the rest of the money. If I'm honest, Andrew, I've set up an appointment with the estate agents to value this place to give me a clearer picture before I sell it.'

'And your plan now?'

Grace shrugged, 'It's home. I'm torn ... but if I sold it, I wouldn't be struggling.'

Andrew was quiet for a moment. 'Let me help you?'

'It's very kind of you but, honestly, we don't need help.'

'I'll buy the Castle from you. Whatever the valuation says, I'll give you exactly that. I'll make the process as simple as possible, then you can take the money and set up a home for you and your boys. I'm being genuine here. Let me help you.'

Grace was taken back by the offer. 'And that's half the problem – the boys. They don't care that we don't have a penny to our name. They don't care that we don't have large TVs, game consoles or fancy toys. They've been so happy since we've arrived, playing out in the fresh air, picking fruit from the orchards, filling wellington boots up with water. I can see the sparkle back in their eyes, their laugher is non-stop. This place is good for them.'

Andrew nodded.

'But thank you for your offer.'

'At least think about it?'

'I will.' Grace looked around the room. Even in such a dire state she'd become so comfortable with her surroundings in the last few days that it didn't actually seem as bad anymore. 'And thank you for today, the boys have loved it.'

'No, thank you, I really enjoyed their company. You have a lovely family, Grace, and one you should be proud of.'

Grace wasn't sure, but she thought Andrew's voice

cracked a little as those words left his mouth. 'I am very proud, we have been through so much together.'

They both sipped their tea in silence. Andrew was still staring at the chart, but didn't say any more. Grace knew he was shocked by the state of the Castle and her revelations about the past, but now it was out in the open and she felt better about that. She had nothing to be ashamed of. She might be rich in assets, but the reality was that everyday life was hard. Still, she wasn't going to give up without a fight. If there was no other way to keep hold of the Castle without selling it, that's exactly what she would do, but for now, there was no harm in getting the valuation.

When Andrew finished his tea, he placed his cracked mug on the table. 'I need to go,' he said, standing up. 'I have a function I need to be at tonight, but I just want to say I really have had the best day, despite those pesky birds eating the lunch!'

Grace smiled. 'But out of every bad situation comes a good one. The boys had so much fun fishing... You just have to look for those positives.'

'And that's what I like about you.'

'It's the mother in me,' she said with a grin.

For a second Grace noticed Andrew's smile slip. 'Have I said something wrong?' she asked, having a feeling Andrew was holding back about something.

He shook his head. 'No, honestly you haven't. From what I've seen today you are an exceptional mother.' He walked towards the back door and Grace followed him.

He paused as he opened the door, his presence so close

to her that Grace looked up and their eyes locked. 'Just have a think about my offer. This is no way to live.'

Grace nodded and shut the door behind him. She knew Andrew had been shocked that everyone didn't live with the same extravagance. Maybe he'd never seen the struggle of real life. But she was glad she'd opened up about the past as it really did affect the future of her and the boys. Placing the two mugs in the sink, Grace climbed the stairs to check on the boys with Andrew's offer still very much on her mind. For the first time in a long time she was happy. This was her home. Granted, the Castle needed work, but wasn't that half the fun, making the place their own? Tomorrow, she would check out the state of the Castle shop. Maybe she just had to stop thinking about the bigger picture and take one step at a time.

All three boys were fast asleep and Grace watched them all for a little while. Each of them looked rested and Grace couldn't help but think that they had fallen asleep with smiles on their faces after such a perfect day.

In her mind she was batting Andrew's proposal back and forth. Should she sell, should she not sell? It would make her life a whole lot easier if she did, but, watching the boys sleeping, she didn't want to cause them any more upheaval. The decision was laying heavy on her heart.

Shutting the twins' bedroom door, she stood on the landing and looked at the door opposite. The only door that she hadn't opened since arriving back at the Castle: the door to her old bedroom. Grace hovered outside and placed her hand on the doorknob. What exactly was she scared of?

It was just a room. But Grace knew the second she opened that door she would discover whether her grandfather had cleared it out, so that it was now vast and empty like all the other rooms in the Castle, or he had left it exactly the way it was, the night she'd left.

'You can't keep the door shut for ever,' she murmured under her breath. 'It's just a room.' But that room held a lot of memories for her. 'Be brave.'

Taking a deep breath, she twisted the knob and pushed open the door – and gasped. Instantly, the burst of colour hit her like a high-speed train. Stepping into the room, she saw that everything had been left just the way she'd left it, the night she ran away. Feeling emotional, Grace looked around. The brightly coloured bedspread and pillow stood out against the pastel-pink wall and curtains. The narrow bed was still pushed up against the wall, her old Doc Martens boots kicked off at the side of the bed. The shelves were packed with books, medals and trophies from school and a framed photo of her mum. Immediately Grace walked over and picked it up. It was a photograph of them both, when she was only a little girl. They were both smiling, standing in front of the fountain. Grace had her arms wrapped around her mother's legs and at a guess was around seven years of age.

She clutched the photo to her chest and sank on to the bed. Blinking back the tears, she was engulfed with fresh guilt. She wondered if her grandfather ever came to this room or if he just closed the door as the pain was too much to bear. Her desk was covered with art supplies alongside make-up brushes and a vanity mirror. There was her hairbrush, hairbands, bottles of nail polish and various perfumes and body sprays. Abandoned on the floor was a pile of dirty clothes that never made it to the washing basket. Her corkboard were filled with posters of her favourite band back then and her favourite teddy was propped up against her pillow. Grace sniffed it hard and hugged it tight. Even after all this time she would recognise that smell anywhere. The fluffy warm comforter providing exactly that, comfort. Standing up, she pulled back the curtains. The River Heart was in view and the bridge still full of tourists and hikers strolling between the village and the town.

With the window now open to let in the cool draft, Grace placed the photo back on the shelf, pulled back the duvet and climbed into bed. Resting her head on the pillow, she closed her eyes. Exhausted, her mind was awash. She knew there were still big changes ahead and her life could be catapulted in a different direction if she accepted Andrew's offer; but on the flip side, Grace had surprised herself. She actually quite liked being back at the Castle. Why was this growing-up lark always so difficult? Grace fell fast asleep on her old bed, with Andrew's offer very much on her mind.

Chapter Fifteen

'Woah! Look at this room.'

Grace woke up to three boys standing over her. She sat bolt upright, forgetting where she was for a second. The boys were already dressed and were now rifling through the drawers of her old desk and looking at the nick-nacks on the shelves.

'Growing up, this was my old bedroom.'

'Who's that?' asked Freddie, pointing at the photograph of Grace and her mum.

'That is your grandmother,' replied Grace. 'Bring the photo here.'

Freddie handed the framed photograph to Grace, and they all climbed on the bed next to her.

'And that is me as a very young girl. You would have loved your grandmother so much,' shared Grace, her voice faltering.

'You look funny,' remarked Freddie, pointing to the photograph. 'What have you done to your hair?'

Grace laughed. 'They are bunches.'

'They look stupid,' added Freddie.

Grace tickled him. 'It was all the rage back then.'

'I'm glad I didn't live in the olden days,' chipped in Joey, placing the photograph back on the shelf.

'Right, let's get breakfast,' said Grace, swinging her legs to the ground.

'We've already had cereal,' said Joey.

'You have? Look at you three, washed, changed and already had breakfast. What's the plan now?' she asked, walking down the stairs.

'Can we go and pick the fruit and sell it at the Castle gates again?' asked Freddie, looking hopeful.

'I don't see why not. Hector should be around somewhere. Do you know where you are going?'

All three boys nodded.

'I'll get myself changed and have a cup of tea, then I'll head over.'

Before Grace had even switched on the kettle, the boys had pulled on their trainers and were skipping across the courtyard hand in hand with Billy in the middle of the twins. She watched and smiled until they were out of sight before making herself a cup of tea.

'Good morning, Ms Power.'

Grace jumped out of her skin and brought both hands up to her chest as she spun round to find Mr Burns standing in the open doorway.

'You frightened me to death.' As soon as Grace realised what she said, she chuckled. 'I suppose that would be good for business.'

With his face still as deadpan as the first time they met, Mr Burns didn't crack a smile. He was holding an urn. 'I'm returning Mr Power to you.'

Grace stared at the urn, teary-eyed. 'Thank you,' she said, taking it from his hands.

Mr Burns disappeared as quickly as he had appeared, as if in a puff of smoke. Grace placed her grandfather on the worktop, the emotion rising inside. Never having been in this situation, she was at a loss as to what to do now. She had no clue about her grandfather's wishes. Did he want his ashes scattered or buried? Maybe the best thing would be to ask Hector.

Grace sat and stared at the urn for twenty minutes, her tea stone-cold, not moving a muscle. Her emotions were all over the place. She placed the urn on top of the cupboard where her grandfather kept his whisky. 'I bet you need a drink, because I think I certainly do,' she said, hearing the boys' footsteps running across the courtyard, shouting her name. The boys crashed through the door.

'We've got forty punnets today,' said Freddie, proudly. He was pulling at Grace's arm. 'Come and look.'

The wheelbarrow was full of an array of colourful fruit and vegetables.

'Lady Grace, I'll take them down to the Castle gate to sell the punnets, if you have things to do,' offered Hector.

'Actually, would you? That would give me time to go and check out the state of the Castle shop.'

'No problem whatsoever, but could I just grab a drink of water?'

'Of course, help yourself.'

Hector stepped inside and the first thing he did was notice the urn. Immediately, he took his cap off and clutched it to his chest.

'Mr Burns just dropped it off.'

Side by side, they stood in silence, staring at the urn for a moment.

'Hector, I've no idea what to do with it. Would you know?'

'Believe it or not, it's something you avoid talking about when you get to my age. It's just a bonus to wake up every day. I do know he had a box of important paperwork somewhere, but I'm not sure where. Perhaps his wishes would be in there somewhere?'

'I've not come across the box but it can't be that hard to find as the Castle isn't exactly brimming with furniture and nick-nacks. I'll have a look later on tonight when the boys have gone to bed.'

After a drink of water, Hector headed towards the Castle gates with three excited boys in tow whilst Grace found the shop keys.

Five minutes later, armed with a bucket full of cleaning products and a pair of Marigolds, she walked out across the courtyard and took the long route along the curved stone path through the wild flower garden which was in full bloom. Inhaling the aroma, she carried on through the walled garden, which was edged with French lavender, and walked past the tiny pond. This pathway took her around the edge of the estate and as she hurried around the next corner she was amazed to see, after all this time, the huge oak tree still standing there, supporting a beautifully crafted ladder leading up to the tree-house. The boys were absolutely going to love this.

Grace placed the bucket she was carrying on the ground and climbed the ladder. She was not a fan of heights, but it felt secure, at least. She climbed the final rung, pushed open the trapdoor above her head and stepped onto a little platform. The walls were still hung with fairy lights and the window was still cut out with cloth nailed over it to make a curtain. There were two old beanbags, and Grace gave a tiny gasp when she set eyes on the 'KEEP OUT' sign that she and Isla had made. They used to pin it to the outside of the trapdoor. There were posters nailed to the wood, a pack of cards and a couple of board games, and a box of notepads and pens which obviously had seen better days. The memories came flooding back. She'd had some great times in this hideaway. The boards squeaked as she walked over them to pull back the makeshift curtain. She squatted down and looked over the rolling countryside and the mountainous terrain. It felt like nothing had changed even though the years had flown by. There was a bucket tied to a rope which Grace had used to carry things up and down to the tree-house.

Hanging on a peg was still a pair of binoculars. If you

looked to the right and focused, you could see the courtyard and the servants' quarters. Grace sat and remembered the past. Secrets were told in confidence inside these four walls. Her friends shared magazines and used to have to shout a password to be let in. Grace smiled. Those days were good days.

Bringing the binoculars up to her eyes she focused on the mountain, where tiny figures were hiking up the path. She shifted her gaze, now looking over to the garden behind the holding room, and altered the focus so she could see. Rose was setting the table when suddenly Andrew appeared. There weren't many men who could pull off looking good in a pair of flip-flops, but he looked sensational. He was dressed only in a pair of shorts and his toned torso was ripped and glistened in the sunshine. She watched as Rose positioned a sun umbrella near him, then his servant appeared and handed him a drink. Andrew lay down on the sunbed and even though Grace knew she was technically spying, she couldn't take her eyes off him. A couple of seconds later she watched him sit up and answer his phone, and he gave a sideways glance in her direction, causing her stomach to flip over and her cheeks to flush pink. Surely he couldn't see her from there. Immediately she placed the binoculars back on the hook and climbed down the ladder. She couldn't wait to show the boys the tree-house; they were going to love it.

Grace carried on walking towards the Castle shop, which was situated on the opposite side of the living quarters. There was a separate entrance for the general public to access the Castle gardens and the shop, with a path that snaked from the main road in the town. There was a kiosk at the bottom for taking the money and handing out the tickets. She felt a little excited and wondered whether the state of the shop would influence her decision about selling the Castle, because this was possibly a business she could relaunch if it wasn't too costly to spruce up.

The sign above the shop reading Heartcross Castle Shop was slanted and rotten. The blinds over the windows were pulled down so at first Grace couldn't see inside, and the 'CLOSED' sign stuck to the glass was clinging on for dear life. Hearing the crunch of gravel, she swung round to see Andrew. 'What are you doing here? I thought you were catching a few rays,' said Grace, then realised: how would she even know that? 'I'm just assuming as the weather is glorious!' she quickly added.

'I was just going to grab some fruit from the gardens when I spotted you up ahead. Are you going in there?' Andrew looked towards the run-down shop.

'Yes,' replied Grace, 'even though I have no idea what I'm about to find, hence the bucket and cleaning stuff.'

'Well, in that case, you may need some help.'

Grace looked over his shoulder. 'Help? Have you sent Rose to help me?'

'Ouch,' replied Andrew, holding up his hands.

'You, you mean you. Really? You are going to get your hands dirty?'

'Well, if you don't want my help?' Andrew turned around to walk away.

'No, stop, you can stick around and be chief spider-catcher. It might be amusing to see Andrew Glossop get his hands dirty.'

'As long as I provide you with some sort of amusement.'

Grace took the yellow Marigolds out of the bucket. 'You better take these, we can't have you getting your hands dirty. I bet you've got those insured for thousands.'

Andrew looked a little sheepish.

'Oh my God, you have, haven't you?'

'No comment and I'm not wearing those!' he exclaimed, looking perturbed at the bright-yellow Marigolds.

'You are definitely not in touch with your feminine side, are you?' she teased.

'How bad is it in there? And what exactly is the plan for this shop?'

Grace shrugged. 'I'm not sure how bad it is until we step inside. I'm trying to gauge whether opening up the Castle gardens will provide an income – which will of course help me make the living area in the Castle more comfortable.'

'But it's still going to be a lot of hard work. Do you really want the hassle of that? Wouldn't it be easier to sell and start afresh with no worries whatsoever?'

'Most probably, but I'm not one for giving up easily and this is my home.' Grace couldn't gauge whether Andrew looked disappointed by her answer but she knew she had to do what was best for her and her boys, and as yet she hadn't made her mind up.

She handed the bucket over to Andrew to hold. His

fingers brushed against hers and they stared at each other for a second until Grace searched the bundle of keys and located the one with the white sticker on which was scrawled in blue Biro 'SHOP'. She placed it in the lock and turned the key.

'Oh shit,' she announced, pursing her lips as she swung open the door.

They both stood outside and stared in.

'Blimey! I think we might need some breathing apparatus,' observed Andrew. 'How long has this place been locked up for?'

'Since a year after I left.'

'And how long is that?'

'A very long time,' Grace replied, blowing out a breath. 'This place once oozed charm.'

'Charm is not the word I would use to describe it. It's more like a haunted house.'

'Are you going in first?' she asked, looking up at him.

'Why should I go in first? Ladies first,' Andrew gestured, holding the door open.

'You are so kind!'

They stepped inside and looked around. Grace had to admit she'd never seen so much dust in her life, and this place housed more spider webs than the toolshed. She shuddered and jumped backwards, bumping into Andrew, when a large spider ran for its life across the floor.

Andrew grabbed on to Grace. She looked at him, amused. 'I thought you were going to be the spider-catcher?'

249

'You said that, not me and I didn't know they would be that huge.'

'You loon,' she said, laughing, and playfully swiped him with a cloth.

'And when would you be hoping to get this shop up and running?' Andrew raised an eyebrow at the hundreds of cobwebs and dead flies that were shrouding the cuddly toys that were sitting on the shelf sporting their Heartcross Castle T-shirts.

'As soon as we clean it up and see what sort of state it's in. Are you sticking around?'

'If I must,' he replied, 'But I think I may just take those gloves after all.'

Grace laughed. 'Come on, we best get cracking.' She watched in amusement as Andrew pulled on the bright-yellow Marigolds.

'And you can stop smiling. I'm not having anyone say I'm not in touch with my feminine side.'

Walking over to the window, Grace pulled on the cord of the blind, which immediately shot up. There was a cloud of dust and still not much light filtering through the grimy windows.

'There's a small staff room at the back of the shop. Go and fill the bucket with water,' instructed Grace as she pulled on the cord of the next blind, which once again mushroomed a cloud of dust into the air, making Grace splutter.

Andrew disappeared with the bucket whilst Grace opened up a bin bag and scooped the cobwebbed teddy bears straight in, along with all the discoloured key-rings. The whole shop used to be colourful and bright and now was lifeless and dingy. Thankfully, the place still looked watertight and hopefully there was no decaying brick work. The ice cream freezer was empty and switched off at the wall, yet the counter in front of the shop till was still full of confectionery. After the initial shock of seeing the place, Grace was beginning to have a good feeling about it. She knew she would struggle to invest heavily in this place. But surely, if it was cleaned out, it didn't have to be full of merchandise – maybe a simple tea and coffee machine. She could even ask Rona from the teashop to make some muffins or ask Isla about the ice cream they made at Foxglove Farm.

After propping open the door, Grace rubbed the dirt from the window to look out over the spectacular gardens. For a moment she struggled with the jammed window, but eventually it opened. Andrew returned with a frothy bucket of water and Grace held up a packet of crisps in each hand.

'Frazzles or Cheese Balls,' she asked, blowing the dust off a packet of crisps that was out of date by over ten years.

'Frazzles every day of the week.'

Grace shook her head. 'Me and you would just never work,' she joked, but caught Andrew looking at her with a glint of possibility in his eye.

Taking the sponge from the bucket, Grace squeezed it at the top of the window and the dirty water dripped on to the floor, whilst Andrew ripped the blinds from the top of the window. As Grace began to scrub the windows, she thought about Andrew's life. What exactly was it like being him?

'What does being famous feel like for you?' Grace was intrigued by the constant attention. 'Is the amount of attention huge on a daily basis?'

'Some days are more manic than usual. With the first episode of the new show being aired tonight, I'll be bombarded tomorrow with constant notifications. I usually end up switching my phone off and not venturing into the wide world for a couple of days.'

'Surely it's a good thing that people want to talk about the show?'

'It depends what they're saying,' said Andrew with a grin. 'There are times when you wish the world around you would go away, but then you remember you are in the limelight because those people have invested in you. But they never really get to know the real me – just the image that is put out there.'

'What was your childhood like?' asked Grace, wanting to know more about the world that Andrew had been brought up in. 'You have a successful mother and father, mansions dotted all over the world ... yachts.'

'You have done your homework.'

'Google,' admitted Grace, 'I was intrigued.'

'If the truth be told, not as glamorous as you think.' Andrew stopped what he was doing for a second, seeming lost in thought.

'I didn't mean to pry,' she added. 'But I bet your parents are as proud as punch.'

Andrew took a breath. 'Disappointment was written all over my dad's face when I said I wanted to be a chef. "That's not going to make you any proper money, I didn't pay for a decent education for you to cook up a full English breakfast in a greasy spoon,"' said Andrew, mimicking his father's voice, 'but sometimes you have to just go with your heart and stand by your dreams. It wasn't easy with successful parents.'

'But surely you had everything you ever wanted?'

'I didn't want for much as a kid, I had all the material things you could ever want...' Andrew stopped talking and looked at Grace. 'But my God, it was lonely.'

'Lonely, in what way?' asked Grace curiously.

'I had various nannies, servants that would run around after me, but I barely even saw my parents. My mother was always flying to New York, my father at some business meeting or another. There was one Christmas I actually sat and ate my Christmas dinner with my nanny,' said Andrew, raising an eyebrow. 'I was packed off to boarding school. Now you could say they just wanted the best education for me and I was worth it, but I think it was more about it fitting with their lifestyle. I'm not saying my parents are bad people, but it wasn't the happy family that you have. The loving bond you have with your boys is obvious to anyone. My parents were driven by success and money. They barely spent any quality time with me. Take, for instance, today.'

'What's today?'

'My mother is arriving sometime today and to the

outside world that looks like she's a supportive parent visiting her son on the day his new TV show is aired.' Andrew was shaking his head. 'It's more to do with her having a business meeting in Glasgow and it's more convenient for her to see me now than to arrange a time when she's not running about everywhere. Sometimes it feels... Even at my age, I'm never put first above business. We certainly don't have the relationship you have with your boys.'

Grace carried on listening, hearing the sadness in Andrew's voice.

'Yesterday, that was real family life. The way you interact with your boys and the way they interact with you. The day was full of fun and laughter, adventure and positives! I've never been to the island with my mother, always a nanny. We've never swum together in the sea, or jumped in puddles, fished... The list is endless. I can remember once sitting on the edge of a fountain – and we had many fountains on our property – and all I wanted to do was take off my shoes and socks and paddle, but my mother would never allow that. Even though at every house I ever lived at as a child there were fountains.'

'Why ever not?'

'Probably because my hair had to be just so, my shoes cost way too much money and I certainly wasn't allowed to get my clothes dirty, heaven forbid.' Andrew looked down at his not-so-white T-shirt and grinned. 'Times must be changing since Grace Power walked back into the Castle. My mother would have a fit.'

Grace laughed. 'Make sure you get changed before she arrives!'

'I'm sure it sounds like I'm saying I had an unhappy childhood. It was just different from how other people live.'

'Like a normal family.'

'Exactly that, like yesterday. Spending quality time together.'

'The boys had the best day and that was down to you. Thank you.'

'And what you find is being me can be hard sometimes. People want to be my friend because of what I do, not who I am, and it's rare you meet people in normal circumstances. Usually my life is full of glitzy events and champagne. People who follow me around all night wanting something from me because I'm "Andrew Glossop", not because I'm Andrew Glossop, if you get my drift.'

'Sounds like hell,' teased Grace. 'I get your drift but just so you know, I don't care which Andrew Glossop is helping me clean up this place as long as it gets done!'

Andrew swiped the cloth at her. 'Cheeky!'

For the next couple of hours they stripped out all of the old faded and out-of-date stock, washed down the walls and shelves, brushed and mopped the floor countless times. They were both covered head to toe in cobwebs. 'What's that?' said Grace, her eyes fixed on something long and green that was sticking out from a crate on the floor. 'Oh my God, it's a snake,' she screamed, and jumped straight on to the serving counter, which wobbled, so Andrew had to steady her. Her heart was beating nineteen to the dozen as she pointed to the floor.

Andrew took a step forward then howled with laughter. 'And breathe! It's one of those rubber toy snakes.' He bent down and picked it up, then waggled it in front of her.

She exhaled, and grabbed Andrew's hand as he helped her down from the counter.

They both stood back and admired their hard work. 'It's quite roomy in here,' observed Andrew.

'You know what, with a lick of paint, colourful bunting and maybe tea, coffee and cold drinks, it might be possible to open this up again. Do I actually need teddy bears with a logo of the Castle or key-rings? Low-cost and simple is the way,' she declared. 'I think this is actually doable.'

'Just think about it carefully, don't go biting off more than you can chew.'

'Aww, for a moment there, it sounded like you cared.'

Andrew rolled his eyes.

'Let's leave those bags of rubbish there for now. I'll bring the barrow up in the morning and get them shifted.'

'You really aren't averse to hard work, are you?' said Andrew, emptying the last bucket of dirty water down the drain. 'I'm quite impressed.'

'Sounding like you cared a second ago and now paying me a compliment. Are you paying me a compliment?' Grace teased, with a sparkle in her eye.

'I might be.'

'Are you actually though?'

'Oh, so needy. Actually I am.'

'Well, thank you,' she replied. What was wrong with accepting a compliment?

'What about you, Grace Power, what do you aspire to be?'

'Apart from a good mum, that is a very good question.'

Grace knew she didn't want to be merrily plodding along for the rest of her life. She was ambitious, but what actually did she want from life? She wanted to be successful in her own right, leave her mark, make a little bit of the world go round.

'I'm not sure where my journey is taking me yet, but I'll be sure to let you know as soon as I figure it out,' she replied light-heartedly.

She threw the sponge into the bucket and took another look around. 'I think that's enough for today. I'll keep the windows open for ventilation. Thank you.'

'You're welcome,' replied Andrew, peeling off the wringing wet Marigolds. 'I've quite enjoyed myself.'

They threw the last bin bag outside and Grace locked the door behind them. They stood in the sunshine for a moment, then Grace burst out laughing. 'You seem to have a spider's web for a hair net.'

Instantly, Andrew jigged up and down on the spot, brushing his hands frantically over his hair. Grace watched in amusement as he shook his head wildly. 'I was only joking, you're all good,' she said, her eyes sparkling playfully.

He swiped her with the Marigolds. 'You bugger!'

With the sun still beating down they walked side by side

back through the grounds towards the Castle. Grace noticed the water from the fountain was shooting into the air, the sunlight glittering on the water droplets as they fell into the shale at the bottom of the pool. She walked over and immediately noticed the fantastic job Hector had done cleaning it out.

She looked at the fountain, then Andrew. 'Go on. I dare you.' The wicked glint in her eye said it all.

'Dare me?'

'You said you would never have been allowed to jump into a fountain. Here's your chance!'

Andrew looked at the fountain and back at Grace. 'You are crazy! I can't do that!'

'Why not, who's going to stop you?' Grace swung around. 'There's nobody in sight. What are you afraid of?'

Once more, Andrew looked at Grace like he was admiring her carefree attitude.

'Dancing in the fountain costs absolute nothing,' she encouraged.

For a split second Andrew hesitated, then, taking Grace by surprise, he kicked off his shoes and tugged his T-shirt over his head. Immediately her eyes ran up and down his tanned chest as he made for the fountain.

'Come on then!' Andrew urged, as he placed both hands on the rim of the fountain wall, swung his legs over and landed in the pool of water.

'If your mother could see you now!' joked Grace. 'You daredevil, you.'

Andrew stood directly under the fall of the fountain,

tilting his head back and running his hands through his hair. 'She would have an absolute fit!'

Grace couldn't take her eyes off him. He stretched out both hands towards her and she reached back. As soon as his fingertips touched hers, they tingled with adrenalin. He gently pulled her into the water and under the fountain.

'Eek!' she squealed at the shock of the freezing cold water.

'Let the water fight commence!' announced Andrew, leaning over the side of the fountain and picking up a couple of empty plant pots that Hector must have left lying there.

For the next five minutes they scooped up the water and ran round and round the fountain, laughing and joking, chasing each other like a couple of kids. Grace couldn't remember the last time she had fun like this. She felt relaxed in Andrew's company. They continued to playfully throw water at each other and chase each other around, the cool water splashing up their legs.

'You bugger!' exclaimed Grace, dodging a pot full of water that Andrew had just thrown at her. In that second, she stumbled and gasped. Reaching forward, she grabbed hold of Andrew's arm to steady herself.

He gave her a lopsided grin. 'Are you falling for me?' he joked, catching her eye and causing her heart to pound. They were centimetres apart, Grace still gripping his strong, strapping arm.

'I must have gone weak at the knees,' she replied, eyes

sparkling, and she noticed the glint in his eyes. Reluctantly, she let go of his arm.

'You've got a leaf stuck in your hair.' Andrew reached forward, his arm brushing against hers, leaving a tingling pulse racing through her body which she couldn't control. But it was just a ploy, as Andrew splashed water over her. Grace pushed against his chest and turned in the opposite direction, but he caught hold of her and spun her round. Grace could feel her heart hammering against her chest. They were looking straight into each other's eyes, and the sparks between them could light up the whole of the town. He had an air of confidence and a twinkle in his eye, and he was making Grace's pulse race. She poured one last plant pot of water over his head and giggled uncontrollably. He pulled her back towards him, their eyes still locked. All the time he was staring at her he had a smile on his face and its warmth radiated through her body. He was looking at her in a way that only meant one thing to Grace: they were flirting – just a little.

'What the hell do you think you are doing?'

Grace's eyes pinged wide open as she swivelled her head towards the voice.

Standing right in front of them was Magdalene Glossop, Andrew's mother. Grace recognised her in an instant from her Google search and immediately noticed the lack of a smile on her face. She dismissed Grace and stared straight at Andrew.

'It's your mother,' whispered Grace under her breath, causing Andrew to stifle his laughter.

'I know it's my mother,' he whispered back. 'I can see her.'

'She's not looking too impressed.'

'I can see that.'

'Shall I shut up?'

'Probably best.'

'What are you doing?' Magdalene asked again, her disgruntled tone obvious to all.

'Dancing in the fountain,' replied Andrew, with a huge beam on his face, but Magdalene still didn't crack a smile – unlike Andrew, who kicked water at Grace one last time. 'It's very liberating.'

'Stop it,' said Grace, swiping his arm playfully.

'You have a room full of important people waiting for you. Have you forgotten this afternoon's press conference before the show is aired tonight? The holding room is full of journalists and photographers and they can't see you like this. Whatever will they think? Look at your shorts, they'll be ruined.'

'They'll dry,' threw back Andrew before turning to Grace, his voice low and discreet. 'Thanks for another fantastic afternoon.'

'You're very welcome.'

Still grinning, Andrew stepped out of the fountain, slipped his wet feet back into his loafers before extending his hand to help Grace out of the water, then picked his T-shirt up off the ground.

Magdalene tutted, and took the crumpled-up, dirty T-shirt from his hands and shook it out. 'What the hell have you been doing? Rolling in the mud?'

'I can neither deny nor confirm,' replied Andrew. His eyes sparkled, but his mother gave him that look that mothers do – the death stare.

'And why weren't you there to welcome me?' Magdalene was still grumbling as they walked away.

Andrew looked over his shoulder as he went, giving Grace a mischievous wink. She winked back, sitting on the edge of the fountain and swinging her legs back and forth like a naughty child.

As they disappeared out of sight, Grace looked up at the magnificent Castle and smiled. Even though the last couple of hours had been hard work, she'd had so much fun. She realised that Andrew had had his own struggles growing up. He might have great wealth but he'd never had what she'd had: constant quality time with her mother and her grandfather. Her heart had softened towards him. She was beginning to see the real Andrew Glossop when all the lights, camera, action were stripped away. She admired how honest he had been.

Jumping from the edge of the fountain, Grace looked down at her own dirty, dowdy clothes. Her sodden, bobbled, grey jogging pants were covered in dust and grime and her T-shirt too was smeared with dirt. There was plenty of time to have a shower before she made tea for the boys, and right now she was excited to tell Hector all about the shop. With a spring in her step she walked through the walled gardens and pinged a text over to Isla: 'I'm thinking of opening up the Castle gardens to the public again, but am in need of ice cream! Is there a deal we can do?'

Almost immediately, Isla's name flashed on her screen: 'Absolutely we can!'

Grace stopped walking, flung her arms open wide, tilted her face to the early afternoon sun and spun round like a child. Was living in a run-down castle really that bad? For the last few years in particular she'd felt like she'd spent every day moving through fog, and it was only now she had made the break from her past that she was beginning to see the next step in front of her: Heartcross Castle. She felt as happy as the boys did in their safe place, and even though Andrew's offer to buy the Castle was on the table, she wasn't sure she could ever accept, however tempting it was.

Chapter Sixteen

When Grace walked into the kitchen Hector and the boys were standing around the budget chart, smiling. Billy was pointing at a pile of coins.

'Another forty pounds,' declared Freddie, high-fiving Hector.

'Wow, this is amazing, you've done so well. Come here.' Grace opened her arms to give the boys a hug, but they all took a step back. She remembered how filthy she was. 'Oops, sorry, I probably need to go and cleaned up,' she said.

Billy was pointing to the far end of the kitchen and Grace looked over. The table was set, with place mats drawn by the boys, and was laden with egg salad, fresh bread, baked potatoes and, to cap it all, a delicious fruit salad they'd made of fruit from the orchard.

'We thought the last thing you would want to do after cleaning up the shop was make lunch,' said Hector.

Grace's eyes shone proudly. 'This is just fabulous, thank you,' she said graciously, accepting a glass of homemade lemonade from Billy.

'And what has happened to you? Was there a leak at the shop? You are soaking wet.' Hector was looking Grace up and down and handed her a towel.

'I had a date with a fountain,' replied Grace with a grin, leaving Hector to inquisitively narrow his eyes at her.

'Hector showed us how to make lemonade, it's delicious,' exclaimed Freddie, interrupting the conversation excitedly.

Grace took a sip. 'I agree! This is just want I needed. I'll drink this and then maybe have a quick shower.'

'The boys have got other ideas,' said Hector, nodding in their direction.

'We will be five minutes,' shouted Joey, pulling at Freddie and Billy's arms. They immediately ran off, and Grace could hear their feet echoing up the stairs.

Puzzled, Grace looked towards Hector. 'What have you done with my boys?'

'They are such a joy, aren't they?' Hector's voice faltered.

'Hector, what is it?' asked Grace tentatively, noticing Hector's eyes well up with tears.

'Oh, forgive me, Lady Grace, I've just had such a good afternoon. It's been a long time since I've had some proper company. They make me feel young again.'

'You can borrow them any time,' replied Grace softly.

'I'll keep you to that. Now, how was the shop? What was the state of it?'

'Not too shabby after a good clean. Hector, I'm thinking we could possibly open the gardens again to the public. With a little bit of marketing I'm sure tourists would flock back in their droves.'

'We?'

'Yes, we! Me and you. After all, you are the chief gardener and if it wasn't for you keeping the gardens in such a fabulous state it wouldn't even be doable.'

'I think it's a wonderful idea, Lady Grace. This place needs some love and attention and I know it sounds daft but you and those boys are breathing life back into it. Let's talk later.' Hector pointed to Freddie who'd appeared at the door.

'We are ready for you,' Freddie declared, taking Grace by the hand and leading her out of the kitchen, down the hallway towards the stairs.

'Lunch will be served in forty minutes,' shouted Hector after them. 'Oh, and before I forget, Dougie popped in to tell us that Andrew's show will be aired on TV tonight if you fancy watching it together.'

'I'd love to, Hector,' shouted Grace from halfway up the stairs.

Freddie was still holding Grace's hand as he led her to the bathroom. Joey and Billy were waiting by the door. There was a crayoned sign stuck to the door, 'Do not disturb,' which made Grace smile. Joey flung open the door and all three boys stood there as Grace stepped inside. The bathroom had been cleaned, and the bath filled with water and bubbles with a gorgeous aroma of lavender. All around the room were jam jars filled with wild flowers.

'It didn't cost a penny to make it this pretty,' declared Joey. 'We picked the flowers from the meadow and the gardens.'

'And we found the jam jars in the outbuilding. Hector helped us to wash them out,' chipped in Freddie.

For a second, Grace was too emotional to speak; her hands were on her heart, her eyes brimmed with tears. 'I have just the best boys.'

Billy handed Grace a towel.

'Forty minutes until lunch,' reminded Freddie, gently putting his hands on the bottom of Grace's back and pushing her into the room.

Shutting the door behind her, she heard the boys running down the stairs.

Lying in the bath was bliss. She closed her eyes and thought of Andrew: how he'd helped clean the shop and how he'd opened up to her just like she'd done last night. He was right when he said how loving she was to the boys and they were to her. Just running her a bath and picking the flowers melted her heart. She thought about the moment when she and Andrew were face to face in the fountain, and how she had known then that there was a fizz of chemistry between them. She sank her shoulders under the warm water. She couldn't wait to talk to Hector about the shop in more detail. With Isla on board at least they could sell ice cream... But she was still going to give the go-ahead for the valuation, even if it was more out of curiosity than anything else.

Thirty minutes later, Grace was clean, dressed and sitting at the table enjoying the meal prepared for her. She watched the twins chatting to Hector, who was teaching them how to speak in a Scottish accent, which made Billy erupt in a fit of giggles. This was everything Grace ever wanted from a family: chatter and laughter that filled the room, not the atmosphere of fear and terror that they had endured for the past few years. She'd had enough of not ever being enough. It took a lot of hard work to create the perfect family, but judging by the boys' smiles she was well on her way.

Hector was now educating them in the art of growing fruit and veg, telling them all about the different times of the year for sowing the seeds, and in what months of the year you could harvest the different fruits and veg. The boys were hanging on to his every word. Hector looked at the near-empty bowl of fruit salad. 'There's not much left,' he said, looking at Grace and holding the bowl towards her. 'You have it.'

She relented. 'Go on, just another spoonful,' she said, smiling.

'And today's lunch hasn't cost anything. We baked the bread, made the lemonade, the salad, eggs and fruit salad came off the land. I noticed you are running a very tight ship.' He nodded towards the budget chart.

'We are and we are managing just fine. Aren't we, boys?' replied Grace. She stood up to clear away the empty plates but Hector was having none of it. 'Come on, boys, it's your mum's afternoon off.'

Grace was stunned as the boys cleared away the plates from the table. Freddie filled the bowl with water and washed them, while Joey dried them and passed them to Hector and Billy to put away in the cupboards. It was all about the teamwork.

'You can definitely come around more often. They've fallen under a magic spell,' said Grace enthusiastically, looking at Hector. 'And what are we going to do this afternoon?'

All the boys looked at Hector and then at Grace.

'What's going on?' she asked, scrutinising them.

'Hector has cleaned out the fountain so we were hoping we could go and play in it this afternoon?' asked Freddie.

All three boys were poised with their fingers crossed behind their backs.

Grace burst out laughing. 'Of course. You might find some plant pots knocking about by the edge of the fountain. They'll be great fun for scooping up the water.'

'You sound like you know what you're talking about, Lady Grace,' remarked Hector.

'Maybe I do, Hector,' she said with a wink.

With their towels under their arms, all three boys ran towards the fountain. Kicking off their shoes and pulling their T-shirts over their heads, Joey and Freddie pulled themselves up and over the edge of the fountain and stood on the shale. They turned back around and each extended an arm towards Billy, lifting him clean from his wellies, and hauled him over the edge. Within seconds they were running around in circles and attempting to catch the water shooting from the top with their pots.

'That should keep them entertained for a short while,' said Grace with a chuckle. The boys were already soaked to the skin.

'They certainly bring life back into this place,' shared Hector. 'Your grandfather would have loved to meet them.'

'I know, Hector, it breaks my heart just thinking about it. Did you ever want children?' she asked.

'Yes, I always wanted children but it wasn't an option for me, Lady Grace. I couldn't have them.'

Grace noticed his voice falter and tears in his eyes. She linked her arm through his and rested her head on his shoulder. She didn't question him further.

'Well, you can borrow these three anytime,' she joked. 'You are the closest thing they have to a grandfather and I'm sure my grandfather would love the fact that his oldest friend is a part of their lives.'

Hector took his cap from his head and held it in his hands. 'I'd like that. You don't know how much that means to me.'

The boys were having the time of their lives out on the fresh air. Grace and Hector stood there in silence, watching them have fun.

'Hector! Come in with us! Please!' Freddie was beckoning Hector to join them in the fountain and he didn't need asking twice.

'We can't let the youngsters have all the fun, now, can we?'

Grace laughed as Hector kicked off his shoes and rolled up his trousers to his knees. Within seconds he was standing in the fountain. She watched as Hector held out his arms towards Billy, then scooped him off his feet and swung him around under the falling water. Billy was giggling uncontrollably.

The boys were already making memories at the Castle. They had the perfect outdoor space to be boys and were safe in the Castle grounds. With every second that ticked by Grace knew it would be harder to even think about taking this place away from them – and Hector too. Taking her phone out of her pocket, she walked out of earshot and rang the estate agent.

'Hi, it's Grace Power from Heartcross Castle. I have a valuation booked in, but I'd like to cancel it, please.'

'Ms Power, before you cancel the valuation I think I should let you know that we have already received a phone call about the property and if it does go on the market an offer has already been made by Mr Andrew Glossop.'

Grace wondered how much the offer was. In that moment her head was fighting her heart. Did she actually *want* to know? Did it matter, if she had no intention of selling?

'Five million,' added the estate agent. 'And we think that's a pretty good offer, in fact a damn good offer – possibly 1.5 million over the asking price.'

Grace couldn't believe her ears. That was an

extraordinary amount of money. She was dumbfounded. Her thoughts tumbled quickly over each other. Five million. This was the chance of a lifetime. That amount of money could change her life. She and the boys would never struggle financially again.

After bringing the conversation to a close, Grace still couldn't get her head around the offer. The adrenalin was pumping inside her. Only a few hours earlier, she'd been convinced that her destiny was Heartcross Castle and that she was about to build her for ever home with her boys. And now, suddenly, she wasn't sure.

As she watched the boys having the best time splashing about in the fountain with Hector, Grace felt excited, terrified and simply confused.

Chapter Seventeen

'**B**loody hell' were the only words Grace could muster up under her breath. She hadn't mentioned the offer to anyone. She wanted to get things straight in her own mind but an offer like that was very tempting. She knew at some point she needed a proper conversation with Hector and the boys and it was one she wasn't looking forward to. She knew how much this place meant to them all. If she was being honest with herself, she didn't know exactly how *she* was feeling about it, but she was thinking deeply about the offer. It could be incredibly exciting for them, and lead to fantastic opportunities for her and the boys.

'You okay?' asked Hector, sitting down on the settee next to the boys. 'You seem a little quiet.'

Grace felt a little guilty she hadn't told Hector about the offer but, deep down, she knew it would unsettle him, and what was the point of that when she had no clue what she was going to do?

'I'm just thinking about the Castle gardens. Do you know how many visitors it attracted every year?'

'Oh, I do. On average it pulled in no less than 200,000 tourists a year. Most of the time it was more.

Grace let out a low whistle. 'Are you serious?'

'Those gardens were the making of this place.'

'And if a ticket was fifteen pounds...' said Grace, thinking aloud.

'That's a hell of a lot of money, but don't forget you'd have quite a few costs. You will need more staff. At my age now, I couldn't manage the upkeep of those gardens by myself. It's only in the immaculate state it is at the moment because I spent a month on each section and then start the process again. You will need to employ gardeners, cleaners, shop staff... We used to have children's entertainers, balloon stalls, drinks and food stalls. The rose garden was very popular, and the maze for the children.'

'The Earth Garden was a huge hit with the children. I used to love to weave through the bamboo tunnel and slide down the wormhole tubes,' Grace reminisced.

'Tourists used to make a day of it. They'd bring picnics, and some of them portable barbecues. My favourite part of the garden is the Waterlily House.'

'But, Hector, with all the costs, that would still be a profitable business, wouldn't it?'

'Oh, yes. Your grandfather used to plough the money back into the gardens and he used to donate a lot to charity. His downfall was that he didn't make a plan for if the gardens ever closed. He'd hoped you might think of taking it over one day and keep it in the family, so to speak.'

Talking to Hector had planted lots of seeds in Grace's mind. But the main problem was employing the staff and getting everything in order.

'And since the village of Heartcross was catapulted all over the news, the tourist industry has increased. Don't forget there's all the guests at Starcross Manor and elsewhere – even Julia had to extend the B&B as business was booming. The town's hotels are always full and many people take day trips to this area now. I'm sure Andrew Glossop making his TV show here would also attract visitors.'

Grace was taking on board everything that Hector was saying. The Castle had the potential to make more money than what Andrew was offering to purchase the property. All Grace had to determine was: was she brave enough to take the risk?

'Switch the TV on, Freddie,' she said, realising the time.

They were all sitting down ready to watch the first episode of Andrew's TV show. Grace knew that Andrew must be having guests over to watch the screening, as the courtyard was jammed with more posh cars than a luxury garage, and, according to Hector, Andrew's mother had arrived by limousine with a huge entourage.

'Here we go,' exclaimed Grace.

Within seconds the theme tune played out and Joey pointed at the screen. 'There's Heartcross ... the town... our Castle.' He rushed over towards the screen for a closer look.

'Doesn't it look magnificent when you see the Castle like that?' Grace was in awe. The Castle looked stunning and the cameras swooped over the gardens.

'And you are telling me that tourists are not going to want to visit this place. That there,' said Hector, pointing at the screen, 'is the best marketing you'll ever have. Heartcross Castle is on prime-time TV.'

Grace looked across at him. He was spot on. Heartcross Castle was being shown on so many TV screens across the country. This was a perfect marketing opportunity.

'There's our home on the TV,' said Freddie excitedly. 'It looks huge!'

Grace smiled at the boys' excitement. Joey sat back down and squeezed in between Billy and Freddie. They resembled meerkats as they all sat up straight, waiting to see what was coming on the screen next.

The excitement was short-lived. After the programme's opening, the Castle was no longer featured, and within five minutes the boys were itching to leave.

'Can we go and play?' asked Freddie, bored.

'Of course,' replied Grace.

The boys didn't need telling twice, and rushed out of the kitchen and ran upstairs.

Grace and Hector sat in silence and watched Andrew on the screen. There was no denying that he had star quality and was on top of his game, but Grace shifted slightly in her seat and turned her gaze to Hector, who raised an eyebrow.

'What are you thinking?' she asked.

They both looked back at the TV screen.

'Well, it's a nice kitchen,' declared Hector, causing Grace to laugh.

'Oh my days, this is bad, isn't it? I know I shouldn't say anything if I have nothing nice to say, but...'

'It's bad,' agreed Hector.

'There's no oomph. It's falling flat. I mean, he's got the content all wrong. This programme isn't family friendly, it's more for the elite. Is lobster your favourite?'

Hector gave a chuckle, 'I'm not sure I have ever eaten lobster. There doesn't look to be enough meat to fill me up, never mind a family.'

'I agree. This wasn't what I was expecting. Andrew needs to cook dishes that we can all follow, that the kids can get involved in. "Pick a lobster from your tank,"' Grace quoted. She looked around the kitchen. 'How many people have fresh lobster milling about in their kitchen?'

'Definitely not me,' replied Hector.

'Can you imagine me saying to the boys, "Hey, kids, tonight we have a light cream and dry vermouth sauce slightly flavoured with parmesan cheese and mustard, new potatoes and mixed salad leaves?'

Hector chuckled. 'They would have no clue what that was.'

'And no doubt would just want a fish finger sandwich with lashings of tomato sauce.' Grace googled the price of lobster on her phone. 'Jeez! To cook that for two people – go on, guess how much?'

'Twenty-five pounds,' guessed Hector.

'And the rest, nearly one hundred pounds for two.'

Grace looked over to her budget chart. 'Andrew really isn't living in the real world, is he?'

'And I'm not sure if I was the richest person on the earth that would be my go-to dish.'

They endured another twenty minutes before the credits rolled. Grace blew out a breath. 'I'm not sure that has done Andrew any favours at all. It made him look a little pompous.'

'I agree. Would you tune in to the next show?'

Grace was shaking her head. 'I think not, but that's between me, you and these four walls. A bit of an anti-climax,' she admitted. Hearing raised voices filtering across the courtyard, Grace looked out of the window. 'Oh my.'

Andrew was pacing up and down, whilst having what looked like a fraught conversation with his mother. He threw his arms in the air then looked back at his phone. A crowd of people were filtering out of the servants' quarters, giving Andrew a few nods and mumblings as they began to climb in their cars and drive away.

'What do you think is going on?' asked Hector.

'I think Andrew isn't happy with the show and now it's been aired to the nation, look how despondent he looks.'

Dougie appeared and spoke to Andrew and his mother, then Magdalene disappeared back inside. Andrew's eyes were firmly fixed on his phone whilst Dougie was looking at it over his shoulder.

'They definitely aren't happy,' observed Grace, picking up her own phone. She was quiet for a second before turning to Hector, who'd stood up and come to look for himself. 'And I'm not surprised. Andrew is getting slated on all social media. There are people saying he's lost all sense of reality et cetera. I'm so glad I'm not famous. Could you imagine everyone having an opinion about you? Oh no, they've spotted us watching.'

For a second Grace felt a little awkward and then gave a tiny wave. 'And now they are coming over.'

'And that's my cue to leave. Thank you for a lovely afternoon, Lady Grace.'

'You can't leave me now, Hector,' she whispered under her breath as he opened the door. 'Good evening,' she said, looking at a somewhat harassed Andrew and Dougie.

'I'm just leaving,' said Hector and placed his flat cap firmly on his head. 'I'll see you all tomorrow.'

Grace waited until Hector was out of sight before speaking. 'Are you pair okay? You look kind of...'

'Sorry to descend on you like this. It's a little stifling over there. Can we take a breather over here?'

'Of course.' Grace opened the door wide and was glad the atmosphere wasn't contagious as they both stepped inside.

'Has something happened?' she asked, thinking it was easier to play dumb. 'Would you like a drink? I can only offer water, homemade lemonade or tea and coffee.' Grace gestured for them to sit down as she got them a glass of water each.

Dougie, who was sitting on the settee next to Andrew, went straight to the point. 'Grace, can we ask, did you watch the show tonight?'

Grace perched on the armchair and looked at them both. 'I did,' she replied, slowly.

'And your thoughts?' asked Dougie.

'Can we really put Grace on the spot like this?' asked Andrew.

Dougie was quick to retaliate. 'You are assuming she didn't like the programme or you don't want to face the criticism. It can't be any worse than what's trending on Twitter. Grace is the ideal woman.'

'I do know I am the ideal woman,' joked Grace, trying to ease the tension, 'but I'm assuming this isn't a marriage proposal.'

'You are a mum of three, you cook for a family. Give us your honest opinion. Grace is the target market. What did you think of the programme?'

Grace took a deep breath. She knew exactly what she thought about the content of the programme, but she wasn't sure it was her place to give her opinion to a global superstar. 'You were good,' she replied, turning to Andrew, 'very professional.'

Andrew was staring at her and began to wind his hand around in circles, indicating that Grace should carry on.

Grace felt a little apprehensive, but it didn't look like either of them were budging until she gave her opinion. 'Okay, this is my opinion but I'm not sure what it's worth.' She took a breath. 'I know this isn't want you wanted to hear, but it was car-crash TV. That about sums it up,' she admitted quickly. 'I know that sounds brutal. I'm sorry... I'm sorry,' she repeated.

Andrew looked like his whole world had come crashing down. The pained expression on his face deepened.

'But your kitchen looks fantastic on the screen. I loved the bunting. I could do with getting some in here to brighten up this room.'

'You loved the bunting?' Andrew replied wide-eyed. 'Well, that's okay then, isn't it?'

'You do know you are trending on Twitter?' she asked, not really wanting to add fuel to the fire.

'Oh, I know. "We cannoli take so much." "Oh, it's a clam-ity!" "Tonight's show was a huge missed steak." "Glossop's new show didn't pan out well."'

Grace tried her best not to laugh, but she couldn't help it. Some of the comments were hilarious, though maybe not if you were on the receiving end of them. 'Sorry, sorry. I didn't mean to laugh, but surely you don't dwell on these comments? What's the saying... there's no such thing as bad publicity?' shared Grace. 'What's the worst that can happen?'

'If the ratings fall next time and the reviews are as bad as tonight, the show will get axed,' declared Andrew.

'So you don't let that happen. Just do the next show differently next time.' Grace's voice was upbeat. 'It's simple.'

Both Andrew and Dougie narrowed their eyes at her.

'Go on,' encouraged Dougie. 'What do you mean?'

'What exactly was your target audience and what were you trying to achieve?' asked Grace.

'To create new and exciting dinners for families.'

'Let me help you out here. How many average families would be able to afford lobster? It might be okay for a special dinner party, but not your everyday evening meal after a hard day at work. Think about the footage when the boys stormed your kitchen.'

Grace had their attention, 'It was comedy gold. The boys lit up the screen when they were interacting with you, and, my God, it was funny when Freddie spat out the food.'

'I can't have people spitting out my food on TV.'

'That's not what I'm saying, but think about the brand you are trying to create. That brand being you – Andrew Glossop.'

'You've lost me,' replied Andrew.

'Think of a different type of show that would appeal to a wider audience. Think of the types of families that are out there. Look at me, on my own with three boys. Everything is on a budget.' Grace pointed towards the budget chart and noticed the surprised look on Dougie's face. 'The best way to get kids eating different types of food is to get them involved. Ask them what they want, get them to grow the fruit and veg. Take this dinner time, we had fresh eggs from the chickens, and a fruit salad with fruit from the orchards that the boys had picked themselves. There wasn't a scrap of food wasted and it cost us next to nothing. Now, not everyone has home-grown produce, but not everything has to be about fancy food that isn't accessible to everyday families.'

Dougie and Andrew were listening intently.

'Pitch a different type of cooking show. Ask people to

apply to the show, bring on their children, even take the family shopping... Cook to a budget. Get the kids involved and let them taste the food after they've all cooked it together. Kids are funny, they say what they think. You could have so much fun on screen. Give normal families access to Andrew Glossop's talent and wisdom and you learn from them too.'

Grace noticed that Andrew and Dougie were looking at each other, mulling over everything she had just said.

'Set a reasonable budget for each meal,' suggested Grace, 'and maximise those kitchens.'

'What do you mean, maximise the kitchens?' asked Andrew.

Grace was getting in her stride, brimming with ideas, 'Multi-generational cooking. You have the talent to create a warm and loving home with meals that are nutritious and affordable. Just think of all those traditional family recipes they can share with you.' Grace knew she was positively glowing, there was an excitement to her voice. 'There must be at least seven bedrooms in the servants' quarters?' she queried.

Andrew nodded.

'And over at Starcross Manor, you provided masterclasses. People booked on to your afternoon class to learn how to bake bread, et cetera. Go the extra mile – Andrew Glossop's residential cooking school. They book for a week and come and stay in this fabulous place and you have the most amazing kitchens to cook up a storm with them. Heartcross is a tourist village with plenty of things to see and do… Win-win. Food is your passion. Share that passion and knowledge.'

'I think Grace is on to something. Cooking on a budget, getting the children involved. A residential cooking school is a good idea. What do you think, Andrew? I think it could work,' said Dougie, nodding his head in agreement.

'And use those people to film your show. Granted, it may not be easy to set up for the rest of this series, but just think how many families are out there in the same situation as me.'

Andrew hadn't said a word. He was lost in thought.

'Surely the TV company would point you in the right direction?' quizzed Grace.

'I am the TV company.' Andrew rolled his eyes.

'Oh, I see. How about a challenge?' suggested Grace, looking straight at Andrew.

'Go on,' he acknowledged, looking curiously at her.

'How do you feed a family of four on a very small budget? From what I can see, you shop in delis, not supermarkets. Everything you cook is lavish, over the top. Bring it back to basics. Let me and my boys show you how it's done. Why don't you come shopping with us? Let's set a budget and cook a meal together. See what life is like for the average family out there. There's nothing to lose.'

'I think this TV show needs saving and Grace is right, we have nothing to lose,' reassured Dougie, looking at Andrew.

'Come on, you can't be frightened of a few kids,' teased

Grace. 'Just because they didn't like your lobster paste,' she added playfully.

Andrew was staring straight at her.

'The boys will love it.'

Andrew threw up his hands in defeat. 'Okay, okay. After being slated on social media... It's not as though the boys can dent my ego any more. Tomorrow will be even worse. I'm just dreading the onslaught. Tomorrow's newspapers, the food critics,' he admitted.

'So don't read them. Who cares what people think?'

'I do,' he replied, 'and my mother will be scrutinising every article.'

Grace had no clue what it was like to live in the public eye or how anyone would cope with reading negative comments about themselves. It wasn't for the faint-hearted – but she was sure that if anyone could change the public's perception of Andrew, it was Andrew himself.

'Tell her not to. You don't need validation from anyone. You cook for you because that's your passion. If other people enjoy that, then embrace it. If they don't, that's their loss. We can't please everyone all of the time. Don't take criticism unless it's from someone you respect in your own field. It's simple.'

'When you put it like that, Grace Power, you talk a lot of sense. Thank you,' he said, the warmth showing in his eyes.

'You are very welcome,' she said smiling. 'As long as I've given you some food for thought.' She held up her hands 'No pun intended. But now, if you don't mind, my boys are extremely quiet, which normally means they are up to some sort of mischief. They've been dancing in the fountain this afternoon, and they've had so much fun.' For a second Grace and Andrew caught each other's eye and grinned. Then Andrew stood up. 'We'd better go and find my mother. She's a bit like your boys – leave her on her own and she too will get up to a lot of mischief.'

Dougie touched Grace's arm on the way out. 'You have been a great help and pointed us in the right direction.'

Thankfully, Andrew seemed a lot calmer than when he arrived and didn't look as frazzled. Just as he was about to walk out, he said, 'Grace, I was wondering – Saturday evening, I'm having a few drinks with some of my friends and colleagues in the garden. Would you like to join us?'

'If I can get Hector to babysit, that would be perfect. I'll let you know.'

'And this shopping trip—'

'Don't you worry about the shopping trip,' interrupted Grace. 'It'll be a lot of fun. We will go easy on you and I'll set the budget. It'll help you to know what it's like to live in the real world.' Grace gave him a cheeky smile. 'Oh and, Andrew…'

'Yes?' he replied, still holding her gaze.

'You left your front door open. Delia has just snuck in!' Grace had a huge beam on her face she couldn't hide.

'Oh, my mother is going to love that.' Andrew hurried across the courtyard shouting for Rose.

Grace watched Andrew and Dougie disappear out of sight. She was quite surprised to find that Andrew had a sensitive side and worried about what people were saying about him on social media platforms. She supposed it didn't matter how much money he had, he was only human. Andrew really did need to tweak his TV show and she knew she and the boys would help him to make it a success. Admittedly she was looking forward to spending some more time with him, and her heart gave a little leap at that. There was something about Andrew Glossop that got her attention every time.

Chapter Eighteen

The following morning Grace woke up in her old bedroom, full of energy. She jumped out of bed and threw back the curtains to witness the cloudless cobalt sky and the magnificent view of the glistening River Heart flowing under the bridge. After opening the window and inhaling the fresh air, Grace checked the time. It was just past 9 a.m. After pulling a brush through her hair she admired her skin in the mirror, the long line of freckles dotted across her nose and the sun-kissed glow that had suddenly appeared after yesterday's sunshine.

Hearing the boys' voices filtering from downstairs, she quickly tied her hair in a loose bun on top of her head and pulled on a pair of shorts and a T-shirt. She was surprised to find Hector in the kitchen with the twins, sitting at the table eating their breakfast. There was toast on the table and tea in the pot.

'Good morning. I hope you don't mind me being here. I just popped over with today's box of delicious vegetables and the boys spotted me. You have a busy day today, haven't you?'

'Yes, Isla and the gang are all coming over!' Grace was excited, but still a little nervous as even though they'd swapped text messages she still hadn't come face to face with Allie yet. 'We are decorating the boys' rooms and having a barbecue on the courtyard. You must come and join us.'

'Thank you, Lady Grace, I may just do that, but I want to take a look over at the bamboo garden and make sure that it's up to scratch.'

'You work so hard, Hector.'

'And if you are seriously thinking about opening the place again, you will need to think about hiring staff.'

'I've done nothing but think about it,' she replied. 'I'm going to take some time tomorrow and have a proper look at everything. Oh and, Hector, would you be able to babysit the boys for me on Saturday night?'

'It will be my pleasure. By the way, Billy is in the garden with Delia. You have a good day and fun with your friends.'

'It's a painting and barbecue day,' announced Joey. 'It's going to be so much fun.'

'It is,' replied Grace, checking her phone. She read a text message from Isla. 'Today's mission, to paint three bedrooms and throw some meat on the BBQ! See you a little after 9 a.m.'

'There's no way we are going to being able to paint three rooms in one day. I know Isla may think we are superwomen but...'

'You will if most of the community are on board,' replied Hector, with a broad grin. 'I think Isla's managed to recruit most of the village.'

Billy ran into the kitchen and began tugging at Grace. She followed him outside and couldn't believe her eyes. The Castle gates were swung open and there was Drew driving the tractor with Fergus sitting next to him, and they were pulling a trailer with all her old friends on board. This was community spirit at its best.

'All this for me?' Grace turned around towards Hector.

'You better believe it,' he said and grinned.

They watched as the tractor climbed its way up the path and came to a halt in the courtyard. Grace had to laugh when Drew parked the muddy vehicle right next to Magdalene's clean, shiny black limousine.

The first person Grace locked eyes with was Allie. 'Come here,' Allie cried, jumping off the back of the trailer and launching herself at Grace with her arms wide open. 'I can't believe it's you – and look at your hair.' Allie's face was beaming. 'And back at the Castle, which I believe is not in the best state.'

'You just wouldn't believe,' said Grace, pulling Allie in for another hug. 'Did you miss me?'

'Maybe, just a little,' said Allie pinching her thumb and forefinger together.

'And you're with Rory. Who ever saw that coming?'

'Well, not him, to be fair,' chuckled Allie. Allie had arrived in the village of Heartcross at the age of eight when her parents had settled at The Grouse and Haggis. Even though Allie had known Rory at primary school, it wasn't until he'd returned from university that Allie had taken a real interest in him.

'I really didn't see it coming,' said Rory with a grin, extending a hand.

'Don't shake her hand, give the woman a hug. I'd get in there before she disappears for another ten years,' joked Allie as Rory laughed and pulled Grace in for a hug.

Everyone began to jump down from the back of the trailer. There were a few faces Grace didn't recognise.

'Let me introduce you to Julia and Flynn. Julia owns the B&B and Flynn, Starcross Manor, The Boathouse, The Lake House... In fact, he's just greedy!'

Flynn extended his hand, whilst shaking his head at Allie's introduction. Grace couldn't quite believe millionaire Flynn Carter was standing in front of her and about to muck in for the day. Julia hugged Grace and handed over a bag of supplies. 'I'm Julia, owner of the B&B. I've heard so much about you. Not all good, I'm afraid!' she joked.

Isla and Allie burst out laughing.

'We have drinks, snacks and food for the barbecue,' added Julia.

'This is just amazing, I've come over all emotional,' said Grace, flapping a hand in front of her face.

Aggie and Martha were helped down from the back of the trailer, carrying a sewing machine between them. Rory handed Drew a barbecue. Fergus was carrying a huge cool box full of food. Isla unloaded tins of paint whilst Finn, Angus and Esme had spotted the boys and were already off running towards the gardens, to no doubt jump in the fountain.

'This is Eleni and Jack,' introduced Julia. 'Eleni is my right-hand woman at the B&B and Jack, her boyfriend, is a local builder.'

Grace smiled.

'And this is Molly and Cam, Molly's a vet, Cam is the baker over at The Old Bakehouse,' continued Julia.

Grace narrowed her eyes. 'Cam from Bumblebee Cottage. Your grandmother is Dixie.'

Cam grinned. 'The very one!' he replied, giving Grace a quick hug.

A vivid memory suddenly flooded back to Grace. 'We used to fish at the lake. You were with your grandfather, I was with mine.'

'We did. Those were the days,' he said with a huge grin.

'This is so surreal, more than surreal. I feel like we've all gone back in time but been transported into the future, if that is even possible?' Grace looked between her old and new friends.

'Very surreal,' admitted Allie, 'considering we never really knew what the hell had happened to you. One minute we are sneaking Lambrini from the bar at my mum and dad's pub and the next we are trawling the mountain and the River Heart looking for any clues. Then the letter arrives.'

Grace knew that out of her oldest friends Allie was the feisty one, the one who always said it how it was and was sometimes a little stubborn. 'I'm so sorry, Allie, really I am. If I could change things I really would.'

Allie smiled. 'Just don't do it again, I'm not sure any of us can go through that again.'

'I promise I won't.'

With the look that Allie had given her, Grace knew that things were okay between them. Time had moved on. No judgements were made.

'Felicity and Rona can't be here because of the teashop, but they've sent cake, gingerbread men and pasties for the kids,' said Fergus, handing over a carrier bag, 'and the cool box is full of meat for the barbecue.'

Once the introductions were over, Drew and Fergus set up deckchairs on the courtyard and placed the barbecue on the grass verge. Hector had brought out a table and an extension lead and in no time at all Martha had set up the sewing machine. Aggie was armed with a tape measure and bags of material. They were ready to transform the kids' bedrooms.

'The paint is all the same colour,' said Drew. 'Polished pebble – it looks fab with the multi-coloured dinosaur material that was Finn's old bedspread.'

'We will have those curtains whipped up by mid-morning,' confirmed Aggie, raring to go. 'You better show us the way,' suggested Isla.

As Grace led her friends through the Castle kitchen, everyone began to chatter, sharing their own memories of the Castle. Each and every one of them was amazed to see the vast, dowdy spaces that had once been a glorious place to live. The first bedroom about to be decorated was Freddie's. Drew flung open the window and took a look around before pulling up the edge of the old threadbare carpet, which stank to high heaven.

Drew and Fergus rolled up the carpet, then Drew looked out of the window and shouted, 'It's all clear!' They flung it out of the window to Rory and Flynn, who were waiting at the bottom. It hit the ground like an atomic bomb, a huge cloud of dust mushrooming into the air. As soon as the dust settled, Rory and Flynn hurled the carpet into the back of the trailer.

'Wow, look at that wooden floor,' exclaimed Grace. 'It's an absolute crime to keep that covered up.'

'This will look perfect with a huge rug thrown over it,' said Allie, admiring the room.

Within seconds, everyone set to work, brushing the floor, wiping down the windows and peeling off the old wallpaper. As soon as the bright-white paint hit the skirting boards, the whole room began to burst into life.

With the music from the radio filtering through the room and everyone working hard, Grace looked round at her friends. She couldn't quite believe that they'd given up their day to come and help her.

By mid-afternoon, Grace was amazed at the transformation. 'The boys are going to love this,' she said as Martha and Aggie appeared in the doorway with curtains that fitted the windows perfectly. Everyone had pulled together and Grace was standing back admiring the room. In the warm summer's air, the paint had dried almost instantly. It looked light and airy, clean and bright.

A few hours later, 'I think we all deserve a drink and some food. Shall we go and sit on the grass outside?' suggested Grace.

No one needed asking twice. Immediately, everyone downed tools. Outside they were greeted by Jack and Eleni, who'd already fired up the barbecue, and there was a welcome aroma of sausages and burgers sizzling away. The children appeared with Hector, armed with baskets of fruit. Julia had brought a trestle table from the B&B and a linen tablecloth had been thrown over the top. Jack began to pile up the burgers on paper plates.

Everyone flopped on to the grass and tilted their faces up to the sun.

Out of the cool box came a delicious-looking salad and homemade coleslaw from the teashop, alongside cans of lemonade. There were extra thick wedges of shortbread, gingerbread men and a Tupperware box full of homemade scones.

Everyone had been working so hard.

'Drinks for the workers.'

Grace looked up to see Andrew, Rose and Dougie standing in front of them, each holding a tray of cool beers.

'You beauty.' Fergus was up on his feet, helping to hand out the drinks.

Andrew gave Grace a warm smile as he handed her a beer. 'Party in the courtyard? Where was my invite?'

'I thought you would have had enough of me after dancing in the fountain,' said Grace, 'I wouldn't want another telling off from your mother,' she quipped, giving Andrew a cheeky smile then catching the eye of Isla, who'd cocked an eyebrow.

'Maybe, maybe not,' replied Andrew, with a glint in his eye.

How things had changed in little under a week. Grace would never have imagined she'd be living in a castle, feeling relaxed and happy and dancing in the fountain with a world-famous chef. You just never know what is around the corner.

Grace watched as Andrew was chatting away with Flynn. She noticed the way he would often push his fringe to one side out of his eyes. He had the beginnings of a beard and his face was a little tanned from the sun. For a second she wondered what it would be like to be on the arm of Andrew Glossop, but then pushed the thought out of her head. She was a single mother of three boys with barely any money to her name, whilst he was an international superstar from a famous, successful family. Their worlds were miles apart.

Andrew must have felt her watching him, because he looked over in her direction and smiled, sending a swarm of fireflies swirling at top speed around Grace's stomach. 'Don't forget drinks tomorrow night,' he reminded her.

'I won't. It's on the calendar and when any mum writes anything on the calendar it's law.'

Isla touched her shoulder and handed Grace a burger before sitting on the grass next to her. 'Don't think I've not noticed,' she whispered in Grace's ear.

Grace stole another furtive glance in Andrew's direction, then leaned in towards Isla. 'I don't know what you mean.'

'Sexual chemistry,' whispered Isla, giving Grace a knowing look, and nudging her elbow lightly.

'Behave,' whispered Grace, but feeling a flush of warmth as Andrew looked over again and caught them whispering.

'Andrew, Andrew, where are you, darling?'

Magdalene was walking towards her son in one of her own fashion creations and the hugest, floppiest hat that Grace had ever seen.

'We will be late. We have a date with a private yacht and Pimm's,' she announced, then cast a glance over everyone. She wrinkled her nose like it was the most uncouth thing to be doing, sitting around eating burgers and drinking beer.

Grace and Isla watched in amusement as Magdalene tapped her watch and pointed towards the limousine. She checked her phone as the chauffeur appeared.

'Oh, fabulous news, Andrew dear. We have Arabella joining us. You are going to love her. She's an up-and-coming fashion model and from a very wealthy family in New York.' Magdalene linked her arm through Andrew's as they walked to the limousine and when the chauffeur opened the door they lowered their heads and stepped inside.

Grace felt her mood slump a little and a tiny pang in the pit of her stomach. It sounded like the perfect date for Andrew.

Isla leaned in, bumped her shoulder and whispered, 'That Arabella sounds right up her own—'

'Isla!' interrupted Grace, laughing, knowing that Isla was just trying to make her feel better.

Suddenly, the limousine door swung open and Magdalene jumped out in a complete flap, waving her hands in the air like an overzealous traffic warden. 'There's a chicken in the car,' she squealed. 'It's pooed everywhere.'

Billy raced over and snuck under Magdalene's arms, reached out to grab Delia from Andrew and gently placed her on the grass verge.

'How did Delia get into the limousine?' asked Grace, looking at Billy, who simply shrugged but the fits of giggles from Freddie and Joey told their own story. 'Boys, you are meant to be on your best behaviour.' Grace looked across at Andrew and mouthed, 'Sorry.' She noticed he gave Billy a thumbs-up and Billy smiled back.

The chauffeur looked wearily amused, wearing Marigolds and holding a cloth in one hand and anti-bacterial spray in the other. He was busy cleaning whilst Magdalene stood and tutted.

'I bet she's never put a pair of Marigolds on in her life. I shouldn't be mean.' Isla pretended to zip her lips. She squeezed Grace's arm. 'I've missed you, you know – our chats.'

'I was just thinking the same,' replied Grace, looking round at her friends then towards the children, who were sat in a circle tucking in to hotdogs dripping with ketchup. Hector sat on the bench with his cap tipped over his face, taking forty winks to recharge his batteries.

'Come on, we have one room left to transform,' announced Allie, extending a hand and pulling Grace to her feet. 'We need to get a shift on as the weather is going to change tomorrow – a day of torrential rain apparently – and we need to keep the windows open tonight for the smell of the paint to disappear.'

'Oh good,' chipped in Hector, who'd woken up and pushed his cap back on to the top of his head. 'The fruit trees need a good blast of water.'

With their stomachs full, they all stood up ready to decorate the last room. Aggie and Martha began sewing the last of the curtains whilst everyone piled back up the stairs of the Castle. Isla must have noticed the pensive look on Grace's face. She was thinking about Andrew and a supermodel on a date and she had to admit she didn't quite like it.

'Penny for them,' asked Isla. 'Even though I know exactly what you are thinking. You are wondering about those two.'

'How would you even know that?' It was like Isla had just read her mind. 'There's no point me wondering about everything. Look at me, single mum of three boys without a penny to my name. I wear the same clothes all the time, don't even have a car or enough money for a night out. As if he would even look in my direction.' Grace sighed.

'Why would he not look in your direction? I think a single mother of three with ambition and a good work ethic, not to mention gorgeous and humorous, is a very good catch – and you do own a castle.'

Grace looked straight at Isla.

'What's that look for?'

'Between you and me, Andrew has put in an offer on this place. He wants to buy it.' Grace's voice was low.

'You can't sell it. It's your home and the boys love it here.'

'I'm not sure if it's an offer I can refuse, but I've got time to think about it. But I'm also thinking I really can't go tomorrow night for drinks.' She looked down at her clothes. 'What the hell would I wear?'

'Don't you worry about that. Between myself, Allie and Felicity we have three wardrobes to choose from.' She winked. 'And Felicity is good at styling hair too. All heads are going to turn when you walk in that room.'

Grace smiled at her friend. This was what she'd missed out on, all these years: a best friend to confide in, someone to have fun with, and friends who looked out for each other no matter what.

'Grace, I'm not sure what this is,' said Drew, handing over a small cardboard box with a lid. 'I've just found it over there, it must have fallen behind those shelves.'

'I've no idea,' she replied, taking it from Drew then lifting the lid.

'What is it?' asked Isla, glancing over Grace's shoulder.

Grace looked puzzled. 'A key,' she said, placing it in the palm of Isla's hand before opening the folded piece of paper in the box. 'It's a statement from the bank in the town. Box number 21 with my grandfather's name and address. What does that mean?'

'It's a safety deposit box,' observed Drew, looking over it before painting the last patch of white on the ceiling.

'Do you think it's current?' asked Grace, feeling perplexed. 'What do you keep in safety deposit boxes?'

'Important stuff,' chipped in Allie. 'Maybe it's a winning lottery ticket or important papers of some sort. It's got to be current if your grandfather still has the key otherwise the box would have been allocated to someone else.'

'Ring them and ask them,' suggested Julia, leaning on the broom. 'Oooh, exciting, it's like finding treasure.'

Curiosity was getting the better of Grace as she whipped out her mobile phone from her pocket and dialled the phone number on the statement. After three rings the phone was picked up.

'Hi, I'm not sure you can help me but...' said Grace, explaining the situation.

'Let me check,' replied the woman on the other end of the phone, and promptly disappeared for a minute. 'Who did you say you were again?' she asked. 'And please confirm your address.'

'Grace Power,' answered Grace, promptly followed by her address.

Grace could hear the woman tapping on a keyboard and phones ringing in the background. 'Yes, the security box is still current and can be accessed by either Marley Power or Grace Power, along with identification.'

Grace's mind was racing. She hadn't been aware that the box even existed and here was the woman at the bank confirming she was the only other person apart from her grandfather to have access. What the heck was in that box?

'Would you like to make an appointment? We need to make sure a member of staff is available to escort you to the vault,' said the bank assistant.

Grace couldn't help but think it all sounded very cloak and dagger. 'Yes, please,' she replied.

'We have availability the day after tomorrow at 10 a.m. Would that be convenient for you?'

Grace confirmed she would be there at 10 a.m. and hung up.

Everyone was looking at her, waiting in silence. 'Well?' urged Isla, wanting to know more details.

Grace just shrugged. 'I've no idea, but all will be revealed the day after tomorrow just after 10 a.m. Watch this space.' Grace took the key back from Isla and placed it in the box for safe keeping.

Grace didn't know why, but she had an uneasy feeling in her stomach – which was daft as she had no clue what she was going to discover in the box. Maybe it was nothing

CHRISTIE BARLOW

of any significance, but why would whatever it was be locked away in a security box?

Drew's whistling was filtering up the stairs and he appeared in the doorway along with Fergus, Flynn and Rory close behind. Their arms were jampacked with books and toys.

'I don't want you to think we are interfering, but we've all had a good clear-out for the boys. We've got more toys, books and beanbags at the farm. I thought it would brighten up their room.'

'Oh my, that is so kind. Thank you. And what's that?' asked Grace, looking towards Flynn.

'A spare bed from the hotel,' replied Flynn, laying it down on the floor.

'I can't take a bed from you,' exclaimed Grace, looking at the smile on Flynn's face.

'You can and you will. Any mate of these guys is a mate of mine. You are one bed short and here you go.'

'Flynn, I don't know what to say.' Grace swallowed a lump in her throat. Everyone's kindness was overwhelming. Without warning, her eyes welled with tears that began to roll down her cheeks. Her friends' desire to spread joy and make others feel good about themselves choked Grace with emotion.

'Come here, you daft thing,' said Isla, pulling her in for a hug.

'Thank you, everyone, for what you've done for me and the boys today.'

'Whose room is this?' asked Freddie, appearing at the

306

door. 'This looks amazing.' His eyes widened as he stepped inside.

'Don't touch the walls, the paint may still be wet,' Grace warned. 'There are three rooms, all painted, so you can take your pick.'

'And these are the last of the curtains to hang,' chipped in Martha, walking into the room with the curtains draped over her arms.

The boys ran from room to room and each chose their favourite one before running back towards Grace. They flung their arms around her waist and Billy looked up with the biggest and most adorable smile ever.

'I love you all,' murmured Grace, kissing each child on top of his head.

'Is it bedtime yet?' asked Joey. 'I want to go to sleep in my new room.'

Everyone laughed.

'Not quite,' replied Grace, 'but it won't be long. But how about in the meantime we head to the small paddock and have a game of rounders and some homemade lemonade?'

All the kids jumped for joy and ran out of the room. Their footsteps could be heard thundering down the stairs and everyone headed after them except Grace, who hovered in the doorway and took a look around. She smiled. With the boys now having their own space and happy place, she felt so much more at home – and that was down to the wonderful friends she had. Even after she had let them down all those years ago, they were still willing to help out. She was so grateful and she realised how lucky she was.

'Come on, Mum, you're on the kids' team,' announced Freddie, shouting up the stairs.

'I'm coming,' she said, hurrying to catch the others up.

This was the happy family life Grace had always craved, carefree and fun. She was beginning to enjoy her time at the Castle more and more. She wasn't even sure why she had ever felt nervous about returning. With Hector on her doorstep and her friends close by, her life was coming together nicely. She had a lot to thank her grandfather for.

Chapter Nineteen

The next day the weather changed dramatically; the sky was dark and the rain was lashing down. In the distance the sound of thunder boomed across the sky and the rain didn't look like it was easing any time soon. With her coat pulled up over her head, Grace splashed through the puddles up the long drive of Foxglove Farm. It was late in the afternoon and she was taking her life in her hands and allowing the girls to dress her up for tonight's drinks across the courtyard in the servants' quarters. Grace was feeling nervous and she kept telling herself it was daft. Andrew's friends might be rich and famous, but they were just people. Still, that didn't stop her from her from worrying that she might be a fish out of water. She couldn't remember the last time she was in a room full of people enjoying herself. She just hoped she didn't somehow spill her drink, trip up or show herself up in some other way.

The second she knocked on the front door of the farmhouse, it swung open and Grace was greeted by Isla. 'Come on in,' she said, helping to peel the sodden coat from Grace's back. 'Where are the boys?'

'In Hector's capable hands. Honestly, Isla, he's brilliant with the boys, worth his weight in gold. I've left them setting up an old train track of Hector's in the Grand Hall. The boys are so excited.'

'Aww, how lovely… Drink?' Isla asked.

'Cup of coffee, please,' replied Grace, kicking off her shoes and hanging her bag over the bannister.

'Coffee?' Isla was grinning. 'The girls are through there with a bottle of wine.'

'Not too much wine, I can't turn up tipsy tonight. Can you imagine that? And what his mother would say? I'm not even sure she likes me much. Why am I going, again?' Grace was beginning to have doubts. 'Why am I feeling so nervous?'

'You are going because Andrew invited you, so he must want you there. And who needs to fit in with them? Your natural beauty will shine through and let them fit in with you. A glass of wine will help you steady those nerves. It's just drinks … across the courtyard … with a drop-dead gorgeous man.'

'You are not helping me! And I'm not sure if I'm more nervous about walking into a room of Andrew's friends or about how you are going to make me look,' teased Grace, but secretly she was worried about Andrew's highbrow friends. She was just the girl next door who happened to be a single mother of three; that was her everyday life. She had no clue about the circles he moved in.

'The girls are waiting.' Grace followed Isla into the front room. Felicity and Allie were standing in front of the old Victorian fireplace, which, with its original floral embellishments, set the room off perfectly. A bottle of wine was standing on the oak beam mantel. The girls grinned and immediately Allie handed Grace a glass.

'When these pair are finished with you, Andrew will rescue the princess from the Castle and fall madly in love.' Isla brought her hands up to her heart and gave Grace a lopsided grin.

'Are you trying to bag Andrew Glossop?' asked Felicity, her eyes wide.

'I am not,' protested Grace. 'And no doubt this Arabella who his mother has tried to set him up with is beautiful, with a size eight figure, legs like a giraffe, toned arms, her hair just so and big blue eyes that are enhanced perfectly by her bronzer and nude lipgloss.'

'You are definitely trying to bag Andrew Glossop! And tonight when your eyes meet across the crowded room, the rest will be history ... just like Arabella,' teased Felicity, causing everyone to laugh.

'Do you remember the last time we gave you a makeover?' reminisced Felicity.

'How could I forget?' replied Grace, perching on the edge of a chair and taking a sip from her glass.

'That lad you used to fancy from college, the guy from the garage. He thought he was the bee's knees driving up the road with his dodgy exhaust.'

'I went out with him once in that car.' Grace chuckled at the memory.

'And we feared for your life,' added Allie. 'It was a brown Ford Escort, with cream leather seats, dangly dice and an air freshener that stank to high heaven.'

'Those were the days,' added Isla. 'Then there was the guy from the kebab shop in town. He looked over fifty, sleazy and not even a twenty-tequila type of guy.'

This was what Grace had missed out on: girly chats, glasses of wine and good friends. The way they gelled together instantly, it felt like they'd never been apart. She felt sad for a moment, thinking back to how Cole had isolated her. She hadn't had any proper friends for years.

Just then they all looked at the window; the rain was battering against the windowpane. It was coming down heavily, but according to the weather app it was back to glorious sunshine tomorrow.

'We can't give you a makeover then send you out in this,' exclaimed Isla.

'I'll run Grace back in the car on the way home,' offered Allie. 'I'm only having one drink.'

'And if it carries on like this, I'll use the secret passage from the Castle to the servants' quarters – that'll save me getting drenched.'

'Dress code for tonight will be bikini and flippers. Heads will turn,' joked Isla with a chuckle.

'And just think, how handy it'll be using the secret passage to sneak between the two buildings.' Allie gave Grace a mischievous look.

Grace shook her head in jest. 'You'd think we were teenagers again,' she said, trying to play it down but feeling the hairs on the back of her neck standing on end, and goosebumps prickling her skin, every time she thought of Andrew. He was creeping into her thoughts more and more.

Her phone pinged and she looked at the screen. Sheer pleasure mixed with apprehension ran through her entire body.

'Looking forward to seeing you tonight,' read the text from Andrew.

Immediately, the girls noticed the smile that hitched on Grace's face.

'And who was that text from?' probed Allie. 'As if we didn't know.'

'Andrew!' Grace confirmed, showing them the screen.

The girls squealed. 'Let's get you ready!'

The mood was jovial and within minutes the living room resembled the bedroom of a messy teenager, with clothes thrown over the back of the settee, make-up scattered over the coffee table and music playing on Isla's iPhone. Grace was sitting on a chair, without a mirror in sight; her entire look was in the hands of her oldest friends.

Twenty minutes later, 'What do you think?' asked Felicity, standing back and studying Grace's face like she was a professional make-up artist, whilst Isla and Allie ummed and ahhed, tilting their heads from side to side.

'I'm not sure that's the look we are going for,' admitted Isla, throwing a packet of make-up wipes over towards Allie.

'Let me see first,' protested Grace, wondering how bad she actually looked.

Isla passed her a mirror.

'Bloody hell!' Grace stared open-mouthed. 'That is not the look we are trying to achieve. I look dead....'

The girls howled with laughter. 'You look like one of those frightening porcelain dolls stuck on a shelf in a charity shop,' said Isla. 'Less foundation this time.'

'I'll be on the shelf at this rate if I leave this to you. Why did I ever let you talk me into this?'

'It's just a blip, let's start again,' ordered Isla, taking the mirror from Grace and cranking up the music.

'Let's go for the smoky eye look,' suggested Felicity, smudging the eye shadow with her finger. 'And what colour lipstick?'

'Natural? Nude lipgloss. I've not worn lipstick for years, I'll be looking like a clown next.'

'You are going to look hotter than any catwalk model,' reassured Allie.

'Mmm, why aren't I convinced?' replied Grace.

Fifteen minutes later, all three girls stood back to admire their work, making Grace feel nervous once more.

'Pass me some more wine, I think I'm going to need it.' She held up her glass.

'Have faith.' Isla handed her the mirror.

Grace was rendered speechless. She stared at her

reflection and couldn't believe that was actually her staring back. 'Wow, I look...'

'Absolutely stunning,' replied Felicity, giving Isla and Allie a high-five. All three friends looked chuffed to bits.

'Is that actually me?' Grace was still staring at her reflection.

'You better believe it. And now for the outfit... So it's just drinks tonight?' asked Isla.

'Yes, film and production people, I'm assuming.'

Over the back of the settee was a collection of outfits. 'So, posh drinks, do we go for skinny jeans, high heels—'

Grace quickly interrupted Allie. 'I have not worn heels in over twenty years. I'd never be able to walk in heels.'

All three women looked horrified. 'What do you wear on your feet when you go out?' quizzed Isla.

Grace thought about it for a second. 'I can't remember the last time I went out.' She knew how sad that sounded as soon as the words left her mouth.

'Things are about to change,' Isla said confidently, browsing through the clothes. 'What about this dress?'

'Too bright,' chorused Allie and Felicity.

'I'll be quite happy in my jeans and battered old Converses.'

'Not a chance,' replied Isla. 'What about this?' she said, holding up a jumpsuit that resembled an onesie.

'I'll look like I'm going to bed,' said Grace, 'If this is fashion, they can keep it. How soon will this torture be over?' she joked, taking another swig of wine.

'I honestly think we go for the sophisticated Julia

Roberts look. Tumbling locks over a plain white T-shirt, a blazer with a simple necklace, skinny jeans – and what about these heels with a splash of colour?'

Isla handed Grace an outfit. 'Go and get changed in the downstairs bathroom.'

Two minutes later, Grace appeared in the doorway. She gave a twirl and waggled her jazz hands in the air. 'Ta-dah!'

'Perfect!' declared Isla, handing Grace a pair of red high heels.

'I'm not sure about those,' said Grace, looking at the size of the heels.

'These are the height of fashion,' replied Allie.

Holding on to Isla and slipping her feet into the shoes, Grace wobbled from side to side. Letting go of Isla, she attempted to walk around the coffee table but was still wobbling.

'Whoa!' she said, grabbing hold of Allie.

'Okay, maybe ditch the heels for,' Felicity looked at the pile of shoes, 'these leopard-print loafers.'

Grace was relieved they were flat and that she could walk in them without the possibility of breaking her neck. 'These will do!'

The girls chinked their glasses together. 'A job well done,' trilled Isla. 'How long have you got before you have to be at Andrew's?'

Grace looked at her watch. 'An hour – and Hector is feeding the boys, so I don't have to worry about making the tea either.'

'Sit back and relax,' Isla patted the chair, 'whilst we curl your hair – oh, and...' Isla gave Grace two squirts of perfume on her neck then took in the aroma. 'Chanel,' she said with a wink. 'Posh perfume, who can resist that smell?'

'Hopefully, not Andrew,' teased Felicity with a cheeky grin while Grace rolled her eyes.

When Grace arrived back at the Castle, she opened the back door to find the boys sitting around the table with Hector looking very much at home in the kitchen preparing food. He stood and stared at Grace when she stepped in the kitchen. 'I've only walked from the car,' she announced, shaking off the umbrella and propping it outside the back door.

'Lady Grace, look at you ... a princess fit for a Castle. You look beautiful.'

'It makes a change from dirty bobbled joggers and sweat-stained T-shirts,' Grace replied, 'and thank you, despite my reservations the girls have done wonders. And how are the boys?' Grace looked over towards them. All three of them were smiling.

'We've set up the train track and we've been making a model village out of cardboard boxes and plant pots,' announced Freddie. 'It's been so much fun.'

'You certainly have a way with them.' Grace smiled warmly at Hector.

'They've given me a new purpose, I enjoy their company,' he shared, suddenly dabbing a joyful tear from his eye.

Grace touched his arm affectionately. 'They've never had a grandfather figure, and from the look on their faces they enjoy your company too. Are you okay if I make my move over to the servants' quarters for drinks? I'm not going to be too long – maybe an hour or so – just to show my face as Andrew invited me.'

'Of course, you be as long as you want.'

'Thanks, Hector,' said Grace, turning and looking at the dark clouds looming over the mountains. The rain sounded like bullets as it pelted against the window pane.

'I know it's only a short walk across the courtyard, but I'm going to be drenched. I think I'll take the passage through the library. Do you think that's a bit too cheeky, though?' she asked Hector.

He shook his head. 'Not at all, look at that rain.'

After giving each of the boys a kiss, Grace went into the library and swung back the bookcase that revealed the passage leading from the main part of the Castle to the servants' quarters. She felt nervous about the prospect of walking into a room by herself. 'It's just drinks,' she told herself. Why was she feeling so nervy? It wasn't as though they were on a date. 'Stop being ridiculous,' she told herself. It was probable that she would barely see Andrew tonight; no doubt he would be mingling with the TV production crew and his friends.

With the end of the passage in front of her, she pulled the lever that opened the door into Andrew's state-of-the-art kitchen. She stepped inside and took a look around. She had only seen the kitchen from the TV screen, which didn't do the space justice. Everything was top of the range. This would make a perfect residential cooking school. Grace already envisaged wannabe chefs standing behind the workstations preparing meals on a budget to feed their families. She was looking forward to the challenge she'd given Andrew of shopping on a budget, and she knew the boys would enjoy getting involved too. She was just about to head towards the gathering when she heard the raised voices of Andrew and Magdalene coming her way – and getting closer.

Panicking, Grace didn't know what to do. They seemed to be having some sort of argument and instead of just standing there when they walked into the kitchen she did something stupid and found herself crouching down behind a workstation. She held her breath and closed her eyes, willing them not to notice her.

'I've offered way over the asking price for that Castle, there is no doubt it's going to be yours. She would be stupid to refuse such an amount and if she has the audacity to refuse, we offer more. Everyone has their price. Andrew, you need that Castle, it will do wonders for your image and brand, and the revenue that can be generated from that place is huge.'

'Mother.'

'A single mother of three and no servants? She's not our kind. And the Castle is in a state, you say. How will someone like that ever be able to restore it to its beauty?

Look at how much money you have already spent on this place. It breaks my heart that you have to hang around with someone of that class, but needs must. You just make sure you get that Castle.'

Andrew didn't answer, but Grace heard the door open and shut and then there was silence.

She could feel the heat rising through her body as they left the room. She swallowed hard as she stood up and steadied herself, placing both hands on the worktop. Feeling herself shaking, she took a deep breath. Is that what Andrew Glossop was doing? He was being nice to her because he wanted her to sell the Castle to him? She remembered the conversation he'd had with his friends outside the bistro. Andrew had had a game plan all along. With a pounding head she played the conversation back over in her mind. She still couldn't quite believe how anyone could be that calculating. Andrew Glossop was actually playing her? Did he help clean out the Castle shop, and flirt with her, just as a ploy to make her think he liked her? What a complete arsehole. Grace had a good mind to go marching in there and tell him his plan was well and truly scuppered. There was no way on earth she would ever sell the Castle to him now. Feeling a horrible twist in her heart and a pang in her stomach, Grace knew she was attracted to him and he'd played her for a fool. 'Damn that man,' she muttered to herself.

With her heart still hammering against her chest, Grace hurried back through the door of the secret passage and closed it behind her just as her phone pinged. It was Andrew.

'What time are you getting here? I can't wait to see you.'

Grace shook her head in disbelief. The cheek of the man. She ignored the text and switched off her phone. She wasn't playing Andrew Glossop's game anymore.

Chapter Twenty

The next morning Grace woke up and watched the sun rising above Heartcross Mountain from her bedroom window. She was thankful the rain had stopped and it was going to be a sunny day – she didn't relish the thought of walking to the bank and getting soaked in the process. She looked across towards the servants' quarters. There was no sign of life but as the courtyard looked like a car showroom, with all the posh cars lined up, Andrew's friends and colleagues must have stayed over.

After a shower, Grace pulled a brush through her hair and smothered her face in moisturiser, then finally switched on her mobile phone. As soon as it powered up, it pinged into life. Three text messages from Andrew.

'The drinks are in full flow.'

'Are you running late?'

'Text me!'

Still fuming, Grace thought back to last night.

Considering the drinks were in full flow and the room full of guests, he was texting her an awful lot. But of course he wanted her to be there; he was trying to reel her in with his charm, lead her into a false sense of security and try to whip the Castle from underneath her. Grace didn't answer the text; she could feel the anger still simmering inside. The only interesting thing to come out of that conversation was Magdalene's reference to the revenue that could be made from the Castle. She'd obviously done her homework and that's exactly what Grace was going to focus on. She'd show them that she wasn't their kind, she was better than their kind.

Trying to push last night's conversation out of her mind, Grace looked at the clock and wandered downstairs to the kitchen. There was a couple of hours before her appointment at the bank and soon the mystery of the safety deposit box would be solved. Every morning since she had arrived at the Castle Hector had left a box of goodies on the doorstep and today was no exception. She smiled as she opened the door and lifted up a box crammed with fresh homemade bread, runner beans, potatoes and something wrapped in silver foil. Hector had left a note.

'My early morning catch from the river.'

Grace carefully placed the box on the kitchen table and opened the silver foil to uncover four fish. 'Just look at those.' Hector had been busy, up and out on the banks of the river at an early hour. This would be perfect for tea. Maybe it would be possible to build a small fire outside with the boys and roast them in the sunshine? The memory instantly took her back to the day on the island with Andrew. Grace wrapped them up again carefully and placed them in the fridge. Hector was so thoughtful.

She took a quick look at the budget chart. She hadn't spent any money in the last couple of days; living off the land was proving very fruitful. After switching on the kettle for an early morning cuppa, Grace went to shut the back door and there was Andrew across the courtyard, standing checking his phone. He looked up and caught her eye and waved across at her with a warm smile. He started walking towards her. Grace was livid; she ignored him and shut the door. She couldn't help herself, her blood was still boiling from the conversation she'd overheard last night, and now she was cross with herself for not playing it cool, because she knew it wouldn't be long before *he* knew.

Within seconds, Grace heard a knock on the back door and she didn't have to turn around to know who it was. Taking a deep breath, she spun round and walked towards the door. She really didn't like confrontation, but she had a burning desire to say her piece.

Feeling hot under the collar, Grace opened the door.

'You okay? What happened to you last night? I'd told so many people you were coming and there were so many people who wanted to meet you.' Andrew touched her elbow, sending tiny shockwaves through her body. She was mad at herself for still being attracted to him.

Taking a step back, she couldn't help saying, 'Why would anyone want to meet the poor single mother of three who really isn't one of your kind?'

Andrew raised a perfectly arched eyebrow. 'What do you mean?'

Grace was hoping her voice sounded braver than she thought it did. 'So your plan was to use your charm, good looks, maybe flirt a little with me…?'

'So you do think I'm good-looking?' Andrew interrupted with a smile, but was soon brought down when he realised Grace wasn't joking and there was something more serious going on here.

Grace didn't crack a smile. 'You are being nice to me because you think you can sweet-talk me into selling the Castle to you. Was your plan to make me fall head over heels for you, then whip everything from underneath me? You really don't have to humour me any more by actually pretending to like me. Don't take me for a fool.'

Those last words hung in the air. Grace and Andrew stared at each other.

Andrew frowned and gave a short strangled laugh. 'Have you completely lost your mind?' he said, finally breaking the silence. 'What would make you think I don't like you?'

Now Grace felt guilty. She only had one option: to come clean and reveal that she had listened to his private conversation last night. 'I heard you and your mother last night. I'm not your kind, make sure I sell the Castle to you as it will be the best thing for your brand. It breaks your mother's heart that you have to hang around with someone of my class until you seal the deal on this place. Shall I go on?'

Andrew didn't take his eyes off her. He was processing what she just said. Grace had to admit, he looked stunned, his colour pale.

'But do you know what I have, Andrew? I have morals, I'm kind, I don't pretend I'm something I'm not... What you see is what you get, and the love me and my boys have for each other is worth more than any business deal... Oh, and guess what else I have? This Castle.'

Andrew genuinely looked frustrated, his mouth open. 'It really isn't what you think.'

'I was there, Andrew. I heard you talking about me in the kitchen. Do you know what, Andrew? Just go!' Her outburst took her by surprise. She felt the tension growing between them.

'Whatever you may have heard, you've got it all wrong,' he said, 'So, so wrong. For the record, I like you, Grace, genuinely like you and the boys.'

Grace was keeping her wits about her and wasn't going to let anyone sweet-talk her, but Andrew didn't say any more, instead he turned and walked away. She felt exasperated by the whole situation and even more so by the fact that he could stand there and be untruthful. But although she had vowed no man was worth it, somehow Andrew Glossop had managed to get under her skin in such a short time. How the hell had she let that happen?

Chapter Twenty-One

G race took a long walk by the river into the town of Glensheil. She had twenty minutes before she was due at the bank for her appointment. She sat down on a bench and stared out across the water, which was sparkling in some spots and murky in others. The ducks were shaded from the sun in the reeds growing near the bank and Grace noticed a couple of young children standing on the large stones, swooping their fishing nets in and out of the water with their parents standing nearby. There was something tranquil about the sound of running water splashing over the rocks.

Grace turned the safety deposit key over in her hand and thought of Hector and his commitment to Heartcross Castle. After hearing Magdalene talk about revenue, Grace was determined to sit down and devise a plan to re-open the gardens as soon as possible, and advertise for staff. Isla had already agreed to selling of the farm's ice cream, and if

Grace could talk to Hamish or Meredith about sourcing the drinks that would help too.

Checking her watch, she stood up. Five minutes later, she was standing outside the bank, about to discover what was inside the box. Pushing open the glass door she stepped onto the glossy-tiled floor. The space was vast with security guards dotted around the area. There were video cameras on every wall recording everyone's every move. There was a roped area guiding customers to the cashier, and a table to the left with pens on a chain where deposits were filled out. Grace could hear the rustle of papers, the thunk of the stamp on paperwork and the cashier calling out to the next customer in the line.

'Can I help you?'

Grace looked up to see a bank representative smiling at her.

'I'm here to check the contents of a safety deposit box,' she replied, and the woman nodded and led her over to a desk at the back of the room.

After taking a few details the woman checked Grace had the key to the box before she led her through a door to the lift. The woman didn't speak as she stepped inside and pressed a button on the control panel. Grace held on to a handrail as the lift began to move. As soon as the lift stopped, the metal door sprang open and in front of Grace was another door. The bank assistant held a key card up to the electronic keypad on the wall and the door to the room automatically opened. Grace didn't know what to expect inside. She glanced around the clean, clinical room. The white floor tiles gleamed and from ceiling to floor were numbered metal doors that reminded Grace of the lockers in high school. The woman pointed to the right-hand side of the room.

'Your box is halfway down on the right.'

Grace nodded and began to follow the numbers until she saw door twenty-one. Taking a deep breath, she turned the key in the lock and the door opened with ease. Inside was a shoe box with an elastic band wrapped around it. Grace held the box and shook it lightly. There was definitely something inside it. She was tempted to open it there and then, but instead she placed the box inside her tote bag and locked the door.

'I'm not sure I need this security box any more,' she declared, holding up the key and giving it back to the bank assistant.

Hurrying home, Grace took the shorter route to the Castle along the high street then jumped on the moving chairlift from the gatehouse to the top of the steps. The box was inside her bag, which was resting on her knee. Hector had been looking after the boys and was dropping them up at Foxglove Farm for a play date with Isla's boys. Grace was picking them up just after lunch.

As the chair screeched and came to a halt, Grace jumped down and hurried across the courtyard. Rose was in the doorway of the servants' quarters with Delia in her hands. She gently placed her on the ground and looked over towards Grace. 'This chicken seems to like Mr Glossop's shoes,' she shouted across the courtyard towards Grace, holding up an egg before disappearing back inside. Usually, Grace would find this amusing, but she was pre-occupied, just itching to discover what was inside the box.

As soon as she was inside, Grace took the shoebox out of her bag and sat in her grandfather's chair. She looked over at the urn. Maybe the box contained instructions about where to scatter his ashes. She carefully slid off the elastic band, took a deep breath and lifted off the lid. Inside was a bundle of papers and photographs bound together by string, and also her grandfather's war medals. Her heart was pounding as she undid the string and spread everything out on the coffee table in front of her.

The first thing Grace noticed was a very old photograph of two soldiers in uniform, looking handsome and proud. She immediately recognised her grandfather but not the other man. The back of the photograph revealed the names, Marley Power and William Glossop. She looked once more at the photograph. 'Glossop.' Then she realised there was a photograph of the same soldier hanging in the hallway of the servants' quarters. 'Andrew's grandfather.' What were the chances of that? She didn't even know that they'd known each other. They looked like friends and no doubt were brought together by the war; in normal circumstances it was unlikely that their paths would ever cross.

Picking up a newspaper cutting, Grace read the headline. '**Top military honour for Heartcross D-Day war hero**. Ninety-one-year-old Marley Power will join eight other Scots veterans who risked their lives to liberate France in the Second World War, to be made a Chevalier de la Légion d'Honneur today.'

Grace couldn't believe it. Her grandfather had been awarded France's highest military honour for his bravery during the Second World War.

Feeling emotional, she read on. Her grandfather was hailed a hero. He was among thousands of Allied troops who stormed the beaches of France on June 6, 1944, aged only twenty. He had been called up to the Royal Navy as a teenager and joined the Forward Observation Unit as a telegraphist with headquarters at HMS *Dundonald* in Troon.

On June 5, 1944, Marley's unit crossed the Channel before landing on Sword Beach at around 7.30 a.m.

'"That's when all hell let loose,"' Marley was quoted as saying. '"My introduction to D-Day was seeing a soldier lying face up in the water, dead. That soldier was my best friend William Glossop. It's something you never get over. We'd been by each other's side, flak was flying everywhere, snipers were firing from the villas along the beach and William was in the line of fire. I called out and tried to throw myself in front of him but it was too late. The sniper's bullet went straight through his heart. I tried to revive him, but he died in my arms. They continued to fire, and the next bullet missed my heart by about five inches. Fortunately for me, my sixty-inch wireless set on my back took the full force of the shrapnel and I was wounded in my lower back – it was something you never forget."'

Marley spent months, and his twenty-first birthday, in hospital before he was discharged on April 4, 1945.

The tears were flowing freely down Grace's cheeks as she read on.

'Joining Marley at the ceremony today was his best friend Hector Bedford.

'Hector added, "Marley is a hero and my best friend to boot. I'm very proud. I have such admiration for his courage."'

With a trembling hand, Grace placed the article on the table. She was so proud of her grandfather. He must have suffered terribly during that time, especially if he saw his best pal killed. She picked up another photo, of her grandfather when he was around thirteen years of age, working on a farm. Grace had heard over the years that her grandfather was from a farming background, but she didn't know how he acquired his wealth. Placing that photograph next to the other, she unfolded a piece of paper and stared at it. It seemed to be some sort of contract, which was clipped to a handwritten note.

Grace read out loud, 'I owe Marley Power one castle, won fairly in a game of poker,' the note signed by William Glossop. Marley had signed the note too.

The contract was a dated, signed agreement between the two of them with witnesses' signatures. Grace was astounded. A game of poker resulted in William Glossop handing over Heartcross Castle to her grandfather? Surely not. That would be ridiculous – some serious game of poker. She just stared at the contract. Attached to the back was the sale agreement. Who would give away a castle in a game of poker? Surely that had to be some sort of joke? And why had it never been challenged by the Glossop family? Because that would have meant handing over a huge chunk of their wealth.

Grace looked up at her grandfather's urn, wide-eyed, then down at the paper. The Castle would have been in Andrew's family. This wasn't technically her inheritance, it was his. She brought her hand up to her mouth. Surely this wasn't legal? She knew she needed to talk to Hector about this; he must know something.

Grace carried on looking through the box and found other papers, wage slips of some sort. Rummaging through, she discovered another photograph, not of the best quality. It showed a man and a woman cradling a newborn baby swathed in a white blanket, standing on the steps of a cottage hospital, which Grace recognised; it was on the outskirts of Glensheil. She turned the photograph over. Written on the back was 'Hector, Kate and Eleanor'. She was puzzled. Hector didn't have any children but there he was with his beautiful wife Kate and with a baby in his arms. Grace stared at the names and the date. Her heart began to beat fast and her eyes were fixed on the date: her own mother's birthday. It hit her like a high-speed train. The baby had the same name as her mother as well as the same birthdate. The baby that Kate was holding was Grace's mother. Grace blew out a breath and began frantically looking through the rest of the papers in the box.

She knew exactly what she was looking for but she couldn't find it; there was no birth certificate for her mother. But she stumbled across other legal documents, including deeds to the cottage that Hector lived in on the estate. The legal papers were dated the same day as her mother's birthday. Why had her grandfather gifted Hector and Kate Castle Cottage on the day her mother was born? Why would he do that? None of this was making any sense to Grace at all.

Grace's thoughts were swirling with all sorts of possibilities. Was there some sort of significance to her mother's birthday? Why were Hector and Kate holding her mother on the steps of the hospital? 'No way,' Grace whispered. She didn't know if she was adding two and two and making five, but now she was struggling to breathe as the possibility washed over her that Hector and Kate were actually her mother's parents. She frantically searched for some more clues but there was nothing.

'It can't be true, surely it can't be true,' she murmured, wiping away escaping tears of puzzlement. She just didn't understand what was going on here. There was only one person who had the answers – Hector.

'Are you okay?'

Grace jumped out of her skin and spun round to see Andrew standing in the open doorway.

'Please, if you've come for an argument, this isn't the right time,' she said, wiping away tears with the back of her hand.

'I haven't. I've come to make sure you're okay. I didn't want to leave an atmosphere between us, because what you said this morning really isn't the truth.'

'Honestly, right now I have more important things to

worry about,' she replied, knowing that one of the things she had to worry about was that the Castle might not legally belong to her. If it didn't belong to her grandfather in the first place, then the rightful heirs were Andrew and his family.

For a second neither of them spoke. Then Andrew broke the silence. 'Do you want to talk about it?'

'I really don't and I don't mean to sound rude...' All Grace could think about was tracking down Hector and talking to him about the contents of the box.

'Okay, I really don't want to intrude, but can I just say: the conversation you heard was a one-sided conversation. I am not responsible for my mother's actions.'

Grace was still staring at him and didn't say a word.

'Yes, I told my mother about the state of the Castle and that you inherited the Castle from your grandfather and had no other revenue. Maybe I shouldn't have said anything, but I was excited to talk about you and the boys and maybe that's where I went wrong.'

'What do you mean?' asked Grace.

'I mean you are the only woman that I've ever openly told my mother about. I loved hanging out with you and the boys. You brought a smile to my face, and you made me feel ... good about myself, and most of all you and the boys have taught me none of this matters.' Andrew gestured towards the servants' quarters. 'Do you know what does matter? Of course I'm saying this to the wrong person because you do know what matters. You, Grace Power, know the difference between right and wrong and you,

Grace Power, aren't motivated by wealth and materialistic things, you are motivated by the love of your children and you give your children your all and they love you unconditionally.' He took a breath. 'And that's something that money can't buy. I know I'm speaking out of turn when I say this, but my mother wouldn't have a clue how to be a mother like you.'

All Grace could focus on was his words 'You Grace Power know the difference between right and wrong.' She knew she had to find out the legal situation of the Castle and come clean; she could never take what wasn't legally hers.

'Thank you, that's kind, to say that about me and my boys.' She nodded her appreciation.

'Grace, I never put in that offer to the estate agent's, I promise you. Yes, I did mention to my mother that I offered to buy this place, but that's as far as it went. I can see how your boys love living here and I would never dupe you into selling me this place for my own gain. A conversation that I wish you were privy to took place this morning when I asked my mother to leave. We don't have a bond like you have with your boys and that saddens me, but it's the truth. I suppose I'm sad that I wished she'd tried harder to love me unconditionally and to protect me at all costs, but she let me down so many times, and her actions in the last few days haven't been ones I would ever support. In such a short time you've taught me that life is better simple, and those smiles on the boys' faces are worth more than money in the bank.'

Grace wasn't expecting this. 'You are right, no amount of money can ever buy those boys' smiles, and they have been on their faces continuously from the day we arrived.' She was just about to add that the Castle was definitely not up for sale but there was a small worry in the back of her mind. She was sure that if Andrew discovered the truth about the transfer of the Castle between the families, he would try and win it back – and of course, unlike Grace, he had the money for legal costs.

'You're crying.' Andrew handed Grace a tissue from his pocket. 'It is clean,' he said, softly. 'For your eyes.'

Grace nodded her appreciation and dabbed her eyes gently. 'Thank you. I've just got a lot on my plate at the moment.'

'I seem to have got you a bad time. I can come back, if you prefer?' he offered.

Grace exhaled. 'It's okay, I've got ten minutes.' She was itching to go and find Hector; she had so many questions that needed answering. She looked up and attempted a half-hearted smile. 'Why does your mother think I'm so bad? Why has she judged me without even getting to know me?'

Andrew rolled his eyes. 'It's not you, she doesn't know you. Maybe it's her expectations. She's expecting me to go out with a girl that drives a Ferrari, has a multi-million-pound business and no children. Whereas for me it's about the person. You are attractive, funny, kind, a good mother and happy in life for the right reasons, not just because the next designer handbag has been released.'

'Expecting you to go out with a girl?' Grace questioned. 'Is that what you are looking to do?'

Their eyes stayed focused on each other.

'You make me nervous, Grace,' said Andrew, and quickly added, 'in a good way.'

She smiled, feeling a rush of warmth through her body. 'Just say those things about me again,' she teased, biting her lip to suppress her smile.

'I think you are attractive, warm, humorous and have such gorgeous boys…'

'I do have wonderful boys, and I can see such a huge difference in Billy – in the past week I've seen him smile and laugh. The Castle has done wonders for him, the open space, the freedom and he just loves Delia … though I know you aren't too fond of her,' she added with a smile.

'Grace Power, you are one awe-inspiring woman.' Andrew was looking at her with adoration. 'I can't even imagine what you have been through, but somehow you've managed to keep it all together and, for what it's worth, I'm so glad you turned up here.'

'Don't, you'll have me crying again.'

'Well, I can't have that, can I?' he said with a smile.

Grace looked around the kitchen. 'This Castle saved us from our old life and I was looking forward to my next chapter…'

'Was?' interrupted Andrew.

Grace swallowed and leant forward, put everything back in the shoe box and shut the lid. The emotion surged through her body. 'Was, am… I'm not quite sure yet.'

Andrew could see the upset in Grace's eyes.

'What I need to do is go and find Hector.'

Andrew nodded. 'I'm not quite sure what's upset you, but I'm on my own for the rest of the day so if you need company please come and find me... Promise me?'

'I will,' replied Grace. 'And thank you.'

Andrew stood up and, taking Grace by surprise, leaned across and kissed her softly on the cheek. 'You know where to find me,' he said warmly, touching her elbow, then left and closed the back door behind him.

Checking the time, Grace knew she had a couple of hours before she had to pick the boys up from Isla's. This would be the perfect time to talk to Hector. She stood up and brushed herself down. Whatever had gone on in the past, Grace was determined to discover the hidden truths of Heartcross Castle, and she might be about to open a right can of worms.

Chapter Twenty-Two

With a thumping heart, Grace walked towards the greenhouse. She attempted to rehearse the conversation over in her head but had no clue how it was going to pan out. She really didn't want to upset Hector, but the only way to find out the truth was to ask him outright about the photograph and why her grandfather had handed over Castle Cottage on the day her mother was born. In her heart she knew all the evidence was pointing in one direction. Was it actually possible that Hector was her grandfather? But why had it been kept secret and why hadn't he ever said anything? Grace could feel herself shaking and had a nauseous feeling in the pit of her stomach.

'Hector, can I talk to you?' Her voice cracked.

Hector looked up with his usual beam on his face, 'Lady Grace, we have champion carrots this morning, the boys will be able to sell them with no trouble at the gates.'

343

Grace felt her stomach churning as Hector's gaze dropped towards the shoebox in her hand. He immediately slipped his cap from his head like a mark of respect.

There was a pause.

'Hector, do you know what's in this box?'

'Possibly.' Hector managed a nod and pulled out a gardening stool for Grace to sit on. Turning over a wooden crate he sat down next to her and Grace handed him the box. She watched as he took off the lid. The first thing he saw was the photograph of himself and Kate holding the baby on the hospital steps.

'I don't get it, Hector.' Grace could feel her heartbeat quicken.

Hector was still staring at the photograph. 'The past has a way of catching up with you when you least expect it.'

With an uneasy feeling swirling in the pit of her stomach, Grace pointed at the photograph. 'Hector, is that baby my mother?' she asked.

Bleary-eyed, Hector nodded.

Grace exhaled.

'But it's not what you think.'

'Please tell me then because right at this second...' She took a breath. 'You said you couldn't have children but are you my grandfather?'

The adrenalin was pumping through Grace's veins as she waited for Hector to speak.

With a trembling hand he held the photograph. He shook his head, his voice barely a whisper. 'No, I can see what this looks like but, no, your grandfather is Marley.'

'Then why are you holding my mother on the day she was born and why,' Grace reached inside the box, 'and why did my grandfather gift you a cottage on the day she was born?'

Hector swallowed as the tears welled up in his eyes. 'This is painful for me to talk about, Lady Grace, it brings back memories that are both happy and sad.'

Grace sat in silence whilst Hector dabbed his eyes with his handkerchief. 'Your grandfather and I were friends for many years. We met at primary school. Our parents were from the same farming background and we grew up together. Even the war didn't separate our friendship – it cemented it even more when we both returned home. Your grandmother Nancy and my wife Kate were the best of friends too. The four of us went everywhere together, we looked out for each other and each of us knew there was no other woman for him.' He took a breath. 'Kate and I, we tried and tried for a family but with no luck and it turned out I couldn't have children. I was completely devastated but Kate was a brave, strong, independent woman and for her I was enough. "We have each other and that's special enough," she would tell me every day. She was such a special person.'

Hector was visibly upset, and Grace put her hand on his knee. She knew whatever he was going to say next was painful. She could see his hand shaking as he held the photograph.

'Your grandmother Nancy was one of a kind too. We were very lucky men. But your grandmother suffered multiple miscarriages, and she couldn't carry a baby full term. Both your grandparents were devastated, and to see our best friends in so much pain crucified myself and Kate. And that's when Kate offered to be a surrogate.'

'A surrogate?' interjected Grace.

Hector nodded. 'We kept it between ourselves. Kate carried your mother. It was the greatest gift we could ever give our best friends. Your grandfather was like a brother to me.'

The knots in Grace's stomach took her breath away. 'Hector –' Grace was speechless '– you are the most selfless person I know.'

'That's what I said about my Kate. She was one in a million. I was with her when the baby was born.' He looked down at the photograph. We came home that day and I have to admit it was one of the hardest days of my life, I can't deny that, handing over the baby. But she wasn't ours. I can still see the joy on your grandparents' faces. We didn't ask for anything, we simply wanted to give your grandparents a happy ever after. But your grandparents always wanted to repay us for what we'd done and that's when they gifted us the cottage in the grounds. Kate and I didn't have much money and Marley and Nancy wanted to give us a permanent home, as we had begun to look into adoption.'

'And did that never happen for you both?' Grace asked.

The tears rolled down Hector's cheeks as Grace took his hand. 'After your mother was born there were complications with Kate's health. She passed away just over two weeks later.'

Grace couldn't believe what she was hearing. Her eyes welled up with instant tears. And as the tears slid down both their faces, there was such sadness bleeding all around.

'Hector, I'm so sorry. I just don't know what to say except you both did a wonderful thing.'

Hector remained silent, but his eyes were earnest. He dabbed them once more with his handkerchief. 'Your grandparents looked after me, they were wonderful people, and I became a huge part of their family and life at the Castle. For that, I will be for ever grateful. This place gave me a purpose to keep going. I never wanted to make a life with anyone else. No one would ever come close to my Kate.'

For a moment they sat in in silence, lost in their own thoughts. Hector and Kate had done a wonderful thing for her grandparents and Grace knew right there, right then, that family was all that mattered.

She took both his hands in hers. 'I'm glad to have you as my family, Hector, and I know when I say this, the boys are too. They never met their great-grandfather and the pain twists my heart as that was down to my mistake, but you too are our family and I won't ever let you down.'

'That means so much, Lady Grace.'

'Shall we make a pact, Hector?'

Hector looked up.

'We will look after each other.' Grace opened her arms

and hugged him. 'You are truly a wonderful man,' she said, feeling like she was on a roller coaster of emotions.

'Thank you, Lady Grace.'

After a couple of moments, Grace gently pulled away from the hug and looked speculatively at Hector.

'Tell me about this place. Did my grandfather really win Heartcross Castle in a bet?'

Hector smiled, then gave a little chuckle. 'From what I heard, it was one hell of a poker game.'

Grace took the handwritten note from the box and handed it to Hector. 'And Andrew Glossop's grandfather?'

Hector nodded. 'An unlikely friendship. William Glossop was one of the richest men in the country and Marley a farmhand, brought together by war. Most probably they would never have met under normal circumstances.'

He was staring at the photograph and wiped his brow with his handkerchief before he read the handwritten note out loud. '"Heartcross Castle was won in a game of poker by Marley Power." As the story goes, which is what your grandfather told me, there was one too many whiskys drunk that night. The other soldiers had thrown in their cards a couple of rounds earlier and sat back and watched. The stakes got higher and higher until William Glossop declared all or nothing on the very next game. Marley hadn't lost a hand all night, and the IOUs were piled up beside his whisky glass. Apparently this was when William challenged Marley, all or nothing, and the stakes were Heartcross Castle and the money. William thought he had the winning combination, but when the hands were revealed Marley won.'

'And William actually handed over the Castle because my grandfather won at a game of cards?' asked Grace.

'Not quite at that moment. Marley would never have taken the Castle from William. He was happy just keeping the money he had won. But in jest that night they scribbled this note, just so they could look back on the memory and probably tease William over time that Marley had beaten him at cards hands down. William placed this piece of paper in the inside pocket of his jacket.' Hector took a breath. 'This poker game took place before Marley's unit crossed the Channel before landing on Sword Beach and that's when all hell broke loose. William was killed in battle and your grandfather was absolutely devastated. They had become so close. He tried to revive William, but he died in his arms – but not before making a pact that they would look after each other and each other's families, no matter what.'

Grace had both hands on her heart, listening to the story. 'I just can't imagine.'

'The loss of William hit Marley hard, it was something he never got over.'

Hector looked at the handwritten note. 'This note was discovered in William's pocket when all of his possessions were handed over to his wife, Evelyn. During the war she'd received letters from William telling her all about his friendship with Marley, and as William Glossop was a man of honour and true to his word, Evelyn made sure that this place was given to Marley.'

Grace gave a low whistle. 'So that's how Heartcross Castle ended up in the family.'

Listening to the truth, she felt emotionally battered and bruised. 'You are all such good people.' Her voice faltered, knowing she'd put her grandfather through so much by running away.

'And you are too,' replied Hector.

'I'm going to make my grandfather proud.' Grace looked up at the towering Castle in the mid-day sun. 'I can't wait to show the boys these medals and tell them the stories of their great-grandfather.'

Hector placed his arm around her shoulder and pulled Grace in for a hug. 'He was a hero and my hero too. Marley hoped you would come back, and I'm so glad you did, Lady Grace. There's only one way to go now … the future.'

Hector stood up and walked over to a box in the corner of the greenhouse and pulled out two small glasses and a bottle of whisky. 'We have bottles hidden all over this place,' he chuckled.

Grace watched as Hector poured two glasses and handed one to Grace. 'Here's to you, Marley. And, of course, my Kate.' Hector held his glass up to the sky.

'Is that why my grandfather rented the servants' quarters out to Andrew – because of the connection of the past?' asked Grace, thinking out loud.

'Yes,' confirmed Hector.

'Hector…' Grace paused.

'What is it?'

'Technically the Castle isn't my inheritance, is it? This should have been Andrew's inheritance.'

Hector was quiet for a moment. 'It was won fair and square.'

'But this place is worth more than any gambling win.'

'More than a gambling win, this Castle brought you back here, and for that I am truly grateful.'

Hector and Grace sat in a comfortable silence. They drank their whiskies looking up at Heartcross Mountain in the distance. Grace breathed in the fresh air and stared at the meandering trail that passed through the purple heather and bracken. The views were spectacular, the fells rising on each side breathtaking – it was stunning. She felt peaceful.

'Hector.' Grace pointed to the mountain top. 'Would Heartcross Mountain be a good place to scatter my grandfather's ashes? He could fly free above us.'

Hector nodded. 'I think that would be perfect.'

'And maybe place a bench in the Castle gardens with his name on it?' she suggested.

'That too I think is a splendid idea, Lady Grace.'

Grace smiled. Lady Grace had a good, familiar warmth to it and she liked it. 'Do you think you'll always call me Lady Grace?'

Hector smiled warmly. 'Always, Lady Grace.'

Chapter Twenty-Three

'**M**um, we need to buy Billy a birthday present soon.' Freddie's hands were cupped around Grace's ears. 'Can we have a look for a present today?'

Grace nodded and gave Freddie a thumbs-up. 'Of course,' she whispered.

She and her boys were standing in the courtyard waiting for Andrew, who stepped from the servants' quarters looking ready for his shopping day challenge. Today he had the casual look going on; cut-off denim shorts, loafers and a crisp, clean white T-shirt, with a pair of sunglasses balancing on the top of his head. He waved across at Grace and the boys. 'Are we ready?' he bellowed across the courtyard, holding up the shopping bag.

'Oooh, good start,' exclaimed an impressed Grace, pointing to the shopping bag. 'There's ten pence saved already.'

Now standing next to Grace, Andrew was shaking his

head at her sarcasm. Grace discreetly inhaled the masculine woody scent of Andrew's aftershave and a burst of adrenalin electrified her heart. She briefly closed her eyes only to find when she opened them that Andrew was looking back at her, smiling.

Giving herself a little shake, 'Are we ready to go shopping?' asked Grace with a glint in her eyes.

Freddie coughed and held out his hand towards Andrew, who cocked an eyebrow. 'Hand it over,' demanded Freddie.

'Hand what over?' asked Andrew, looking confused.

'Your wallet,' explained Freddie.

'The boys are making sure you don't cheat,' Grace put in.

Andrew held up his arms in mock protest. 'As if I would cheat,' he declared, reluctantly handing his wallet over, but with a sparkle in his eye.

'Turn out your pockets,' ordered Joey. Billy was watching in amusement.

Andrew pulled out the insides of his pockets. 'See, nothing.'

'Okay, we are satisfied,' reported Freddie, looking pleased with himself.

'Gosh, you are all taking this very seriously.'

'You bet, said Freddie, handing Andrew a crisp ten-pound note.

'What's this for?'

'Spends,' replied Freddie. 'That's your budget, you only have ten pounds to spend.'

'Ten pounds per person?' asked Andrew.

'Afraid not, ten pounds to feed a family of four,' chipped in Grace.

Freddie pointed to each of them and then Andrew. 'You can be in our family just for today.' He counted, 'One ... two ... three, four and five.' He looked puzzled and looked up at Grace.

'The challenge just got more difficult. That'll be ten pounds to feed five of us,' added Grace with a chuckle.

A huge grin spread across Andrew's face. 'Thank you very much. I'm up for the challenge if that means I can be part of your family for one day.'

Grace beamed as the words left Andrew's mouth. There was something about the way he said it, and he gave her a look that flipped her heart.

Andrew waggled the ten pounds in the air. 'Are you sure this will be enough?

'Absolutely,' replied Grace, 'And change, too!'

'Enough for an ice cream?' asked Joey, holding on to Billy's hand.

'Let's hope so!' replied Grace.

They all began to walk down the sweeping driveway towards the Castle gates. Thankfully, there were no huge crowds hanging about there, as otherwise Grace was no doubt that Andrew's fan club would be following them around the town all morning.

The boys ran in front and spotted Hector painting the small ticket office at the separate entrance to the Castle grounds. All three of them flung their arms around him and

Grace could see the happiness in his eyes. He already loved those boys with all his might.

'Good morning,' chirped Hector. 'Mind the wet paint.'

Grace had every intention of opening the gardens in the next couple of weeks and Hector was doing his very best to make that happen. She looked at the ticket office. 'You have been busy. This looks amazing.'

'Good job, Hector, this looks like it will be ready to open very soon,' observed Andrew.

'Very soon. Hopefully in the next couple of weeks. I'm going to ring the local paper to see if they will write a feature and set up a Facebook page and maybe get the local TV news involved. It's all go,' replied Grace, still with a little worry in the back of her mind. She hadn't told Andrew how the Castle had come to belong to her family and she wasn't sure what Magdalene would do with the news when she found out. But Grace had checked out the legality of it all with Jaydon Fairbrother, who confirmed all the paperwork in handing over the Castle was legal and above board.

They left Hector painting and walked along the high street of the town, the boys walking in front of them, all holding hands. Andrew turned towards Grace. 'Just look at them,' he remarked, his hand brushing against hers, and for a second their fingers entwined. With a warm, fuzzy feeling inside, Grace looked up at him, and his eyes sparkled as he gave her a captivating smile.

A little further up the high street, Andrew stopped

outside the deli. 'First stop, boys. What is your favourite food?'

'Beefburgers,' the twins chorused in unison and Billy gave a thumbs-up in agreement as they spun around to look in the deli window, which was an array of extravagance: an expansive glass case filled with cured meats, everything from pastrami to chorizo. There were sandwich fixings, lettuce, several types of cheese, pickles and olives and condiments. To the right of the window were trays lined with wax paper containing coleslaw, salads and cooked peppers.

Andrew went to step inside the deli but Freddie stood in front of him and held up his hand. 'What do you think we are going to buy from here?' He put his hands on his hips, causing Grace to giggle.

'This will be the perfect place for coleslaw, tomatoes, cheeses and chopped lettuce. We could get the majority of the ingredients from here.'

Freddie was shaking his head, whilst Joey whipped out a calculator from the bag he was carrying and stared at the produce in the window before punching in numbers. He turned to show Grace.

'Nine pounds and thirty pence.' She mirrored Freddie's action by shaking her head. 'You will have already spent the majority of your budget, and there's no way you can get the rest of the ingredients.'

Billy and Freddie got behind Andrew and began pushing him up the street. Grace watched in amusement, 'This way,' ordered Freddie.

Within five minutes, they walked into the supermarket and Grace picked up a basket. Andrew headed straight for the fruit and veg, but was redirected by the boys. Joey slipped his hand inside Andrew's and led him, with a puzzled look on his face, towards the very back of the supermarket. They stood in front of a tall aluminium trolley.

'What's this?' asked Andrew, looking at all the different varieties of produce crammed on to the shelves.

'Food that is at a reduced price, short shelf-life. Best before today. You can pick up some absolute bargains,' said Grace.

'Mum!' exclaimed Joey, who sounded like he'd won the lottery. 'What about these?' He was holding up a packet of six bread rolls.

'How much?' asked Freddie, searching for the red reduced sticker. 'Thirty-five pence.' Immediately Freddie popped them in the basket.

'Perfect find,' chirped Grace. 'Is there anything else we can see?'

The boys began to search thoroughly whilst Andrew watched them. This was a different way of life to him. He'd never had to think about money or how he was going to feed himself, and never thought twice about throwing food away – something he was beginning to feel a little ashamed about now. He'd taken his whole world for granted; his life was filled with extravagant restaurants, food that cost over the odds, and standing at the reduced section was a first for him.

Grace was watching Andrew watching the boys. 'You really have never shopped on a budget, have you?'

Andrew shook his head and swallowed and emotion swept over him. For the boys this was normal, hunting for a bargain to feed themselves, whilst he never had to think about it.

'You must be proud of them.' His voice faltered and Grace picked up on it.

'You aren't coming over all emotional on me, are you?'

'Of course not ... maybe just a little. I'm guessing this is what real family life is like.'

'I suppose it is when you don't have money to spare. I go without a lot of things so the boys can have things, but they don't do too badly. Look at those smiles – they love hunting for a bargain.'

'Mince, they have mince, reduced to seventy-five pence.' Joey was holding it up in the air then popped it in the basket. 'How much have we spent?'

Freddie did the maths. 'One pound ten pence, leaving us eight pounds and ninety pence.'

After paying for the items, Andrew put the change back in his pocket and followed Grace and the boys down a side street which he hadn't even known existed. Where the street came to an end, it opened out into a small square. There were rows of tables and booths filled with local seasonal produce: bundles of carrots, beets and asparagus, bags of potatoes stacked up, crates of shiny tomatoes and cucumbers and baskets of fruit.

'The farmers' market,' said Grace.

Freddie inhaled. 'Smell that,' he said and sniffed, making Billy giggle. 'It's everything all mixed up.'

'Here, boys ... catch.' The man behind the fruit stall threw peaches to the boys. 'Enjoy!'

'Thank you! Look at this,' exclaimed Freddie in delight, holding up his peach.

With a huge beam on his face Billy had already taken a bite of his, and the peach juice began to drip off his chin and slide down his arm.

'Right, what are we looking for?' asked Grace, looking between the boys.

'Tomatoes, lettuce and potatoes...' replied Freddie, leading them over a table packed with fresh produce.

'And what can I do you for you?' asked the man standing behind the table.

'Five of those juicy tomatoes,' Freddie pointed, 'one cucumber, one of those lettuces and four large potatoes.'

The man placed the tomatoes on the hanging scales, then popped them in a brown paper bag which he spun over to seal it. After placing it and the other items in their carrier bag, the man handed it over to Freddie.

'That'll be three pounds seventy-five, please.'

Freddie began to haggle and Andrew was impressed.

'I'll give you three pounds fifty,' replied Freddie looking hopeful.

'Your son drives a hard bargain.' The man looked directly at Andrew, but before Andrew could set the record straight, the man turned back towards Freddie.

'Three pounds fifty it is.'

Freddie and Joey counted out the money and Freddie handed it over. The man unzipped the pocket on the front of his pinstriped apron, dropped the money into it and gave Freddie a nod.

Looking pleased with himself, Freddie handed the carrier bag over to Grace.

'I am impressed. Who gets away with haggling in this day and age?' asked Andrew as they walked away.

'You must haggle. Surely when you've filmed the TV shows abroad, the road trips, you've haggled?'

Andrew shook his head. 'Never.'

Joey and Freddie were already standing in front of another stall whilst Billy was holding Grace's hand.

'One garlic, one tomato paste and five mozzarella balls, please,' requested Freddie.

'Two pounds,' replied the woman.

'What, no haggling?' probed Andrew.

'Nah, that's a fair price for mozzarella.' Freddie gave him a cheeky grin.

'Have you ever thought about working in the food industry?'

Freddie shrugged. 'I'll have a think about it,' he said, causing Grace to laugh.

As they stood in the corner of the farmers' market, the boys added up how much they'd spent. 'Six pounds and sixty pence,' said Joey, punching the numbers in the calculator, 'leaving three pounds and forty pence towards the next meal.'

All three boys looked chuffed with themselves.

'I am impressed, I would have blown the ten pounds and a lot more at the deli. I've only got one thing to ask you boys now.'

All three of them looked up at Andrew.

'How about we go back to the kitchens and cook up some burgers for lunch?'

All three boys jumped for joy as they headed back towards the Castle.

As soon as they were back in the courtyard, Freddie told everyone to stand still and wait there. They watched as he raced through the gardens in the direction of the greenhouse and within seconds reappeared looking chuffed to bits, holding up a courgette. 'And we didn't have to buy one of these,' he said, 'it's from the greenhouse.'

As they placed the shopping bags on top of the workstation in Andrew's kitchen, Dougie appeared in the doorway. 'And what have you lot been up to?' he asked, taking a swift glance at them all and the bags.

'Challenge Day. We are teaching Andrew everything he needs to know about shopping properly,' announced Freddie.

'We took Andrew proper food shopping and now we are going to teach him how to make the best burgers, Heartcross Castle burgers,' added Joey, tipping out all the food from the carrier bags.

'Castle burgers? They sound delicious.'

'A family budget meal with homemade chips all for the value of ...'

'Six pounds and sixty pence,' interrupted the twins.

'Well, I am impressed,' replied Dougie, smiling at the boys before disappearing from the kitchen.

After the boys had washed their hands and tied aprons around their waists, the twins began to fire orders at Andrew.

'Excuse me, I am the chef,' Andrew teased, pulling up a stool and balancing Billy on top so he could reach the workstation.

'Yes, Chef!' saluted the boys.

'Okay, what's first, boys?' asked Andrew, taking out a large glass bowl from the cupboard and putting a grater on top of the worktop.

Immediately, Freddie began to grate the courgette and placed it in the bowl along with the mincemeat, garlic, tomato paste and a tiny sprinkle of oregano that they pinched from Andrew's spice rack. Billy began to squish all the ingredients together with his hands, the mincemeat squidging between his fingers.

Once it was all mixed together, the twins divided the mixture into five evenly sized balls and began to flatten them in the palms of their hands whilst Grace cut up the potatoes into chips. Once the boys had made patties Andrew placed a mozzarella ball in the middle of each and reshaped the balls so the cheese was hidden in the middle of the burger.

With the chips sprinkled with salt and pepper, doused in oil and thrown into the oven, Andrew brushed a large non-stick frying pan with oil. Once the chips had been in for ten minutes, he would be ready to cook the burgers. Whilst they were waiting the boys washed and chopped up the lettuce and the tomatoes and Grace sliced the buns. With the patties now sizzling in the pan, Andrew gave everyone a high-five. 'Teamwork,' he declared.

The kitchen door opened and Rose appeared in the doorway. 'Are you eating outside? Would you like me to set the table?' she asked, looking at Andrew.

Without hesitation, Andrew replied, 'Rose, I think we can manage, why don't you take the rest of the day off?'

Rose looked pensive. 'A day off? I wouldn't know what to do with myself, Mr Glossop. What about the cleaning up?' she asked, looking around the kitchen.

Grace followed her gaze. She had to admit the kitchen did look like a bomb had hit it, there were bowls, grated cheese, and chopped tomatoes everywhere, but the boys were having so much fun.

'We can manage. I'm quite sure I can wash up and clean up.'

'But ...'

Andrew walked over towards her, and twizzled her towards the door. 'Go and read a book, walk around the grounds, take a trip to the pub, walk along the river ... anything. But just one thing...'

'Anything, Mr Glossop.'

'On your way out, get that chicken out of my house!' Andrew pointed to the hallway where once more Delia had managed to sneak into the living quarters.

Grace looked at the boys, who burst out laughing.

'You've got to love Delia,' exclaimed Grace as Andrew

rolled his eyes.

'Right, boys, knives and forks in that drawer, the table needs setting outside, and help yourself to a drink from the holding room bar.'

Freddie stopped dead in his tracks. 'We need tomato ketchup. You can't have burgers without ketchup.'

'Now wouldn't that have taken us over our budget?' said Andrew.

'Nah, tomato ketchup doesn't count, you always have to have ketchup!' replied Freddie, giving Andrew a lovable grin.

Andrew laughed. 'I'll remember that!' he said, with a chuckle, opening the fridge and handing over a bottle of ketchup.

With a clatter of knives and forks, the boys raced outside to set the table.

Grace was impressed that Andrew had given Rose the afternoon off. Maybe a day out with her and the boys had taught Andrew a thing or two. 'So you are going to clean up. Is that a first for Andrew Glossop? No servants running around after you.'

'Cheeky,' he replied. 'Today there have been a lot of firsts for Andrew Glossop and one of those was having three terrific boys in my kitchen to cook with.'

Grace smiled at the word. 'They are terrific, aren't they?' she said, beaming.

'Their mother isn't too bad either,' he said, nudging her arm playfully. 'And for what it's worth, I've had a great day. You have a wonderful family.'

'I do, don't I?' replied Grace, holding his gaze. 'Today has been a good day.'

'Oh, and before I forget.' Andrew rummaged in his pocket. 'A family meal on a budget, here's the change, we actually have change.' He handed the loose change to Grace, his fingers brushing against hers. Instantly, her whole body tingled as they just stared at each other before she placed the money on the workstation.

Grace knew they'd just had a moment. Her eyes shifted to his lips, then back to his eyes. He was still staring at her. Just at that second the boys burst back through the door, 'Is it ready yet?' asked Joey. Three pairs of eyes were staring at them.

'Go and sit down and we'll bring it out to you in a second,' replied Grace. 'It just needs dishing up.'

The boys didn't need telling twice and disappeared back outside.

'You've got to love family life,' said Grace, her eyes sparkling. She was sure that if the boys hadn't reappeared so soon, they might have shared a kiss. She was excited about that. Andrew was still staring at her with a sparkle in his eye. 'I think we are on to something here.'

'What do you mean?' she asked.

'I think you were right about the cooking school, a residential cooking school. Weeks could be themed to suit the clientele, cooking on a budget, meals made with simple ingredients. Get the public involved in the TV show, if they wish to be filmed. What do you think?'

'I think you are on to a winner,' she replied.

'I think I am.'

The way Andrew was staring at her with such intensity, she wasn't sure if he meant the new business venture idea or her. She was sure he was flirting. Yes, he was definitely flirting. The air was charged between them. Andrew gave Grace the most gorgeous smile. 'Would you like a drink with your lunch? A glass of champagne, maybe?' he asked.

'Absolutely not, it's a dinner on a budget and champagne will take us way over that budget. Water for me.'

He laughed. 'Do you always do everything by the book?' he asked, staring at her intently. Was he actually willing her to kiss him?

'Most of the time,' Grace replied, taking a step closer to him.

'That's a shame,' he murmured.

'Is it?' she replied. Their faces were now millimetres apart.

'The footage is amazing.' Dougie burst through the door with excitement and Grace took a step backwards. 'It's so natural, cooking with the kids, we are on to something here. Come and take a look, come on.' Dougie was gesturing for Andrew and Grace to follow him.

'You go and take a look, I'll bring the food out,' said Grace, unable to take the silly grin off her face.

Andrew followed Dougie, and Grace briefly closed her eyes. She took a deep breath. She was feeling the attraction between them and it was a feeling she hadn't felt for a very long time. When she opened her eyes Andrew had stopped in the doorway, looking over his shoulder, was giving her the most adoring smile. The second the kitchen door shut, Grace exhaled. She was impressed with the way Andrew interacted with the children: he teased them, entertained them, encouraged them, and now they were about to sit down to a meal that they had prepared together. They were all good qualities she liked.

Holding two plates in her hands, Grace made her way out of the kitchen. The boys were patiently sitting down on the settee in the holding room. She stopped and stared for a moment. The scene on the screen was like something from a proper family kitchen. Mum and Dad preparing dinner with the help from the kids. Billy looked so at ease moulding the burgers in his hand, standing on the stool. Everything was picture perfect.

'Mum, look at this!' said Freddie. 'We are on the telly!'

'I know, I'm watching,' she replied with a smile.

'Grace, this is brilliant TV, cooking on a budget,' enthused Dougie. 'I know you didn't know I was filming this, but look how you all light up the screen. I think this is what we need, family life. Look at it, Andrew, what do you think? This will improve the ratings, I'm in no doubt.'

Andrew was quiet for a moment. He'd never worked with children before. He'd always been in charge of his own kitchen, and it was true that when the boys had stormed the kitchen during the last filming he hadn't been happy – but maybe that was because they had brought extra energy to the mix, and Andrew wasn't sure how to deal with it as he'd always been the star of the show.

'You know what,' he said, 'I think we should give it ago.'

Dougie slapped Andrew on the back, 'Good man.'

'But...'

'I'm not sure I like buts...' said Dougie, his eyes wide.

'I want more than just the TV show. I want to use my skills to help other people. Look at this place. I want to do what I do best, help people to cook.'

'So what are you saying?' asked Dougie, still unsure what Andrew was getting at.

'Let's get a date in the diary to open the residential cooking school. I want the guests who book to try new recipes and expand their tastes in food. There are seven bedrooms in this part of the Castle. Surely we could employ a housekeeper to keep the rooms spick and span and so forth. We could do a trial week to see how it pans out?'

'I think it's a good idea. And it'd be brilliant to sell merchandise in the Castle shop.' Dougie looked at Grace. He was always seeing the bigger picture. 'Aprons, Andrew Glossop cookware.'

'But it all depends on Grace.' Andrew looked towards the boys. 'Shall we go and take a seat at the table?'

The boys raced off outside and Grace put the plates down on the table in front of them. 'I'll just get the rest of the food,' she said to the boys, walking back inside.

When she returned, Grace turned towards him. 'What depends on me?'

'I can't put all my energy into a project, advertising to promote a new venture, employing staff, knowing that there's the possibility you could pull the rug from underneath me at any time. Not that I'm saying you will, but you might get fed up of having me around.'

'I doubt that,' she said with a grin.

'What I'm saying is, can we make the arrangement a little more permanent? Maybe sort out a two-year contract?'

'We'd like him to stay,' chipped in Freddie.

'I second that,' added Joey, with Billy nodding furiously.

Grace smiled. 'Obviously it's something we can have a chat about. How about tonight? We could sit out in the courtyard.'

'I'd like that,' replied Andrew. 'Right, let's taste how wonderful these homemade burgers and chips are, and all for the grand price of six pounds and sixty pence.'

The boys all cheered except Billy, who'd already sunk his teeth into the whopping burger and now had tomato ketchup dripping off his chin. Grace grinned. 'I think someone is already impressed with the burger.'

Grace knew she needed to come clean about the history of the Castle to Andrew. She had to know what Andrew thought about it and whether he would have any intention of attempting to claim the Castle even though the solicitor had confirmed the legal documents were in order. Maybe she was worrying unnecessarily, but she needed to make sure everything was out in the open. If Andrew knew the truth about the Castle, he could make up his own mind whether he thought he had some sort of entitlement to claim his inheritance back. Grace could only wait and see.

Chapter Twenty-Four

'And what's with that huge beam on your face?' asked Grace, turning around to see Hector standing in the doorway. She narrowed her eyes.

'I can't quite say, Lady Grace, but I've been instructed to give you this.'

He handed over a blush-pink envelope.

'Well, it doesn't look like a bill,' said Grace, thankfully. 'Where's it come from?'

But Hector wasn't giving anything away. 'I'll be back ten minutes before the time stated on the letter.' He tipped his cap and before Grace could ask any more questions he was gone.

She turned the envelope over in her hand. Her name was written elegantly on the front in old-fashioned black ink. Grace was intrigued. Slipping her finger under the lip of the envelope, she opened it. Inside was an invitation on pale-pink card with a blush-red border.

Grace read out loud, 'Andrew Glossop would love the company of Grace Power for dinner tonight. The time seven o'clock, the location the fountain. Dress code, come as you please.'

She stared at the invitation and took in the aroma of Andrew's aftershave. She knew they'd agreed to sit out in the courtyard tonight, but this was on a different level. Was this actually a date? Grace didn't quite know, but what she did know was she couldn't take the smile off her face. Quickly, she pinged a text to Isla. 'I'm not sure if I've just been asked out on a date.'

'Tell me more,' Isla's text came back instantly.

After she explained the situation, Isla talked her into wearing the same outfit that they'd put together for the evening of drinks at the servants' quarters which of course, Grace hadn't yet returned. She didn't know whether that outfit was jinxed, but it was all she had that at least looked a little sophisticated. After checking on the boys, who were happily playing with the train set in the Grand Hall, she ran herself a bath. With lavender bubbles nearly up to the brim, she slipped into the water and closed her eyes. She thought about everything that had gone on since arriving back at Heartcross Castle and how nervous she had been. But her grandfather must have been certain that once she was back, Grace wouldn't want to leave. Heartcross was her home and her friends were there for her, no matter what. She knew she'd already made the decision that she was going to tell Andrew how her grandfather had acquired the Castle and let him look over the betting letter that she'd discovered in the shoebox, but whatever happened after that, Grace knew she was going to be okay. Somehow all the anxiety of the past had been lifted and she was looking forward to the future.

After a thirty-minute soak in the bath, Grace dried herself and began to get ready. Hector had agreed to make omelettes for the boys once he'd arrived so Grace didn't have to worry about preparing their tea. She was sitting at her old dressing table. All those years ago, she'd been sitting in the very same spot, getting ready for her very first date with a boy whose name she couldn't even remember. But she did remember butterflies swirling around in her stomach at the time, and it was no different now. Every time she thought of Andrew, her heart gave a little flip. After recreating the look that the girls had given her a few days earlier, Grace gave herself a small squirt of perfume and declared herself ready. As she walked into the kitchen she noticed hushed whispers between the boys and Hector.

'And what are you four whispering about?' she asked suspiciously.

The boys looked at each other with slight smiles on their faces.

'Nothing,' said Freddie, picking up the invitation and passing it to Grace. 'We will see you later.'

'Are you trying to get rid of me?' Grace narrowed her eyes at all three of them. 'It really seems to me like you are trying to get rid of me. Are they trying to get rid of me?' Grace turned her attention to Billy, who was frantically shaking his head, but Grace noticed the twinkle in his eye.

'Okay, I'll be going, but I'll get to the bottom of what you are all up to.' She pointed at each of the boys, then tickled their tummies, and they squealed with delight.

Just as Grace was about to leave, she opened the shoebox, which she'd left on the small dresser, and took out the paperwork and the photograph that she wanted to show Andrew.

Hector walked her to the door. 'Are you sure you want to tell Andrew? It was given to Marley fair and square. Does he need to know?'

'I think he needs to know. I just need to be straight and open. The good thing is this Castle has brought us back together and that makes me happy.'

'And me too, Lady Grace. Now go and enjoy your evening,' insisted Hector, 'and don't worry about the boys.'

Grace set off through the gardens towards the fountain. As soon as she set eyes on it, she stopped dead in her tracks and looked around, but there was no sign of Andrew. There were two bay trees swathed in twinkly fairy lights, and between them were two chairs facing each other on either side of a small table. A crisp white linen cloth adorned the table, decorated skilfully with scattered sugar rose petals. Dozens of tea lights were dotted on top of the wall of the fountain. Grace was astounded; she couldn't believe Andrew had gone to all this trouble. Her whole body began to tremble as she walked towards the table. Andrew was still nowhere in sight. Her heart was pounding as she stood next to the table. Andrew had gone to great lengths to set the scene perfectly and it resembled something from a romantic movie.

She went to pull out a chair and jumped out of her skin as Andrew appeared behind her, giving her the warmest of smiles. 'Let me do that?'

'Thank you,' she said, her eyes discreetly looking him up and down. Andrew was dressed casually yet smartly, his features perfect. Grace had already glimpsed strong arms that fitted into his tight pale-blue shirt very nicely. She knew she was staring at him, but couldn't quite help it.

'Dinner for you, a thank-you for today. I can't even begin to tell you how much I enjoyed today.'

'Me too. This looks fancy. I knew you couldn't rein in your extravagance for long,' she teased.

'You'll be surprised,' he replied, not giving any more away.

Grace looked over at the fountain, and up at the mountain towering behind. The setting was stunning and the company perfect.

'Water?' asked Andrew, holding up a carafe of iced water.

'No champagne?' asked Grace, quite surprised.

'No, we are on a budget,' replied Andrew with a twinkle in his eye.

After he'd poured the water, he too looked over at the fountain then back at Grace, and took a breath. 'I do need to talk to you about the servants' quarters. I know when we first met I was a little bit—'

'Of an arse,' interrupted Grace, knowing that the light-hearted comment would make Andrew laugh.

'Okay, we will go with arse,' he said, shaking his head. 'But in my defence, I'm sorry for thinking you were the housekeeper. By the way, tonight you look stunning.'

'Thank you,' replied Grace, accepting the compliment.

'And I'm sorry I didn't know they were your boys when they invaded my kitchen. I shouldn't have shouted and I am sorry.'

'Apology accepted,' replied Grace.

'But this place has become my life too. I'm settled here. Your grandfather was so kind to me, letting me take over the servants' quarters. Do you know what, at first he refused the rent but I insisted and made sure he took it off me, every penny. But the best thing about this place is it's fabulous to have someone else milling around, to hear the boys racing about. It's given the place new life. I want to keep my business here and I'm excited about the cooking school. I want to talk to you about making it more permanent.'

Grace reached across the table and, for a brief second, rested her hand on Andrew's. 'I need to be honest with you about something.'

She could see by the look on his face that he wasn't expecting to hear those words.

'Honest about what?' he asked, looking nervous and taking a sip of his water.

Grace opened her bag and took out the photograph of the two soldiers, then handed it to Andrew.

'My grandfather and your grandfather.' She watched the puzzled look hitch on Andrew's face.

'I'm not quite understanding,' he said, watching her closely. 'I didn't even know they knew each other.'

'It's a very long story, but here's the shortened version...' Grace began to tell the story of their friendship and how their paths had crossed.

Andrew's jaw had dropped wide open. 'I was never expecting that.'

'Me neither,' admitted Grace. 'Their normal worlds were so far apart, a little like us. My grandfather a farmhand and your grandfather one of the country's richest aristocrats.'

She took a deep breath. 'Which brings me on to this place ... Heartcross Castle.' She took a look over her shoulder at the magnificent building towering behind them.

Andrew was looking at her, intrigued. Grace handed over the handwritten letter and the transfer of property deeds. She watched as he perused the documents in front of him.

'As you can see, the Castle was won in a game of poker. This letter was discovered in the pocket of your grandfather's uniform after he was killed. Throughout the war, they looked after each other as best they could. Your grandmother Evelyn discovered this letter when your grandfather's belongings were returned home, and honoured the bet. My grandfather didn't want to take such wealth but she insisted, knowing that William thought so highly of him. My family had no wealth, until your grandmother gave my grandfather all this.'

Andrew let out a long breath and sat back in his chair, a look of astonishment upon his face. 'That must have been one hell of a game of poker and one hell of a friendship.'

'That's exactly what Hector said. True friendship, loyalty, isn't about wealth. They wouldn't have met except for the situation that was thrust upon them and now I'm thinking...' She took a breath. 'This Castle isn't really my inheritance. It's rightfully yours.'

Andrew's eyes met Grace's and he was silent for a moment, taking in everything that she'd had just told him. Then he spoke.

'This bet was honoured by my grandmother, so who am I to argue? Those two men served their country, their friendship cemented by the situation they found themselves in, and I know my grandmother must have wanted to do this. As far as I'm concerned, this is now the home of you and your boys and I wouldn't dream of taking it away from you. As far as I am concerned, we look after each other too. It seems our grandfathers were lucky that their paths crossed. Special friendships are hard to find. The Castle is rightfully yours, Grace, and I'm hoping you are sticking around.'

Instantly, the tears welled up in Grace's eyes. Andrew's words had been so kind and thoughtful. It was generous to say she could keep the Castle. After thinking about their grandfathers' friendship, her thoughts turned to Isla, Felicity and Allie. Andrew was right about special friendships: those girls had welcomed her back with open arms and with no judgement. They had all been there for her and had chipped in to make things a little easier. Good friends were indeed hard to find and Grace had no intention of running or throwing them away a second time.

'I think I just might stick around.'

'Good,' he said. 'You don't know how glad I am about that.'

With a flutter of butterflies in her stomach and a pounding heartbeat, Grace knew she had a silly grin on her face. The eye contact between them was strong, their legs touching under the table.

'But.'

'But what?'

'I thought I'd give you a chance to win the Castle back.'

Andrew raised his eyebrows. 'What do you mean?'

From her bag Grace produced a pack of cards and placed them on the table. 'Fancy a card game? I must warn you, the only game I know is Snap.'

Andrew threw his head back and laughed. 'Luckily for you, the only card game I know is Happy Families – and that's exactly what you have, so I won't be challenging you to a game. But maybe I could win my part of the Castle from you or rent it indefinitely.'

'We can talk about those options.'

'But just not now.' He looked at his watch. 'Are you ready to eat?'

'I am, but why are you smiling like that?' she asked, giving him a quizzical look.

Andrew picked up his phone and punched in a number.

'I think we are ready for you now,' he said, not giving any more away.

Grace raised an eyebrow. 'Ready for who? What's going on?'

Andrew looked towards the main path leading from the Castle. Grace followed his gaze and couldn't believe her eyes. The twins, dressed in crisp white shirts and black shorts, were carrying two silver cloches.

Grace bought her hands up to her heart. 'Well, look at you handsome pair. I hope Andrew is paying you a decent wage for being waiters this evening.'

Freddie and Joey were grinning as they placed one cloche in front of Grace and one in front of Andrew. The boys gave a cheeky grin and, after giving Andrew a thumbs-up, they skipped away.

'I think they like you,' shared Grace, watching the boys until they were out of sight.

'That's good to hear, but, before we enjoy our meal, we need the wine.'

Grace looked over to see Billy walking towards them. She threw back her head and laughed. Billy was holding a bottle of Lambrini. He handed it to Andrew, before turning and running after his brothers.

Andrew held up the bottle. 'Only the best for you!'

'I am impressed,' she said, still laughing. 'I can't wait to see what is under here.' She attempted a tiny peek but Andrew lightly and playfully slapped her hand. 'What are we eating? I'm dying to know.'

'You'll be pleased to know I'm within budget…'

'And the budget being...' she mused.

'The change from today.'

Grace looked down at the cloche. 'This meal cost three pounds forty? I don't believe you!'

'Oh yes, including that wine, which is understandable as it tastes...'

'Don't diss the wine. Lambrini has got me through many situations,' she joked. 'I can't wait to see what's under here.'

Andrew gave her a nod. Grace lifted the lid of the cloche, looked down at the plate in amusement and bit her lip before laughing heartily. 'Beans on toast!'

'Unfortunately there wasn't enough money left for the cheese as the wine took me over budget.'

Grace was still laughing as she picked up her knife and fork and began to scoop up the beans from the top of the toast. 'Mmm, cooked to perfection. You are such a good chef.' She waggled her fork in his direction. 'Michelin-star worthy!'

The night was perfect, the sky glowed soft blue and the sun was still warm. With the sound of the fountain trickling behind them and the branches of the trees swaying in the light breeze, there was a calmness about the place that Grace loved. She knew the past had brought her here and as she sat opposite Andrew she was thankful.

She held up her glass. 'Here's to our grandfathers and Heartcross Castle.'

She clinked her glass against Andrew's.

'Here's to Heartcross Castle and its future,' added Andrew. 'And I have to say I'm quite excited by what the future may hold.' There was that look again that melted her heart. Grace never thought, after everything she'd been through, that she would have these types of feelings again for anyone, but looking across the table at Andrew, she knew she wanted him to hold her, she wanted to get closer to him. The attraction was there and he was giving her all the signs that it was for him too. She glanced nervously towards him. 'I was just wondering…'

'Go on,' he said.

'Have you got any brown sauce? I always have brown sauce on beans on toast.'

Andrew burst out laughing. 'No, because that would take us over budget!'

Chapter Twenty-Five

Two weeks later

Hearing a loud knock on the door, Billy immediately ran to fling it open. Hector was standing outside with a cluster of brightly coloured balloons in one hand and a huge round birthday badge in the other.

'I believe there is a birthday in the Castle. Is it yours, Freddie?' Hector looked towards Freddie, who shook his head. 'Well, if it's not yours it can't be Joey's, being twins and all that.' Hector gave a little chuckle. 'Which means it must be yours!'

Hector handed the balloons over to Billy, then pulled him in for a hug. 'Your birthday present is on the way and hopefully it'll arrive before we open the gates to the Castle gardens. What a day this is going to be.'

'Can I cut the ribbon?' asked Freddie. 'Pleeease!'

'I think we should let Hector cut the ribbon,' said Grace.

'After all it's down to Hector's hard work that the gardens are opening today. What do you think?'

Freddie nodded. 'Okay, but can I give out the first ticket?' he asked, looking hopeful.

'I think you can,' agreed Grace.

Freddie jumped up and down and looked over towards Hector, who nodded. With balloons trailing behind them, they ran down the hallway and appeared with homemade cards.

'For me? But it's Billy's birthday, not mine.' Grace looked down at the cards, hugged them to her chest then looked at them again. 'Good luck with your new business.' The boys had drawn a picture of the Castle with lots of flowers and trees. She planted a kiss on each of the boys' cheeks and each pretended to wipe it off. 'You are never too old to have a kiss from your mother!' she joked. 'And thank you for my cards, I will treasure them,' she said, standing them up next to Billy's birthday cards.

'I'm not sure you had much sleep last night, did you?' Grace looked at Billy. 'Too excited for your birthday. Once the Castle gardens are open, we can enjoy your birthday party this afternoon. Are you looking forward to that?'

Billy smiled and nodded then hugged Grace tightly.

'We have stilt-walkers, magicians, and your birthday present is on its way.'

Grace couldn't believe today was the day that the Castle gardens were opening again to the public. After the local newspaper interviewed her and Grace set up the Facebook page, it was only a matter of seconds before people began to pre-book tickets online. Isla had given Grace an old laptop and helped to create a website. Over the past few days Grace had worked hard marketing the new business. Already, she'd counted up the revenue that the Castle gardens would generate for today and the first thing she was going to do with the money was pay a Hector a wage for all his hard work over the years. It was all down to him that today could actually be happening.

'Is Andrew coming over this morning?' asked Hector.

Grace nodded. 'Any minute.'

The last couple of weeks had been a whirlwind. Whenever Andrew wasn't working he was over at the Castle helping the boys to build dens, playing football in the meadow and sneaking them pop and crisps from the holding room. Grace didn't know who loved it more, him or the boys.

'Oh, no, Hector, what's wrong?' Grace had looked up to see a tear rolling down his cheek. 'Today is meant to be happy.'

'Oh, I am happy, Lady Grace. Your grandfather and your mum would have been full of pride. I never thought this day would come. I'm just feeling a little emotional.' Hector looked towards his photograph, which Grace had framed and put on the wall.

'I'm sure everyone is looking down on us today,' she said, giving Hector's arm a quick squeeze. Since arriving home, everything in Grace's life was going from strength to strength and she was feeling content. 'Here's Andrew now,' she said, opening the door wide. 'How are you this morning?' She walked over and pressed a light kiss to Andrew's cheek.

'I think this day should go down in history. Not only is there a birthday in the Castle,' Andrew gave Billy a wink, 'but today the Castle gardens are opening to the public and...'

'What is it?' asked Grace, with a sprightly rise of her eyebrows. 'The suspense is killing me.'

'The first week of our residential cooking school is already booked up.'

'No way!'

'Yes way,' replied Andrew, lifting Grace clean off the ground and spinning her round, causing the boys to giggle.

After Grace had shared with Andrew about the way she'd inherited the Castle they'd talked in depth about the servants' quarters and the opening of the school. Grace knew now she was back in Heartcross her world was all coming together; she couldn't ever think of leaving this place. The boys loved it here and of course she wanted to share as much time with Hector as she could. Andrew had asked Grace to be his right-hand woman and be a part of the school, in fact the first person that the residents would meet, and Grace had agreed to be a part of the venture.

'Andrew! That is amazing! It's all coming together.'

'And that is down to your brilliant idea. What would I do without you?'

'Luckily you don't have to think about that,' she replied, and nudged him gently.

Just at that moment the drone of Drew's tractor could be

heard driving into the courtyard and Grace gave Hector a secret smile. Billy's birthday present had arrived and she couldn't wait to see Billy's face.

'Billy, come here and close your eyes,' she instructed him. 'Your birthday present has arrived.' She could hear the excitement in her own voice as she covered up Billy's eyes with her hands. Andrew and Hector slipped out of the door to help Drew unload Billy's present off the trailer. 'And no peeping,' she insisted.

Once the present was in position on the small grassy area at the side of the courtyard, Grace guided Billy through the door.

As soon as Billy opened his eyes, everyone started singing 'Happy Birthday' at the tops of their voices. To his surprise, Billy saw in front of him his very own wooden chicken coop. He raced towards it, opened the door and stood inside. The smile on his face said it all.

'This is from me, the twins and Hector – but Andrew has got you a present too.'

Billy looked over as Andrew brought out a small wooden crate and placed it on the grass next to the coop.

'Go on, take a look,' Andrew encouraged Billy.

Everyone was watching as Billy lifted the lid and a smile erupted on his face. He dropped the lid, ran towards Andrew, wrapped his arms tightly around his legs and then looked up with the most adorable eyes.

Andrew ruffled his hair and kissed the top of his head, then bent down and hugged Billy tight. 'Chickens for the best birthday boy I know.'

'Thank you,' exclaimed Billy.

The acceleration of Grace's heart-rate was instant. She honestly thought she was going to melt or combust. She was rooted to the spot, looking at Andrew and then at Hector. Billy was back. How she'd missed the sound of his voice. She swallowed an emotional lump in her throat. The twins ran to him and flung their arms around him. Billy was grinning like Grace had never seen him grin before. He was about to burst with happiness.

As Grace watched her boys hug each other, relief flooded her body and she couldn't help it, the tears began to free-fall down her face. She didn't care that she'd spent hours doing her make-up this morning; this was a breakthrough. Billy had spoken. She was on tenterhooks, waiting to see if he would say anything else. Grace gave him a warm, encouraging smile as Andrew slipped his arm around her shoulder and she snuggled into his chest, still crying tears of happiness. She buried her face in the soft fabric of his shirt, then slowly pulled away, her eyes flitting over the wet patch. 'I'm so sorry,' she said.

'Don't be.' He was smiling.

The boys were all bent down now, looking at the chickens inside the basket.

'You did this. This was your idea. Thank you.' Grace looked deep into Andrew's eyes and her heart constricted at how gorgeous he was. Every inch of her tingled with desire for this man who'd become a huge part of their lives in such a short time. They stayed locked in each other's arms for a moment, then gazed at each other in a contemplative silence. Andrew leaned forward and gently tucked an escaped strand of hair behind her ear. 'Everything is going to be okay,' he whispered.

Grace nodded. 'He's back. The chickens are a winner.' She smiled gratefully.

'And let's hope they never become dinner,' he joked, lowering his lips to hers and kissing her softly.

She swiped his arm playfully and looked at Hector, who was dabbing his eyes with his handkerchief. 'Oh my days, I've never cried this much in years,' he said, swooping down and swathing Billy in the hugest of hugs.

'You have to promise me one thing though, Billy,' said Grace. 'You have to promise me to look after them, and make sure they are cleaned out and give me the odd egg from time to time.'

'I will,' promised Billy.

There it was again, the sound of Billy's voice. She looked up at Andrew, who gave her a comforting smile. They watched as Billy went back to the crate with the twins by his side, Freddie and Joey propped the lid of the basket open whilst Billy scooped down and picked up the first fluffy white chicken from the basket. Freddie was laughing at the chicken's furry feet whilst Joey was pointing to the pompom that flopped on top of its head.

'They definitely have character,' said Grace, turning towards Drew.

'The best breeds for pets,' Drew confirmed. 'Silkies are entertaining and have sweet temperaments – and look how they look. Happy birthday, Billy! I think this is an eggcellent present,' joked Drew with a wink.

Freddie groaned. 'That's a terrible joke.'

Drew ruffled Freddie's hair before waving above his head. 'I'm going to take the tractor back to the farm. We will see you at the ticket office very soon. And you, Billy, enjoy your day.'

They waved Drew off before Hector turned towards Billy. 'The question is: what are you going to call them?' he asked.

Billy shrugged, scooping up the other chicken in his arms.

Behind them was a loud squawk. Everyone spun around. Rose was standing in the doorway of the servants' quarters and once again ushering Delia out of the house on to the courtyard.

Everyone laughed.

'Do you think they will all become friends?' asked Billy.

'Without a doubt,' replied Grace, checking her watch. 'However, I think we better be making a move.'

Andrew agreed. 'But first we need to set up the coop with sawdust, food, and water. Apparently the hens should stay inside the coop for twenty-four hours until they realise that this is their home.'

'Eww, it's going to be full of chicken poo.' Freddie was scrunching up his face.

'And you'll have to clean it out,' said Joey.

'I think we can all help to clean them out.'

Billy pointed at the first chicken. 'Mary,' he said, then pointed at the second chicken. 'Poopins.'

'What brilliant names!' remarked Grace, picking up Billy and placing a noisy kiss on his cheek. 'Welcome to the family, Mary and Poopins.' Her heart was bursting with happiness. 'They are bundles of cuteness, just like you three.'

'Mum!' Joey looked horrified at being called cute. Grace looked adoringly at her children; they seemed so happy here.

Thirty minutes later, after the coop was set up, and Mary and Poopins were settled inside, it was time to head off to the Castle gates for the grand opening of the gardens.

'Are you ready, boys? Shall we go and open the Castle gardens?' asked Grace, looking around for Hector, who had disappeared but was now walking back into the kitchen proudly wearing a straw hat and a striped pinny with the words 'Castle Gardens' embroidered on the front. Hector had asked to work the first shift in the Castle shop. Grace knew there was a method to his madness; it was going to be an extremely busy day but Hector could chat to his heart's content about the gardens and their history.

'Boys, the first ice creams are on me!' announced Hector.

'Does this mean we get free ice cream whenever we want it?' asked Freddie, crossing his fingers in front of him.

'No!' exclaimed Grace.

'Yes!' exclaimed Hector, at the same time.

'It's up for discussion!' added Andrew.

There was an air of excitement as they all held hands

and walked down the sloping drive of the Castle towards the ticket office together. Grace couldn't believe the line of people that were already queuing along the main road. She pointed, 'Are your TV vans trying to get through?'

'They aren't here for me, they are here for you. They're covering the story for local news.' He beamed at her. 'Heartcross Castle is going to be put well and truly on the map and that's down to you.'

'And Hector,' Grace added.

Hector was now walking in front, holding Billy's hand, and the boy was chatting away.

Grace listened in. 'Did he really say he was going to bath his chickens?' She gave a little chuckle. 'I'm sure he said he was going to bath the chickens.'

'Surely not,' replied Andrew, raising an eyebrow, then they both burst out laughing.

Halfway down the driveway, everyone paused. Hector took off his hat to pay his respects. They gathered around the bench in front of them. The plaque read 'In loving Memory of Marley Power. Always in our hearts.' They'd scattered his ashes the previous evening and after taking a moment and looking up at the sky they all continued to walk towards the ticket office, lost in their own thoughts.

As they all approached the end of the driveway, the queue of people waiting on the other side of the gates erupted in cheers. The applause was deafening and Grace curtseyed in grateful acknowledgement.

'I think that cheer is for you this time, not me. What a fantastic turnout.' Andrew squeezed her hand and looked adoringly at Grace. 'You, Grace Power, are amazing. I'm proud of you.'

Looking out over the crowd, she had an overwhelming feeling of triumph. All these people standing at the gates of Heartcross Castle, waiting for it to open. Her heart thumped with excitement as she took it all in.

Then she spotted all the gang gathered at the front of the gates. Isla, Drew and the boys were waving madly at her. Allie and Felicity were behind them. All her old friends and the community of Heartcross were coming together to make this day the best it could be. Grace's eyes shone. 'Everyone is here.' This meant the world to her. The turnout was truly magnificent.

Grace felt Billy's hand slip into hers. 'This is the best birthday! Do you think all these people would like to come to my birthday party?'

Grace smiled at her son lovingly, still feeling the relief that had flooded her the second she heard him speak. It had been Andrew's idea to organise the chickens for his birthday, knowing that animals provided warmth, reassurance and unconditional love, and she couldn't thank him enough.

'I think there will be lots of people wishing you happy birthday today, especially when they see that huge badge you are wearing!'

Billy looked down at the large badge pinned to his chest and beamed with pride.

Andrew gently ushered Grace towards the gates in front of the ticket office. Hector passed her the key and she

CHRISTIE BARLOW

swung open the gates. Standing in front of the red ribbon, Andrew passed her a pair of scissors. She stood in silence for a moment, taking in the view, staring out over the huge crowd. The moment felt surreal. A voice from the crowd shouted, 'Welcome home,' taking her by surprise. Knowing she felt a huge part of this community once again, her heart soared with gratitude to her grandfather.

The boys gathered by Grace's side and they posed for photographs for the press. She noticed that the TV cameras had started to film, too and took a breath to compose herself. The crowd fell silent. Grace had always shied away from public speaking, but today she felt a rush of adrenalin and wanted to make Marley, her mum and Hector proud.

'Thank you all for coming today.' She was thankful her voice sounded calm when her heart was beating so fast. 'Welcome to Heartcross Castle, my family home. Over many decades the Castle gardens were open to the general public, with hundreds of thousands of visitors each year, and today, thanks to our trusted, loyal family friend and chief gardener Hector Bedford, these gardens will be open once more. Please do make a wish in the fountain and meander through the wild flower garden. Children – try not to get lost in the maze! Just in front of the fountain you'll find the Castle shop. Do enjoy an ice cream, a punnet of strawberries and ice-cold drinks – you'll need them on a day like today. Oh, and if any one see a little boy around this high with mousy hair and blue eyes, and wearing a huge birthday badge,' Grace discreetly pointed towards Billy, 'please do wish him a happy birthday.'

At that moment the crowd in front of them burst into song, taking Grace by surprise, and the chorus of 'Happy Birthday' left Billy with a huge smile across his face. As soon as they finished singing, Grace took the scissors and snipped the ribbon. 'I declare Heartcross Castle gardens open.'

The crowd began to move forward whilst Hector and the boys took their places inside the ticket office and opened the window. As the crowd filtered through the gates, the boys were in their element, taking money and giving out tickets, guided by Hector.

Andrew joined Grace and pulled her towards him. He placed his arms around her waist.

'What is it like to be home?' he asked.

'Surreal, just the best,' she replied. 'Home sweet home … and it's a relief to know my boys are going to have the best home to grow up in, in the best town with just the best people.'

'And do those best people include me?' asked Andrew with a glint in his eye.

'Absolutely they do.'

Andrew tilted Grace's head to his and kissed her on the lips. She felt happiness like she'd never felt before. Her life had finally come together and she couldn't want for anything more. She was right at the start of her romantic journey with Andrew and for the first time in a long time she couldn't wait for the future.

'Mum, you need to take over,' shouted Freddie. 'We need to sell ice cream.'

Grace saluted. She and Andrew stepped inside the office and took over the ticket sales whilst Hector and the boys followed the crowds of people and the balloon sellers along the path towards the Castle shop.

As Andrew began to take money and hand out tickets, he pointed to a gift bag at the back of the office. 'There's a present there for you. I couldn't let the grand opening pass us by without a toast.'

Grace quickly peeped inside the bag and burst out laughing. 'Only the best for me – Lambrini!'

She quickly poured the wine into two plastic glasses, which they clicked together before resuming dishing out the tickets.

'Do you know what I'd love at this moment?' declared Andrew, placing his cup down.

'What's that?' asked Grace.

'A decent glass of champagne!'

'After today, I think our budget can stretch to one bottle,' Grace replied. 'Here's to the future.'

'Here's to the future,' echoed Andrew, leaning in and kissing her.

Grace took a quick glance at the fairy-tale Castle. It really was a place where dreams came true. She was thankful it had given her a second chance. This was her forever home, and she couldn't wait to see what the future held.

Acknowledgments

Can you believe my fourteenth book has just been published? Me neither! It's so exciting!

It's thank you time again and I have a long list of truly wonderful folk to thank. First up, I could never have written this book without the support of my brilliant editor Emily Ruston who in the most amazing way makes my books the best they can be. Thank you Emily!

Writing is a huge team effort and even though my name might be on the cover a lot of hard work goes on behind the scenes. As always thank you Charlotte Ledger who is without a doubt the best boss I have ever had the pleasure of working with. I'm so grateful to you for turning my stories into books.

Thank you Charlie Redmayne, an encouraging CEO. You captain a great ship!

Biggest thanks goes to my children, Emily, Jack, Roo and

Mop. They are my greatest achievement with my books coming a close second!

Much love to Woody (my mad Cocker Spaniel) and Nellie (my bonkers Labradoodle), you are both my partners-in-crime and are always by my side.

Love to my brother Graham, this year has been a challenge not only due to a global pandemic but has been difficult for personal reasons. He was there for me at a time I needed him the most. Thank you.

Thank you Anita Redfern, who is my epic friend, a friend like no other. My best friend for nearly thirty years. Love you BMITWE.

A massive thank you to Catherine Snook with twenty-two years of friendship under our belts, here's too many more.

A special mention to Kim Smith, a gorgeous human being who lifts everyone's spirits no matter how hard life gets. A truly inspirational woman who champions my books at every opportunity and I have the honour of calling you my friend.

Group hug to a lovely bunch of authors who support each other daily: Glynis Peters, Deborah Carr, Terri Nixon, Bella Osborne and Erin Green. Thank you for the texts, chats, RT's and shout outs – I appreciate you all.

A special shout out to Joanne Goostrey, it doesn't matter where I move to in the country, she still turns up with her ice-pack and recliner to put a smile on my face!

High fives to all the staff at The Health Club and Spa at St George's Park especially Mark Kelly, Chris Wathall,

George Shorter and Ben Winson who without knowing have given me a purpose and a safe place to go where I can just be me and forget the rest of the world.

Thank you Julie Wetherill, who is helping me to write my new chapter. Just keep swimming!

Much love to Novels@Night Y Lolfa GCG Library. These lovely bunch of ladies who continually flag wave my books. Here's to many more fun Zoom calls and hopefully one day we will finally meet! Thank you Lucy Harrison, Emma Louise Aue, Sian Davies O'Connor, Emma Louise Davies, Helen Spedding, Bethan Williams, Sara Wigglesworth, Debbie Ware, Hannah Pike, Hardeep Kaur, Kath Pugh and Caroline Howells.

Deep gratitude to these fabulous readers who pop up time and time again on my author page supporting my books. Thank you, Carmel Barclay, Alma Stelfox, Emma Bakewell, Liz Cubbin, Emma Jane Lambert, Meena Kumari, Cheryl Wood, Michelle Brown, Nicola Clough, Gemma Louise Smith, Gill Bower, Adele Blair, Emma Vale, Joanna Mitchell and a special mention to Grace Power who kindly allowed me to use her name as the main character in this book. Obviously the storyline is completely fictional and doesn't bear any resemblance to Grace's personal life, except her name is Grace!

A virtual group hug to all my readers, the wonderful bloggers, reviewers, retailers, librarians and fellow authors who have supported me throughout my career. Authors will be lost without you, and I'm so grateful for your support.

I have without a doubt enjoyed writing every second of this book and I really hope you enjoy hanging out at Heartcross Castle with Grace and Andrew. Please do let me know!

Warm wishes,

Christie xx

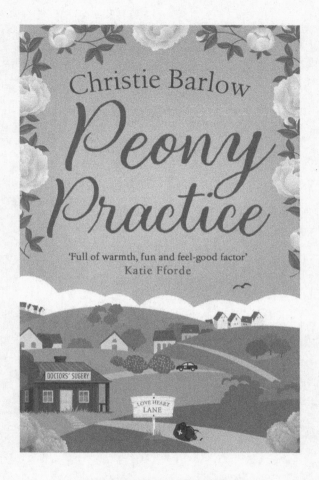

Christie Barlow

Peony Practice

'Full of warmth, fun and feel-good factor'
Katie Fforde

Don't miss *Peony Practice*…

**The next heartwarming instalment in the Love Heart Lane
series by Christie Barlow!**

Where friends are there for you no matter what…

ONE MORE CHAPTER

YOUR NUMBER ONE STOP

FOR PAGETURNING BOOKS

One More Chapter is an
award-winning global
division of HarperCollins.

Sign up to our newsletter to get our
latest eBook deals and stay up to date
with our weekly Book Club!
<u>Subscribe here.</u>

Meet the team at
<u>www.onemorechapter.com</u>

Follow us!

 <u>@OneMoreChapter_</u>
 <u>@OneMoreChapter</u>
 <u>@onemorechapterhc</u>

Do you write unputdownable fiction?
We love to hear from new voices.
Find out how to submit your novel at
<u>www.onemorechapter.com/submissions</u>

Rüdiger Safranski was born in Germany in 1945 and is one of the most renowned scholars of German philosophy in the ███████ previous books include *Schopenhauer and the Wild Ye███████* ███1) and *Martin Heidegger: Between Good and Ev███*

Shelley Frisch has taught G█████████████████████ olumbia University, Haverford College ███████████████████ versity. She lives in Princeton, New Jersey.

'A highly readable narrative coupled with intelligent and perceptive accounts of his subject's work' AC Grayling, *Guardian*

'Safranski produces a considered and thorough analysis of Nietzsche's writing . . . this book provides engaging and informative philosophical scrutiny' *Scotsman*

'Safranski's biography is on an altogether higher plane. This is a history of Nietzsche's inner life; events and relationships enter into it only in so far as they influenced the course of his thinking' *New Statesman*

'Thorough, readable and respectable' Roger Scruton, *The Times*

'Rüdiger Safranski's study is advisedly chaste. Concentrating on Zarathrustra's philosophical progress, it finds plenty of refreshing, and relevant, life in the old dog' *Literary Review*

'"All of us who regard thinking as a central concern of life will keep coming back to Nietzsche." For those who do come back this biography will be vital to their understanding' *Contemporary Review*

Also by Rüdiger Safranski

Martin Heidegger: Between Good and Evil
Schopenhauer and the Wild Years of Philosophy

Nietzsche

A Philosophical Biography

Rüdiger Safranski

TRANSLATED BY
Shelley Frisch

Granta Books
London

Granta Publications, 2/3 Hanover Yard, London N1 8BE

First published in Great Britain by Granta Books 2002
This edition published by Granta Books 2003

Originally published in Germany as *Nietzsche. Biographie Seines Denkens*
by Carl Hanser Verlag München Wien, 2000
Published in the US by W.W. Norton & Company, Inc., 2002

Copyright © 2002 Carl Hanser Verlaf München Wien
English translation copyright © 2002 by Shelley Frisch

Rüdiger Safranski has asserted his moral right under the Copyright,
Designs and Patents Act, 1988, to be identified as the author of this work.

A CIP catalogue record for this book
is available from the British Library.

1 3 5 7 9 10 8 6 4 2

Printed and bound in Great Britain
by Mackays of Chatham plc

It is absolutely unnecessary, and not even *desirable,* for you to argue in my favor; on the contrary, a dose of curiosity, as if you were looking at an alien plant with ironic distance, would strike me as an incomparably more *intelligent* attitude toward me.

—Nietzsche in a letter to Carl Fuchs, July 29, 1888

Contents

Translator's Preface

THE GERMAN satirist Kurt Tucholsky once quipped: "Tell me what you need, and I'll supply you with the right Nietzsche quotation."[1] Nietzsche has proven fascinating to readers of all persuasions. Each of us can discover a different Nietzsche to admire and/or detest. Beyond his many published works, Nietzsche left behind a voluminous literary estate (*Nachlass*), from which we can now pick and choose "our" Nietzsche. Access to the full range of his writings was not always possible in the past. Over the course of decades, readers' choices were dictated by the censoring hand of Nietzsche's sister and literary executor, Elisabeth Förster-Nietzsche, who suppressed and falsified his writings to assure her own prestige and finances and to secure Nietzsche's appeal among the radical right.[2] The twenty-volume edition of Nietzsche's works compiled under her supervision served as the standard edition into the middle of the twentieth century.

[1] Tucholsky, "Fräulein Nietzsche," in *Gesammelte Werke,* vol. 10 (Hamburg: Rowohlt, 1960), p. 14.
[2] H. F. Peters's *Zarathustra's Sister* (New York: Markus Wiener Publishers, 1985) provides a fascinating account of Elisabeth Förster-Nietzsche's manipulative will to power after Nietzsche's death. See also Walter Benjamin's scathing indictment of Förster-Nietzsche in his 1932 essay "Nietzsche und das Archiv seiner Schwester," in Benjamin, *Gesammelte Schriften,* ed. Hella Tiedemann-Bartels, vol. 3 (Frankfurt: Suhrkamp, 1972), pp. 323ff.

In 1967, the Italian scholars Giorgio Colli and Mazzino Montinari began publication of a groundbreaking complete critical edition of Nietzsche's published and unpublished works, followed by an eight-volume edition of his letters. These editions have allowed readers of German to examine all extant writings by Nietzsche, and have provided the foundation for subsequent Nietzsche scholarship in all parts of the world.

Unfortunately, there is as yet no English counterpart to this critical edition of Nietzsche's works. Walter Kaufmann's English renderings of a series of individual texts and compilations and his influential scholarly analyses represented a milestone in Anglo-American Nietzsche scholarship, but they predate the critical edition. Several additional translations by Kaufmann's collaborator R. J. Hollingdale appeared in the series Cambridge Texts in the History of Philosophy. Among the more recent noteworthy translations of individual texts are those by Marion Faber, Carol Diethe, Douglas Smith, and Duncan Large.

A promising new development in Nietzsche studies is a planned twenty-volume set of *The Complete Works of Friedrich Nietzsche*, which was launched under the editorship of Ernst Behler. Three volumes of this set *(Unfashionable Observations, Human, All Too Human I,* and *Unpublished Fragments from the Period of Unfashionable Observations)* have appeared in outstanding translations by Richard T. Gray and Gary Handwerk. Owing to Behler's untimely death, the project was on hiatus, but additional volumes are now in preparation.

When I first embarked on the translation of *Nietzsche: A Philosophical Biography*, I planned to cite published English translations for the Nietzsche passages wherever these were available. As the project progressed, this approach proved ill-advised for two reasons. First, the wording of the available translations too often clashed with the particular nuances of Rüdiger Safranski's interpretations and therefore tended to detract from an understanding of the texts under discussion. Second, translations that predated the Colli/Montinari critical edition failed to include key passages because these passages had been expunged by Nietzsche's sister. In *Ecce Homo*, for example, Nietzsche aimed a series of barbs at his mother and sister, calling them a "consummate machine of hell" of "unfathomable vulgarity." He went so far as to decry his cherished theory of eternal recurrence because it might force him to reencounter his family members (6,268; *EH* "Why I Am So Wise" § 3). Elisabeth Förster-Nietzsche justified her excision of these scathing remarks by calling them the product of her brother's febrile delirium and deeming it imperative that they be destroyed before he recovered. She contended that her brother actually loved her dearly, citing as evidence his affectionate references to her as "llama," an animal featured in one of their favorite children's books. In fact, the book in question depicted the llama in downright repulsive terms: "The llama, as a means of defense, squirts its spittle and half-digested fodder at its opponent."[3]

Under the circumstances, I opted to provide new translations of all Nietzsche passages in *Nietzsche: A Philosophical Biography*, with the single exception of a poem that opens the fourth book of *The Gay Science*, for which I have relied on Walter Kaufmann's felicitous rendering. To allow for ready access to all passages in both the German critical edition and any English editions, I have supplied bracketed references in the text that provide the volume and page of the German critical edition as well as the name and section number of each cited text.

The unique publication history of *The Will to Power* merits separate attention. Although Nietzsche had planned to write a book called "The Will to Power," he never did so. After Nietzsche's death, his sister and his friend Heinrich Köselitz, whom Nietzsche called Peter Gast, picked through and contrived their own selection from Nietzsche's many jottings, and published a book with this title. The critical edition does not recognize this compilation as a work by Nietzsche, and restores the mate-

---

[3] Cited in Walter Kaufmann, *Nietzsche: Philosopher, Psychologist, Antichrist* (Princeton: Princeton Univ. Press, 1974), p. 55.

rials so assembled to their original fragmentary form.[4] In those instances in which Nietzsche passages found their way into this fabricated work, I have noted the section number of *The Will to Power* for readers wishing to locate the corresponding passages in Kaufmann's translation.

Rüdiger Safranski excels at the art of philosophical narration, as evidenced in his earlier biographies of Schopenhauer, Heidegger, and E. T. A. Hoffmann, and amply confirmed in this latest offering on Nietzsche. Safranski's presentation is informed first and foremost by Nietzsche's thought as expressed in his published and unpublished writings, and only secondarily by the facts of his life, which are brought to bear where they shed light on Nietzsche's thinking. Nietzsche's many physical ailments, for example, which significantly shaped his philosophical attitudes, are described in fitting detail, whereas his final descent into madness and catatonia receives accordingly less attention. Readers in search of the sort of tell-all memoirs and scandalmongering that litter bookstore shelves will encounter only intermittent references to topics that another biographer of Nietzsche might have seized on—sexual proclivities, romantic entanglements, and graphic details of the final decade of madness. They will find instead subtle, yet riveting, descriptions of the major junctures in Nietzsche's life that served to mark turning points in his philosophical orientation, most notably in Safranski's sensitive portrayal of Nietzsche's dashed hopes for a new musical era at the Bayreuth Festival, when it became painfully evident to him that Richard Wagner's fawning hypocrisy and showmanship had overshadowed the composer's once lofty visions of new mythology of art. *Nietzsche: A Philosophical Biography* provides a sweeping panorama of the philosophical currents that converged in Nietzsche, from the pre-Socratic period to the mid-nineteenth century, and devotes a final chapter to the resonance of his philosophy throughout the century following his death.

[4] Karl Schlechta's edition of Nietzsche's writings, *Werke in drei Bänden* (Munich: Hanser, 1954–56), was the first to consign "The Will to Power" to the status of fragments from the 1880s.

Safranski vividly portrays Nietzsche's many attempts to try on identities and masks. Nietzsche played the free spirit, the moralist, the scientist, the antiscientist, the prophet, and the fool. Particularly when he lived in Genoa for several periods in 1880–82, he fancied himself a new Columbus of the mind, exploring territory as yet uncharted by human cognition. Throughout all of his forays, he clung to music as his anchor, whether he was looking to Wagner, Dionysus, or his own sense of the colossal power of music.

The author does not succumb to the temptation to homogenize Nietzsche's multifaceted philosophy.[5] He invites the reader inside the workings of Nietzsche's highly complex and often discrepant philosophical byways. Nietzsche struggled to overcome his own compassion and embody the *Übermensch* he championed, by creating what he called a "second nature." In the end, however, he never quite managed to escape his first nature, which was anchored in the "human, all too human."

I would like to thank my students at Rutgers, primarily those enrolled in my translation methodology seminars; their diligent and at times resplendent renderings of their texts have continued to provide me with fresh perspectives on my own work. Several students also steered me to just the right websites when my more traditional (paper-based) means of fact gathering stalled out. Professor Christian Wildberg of the Princeton University Classics Department was kind enough to clarify several perplexing issues concerning Greek antiquity. I am grateful to my good friend Anthony Heilbut for introducing me to this project; his sparkling writing style inspires my own efforts. Thanks also go to Robert Weil, my

[5] For a provocative and influential discussion, written during World War II, of two major "camps" of Nietzsche reception, which pits the "gentle Nietzscheans" against the "tough Nietzscheans," see Crane Brinton's *Nietzsche* (Cambridge: Harvard Univ. Press, 1941). Safranski refrains from entering into this debate.

editor at Norton, whose encouraging and enlightening e-mails always came at the right moments, and to his able assistant, Jason Baskin. My greatest debts of gratitude go to my husband, Markus, and our sons, Aaron and Noah. They now know far more about Nietzsche than any of them would have wished, and I appreciate their boundless tolerance for all of the time I spent in libraries and before a computer screen.

—Shelley Frisch
Princeton, New Jersey
May 2001

Reference Key to Nietzsche's Writings

Collected Editions Cited in Text

The following critical edition of Nietzsche's works is cited parenthetically in the text by volume and page:

Sämtliche Werke: Kritische Studienausgabe. Edited by Giorgio Colli and Mazzino Montinari. 15 vols. Munich: Deutscher Taschenbuch Verlag, 1980.

The following editions are also cited in the text by volume and page and the abbreviations indicated:

B *Sämtliche Briefe.* Edited by Giorgio Colli and Mazzino Montinari. 8 vols. Munich: Deutscher Taschenbuch Verlag, 1986.

J *Frühe Schriften, 1854–1869.* Edited by Hans Joachim Mette. 5 vols. Munich: Deutscher Taschenbuch Verlag, 1994.

N/W *Nietzsche und Wagner: Stationen einer epochalen Begegnung.* Edited by Dieter Borchmeyer and Jörg Salaquarda. 2 vols. Frankfurt: Insel Verlag, 1994.

Individual Works Cited in Text

A *The Antichrist*
BGE *Beyond Good and Evil*

BT	*The Birth of Tragedy*
CW	*The Case of Wagner*
D	*Daybreak*
DS	"David Strauss" (*Untimely Meditation* I)
DW	"The Dionysian Worldview"
EG	"Exhortation to the Germans"
EH	*Ecce Homo*
FE	"On the Future of Our Educational Institutions"
GM	*On the Genealogy of Morals*
GMD	"Greek Music Drama"
GS	*The Gay Science*
HC	"Homer's Contest"
HH I	*Human, All Too Human,* vol. I
HH II	*Human, All Too Human,* vol. II
AOS	"Assorted Opinions and Sayings" (part 1 of vol. II)
WS	"The Wanderer and His Shadow" (part 2 of vol. II)
HL	"On the Benefits and Drawbacks of History for Life" (*Untimely Meditation* II)
PTA	"Philosophy in the Tragic Age of the Greeks"
SE	"Schopenhauer as Educator" (*Untimely Meditation* III)
ST	"Socrates and Tragedy"
TF	"Truth and Falsehood in an Extramoral Sense"
TGS	"The Greek State"
TI	*Twilight of the Idols*
WB	"Wagner in Bayreuth" (*Untimely Meditation* IV)
WP	*The Will to Power* (compilation by Elisabeth Nietzsche and Peter Gast)
Z	*Thus Spoke Zarathustra*

The Drama
of Disillusionment

*Music and the colossal power: A double passion • How to
live when the music stops • Postsirenian melancholy •
Disillusionment • Attempts and temptations*

*N*IETZSCHE EXPERIENCED music as authentic reality and
colossal power. Music penetrated the core of his being, and it meant
everything to him. He hoped the music would never stop, but it did, and
he faced the quandary of how to carry on with his existence. On
December 18, 1871, Nietzsche traveled from Basel to Mannheim to hear
Wagnerian music conducted by the composer. Upon his return to Basel,
he wrote to his friend Erwin Rohde: "Everything that . . . cannot be
understood in relation to music engenders . . . downright aversion and
disgust in me. And when I returned home from the concert in
Mannheim, I actually had a peculiarly exaggerated weary dread of everyday reality, because it no longer seemed real to me, but ominous" (*B*
3,257; Dec. 21, 1871).

His return to a daily routine devoid of music was a problem that
Nietzsche pondered incessantly. There is such a thing as life after music,
he deliberated, but can it be endured? "Without music, life would be an
error" (6,64; *TI* "Maxims and Arrows" § 33).

Music, Nietzsche declared, imparts moments of "true feeling"

(1,456; WB § 5). It could be claimed that his entire philosophy was an endeavor to cling to life even when the music stopped. Although Nietzsche attempted to make music with language, thought, and ideas as much as humanly possible, displeasure was his constant companion. "It should have sung, this 'new soul'—and not spoken!" (1,15; *BT* "Attempt at Self-Criticism" § 3), Nietzsche wrote in a later self-critical preface to *The Birth of Tragedy*. His discontentment continued to dog him. Among his fragments written in early 1888, the following remark appears: "The fact is 'that I am so sad'; the problem 'I don't know what that means' . . . 'The tale from the distant past'" (13,457). Nietzsche was on the trail of Heinrich Heine, recalling lines from Heine's famous poem "The Lorelei," in which a beautiful woman seated on the cliffs lures sailors to their deaths with the allure of her song. Having heard the siren song, Nietzsche grew dissatisfied with a culture in which the sirens had fallen silent and the Lorelei was nothing more than a tale from the past. His philosophy originated in postsirenian melancholy. He strove to preserve at least the spirit of music in words and an echo of farewell while tuning up for the possible return of music, so that the "bow" of life "does not break" (1,453; WB § 4).

Over the course of many years, Nietzsche used the music of Wagner to gauge his aesthetic pleasure. After hearing the overture to the *Meistersinger* for the first time, before his personal encounter with Wagner, he wrote to Rohde: "Every fiber and nerve of my being is tingling. It has been a long time since I experienced such a sustained feeling of rapture" (*B* 2,332; Oct. 27, 1868). This feeling was heightened when he improvised on the piano. He could surrender himself to the lure of the piano for hours at a time, forgetting himself and the world. One famous and infamous scene described by his childhood friend Paul Deussen refers to this rapture. "Nietzsche," reported Deussen, "traveled alone to Cologne one day, took a guided tour of the sights, and then asked the tour guide to take him to a restaurant. The tour guide took him instead to a house of ill repute. Nietzsche told me the next day, 'I suddenly saw myself surrounded by a half dozen apparitions in tinsel and gauze, staring at me expectantly. I was speechless at first, but then I went instinctively to a piano, as if it were the only being in the group with a soul, and struck several chords. They broke the spell and I hurried outside . . .'" (Janz 1,137).[1]

Music, even when limited to a few improvised chords, triumphed over lust. In 1877, Nietzsche devised a hierarchy of things according to the degree of pleasure they afforded. Musical improvisation was placed at the pinnacle, followed by Wagnerian music. Lust was placed two rungs lower (8,423). In the bordello in Cologne, two chords were all he needed to transport him to another realm. They ushered in what he hoped would be a never-ending flow of improvisation in which to drift. Nietzsche treasured Wagner's unending melodies for the same reason. They keep unfolding like an improvisation and begin as though they had long since begun, and when they stop, they are still not truly finished. "The unending melody—you lose the shore and surrender to the waves" (8,379). Waves, which spill ceaselessly onto the shore, carrying you and pulling you along, and perhaps even pulling you under and submerging you, were Nietzsche's symbol of the depths of the world. "This is how the waves live—just as we live, the desirers! I will say no more . . . how could I ever betray you! Because—heed my words!—I know you and your secret, I know your type! You and I are of one and the same type!—You and I, we have one and the same secret!" (3,546; *GS* § 310). One of these secrets is the intimate relationship of wave, music, and the great game of life that Goethe called "expire and expand." It is a game of grow and fade, rule and be overruled. Music transports you into the heart of the world, but in such a way that you do not die in it. In *The Birth of Tragedy,* Nietzsche called this ecstatic life in music the "rapture of the Dionysian state, which eradicates the ordinary bounds and limits of existence" (1,56; *BT* § 7). As long as the rapture persists, the everyday world is carried off, only to be regarded with disgust when it returns to

---

[1] Parenthetical references within the text that are not keyed to works by Nietzsche can be found in the Bibliography. —Translator

one's consciousness. The sobered ecstatic succumbs to a "will-nullifying frame of mind" (1,56). At this moment, he resembles Hamlet, who is similarly revolted by the world and can no longer brace himself to act.

At times the experience of music is so overpowering that one fears for one's poor ego, which threatens to be submerged in the pure rapture of music, in an "orgiastic celebration of music" (1,134; *BT* § 21). It is therefore essential that a distancing medium be inserted *between* music and the listener receptive to Dionysian influences: a myth of words, images, and the action onstage. A myth understood as such "protects us from the music" (1,134; *BT* § 21), which is relegated to the background. From this position, music bestows such an intensity and significance on the actions, words, and images in the foreground that the viewer hears the whole thing "as though the innermost abyss of things were speaking to him perceptibly" (1,135; *BT* § 21). It is difficult to imagine any person, claimed Nietzsche, capable of experiencing the third act of Wagner's *Tristan and Isolde* "without the aid of word and image, simply as a mighty symphonic movement, without drawing his final breath in a spasmodic spreading of all wings of the soul" (1,135). Hearing this music puts our ears "virtually up to the heartbeat of the world will" (1,135), and only the graphic action in the foreground saves us from losing consciousness of our individual existence altogether.

But surely Nietzsche was overdoing the pathos here? Undoubtedly. Still, Nietzsche allowed art to be pathetic. In its triumphant moments, art provides a totality, a universal whole that can be beautifully endured. Succumbing to the sensation of art allows one to share in the pathos of the universal resonance. "We tolerate pathos only in art; actual living beings are supposed to be straightforward and not too loud" (8,441; 1877). An uncomplicated person can carry out scientific tasks without a trace of pathos, and is capable of showing "how pointless it was for man to have worked his way into this pinnacle of feeling" (8,428; 1877). Suddenly, the world of pathos appears in a different light. All affects and passions reveal their unappealing and even laughable origins. The same applies to the elation of music, which can relinquish the magic of its psychological and physiological enchantment. From this perspective, the way in which music provides a bond to one's innermost being appears to be nothing but a function of organic processes. Here Nietzsche employed arguments that were antithetical to pathos to grapple with his own tendencies in this direction, and experimented with a mode of thought that made a mockery of his passions.

Man, Nietzsche contended, is a being that has leapt beyond the "bestial bounds of the mating season" (8,432) and seeks pleasure not just at fixed intervals but perpetually. Since, however, there are fewer sources of pleasure than his perpetual desire for pleasure demands, nature has forced man onto the "path of pleasure contrivance." Man, the creature of consciousness whose horizons extend to the past and future, rarely attains complete fulfillment within the present, and for this reason experiences something most likely unknown to any animal, namely boredom. This strange creature seeks a stimulus to release him from boredom. If no such stimulus is readily available, it simply needs to be created. Man becomes the animal that plays. Play is an invention that engages the emotions; it is the art of stimulating emotions. Music is a prime example. Thus, the anthropological and physiological formula for the secret of art: "Flight from boredom is the mother of all art" (8,432).

Not a trace remains of the pathos of art when it is viewed in this manner. Could the so-called secret of art be any more trivial? Must the ecstasy of enthusiasm for art be reduced to a flight from the unalluring desert of the ordinary? Is art being degraded to mere entertainment? Nietzsche flirted with this demystifying viewpoint devoid of pathos. He sought to desecrate art, which had been sacrosanct to him, and to cool his fervor in "antiromantic self-treatment" (2,371; *HH* II Preface § 2) to determine "how these things look *if* they are turned around" (2,17; *HH* I Preface § 3). This process involves not only an inversion of the order of precedence of moral values but also a shift from a metaphysical to a physical and physiological outlook.

However, even "boredom" has its aura of mystery and is imbued with a singular pathos by Nietzsche. Boredom, from which art provides a refuge, becomes terrifying—the yawning abyss of being. When people are bored, they regard the moment as an empty passage of time. External events, as well as people's sense of self, become inconsequential. The phases of life lose their intentional tension and cave in on themselves like a soufflé removed from the oven too soon. Routines and habits that otherwise provide stability suddenly prove to be nothing more than façades. Finally, the eerie scenario of boredom reveals a moment of true feeling. When people find nothing to do with themselves, nothingness besets them. Against this backdrop of nothingness, art performs its task of self-stimulation—a virtually heroic enterprise, because people on the verge of a breakdown need to be entertained. Art steps in as a bridge to prevent succumbing to nihilist ennui. Art helps us live; without it, life cannot stem the onslaught of meaninglessness.

The formula of art as "flight from boredom" is rich in significance, assuming we take boredom to be an experience of nothingness. If we do so, however, we switch from the physiology of self-stimulation to the metaphysics of the *horror vacui*. Nietzsche was a virtuoso of this leap from physics to metaphysics. He knew how to imbue his physiological disenchantments with a new metaphysical magic. For him everything was ultimately colossal.

Anything can take on colossal proportions—one's own life and perceptions or the world as a whole. Music is so attuned to the colossal power that it helps us endure despite everything. Colossal power became Nietzsche's lifelong theme.

CHAPTER 1

Inventing
a Life

A boy writes • The divided self • Lightning and thunder •
Finding and inventing life stories • Prometheus and others
• First attempt at philosophy: "Fate and History" • Ocean
of ideas and nostalgia

THE FIRST colossal power to intrude upon the young Nietzsche was his own life. During his high school and college years, from 1858 to 1868, he penned no fewer than nine autobiographical sketches, each following the general theme of "How I became what I am." Later he switched over from the epic genre to something more dramatic in nature, and combined writing about his own life with grand gestures of proclamation. By that point, he had concluded that his life was exemplary. At first he simply wrote about his own life; then he wrote with all of the life force he could muster, and ultimately he wrote to stay alive.

Those who commit their lives to paper at such an early age are not always narcissistic, and often they do not necessarily regard themselves as highly problematic. Factors of that sort are more likely to work to a writer's disadvantage, because extreme entanglement in one's own problems or an excess of self-love generally precludes a writer's ability to maintain an essential distance. Nietzsche's autobiographical writings presuppose his ability to experience himself not only as an indivisible *"individuum"* but also as a *"dividuum"* (2,76; *HH* I § 57) that can be split apart.

There is a time-honored tradition of referring to the "individual" in terms that suggest an indivisible human nucleus. From an early age, however, Nietzsche set about experimenting with the nuclear fission of the individual. Self-portraiture generally implies a preoccupation with the difference between "ego" and "self." Not everyone sees the world in this way: curiosity and an abundance of thought are necessary components, as are self-love and self-loathing. Alienation, euphoria, and despair have to have fostered or provoked the self-splitting of the indivisible, the "dividualization" of the individual. Friedrich Nietzsche, in any case, considered himself divided to the point that he could sustain an extremely subtle relationship with himself, one that, as he later reported, served him well in his self-portrayals. "We, however, wish to be the poets of our lives" (3,538; *GS* § 299). His development would demonstrate that the "poet" of his life would lay claim to his work. The characteristic traits of his being were to become his work. He wished to credit himself for what he was and what he had made of himself.

Nietzsche formulated his imperative for self-configuration as follows: "You should become the master of yourself and also the master of your own virtues. Previously, they were your masters, but they must be nothing more than your tools, just some tools among others. You should achieve power over your pros and cons and learn how to put them forth and hang them back in accordance with your higher aim. You should learn to recognize the perspectivism inherent in every appraisal" (2,20; *HH* I Preface § 6). He did not accept the "innocence of becoming," nor would *amor fati,* the love of one's own fate, suffice to make a person the author of his life history. An intervening, planning, constructive outlook was required, even an outlook of "excess and surplus." Nietzsche fashioned himself into an athlete of alertness and presence of mind. All of his impulses, endeavors, and actions were pulled into the glaring spotlight. His thinking became tense self-observation. He was determined to monitor his own thought so as to experience the workings of his multi-layered world of ulterior motives, self-deception, and fraud.

Nietzsche was able to track himself masterfully from an early age. During his military service in 1867, he noted: "It is a good ability to be able to observe one's condition with an artistic eye and even in pain and suffering, awkwardness, and matters of that sort to have the Gorgon gaze that instantaneously petrifies everything into a work of art: that gaze from a realm without pain" (*J* 3,343).

Distancing oneself from one's own life can freeze that life into an image, giving it the semblance of a work of art but depriving it of vitality. For this reason, Nietzsche opted for the epic method. "Another good ability is being able to recognize and assess everything that is personally relevant for us as a step toward refinement" (*J* 3,343).

The young Nietzsche undertook his first autobiographical sketches as a narrative strategy for mapping out his life and the course of his intellectual maturation. The prospect of transforming a life into a book fascinated him and he concluded his first autobiography of 1858 with this lament: "If only I could write quite a few of these little volumes!" (*J* 1,32).

As a young boy, Nietzsche began to discover his keen delight in writing, which he indulged even while playing children's games. Barely able to contain his eagerness to record his experiences, he always rushed to note down in his "little book" every detail of his games and have his playmates read his compositions. The game itself paled in comparison with his account of the game. For Nietzsche, games provided the stimulus and raw material for his later jottings. As his experiences unfolded, he was already crafting his narratives of them. He captured the fleeting moment and infused the present with imminent meaning.

Nietzsche held to this method when structuring his later life as well. He would not settle for producing a series of quotable sentences; instead, he sought to organize his life as a quotable foundation for his thought. All of us ponder our existences, but Nietzsche strove to lead the kind of life that would yield food for thought. His life was a testing ground for his thinking. The essay was a mode of living.

Nietzsche made an explicit and emphatic point of expressing his ideas in the first-person singular, yet, paradoxically, he insisted that the process of thought was fundamentally anonymous—he considered it a mere quirk of grammar that people say "I think." Like every predicate, the predicate "think" requires a subject, which misleads readers into concluding that because "I" is the subject, it is in fact the agent. Quite the opposite applies: the act of thinking gives rise to the consciousness of an "I." The basis of thought is first and foremost the act, and only secondarily the agent (5,31; *BGE* § 17).

Nietzsche could easily envision thinking without the first-person subject, and yet, with the possible exception of Montaigne, no other philosopher has employed the pronoun "I" as often as Nietzsche. The reason is evident: Nietzsche knew that he was Nietzsche. He considered himself exemplary. It was worth his while to be himself, and he believed that it would be worth our while to share in his experiences. He consciously crafted his work with all of mankind in view. His late writings brimmed with unmistakable pride and confidence. "I know my destiny. Someday my name will be associated with the memory of something tremendous, a crisis like no other on earth, the profoundest collision of conscience, a decision conjured up against everything that had been believed, required, and held sacred up to that time" (6,365; *EH* "Why I Am a Destiny" § 1).

When writing about himself, Nietzsche aspired to several simultaneous and consecutive goals. His first objective was to wrest abiding images of memory from evanescent moments of time. He sought to engage his friends and family in this project of memory and found it most compelling to communicate memories to people who had some direct connection to the scenes he was recalling. Although Nietzsche wrote for these readers, he himself remained the primary intended audience for his chronicles. He supplied material for retrospection that would elevate his self-esteem to epic proportions. In the moment of composition, he was in the grip of an event, but later, when he read the notations, he hoped that a story of some significance might emerge. His quest was for significance. Nietzsche sought to shed the light of retrospective analysis on the haze of the experienced moment. He tried to come upon a glimmer of future understanding even as the experience was taking place. As subtle as this process may be, it is essentially a matter of applying techniques of self-thematization and self-description that any modestly gifted diarist has at his disposal.

Nietzsche was convinced that his life, anguish, and thought were exemplary in nature and consequently worth the while of "all and none" (4,9; *Z*), as the subtitle of *Thus Spoke Zarathustra* indicates. He envisioned himself as Atlas, vicariously hoisting the problems of the world (or, more specifically, the problems of existence in the world) onto his shoulders and then managing to romp and gambol with his heavy burden. He wanted to make matters difficult for himself, but still present himself as the acrobat of relief. All of this was made possible by language, which sustained him, and was even quicker and nimbler than thoughts. His buoyant language conveyed him along, and with growing amazement he registered its effects on him. In this way, his own self, the "dividual individual," became the scene of his internal world history. Anyone wishing to scrutinize it needed to join with him as an "adventurer and circumnavigator of the inner world known as 'human'" (2,21; *HH* I Preface § 7). Human beings, however, are situated in time. Nietzsche's inquiries are capable of engaging us only because his time frame comprises our time as well.

Let us now return to the fourteen-year-old Nietzsche, ensconced in the dark downstairs living room of his house in Naumburg, filling page after page with his meticulous penmanship in a quest to recount his life to himself. He began like an elderly man, faintly recalling the distant past. He was exasperated by his lapses in memory. His life seemed like a "muddled dream" (*J* 1,1). The boy sought to triumph over the ephemeral nature of time by assembling bits and pieces of elapsed memory and constructing an artistic whole like a "painting." Not satisfied simply to recall the past, he strove to capture the future as well. He contentedly pictured himself poring over his chronicle in the future. He imagined himself as the future reader of himself. "It is exquisitely beautiful to convey the first years of your life before your soul and thereby to discern the evolution of your soul" (*J* 1,31). He knew that he was slipping away from himself in the experienced moment, and could discover himself only in retrospect. Only then would he fully grasp what had shaped and unconsciously guided him. At this point in his life, he was certain that the "almighty hand of God" (*J* 1,1) was at work. Convinced that nothing is pure chance, he tried to establish meaningful links. Sharing his late father's passion for improvisation on the piano maintained one of these links.

The early death of his beloved father left Nietzsche "solitary," but because he got along well on his own, he was not dejected when alone. He realized that he was too serious for his age, but how could it be otherwise? He had had to cope with the deaths of his father, his younger brother, an aunt, and his grandmother, and the experience of leaving behind the tranquil world of the village parsonage in Röcken and moving to Naumburg after the death of his father tore him apart. How could he not turn solemn? He was proud of his earnest attitude, even though his fellow students often teased him for it. On one occasion, when he strode across the marketplace during a downpour with the ramrod posture prescribed by the school, the children tauntingly dubbed him "the little pastor."

Nietzsche considered his own gravity a mark of distinction. One self-description written in October 1862 closed with the following words: "Serious, tending to extremes, I would say passionately serious, in a variety of circumstances, in joy and in sorrow, even in play" (*J* 2,120). Observing himself from without as a nineteen-year-old, he fancied himself "a plant, born near the churchyard." Far from striving to be pious and well-behaved, however, he dreamed of a path in life that would pull him about and enable him to indulge his wild streak. He sought out the "free temple of nature" (*J* 1,8) and took great delight when lightning, thunder, and rainstorms poured down from the heavens, igniting his fantasy. He pronounced such moments "deliciously ferocious."

In July 1861, at boarding school in Pforta, Nietzsche composed an essay on Ermanarich, king of the Ostrogoths. He considered this essay his finest work well into his college years. The essay positively reveled in tumultuous images of the forces of nature. Every word in the Germanic sagas was said to be "like lightning, powerful and full of significance." He was analyzing literary texts here, but these were also the dreams of a pubescent schoolboy who recognized that language can pierce its way into life. Nietzsche sought the words that would wield the magical power to "shatter his audience" (J 2,285). He took pleasure in quoting a verse from the saga: "We have fought beautifully: we sit on corpses / That we felled, like eagles on branches" (J 2,289).

Deaths in the family were described in elaborate detail, with occasional religious overtones. In his first autobiographical endeavor, which depicted the circumstances under which he learned about the death of his aunt, he wrote: "I awaited the news with some trepidation, but once I had heard the beginning, I went outside and cried bitterly" (J 1,20). Shortly thereafter, he relinquished this biblical style in both prose and poetry, which he frequently annotated, critiqued, and categorized as a series of creative periods. In September 1858, he declared that his earliest poems had been profound, but unwieldy. The next period was marked by a lighter tone, giving greater priority to ornamentation than to ideas. His third period began on February 2, 1858, the day his grandmother died. He finally discovered how to couple poetic agility with richness of thought, "loveliness with vigor" (J 1,27). He was now determined to create a new poem every night in this new mode and prepare a catalog of his lyrical works. It was evident that he planned to fashion a life out of jaunty words.

Nietzsche was bent on ordering and classifying his life as well as his literature. The young author's pre-university life, as of 1864, fell into three distinct stages. The earliest period ended when he was five, with his father's death and the family's move from Röcken to Naumburg.

Nietzsche provided details of these childhood years in his earlier auto-biographical sketches. Subsequently, however, he began to wonder whether he had actually experienced these incidents or was merely par-roting what others had told him. Finally, unable to reconstruct his own experiential perspective, he opted to omit this phase.

For the following period, he placed particular emphasis on the cir-cumstance that the "death of such an outstanding father" brought him under the exclusive care of women, thus depriving him of male super-vision, which he sorely missed. As a result, "a yearning for something new, perhaps also a thirst for knowledge" (*J* 3,67), led him "to the most diverse educational materials in a highly chaotic manner." Between the ages of nine and fifteen, he strove to acquire "universal knowledge." With the same "almost doctrinaire fervor," he continued to record every last detail of his childhood games. He also claimed to have devoted the same diligence to the "horrendous poems" he composed during this period. At the age of twenty, Nietzsche came to understand that he knew how to construe this diligent, yet eccentric, characteristic of his intellectual enterprises. This exuberant prodigy took an awkward and precocious stab at self-discipline, since there was no paternal authority to impose discipline on him. Once he was accepted into the boarding school at Pforta, however—an event that signaled the second phase of his young years—the teachers put an end to his "aimless wandering." A similar development from boundless meandering to rigorous discipline was evident in his early passion for music and composition. In the Pforta school, he took pains "to work against the trivializing effect of 'improv-isation' by gaining a thorough mastery of writing methods" (*J* 3,68). His teachers initially supported him in this effort, and later he pursued his passion for writing on his own.

Although he would sometimes forbid himself to improvise while playing music, when it came to writing about subjects other than his own life, he gave free rein to his fantasy and used his characters to experiment with his passion for writing. In April 1859, for instance, Nietzsche drafted a free verse drama about the Titan Prometheus, who would not stand for people bowing to the rule of Zeus. Prometheus wanted them to be free like himself and proudly recalled having placed Zeus on the throne. The young Nietzsche idolized the gods far less than those who *make* gods. The drama closes with a chorus of people who proclaim to the world that they will submit only to gods who are free of guilt—the culpable gods must die like people and hence cannot offer any consolation: "They sink down to Orcus like reeds buffeted by deadly tempests" (*J* 1,68). Even as a young author, Nietzsche reflected on what he had written, and annotated his work on the spot. Why Prometheus? he asked. "One would like to re-create the era of Aeschylus, or are there no humans left and we have to make the Titans appear once again!" (*J* 1,69).

The young Nietzsche could not tear himself away from the Titans. Several weeks later, he portrayed two intrepid chamois hunters high up on a Swiss mountain who get caught in a terrible storm but do not turn back; "the awful danger gave them immense power" (*J* 1,87). Like Prometheus, they meet a dire end. The moral that pride goes before the fall is still valid here, but it was becoming evident that the young author valued pride over the consequences of morality. One evening in Pforta, after he read Schiller's play *The Robbers,* his imagination went soaring. Here, too, he saw a "battle of the Titans," but this time the battle was being waged "against religion and virtue" (*J* 1,37). For the time being, however, he felt a greater affinity with the founders of religions than with their assailants. In an essay entitled "The Childhood of Peoples," the seventeen-year-old immersed himself in the genealogy of world religions and concluded that they were indebted to "profound men who, carried away by the soaring of their unbridled fantasy, claimed to be envoys of the highest gods" (*J* 1,239).

After sketching out this history of religion and religious founders in early 1861, Nietzsche drafted yet another version of his life story. Having dealt with the "moral and intellectual development" of mankind, he now returned to delineating his personal development. However, he was not able to sustain the switch of inquiry from mankind to one specific individual. After just a few sentences, the autobiography glided back into the territory of religious philosophy. The 1859 autobiography had concluded with this devout formula: "God has guided me safely in everything as a father would his weak little child" (*J* 1,31). By May 1861, however, this guiding hand of God was subjected to intricate analysis. Nietzsche wrote that the rationale of the "power that metes out" our destinies (*J* 1,277) is unfathomable; there is too much injustice and evil in the world, and even coincidence plays a major, often wicked role. Is the basis of it all a blind or perhaps even evil power? That cannot be the case, because the origin and essence of the world cannot be beneath the human mind, which seeks sense and meaning and is receptive to goodness. Thus, the world as a whole cannot be meaningless, let alone ruled by an evil principle. The essence of the world cannot be more arbitrary than the human mind that seeks to fathom it. "Chance does not exist; everything that happens has meaning" (*J* 1,278). The text, which began as a sketch of his life, breaks off with these words. Shortly thereafter, Nietzsche took up the task of outlining his life story once again, but his overwrought search for "meaning" obviously discouraged him, and he abandoned it yet again. "The things I know about the first years of my life are too insignificant to be told" (*J* 1,279). A third attempt followed soon after, in the form of a narrative centering on the death of his father and the family's departure from Röcken. He depicted these events in terms that suggest an expulsion from paradise. "That was the first, fateful period, which reshaped my whole life to come" (*J* 1,280). A wistfulness coupled with a "certain sense of tranquillity and serenity" (*J* 1,281) stole over him, as did a feeling of alien existence in the world beyond paradise, a feeling of desolation. He was on the lookout for figures with whom he felt some spiritual bond or who roused him to self-empowerment: he immersed himself in studies of Hölderlin, Lord Byron, and Napoleon III.

Nietzsche had to defend his Hölderlin against the teachers who wanted nothing to do with "the ravings of a lunatic" (*J* 2,2). He praised the "music" of his prose, the "soft melting timbres" that resonate like uncanny dirges yet wax triumphant in "divine majesty" (*J* 2,3). He considered Hölderlin the king of an as yet undiscovered empire, and himself Hölderlin's apostle, bringing light to the darkness; however, the darkness was unable to fathom it.

Lord Byron needed no advocate. In characterizing Byron's character Manfred, the young Nietzsche employed for the very first time an expression that later took on a life of its own. He called Manfred an "*Übermensch* who commands the spirits" (*J* 2,10). How did Manfred, and by extension Byron, become such an *Übermensch* in Nietzsche's eyes? Byron led his life the way others might tell a story: he became the poet of his life in an eminent sense and transformed the members of his magic circle as though they were characters in a novel. Nietzsche admired Byron's staging of life and his metamorphosis into his own works of art. The young Nietzsche, who aspired to impart meaning to his own life through the inner stage of his diaries, revered geniuses who not only turned inward but portrayed themselves and authored their own lives for the public at large. Since Byron's life lent itself to story-telling by others, he was a worthy subject for narratives.

The sixteen-year-old Nietzsche selected another figure he considered equally deserving of narrative treatment, namely Napoleon III, and wrote an essay about him in 1862. The essay contended that Napoleon was capable of ferreting out the hopes and dreams of the people with unerring instinct and fulfilling them in such a way that, ultimately, "his boldest coups appear to be the will of the whole nation" (*J* 2,24). It is unclear whether Nietzsche actually had Napoleon Bonaparte in mind rather than Napoleon III. In any case, Nietzsche claimed that the latter also had an effect on the people he governed that made it seem that he was the historical destiny they had chosen. In his dealings with these figures, Nietzsche thought his way into their mentalities. With Hölderlin, he examined the covert potency of impotence. Lord Byron's artistic and full life captured Nietzsche's fancy, as did the magic of political power he recognized in Napoleon III. In all three of these cases, power amounted to self-assertion in the domain of fate.

"Fate and History" was the title Nietzsche gave to an essay composed during his Easter vacation in 1862. He considered this essay so bold that it set him trembling. He felt as though he were impelled into the distance of a "boundless ocean of ideas" (*J* 2,55), with neither compass nor guide—a pure folly and devastation for "undeveloped minds." (Nietzsche did not include himself in this category.) He attempted to brace the outcome of his "youthful brooding" so as not to be "drawn off course" by the "storms." Nietzsche created an uncommonly dramatic atmosphere on an imaginary stage before broaching his ideas, which centered on the question of how our view of the world might change if there were no God, immortality, Holy Spirit, or divine inspiration, and if the tenets of millennia were based on delusions. Might people have been "led astray by a vision" (*J* 2,55) for such a long time? What kinds of reality are left behind once religious phantasms have been taken away? The schoolboy in Pforta trembled with courage at the very act of posing this question. His answer was nature, in the form of the natural sciences and a whole universe of natural laws. Also left behind is history—a succession of events in which causalities and coincidences occur in the absence of a recognizable larger goal. God was the essence of meaning and goals; if this essence vanishes, meaning and goals in nature and history fade accordingly. We are then faced with an alternative: either we accept the fact that this kind of overarching meaning of life is altogether unnecessary, or we stop looking for it in transcendence, where our imaginations situated it for so long. Nietzsche did not wish to forgo meaning and goals; thus, the first option was not tenable for him. He was not, however, prepared to go on accepting meaning and goals as postulates. He now tended to regard them as assignments delegated to us. He was intent not on faithful acceptance but on enthusiastic production.

This essay was the young Nietzsche's first attempt to explore the will to life enhancement as immanent transcendence. His presentation was a far cry from the pious feelings straining toward the beyond that had typified his predecessors. The essay underscored his intense desire to structure life creatively, but how could this desire hold up against the worldview of what were then called the modern sciences, based on determination and causality? The young Nietzsche "solved" this problem quite simply, in the very manner that it had already been "solved" by idealist philosophy at the beginning of the nineteenth century, although he was still a pupil at the Pforta school and barely acquainted with idealism. He reflected on the circumstance that reflecting reason is sufficiently free to allow the problem of freedom to emerge in the first place. Even the question itself—"How is freedom possible?"—manifests a "free will." Although free will does belong to the universe of determination, it is still free enough to be able to distance this whole world conceptually. To this liberated consciousness, the world appears as the grand Other, the universe of determination. Nietzsche called it "fate." Free consciousness experiences this world as resistance, struggles to establish its own latitude within it, and in doing so experiences itself as "free will." However, this will is free only in the self-perception of consciousness. Later Nietzsche was to call a person who had achieved this latitude the "undetermined animal" (5,81; *BGE* § 62)—one that seeks conclusions and dubs them "truths." "Truths" are regarded as morality to guide our actions and as the recognition of laws in nature and history; they provide us with an orientation. This brilliant boyhood essay did not, of course, fully develop Nietzsche's perspectives on truth, but further explications would follow in due course. Fate, explained the young Nietzsche, is the stable element, and freedom is the singular open and mobile element in this determined world. He called free will the "highest power of fate" (*J* 2,59), which is realized in its antithesis, namely in the medium of freedom of will. Nietzsche did not know Kantian philosophy at this time; if he had, he might have cited Kant's causality in freedom. Nietzsche hoped to avoid seeing the world split apart into a dualism of determination and freedom; "uniformity" should somehow be kept intact in a polar tension. Only freedom can experience fate as a compelling power, and only the experience of fate can prod "free will" into liveliness and enhancement. Unity lies in dissonance.

Nietzsche rejected any interpretation that considered fate a manifestation of benevolent divine providence. Fate, he insisted, is faceless and does not target individuals. It is a blind coincidence from which we wrest meaning with our own actions. He considered belief in benevolent providence a "degrading sort" of "surrender to God's will," which does not dare to "confront destiny head on" (*J* 2,60). He regarded fate as a contingency, an inane coincidence, and a necessity. Nevertheless, in the final analysis, there is a kind of goal, even if the course of the world is not intentionally oriented toward it. When the young Nietzsche wrote his essay, the idea of evolution was in the air. Because Darwinism had already begun its triumphant advance, Nietzsche was drawn to experiment with the idea that natural history culminates in human beings. The arena of consciousness is unveiled in humans, and life itself becomes vivid theater. Nietzsche was quite taken with theatrical metaphors. "The curtain falls," he wrote, "and man rediscovers himself like a child playing with worlds, like a child awakening at dawn and laughingly wiping his awful dreams from his brow" (*J* 2,59). The "awful dreams" refer to the notion that we do not so much live life as get lived *by* it, that we do not act consciously, and that thus everything originates in "unconscious action." However, once we awaken to consciousness, we cannot be sure whether we are truly awake or have simply exchanged one dream for another, and whether the supposed freedom will not in fact turn out to be a somnambulistic dream. "I have *discovered* for myself," Nietzsche later wrote, "that the past of both humans and animals and indeed of all of the entire primeval era and past of all sentient being in me keep on creating, loving, hating, and conjecturing—I suddenly woke up in the middle of this dream, but only to the awareness that I am dreaming and that I will *have to* keep dreaming so as not to perish, just as the sleepwalker must keep dreaming so as not to fall" (3,416; *GS* § 54).

This later perspective expanded Nietzsche's earlier insight into the mystery of freedom, which he viewed as the "highest power of fate." But what did all of this amount to for the young Nietzsche? If the relationship between freedom and fate is constituted such that it depends on the individual to connect the two spheres in his own life, every individual becomes an arena of the world as a whole. Each individual is a case in point of the link between fate and freedom. The two concepts blend, Nietzsche wrote, into the "idea of individuality" (*J* 2,60). The true individual stands between a God who would have to be conceived as absolute freedom and an "automaton" who would be the product of a fatalistic principle. The individual must not bow to God or nature and should neither negate nor objectify himself. False spirituality and false naturalness were the twin dangers of which even the young Nietzsche was wary.

With thoughts of this sort, the seventeen-year-old schoolboy created an impressive internal scenario for the heady task of self-configuration. During his Easter vacation in 1862, Nietzsche contemplated God and the world, cruised on his "boundless ocean of ideas," and imagined where the trip would lead him, deciding that it would be crucial to become an individual who shapes himself to achieve wider horizons and self-enhancement. He sought to accelerate the process of self-configuration. In a concluding remark of his train of thought, he attempted to reconcile the idea of self-configuration with Christianity, which involved modifying Christian theology to meet his specific concept. What does the idea that God became a human being in Christ actually mean? It signifies that we can be assured that it is worth being a human being. But we are not humans from the start; we need to become human. Toward this end, we need the insight "that only we are responsible to ourselves, that accusations that we have missed our life's calling can be directed only at us, not at some higher powers" (*J* 2,63). We are in no need of the delusion of a supernatural world, because the very task of becoming human is the truly colossal achievement.

In the realm of everyday reality, the schoolboy of Pforta had strict limitations on his freedom of movement. He was alternately subject to the rigid regulations of boarding school life, vacations at home with his mother and sister in Naumburg, an occasional trip to his relatives in Pobles, and brief weekend excursions, notably to Bad Kösen, where he drank too much beer, returned inebriated, and was plagued with a bad conscience for days. Nietzsche broadened his narrow horizons of reality with the help of the stage, which unlocked his fantasy. He began to write a novel as a means of trying out new roles. The narrator of this work was a cynical nihilist, a villainous figure vaguely reminiscent of Lord Byron or of William Lovell, the title character of a novel by Ludwig Tieck. The problem facing Nietzsche's narrator is that life has lost its mystery. "I know myself through and through. . . . And now, like a rattle on the treadmill, I lug the rope they call fate at a nice leisurely pace" (*J* 2,70). Reveling in adolescent and dallying fantasies, the wicked Euphorion relates how he has made a thin nun "fat" and her fat brother "gaunt as a corpse" (the narrator adds the last phrase so that the murderous point cannot possibly be missed). This attempt at writing a novel came to a halt after two manuscript pages. Nietzsche had wanted to create a character who suffers from too much self-transparency, though that was not his own situation. The charm of Nietzsche's own self-referentiality was that he remain a secret to himself. He was altogether determined to keep things that way. He sought the vistas of the unforeseeable; thus, music was his priority. A few days after breaking off his novel project, he noted: "Our emotional life is least clear to ourselves." For this reason, it is imperative to listen to music, because music makes the strings of our inner life resonate. Even if the result is not complete self-realization, at least we can still feel our essence in the "resonance" (*J* 2,89).

A person can be creative only if he remains an enigma to himself. Nietzsche later called himself a "fan of puzzles who does not wish to lose the enigmatic character of things" (12,144). But his own puzzling nature was not always a source of satisfaction to him. In September 1863, he wrote to his mother and sister: "When I am able to think over what I want for a few minutes, I seek words to a melody I have and a melody to words I have, yet both together fail to mesh, even though they came from a single soul. But that is my lot!" (*B* 1,153).

On New Year's Eve of 1864, Nietzsche, now a university student in Bonn, rummaged through manuscripts and letters, mixed himself a hot punch, and played the requiem from Schumann's *Manfred*. Having struck the proper mood, he was anxious, according to an entry in his diary, to "leave aside everything else and to think only of myself" (*J* 3,79). Describing his New Year's Eve to his family, he wrote: "In hours such as these, decisive resolutions are born . . . . For a few hours, one is elevated above time and virtually steps outside of one's own development. One secures and documents the past and gathers the courage and resolve to continue on one's path" (*B* 2,34). This account to his mother and sister is fairly conventional, tailored to their preconceptions, and not an accurate reflection of the holiday's subtle events, which he related to his diary as a quasi-supernatural scene. In that account, Nietzsche was sitting in the corner of the sofa in his room, his head resting on his hand, his mind's eye reviewing scenes from the past year. Absorbed in the past, he suddenly became aware of his surroundings and saw someone lying on his bed, softly moanly and gasping. A dying man! Shadows whispered and murmured to the dying man from every direction. And then he knew: the old year is dying. A few moments later, the bed is empty. It gets light again, the walls of the room recede, and a voice says: "You fools and idiots of time, which is nowhere but in your heads! I ask you, what have you done? If you want to be and have what you hope for, what you await, do it" (*J* 3,9). In his diary, Nietzsche described this vision and interpreted it on the spot. The gasping figure on the bed, he concluded, is time personified, whose death remands the individual to himself. One's own creative will, rather than time, is what transforms and develops a person. Objective time cannot be relied on, and the project of fashioning one's own identity must be carried out by oneself.

CHAPTER 2

Schopenhauer and the Will to Style

Self-examination • Philological diet • The Schopenhauer experience • Thinking as self-transcendence • Transfigured physis and genius • Doubts about philology • The will to style • First encounter with Wagner

THE YOUNG Nietzsche was hardly unaware of the problems that came along with focusing so much attention on himself, since he had already penned several sketches of his life and other reflections on himself in his diary. In 1868, he jotted under the heading "Self-Observation" the following sentences: "It is deceiving / Know yourself. / By action, not by observation. / . . . Observation saps your energy: it corrodes and crumbles. / Instinct is best." He paused and thought over what he had written. Did self-observation really just impede and subvert? After observing his self-observation, he realized that it had worked to his benefit. "Self-observation a weapon against influences from without," he appended (*J* 4,126).

Self-observation allowed Nietzsche to differentiate between internal and external impulses, and to distinguish what he himself wanted from what others wanted from him. But this clean division was not always possible. Inherent in our own enigma is the fact that we do not always know what we want. How can we recognize our own volition? Perhaps we cannot know ourselves absolutely until we take action. Nietzsche pondered this issue in early 1869, when he learned of his appointment to Basel and was reviewing his prior development to figure out how he ought to react to this offer of a professorship. He was now committing himself to a future in classical philology. But how did he end up in philology? Was it a "baroque caprice" of external fate? He had had exemplary, inspiring teachers of philology, the special aura of Pforta, talent, diligence, and a love of combinations and conjectures—but none of this sufficed to explain his own development. Shortly before moving to Basel, he opted for a particular path to self-understanding: "The feeling of not getting to the basis of universality drove me to the arms of exacting scholarship. Then the longing to escape from the abrupt mood swings of artistic inclinations into the harbor of objectivity" (*J* 5,250).

Self-scrutiny brought him to the realization that it was not external pressure or the prospect of a career and professional security, nor passion for philology, that determined his choice of education. Rather, he had chosen philology as a means of discipline in the face of temptation by the enormous horizons of perception and artistic passions. The "groping hand of instinct" (*J* 5,250) had obviously not led him to travel out onto the open sea, but instead recommended that he be content with looking out onto the horizon from the shore. His feelings warned him to beware his own longings, and hence he was prepared to bow to self-elected constraints.

First he acceded to the wish of his mother, who wanted him to become a pastor and follow in the footsteps of his deceased father. But after only a single semester in Bonn, he broke off his study of theology and turned to the exclusive study of classical philology. Of course, he was far from finished with Christianity, but the Christian dogmas of resurrection, grace, and vindication by faith no longer had any binding force. When he returned to Naumburg during the first semester break in early 1865, his mother was horrified to see her son demonstratively refusing to take communion. An emotional quarrel ensued. Finally, she broke down in tears and was consoled by one of his aunts, who pointed out that all great men of God had to overcome doubts and temptations. She calmed down for the moment, but demanded that her son show considerate restraint in the future. He was not to mention any doubts about religion in her presence. His mother wrote to her brother Edmund: "My dear old Fritz is a noble person, despite our differences of opinion. He truly interprets life or, more accurately, time and appreciates only the lofty and good and despises everything crude. Yet I am often worried about this dear child of mine. But God looks into our hearts" (Janz, 1,147).

For the time being, though, his mother did not really want to know exactly what was going on in the heart of her rebellious son. The young Nietzsche, in turn, complained about the restriction she imposed on him to write only about "the latest news," and implored her in a letter of May 3, 1865: "Let us choose other subjects to write about" (*B* 2,51). He was candid when writing to his sister. On June 11, 1865, he gave Elisabeth an update on his thoughts concerning religion and faith. He wrote that while it would be easy to stay with comforting beliefs, the truth is difficult to pursue, because the truth is not necessarily in league with the beautiful and the good. A lover of truth cannot aim at tranquillity, peace, and happiness, because truth can be "detestable and ugly in the extreme" (*B* 2,60). Thus, people need to choose one of two paths: "If you want to attain peace of mind and happiness, then you should have faith; if you want to be a disciple of truth, then you should probe" (*B* 2,61).

As a student of classical philology, Nietzsche initially forwent the search for grand truths and remained satisfied with the little nuggets his scholarly field offered. Delving into scholarship had a positive effect on his disposition; his sustained project gave him "peace of mind and an uplifting feeling" (*B* 2,79). He was also gaining considerable recognition throughout the academy. Friedrich Ritschl, the leading classical philologist of the time in Leipzig, encouraged Nietzsche to work on scholarly editions at an early stage in his career and submit essays to professional journals. Ritschl also awarded one of his essays a prize in a competition.

Nietzsche's mentor heaped praise on his protégé, declaring that he had never had such a talented student. The philological protégé remained cautious, however. "How easy it is," he wrote on August 30, 1865, "to be guided by men like Ritschl, to get pulled away on perhaps the very paths most alien to one's own nature" (*B* 2,81).

From the moment he held the writings of Schopenhauer in his hands, philosophy, rather than philology, became the force that pulled him away on these paths. In October 1865, Nietzsche discovered the two volumes of *The World as Will and Representation* in a secondhand bookshop in Leipzig. He purchased them on the spot and perused them as soon as he got home. As he reported in one of his autobiographies, he was walking on air. He read in Schopenhauer that the world construed by reason, historical meaning, and morality is not the actual world. True life, namely the will, roars behind or underneath it.

In letters and diaries of his years in Leipzig, between 1866 and early 1868, an attitude of deep emotion manifested itself, one that could almost be called a conversion. The notion that the essence of the world, its very substance, was based not in reason or logic but in dark, vital instinct was immediately apparent to him. First and foremost, however, he had found confirmation for his passion for music in Schopenhauer's idea of redemption through art. The young Nietzsche interpreted the very fact that people wax enthusiastic about art as a triumph of the human mind over the strictures of nature. If such a triumph is possible, one can set the goal of the "sanctification and modification of the entire essence of man" (*J* 3,298). One has to gain control over one's own life by means of self-denial. For a period of two weeks, Nietzsche forced himself to go to bed no earlier than two in the morning and to get up no later than six. He prescribed himself a strict diet, created his own cloister, and lived like an ascetic. He shocked his mother by providing chilling details from his ascetic workshop, writing to her on November 5, 1865, that a person needs to decide whether to be stupid and content or clever and full of renunciation. We are either a "slave of life" or its master. The latter is possible only if we discard the "goods of life." Only then is life bearable for those of us who do not wish to remain trapped in animal existence, "because our burden is dispelled and no strings bind us to life anymore. Life is bearable because it can be disposed of without pain" (*B* 2,95f.). As Nietzsche wrote to Rohde in October 1868, the "ethical air, the Faustian odor, cross, death, and grave" (*B* 2,322) were what fascinated him about Schopenhauer. "Cross, death, and grave" did not depress him; on the contrary, they seemed to be an elixir of life. Nietzsche found Schopenhauer's gloomy outlook enticingly provocative. He absorbed it into himself to test how much of it he could bear without losing his lust for life. Terminologically, his early jottings while caught up in reading Schopenhauer were not framed as a "Will to Power," but in practice he was already experimenting with this will to power, because, in his view, Schopenhauer's negation of the will was not denial but extreme affirmation. It signaled the victory of the mental will over the natural will.

Nietzsche considered both internal and external forces of life sublime when regarded from a Schopenhauerian perspective. Describing the impression a thunderstorm made on him, he wrote on April 7, 1866: "How different the lightning, the storm, the hail, free powers, without ethics! How happy, how powerful they are, pure will, untarnished by intellect!" (*B* 2,122). He even saw his neighbors in a different light. Since Schopenhauer had removed the "blindfold of optimism" from his eyes, his vision had grown keener, and life seemed "more interesting, albeit uglier," he wrote to his friend Hermann Mushacke on July 11, 1866 (*B* 2,140). When his friend Carl von Gersdorff was in the depths of despair over the death of his cherished brother, Nietzsche wrote to him on January 16, 1867: "It is a period in which you yourself can put to the test what is true in the doctrine of Schopenhauer. If the fourth book of his major work now leaves an ugly, dreary, annoying impression on you, if it does not have the power to lift you up and to lead you out from the outward intense pain to that melancholy but happy mood we experience when listening to noble music, in which you see the earthly veils fall away: then I will have nothing further to do with this philosophy. Only a person who is filled with pain may pronounce a decisive judgment: the rest of us, standing in the stream of things and of life, only longing for that negation of the will as an island for the fortunate, we cannot judge whether the consolation of this philosophy would also gratify us in times of deep mourning" (*B* 2,195). Schopenhauer's consolation worked for his friend, which kept the two of them, Friedrich Nietzsche and Carl von Gersdorff, united in the spirit of philosophy.

In an essay on Schopenhauer that Nietzsche wrote five years later, he insisted that Schopenhauer was not only a teacher but above all an "educator." In this essay, he defined the true educator as a "liberator" (1,341; SE § 1) who helps a "young soul" discover the "fundamental workings of one's true self." The liberator is also a reviver. Nietzsche considered himself greatly in need of revival at the time of his initial encounter with Schopenhauer's writings, and outlined his shortcomings in 1872, in the fifth address in his lecture series "On the Future of Our Educational Institutions." Drawing on his own experience, he deduced that students appear to live freely and independently and feel as though they were in a dream in which they think they can fly, but are held back by inexplicable impediments. Nietzsche noted "that he cannot lead or help himself." Although "proud and noble resolutions" germinate in him, they lack the power to prevail. Thus, he plunged "despairingly into the world of the day and daily grind," but after a short while was gripped by the horror of it. He did not wish to lapse so early in life into "narrow-minded pedantic professionalism." But pedantry would be his inevitable fate, were he to suffer the "lack of a guide to cultivation" (1,744f.; FE Fifth Lecture). For Nietzsche, Schopenhauer was just such a "guide," who radiated what one expected from a "true philosopher," namely that one "could obey him because one would trust him more than oneself" (1,342; SE § 2). This level of trust does not imply agreement with every last detail of these teachings. Personal credibility was more important to him than factual content. For this reason, his trust in Schopenhauer was unshaken after a second, critical reading yielded doubts and objections.

This second reading was influenced by Nietzsche's encounter with the writings of Friedrich Albert Lange. Lange's *Geschichte des Materialismus*

(History of Materialism, 1866) was an attempt to link materialist and idealist thought. This book was extraordinarily influential at that time. By reading Lange, Nietzsche learned about Kant's critique of knowledge, ancient and modern materialism, Darwinism, and the basic outlines of the modern natural sciences. With a heightened sense of attention, he now discovered several theoretical weaknesses in Schopenhauer's system. Nietzsche concluded that one should not make any assertions concerning the unknowable "thing in itself," not even the assertion that all labels we place on the world of appearances, such as space, time, and causality, would have to be removed from this "thing in itself." The unknowable must not be reinterpreted as a negative image of the knowable, otherwise one runs the risk of using the logic of the antipode to project determinations of the knowable world onto what is indeterminable. It is essential not to interpret the "thing in itself" as will, which accords far too much specificity to the indeterminate essence of the world. Nietzsche acknowledged that the "will" is an elemental, perhaps even *the* primary life force, but criticized the notion that man allows the "will" to occupy the categorical space Kant had reserved for the "thing in itself."

This neo-Kantian critique of Schopenhauer, which Nietzsche developed in accordance with Lange, did nothing to alter his agreement with two basic ideas of Schopenhauerian philosophy. One was the idea that the inner nature of the world is based not on reason and intellect but on impulses and dark urges, dynamic and senseless, measured by the scale of our reason.

The second basic idea to which Nietzsche adhered is the possibility of transcendent knowledge, described by Schopenhauer under the rubric "negation of the will." At issue here is not transcendence in the religious sense of visions of a God in heaven. Transcendence could be achieved by assuming an attitude of composure that supersedes the usual egoistic disposition. Liberation from the power of the will, a process bordering on the miraculous, was also described by Schopenhauer as a state of ecstasy. Nietzsche was fascinated not so much by the "no" in this mysticism of negation as by the power of a will that turns against itself, against its usual impulses. Later, in the third *Untimely Meditation,* on Schopenhauer—from which we can quote in this context because Nietzsche himself explained that this 1874 text harked back to ideas from his student days—Nietzsche designated the ultimate elevation of the will to the point at which it turns against itself as an emancipation from "animal existence." The "no-longer-animals" succeed in this process, namely the "philosophers, artists, and saints" (1,380; SE § 5). The egos of the latter are "completely melted away, and their life of suffering is felt as no longer, or scarcely any longer, individual, but as a most profound sensation of identity, compassion, and unity with all living things: the saint in whom that miracle of transformation takes place, which the game of becoming never hits upon, that ultimate and supreme becoming human to which all of nature presses and drives to its redemption" (1,382; SE § 5).

Nietzsche later construed this inversion of the will as ascetism and as the triumph of a will that prefers nothingness to not wanting. He then regarded this "nothingness" as a negation of practical, serviceable attitudes fixated on self-assertion. Joie de vivre was replaced with overexertion, domination with surrender, reining in with broadening out, and individuation with mystical union. Nietzsche took up Schopenhauer's thought at the very point at which his own philosophy was agitating for a transformed life.

As is well known, Schopenhauer had made only passing reference to illumination and transformation. He was himself no saint or "Buddha of Frankfurt." He rose "only" as far as philosophy and the love of art. For Schopenhauer, philosophy and art lay halfway along the path to redemption by creating a distance from the world through contemplation. His was an aesthetic stance. His philosophy was a metaphysics of aesthetic distancing, and Nietzsche used it in this sense for his own visions. In contrast to traditional metaphysics, the liberating aspect of Schopenhauer's aesthetic metaphysics is not located in the content of what is discovered as "essence" behind the world of appearances. In traditional metaphysics, this recognition of the "essence" penetrates to the basic good in the world and uncovers firm foundations. For Schopenhauer, however, the core of the world was not solid ground but an abyss, the depths of the will, tormenting existence, the heart of darkness. "Just try to be all nature—it is intolerable," Schopenhauer noted. Liberation lies not in the "what" of the discovered being but in the act of distancing cognition, which is to say in the "how." Aesthetic distance from the world means regarding the world while "absolutely not being actively involved in it." This aesthetic distancing opens up a locus of transcendence that must remain empty. Not volition, not obligation, only being that has become completely visual, the "eye of the world."

Nietzsche called this Archimedean point of Schopenhauerian cosmic alleviation "transfigured *physis*" (1,362; SE § 3). When he coined this term, he had already developed his theory of the elemental life forces of the Dionysian and Apollonian. In "transfigured *physis,*" we reencounter his idea of Dionysian nature subdued and refined by Apollonian influence. Unlike Schopenhauer, Nietzsche was powerfully attracted to Dionysian nature; he sought to step right up to the abyss because he envisioned even more alluring secrets there and considered himself impervious to vertigo. At this point, his divergence from Schopenhauer did nothing to dampen his enthusiasm to make Schopenhauer his model.

What did Nietzsche consider exemplary in Schopenhauer? He admired the perfectly self-assured, domineering posture of this philosopher, who, in defiance of the spirit of his age, pronounced his judgments and sentences as a "judge of life" and at the same time acted as a "reformer of life" (1,362; SE § 3) through his philosophy of negation. Nietzsche later called Schopenhauer's endeavor a "revaluation of values." To which values did he take exception? Nietzsche described his own era when portraying the world that Schopenhauer wished to assail and transcend. According to Nietzsche, this world was populated by those who think of themselves with haste and exclusivity, "as people have never before thought of themselves; they build and plant only for their day, and the hunt for happiness will never be greater than if it must be seized today and tomorrow: because by the day after tomorrow, perhaps the hunting season will have come to a permanent end. We live in the age of atoms, of atomistic chaos" (1,367; SE § 4). Nevertheless, who will be in a position to raise up the "image of man" in the midst of an "atomistic revolution" that leads us down into "bestiality" or "rigid mechanization"? (1,368; SE § 4).

Nietzsche considered three such images in recalling mankind's loftier visions for man, namely those of Rousseau, Goethe, and Schopenhauer. Rousseau focused on reconciliation with nature and restoration of civilization to a state of nature. Goethe's man was contemplative and made his peace with the circumstances of his life in wise resignation and a sophisticated sense of style. The Schopenhauerian man discovered that all human structures are designed to keep the tragic and senseless design of life from being palpable. Everyday life is pure diversion. Although it can plunge him into despair, the Schopenhauerian man aspires to lift the veil of *maya* (illusion) and take the "voluntary" "suffering of truthfulness upon himself," which serves "to destroy his individual will and to prepare for the complete upheaval and reversal of his being, the achievement of which is the true meaning of life" (1,371; SE § 4). Nietzsche called this approach to life "heroic" (1,373; SE § 4). At that time, he was unaware of a confessional letter Schopenhauer had written to Goethe, in which the philosopher expressed himself in precisely this "heroic" vein. The passage in the letter reads: "The courage not to keep any question just in one's mind is what makes a philosopher. Philosophers must be like Sophocles' Oedipus, who tirelessly searches for enlightenment about his own terrible fate, even if he already suspects that he will be horror-struck by the answers." Schopenhauer really did consider himself as heroic as Nietzsche regarded him when he called Schopenhauer a "genius" in his 1874 essay.

What constitutes a genius? Nietzsche contended that a philosophical genius reassesses the value of existence and is a "legislator for the measure, coinage, and weight of things" (1,360; SE § 3). For the young

Nietzsche, philosophy was an enterprise with a decided impact on life. Philosophy went well beyond a contemplative, reflective portrayal of life; it both induced and embodied this transformation. Thought is action. Certainly, this transformation did not apply to every thought process and thinker. A certain charisma on the part of the thinker and a vitalizing power of thought is an essential component to ensure that truths are not simply detected, but actualized. One decade later, Nietzsche called the philosophers who could realize their ideas the "tyrants of the spirit" (2,214; *HH* I § 261).

The finest examples of "tyrants of the spirit" could be found in ancient Greece. Parmenides, Empedocles, Heraclitus, and Plato all wanted to reach the "core of all being with a single leap" (2,215; *HH* I § 261). We should not be misled by their sometimes intricate and long chains of argumentation. These "tyrants" did not uncover their truths in these ways. Those extended arguments were merely supplementary demonstrations, verbose intimidations, and logical excesses, preliminaries and postliminaries. In point of fact, the heroes of philosophy wanted to risk the leap into the public arena after their leap into truth and to communicate their powerful messages, which were designed to induce either particular individuals or an entire society to see, experience, and lead their lives differently from the way they had before. But the time for such tyrants was now past; only the "gospel of the tortoise" (2,216; *HH* I § 261) remained. "Truths" could no longer be captured in a single leap, and they were no longer forced imperiously upon people. Philosophy had lost the will to power, and a new breed that merely picked apart grand old "truths" with philological and historical analysis was in the ascendant.

This is how the young Nietzsche, who had studied the great philosophical deeds of antiquity as a philologist, pictured the situation in the moment of experiencing, through the lens of Schopenhauer, the unexpected return of a "tyrant of the spirit." His involvement with Schopenhauer had a significant impact on his philological writing. "It is a terrible thought," Nietzsche wrote in late 1867 in his log, "to contemplate that an immense number of mediocre thinkers are occupied with really influential matters" (*J* 3,320). Nietzsche planned an essay on Democritus and on the "history of literary studies in antiquity and modernity." The goal of this essay, he wrote to Erwin Rohde on February 1, 1868, would be to tell "the philologists a number of bitter truths" (*B* 2,248). He planned to demonstrate that we have received "all enlightening thoughts" from only few "great geniuses" and that this "creativity" stems from people who most assuredly did not pursue philological and historical studies. Unlike philologists, who merely annotate, compile, explicate, organize, and enshrine other authors, geniuses themselves contribute something to the world. Authors of primary texts make assertions and assert themselves, whereas writers of secondary literature, namely philologists and historians, diminish great things by working them into little bits; they are "devoid of the creative spark" (*B* 2,249).

By the fall of 1867, Nietzsche was yearning to emerge from the ranks of commentators and compilers and to become a creative author, while remaining in the field of philology. In his notebooks, he vented his displeasure with the routines of the business of philology. It is finally time, he contended, to stop poking through the "coffer" of tradition; "we must stop rehashing" (*J* 3,337). Philology should recognize that its stock of truly interesting objects will be exhausted, and that the time has come to forge something new and forward-looking from the old by means of a few "great thoughts: the best thing that can be accomplished is a deliberate poetic re-creation of minds, events, characters" (*J* 3,336).

Nietzsche had not yet reached the point where he could regard himself as a genius. In retrospect, at any rate, he would claim that his essay "Schopenhauer as Educator" could just as well have carried the title "Nietzsche as Educator." In 1867, his thoughts had not taken this direction, but his philological endeavors were falling far short of his aspirations. Nietzsche had a distinct premonition that he would someday become an author, but noted with a shock of recognition that he was lacking in style. "I have lived far too long in stylistic innocence" (*B*

2,208), he wrote in a letter to Carl von Gersdorff on April 6, 1867. A "categorical imperative" aroused him with the directive: "You should and must write"; in this instant he recognized to his horror that he was unable to do so. "Suddenly the pen froze in my hand." He perused Lessing, Lichtenberg, and Schopenhauer for stylistic guidance, but "the Graces" seemed unwilling to approach him. How would he find the key to unleash "some gay spirits" in his style? Perplexed but determined, he resolved to work on himself, keeping in mind that he had yet to cross the threshold. He forced himself to interpret the troubling recognition that "I have simply no style at all in German" as a gift, reasoning that anyone wishing to become an author had to admit the "blank slate of our stylistic arts into our conscience" (*B* 2,214).

For the time being, Nietzsche remained within his chosen field of philology, which continued to captivate him when he was offered a distinguished professorship in classical philology in Basel before he had even concluded his doctoral dissertation. However, as a philologist who had looked over the fence of his discipline and discovered his passion for writing and philosophizing, he felt confident that he had the power to breathe life into his field.

Nietzsche called the process of transforming the established canon and strictures of his field into something personally meaningful the creation of a "second nature" (*J* 3,291). He described this concept in an autobiographical sketch, written in 1867 after his military service, by citing the example of the foot soldier who initially fears that he will forget how to walk during drills "if he is taught the consciousness of lifting his foot." However, once marching has been integrated into his flesh and blood, "he can walk just as freely as before" (*J* 3,291). The concept of "second nature" would acquire a pivotal significance for Nietzsche. When in 1882 his friends chided him that his free-spirited conduct was out of line with his nature and that he had gone too far with it, he defended himself in a letter to the pianist and composer Hans von Bülow, who was Cosima Wagner's first husband: "True, it may be a 'sec-

ond nature': but I hope to prove that I have only now taken true possession of my first nature with this second nature" (*B* 6,290).

"First nature" reflects the manner in which people have been brought
up and what inheres in them and their backgrounds, milieus, and characters. "Second nature" is what people do with their potential. The
young Nietzsche discovered that language and writing would enable him
to make something of himself.

Self-configuration through language became a passion for Nietzsche.
It contoured the unique style of his philosophy, which blurred the
boundaries between detection and invention. Since he considered philosophy a linguistic work of art and literature, thoughts were inextricably bound to their linguistic form. The magic of his linguistic virtuosity
would suffer considerable loss if his words were to be expressed any
other way. Nietzsche was well aware of the degree to which his insights
depended on their singular formulations. He therefore harbored doubts
as to whether it would be possible for him to form a "school." He considered himself, and what he had made of himself, inimitable. He felt at
home on the boundary of communicability, which is where he chose to
conduct his experiment with self-configuration.

Nietzsche's remarkable language combined with his extraordinary
ideas would initiate his self-configuration and the creation of a "second
nature." A second nature, in turn, would imbue them with the requisite
"secret spices" (5,239; *BGE* § 296). The reader cannot fail to notice
Nietzsche scrutinizing his ideas to measure their effect on him. His
works present both the thought and the man engaged in the thought
process. Nietzsche would not restrict himself to developing ideas;
instead, he demonstrated how these thoughts originated from life and
struck back into life and transformed him. He tried out their power to
ascertain whether they could hold their ground against the physical
pains from which he was suffering. Thoughts would have to be incorporated, he demanded—only then would they have value and significance for him. A person who is always asking himself, "How do I form

my thoughts, and how do my thoughts form me?" inevitably becomes the self-portrayer of his thinking.

Nietzsche began to see himself as a philosophical writer who had moved beyond the confines of philology to a state of "drifting" into the "unknown with the restless hope of at some point finding a goal at which to rest" (*J* 3,336). During this period, he made the personal acquaintance of Richard Wagner. Just a few weeks before this encounter, he had written quite critically about Wagner in a letter to Rohde. He portrayed the composer as the "representative of a modern dilettantism that ingests and digests all kinds of artistic interests" (*B* 2,322; Oct. 8, 1868). The qualities he cherished in Schopenhauer—"the ethical air, the Faustian odor, cross, death, and grave, etc."—turned out to be the very ones he revered in Wagner. Three weeks later, he attended a concert in which the overtures to *Tristan and Isolde* and *Die Meistersinger* were performed. He resolved to keep his distance, but to no avail. "I cannot find it in my heart to keep a cool critical detachment from this music: every fiber and nerve of my being is tingling, and it has been a long time since I experienced such a perpetual feeling of rapture" (*B* 2,332; Oct. 27, 1868).

Wagner heard about the talented student and connoisseur of music Friedrich Nietzsche during a visit to the home of Heinrich Brockhaus, an Orientalist in Leipzig, and expressed his wish to meet the young classical philologist. Nietzsche was bursting with pride when he received his invitation to meet the great composer. He ordered a new suit from the tailor, which was delivered without delay, but he did not have the money on hand to pay for it. The tailor's assistant wanted to leave with it, whereupon Nietzsche seized the assistant and a scuffle ensued, with both men pulling at the trousers. The assistant prevailed, and fled with Nietzsche's outfit. Nietzsche described this scene to his friend Rohde: "I sit on the sofa brooding in my shirtsleeves and examining a black cloak, trying to decide if it would be good enough for Richard" (*B* 2,340; Nov. 9, 1868). He put it on in a "heightened mood of fiction."

At the Brockhaus home, Nietzsche encountered a cozy family circle. Wagner walked up to him, made a series of complimentary remarks, and inquired how the young man had become acquainted with his music. The conversation quickly turned to philosophy. With "indescribable warmth," Wagner spoke of Schopenhauer and called him the only philosopher to have "grasped the essence of music." Wagner played several passages from the *Die Meistersinger* on the piano. Nietzsche was enchanted. When the party ended, the maestro shook his hand warmly and invited Nietzsche to visit his home in Tribschen, near Lucerne, "to make music and discuss philosophy" (*B* 2,340; Nov. 9, 1868).

Nietzsche's move to Basel put him in the vicinity of Tribschen, providing the opportunity for a visit to Wagner. He was received with great cordiality, especially since Wagner gratefully welcomed any proselyte. After this first visit on Whit Monday of 1869, Nietzsche wrote to Richard Wagner: "My esteemed Sir, I have been intending to express to you for some time now the degree of gratitude I feel for you, in forthright terms, since I connect the best and loftiest moments of my life with your name, and I know of only one other man, your great spiritual brother Arthur Schopenhauer, whom I hold in the same degree of reverence, even *religione quadam*" (*B* 3,8).

There are many anecdotal descriptions of the series of blithe sojourns at Tribschen that followed this first visit. Nietzsche happily recalled the walks they took together at the lake, Cosima Wagner strolling arm in arm with Nietzsche. There was a cozy family evening in which the whole group read E. T. A. Hoffmann's story "The Golden Pot." Wagner dubbed Cosima the enchanting Serpentina of Hoffmann's story, himself the demonic Archivarius Lindhorst, and Nietzsche the dreamy and clumsy student Anselmus. For his Christmas visit, Nietzsche went to great lengths to supply just the right wine glasses, tulle streamers with gold stars and polka dots, a carved Christ Child, and a set of puppets. He dutifully assisted with the Wagners' Christmas ritual of gilding apples and nuts, and just as dutifully perused the galleys of Richard Wagner's autobiography. On the morning of the first day of Christmas in 1870, a little orchestra assembled in the stairwell to perform Wagner's new composition, the *Siegfried Idyll,* in honor of Cosima's birthday. Nietzsche improvised on the piano, while Cosima listened politely and Richard Wagner left the room, barely able to contain his laughter.

Wagner made a quick assessment of Nietzsche's abilities and noted some good qualities that he supposed would come in handy for his own purposes. He wrote: "You could take over quite a lot for me, perhaps one entire half of my calling!" Wagner went on to maintain that he was grappling with philosophy but had little to show for his efforts. Philology, by contrast, was as important to Wagner as music to Nietzsche. The two could complement each other perfectly. Nietzsche should remain a philologist and "conduct" him, and the philologist in turn could be guided and inspired by the musician. Wagner wrote on February 12, 1870: "Now you must demonstrate the purpose of philology and help me to usher in the 'Renaissance' in which Plato embraces Homer, and Homer, filled with Plato's ideas, really does become the greatest possible Homer" (*N/W* 1,58).

Wagner encouraged the young professor to undertake a bold endeavor in classical philology. Nietzsche, who was captivated by the idea of contributing to the "great Renaissance" of which Wagner had provided vague hints, began to write his book on tragedy, surmising that while it would most likely not move him ahead in his profession, it would afford him a better understanding of himself. This book would make for an extravagant digression within the field of philology and adopt the style of the "adventurer and circumnavigator of the inner world called 'human'" (2,21; *HH* Preface § 7). Still grounded in philology, but overpowered by the will to dance, Nietzsche wrote his first masterpiece: *The Birth of Tragedy.*

CHAPTER 3

The Birth of
The Birth of Tragedy

*The vortex of being • Fundamental cruelty • Nietzsche
goes to war • Slaves • Moral vs. aesthetic thinking • Fear
of uprising • Glimpses into the innermost secrets of culture
• Bright lights and blinders in the face of enormity •
Dionysian wisdom*

O_N *JULY 2, 1868,* Nietzsche confessed to Sophie Ritschl, the
wife of his esteemed teacher of classical philology and sponsor, that he
was seeking an opportunity to combine philology and music. "Maybe I
will find a philological subject that can be treated musically, and then I
will babble like an infant and heap up images like a barbarian who has
fallen asleep in front of an antique head of Venus, and still be in the right
despite the 'flourishing haste' of the exposition" (*B* 2,299). This letter
was written before Nietzsche met Wagner. The young classical philologist, who had already mastered his profession to the point that it bored
him "to write down sober trains of thought with the requisite discretion
and *alla breve*" (*B* 2,299), began to indulge in daydreams of this sort.

Treating philological material "musically" implies more than simply
introducing musical themes. It requires the production of music, "which
happens to be written with words instead of notes" (*B* 2,298). Nietzsche
sought a theme that would allow him to create music with words. After

meeting Wagner, he discovered that the theme had been right in front of his nose all along. It was Greek tragedy. Even before his encounter with Wagner, Nietzsche had dealt with this topic, but only now did he discover the "vortex of being" that it offered, as he stated in a draft of a preface to *The Birth of Tragedy* (7,351).

Nietzsche wrote this first book while still beholden to the philological profession and wanting to vindicate his premature academic appointment, when he had neither doctorate nor postdoctoral thesis in hand, with a dazzling publication. Later, in his "Attempt at Self-Criticism," written in 1886, he put these motives behind him. In retrospect, Nietzsche described himself as a "disciple of an as yet 'unknown God,'" who, under the "cloak of the scholar," had nothing in mind but seeking "fellow revelers and luring them into new secret alleys and dance floors" (1,14; *BT* "Attempt at Self-Criticism" § 3).

Greek tragedy became a dance floor on which one could be pulled into the "vortex of being."

The individual stages of *The Birth of Tragedy* can be readily distinguished. First came two public lectures, "Greek Music Drama," which was delivered on January 18, 1870, and "Socrates and Tragedy," on February 1, 1870.

In the first of these two lectures, Nietzsche developed his thesis that Greek tragedy originated in Dionysian festivals. This lecture remained entirely within the framework of contemporary classical philology. Nietzsche had borrowed a standard work on Greek tragedy, Karl Otfried Müller's *Geschichte der griechischen Literatur* (History of Greek Literature, 1857) from the university library in Basel. Müller's book referred to the cult of Dionysus as the germ cell of Greek drama. His book provided many revealing details concerning the dancers' goat and deer hide costumes, their masks, and their "need to emerge from themselves and become alien to themselves" (Latacz 38). Nietzsche, however, wished to move well beyond the typical parameters of classical philology, which kept a strict distance from its subject matter, and to immerse himself in the delirium of these festivals. The "impediment" of scholarship is more of a hindrance, Nietzsche argued, because its ideal of clarity can only impair our receptivity to darker forces: "all growth and evolution in the sphere of art must take place in the depths of night" (1,516; GMD).

Nietzsche wanted to lead his readers straight into this night. He depicted the ecstasies and excesses of agitated, frenzied crowds, comparing them to the Saint Vitus dances in the Middle Ages, which some scholars dismissively label a "folk epidemic" (1,521; GMD). Evidence that their negative assessment is misguided lies in antiquity, where this so-called folk epidemic of Dionysian excess gave rise to Greek drama and endowed it with authority. Nietzsche declared that it was the misfortune of modern arts "not to have flowed from such a mysterious source" (1,521). But how do excess and ecstasy result in tragedy on the stage? Nietzsche outlined the individual phases of the process. The individual loses any consciousness of his individuality when seized by this frenzy; he disappears into the excited crowd of revelers and blends with it. Individuals excite one another once they blend into the aroused group, which shares a set of visions and images. The "Dionysian revelers" believe that they are seeing and experiencing as one. Then, however, and every time the moment of awakening from this frenzy arrives anew, each person falls back into his isolation. This is the difficult and risky transition to sobriety, a transition that demands a ritual accompaniment and support. The performance of a tragedy at the conclusion of the Dionysian festivals is this very ritual of transition from the collective frenzy into the everyday life of the city. Attic drama, Nietzsche explained, was made possible only because "some of this Dionysian natural vitality" was preserved on the stage of the theater.

Which aspects of Dionysian natural vitality were retained? The ritual play stages both integration into collective experience and isolation. There are the protagonists on the stage, and there is the chorus. When the individual in the tragedy meets his doom, he is doing penance for the guilt of being an individual. It is the chorus that will outlive the individual, which is why the protagonists onstage appear as though they were a vision of the chorus. And, Nietzsche declared, the chorus allows the writer of tragedy to bring the audience and its visions up onto the stage. Attic theatergoers sought a state of reverie when settling down under the open afternoon sky on the stones of the wide rotunda, and their wishes were fulfilled. They were in a festive mood and prepared to be transformed and to step outside of themselves. Then the music sounded, the rhythmic song of the chorus, which set the bodies of the singers and listeners in motion. An expectant atmosphere arose, and when the individual figures took the stage, it was as if a common vision had been born from this atmosphere. The protagonists acted in front of the chorus, first just one, then several at a time.

But some individuals asserted their individuality against the collective chorus, coming to the fore and embodying "living dissonance." As is typical of dissonance, a dramatic tension ensued onstage. The protagonists detached themselves as a single voice from the chorus, developed their dissonant role, and were resubmerged into the unison of the chorus. The dissonant individual could not hold up for long, and when he foundered, he returned to the lap of the music and the chorus reabsorbed him. The characters and their actions stood out from the music like an island from the ocean. The chorus and its music were omnipresent. The action onstage was public, in the full light of day. Nothing remained hidden from the chorus. The individual had nowhere to hide; the music of the world would devour him. For the Greeks, insisted Nietzsche, the task of music was to "transform the suffering . . . of the heroes into intensely strong sympathy from the audience" (1,528; GMD).

Greek tragedy dramatized power plays. The protagonist controlled the words, but it was the choral music that controlled the maker of words. Words are subject to misunderstandings and misconceptions; they do not originate in our innermost being, and they also do not reach that far. They hover at the periphery of being. Music is different. It "goes right to your heart, as the true universal language that is understood everywhere" (1,528f.; GMD).

This first lecture already indicates that words bring about the demise of tragedy. Logos defeats the pathos of tragedy. Tragedy comes to an end when language is emancipated from music and overwhelms it with its own logic. What is language? An organ of consciousness. Music, however, is being. With the decline of tragedy, being and consciousness no longer mesh. Consciousness is closed off from being and becomes flat. For Nietzsche, the demise of the ancient tragedy of pathos signals the beginning of the new tragedy of Logos, which, according to him, is where we still find ourselves today.

Regarding the derivation of tragedy from the festivals of Dionysus, Nietzsche was still within the boundaries of the classical philology of his contemporaries. But the main argument of his second lecture, which was already suggested at the end of the first lecture with a reference to the "decomposition" (1,530; GMD) of tragedy through intellectualization, had to have provoked the philological establishment. For this reason, Nietzsche tried to prevent this lecture from coming to the attention of his teacher Ritschl. Ritschl did ultimately hear about it and, as one can imagine, was hardly pleased. As though Nietzsche needed to atone for his overly freewheeling jaunts, he offered his teacher a traditional philological essay for inclusion in an anthology published by the professional organization Meletemata Societatis philologicae Lipsiensis.

As Nietzsche reported to his friend Rohde in mid-February 1870, the lecture entitled "Socrates and Tragedy" "aroused terror and misconceptions" (*B* 3,95). What could have been so terrifying and open to misconceptions about this lecture?

Nietzsche criticized the high esteem accorded to consciousness, particularly the consequences of Socrates' disastrous idea that "everything must be conscious to be good" (1,540; ST). First, this idea destroys the essence of tragedy, and then it proceeds to diminish and impede the creative unconscious as a whole. Socrates ruptured the power of music and replaced it with dialectics. He was a disaster who ushered in a rationalism that wanted nothing further to do with the depths of being. He marked the beginning of knowledge devoid of wisdom. In the domain

of tragedy, the pathos of fate was displaced by intrigues and calcula-
tions. The representation of life forces became the staging of cleverly
devised machinations. The mechanism of cause and effect dislodged the
link between guilt and expiation. On the stage, discussion took the place
of song. The action onstage forfeited its mystery, and the protagonists
suffered because of banal miscalculations. The prevailing mood of
tragedy was lost. "We get the feeling," Nietzsche concluded, "that all of
these characters met their end as a result not of tragedy but of errors in
logic" (1,546; ST).

Nietzsche treated Socrates as a symptom of a radical and momentous
cultural transformation that had carried over into his own era. The will
to knowledge overwhelmed the life forces of myth, religion, and art.
Human life breaks away from the obscure roots of its instincts and passions as if being had to justify itself to consciousness. Life strained
toward the light, and dialectics triumphed over the dark music of fate.
An optimistic hope was aroused that life could be corrected, steered, and
calculated by consciousness. Music drama might have died of "delusion,
will, and woe" (1,132; *BT* § 20), but its death would not be permanent.
Nietzsche's lecture concluded with hints of a possible rebirth of Greek
tragedy. Richard Wagner was not mentioned by name, but it is likely that
all audience members would have realized that he was meant.

Will the renewed music drama be able to take hold, and will it be able
to reawaken a feeling for the tragic abysses in an age of optimism that
had been steered by the sciences? These were the questions Nietzsche
pondered at the close of his lecture. He indicated that the fate of the
music drama in the present era would depend on the strength of its
antagonist, the "Socratism of our days." His original lecture manuscript,
which he sent to the Wagners in Tribschen, concluded with the sentence
"This Socratism is the current Jewish press: need I say more?" (14,101).

Classifying subversive knowledge as a "Jewish" principle reflected a
basic conviction in the Wagner household. Perhaps Nietzsche had
adopted it from the Wagners. Even so, Cosima Wagner considered it
necessary to warn this young admirer. "I do have one request for you

now," wrote Cosima on February 5, 1870, "namely, not to stir up this hornets' nest. Do you follow me? Do not mention the Jews, especially not in passing. Later, when you want to take up the bitter fight, in God's name, but not from the beginning; you want to avoid having everything on your path turn confused and chaotic. . . . You do, of course, know that from the bottom of my soul I agree with your claim" (*N/W* 1,52).

Richard Wagner also applauded Nietzsche's lecture. He concurred with each of its points, but admitted to reacting with "shock" to the "boldness" with which Nietzsche "communicates [his] very new ideas" (*N/W* 1,50). Wagner, like his wife, counseled caution. "I am worried about you," he wrote, "and hope from the bottom of my heart that you do not suffer any consequences." He then offered the suggestion that Nietzsche develop his ideas in a "large comprehensive work" (*N/W* 1,50).

There are indications that Nietzsche conceived the plan for *The Birth of Tragedy* in response to this suggestion. He began to have a strange premonition of great things to come and of what he would create. In mid-February 1870, he wrote to Rohde: "Scholarship, art, and philosophy are now growing together in me so fully that someday I am sure to give birth to a centaur" (*B* 3,95).

Early in the summer of 1870, Nietzsche encountered an idea that would guide his understanding and evaluation not only of the culture of antiquity but of the dynamism and vividness of culture as a whole. This idea was the discovery of the interplay of fundamental polar forces of culture, to which Nietzsche assigned the names of the two gods Apollo and Dionysus. In "The Dionysian Worldview," written in the summer of 1870, he began employing the contrastive pair "Apollonian-Dionysian" to interpret Greek tragedy.

The reflections developed in his first two lectures led him right to the threshold of this discovery. The first lecture treated the origin of tragedy in Dionysian festivals; the second discussed the "Apollonian clarity" (1,544; ST) of Socrates. Now he recognized that tragedy represents a compromise between these two basic drives. Passions and music are

Dionysian; language and dialectics on the stage are Apollonian. A combination of the two yields an enlightening performance of the dark forces of fate.

Nietzsche began by viewing the Apollonian and Dionysian as artistic elements of style. Apollo is the god of form, clarity, solid contours, bright dreams, and, above all, individuality. Sculpture, architecture, the Homeric world of the gods, the epic spirit—all of these are Apollonian. Dionysus, by contrast, is the wild god of transport, rapture, ecstasy, "the orgiastic." Music and dance are the preferred forms. The appeal of the Apollonian lies in the fact that the artifice is never forgotten for a single instant and the awareness of distances is retained. In the Dionysian arts, by contrast, boundaries are fluid. A person in the thrall of music, dance, or other such artistic exploit loses his distance. The "Dionysian reveler" does not see himself from without, whereas the Apollonian remains reflexive; he enjoys his enthusiasm without succumbing to it. The Apollonian celebrates individuality, whereas the Dionysian breaks down the confines of the individual.

What had begun as an analysis of aesthetic principles broadened out to a first, bold sketch of the basic metaphysical conditions of human existence. This is where Schopenhauerian philosophy came into play for Nietzsche, because the Dionysian was held to be the world of the compulsive will, and Apollo was responsible for ideas and awareness. For Nietzsche, as a follower of Schopenhauer, it was unquestionably evident from this constellation that the Dionysian represented the primary, elemental life force, and that this facet of life, while creative, was also cruel and unholy, just as Schopenhauer had construed the world of the will as creative, cruel, and unholy.

By reinterpreting the artistic and stylistic traits of the Apollonian and Dionysian as metaphysical life forces, Nietzsche had taken the first decisive step in his intellectual biography. From this point on, he believed that he held the key to unlock the innermost secret of cultures, their past and their future.

The Dionysian, in Nietzsche's vision, is the colossal course of life itself. Cultures are the fragile and always precarious attempts to create a zone of habitability within it. Cultures sublimate Dionysian energies; cultural institutions, rituals, and explanations are representations that live off the actual substance of life and yet hold it at a distance. The Dionysian lurks before and under civilization. It is the dimension of the colossal power that both threatens and allures.

Alluring in the Dionysian is a threefold dismantling process, a threefold transcendence of the *"principium individuationis"* (1,554; DW). Man steps beyond his confines to blend with nature. He emerges from his detachment to join with his fellow man in the "orgiastic" experience of love and the frenzy of the masses. The third barrier is set aside from within the individual. Consciousness opens up to admit the unconscious. An ego that anxiously clings to its identity must perceive this threefold dismantling as a threat. A Dionysian, by contrast, would be receptive to the experience of a pleasurable demise.

When Nietzsche wrote his essay "The Dionysian Worldview" in the summer of 1870, the Franco-Prussian War had just been declared. He regarded the outbreak of the war as a Dionysian breakthrough complete with tragic-heroic atmosphere. "Our entire threadbare culture is plunging at the breast of the horrible demon," he wrote to Rohde on July 16, 1870 (*B* 3,130). The word "demon" is meant as a label not for France but rather, as Nietzsche stated elsewhere, for "military genius" (1,775; TGS). "Military genius" breaks through the thin crust of civilization; it appears when life turns serious. Nietzsche's reactions to the war make explicit what he had been hinting at in his perception of the Dionysian world. This world of the elemental will is also the Heraclitean world of war, which, in turn, is the father of all things.

In this hour of truth, as the "terrible foundations of being are revealed" (*B* 3,154; Nov. 7, 1870), Nietzsche felt that he could not simply remain at his desk. He reported to the front as a medical orderly, even though Cosima Wagner advised him against it and recommended that he send the soldiers cigars rather than himself (*N/W* 1,96; Aug. 9, 1870). Nietzsche spent a mere two weeks in September at the western battlefields. He witnessed the dead being gathered from the fields, and he accompanied a transport of the wounded. In the process, he contracted both dysentery and diphtheria. He wrote to Richard Wagner on September 11, 1870: "So, after a brief run of four weeks, working on the world at large, I am already thrown back upon myself" (*B* 3,143). He was unable to shake off the "ghastly images" (*B* 3,146) of dying and mutilation on the fields of corpses. When he called the "Dionysian worldview" a "glorification and transfiguration of the horrific and dreadful aspects of existence as remedies of existence" (1,570; DW), he knew the feeling from personal experience. In a draft of a preface to *The Birth of Tragedy*, addressed to Richard Wagner in February 1871, he declared: "I have hopes as well, which enabled me, while the earth trembled under the thudding strides of Ares, to remain aloof and engaged with my theme even in the midst of the terrible direct effects of the war; indeed, I recall lying together with wounded men in the freight car in the lonely night, and although I was charged with their care, my thoughts turned to the three abysses of tragedy: their names are 'delusion, will, woe'" (7,354).

Nietzsche pinned his hopes on a revival of culture, which had become blunted in the "sunset glow of peace" (*B* 3,130) and had dislodged the Dionysian-Heraclitean solemnity of life. Chances for a revival would be good because "military genius" had invaded bourgeois reality as a Dionysian force.

The role of war as a life force was more prominent in the original plan for *The Birth of Tragedy* than in its final version. Nietzsche opted not to include a lengthy passage about war and slavery in Greece, but instead reworked this passage into a preface to a book he planned to write called "The Greek State." In this text, the Dionysian world and the world of Heraclitus merge. The Dionysian life force is identified with war as the father of all things. A similar train of thought is manifest in "Homer's Contest," an essay written at the same time. The world of the will, seen in Schopenhauerian terms, which Nietzsche identified with the Dionysian facet of life, had a military dimension. Schopenhauer had conceived of the world will as a unity of mutually hostile embodiments of the individual will. It is therefore not surprising that Nietzsche discovered this hostility in the elemental facet of life and in the foundation of culture as well.

The Dionysian in general and its bellicose aspect in particular are subject to cultural transformations by means of ritualization and sublimation. Nietzsche interpreted the ancient institution of contests as one such cultural metamorphosis. According to him, the Greeks had a "streak of cruelty, a tigerlike desire to annihilate" (1,783; HC). In the Homeric epics, for example, we gaze into "abysses of hate" (1,784; HC). The *Iliad* depicts the wrath of Achilles when he drags the corpse of Hector through the city on a chariot as though it were not offensive and simply a natural outgrowth of heroism. In Nietzsche's view, this example reveals the dimensions of a shocking archaic cruelty that had already been mitigated by the time of Homer. In the "pre-Homeric world" (1,785; HC), it must have been far worse. The little we know of that world would indicate "night and horror" (1,785; HC).

Greek culture also exemplified how this militant cruelty could be sublimated by contests. Contests in the areas of politics, social life, and art could be found throughout Greece. Nietzsche quoted from Hesiod, whose didactic poem *Works and Days* opened with the description of the dual Erises, one the goddess of discord and the other the goddess of envy. One Eris, who arises from the dismal night, promotes wicked feuding and evokes our desire for strife. But Zeus placed a second Eris at her side, who redirects the resultant discord in a productive manner by inducing people to compete rather than murder. Their very rivalry serves to elevate mankind. Nietzsche quoted Hesiod: " 'She [the second Eris] impels even the most shiftless man to work; and if someone who lacks possessions sees someone who is rich, he hurries to sow and plant and manage his household in the same way; neighbor competes with neighbor, striving for prosperity. This Eris is beneficial for mankind'" (1,786; HC).

Jacob Burckhardt had brought the agonistic feature of Greek culture to Nietzsche's attention, and Nietzsche inserted this concept of the transformation of war into contests into his framework of the transformation of Dionysian energies into a livable Apollonian form. There is the danger, however, that Dionysian energy dissipates once it has assumed Apollonian forms. Therefore, Nietzsche concluded, in order to preserve culture it is imperative that its formidable foundation break forth and, like the lava of a volcano, revive the soil to a state of even greater fertility. This is how he understood the culturally productive power of "military genius" (7,347; TGS).

Nietzsche's highest goal was always the flourishing of culture. Of Burckhardt's three major forces of existence—namely state, religion, and culture—culture was the highest objective for Nietzsche, who wanted everything to revolve around it. He was outraged by even the slightest hint that culture had been subordinated to the objectives of the state or the economy.

His 1872 lecture series entitled "On the Future of Our Educational Institutions," gave eloquent expression to this outrage. Here Nietzsche attempted to defend the ideal of development of character against the economic and political instrumentalization of character formation, which, in his eyes, had degenerated into mere instruction. Everything should be subordinated to culture, including the Franco-Prussian War, which Nietzsche had initially hailed, hoping that it would be able to revive culture. He wrote to his friend Rohde after deciding to participate in the war effort: "we will once again need monasteries" (*B* 3,131). Nietzsche was not motivated by the triumph of Prussia, the birth of a strong nation-state, or even chauvinism or hatred of France. When it became clear to him that victory in war worked to the advantage not of culture but of the state, money-making, and military conceit, he distanced himself. On November 7, 1870, he wrote to Gersdorff: "I am terribly concerned about the impending state of culture. If only we do not have to pay too dearly for the tremendous national success in an area in which I, for one, do not want to face any loss. Between you and me, I now consider Prussia a power that is extremely dangerous for culture" (*B* 3,155). One month later, he confided to his mother: "My sympathies for the current German war of conquest are gradually fading. I think the future of our German culture would appear to be in greater jeopardy than ever" (*B* 3,164).

Greek antiquity served as Nietzsche's model of how war benefited culture. The shift of martial impulses to the culturally productive form of the contest was exemplary in ancient Greece. But war is even more fundamentally linked to the destiny of culture. In the essay "The Greek State," Nietzsche employed the Hobbesian argument of "nature" and the "bellum omnium contra omnes" ("war of all against all") to demonstrate that the state arises from attempts to subdue war within its boundaries, however these may be defined, and to redirect it outward to other communities. There will always be periods of "terrible thunderstorms of war" between nations, but in the "intervals," society has the time and opportunity to produce "the radiant blossoms of genius" of culture in "the concentrated effect of that *bellum,* turned inward" (7,344; TGS). Periodic war as a test case and as a re-immersion in the Dionysian-Heraclitean element is indispensable in order for culture to blossom. Culture requires a foundation of cruelty; it is a beautiful culmination of the appalling. The necessary association of "battlefield and artwork" (7,344) reveals the truth about culture.

Culture requires more than just the cruelty of war. According to Nietzsche, a second form of cruelty is a necessary precondition. In his discussion of the cultural nation in Greek antiquity, which he considered exemplary, he unabashedly put a name to the form of cruelty that he was advocating: slavery.

Every advanced culture needs an exploitable, working class, a "slave class" (1,117; *BT* § 18), Nietzsche declared without mincing his words. He went on to write: "There is nothing more dreadful than a barbaric slave class that has learned to regard its existence as an injustice and sets about taking revenge not only for itself but for all generations" (1,117).

Nietzsche penned these words in early 1871 in a preface to an unwritten book called "The Greek State," a text he presented to Cosima Wagner in a private printing but did not publish in any other form. The

newspapers reported from Paris in May 1871 that insurgents had pil-
laged and destroyed the Louvre (in actual fact, there had only been a fire
in the Tuileries). Nietzsche interpreted the event as a beacon of impending barbarism. On May 27, 1871, he wrote to Councillor Wilhelm
Vischer-Bilfinger in the context of excusing his absence from a university meeting: "The reports of the past few days have been so awful that
my state of mind is altogether intolerable. What does it mean to be a
scholar in the face of such earthquakes of culture! One feels so atomistic! You use your entire life and the best of your power to deepen your
understanding of and learn to explain a period of culture; how does this
profession seem if a single unfortunate day reduces to ashes the most
precious documents of these periods! It is the worst day of my life" (*B*
3,195).

   Nietzsche regarded the fire in Paris as a precursor of major crises to
come. He attributed these social conflicts to an increase in demands
owing to a heightened awareness of suffering among the masses rather
than to any deterioration of their standard of living. He watched the
masses stepping onto the political arena, with incalculable repercus-
sions. When he learned in the fall of 1869 that a convention of the
International Workers Association was being held in Basel, of all cities,
Nietzsche was filled with alarm. A few years later, he was seized with the
suspicion that the "International" was scheming to prevent the Bayreuth
Festival. He considered efforts to solve the "social question" with reference to the workers a threat to culture. He accused "democrats" of
wanting to emancipate the masses and leading them to believe in the
"dignity of labor" and the "dignity of man" (1,765), with the result that
the masses only then would perceive their situation as a flagrant injustice
and demand equity. They would compare their depressed circumstances
to the glitter of high culture, which they abhor because it is not intended
for them and because they do not figure in it, although they have
wrought the material preconditions for it with the labor of their own
hands. But are the claims to social justice and liberation from exploitation not justified, and is it not understandable to hate a culture that the

masses view as nothing more than vile luxury? Nietzsche asked himself these questions and found himself pondering the connection between culture and justice. He drew a set of conclusions that would endure, some vacillations notwithstanding, until his final creative period of his work on *The Will to Power*.

Life, as we saw earlier, is tragic. It unfolds with enormous suffering, death, and cruelty of all kinds. In *The Birth of Tragedy*, Nietzsche coined the famous formula "Existence and the world are eternally justified solely as an aesthetic phenomenon" (1,47; *BT* § 5). In "The Greek State," and in other fragments from this period that addressed issues pertaining to the social mass movement and Nietzsche's fear of the Paris Commune, the implicitly political meaning of this formula came through more clearly than in *The Birth of Tragedy*, which had muted this topic. In his notes, Nietzsche sharpened the problem of the link between culture and social justice. When it comes to culture, he contended, a decision must be made as to its essential aim. The two major options are the well-being of the greatest possible number of people, on the one hand, and the success of individual lives, on the other. The moral point of view gives priority to the well-being of the greatest possible number of people, whereas the aesthetic view declares that the meaning of culture lies in the culmination of auspicious forms, the "peak of rapture."

Nietzsche opted for the aesthetic view. In the fall of 1873, he noted in a fragment that individuals must bow to the "good of the highest individuals," namely "creative people" (7,733). The latter produce great cultural achievements in art, philosophy, and the sciences; these achievements are the direct fruits of exploitative labor. In some cases, creative individuals are themselves works of art that merit our attention. These heroes of creativity are justified not by their social usefulness but by their superior existence. Although they do not improve mankind, they embody and display its better possibilities. Culture and states are justified if these "highest exemplars can live and create" in them (7,733). These "highest exemplars" are, according to *The Birth of Tragedy*, the "bright lights" (1,65; *BT* § 9) in the dark night of the tragic sense of being alive.

If happiness and freedom of the greatest possible number are given higher priority, Nietzsche claimed, the result is a democratic culture in which mass taste triumphs. The orientation of a democratic state to comprehensive welfare, human dignity, freedom, egalitarian justice, and protection of the weak impedes any prospects for development of great personalities. The "bright lights" vanish from history and along with them any last vestige of meaning.

In his quest to defend aesthetic significance in history, Nietzsche assailed democracy as far back as the early 1870s, even before his shrill attacks on the "complete appeasement of the democratic herd animal" (11,587; *WP* § 125) some years later. Nietzsche considered the ancient Greek slaveholder society the paragon of culture for the very reason that it disallowed concessions to the "democratic herd animal." He extolled antiquity for being honest enough not to have covered up the terrible foundation from which its blossom grew. The ancient Greeks freely confessed to the need for slaves. We can certainly find evidence in Plato and Aristotle just how staunchly and aggressively the need for slavery was defended in the name of the continued existence of culture. Just as people need brains and brawn, Nietzsche argued, society needs the hardworking hands of laborers for a privileged class, allowing that class "to engender and fulfill a new world of needs" (1,766; TGS). Slave society is an especially crass example of how refinement and culture rest on an "awful premise. In order to have a broad, deep and fertile soil for artistic development, the overwhelming majority must be slavishly subjected to the necessities of life in order to serve a minority beyond the measure of its individual needs" (1,767; TGS). More recent eras have glorified the world of work, but glorification is self-deception, because even the "terminological fallacy" of the "dignity of work" does not alter anything in the fundamental injustice of life, which metes out mechanical work to some and creative activity to the more highly gifted. Slave societies were brutally frank about their inequities, whereas our modern times feign contrition but are unwilling to forgo exploitation in the service of culture. Thus, if art justifies our existence aesthetically, it does so on the foundation of "cruelty" (1,768; TGS).

This "cruelty in the essence of every culture" confirmed for Nietzsche that existence is an "eternal wound" (1,115; *BT* § 18). The remedy of art, which is its aesthetic justification, holds the wound open. People are sacrificed for the beauty of art, which is why the existence of art adds a further injustice to the wretched state of the world. For this reason, Nietzsche was also prepared to experience guilt in defending slavery, because he was one of those privileged few who could enjoy the aesthetic justification of the world. He knew that his own existence was built on the sacrifice of others. In a letter of June 21, 1871, he rebuked his friend Gersdorff, who had arrogantly railed at the culturally hostile mob in Paris. Nietzsche wrote that scholarly and artistic life seemed an "absurdity" in view of the fact that the brilliant works of centuries could be undone by an act of vandalism within minutes. He had clung to the "metaphysical value of art, which cannot exist merely for the sake of poor human beings, but instead must fulfill higher missions." "However," he went on to write, "even when my pain was at its worst, I was unable to cast a stone against those villains, who struck me as nothing more than bearers of a general guilt, which ought to give us food for thought!" (*B* 3,204).

Nietzsche applied the expression "general guilt" to the iconoclastic Paris Commune in this particular instance, but he also extended it to the culpability of art in general, which profits from the injustice of the world and even from "slavery." He did not sidestep the problem, but openly avowed the postulate that if we wanted to do away with this guilt-ridden entanglement of art, we would have to destroy the principle of every advanced culture. One thing was certain: the principles of equality and justice, taken to their logical conclusion, would unleash hostility on culture. But because art also profits from injustice, those who enjoy the privilege of partaking in art have no right to lapse into arrogance. They need to remain aware of the link between art and guilt.

Nietzsche was touching on an old issue, namely the question of theodicy, which was once applied to the relationship between God and the world and was now being reframed in terms of the relationship between art and non-artistic reality. By formulating the aesthetic justification of the world in the way he did, he was explicitly reworking the classic theodicy question, which had been posed as far back as Job and continued to be pondered by Leibniz: How can the existence of God be justified when there is evil in the world? Once the ancient God was no longer in the picture, the theodicy question could be applied to art in roughly the following terms: How can the relatively luxurious enterprise of art be justified when there is evil in the world? The fact that some produce art while others suffer is surely a scandalous proof of injustice in the world. The misery of the world and the incantation of art—how can they fit together? The young Hugo von Hofmannsthal later wrote a celebrated poem on this theme: "Many truly down below must perish / Where the heavy oars of ships are passing; / Others by the helm up there have dwelling, / Know the flight of birds and starry countries" (Hofmannsthal 34–35).

Nietzsche's notion that art grows out of a dark foundation of injustice and that "cruelty" and sacrifice are essential components of culture would provoke anyone who would prefer to see art paired with social progress. Nietzsche welcomed this provocation because he regarded social progress as a threat to art. One day, he wrote, there would be a "rebellion of the oppressed masses against drone-like individuals." It would be "the roar of sympathy that would knock down the walls of culture. The urge for justice, for equal sharing of suffering would engulf all other ideas" (7,340).

This is precisely what happened. In the revolutionary social movements of the twentieth century, there occurred a large-scale betrayal of art motivated by solidarity with suffering. Heinrich Heine had predicted this turn of events along with Nietzsche. In 1855, Heine described the communists, with whose goals he sympathized, as follows: "with their red fists they are smashing all of the marble structures of my beloved art world . . . the shopkeepers hawking their goods will use my *Book of Songs* for shopping bags, to store coffee or snuff for the old wives of the future" (Heine 5,232). Other artists were prepared to dispense with the restrictions of cultural life. Tolstoy, for example, in reaction to the ocean of social ills that surrounded him, stopped writing toward the end of his life and called upon writers to contribute to society in more practical ways than by fabricating stories. His decision marked a prelude to the epoch of the great destruction of culture in the name of social revolution.

Nietzsche was convinced that his era posed a twofold danger to art. Art could be destroyed by social revolution, or it could lose its dignity as an end-in-itself by conforming to social utility. Either it would be swallowed up by a socially oriented movement, or it would join forces with it and degenerate to political engagement. In either case, bad times loomed ahead for the muses.

Not all of these reflections were developed in *The Birth of Tragedy*. Ideas pertaining to the cultural necessity of war and slavery were only intimated and not stated with the provocative directness of the notes. Nietzsche pondered the consequences of his conviction that the underbelly of life was Dionysian-Heraclitean, cruel, vital, and dangerous. Life was monstrous and not at all the way gentle humanism pictured it. In his 1872 essay "On Truth and Falsehood in an Extramoral Sense," Nietzsche depicted the relationship of consciousness to the underbelly of life as follows: "Woe to the portentous curiosity that could manage to look out of and down from the chamber of consciousness through a slit and that now began to realize that man rests on the heartless, the greedy, the insatiable, and the murderous in the indifference of his ignorance, hanging in dreams, as it were, on the back of a tiger. In this constellation, where in the world does the urge for truth originate?" (1,877; TF § 1).

Nietzsche used the term "Dionysian wisdom" (1,67: *BT* § 9) to designate this mode of perception, which problematizes the very act of cognition in view of the monstrous process of life. When he later credited *The Birth of Tragedy* for having presented "science for the first time as problematic and questionable" (1,13; *BT* "Attempt at Self-Criticism" § 2), he cited "Dionysian wisdom" as the inspiration for this book.

"Dionysian wisdom" was indeed the decisive step forward of *The Birth of Tragedy*. It was an intellectual operation entirely within the tradition of transcendental philosophy. Nietzsche anticipated a horizon that would comprise all knowledge and serve as a backdrop to all of life's activities. He was reaching out to the absolutism of reality that can never be grasped. This is no speculative beyond, but the embodiment of all reality in which perception, life, and art take place. The transcendental act does not construct transcendence, but rather is the attempt to capture and relativize to what extent the inexhaustibility of reality can be recognized.

The inexhaustible is, of course, not recognized. How could it be? It is unknowable! But the inexhaustible is experienced in the moment that it becomes evident that knowledge cannot exhaust life in its tremendous abundance. However, the need to conceptualize the inexhaustible and not just give it a name is the age-old allure of metaphysics, and it was irresistible to Nietzsche. Kant had warned against this allure. In his otherwise dry-as-dust *Critique of Pure Reason,* he contrived a poetic image for this allure: "We have not only traveled around . . . but actually traversed the land of pure intellect, and defined everything in its place. However, this land is an island . . . surrounded by a wide stormy ocean . . . where many banks of fog and a great deal of ice beginning to melt pose as new lands, and by incessantly fooling the sailor who is eagerly moving about filled with false hopes in quest of discoveries, entangles him in adventures from which he will never desist and yet will never be able to complete" (Kant 3,267).

Kant remained on the island and called the "stormy ocean" the ominous "thing in itself." Schopenhauer ventured out farther by calling the ocean the "will." For Nietzsche, absolute reality was "Dionysian." In the words of Goethe, whom he quoted, reality is " 'an eternal ocean, a mutable weaving, a glowing life'" (1,64; *BT* § 8). When the Dionysian is understood in this way, it is not merely one aspect of reality but its very core. As if wanting to respond directly to Kant's metaphor of the ocean of the unknowable, Nietzsche the Dionysian wrote in his later *Gay Science:* "Finally our ships may once again set sail, sailing out no matter what the danger; any risks taken by the lover of knowledge are permitted once again; the ocean, *our* ocean, lies open there once again. Perhaps there has never been such an 'open ocean'" (3,574; *GS* § 343).

Nietzsche did not always use the expression "Dionysian" in a strictly terminological sense to designate absolute reality. "Dionysian" was also his way to describe the "barbarism" of precivilized violence and sexual excesses (1,31; *BT* § 2) as well as subcivilized instincts. When Nietzsche employed the term "Dionysian" in the sense of precivilization or sub-civilization, this cultural-historical or anthropological use of the term continued to refer to its essential ontological and metaphysical meaning. The Dionysian is the "primordial unity" (1,38; *BT* § 4), an all-encompassing being that is ultimately incomprehensible. The concept of the Dionysian naturally implies a theoretical choice that, in turn, goes back to a defining experience. Even for the young Nietzsche, being was something precarious, at once threatening and enticing. He experienced it in "lightning, storm, and hail," and in his early notes there are references to the "world child" of Heraclitus, who playfully forged and destroyed worlds. It is indeed necessary to have experienced being as a monstrosity. Life that is roused to consciousness should be wary of being. Being turns Dionysian when familiar things turn eerie.

"Dionysian wisdom" is the power to endure Dionysian reality. A twofold endurance is involved, combining "hitherto unknown pleasure" and "disgust." Dionysian integration of the individual consciousness is a pleasure because the "bounds and limits of existence" are eradicated (1,56; *BT* § 7). However, when this condition has passed and everyday consciousness has resumed its domination over thinking and experience, "disgust" comes over the disillusioned Dionysian. This disgust can escalate to the point of horror: "In man's awareness of the truth he has now seen, only the horror and absurdity of existence are evident to him" (1,57; *BT* § 7).

What is going on here? Where is the horror manifest? Is the "truth" of the Dionysian the horror, or is it everyday reality that assumes a horrifying appearance because one has experienced the bliss of Dionysian transgression? Nietzsche means horror emanating from both directions. From the vantage point of everyday consciousness, the Dionysian is horrifying. By the same token, the Dionysian perspective regards everyday reality as horrifying. Conscious life moves between both outlooks, and this movement is tantamount to being torn in two. One is simultaneously transported by the Dionysian, with which life must retain contact to avoid becoming desolate, and dependent on the protective devices of civilization to avoid being sacrificed to the disintegrating power of the Dionysian.

It is hardly surprising that Nietzsche found the symbol for this precarious situation in the fate of Odysseus, who had himself bound to a mast in order to hear the song of the sirens without having to follow it to his own destruction. Odysseus embodies Dionysian wisdom. He hears the voice of temptation, but accepts the fetters of culture in a quest for self-preservation.

Nietzsche developed a typology of cultures from the perspective of how various cultures have succeeded in organizing life in the face of temptation. He formulated his question as follows: What system of blinders does each culture rely on to shut out the threatening power of the Dionysian and to channel essential Dionysian energies? Nietzsche posed this question fully aware that he was touching on the innermost secrets of each culture. He traced the surreptitious ways of the will to live and discovered how culturally inventive this will to live could be. To keep its creatures "clinging to life" (1,115; *BT* § 18), it wraps them in illusions. It ensures that some choose the "veil of beauty in art" and that others seek metaphysical solace in religion and philosophy in order to be reassured "that under the whirl of phenomena eternal life keeps flowing indestructibly." Still others are captivated by a "Socratic love of knowledge" and are deceived into thinking that knowledge can "heal the eternal wound of existence" (1,115). A mixture of these ingredients yields what we call culture. According to the proportions of the mixture, a culture will be predominantly artistic, such as that of Greek antiquity, or religious and metaphysical, as in the heyday of the Christian West and the eastern Buddhist world, or Socratic, emphasizing knowledge and science.

The latter type has dominated the modern era. The principle of Socrates brought us science and enlightenment, the long-term consequences of which were the ideas of democracy, justice, and equality. Knowledge would be the key to comprehending and turning around our fate. In all areas, people could themselves shape and determine the history of which they are a part. Nature, which reigns so unjustly by producing unequal talents and destinies, could be corrected or at least compensated for. There could be an end to the exploitation and enslavement of people. Nietzsche saw these consequences in the Socratic culture of knowledge and cognition, and he therefore made his own (and our) here and now begin with the Socratic victory of optimistic knowledge over a tragic approach to life, as we will see later.

It is important to keep in mind that both Dionysian and Apollonian forces were in play in all of the types of culture Nietzsche discussed. Art, religion, and knowledge are Apollonian forms in which Dionysian reality is both warded off and channeled. In this context, Nietzsche formulated a fundamental ontological principle for the relationship between the Dionysian and Apollonian in the final section of his *Birth of Tragedy*. "The consciousness of the human individual may receive just enough of the foundation of all existence, the Dionysian substratum of the world, as can be surmounted by the Apollonian power of transfiguration" (1,155; *BT* § 25).

Nietzsche derived his concept of strength and status from this ontological principle. People and cultures that can incorporate a major dose of Dionysian elemental force without cracking are strong and high in status. This strength also implies that the Apollonian power of transfiguration be equally predominant. Strong cultures and individuals wring beauty out of shocking elements. Greek culture is strong in this sense. We should not be misled by the cheerfulness of the Greeks; their prevailing sentiment was tragic and pessimistic. When Greek life awakened to consciousness, it gazed into the abyss. Horror was the precursor of the advance of the mind. Nietzsche cited the wise Silenus, the companion of Dionysus, who, according to an old story, replied to Midas's question of what would be the very best and most desirable for people: "You wretched species, children of chance and drudgery, why do you force me to tell you what you would greatly benefit from not hearing? The very best is far beyond your reach: not to be born, not to be, to be nothing. The second best for you, however, is to die soon" (1,35; *BT* § 3).

The underlying tragic sentiment of Greek culture went along these lines. Apollonian affirmation was based on a bold, vital "nonetheless." The Olympians owed their genesis to the same "drive that inspires art, as the completion and consummation of existence, enticing us to go on with our existence" (1,36; *BT* § 3); this artistic sphere resembled the ecstatic visions of a tortured martyr. The Apollonian will to culture erected a shield or, to use military terminology, a "perpetual military encampment" (1,41; *BT* § 4) against the elemental life forces. In the foreground or in the interior of the fortress, it situated the theater of life with all of its local gods, laws, virtues, artworks, tales, and political shrewdness. The Dionysian, however, as expressed in orgiastic cults and festivals, sacrificial rites, music and exhilaration, was perched far closer to the horrendous abyss of life, even though it also represented sublimation and cultivation. In short, the Dionysian life forces of pain and pleasure and "expire and expand" were still manifest in ancient art. Nietzsche's *Birth of Tragedy* closes with this rhetorical declaration: "How much must these people have suffered to achieve such beauty!" (1,156; *BT* § 25).

Nietzsche circled around the Dionysian and left its fundamental ambiguity in place. He regarded it as the absolute reality in which the individual enthusiastically disintegrates or goes down in horror, and considered it a grave error to approach the overpowering force of life without protective devices, namely the intermediaries of religion, scholarship, and art. Here again, Nietzsche brought up the subject of Oedipus. Oedipus had ventured forth too far, answering the questions of the sphinx and solving the "riddle of nature" (1,67; *BT* § 9). However, this solver of riddles was also the murderer of his father and the husband of his mother, thereby violating the "holiest order of nature." According to Nietzsche, "myth seems be whispering to us that . . . Dionysian wisdom is an abomination of nature, and that those who plunge nature into the abyss of annihilation by dint of their knowledge must themselves also suffer the disintegration of nature" (1,67). With his subsequent citation from the myth that "the edge of wisdom turns against the wise" (1,67), Nietzsche took the problem of truth to its logical extreme. How much truth can a person endure without being destroyed by it? Do we not also need the knowledge that allows us to discern how much life is in knowledge? If *The Birth of Tragedy* could be summarized in one sentence, it would read roughly as follows: it is better to approach the enormity of life with art, and best of all with music.

Nietzsche sought to achieve a paradox with *The Birth of Tragedy*. He shifted the Dionysian into the light of knowledge and at the same time undid the sobering effects of knowledge, later claiming that the book was composed for a singing voice. Perhaps his colleagues' harsh indictments stemmed from his attempt to pass off this book as classical philology. In any case, the philological establishment never quite forgave its pampered prodigy. Professor Ritschl, Nietzsche's former teacher and mentor, called the book "witty carousing." Ulrich Wilamowitz-Moellendorf, who later became the pope of classical philology, published a devastating critique in 1873, which closed with these words: "Let Mr. N keep his word, let him take up the thyrsus and move from India to Greece, but he should step down from the podium from which he is supposed to be teaching scholarship; let him gather tigers and panthers at his knees, but not Germany's young generation of philologists" (Janz 1,469).

Overnight Nietzsche had forfeited his philological reputation. Philologists do not get off lightly when they lure us onto secluded "dance floors" (1,14; *BT* "Attempt at Self-Criticism" § 3). The students in Basel deserted him. In Tribschen, by contrast, he was hailed. Richard Wagner was pleased with what he took to be an authentic portrait of himself as Dionysus. It escaped the attention of this egomaniac that Nietzsche was also portraying himself and his own passion for this "unknown god" (1,14).

Nietzsche had gotten involved with the Dionysian power of life from the relatively secure perspective of aestheticism. Now the game was turning serious, and Nietzsche would have to bear the social consequences of his stance, namely dissociation from the academy, which considered him "dead." His professorship in Basel became onerous, and he fell ill. Nonetheless, now that he had entered onto this path, he had every intention of sticking to it. Nietzsche built his critique of the will to knowledge around a Dionysian view of life. His 1872 essay "On Truth and Falsehood in an Extramoral Sense" opened with the following narrative: "Once upon a time, in a faraway corner of the universe, poured out and glistening in infinite solar systems, there was a constellation on which clever animals invented knowledge. It was the most arrogant and devious minute of 'world history': but still only a minute. After just a few breaths that nature took, the constellation froze, and the clever animals had to die. Someone could invent a fable of that sort and still not illustrate adequately how wretched, how shadowy and volatile, how purposeless and random human intellect appears within nature" (1,875; TF § 1).

Life requires an "enveloping atmosphere" (1,323; *HL* § 9) of ignorance, illusion, and dreams in which to ensconce itself to make living endurable. Most of all, however, life needs music, ideally the music of Richard Wagner.

CHAPTER 4

Redemption
through Art

*Nietzsche and Wagner: Collaboration on the myth •
Romanticism and cultural revolution • The* Ring *•
Nietzsche on Wagner • The return of Dionysus • Visions of
destruction and the "peak of rapture" • Disillusionment in
Bayreuth*

*W*AGNER'S MUSIC drama awakened the young Nietzsche's hope
of resurrecting German intellectual life, which, in his view, had been
severely damaged by materialism, economism, and historicism, as well as
being politically harmed by the founding of the German empire in 1871.
In the first of the *Untimely Observations,* Nietzsche decried the "defeat
and even the extirpation of the German mind for the sake of the
'German Reich'" (1,160; DS § 1), by which he meant the triumph of
national chauvinism, profit orientation, and belief in progress. As we
have seen, he had nothing against the success of "military genius"
(1,775; TGS), but he wanted militarism to culminate in a heroic invigor-
ation of culture. The enrichment of culture should remain the loftiest
goal even in moments of military triumph. For Nietzsche, war signaled
that the Dionysian-Heraclitean world was penetrating into politics and
restoring the gravity of life, which would result in the fertilization of culture. When it became evident, however, that military victory served to

further the prosaic aims of bourgeois society, Nietzsche reacted with bitter disappointment. The strengthening of the economy, the state, or a religion beholden to the state was light-years away from his vision of the renaissance of the German mind. In *The Birth of Tragedy*, this rebirth seemed to him more like the image of Wagner's Siegfried: "Let us contemplate a rising generation with this intrepid vision, with this heroic procession to the colossal; let us imagine the bold step of these dragon slayers, the proud audacity with which they turn their backs on all the feeble doctrines of optimism, opting to 'live resolutely' in the fullness of being: would it not be necessary for the tragic individual of this culture, steeled to face severity and terror . . . to desire a new art, the art of metaphysical solace?" (1,21; *BT* "Attempt at Self-Criticism" § 7).

Nietzsche was still banking on metaphysical solace at this time, but later, after he broke with Wagner, he was on the lookout for a perspective on life that would transcend any need for solace. He began to turn away from Wagner in his mind at a time in which he was "officially" still a follower of the composer. Nietzsche later explained that the fourth *Untimely Meditation*, on Richard Wagner, reflected a train of thought that had already been superseded by the time of composition. We will later trace this inner evolution in his thinking. In *The Birth of Tragedy* and in "Richard Wagner in Bayreuth," Nietzsche continued to ponder "metaphysical solace" in the sense of a revitalization of myth and activation of the myth-building potential of consciousness. He sang the praises of Wagner's works, which were forging powerful new myths.

In *The Birth of Tragedy*, Nietzsche defined myth as a "concentrated image of the world" (1,145; *BT* § 23) in which life is thrust into the light of a higher significance. Its meaning is not merely individual but also yields a social and cultural context. "Without myth, however, every culture loses its natural healthy creative power: only a horizon encircled with myths can mark off a cultural movement as a discrete unit" (1,145). Creativity and thought are spared "indiscrimate rambling" (1,145) by myths. Nietzsche concluded that the current lack of myths consigns modern man to deracination. Modern people seek to anchor themselves with possessions, technology, science, and the archives of history. In the second *Untimely Meditation,* Nietzsche would subject historicism as a means of grappling with the problems of life to detailed analysis. However, he broached the subject in *The Birth of Tragedy* by posing this question: "What can be the significance of the incredible compulsion for history on the part of our malcontent modern culture, our devoted amassing of countless other cultures, our consuming desire for knowledge, if not the loss of myth, the loss of a mythic homeland, of a mythic womb?" (1,146; *BT* § 23). Nietzsche turned to myth because he could not sustain religious faith, and because he did not believe rationality capable of giving direction to life.

Myths and mythologizing are means of conferring visual significance on otherwise meaningless phenomena. The indifference of the world provokes the mythmaking potential of our consciousness. We resist the notion of a world in which we cannot feel sure that we are somehow "intended." A person who understands would like to be understood in turn, not only by other people, but by a cosmos abundant with meaning. Although people are themselves a part of nature, their consciousness creates a sense of distance that impels them to expect that nature must offer some counterpart to their own consciousness. People are uncomfortable with the thought of standing isolated with their consciousness, and seek a response in nature. Myths are attempts to engage in dialogue with nature. Events in nature are vital for mythical consciousness. Nature expresses something, even if only an elemental will is manifest, as it was for the Schopenhauerian Nietzsche. After braving a storm with lightning and hail, the young Nietzsche declared in a letter: "How happy, how powerful they are, pure will, untarnished by intellect!" (*B* 2,122).

Hölderlin, whom Nietzsche greatly admired, had sought to update our modes of expression for mythical experience in a strikingly urgent and eloquent manner. Hölderlin was deeply pained by mankind's loss of facility and ease in this realm of experience, which had been a matter of everyday awareness for the Greeks. According to him, this loss makes us sacrifice an entire dimension in which reality could truly be revealed to our gaze and experience. We therefore fail to see the earth or hear the sound of birds, and language becomes parched. Hölderlin called this state of affairs the "night of the gods," and warned of the "hypocrisy" with which mythological themes and names are misappropriated for pure artificiality. For Hölderlin, and then for Nietzsche, it was critical to see the mythical as a life force that returns a festive bounty to being. The most effective way to create a zone that nourishes the senses amid the indifference of nature is through culture. Culture enables us to experience mutual regard in our interpersonal encounters and to forge bonds of solidarity and trust in the rules and institutions that govern meaningful connections between people. Culture represents an effective and perpetual effort to surmount the indifference of the world, at least in an inner domain. For both Nietzsche and Hölderlin, the "night of the gods" was overshadowing culture. Overwhelming indifference had permeated the core of culture and was causing personal relations to atrophy. It was therefore imperative that mythical energies be activated in an attempt to establish binding values of coexistence. Myths create a basis on which to establish a profound level of understanding in society. In doing so, they provide a response to the great silence of nature and the erosion of meaning in society.

Richard Wagner and Friedrich Nietzsche judged their era to be in a dire social situation brought on by a sensory deficit, and therefore set about finding or inventing new myths. Nietzsche looked back to the Greek gods Dionysus and Apollo in order to understand their elemental life and cultural forces and used them as a "compression of phenomena" (1,145; *BT* § 23)—his definition of myth. Nietzsche and Wagner each attempted to resuscitate myth, and refused to put up with what Max Weber later called the "disenchantment" of the world by rationalization, technology, and a bourgeois economic outlook. They agonized at the mythlessness of their times and saw in the sphere of art an opportunity to revitalize or re-create myths. At a time in which art had started to become a pleasant trifle under the prevailing economic constraints, they fought to raise the status of art, which they placed at the pinnacle of all possible hierarchies. For Wagner, art assumed the place of religion. This idea intrigued Nietzsche, but ultimately struck him as too pious, and he retreated from it in favor of an artistic approach to life. He sought enhancement of life in art, not redemption. In a borderline case—and Nietzsche always had borderline cases in view—one should fashion an unequivocal work of art out of one's own life.

Nietzsche and Wagner ultimately parted ways over their disagreement as to the function of myth. For Wagner, myth laid claim to religious authority; for Nietzsche, myth was an aesthetic game to foster the art of living. Before they reached this impasse, however, Nietzsche concurred with Wagner's attempt to establish a new mythology from the spirit of music.

Nietzsche followed in Wagner's footsteps by adopting impulses from early German Romanticism at the turn of the nineteenth century. The early Romantics had already dabbled in originating myths.

A key document in understanding early Romantic myth was a brief essay later given the title "The Oldest Systematic Program of German Idealism." Most likely written in 1796, it has been variously attributed to Schelling, Hegel, and Hölderlin. Some consider it a collaborative effort of all three. The text concluded with the following announcement: "I will offer an idea that has never entered anyone's mind, as far as I am aware—we must have a new mythology, but this mythology must stand in the service of ideas and must become a mythology of reason" (Hölderlin 1,917).

Two motives impelled the search for a new mythology. The first was that reason had become subject to considerable self-doubt toward the end of the Enlightenment era. Reason is strong when it questions and casts a critical glance on moral and religious traditions. "The critical spirit," Friedrich Schlegel wrote, "has become overtly political and has attempted a revolution of the bourgeois world, but it has purified and clarified religion for such a long time that it finally evaporated altogether and vanished in its own clarity" (Schlegel 3,88). This clarity was held to be negative, and the need for a higher meaning and purpose continued even if it amounted to nothing more than a delusion. Ideally, reason and imagination should go hand in hand to create a new synthesis of meaning. The authors of this essay called their project "mythology of reason." The early Romantics conjectured that it would grow out of a collaborative effort of poets, philosophers, musicians, and painters and take the place of established religions, which had lost their vigor. This "mythology of reason" was to be fashioned "from the most profound depths of the mind . . . like a new creation straight from the void" (Schlegel 301).

The second motive for the quest for new myths stemmed from a traumatic experience of social upheaval in the early nineteenth century. Late feudal society was collapsing, and there was a sense of the painful loss of an overarching idea of social life. Mindless egoism and economic utilitarianism dominated the field; a new mythology could carry out the task of "uniting people in a common view" (Frank 12).

The Romantics imagined that the experiment with new myths would provide a foundation, orientation, and set of bounds for reason and bring about social unity. They were convinced that myths of this sort could be created with great artistry, even if serviceable traditions were wanting. From tradition, they had learned that people cannot manage without myths. The spirit of their era, which held that all things are possible, infused them with the confidence to imagine themselves capable of crafting myths of this kind. And yet they were unable to move beyond the initial stages and soon had recourse to tradition. The Grimm brothers collected fairy tales and compiled materials for a *Deutsche Mythologie* (German Mythology, 1835). Clemens Brentano and Achim von Arnim edited an anthology of folk songs called *Des Knaben Wunderhorn* (The Boy's Magic Horn, 1805–8), and Hölderlin conjured up the heaven of the Greek gods. Nietzsche admired the boldness of a venture to establish a new mythology. It was Wagner, half a century after the early German Romantics, who was equal to the task of carrying out this venture. His plan took shape at the barricades of the Revolution of 1848 in Germany.

Wagner had conspired with Mikhail Bakunin in Dresden and had participated in street fights. After the uprisings had been suppressed, he fled to Switzerland, where he wrote an essay entitled "Art and Revolution." Nietzsche reacted to this essay by exclaiming: "Down with all art that does not by its very nature urge on to the revolution of society and the renewal and unity of the people!" (8,218).

Wagner's "Art and Revolution" laid the foundations for his project on the *Nibelungen*. Using the perspective of early socialist anticapitalism, he contrasted the idealized culture of the ancient Greek polis with the cultural situation of modern bourgeois society. In the Greek polis, Wagner contended, collective and individual interests coalesced, as did the public and private spheres. Art was a truly public affair, an event that exposed people to the meaning and principles of their life as a community. In the modern era, by contrast, this public aspect of art no longer exists. The public arena has been reduced to a market, and art has succumbed to the pressures of commercialization and privatization. Art is being marketed and sold as a commodity like any other product. Artists, in turn, are now producing art purely for the sake of profit. This is a scandalous process, since art, which is the expression of human creativity, ought to possess inherent value. The "slavery" of capitalism has stripped art of its dignity and reduced it to a means to an end, rendering art an instrument of entertainment for the masses and a sumptuous indulgence for the rich. At the same time, art is being privatized in the same measure "as the public spirit is frittered away in a thousand egoistic directions." Only superficial originality remains. Those who want to stand out have to differentiate themselves from their competition. Art does not answer to a higher truth but is intent only on "developing independently as a solitary and egoistic enterprise" (Wagner, *Denken* 132).

Wagner took the view that the corruption of society has also corrupted art. Without a revolution in society, art will be unable to find its way back to its true essence. The individual artist has no need to wait for a revolution, however. Artists can work toward the emancipation of society by initiating the task of liberation in their own domain. Art can convey the true meaning of existence, which, according to Wagner, is the display of human creativity. He stated unequivocally: "The highest purpose of mankind is artistic" (Wagner, *Denken* 145). Because revolution stands in the service of art, art should stand in the service of revolution. Because artists are truly free, they are also revolutionary.

Wagner's mythic *Ring des Nibelungen* developed an image of free individuals. Wagner intended this work to contribute to the project of political liberation, yet he remained convinced that his creation could be understood properly only once a revolution had taken place. However, no successful revolution was forthcoming. Wagner therefore had to settle for communicating at least the necessity of a future revolution. In the last decade of his life, during the years of his friendship with Nietzsche, Wagner was disenchanted with politics but believed so fully in his art that he thought it capable of compensating for or even replacing the aborted revolution. The experience of art ought to be able to conjure up a temporary moment of redemption from the evils of life and even become a harbinger and promise of the great redemption at the end of all time.

The composition of the *Ring* cycle took Wagner a full quarter of a century. In November 1874 he finished *Götterdämmerung*. "I will say nothing more," he noted on the last page of the score of the tetralogy.

In 1876, the entire *Ring* cycle premiered over the course of four days to inaugurate the Festspielhaus in Bayreuth. This event marked the climax of Wagner's artistic career. Even after his break with Wagner, Nietzsche called it the "greatest victory an artist has ever achieved" (2,370; *HH* II Preface § 1).

The *Ring* tells the story of the demise of the gods and the birth of free people. The gods perish because of their own lust for power. From the very beginning, they brought the world to ruin by their inability to reconcile the two basic principles of life, namely love and power. Instead, they pitted the two principles against each other. The gods became ensnared in hostile life forces. They longed for a new beginning, which would be possible only if the power of the gods ended with the freedom of mankind. Valhalla, the castle of the gods, goes up in flames when Brünnhilde returns the ring, the symbol of power, to the element of water and the innocence of nature. Her actions put an end to power that has been torn away from love, and the original, just order of being is reestablished. Preserving this order of being is the task of human liberty.

The prelude to *Das Rheingold,* which was often lauded by Nietzsche, opens with the famous E-flat major triad, the acoustic equivalent of the origin of all things, namely the turbulent primal element of water. Nietzsche would return to this musical image of water in his later writings as well. The flowing, surging element becomes a symbol of the turbulence of life: "This is how the waves live—just as we live, the desirers!" (3,546; *GS* § 310)

Wagner's entire *Ring* cycle evolves from its first chord. It is possible to discern the very moment of creativity when the chord symbolizing the sun follows. The fire of the sun makes the water shine like gold. There is also gold at the bottom of the water. It is, however, pure beauty, not something of material value, not part of the fateful succession of power and possessions, as yet untouched by the greed of exploitation. The Rhinemaidens guard the treasure by frolicking around it.

Now comes the "black Alberich," a prince of darkness and lord of the Nibelungs. He has no feeling for the beauty of the treasure. He cannot leave it as is, and must possess it to enhance his power. He profanes its value by attempting to exploit it. Heartlessness lies at the root of his will to exploitation. Alberich must renounce any love he harbors and prove callous before he is able to carry out the theft of the treasure. Only a cold heart can capture the metallic treasure.

This opening scene encapsulates the whole conflict of the drama. The tension between power and love, greed and sacrifice, play and compulsion will define the tetralogy all the way to the finale.

In the realm of the Nibelungs, a ring is fashioned from the treasure of gold that confers unlimited power on whoever wears it. Clearly, Wagner intended the Nibelungs to embody the demonic spirit of the industrial age. When visiting the docks in London, he described his impressions to Cosima as follows: "The dream of Alberich has been realized here. Nibelheim, world domination, activity, labor, everywhere the pressure of steam and fog" (Cosima Wagner 1052).

Wotan, the head of the gods, who refers to himself as the "light Alberich," became entangled in the world of power and possessions. He too will refuse to give the ring back to the Rhinemaidens after he has captured it, having struck a bargain with the Nibelungs to hand it over to them instead. He is therefore unable to restore the innocence of being. Consequently, Erda, the chthonian Earth Mother, refuses to acknowledge him: "You are not / what you call yourself " (Wagner, *Ring* 240). The excesses of power, gold, and bargaining triumph over the natural order of things.

The mythic world of Richard Wagner takes place on three physical planes, the lowest of which is the original existence of beauty and love, embodied by the Rhinemaidens and Erda, the Earth Mother. Above this plane is the world of the Nibelungs, in which power and possessions are sovereign. Higher still is the third plane, the world of the gods, now estranged from their chthonian origins. This world is disastrously entangled in the previous plane. At the end of *Das Rheingold,* the Rhinemaidens lament: "Tender and true it is only in the depths: / false and fainthearted / is what frolics above!"

Next Siegfried, who is descended from a complex genealogy, takes the stage. He kills the dragon, innocently takes the treasure, and gives Brünnhilde the ring as a token of his love. However, Siegfried is lacking in wisdom and knowledge, and falls victim to a cabal of envy, lust for power, and greed. Hagen, the son of Alberich, murders him. The task is not quite finished. Brünnhilde completes their duty of restoring the ring to the Rhine. Valhalla goes up in flames, and the gods are apparently consumed by fire.

The gods are thus implicated in the widespread corruption in the world. Salvation will not come from them. Only a free human being can bring salvation, someone who has broken free from the fateful succession of power, possessions, and dubious bargains. A new beginning occurs without the gods, who can die, exhausted from their flawed creation, when man awakens to love and beauty.

The old world of the will to power and of greed is destroyed when the new world is born of love and beauty. Wagner intended to contribute to this new beginning with his cosmic mythological play. Should we regard this mythical apparatus as anything other than fiction? Did Wagner merely rework mythological material that was no longer animated by belief? Was his work designed solely for aesthetic reception, and was the mythical effect neutralized in the process?

Wagner was well aware of the difficulties he faced, as is evident in his numerous theoretical essays. These essays assert his intention to expand the limits of pure aestheticism and to create a state of consciousness that could be referred to as "mythical." Wagner himself called it "religion." He justified the use of this term as follows: "It may be claimed that when religion becomes artificial, it falls to art to salvage the essence of religion" (Wagner, *Denken* 362).

Wagner distinguished the "essence of religion" from its "mythical apparatus" with its complex and disputed dogmas and ceremonies—the whole fund of religious tradition that survives only where it is supported by customs and safeguarded by political power. The essence of religion, however, which his artistry was called upon to rescue, Wagner defined as "recognition of the frailty of the world and the consequent charge to liberate ourselves from it" (Wagner, *Denken* 363). He saw the world through the eyes of Schopenhauer. What he called the frailty of the world was for Schopenhauer a world in which the individual embodiments of the will girded themselves for a hell in battle and mutual destruction. This holds for both nature and humanity, for the whole battle of life. Art was a redemptive force for Schopenhauer as well; he wrote that when we experience true pleasure in art, "we are delivered from the miserable pressure of the will; we celebrate the Sabbath of the penal servitude of willing; the wheel of Ixion stands still" (Schopenhauer 1,196).

With Schopenhauer's ideas in mind, Wagner formulated his concept of redemption through art: "In solemn hours, when all possible appearances dissolve away as though in a dream full of foreboding, we already seem to be partaking of this redemption in anticipation of it: we are no longer alarmed by the image of the yawning abyss, the gruesome monsters of the deep, all of the grasping debris of the will that devours itself, as the day—alas!—presented the history of mankind to us: then only the cry of nature, fearless, hopeful, mitigating everything, redeeming the world resounds to us in all of its purity and longing for peace. The soul of mankind, rendered pure in this cry, made aware by this cry of its high office of redemption of the whole of nature, which suffers with it, soars up from the abyss of appearances, and, freed . . . the restless will feels . . . liberated from itself" (Wagner, *Denken* 396).

If art is to rescue the essence of religion, it must succeed in bringing about a lasting inner transformation of people. Ephemeral pleasure in art will not suffice. The will to art as religion pushes at the boundaries of the merely aesthetic event, which is a source of great distress to artists who, like Wagner, regard themselves as founders of a religion. An explosive potential for hostility is brewing in this conflict: hostility with a world that is ruled by money and in which no one expects anything of art but art plain and simple, or possibly even just entertainment. The roots of Wagner's sometimes fanatical anti-Semitism lay in the hostility of art's emphatic will toward the secular and perhaps also banal world. Wagner saw the Jews as the personification of the economic principle and of vacuous entertainment.

Wagner sought to achieve a sacral, redemptive effect by means of his *Gesamtkunstwerk*. Art must mobilize all of its power. The music supplies a language for the "inexpressible," which comprehends only feelings, and combines with the action on the stage, the gestures, the facial expressions, the set design, and, above all, the solemn ritual of the festival days in which people gather around the altar of art.

Wagner had to pull out all the stops in order to emerge from the preserve of the merely pretty arts and to devise a mythical experience on the order of a religious event. In this endeavor, he became an exponent of the very art industry that he despised. As his contemporaries were already beginning to remark, his art was turning into a comprehensive assault on all of the senses. Although his work was intended as a protest against capitalist modernity, it took a peculiarly modern approach. The primacy of its impact and intended effect is characteristic of modernity. The general public is organized as a market, and artists are put into the position of competing against one another. The result is a mania for originality and sensationalism. Baudelaire, one of the first Wagnerians, recommended that artists in this situation learn from the spirit of advertising: "Step up the level of interest with new methods . . . double, triple, and quadruple the dose" (Oehler 48). The market has brought the public to a position of power. It demands heroes in both politics and art. The public wants to be wooed, seduced, and even overpowered. Everything that comes onto the market has to have a captivating theatrical aspect. The great era of commodification has commenced.

Of course, art has always been tailored to the public, but in the modern era the accent has clearly shifted to the goal of creating a splash. It goes without saying that a countermovement sprang up, a deliberate esotericism, in "l'art pour l'art" and symbolism. A tendency toward the obscure rendered understanding more difficult and impeded accessibility to the public. However, the prevailing tendency of the Wagner era was an ongoing endeavor to win over the public by means of accommodation, provocation, or mystification. The sensuous paintings of Nietzsche's contemporaries Hans Makart and Franz Stuck, the desire for provocation by the naturalists, and the pleasantry of the realists are examples of this tendency. Art was directed outward and defined by its public impact. Anything that lacked effect did not exist. This was the epoch in which Richard Wagner became the hero of art. In this era, Descartes's axiom might well have run along the following lines: I have an impact, therefore I am.

Richard Wagner was quite shrewd in establishing his own person as a public myth. There appears to have been a compelling connection between the modern production of myth and a self-mythologizing on the part of the producer. For instance, Wagner launched his campaign to conquer the Parisian music scene not with the performance of his works but with the rental of a lavish apartment that he was absolutely unable to afford. His intention was to rouse interest in himself; the effect was what counted. Wagner stopped at nothing that held out the hope of enhancing his image. The modern founder of a religion, Wagner was also a gifted strategist in marketing his art. Nietzsche recognized Wagner's cheap showmanship and flashiness quite early on. His notebooks of 1874 contained an entry about Wagner's "theatrical nature" (7,756). Nietzsche was not adopting the disparaging tone here that he employed later, but a skeptical undertone was already apparent. After they had parted ways, he used harsher language for the composer whom he now considered a swindler, calling Wagner a "Cagliostro of modernity" (6,23; *CW* § 5). Wagner's music was calculated to appeal to listeners whose taste followed the maxim "Whoever throws us over is strong; whoever elevates us is divine; whoever plants suggestions in us is profound" (6,24; *CW* § 6).

During the earliest stages of composing the *Ring* cycle, Wagner became convinced that this music drama ought not to be performed in the customary opera houses. He needed a space that would direct all attention to the action onstage, captivate the audience, and convey the appropriate gravity. He envisioned the audience being drawn out of everyday life and gathered over the course of several days in a place that existed for this sole purpose. For a specified period of time, a transformed communal life would be organized around the stage, as a preview of life in "the free beautiful public sphere." Wagner anticipated that entrance fees would not be required; he was counting on government subsidies and private sponsors to cover the expenses. Initially he wanted to establish his theater on the Rhine and proclaim the foundation of a "great dramatic festival" (Müller/Wapnewski 592). Eventually, he settled on Bayreuth, which fell within the dominion of his patron, King Ludwig II of Bavaria, whose support would be crucial. Friedrich

Nietzsche was in attendance at the ceremonial laying of the foundation stone on May 22, 1872, Richard Wagner's fifty-ninth birthday. In the fourth and final *Untimely Meditation* of 1876, he wrote that for an undertaking like the Bayreuth Festival there had been no "divinations; . . . it is the first circumnavigation of the world in the sphere of art; as it appears to have turned out, it was not just a *new* art, but art itself that was discovered" (1,433; WB § 1).

Nietzsche concluded that Wagner was returning art to its origins in Greek antiquity. It was becoming a sacral event in society once again, celebrating the mythical meaning of life. Art was regaining the arena in which a society could come to an understanding of itself and in which the significance of all activities would grow evident to the community at large.

Nietzsche did not dwell on the mythological details of Wagner's text. He focused on the mythical dimension of Wagner's art almost exclusively in his music, which he called a language of true feeling, and contended that it would be necessary to have suffered through the infirmity of our culture to embrace Wagner's music with a sense of gratitude. For Nietzsche, music drama was a redemption from his displeasure with our culture. "Art exists so that the bow does not break" (1,453; WB § 4). Nietzsche wrote that Wagner had diagnosed a poor state of health for language. Scientific progress had undermined clear-cut views of life, and the realm of thought had become murky. At the same time, civilization was becoming ever more complex and elaborate. Specialization and division of labor were on the rise; the chains of events through which each individual was linked to the whole were growing longer and longer and getting tangled in the process. Those who tried to grasp the totality of their existence found that language failed them. This excessive overreaching drained civilization as a whole, and language in particular, and people were barely capable of achieving their real functions, namely communication of the "barest necessities of life" (1,455; WB § 5). Language no longer comprised the totality of which we are a part and no longer reached into our innermost selves. It proved to be impoverished and limited. A feeling of inadequacy was evident in language, but at the same time, it wove the fabric of society more tightly together, and language was undergoing an obvious upsurge in power. Public discourse had turned ideological, which Nietzsche called the "lunacy of general terms" (1,455; WB § 5) that grab and push individuals in directions they were not intending "as though they had arms of ghosts" (1,455; WB § 5). Word and deed may accord, but there is no correspondence of feeling. Nietzsche wrote: "Now, when the music of our German masters resounds in a humanity that is so severely handicapped, what is actually resounding? Precisely this true feeling, the enemy of all convention, all artificial alienation, and incomprehension between one individual and another: this music is a return to nature, yet at the same time a purification and transformation of nature, since the need for this return to nature arose in the soul of the most loving people, and it is nature transformed into love that we hear in their art" (1,456; WB § 5).

Nietzsche considered this "true feeling" a mythical Dionysian life force. He expected Wagner's music drama to furnish a Dionysian reunion in the depths of feeling, a communion through art in the way he had portrayed Greek tragedy. "The bond between one person and another is forged once more by the spell of the Dionysian. . . . Now . . . each person finds himself not only united, reconciled, and blended with another but altogether fused, as though the veil of *maya* had been torn asunder and was only fluttering in shreds before the primordial mysterious unity" (1,29f.; *BT* § 1). Nietzsche experienced Wagner's music drama as a great Dionysian cosmic game. To bring this experience to the level of consciousness, he applied his distinction between the Apollonian and Dionysian to Wagner.

The destinies and characters of individual figures are Apollonian, as are their speeches, actions, conflicts, and rivalries. The resounding foundation, however, is Dionysian. Although there are variations, which the Wagnerian technique of leitmotifs explicitly emphasizes, all divergences sink back into the resounding ocean. Dionysian musical ecstasy melts away the masks representing specific characters to expose an empathetic sense of unity. Wagnerian music was a mythical event for Nietzsche; it gave expression to the bracing unity of life.

Nietzsche became a Wagnerian because he saw Wagner's music drama as a return to the Dionysian and a means to grant him access to the elemental strata of life. His philosophy of music in reference to Wagner was the attempt to understand the musical world of sound as the revelation of an inscrutable human truth. Nietzsche's inquiries raised issues that Claude Lévi-Strauss later revisited in his major work, *Mythologica,* with the claim that music and especially the nature of melody hold the key to the "ultimate secret of man." Music is the oldest universal language, intelligible to all people, and yet impossible to translate into any other idiom.

Music predates the Tower of Babel. If we consider that music, from Bach to pop, is the only universal mode of communication, we can regard it as a power that has triumphed over the confusion of tongues. The related notion that music is closer to our essence than any other product of our consciousness goes back to the beginnings of history. This notion underlies both Orphic and Pythagorean doctrines. Kepler used it in calculating his laws of planetary motion. Music was regarded as the language of the cosmos and as figured meaning. Schopenhauer pronounced music the direct expression of the world will.

If Logos were to break the silence of speechless objects and their inexhaustible being still failed as a concept, and if myth were capable of expressing what Logos cannot grasp, music would have to maintain the most profound relationship to the mythical realm. Perhaps it is that mythical residue that has vigorously asserted itself in the current era's ubiquity of music, which has been made possible by technological progress. Music is all-pervasive as white noise, atmosphere, and milieu, and has become the acoustic backdrop of our entire existence. Anyone who listens to a Walkman while sitting in a subway or jogging through the park is straddling two worlds. Traveling and jogging are Apollonian activities; listening to music is Dionysian. Music has socialized the act of transcendence and turned it into a sport for the masses. Discotheques and concert halls are today's cathedrals. A substantial portion of the population between the ages of thirteen and thirty now lives in the extralinguistic and prelinguistic Dionysian spheres of rock and pop. The inundation of music knows no bounds. It erodes political terrains and ideologies, as was evident in the upheavals of 1989. Music establishes new communities, alters our consciousness, and reveals a different form of being. The acoustic sphere encloses the individual and shuts out the outside world, yet on another level music also unites all who listen to it. People may have turned into windowless monads, but they are not isolated if they all partake of the same music. Music provides the means for profound social coherence in a stratum of our consciousness that used to be called mythical.

Nietzsche cited Schiller's "audacious convention" (1,29; *BT* § 1), which erects boundaries between people and provokes them to animosity, and echoed Schiller's hope that the "beautiful divine spark" could once again bring about the great project of unity. He considered Wagner's music drama capable of realizing this project of unity and removing the "rigid, hostile barriers" in a new "gospel of universal harmony" (1,29).

Universal harmony? But surely the myth that Wagner brought to the stage was a tragic one!

Nietzsche attempted to address the misapprehension that a combination of tragic consciousness and universal harmony would invariably clash. Dionysian life, according to Nietzsche, is tragic, because it unfolds with Goethean "expire and expand," the "rose bursting from the thorns" (1,36; *BT* § 3), the withering of blossoms and the ripening of fruit. Universal harmony lies in the consciousness of the necessity of destruction and sacrifice; it is a consciousness on which the "primeval unity, as the eternally suffering and contradictory" (1,38; *BT* § 4), has dawned and to which "the playful construction and destruction of the individual world" is shown to be "an emanation of a primordial pleasure . . . in a manner that recalls the dark Heraclitean comparison of the world-building force to a child that places stones here and there and piles the sand up high, only to smash it down once again" (1,153; *BT* § 24).

Spectators at a tragedy or a music drama identify with the tragic hero—Siegfried, for example—but see him as a surface phenomenon, a "bright light" on the dark background of Dionysian life. From this focal point, as a "bright light" in the night, life appears "at the bottom of all things indestructably mighty and pleasurable despite any change in appearances" (1,56; *BT* § 7). The dark background of Dionysian life resounds in music. In *The Birth of Tragedy,* Nietzsche coined the term "musical ecstasy" (1,134; *BT* § 21). He felt music, especially Wagnerian music, so strongly that he saw the action on the stage of the music drama and the myths staged there not only as a "bright light," but also as a shield against the devouring force of pure, absolute music. That "other existence" (1,134), into which music has the power to pull us, would be almost unbearable. Alleviating intermediaries must intervene. These intermediaries are the embellishments and scenery from events on the stage and in society, particularly the stage settings, artistic vanities, interpretations, and conventions of taste—in other words, the whole range of the culture industry. When all of this does not predominate, it creates a situation in which we can listen to the siren song of music without losing our senses. The necessary distance is then provided, enabling the sensible enthusiast to listen "as though the innermost abyss of things were speaking to him perceptibly" (1,135; *BT* § 21).

Dionysian consciousness, for which art prepares us, is a sanctification of life, an emphatic affirmation despite, or precisely because of, the vision it provides of the dark abysses that yawned open for Nietzsche under two aspects: the "terrible destructiveness of so-called world history and the cruelty of nature" (1,56; *BT* § 7). Dionysian consciousness gets involved in the uncanny mystery of life with the understanding, facilitated by the artistic intermediary, that there is no earthly solution to the great dissonance of life. Life will always be unjust to the individual, whose only hope lies in mitigating communion with the process of life as a whole. For Nietzsche, that is the "metaphysical solace" (1,56) bestowed by art. It is purely aesthetic in nature; that its effect is only temporary is ample evidence of this. "Our evaluation of things is altered as in a dream, as long as we sense that we are under the spell of art" (1,452; WB § 4). But only for the moment; "the total dramatist is exactly what we need to release us, even if it is only for a few brief hours, from the awful tension" (1, 469; WB § 7). The "metaphysical solace" of art does not feed our hopes for a world beyond, with its compensations and exonerations and its promise of a future realm of great justice.

This "metaphysical solace" stands in sharp contrast to a metaphysical and religious justification of the world. However, this tragic Dionysian formula, "because existence and the world are justified externally only as an aesthetic phenomenon" (1,47; *BT* § 5), also contrasts with a moral outlook. Morality, even when applied to the individual, is intent on improving the world and smoothing over its conflicts. According to Nietzsche, morality has become the true "deus ex machina" (1,115; *BT* § 17) of secularized modernity. Since "Dionysian wisdom" is lacking, moralistic attitudes generally steer clear of a good hard look at life, which would reveal that any attempt to have justice prevail here and now invariably results in injustice elsewhere. The process as a whole is a formula for guilt and victimization. Any happiness a person may experience in the moment is actually scandalous when pitted against suffering in the world. Someone lays claims to achievement although everything is still in a sorry state. "We cannot be happy as long as everything around us is suffering and making itself suffer; we cannot be moral as long as the course of human events is determined by violence, deception, and injustice" (1,452; WB § 4). Nietzsche did not dismiss morality, but he did criticize self-righteousness and the characteristic starry-eyed idealism that tends to accompany it. In any case, however, he found that a moralistic attitude narrows the confines that "Dionysian wisdom" opens up.

"Dionysian wisdom" articulates the "gospel of universal harmony." It comes across as neither religious nor moralistic, but rather aesthetic. Although, Nietzsche added, the truly "aesthetic audience" (1,143; *BT* § 22) that is receptive to its message has yet to be created, great works of art, notably Greek tragedy and Wagner's music drama, have the power to conjure up a public that is appropriate and suited to them.

Contemporary audiences need quite a bit of refinement before they are able to take art seriously. A serious approach to art—receptivity to its charms and the achievement of a higher level of cheerfulness—requires an altogether different kind of solemnity. One must be in a tragic frame of mind to prove worthy of aesthetic cheerfulness. It is necessary to shake off illusions and yet remain passionately in love with life, even after its great futility has been revealed. Nietzsche demanded a great deal from those he would deem suitable for tragedy. They must, first of all, be receptive to horror and terror; next, they must unlearn their "terrible anxiety" all over again once they recognize that "in the blink of an eye, in the tiniest atom of their life, they may encounter something holy" (1,453; WB § 4). The aesthetic moment is precisely this sort of atom of happiness, which more than compensates for all struggles and adversity. Nietzsche concluded this train of thought as follows: "Even if all of mankind should need to perish—and who could doubt this!—man has been charged with a goal, as the loftiest task for all time to come, of growing together into oneness and commonality so that mankind can confront its impending doom as a united entity and with a sense of the tragic. This loftiest of all tasks encompasses the sum total of the ennoblement of mankind" (1,453).

This lofty task therefore entails producing or seizing on moments of a person's or a work's greatest achievement. Nietzsche chose a singular expression to describe this type of moment: "the peak of rapture of the world" (7,200). He employed this expression only one time in his notebooks, to apply to the kind of moment when, in the height of danger, the "mind of a drowning man," for example (7,199), experiences all of eternity condensed into a single second; the supreme agony and ecstasy of life flashes up one final time before it is submerged. The bright lights and illuminations of genius are of this nature. Just as the individual comprehends his whole life in this moment and can pronounce it legitimate, a whole history of man is illuminated and warranted by the light of these beaming images. Culmination in this "peak of rapture" fulfills the meaning of culture.

Wagner's music drama was this kind of "peak of rapture" for Nietzsche; initially, at least, Wagner himself was one as well. Nietzsche admired the boldness with which Wagner placed art at the pinnacle of all possible hierarchies of bourgeois life, the immodesty with which he refused to see art as a pleasant trifle, and the sheer force of will with which he virtually compelled society to take note of his art. Nietzsche admired this Napoleonism coupled with enchantment, magic, and priestliness. By contrast, he regarded David Friedrich Strauss as the prosaic counterpart to Wagner. The first of his *Untimely Meditations* showcased Strauss as a negative example of how the sublime could turn banal. Nietzsche's polemics against Strauss were aimed not at him personally but at a symptomatic and representative outlook in the juste-milieu of the expanding German bourgeoisie. Nietzsche anticipated that an outlook of this kind would inevitably be superseded by Wagner and the Bayreuth project. Shortly before the opening of the first Bayreuth Festival, Nietzsche again depicted the decay of art in the bourgeois world: "A strange clouding of judgment, an ill-disguised craving for amusement and entertainment at any cost, scholarly considerations, pomposity and affectation with the solemnity of art on the part of the performers, brutal financial greed on the part of the proprietors, hollowness and thoughtlessness of a society . . . all of this in combination yields the oppressive and ruinous atmosphere of the current situation of art" (1,448; WB § 4).

To Nietzsche's great disappointment, Bayreuth did nothing to alter this situation. On the contrary: Nietzsche, who traveled to Bayreuth in late July 1876 to see the rehearsals and experience firsthand the whole whirlwind of activity, was horrified, annoyed, and even nauseated to witness the ostentatious arrival of Kaiser Wilhelm I, Richard Wagner's fawning demeanor on the festival hill and at Wahnfried (the Wagners' villa in Bayreuth), the unintended comicality of the staging, the racket made about the mythical enterprise, and the high-spirited, prosperous spectators to this artistic event who were in search not of redemption but of a good meal—they made a mad dash to the restaurant after each performance. Nietzsche returned home from Bayreuth after just a few days. Before visiting Bayreuth, he had written: "Here you will find qualified and dedicated spectators, the ardor of people who are at the zenith of their happiness and who feel that their whole being is condensed in this very state of happiness, which invigorates them for further and higher aspirations" (1,449; WB § 4). Once he had attended the event, he was forced to conclude that his ideal spectators had been a mere figment of his imagination and had no counterpart in reality.

Had he perhaps expected altogether too much of Wagner's music and music drama? After the disappointment of Bayreuth in 1876, Nietzsche began his work on the book *Human, All Too Human* in order to inure himself to disappointment for the future.

However, between 1872 and 1874, when Nietzsche wrote the first three *Untimely Meditations,* he had not yet reached this point. He still considered Wagner's project capable of "enigmatic profundity, even infinity . . . a comet's tail pointing into the uncertain, defying clarification" (1,80f.; *BT* § 11), and believed that this project would succeed in falling under the spell of "monstrosities" (1,81; *BT* § 11), perhaps with his assistance. He hoped that a sense of the great "incommensurability" (1,81) of being would reawaken. In his *Untimely Meditations,* Nietzsche was to take issue with a zeitgeist that replaced "metaphysical solace" with "an earthly consonance and even its own special deus ex machina, the god of machines and crucibles" (1,115; *BT* § 17).

CHAPTER 5

Untimely Meditations

The spirits of the epoch • *Thinking in the workhouse* •
Grand disenchantments • Untimely Meditations • *Against
materialism and historicism* • *Coups and detoxifications* •
Nietzsche and Stirner

NIETZSCHE CHERISHED the colossal power of music and
yearned for the return of a tragic outlook on life that would value
Dionysian wisdom over science. However, he found himself in the middle of an epoch that was celebrating one scientific triumph after another.
Positivism, empiricism, economism, and utilitarian thinking defined the
age. Optimism reigned supreme. Nietzsche indignantly noted that the
founding of the new German empire was widely hailed as a "devastating blow to all 'pessimistic' philosophizing" (1,364; SE § 4). Nietzsche
pronounced his epoch "open" and "honest," but crude, and "more submissive to any sort of reality and more faithful," privileging theories that
would justify "subjugation to the real."

Nietzsche was aghast at the petty bourgeois, and even pusillanimous,
aspect of this approach to reality. The realism that had predominated
since the middle of the century subjugated itself to the real only in order
to control it more fully and transform it according to its own design.
Nietzsche's subsequent proclamation of a "will to power" was already in
evidence, not in the lofty form of the *Übermensch,* but in the busy beaver-
like activity of a civilization that applied science to all practical matters.

This orientation applied equally to the bourgeois milieu and the workers' movement, whose powerful slogan was "Knowledge is power." Education would bring social mobility and provide resistance to deceit of any kind: if you know something, you cannot be fooled as easily. The impressive aspect of knowledge is that we no longer need to be impressed. The ultimate knowledge would guard against the temptations of "enthusiasm" (1,169; DS § 2). Effusiveness was discouraged; dry and sober methods prevailed and assured a gain in sovereignty. There was a drive to reduce things to one's own lowest common denominator.

It is quite astonishing how, after the idealist flights of the absolute spirit in the early part of the nineteenth century, the desire suddenly arose to make people small. The thought pattern "man is nothing but . . ." began its advance. The Romantics had imagined that just by uttering the magic word, the world would break into song. The breathtaking project of poetry and philosophy in the first half of the century was to create and re-create new words to evoke magic. That era demanded effusion. Nietzsche, by criticizing the prosaic attitude of his age, was moving onto Romantic ground more emphatically here than his later outlook would allow. Even as a schoolboy, he had defied his schoolmaster and defended Hölderlin, his favorite Romantic poet. The spirit of the second half of the century was no longer amenable to the matadors on the enchanted stage of the mind. They seemed like children when the realists appeared with their penchant for facts, armed with the formula "nothing but." The idealists and Romantics had had their fun and tossed everything about, but now it was time to clean up. Life was about to turn serious; the realists would see to that. This realism in the second half of the century was able to accomplish the trick of thinking little of people while undertaking great things with them, if we should call the modern scientific civilization that has benefited all of us "great." In any case, the final third of the century ushered in modernism, which was predicated on the conviction that everything extravagant and fantastic was repugnant. Nietzsche was one of the few to suspect what monstrosities would result from the spirit of positivist sobriety.

By about the middle of the century, an extremely stodgy form of materialism had sapped the energy of German idealism. Breviaries of sobriety suddenly attained the popularity of best-sellers. Notable among these were Karl Vogt's *Physiologische Briefe* (Physiological Letters, 1845) and his polemical pamphlet *Köhlerglaube und Wissenschaft* (Simple Faith and Science, 1854), Jakob Moleschott's *Kreislauf des Lebens* (Circulation of Life, 1852), Ludwig Büchner's *Kraft und Stoff* (Force and Matter, 1855), and Heinrich Czolbe's *Neue Darstellung des Sensualismus* (New Portrayal of Sensualism, 1855). Czolbe characterized the ethos of this materialism of force, thrusting, and glandular function as follows: "It is proof of . . . arrogance and vanity to wish to improve the world we know by inventing a transcendental world and to lift man above nature by attributing to man a supersensory aspect. Yes, of course—dissatisfaction with the world of appearances, the deepest root of the supersensory outlook is . . . moral weakness. . . . Be content with the world as it is" (Lange 2,557). But what was this "as it is" to a mentality of this sort! The world of becoming and being was nothing but the flurry of bits of matter and the transformation of energy. Nietzsche found himself challenged to defend the world of the atomist Democritus against contemporary materialists. Obviously, there was no further need for the *nous* of Anaxagoras and the ideas of Plato and most certainly not the God of the Christians, nor was there any useful application for the *substance* of Spinoza, the *cogito* of Descartes, the *I* of Fichte, or the *mind* of Hegel. According to this logic, the human mind is nothing but a function of the brain. Thoughts are to the brain as bile to the liver and urine to the kidneys. Hermann Lotze, one of the few survivors of the formerly strong band of metaphysicians, called these ideas "somewhat unfiltered."

The triumphant advance of materialism could not be impeded by clever objections, especially because it featured a metaphysical belief in progress. If we analyze things and life down to their basic components, we will, according to this belief, uncover the innermost secrets of nature. If we can find out how things are made, we will be able to copy them. This attitude seeks to get to the bottom of everything, even nature. If we can catch nature in the act, we will be able to determine its essence.

This outlook provided a crucial impetus to Marxism in the second half of the nineteenth century. Marx painstakingly dissected the framework of society and identified capital as its soul. Ultimately, it was no longer altogether clear whether the messianic mission of the proletariat (Marx's pre-1850 contribution to German idealism) would stand any chance at all against the unshakable law of capital (Marx's post-1850 contribution to the spirit of determinism). Marx also wished to scrutinize the spirit that had once reigned supreme. He traced back its superstructure to the basis of the work done by society as a whole.

Work had become a reference point well beyond its practical significance. More and more aspects of life were interpreted and evaluated in relation to work. Society was a society of work, and, in it, you were what work you did. Even nature was at work in the process of evolution. Work became a sanctuary, a myth to knit together the fabric of society. The image of the great machinery of society—which turns individuals into cogs and bolts—took over people's images of themselves and provided a horizon of orientation. This view was Nietzsche's focus in his critique of David Friedrich Strauss, the popular enlightener of the second half of the century. With his first book, *Das Leben Jesu* (The Life of Jesus, 1835), Strauss had brought rationalist criticism of Christianity to the attention of the public at large, and decades later, as an old man, he published a widely read confessional book *Der alte und der neue Glaube* (Old and New Faith, 1872). Strauss was a sworn enemy of Wagner's new mythology of art and of all attempts to elevate art to a replacement for religion. For this reason, he was instantly hated by Wagner. Wagner, in turn, inflamed Nietzsche to disparage this author in the first of his *Untimely Meditations*. In that essay, Nietzsche called Strauss a symptom of the prevailing work-driven scientific and utilitarian culture.

Strauss declared that there is every reason to be satisfied with the current era and its many achievements: the railroad system, vaccinations, blast furnaces, biblical exegesis, the founding of the German empire, fertilizers, journalism, and the postal system. There are no further grounds to dodge reality and pursue metaphysics and religion. If physics takes flight, the highfliers of metaphysics come crashing down and should therefore resign themselves to live respectably on the flat earth. A sense of reality will produce the wonders of the future; we should not be carried away by art. In small doses, art is certainly useful and good, even indispensable. Precisely because our world has turned into one huge machine, the following metaphor also applies: "there are not only callous wheels at work in it; soothing oil pours out as well" (1,188; DS § 6). Art is just this sort of soothing oil. Strauss calls the music of Haydn an "honest soup"; Beethoven is a "confection." When he hears the *Eroica,* Strauss gets the irresistible urge "to kick over the traces and seek adventure" (1,185; DS § 5), but he soon returns to the bliss of the commonplace in the fever and excitement of a united Germany. Nietzsche heaped mockery and scorn on this "creeping enthusiasm in felt slippers" (1,182; DS § 4).

We sense in Nietzsche all the indignation of a man who fancies himself in the heart of the world when contemplating art, especially music, and who finds his true essence "under the spell of art" (1,452; WB § 4). For this reason, he opposed the attitude that art is a pleasant trifle—possibly even the most pleasant of all trifles, but still just a trifle.

The German Romantics delighted in casting aspersions on bourgeois desecrators of art, whom Nietzsche later called "cultivated philistines." E. T. A. Hoffmann's musical conductor Kreisler breaks up a musical evening that promises "pleasant entertainment and diversion" with a fast and furious rendition of the Goldberg Variations. In Hoffmann's well-known detective story "Mademoiselle de Scudéri," the artist figure is a goldsmith whose disdain for the public escalates from derision to homicide. These Romantic stories portray the war of art against the philistines of art and their utilitarian outlook. Nietzsche's critique of David Friedrich Strauss was firmly situated in this tradition. Nietzsche reveled in the vindictiveness of an indignant art lover: "woe to all vain masters and the whole aesthetic kingdom of heaven if ever the young tiger . . . were to go out in search of prey!" (1,184; DS § 4). The young tiger had already made his appearance in *The Birth of Tragedy* as a symbol of the spirit of wild Dionysian art. It enraged Nietzsche to watch the educated classes recast feral forces in a cozy light.

Nietzsche's indignation was directed at their view of nature as well. Strauss played down Darwinism, which was becoming extraordinarily influential at the time, and failed to recognize its momentous consequences, as Nietzsche noted critically. People tended to use Darwinism as a source for atheism, and the monkey replaced God as an object of inquiry. Although Strauss draped himself "in the shaggy garment of our monkey genealogists" (1,194; DS § 7), he stopped short of realizing the ethical implications of this genealogy of nature. Had he been daring, he would have been "able to derive a moral code for life from the *bellum omnium contra omnes* and the privileges of stronger individuals" (1,194; DS § 7), thereby inciting the "philistines" against himself. To satisfy their need for security and comfort, Strauss sidestepped the nihilist consequences of materialism and gave his deliberations a cozy and heartwarming twist by discovering in nature a new "revelation of eternal goodness" (1,197; DS § 7). For Nietzsche, by contrast, nature was the epitome of ferocity.

In the third *Untimely Meditation,* Nietzsche outlined his Dionysian interpretation of nature, which he contrasted with the insipid, optimistic view of nature advanced by the cultivated philistines. His aim was to distinguish himself from naturalists and materialists. Nietzsche considered it utterly incredible that out of the entire hierarchy of nature, from the inanimate to the vegetative and the animal, it was in man that consciousness had emerged. Why did nature use man as a forum for consciousness? A stone does not know that it exists. An animal is aware of its environment, but remains inextricably bound to that environment. Only in man does the awareness of awareness come into play, and with it a distancing consciousness. Man does not merely exist in his environment; he experiences it as a wide panorama. Man emerges from the dazed state of animal existence, and in this moment the world takes on a singular transparency. The drivenness of all living things is revealed to conscious life, as is our own "revolting greed" and how "blindly and madly" (1,378; SE § 5) we yearn to consume and destroy other life. Thus, consciousness does not initially experience pleasure in the world of appearances, but first encounters the torments of existence. Are we hit with consciousness the way we catch a disease? Is natural existence the least bit bearable in the mirror of consciousness? Is consciousness ultimately a disaster? "In this sudden brightness, we gaze around us and behind us and tremble: this is where the refined beasts of prey are running, and we are in their midst. The tremendous mobility of humans on the great desert of the earth, their founding of cities and states, their waging of war, their restless assembling and scattering, their muddled running, their copying of one another, their mutual outwitting and stamping down, their cries of distress and their howls of joy in victory— everything is an extension of their animality" (1,378; SE § 5). Consciousness recoils at this sight of awakening from a daze and longs to return to the "unconsciousness of instinct" (1,379; SE § 5). In the everyday conduct of our lives, is it perhaps better "not to arrive at a state of reflection" (1,379)? Reflection can work to undermine practical and efficient realism. Nietzsche was compelled to wonder what purpose nature had in opening men's eyes and having them see their existence mirrored in human consciousness.

By posing this question, Nietzsche was affirming a teleology of nature: "if all of nature presses toward man, it thereby intimates that man is crucial to its redemption from the curse of animal existence and that finally existence holds up a mirror to itself in which life no longer appears senseless but rather comes into view in its metaphysical significance" (1,378; SE § 5). What is this metaphysical significance?

Metaphysical significance is not universal harmony at the foundation of things, nor is it an all-encompassing metaphysical order and justice, but simply nature making "its only leap, which is a leap of joy" (1,380; SE § 5) in life that has awakened to consciousness. Nietzsche continued his teleological argument with the puzzling statement that "nature feels for the first time that it has attained its goal, realizing that it must unlearn the notion of having goals and that it has played the game of living and becoming with stakes that were too high" (1,380). This argument is open to misinterpretation. Nietzsche was well aware that nature is not a "subject" that can learn or unlearn or set its stakes too high. He had no desire to read God into nature. His references to learning and unlearning on the part of nature applied to reflexes in the consciousness of man. Nature is manifested in human self-awareness as a goal-oriented drive that must remain perpetually unfulfilled. This drive recognizes at every goal that it, in fact, wanted to attain not the goal but only itself, and will therefore continue driving on. When consciousness holds a mirror up to the drive, it may well expire. The cause is not exhaustion or despair but the realization that in the end there is no goal; we are always already at it. The fulfilled moment does not lie in the future, but is always there already; it is up to us to seize it by learning to be alert and sharp-witted. The "game" of life has set its stakes too high if they need to be paid out in an ominous future. We may gamble with life in this way, but life itself does not play by these rules. Life does not follow the principle of linear accumulation and progressive enhancement, but instead revolves in a cycle of expiring and expanding. Any point along the circumference of the circle is equidistant from the center. For this reason, life is always already at its goal or remains equally remote from it, which ultimately amounts to one and the same thing. Nature within man, Nietzsche explained, "is transfigured with this knowledge" (1,380). He called this puzzling "emotion devoid of agitation" (1,381; SE § 5) the "great enlightenment," which illuminates the "beauty" (1,380; SE § 5) of reality.

Nietzsche's line of reasoning, which evolved from his study of Schopenhauer, aimed at a transfiguration of reality requiring not a new "revelation of eternal kindness" in nature, as it had for his adversary David Friedrich Strauss, but a transformation in the man of knowledge. Instead of observing reality with an eye to one's own interests and desires, consciousness loosens its ties to the will and adopts a composed attitude toward the world. "Metaphysical significance" lies solely in this shift of perspective from peering around at objects of desire to taking a good look at things. Here Nietzsche was still indebted to Schopenhauer's concept of metaphysics, according to which metaphysical consciousness is awakened from its dazed state by man's will, and the world thus appears in a different light. It is therefore a matter not of discovering a metaphysical world behind or above our world, but rather of experiencing another, extraordinary condition, namely the aforementioned "puzzling emotion devoid of agitation."

In these reflections, Nietzsche continued to adhere so closely to his mentor Schopenhauer that he adopted the latter's idea of overcoming desire as a precondition for altering our perspective on the world. But Nietzsche placed the emphasis elsewhere by stressing the active moment of this process. The will is not extinguished; something within man makes this "leap" and triumphs over the ordinary will. It is this something within man that rules the other restless and oblivious something. Ultimately, this calming something is nothing other than an extraordinarily strong will, which puts the foolishness of life devoid of consciousness in its place. "Dionysian wisdom," with which we are already quite familiar, is strong enough to endure a gaze into the abyss; it does not shatter, but maintains a mystifying, almost cheerful tranquillity.

In his 1873 essay "Philosophy in the Tragic Age of the Greeks," Nietzsche described this type of "Dionysian wisdom" by using the example of Heraclitus. "The eternal and exclusive process of becoming, the utter evanescence of everything real, which keeps acting and evolving, but never is, as Heraclitus teaches us, is a terrible and stunning notion. Its impact is most closely related to the feeling of an earthquake, which makes people relinquish their faith that the earth is firmly grounded. It takes astonishing strength to transpose this reaction into its opposite, into sublime and happy astonishment" (1,824f.; PTA § 5). Withstanding tumultuous existence in a particular type of perspective is a matter not simply, as Schopenhauer thought, of contemplating and eliminating the will but rather of activating another will: the will to configure. To overpower or be overpowered—that is the question. There is an agonistic ontological relationship here. The extremely active will to configure dares to enter into a bet with the life force of oblivious overpowering. This will to configure is an artistic one, which serves a will to live that is enhanced beyond unconscious urges. For this reason, Nietzsche found it appropriate to call Heraclitus an "aesthetic man who has learned from artists and the genesis of artworks how . . . necessity and playfulness as well as opposition and harmony must pair to create a work of art" (1,831; PTA § 7).

The artistic will to configure is also concerned with capturing the whole in a single image. And what is the function of this image—this Heraclitean image of the world—if not to compress the entire course of time into a moment? History is eradicated in the experience that allows for this sort of compression into an image, and we realize that it is unnecessary to have goals because we are already at the goal.

After taking issue with materialism, Nietzsche quarreled with a second aspect of the spirit of his era and waged a battle against the prevailing, overpowering emphasis on history. For him, historicism was also a consequence of the Socratic-Alexandrine culture of knowledge, which had taken a particular turn in Germany during the period of unification. Historicism looked back into history to admire how nicely humanity had progressed. At the same time, people wanted to compensate for the great uncertainty surrounding bourgeois existence. They were not altogether sure who they were and what they wanted. This historicism was expressed as pleasure in the epigonal and inauthentic. The spirit of "as if" was triumphing.

"Impressive" was defined as something that resembled something else. Every material used was intended to pretend to more than it was. It was the era of fake materials. Marble was painted wood, glistening alabaster was plaster of Paris. New things had to look old. Greek columns graced the entrance to the stock exchange, factory grounds resembled a medieval castle, and ruins were newly constructed. Historical associations were all the rage. Courthouses resembled the

Doge's Palace, bourgeois living rooms contained Luther-style chairs, pewter tankards, and Gutenberg Bibles that turned out to be sewing chests. Once the "German Emperor" had been announced in Versailles's Hall of Mirrors, which featured Talmi gold, political power shone like gold as well. This will to power was not altogether genuine; it was more will than power. The point was to stage things. No one knew that better than Richard Wagner, who pulled out all the theatrical stops to bring early Germanic history onto the stage. All of this was consistent with an efficient approach to reality, one requiring that everything be prettified, ornamented, draped, and enshrined to look like something and count for something.

Nietzsche could not shake the suspicion that historicism was trying to compensate for a lack of vitality. Vitality had been weakened because it had lost a meaningful societal anchor in the Socratic culture of knowledge. In *The Birth of Tragedy,* Nietzsche wrote: "Let us imagine a culture that has no firm and consecrated primordial seat, but is condemned instead to exhaust all possibilities and eke out nourishment from all cultures—that is the current era, which results from Socratism bent on the destruction of myth. . . . What can be the significance of the incredible compulsion for history on the part of our malcontent modern culture, our devoted amassing of countless other cultures, our consuming desire for knowledge, if not the loss of myth, the loss of a mythic homeland, of a mythic womb?" (1,146; *BT* § 23).

This historicism provided Nietzsche with an imposing example of the way in which knowledge and insight serve to undermine vitality. The second *Untimely Meditation,* entitled "On the Benefits and Drawbacks of History for Life," describes the process by which life can fall ill from an excess of historical consciousness. In this essay, Nietzsche developed a bold concept that no longer seems so out of the ordinary to us today only because it helped him achieve an important breakthrough. He realized that life needs an "enveloping atmosphere" (1,323; *HL* § 9) of illusions, passions, and love in order to stay alive. This notion drew on a critique of realism, which submits to the supposed hard facts. Full of resignation, devoid of strength, or cynical, it culminates in an attitude of nihilistic egoism altogether indifferent to everything that is not useful in an economic sense.

Nietzsche began with a problem that would at first glance appear to interest only the world of scholarship and education—namely his era's fixation on history, on things that happened and developed, the inundation of historical information, and the endless squandering of effort on picayune issues that served no purpose other than the self-preservation of the scholarly enterprise. Nietzsche used the appeal of historicism in the scholarly world as a point of departure for his critique of the era as a whole. He countered with an emphatic defense of life. The philosophy of life that he developed in the coming decades originated in this essay, a seminal Nietzschean text.

Centuries of historical and scientific research have produced a vast quantity of knowledge. Since erudition and knowledge were proclaimed the highest ideals, educated contemporaries want to take in as much of it as possible, with the result that "in the end, modern man drags around with him a huge quantity of indigestible stones of knowledge, which then, on occasion, rumble around inside his body, as they say in fairy tales. This rumbling reveals the fundamental characteristic of modern man: the curious disparity of an interior with no corresponding exterior, and an interior with no corresponding interior—a disparity that was alien to ancient peoples" (1,272; HL § 4). Nietzsche considered this opposition between interior and exterior a fundamental characteristic of German culture. A time-honored German tradition regards its undigested knowledge as profound introspection and forgoes style and wit on the outside. People foster "inward cultivation for outward barbarians" (1,274; HL § 4), only there is no actual inward cultivation. It does not take shape in life; it is not, to use a favorite Nietzschean expression, "incorporated." Gaudiness, cheap showmanship, epigonalism in art and architecture, and boorish manners in the social sphere characterize this attitude. People take pride in their rough edges and consider their culture superior to French civilization and refinement, and yet "in our belief that we were retreating to a natural state, we were only opting for letting ourselves go, for comfort and for the smallest possible degree of self-transcendence" (1,275; HL § 4). Nietzsche took a stand against the pretentiousness of amorphous introspection that passed itself off as culture. He sided with civilization, which, however, he also subjected to criticism as mere social convention from the perspective of fresh creativity. In the later debate about the difference between German "culture" and French "civilization," the opposing sides were able to cite Nietzsche in equal measure.

The undigested "stones of knowledge" that keep an individual from cultivating a true personality stem from the basis of history and the popularized natural sciences. As for the excess of history in society, Nietzsche considered it the aftereffect of a simplistic take on Hegelianism that regarded historical power as reasonable precisely because it was powerful, and therefore demanded respect for the power of what existed as well as diligence in appropriating history.

Hegel meant all of that in a different way, as Nietzsche was well aware. Hegel was a philosopher in love with history. The besotted Hegel considered history rational, but at the same time captivating and infectious; he called it the "Bacchantic giddiness in which no member is not drunk" (Hegel 39). It had all begun in the abbey in Tübingen, when Hegel and his roommates Schelling and Hölderlin planted a freedom tree on the meadow of the Neckar River after hearing the news of the storming of the Bastille. This was youthful enthusiasm that sought to take history into its own hands and both understand it and inject it with a lively dose of reason. It was precisely that kind of youthful protest that Nietzsche now demanded for his era, which was suffering from an excess of historical interpretation and scholarship. Hegel's generation discovered a revolutionary spirit in history; the act of appropriating history spurred it on. History had verve. It did not weigh you down, but rather swept you along on a journey of adventure. However, in the quarter century after the French Revolution, history had brought great disappointment to many of its enthusiasts, and the image of the reason of history was transformed. It was crucial for the older Hegel to do everything in his power to avoid being disappointed ever again. The betrayed lover consoled himself by becoming complicit in the tricks of reason. He focused squarely on designing a system of the reason of history that would be impervious to disappointment. Reason comes into history, and history ultimately passes on to reason by way of a series of painful contradictions. In Hegel's system, this process is described and imprinted on human self-awareness. The mysteries of history are thus revealed in the consciousness of Hegelian philosophy.

In Nietzsche's view, Hegel had pulled off a remarkable trick. Hegel had taken lamentations about the end of heroic history—represented by the fight for freedom as well as the consciousness of a "latecomer" who only remembers but does not act—and transformed them into marks of distinction. Evidently, it should have been the purpose of history to lead into knowledge of such latecomers. Consciousness of misery is equated with the fulfillment of world history. Since that time, Germans have come to view things in terms of the "historical process," and they see the present as its inevitable result. Nietzsche noted: "This way of viewing things has put history in the place of the other powers of the mind, namely art and religion, making it the sole sovereign power, inasmuch as it is 'the self-realizing concept' and also the 'dialectic of the spirit of nations' and the 'Last Judgment'" (1,308; HL § 8).

Hegel not only ennobled history in philosophical terms but also conferred philosophical dignity on diagnosing the current events of an era. He encouraged further philosophizing for the political fray and for the future as well. Thus, his famous and infamous proposition "What is rational is actual, and what is actual is rational" had direct political implications—in contrary directions. Some interpreted his statement as a justification of existing conditions; others, like Arnold Ruge, Bruno Bauer, Friedrich Engels, and Karl Marx, took it as a challenge to make what merely existed into reality to bring it into accord with a rational construct. For some, the proposition described things as they were; for others, things as they should be. They shared, however, the conviction that society and history represented dimensions of truth.

In the pre-Hegelian tradition, this conviction was not as self-evident as it appears today. Before Hegel, people thought in binary oppositions of God and the world, man and nature, man and being. After Hegel, an intervening world of society and history was inserted between these pairs. This intervening world subsumed everything into itself. The old metaphysics of the whole—God, being, man—was transformed into a metaphysics of society and history, and talk of the individual became meaningless and pointless because the individual was seen as determined by society and history. The intervening world of society and history allowed for only a single point beyond, which was nature, both human and nonhuman. As a creature of nature, though, man was, of course, even much less than an individual creature; he was only an exemplar. Metaphysics had been an endeavor to create a spiritual expanse for man. Now the expanse was narrowing. People wriggled about inside the harness of social and historical and natural exigency. The debate in the second half of the nineteenth century was ultimately about which of the exigencies would predominate. Hegel, and later Marx, believed in the victory of social and historical necessity. Hegel spoke of the "spirit that finds itself" and Marx of the "abrogation of naturalness." For both, these were paths to freedom, which they regarded as a social product of history. The materialists, on the other hand, believed in the superiority of natural necessity. They too, however, generally secularized the old metaphysical promise of salvation and interpreted the evolutionary history of nature as an upward development.

Thus, philosophical thought at the onset of the machine age saw the remaining dimensions of being, nature, and history beginning to evolve into a kind of machine. One could entrust the production of the successful life to "machines," according to the optimists among Nietzsche's contemporaries, assuming that one behaved accordingly. Nietzsche subtly depicted how the Hegelian "historical process" had been converted into machinelike developments and factory-style institutions in his own scholarly field of philology. We educate young people to supply them to the scientific "labor market." Each worker is there assigned a picayune topic and a petty issue to belabor. The whole enterprise is a "scientific factory." No one can tell what the products of this zeal are good for, but their practitioners make a good living. In describing these circumstances, Nietzsche paused at one point to question the terms he was employing: "but we cannot help letting the words 'factory,' 'labor market,' 'supply,' 'productivity'—and whatever auxiliary verbs of egoism there are—spring to mind when we wish to describe the latest generation of scholars" (1,300f.; HL § 7).

Nietzsche considered Eduard von Hartmann, a widely read philosopher of the time, to be a caricature of this busy-bee approach to the historical process. Hartmann sought to augment the doctrines of Schopenhauer by demanding a complete surrender of personality to the historical process. Nietzsche, who greatly admired Schopenhauer, found Hartmann's approach offensive. Curiously, Hartmann's historical process was one long course of denial. Eduard von Hartmann, a discharged officer, was determined to systematize denial of the will, which to Schopenhauer was a mystery to be fathomed only by great ascetics and saints. Hartmann looked to Hegel to develop such a system. The result of this synthesis of Schopenhauer and Hegel was a massive work, *Die Philosophie des Unbewußten* (The Philosophy of the Unconscious, 1869), which laid out an intricate three-stage theory of the disillusionment of the will to live. The book's essential argument was that the individual will to live would be incapable of negating itself of its own accord, and this task would have to be left to the historical process, in good Hegelian fashion. Hartmann hailed the strength of the pessimistic consciousness of mankind, predicting that although it was now still operating on an unconscious level, this pessimistic outlook would come into its own as soon as it had eliminated all illusions of happiness—the illusion of happiness in the beyond, in the future, and in the here and now—and thereby would reclaim the world for itself and vanish. In

Hartmann's work, this zeal for labor on the part of the pessimistic world spirit comes across as comical, as does the optimistic eagerness with which he hastens to achieve his denial, and the simple pedantic precision with which men's illusions are shattered on the path from yes to no. And when this author has finally arrived at the great denial and makes the historical process end there, an oddly conventional contentment takes over. All this talk about "historical process" is distorted beyond recognition. Hartmann makes the world process culminate in a void and thereby demonstrates, with unintended humor, that the "historical process" is a meaningless cliché.

Nietzsche kept returning to his central idea of how knowledge of and belief in the power of the past had worked to the detriment of vitality. His antidote lay in inversion, turning the principle of history against history and breaking the power of history through historical knowledge. In Nietzsche's words: "history must itself resolve the problem of history" (1,306; HL § 8).

Nietzsche turned history against itself by going back to Greek antiquity to seek an era that had not yet begun to think in historical terms, and from there adopting his criteria for an art of living that would know how to protect itself from being overwhelmed by history. He reminded us that the Greeks were also exposed to the chaos of history; Semitic, Babylonian, Lydian, and Egyptian cultures and traditions made inroads into Greek traditions, and the Greek religion was a "veritable battle of the gods throughout the East" (1,333; HL § 10). All the more remarkable is the vigor with which Greek culture learned "to organize the chaos" (1,333) and achieve its true richness. Greek culture succeeded in forming a spacious, yet delimited, horizon. The Greeks described a circle that life could fulfill and in which it could fulfill itself.

When Nietzsche wrote that "history must itself resolve the problem of history," it dawned on him that he had found a formula applicable not only to history but to the problem of knowledge as a whole. How can we avoid being overwhelmed by the momentum of knowledge and supposed truths? How can life be protected from being smothered by knowledge? Nietzsche provided the answer in the sequel to the sentence just cited: "knowledge must turn the goad back onto itself" (1,306; HL § 8).

Nietzsche once confessed to a friend that he would have liked to live in the 1840s. At that time, one author in particular had taken a stand against the machinists of historical and naturalist logic. Max Stirner, the author in question, wrote that the free and lively spirit "knows that people stand in a religious or believing attitude not only toward God, but toward other ideas as well, like right, the State, law; he recognizes possession in all places. So he wants to break up thoughts by thinking" (Stirner 148). Stirner was a philosophical agitator who experimented with the notion of inversion years before Nietzsche did. This philosopher expressed his anarchic protest against the supposedly ironclad logic of nature, history, and society in a work that was published in the year of Nietzsche's birth. Under the pseudonym Max Stirner, Johann Caspar Schmidt, who was a teacher at the Educational Institution for Young Ladies in Berlin, published his book *Der Einzige und sein Eigentum* (The Ego and His Own, 1844), which caused quite a sensation at the time and, owing to its individualist and anarchist radicalism, was officially dismissed by the juste-milieu of philosophy, as well as by dissidents, as scandalous or crazy. Privately, however, many readers were mesmerized by this author. Marx was prevailed upon to write a critique of this work. His critique grew longer than the book under discussion, and in the end he did not publish it. Ludwig Feuerbach wrote his brother that Stirner was "the most brilliant and open writer I have ever encountered" (Laska 49); however, he said nothing about this writer in public. This secrecy surrounding Stirner persisted later as well. Edmund Husserl once referred to the "tempting power" of Stirner, but failed to mention Stirner in his own works. Carl Schmitt was deeply impressed by Stirner as a young man and was again "haunted" by him in 1947 in his jail cell. Georg Simmel refused to have anything to do with this "strange type of individualism."

There seems to have been a remarkable silence on Nietzsche's part as well. At no point in his works did he mention the name Stirner; just a few years before his collapse, however, a major debate flared up on the question of whether Nietzsche had known Stirner and was inspired by him. The most extreme position in this debate—in which Peter Gast, Nietzsche's sister, Nietzsche's longtime friend Franz Overbeck, and Eduard von Hartmann were embroiled—was adopted by those who accused him of plagiarism. Hartmann, for example, argued that Nietzsche had known Stirner's works, since the second *Untimely Meditation* criticized the very passages of Hartmann's work that dealt with an explicit rejection of Stirner's philosophy. Nietzsche had to have known about Stirner in at least this way. Hartmann also pointed up parallel lines of thought and posed the question as to why, if Nietzsche had been inspired by Stirner, he had systematically failed to mention him. The answer, obvious in his day, was formulated by one contemporary as follows: "[Nietzsche] would have been permanently discredited in any educated milieu if he had demonstrated even the least bit of sympathy for Stirner, a coarse and ruthless man who insisted on naked egoism and anarchism; the censorship in Berlin, which was a general source of embarrassment, allowed the publication of Stirner's book for one reason alone: the thoughts it presented were so exaggerated that no one would concur with them" (Rahden 485).

Given the unfavorable reputation of Stirner, one could easily imagine that Nietzsche had no desire to be mentioned in the same breath as this philosophical outcast. Franz Overbeck's inquiries revealed that Nietzsche had sent his student Adolf Baumgartner to borrow Stirner's works from the Basel library in 1874. Was it perhaps a precautionary measure to have the student bring them? In any case, that is how the news was received by the public, an interpretation that was supported by the memoirs of Ida Overbeck, a close friend of Nietzsche's in the 1870s. She reported: "On one occasion, when my husband had gone out, he [Nietzsche] talked with me for a little while and named two particular eccentric characters who were on his mind and in whose works he saw an affinity with his own. He was quite elated and happy, as he always was when he became aware of inner associations. A bit later he saw a copy of Klinger lying in our living room. . . . 'Oh,' he said, 'I was really fooled by Klinger. He was a philistine; no, I do not feel drawn to him, but to Stirner, yes indeed!' A solemn expression spread over his face. While I gazed at him intently, his countenance changed again. He made something like a shooing-away, defensive movement with his hand and said in a whisper: 'Now I have told you, and I did not want to mention it. Forget what I said. People will claim that I am a plagiarist, but you will not do that; I know it' " (Bernoulli 238). According to Ida Overbeck, Nietzsche described Stirner's work to his student Baumgartner "as the boldest and most consequential since Hobbes." Nietzsche, as we know, was not a patient reader, but he was quite thorough. He rarely read books from cover to cover, but he read through them with an unerring instinct for the aspects that were revealing and stimulating. As Ida Overbeck reported: "He told me that when reading an author he was always struck by short sentences; he would attach his own thoughts to them and build a new structure on the existing pillars that presented themselves in this way" (Bernoulli 240).

What was it that made Stirner such a pariah in philosophy, yet at the same time so attractive to Nietzsche? Perhaps Nietzsche saw his own philosophy confirmed in Stirner's. Later he flirted with the aura of depravity on his own; in Stirner's work, he could preview his own enterprise through the lens of the ostracized.

In the philosophy of the nineteenth century prior to Nietzsche, Stirner was without doubt the most radical nominalist. The consistency with which he pursued nominalist destruction might appear foolish even today, particularly to the philosophical establishment, but it was nothing short of brilliant. Stirner concurred with medieval nominalists who designated general concepts, especially those pertaining to God, as nothing more than breath devoid of reality. He discovered a creative power in the essence of man that creates phantoms, then winds up oppressed by its own creations. Ludwig Feuerbach had already developed this idea in his critique of religion, and Marx had applied this structure of productivity—which becomes a prison for the producer—to work and society. To this extent, Stirner remained within the tradition of left Hegelianism, which regarded the emancipation of man as a liberation from subjugation to self-created phantasms and social circumstances, but he stepped up the level of critique. Although acknowledging that man had destroyed the "other world outside of us"—namely God and the morality that is allegedly based on God, thereby achieving the project of the Enlightenment—Stirner contended that the evaporation of the "other world outside of us" had done nothing to undermine the "other world in us" (Stirner 154). We have pronounced God dead and have recognized that he is a phantom, but now there are even more pertinacious phantoms to haunt us. Stirner accused the left Hegelians, who had seen to the vanquishing of God, of resolutely replacing the accustomed "other world" with an "other world in us."

What did Stirner mean by "the other world in us"? On the one hand, it designates what Freud would call the "superego." In this sense, the term refers to the heteronomous burden of a past ingrained by family and society. On the other hand, it connotes the reign of general concepts such as "mankind," "humanity," and "freedom," which are erected within us. The self that has been awakened into consciousness finds itself trapped in a network of such concepts, which have normative power. The self uses these concepts to interpret its nameless, nonconceptual existence. Stirner affirmed the existential principle that existence comes before essence. It was his impetus to bring the individual back to nameless existence and to liberate people from essentialist prisons.

First and foremost among these prisons were the religious ones. They had, however, already been subjected to ample criticism. By contrast, the hold of other essentialist phantasms had yet to be scrutinized, particularly the alleged "logic" of history, the so-called laws of society, and the ideas of humanism, progress, and liberalism. For the nominalist Stirner, all of those were universals that lack reality, yet when we are obsessed by them, they can give rise to baneful realities.

Stirner was especially irked by well-intended discussions about "mankind." There is no such thing as mankind, he insisted; there are only countless individuals. Concepts of mankind do little to clarify any individual existence. What, for example, is the meaning of the "equality" of mankind? That everyone must die? No one ever experiences the necessity of dying in general, but only one's own individual death. I will never know how another person experiences his necessity of dying, even if he is quite close to me. I cannot emerge from myself. I only experience things about the experience of others, but I do not experience the experience of others myself. "Fraternity" is yet another general concept of "mankind." How far can I really expand this feeling, far enough to comprehend the entire earth and all of mankind? No feeling can endure that much expansion; the ego has simply evaporated into a figure of speech. "Freedom" is another prominent general concept that took the place of the idea of God. With biting irony, Stirner describes the process-oriented thinkers who construct a societal and historical machine that is expected to conclude its clattering business with the production of "freedom" as though it were a commodity. Until such time, however, we remain slaves of this machine of liberation in the capacity of party workers. The will to freedom thus turns into willingness to stand in the service of logic. The history of Marxism has abundantly demonstrated what destructive consequences this belief in historical logic can have. In his critique of the universalist constructions of liberation, Stirner has surely prevailed against Marx.

Stirner's nominalism set out to "break up thoughts by thinking" (Stirner 148). It is important not to misinterpret his aim in doing so. He sought not an absence of thought but rather the freedom to think creatively, which means that we do not accede to the power of our thoughts, but remain their creator. Thinking is creativity, the thought is a creation, and freedom of thought means that the creator stands above his creation. Moreover, thinking constitutes power and thus rises above what is thought. Active thinking must remain wary of falling captive to thoughts. "As you are at each instant, you are your own creature, and in this very 'creature' you do not wish to lose yourself, the creator. You are yourself a higher being than you are, and surpass yourself" (Stirner 37).

Medieval nominalism had defended the boundless creative Almighty against the kind of rationality that sought to ensnare him in a web of concepts. Stirner, in turn, defended the boundless creative ego against religious, humanistic, liberal, sociological, and other general concepts. And just as for medieval nominalists God was that colossal power who created himself and the world from the void and was free to stand above any logic, even above truth, for Stirner the *individuum ineffabile* similarly constitutes a state of freedom emanating from a void. This ego is also the colossal power, as God once was, because, according to Stirner, "I am not nothing in the sense of emptiness, but the creative nothing, the nothing from which I myself as the creator create everything" (Stirner 5). With cheap derision, Marx was able to reproach the petty bourgeois Schmidt/Stirner with his social situation, which did place narrow constraints on creativity. In doing so, however, Marx did not consider the ancient Stoic maxim that we are not influenced by things themselves as much as by our views of things. Marx's actions were ultimately guided not by the proletariat but by his own visions. Stirner was therefore quite right in emphasizing the creativity of the ego, because it is this vision that produces the latitude to support it—at least hypothetically.

Stirner's philosophy was an ambitious maneuver, albeit peculiar and ludicrous at times. It was also consistent in a very German sense. Nietzsche quite likely appreciated Stirner's ambitiousness because he was attempting to map out his own philosophy while pondering the problem of knowledge and truth for the sake of life and figuring out how "the goad of knowledge" could be turned against knowledge.

Nietzsche was certainly aware of one major area of disagreement with Stirner. No matter how much Stirner emphasized the creative act, he was still a petty bourgeois at heart, for whom property was everything, as was obvious from his obstinacy in embracing the concept of property per se. Like Stirner, Nietzsche sought to liberate himself from phantoms and use his thinking to do everything possible to "take true possession" (*B* 6,290) of himself. But Nietzsche's actions were less defensive than Stirner's. Nietzsche wanted to unleash himself on himself. Stirner was bent on disclosure; Nietzsche, on advancement. Stirner was determined to demolish, whereas Nietzsche sought a new beginning.

Turning the goad of knowledge against knowledge implied that knowledge had stopped deluding itself about the fact that it is itself a protective device against the void. Knowledge that goes beyond its boundaries not only senses these boundaries but also experiences feelings of giddiness. As we have already learned, Nietzsche called this type of supplementary knowledge "wisdom" or "Dionysian wisdom." How does the totality appear to this "wisdom"?

First and foremost, it comes across as tumultuous becoming that is always at its goal because there is no final goal. In addition, as we know from the essay "On Truth and Falsehood in an Extramoral Sense," it comes into view as a constellation in the universe on which some "clever animals invented knowledge" (1,875; TF § 1)—for a brief period.

The great silence of the cosmos will ultimately put an end to the "historical process" that was so confidently devised. This prevailing tragic mood forms the backdrop to a call for "fire, defiance, self-disregard, and love" (1,323; HL § 9), which brings the essay "On the Benefits and Drawbacks of History for Life" to its conclusion. The typical construct of his later years is already coming to the fore, namely that stimuli and thoughts get more reflexive as the will to immediacy intensifies. Ultimately, almost any stimulus is connected to the formula "will to . . . ." The will to cheerfulness, the will to hope, the will to life, and the will to affirmation—these are all preludes to the will to power. Nietzsche was already at work on a "hygiene of life" (1,331; HL § 10) that features the principle of mediated immediacy, which would recast the first nature into a second nature. "We cultivate a new habit, a new instinct, a second nature so that the first nature withers away" (1,270; HL § 3). This second nature should relearn "the unhistorical and suprahistorical" (1,330; HL § 10). The unhistorical is living immediacy, and Nietzsche defined the suprahistorical as that "which grants existence the character of the eternal with a fixed meaning" (1,330). It is therefore metaphysics. But after everything we have heard about Nietzsche up to this point, it can only be a "metaphysics as if." This metaphysics is not valid in an absolute sense. We use it as another vantage point during the brief moment on the little star in the cosmic night.

Nietzsche described the emotions aroused by Wagner's music at Siegfried's death in a larger context of the inevitability of death. Since death is a universal experience, Nietzsche mused, it is all the more astonishing that the individual gains access to this experience by means of music: "in the tiniest atom of life," the individual "may encounter something holy that amply compensates for all the fighting and deprivation" (1,453; WB § 4).

Something holy? We will be hearing more about that. For now, Nietzsche finds it in music. An animal that can make music is a metaphysical animal. Anyone who knows how to listen properly, however, also hears it come to an end. True music is a swan song.

CHAPTER 6

The Panacea
of Knowledge

Rift with Wagner • Hooked on Socrates • The panacea of
knowledge • Necessary cruelties • Staying cool • Falling
atoms in empty space • Human, All Too Human

*I*N THE SUMMER of 1878, when the first volume of *Human, All*
Too Human had just been published and his rift with Wagner was a fait
accompli, Nietzsche wrote in his notebooks: "Wagner's nature makes
poets out of us and we invent an even higher nature. This is one of his
most splendid accomplishments, which ultimately turns against him"
(8,543). One feature of this "higher nature," which Nietzsche had
devised under the influence of Wagner, was an ability to experience and
conceptualize the "suprahistorical" as a metaphysical vision that may
not conjure up any heavenly order, but discovers the "character of the
eternal with a fixed meaning" (1,330; HL § 10) in existence. In his unfin-
ished "Philosophy in the Tragic Age of the Greeks," written in 1873,
Nietzsche used the pre-Socratic Thales to illustrate the suprahistorical
viewpoint. "When Thales says 'Everything is water,' we jerk up from the
wormlike probings and creepings of the individual sciences, sensing the
ultimate solution of things and using it to surmount the vulgar limitations of the lower levels of knowledge. The philosopher seeks to hear
within himself echoes of the entire sonority of the world" (1,817; PTA

§ 3). Anyone who wishes to hear within himself the echoes of the "entire sonority of the world" and requires true philosophy to replicate this sonority "conceptually" will also be on the lookout for an actual, not just metaphorical, music in which this perceived inner connection of the world resounds. We are already aware that, for Nietzsche, this world of music was Wagnerian.

In the mid-1870s, three aspects of Nietzsche's philosophy coalesced. The first was his insistence that knowledge turn against knowledge, in the manner of Stirner, to make direct experience possible, thereby realizing the "unhistorical," and pulling thought up into the domain of the "suprahistorical." This is the second aspect. Stable structures and connections become apparent from the bird's-eye view. We should not imagine the description of life from this vantage point in overly discursive terms, or expect its "object" to be overly intelligible, because—and this is the third aspect—Nietzsche regarded this sort of conceptual description as an inferior version of an experience that is better sung in the language of music. "Intuitive knowledge" is his name for this idea, which has devised a "higher" nature under the influence of Wagner. But the 1878 reflection cited earlier suggests that the inversive dynamics of the influence of Wagner, which Nietzsche declared its "most splendid" aspect, "ultimately turns against him" (8,543). How are we to understand this?

Nietzsche wrote to Malwida von Meysenbug on January 14, 1880: "I think of him [Wagner] with undying gratitude because it is to him that I owe some of my most powerful incitements to intellectual independence" (*B* 6,5). If we consider this statement in combination with a notation made in 1878, which at first blush appears to contrast with it, "Wagner does not have the power to make man free and great" (8,496), the "incitement to intellectual independence" can apply only to Nietzsche's need to mobilize all of his power to step outside Wagner's magic circle. Nietzsche was therefore grateful to Wagner's powerful sway over him because it enabled him to attain a state of independence. At the end of his Wagner phase, he was proud that he had finally found the exit from Klingsor's garden and discovered himself in the process of matching wits with the magician. In the summer of 1877, Nietzsche entered the following resolute words in his diary: "I wish to declare explicitly to the readers of my earlier works that I have relinquished the metaphysical and artistic views that essentially dominated those works: they are agreeable, but untenable" (8,463).

One decisive idea and one decisive experience had brought Nietzsche to the brink of relinquishing his "metaphysical and artistic views."

Let us begin with the decisive experience that propelled his departure from artistic metaphysics. Nietzsche made note of this disillusioning experience during the first days of the Bayreuth Festival in the summer of 1876 and wrote in his diary two years later: "My portrait of Wagner went beyond him. I had depicted an ideal monster, who was, however, quite possibly capable of inflaming artists. The real Wagner, the real Bayreuth struck me as the mediocre final print of an engraving on inferior paper. My need to see real people and their motives was exceedingly stimulated by this humiliating experience" (8,495). Was Nietzsche now casting aside "the entire sonority of the world" to condescend to the "lower levels of knowledge," as he had called them in his characterization of Thales, and had he opted for the "wormlike probings and creepings" in writing *Human, All Too Human*? We will see. In any case, he registered his experience in Bayreuth in 1876 as an incident that awakened him from a dream. But his disappointment had not come overnight. Let us examine the various stages of his complex relationship with Wagner.

Nietzsche's deep bond with Wagner was most apparent while he was working on *The Birth of Tragedy* and immediately after the book was published. On January 28, 1872, he wrote to Rohde: "I have formed an alliance with Wagner. You cannot imagine how close we are now and how fully our plans mesh" (*B* 3,279). Just as he had two years earlier, in the euphoric phase of their initial encounters, Nietzsche pursued the plan of offering his services to the Bayreuth Festival as a freelance writer. He wanted to travel around giving lectures, heading sponsorship groups, writing, editing, and locating strategic placements for articles, and perhaps also founding a journal. He abandoned these plans once and for all in the fall of 1873, after realizing that the Wagner community was too small-minded and prosaic to endorse his draft of "Exhortation to the Germans," in which he insisted "that people need cleansing and consecration by means of the sublime crafts and terrors of genuine German art now more than ever" (1,897; EG). This "exhortation" was designed to win over patrons and subscribers for the Bayreuth Festival, yet it was phrased like a reprimand. The taste of the masses was denounced. Readers were reminded of their national glory and cultural prominence, and counseled in strong language to prove themselves worthy of Wagner's great cultural achievement. After the Wagner Society's convention in Bayreuth, during which Nietzsche's draft was rejected, Cosima Wagner wrote in her diary: "The societies do not feel justified in using such bold language, and who besides them would sign their names to that?" (*N/W* 1,187).

At this time, the Wagners were still firmly committed to Nietzsche and were more inclined to snicker at the small-mindedness of the "community" than to direct any barbs at him. Richard Wagner's declaration to Nietzsche on June 25, 1872, was absolutely sincere: "Strictly speaking, you are the only benefit apart from my wife that life has brought my way" (*N/W* 1,190). Especially on Christmas holidays and New Year's Day, Nietzsche was an eagerly awaited guest, but the Wagners could turn chilly if he failed to accept their invitations. Cosima Wagner took painfully exact note of even the slightest hints of reserved demeanor on his part. On August 3, 1871, she wrote after Nietzsche had spent several days vacationing in Tribschen that he was certainly the most talented of their family friends, "yet in many ways downright unpleasant, owing to a somewhat unnatural reserve in his manner. It is almost as though he is guarding himself against the overwhelming impression of Wagner's personality" (*N/W* 1,168). Cosima had gauged the situation correctly. Nietzsche was indeed keeping a certain distance, which he required to preserve his own freedom vis-à-vis the maestro. When Richard Wagner once again chided him for having missed a New Year's visit, Nietzsche wrote to his friend Gersdorff: "I cannot imagine how anyone could be more loyal to W. in all the ways that count and be more devoted than I. . . . But in small unimportant matters and by maintaining a certain reserve from more frequent personal interaction, which is essential for me and could almost be thought of as 'sanitary,' I must retain my freedom so that I can maintain my loyalty in a higher sense" (*B* 4,131).

Nietzsche's first, cautious insubordinations began to develop out of this sanitary reserve. In the spring of 1874, Nietzsche attended a performance of Brahms's "Triumphal Song." He was so impressed by this piece that he brought the score along to Bayreuth when he came for a summer visit, and played excerpts from it for Wagner, knowing full well that the latter held Brahms in low esteem. The Wagners were furious. Cosima noted in her diary: "In the afternoon we play the 'Triumphal Song' of Brahms. Great shock about the poor quality of this composition that is praised to us by our friend Nietzsche. . . . Richard gets quite angry" (*N/W* 1,191). Four years later, thinking back to the quarrel about Brahms, Nietzsche noted down that Wagner had a "profound jealousy of anything great . . . hatred of what he cannot himself attain" (8,547).

As long as Nietzsche continued to cling to Wagner, he was clearly and at times painfully aware of the latter's imperious streak, but he tolerated it, recognizing that such inconsiderate behavior on the part of a genius like Wagner simply had to be indulged. It is striking that Nietzsche reacted more and more frequently with illness when a visit to the Wagners was due. The worst of his bouts came during the summer of 1876 in the weeks preceding the first Bayreuth Festival. The fourth *Untimely Meditation,* an essay on Wagner, had just been published, and Wagner had reacted to his advance copy with great enthusiasm: "Your book is tremendous! How did you get to know me this well?" (*N/W* 285). Nietzsche could therefore count on a cordial reception from Wagner. Nonetheless, his body rebelled. On the day before his departure for Bayreuth, he wrote to Gersdorff: "My everyday health is wretched!" (*B* 5,178). When he heard how Bayreuth was preparing for the onslaught of visitors, a suspicion stole over him that this festival was not likely to usher in the rebirth of the Dionysian spirit. The "dedicated spectators" he had described in the fourth *Untimely Meditation* would evidently not be in attendance.

Nietzsche had anticipated that Bayreuth would put an end to the mistaking of "entertainment at any price" for art (1,448; WB § 4). As it turned out, outrageous prices were being charged for food, lodgings, and carriage rides between the city and the festival hill. Monarchs, princes, bankers, diplomats, and women of ill repute were the center of attention. These people typically languished during the performances, but perked up at social events. Later Nietzsche wrote about Bayreuth: "It was not just that the complete indifference and illusion of the Wagnerian 'ideal' was palpably evident to me at that time; more than anything else, I saw how even to the inner circle the 'ideal' was not the point, that entirely different matters was considered weightier and more passionate. Moreover, the pitiful assemblage of patrons and little patronesses. . . . The entire idle dregs of Europe coming together, and every prince racing in and out of Wagner's house as though it were more of a sporting event" (14,492). Nietzsche was witness to rehearsals, pompous arrivals of crowned heads at the train station, and stylish receptions hosted by the Wagners. All the while, he remained confident that his essay on Wagner represented the most significant intellectual contribution to the festival. It therefore cut him to the quick when Wagner failed to grant him due attention in all of this hustle and bustle. In Cosima's diaries, Nietzsche's visit was given only a single, brief mention. He was playing an inconsequential role and did not wish to put up with it. After a few days he left, in a state of turmoil, for the small, remote village of Klingenbrunn, but did return to Bayreuth on August 12, 1876, for the first performances.

Nietzsche endured the appalling situation in Bayreuth until the end of August. He beat a quick retreat from the few performances he attended. "I dread every one of those long artistic evenings," he wrote to his sister even before the rehearsals had begun (*B* 5,181; Aug. 1, 1876). In *Ecce*

Homo, he reported that he had found consolation with a "charming Parisian woman" (6,324; *EH* "Human, All Too Human" § 2). This woman was most likely Louise Ott, who had come from a well-to-do Alsatian family and had moved to Paris after the German annexation of Alsace. She was a passionate Wagnerian and had also admired Nietzsche's essay on the composer. They continued to exchange letters after the festival was over. On September 22, Nietzsche wrote to Ott: "This new friendship is like new wine, quite pleasant, but perhaps a bit dangerous. For me, at least. But for you as well, when I consider the sort of free spirit you have met up with! A man who wants nothing more than to lose some comforting belief on a daily basis and who seeks and finds his happiness in the daily addition to the liberation of his spirit. Perhaps I want to be even more of a free spirit than is possible for me!" (*B* 5,185f.).

Nietzsche's disillusionment at the Bayreuth Festival triggered his rediscovery of the true nature of human beings and their motives, and set him on the path to the "free spirit."

A pivotal new idea was gradually ripening within Nietzsche at the same time, which was to give his philosophy a new direction and pull him away from Wagner's intellectual milieu. This idea had begun to take root before 1876, but only after this point could he resolve and formulate it with provocative clarity. In a letter of July 15, 1878, to Mathilde Maier, who, like Louise Ott, was an admirer from the Wagner clique, Nietzsche wrote that the "metaphysical befogging of all that is true and simple, the battle of reason against reason, which seeks a miracle and an absurdity in all things" (*B* 5,337f.), had been a fateful and sickening error. At first blush, this wording appears to recall the formula for knowledge that turns its goad against knowledge, which was inspired by Stirner. With this formula, Nietzsche had hoped to give life the latitude to gain a second immediacy. The formula had a vitalist meaning. In order to stand in the service of life, the power of cognition and knowledge needed to be delimited. However, he now regarded this maneuver of disabling knowledge with knowledge as self-deception on the part of reason. He found it dishonest to pit reason against reason.

In his enthusiasm for myth (and for Wagner), Nietzsche discovered the will to purposeful, mythical, and aesthetic self-enchantment. In *The Birth of Tragedy,* he had written: "Only a horizon encircled with myths can mark off a cultural movement as a discrete unit" (1,145; *BT* § 23). But what conditions are required for myths to develop this degree of power? Surely, they can do so only if they are considered to have truth value. If an epoch has thought beyond the realm of myths, and knowledge is amassed that is no longer compatible with myths, a breach has occurred, which fundamentally alters a society's relationship to myths. Their truth value dwindles and is perhaps replaced by aesthetic value. However, myths considered from an aesthetic point of view cannot maintain the impact required to consolidate a "cultural movement" into a state of unity. That is possible only for intellectual constructs that go beyond aesthetic realism and lay claim to the entire sphere of knowledge, as was the case for Christianity in its prime, when it still comprised art, knowledge, and morality. The same applies to ancient Greece when it was still under the sway of myth. Nietzsche grew aware that these eras of the past could be conjured up in the mind, but their renaissance could be enacted only at the cost of self-deception. A modern mythical consciousness is hollow; it represents systematized insincerity. Wagner had the gods die onstage—a great achievement, in Nietzsche's view. But Wagner clung to the will to enchantment by means of myth. Nietzsche concurred with him until he realized that once the gods have died, only the aesthetic event remains. Aesthetics can be decked out in myth, but not transformed into a religious event.

Making a religion of art was not the answer. Nietzsche began to recognize this clearly even before the shock of Bayreuth in 1876, when he experienced firsthand how a hallowed art event could deteriorate into banality. He now contested the central proposition of the entire Wagner project. In an essay called "On State and Religion," Wagner had claimed that when reality turns distressing, it is the power of the work of art "to put deliberate madness in the place of reality." Wagner went on to say that a person enchanted by art is so deeply engrossed in the game of art that he experiences the so-called gravity of life only as a game. A work of art can make us "soothingly dissolve reality into a delusion in which this earnest reality itself, in turn, seems like nothing but delusion" (Wagner, *Denken* 315). Nietzsche had on March 2, 1873, recommended that his friend Gersdorff read this essay by Wagner, calling it "among the most profound of his literary products" and "'edifying' in the noblest sense" (*B* 4,131). Two years later, in the notebooks of 1875, Nietzsche rejected the idea that it is possible to lie our way into "deliberate madness" without suffering a loss of intellectual integrity. We should examine the forces that shape art without any illusions: "the pleasure in lying, in the obscurely symbolic" (8,92).

From this point on, Nietzsche no longer wanted to allow himself to employ sophisticated reflection—that is, reason—to nullify reason and dream his way into an aesthetic myth that would ultimately have him believing that he believes. He explained his unwillingness as follows: "In a religious cult, an earlier degree of culture is retained as 'leftovers.' The eras that celebrate it are not the ones that devise it" (8,83). How much further removed from the origin are the times in which the "cult" of tragedy was not even celebrated, but only enjoyed aesthetically! We are just fooling ourselves with all of this allure of tragedy. Nietzsche thickly underlined key phrases in the following note, as though trying to drum them into his head: "The fact that the essence of *ancient culture* has become thoroughly *decrepit* for us *severs us* from that culture permanently. A critique of the Greeks is also a critique of Christianity, because the basis in a belief in spirits, in the religious cult, in the enchantment of nature, is the same" (8,83).

When Nietzsche looked back one decade later at the period of his dreams of a renaissance of myth and tragedy in the wake of Wagner, he wrote in his notebook: "Behind my first period smirks the face of Jesuitism, by which I mean conscious clinging to illusions and forced incorporation of them as the basis of culture" (10,507). As early as the mid-1870s, before even one decade had elapsed, Nietzsche took resolute clinging to shattered illusions to task. He wrote that "impure thinking" is immersed in events of the past and acts as though it can undo the breach of naïveté ushered in by rationalism and the Enlightenment. If we take a candid look at the way things are, they prove to be different from the way the longing for myths would have them: "Phantasm upon phantasm. It is strange to take everything so seriously. All of ancient philosophy as a curious stroll through the labyrinth of reason . . . " (8,100).

This passage comes from the notes for "We Philologists," an essay Nietzsche was planning in 1875 as a fifth *Untimely Meditation*. It was starting to dawn on Nietzsche that his essay "Richard Wagner in Bayreuth," partly complete at the time, would be "unpublishable" (*B* 5,114; Sept. 26, 1875). "We Philologists" was intended to come to terms with classical philology. Nietzsche hoped to make clear that the prominent role of this discipline was based on a false understanding of antiquity, which classical philology continued to perpetuate even in the face of compelling evidence to the contrary in order to maintain its position of power in the educational establishment. Johann Joachim Winckelmann's image of antiquity as noble simplicity and calm grandeur continued to hold sway and justify the educational mission. Ancient Greece was the idealized locus of the classical union of the good, beautiful, and true. Nietzsche's contention that the gentle humanity of antiquity was a mere illusion would have come as no surprise to readers of his *Birth of Tragedy*. In that earlier book, Nietzsche had already disputed Winckelmann's image of antiquity and emphasized the wild, cruel, and pessimistic aspects of Greek culture. The new direction suggested by the notes for "We Philologists" was a shift in interpretation of the meaning of knowledge and its connection to myth and religion. Nietzsche advised readers not to "be unfair to knowledge" (8,47). Thus, even before his rift with Wagner, he was already beginning to turn the tables. Would Socrates, who was portrayed as the embodiment of the will to knowledge in *The Birth of Tragedy* and held responsible for the decline of tragedy, now resurface as the stone guest? Nietzsche jotted down in the summer of 1875: "Socrates, I must confess, is so close to me that I am almost always fighting a battle with him" (8,97). In order to investigate Nietzsche's changed relationship to Socrates, let us examine his portrayal of him in *The Birth of Tragedy*.

In *The Birth of Tragedy*, Socrates was depicted as a man who expected the most from knowledge. He not only considered it possible to live with truth but held that a life devoid of truth was not worth living. For Nietzsche, Socrates was the progenitor of the Western tradition of knowledge and the will to truth. This Socrates embodied a principle of knowledge and truth that was directed against tragedy, because it claimed "not only to know being but even to *correct* it" (1,99; *BT* § 15). If being can be corrected, pain, fear, suffering, and injustice no longer have to be tolerated. They can be eliminated, perhaps even instantaneously. Knowledge produces composure and happiness. For Socrates, correcting existence meant transforming one's own being and in the process shedding so much light on the nature of the world that life can be led free of fear and full of trust in existence. Nietzsche's Socrates was a genius of a science based on the "belief that nature can be explicated and that knowledge is a panacea" (1,111; *BT* § 17). We need not speculate as to how the historical Socrates would have viewed this spirit of science; our focus here is on how Nietzsche used Socrates to exemplify a particular stance.

"The belief that nature can be explicated" implies that nature is essentially cast from the same mold as the human mind. It is intelligible; or, as Plato would have it, like recognizes like. The corporal senses respond to the corporeal aspect of the world, and the mind reveals the ideas that form the perpetual models of the world. In the moment of insight, human beings connect to their true essence and become what they already are. They arrive home. This emphatic notion of insight is predicated on consonance between perceptions and the world. For Plato, all of this takes place in a world of thought, not as an empirical expropriation of the world, which would soon follow.

According to Plato's Socrates, the idea that "knowledge is a panacea" is borne out at the time of one's death. The narrative of the death of Socrates is a fundamental document of Platonism. The knowledgeable mind is put to the ultimate test. The dying Socrates triumphs over tragedy, surmounting his fear and dread in the process. Nietzsche called the image of the "dying Socrates," a man who is liberated from the fear of death by knowledge and reasoning, an "emblem over the portal of science to remind each of us of its mission, which is to make existence appear comprehensible and thereby justified" (1,99; *BT* § 15). It is, of course, comprehensible and justified only because Socrates' knowledge was more than just empirical, naturalistic, and mimetic. It did not investigate unknown states of affairs and was not goal-oriented like modern science. When Nietzsche called knowledge a panacea, he was referring first and foremost to the spirit of participation, which the Platonic Socrates quite vividly brought to bear when it came to his death. Perception, as Socrates demonstrated, is participation in a spirit that extends beyond the empirical ego. We are always conjoined with this spirit, but it is a matter of discovering it within ourselves and granting it dominion over our own lifestyle to the end of our lives. Socrates called this self-discovery of a spirit in which we participate, but which also reaches beyond us, "having a soul all to oneself." If we return to the soul from this standpoint, it is not a matter of separation from the world, or sinking into unworldly inwardness, but a link to a universal being from which the body, as a discrete entity, separates us. As we would say today, the soul represents objectivity and, therefore, what is meaningful and what really holds the world together. The body and our sensuality are merely subjective and ephemeral, devoid of essence and thus not grounded in the world. If we retreat into our souls, as Socrates teaches us, we do not become unworldly. Just the opposite occurs. Until we collect ourselves within our souls, we cannot really approach or join the world. Plato's depiction of the death of Socrates is designed to demonstrate that we do not die in solitude. Death is not the moment of greatest isolation. Socrates is not alone. In the self-awareness he gains by thinking and learning, he is assuring himself of a Being that supports him. He will continue to belong to it long after his death as an individual.

The various proofs of immortality that Socrates cites in his last conversation with his students are of lesser consequence here. The very fact that there are several "proofs" undermines the credibility of each individual proof. Socrates calls them a vessel we use to journey through life. The mind undergoes a process of self-discovery that brings living beings beyond the boundaries of isolation imposed by the body. It is not necessary to extend this confidence of the mind to all of its manifestations. In other words, the truth lies in the act of self-discovery of the thought process, not in the various, more or less illuminating arguments we can contrive. It is for precisely this reason that individual "proofs" of immortality are of only limited reliability, which is why Socrates did not hesitate to fall back on myth. According to him, once you have engaged your powers of reason, you can also "risk" believing in myth. He called belief in myth, especially the myth of the transmigration of souls, a "noble risk" and contended that "we should use such accounts to inspire ourselves with confidence" (Plato, *Phaedo* 114d). There is no fundamental contradiction between the self-discovery of thinking and reason, on the one hand, and myth, on the other. The rational mind led him to the deepest foundations of being, and he sought confirmation in myth.

Nietzsche called this Platonic Socrates a "mystagogue of science" (1,99; *BT* § 15) because of this link between the self-assured mind and myth, which in combination ought to yield crucial insights into existence. For Nietzsche, the difference between Socratic and tragic knowledge lay in the fact that Socrates was not aware of the point at which knowledge "gazes into what defies clarification" (1,101; *BT* § 15). The Socratic universe of the mind is always brightly illuminated; any obscurities are considered temporary. Socratic optimism claims confidence that someday even darkness will become bright. This confidence stems from the Socratic-Platonic intuition that the essence of the world is good. The only possible cause of darkness and obscurity would be a cognitive deficiency.

Cognition is not explicitly intent on an empirical and practical control of the world in the Platonic Socrates. For Nietzsche, however, this development was implicit in Socrates' confidence that knowledge is a "panacea." By the time of Aristotle, one generation later, this connection between knowledge and the command of nature had become more apparent. The formula Nietzsche used to link Socratic-Platonic ontology with our modern grasp of nature was "earthly consonance" (1,115; *BT* § 17), meaning that the subject and the object of knowledge are of the same type with respect to their common basis in mind or matter. There is no unbridgeable gap or abyss.

Modern progress in understanding nature is powerfully driven by a presumption of "earthly consonance" until the point is reached that the old god of metaphysics becomes the true "deus ex machina" who no longer requires tragedy, but instead functions as the "god of machines and crucibles," promising a highly practical "corrective of the world by knowledge" (1,115; *BT* § 17). The ideal of a life guided by science then predominates, and henceforth mankind revolves in a circle of tasks that appear capable of fulfillment. The optimism of knowledge attains complete fruition. Belief in the basic discernibility of the world and its intelligible character presupposes a fundamentally consonant relationship. Dissonances and obscurities appear surmountable, either now if the proper method is used or in a more distant future with the advancement of knowledge. If the Socratic principle is coupled with the idea of historical development, nothing ought to stand in the way of the triumph of theoretical curiosity. According to Nietzsche, however, if reality is regarded as increasingly penetrable and controllable, if the first material successes of this culture of knowledge occur in the areas of technology, production, medicine, and the social sphere, and if the hitherto alarming phenomena of natural forces become natural and thus calculable and theoretically controllable causalities, a feeling of optimism extends right down to those in the lower social strata, who will now begin to share in the dream of the "earthly happiness of all" (1,117; *BT* § 18). If it becomes increasingly more feasible to control nature by means of the sciences, why should it not be possible to eliminate the injustice that is inherent in society as well? If we make strides toward solving the mystery of nature in terms of causality and can grasp at least part of the chain of cause and effect, why should it not be possible to end the power of social destiny at the same time? From time to time, sabotages of destiny are successful, and consequently the sense of entitlement grows among those who previously had to bow to destiny and who now hope to reap all of the benefits that make our lives more comfortable. The distribution of opportunities for the pursuit of life and advancement becomes a question of just versus unjust organization. The unfortunate begin to see their destinies as injustices that can be litigated.

Nietzsche regarded the close affiliation between science and the rebellious spirit of democracy not just in terms of specific outcomes but in their overall ethos, as evidenced by Socrates' lack of respect for the prevailing opinions of his time. Violence entered the arena of argumentation. Claims to truth that came armed to the teeth were disarmed in the pros and cons of the dialogue. Dialectics did not allow for authoritarian stances. The Socratic Logos distrusted "incommensurability," and the "monstrosities" (1,81; *BT* § 11) of tragedy were considered injustices. Surely, such injustices have always sought obscurity to elude discovery! The dark is therefore an object of suspicion to the Socratic spirit. When someone speaks of "matters that defy clarification" (1,101; *BT* § 15), does this not indicate an attempt at concealment? Nietzsche eventually came right out with it: the democratic spirit was incubated "in the womb of this Socratic culture" (1,117; *BT* § 18). In Socratic science, truth is valid without regard to the individual. Although geniuses and renowned researchers have a major role in the sciences, scientific truths and discoveries are valid "intersubjectively," as we say these days. The meaning of truth is valid on its own and must stand up to scrutiny. Specific results that do not lend themselves to generalization cannot claim the status of truth. Truth is constituted in such a way that it can be grasped by everybody. Everyone is equal before the truth. There are no privileged routes of access.

Nietzsche regarded the Socratic spirit, scientific progress, and democratic upheaval as linked together in this manner. Why, then, was this state of affairs so unappealing to him? Why was he afraid of democracy? We have already seen the answers to these questions in our earlier discussion of his defense of slavery. The following statement from his essay "The Greek State" should be noted here once again: "In order to have a broad, deep, and fertile soil for artistic development, the overwhelming majority must be slavishly subjected to the necessities of life to serve a minority beyond the measure of its individual needs" (1,767; TGS). Nietzsche feared that if knowledge and learning were to become available to the majority of people, a horrifying, culturally devastating uprising would ensue, because the "barbaric slave class" would plan revenge "not only for itself but for all generations" (1,117; *BT* § 18). For him, this awful revenge was a "calamity slumbering in the womb of theoretical culture" (1,117).

Nietzsche contended that the order of ancient or modern slaveholder societies could be preserved only if everyone accepted the basic tragic constitution of human life as a consequence "of the natural cruelty of things" (1,119; *BT* § 18). The slaves put up with cruelty, which is one aspect of Dionysian wisdom, and the cultural elite is aware of this cruelty and seeks refuge behind the shield of art, which is its other aspect. How could Nietzsche possibly have failed to notice the obviously cynical implications of this idea? Most likely, he was convinced that the cultural elite—if it is really the elite that it alleges to be—also suffers from the cruelty of existence and spreads out the protective shield of art only in light of this tragic insight. The slave class in the cruel underworld of society lives and breathes tragedy, and the cultural elite is cognizant of tragedy, which makes for a kind of equilibrium. The one group *is* the misfortune, and the other *observes* it. Nietzsche applied his view of tragedy to everyday concerns as well. He was against shortening the length of the workday from twelve hours a day to eleven in Basel. He was a proponent of child labor, noting with approval that Basel permitted children over the age of twelve to work up to eleven hours a day. He opposed educational groups for workers. Still, he felt that cruelties should not exceed a certain limit. A worker needs to feel tolerably well "so that he and his descendants also work well for our descendants" (2,682; *HH* II WS § 286).

Nietzsche's portrait of Socrates, who comes off sounding almost like an ancient social democrat, did not come close to solving his problem with his philosophical forebear. He was not finished with Socrates, and he would never be quite finished with him. Nietzsche's declaration that he was "always fighting a battle with him" (8,97) applies even to writings as early as *The Birth of Tragedy*, which he originally intended to conclude with a reflection on the merits of Socrates, in the fifteenth chapter. Ten additional chapters were added, dedicated in large part to Wagner's renewal of Dionysian tragedy. These chapters were harshly critical of Socrates. In the fifteenth chapter, however, the end of the original version, Nietzsche used conciliatory language. He there indicated that in a certain sense we can also feel gratitude toward Socrates. Socrates is a "turning point and vortex" (1,100; *BT* § 15) of world history because he associated destructive energies with the pleasure of knowledge. The astonishingly high "pyramid of knowledge in our era" is also a dam against the danger of human self-annihilation. Nietzsche invited us to imagine what might have happened had the sum total of power been applied not "in the service of knowledge" but to "practical, i.e., egoistic ends of individuals and nations. . . . The instinctive lust for life would have been so weakened by universal wars of annihilation and perpetual migrations of peoples that suicide would have become a matter of course, and individuals, in a final remnant of a sense of duty, might have become like the inhabitants of the Fiji Islands, where sons strangle their parents and friends strangle their friends" (1,100). Socratic pleasure in knowledge had achieved nothing short of averting the "stench of practical pessimism, which could have generated a gruesome ethic of genocide based on pity" (1,100).

When Nietzsche exhorted himself, in his notebooks of 1875 and in later writings, not to be "unfair to knowledge" (8,47), he was giving Socrates a more charitable assessment, since Socrates represents theoretical curiosity, but Nietzsche sought and found other bases on which to criticize him. When he compared Socrates with other philosophers of antiquity, it was primarily Democritus that Nietzsche played off against him. Why Democritus? He was cold, practical, genuinely scientific, not as "individual and eudaemonistic" as Socrates, and lacked the latter's "loathsome pretension to happiness" (8,103).

Democritus had experimented with a worldview that closely resembled the modern approach of the natural sciences. Nietzsche was now finding it more and more appealing. In *Ecce Homo,* he looked back on the period of his life after he had parted ways with Wagner. "Regarding myself full of pity, I saw that I was quite emaciated, quite starved; *realities* were altogether lacking in my knowledge, and my 'idealities' were not worth a damn!—An absolutely burning thirst took hold of me: from then on I actually pursued nothing more than physiology, medicine, and the natural sciences" (6,325; *EH* "Human, All Too Human" § 3). Nietzsche, a classical philologist by training, had initially made his way to the modern natural sciences by means of the ancient natural sciences. The atomist Democritus had inspired him with his iciness.

Democritus did indeed break away from anthropomorphism in an incomparably bold manner, extracting all moralist projections from his view of life and making it appear neutralized, objectified, and hence "cold." There are only falling atoms and empty space. Since the diverse size of the atoms makes them fall at differing rates, they hit one another like billiard balls, jostle one another, and form random figures. The human soul and mind are also only concatenations and jostlings of exquisitely minute atoms. Democritus taught us that "nothing exists but atoms and empty space; everything else is opinion" (Lange 1,18).

One of the opinions that buzz about but never alight on the essence of things stipulates that nature is determined by goals. Democritus exposed this kind of teleology as an anthropomorphic projection. People imagine the universe in the same way that they set and pursue goals. Democritus cautioned us not to do so. Although it is true that the way the atoms fall, collide, and become linked happens with causality, these are only effects and not causes, occurring as a "blind" necessity devoid of teleology and "meaning." Democritus's universe of atoms is meaningless. In Nietzsche's words: "The world is entirely without reason and instinct, shaken together. All of the gods and myths are useless" (8,106). The sense of meaning that people impose on things is misleading. "Only in opinions," contended Democritus, "do sweetness, coldness, and color exist; in truth, nothing exists besides atoms and empty space."

With this phrase "in truth," Democritus was exploding the entire familiar world, just like today's natural sciences. We see the sun rise, but are aware that this is not really occurring. Science, from Democritus to modernity, teaches us that we cannot trust our senses. The atomic substance of the world is not perceptible; it is at best calculable. Democritus placed a high value on mathematics. Of course, people would go on feeling and having moral convictions, but he explained that these were only intricate motions of atoms. In his universe, there is no spirit that holds together and guides everything and has a moral significance. Good and evil are not cosmic reality, but occur only in human moral illusions. Democritus's image of the world is nihilistic, since it denies the existence of a universal teleological meaning based on morality. Nietzsche understood it as such, and so did the idealist opposition of the time, namely Plato. It is said that Plato burned the works of Democritus.

Plato's response to the lifeless universe of Democritus was his theory of forms, according to which general concepts are considered to be substances and hence more real than the reality from which they are abstracted. The idea of a tree is more real than each individual tree. Goodness is more real than any individual good deed, beauty is more real than any individual thing of beauty, and so forth. These ideas are elevated so high above sensuality and the reality that can be grasped with the senses that they become more and more empty. However, since Plato seized upon them so intensively in his quest to revolutionize ethical life, he inevitably draped these ideas in mythical images and developed a curious mysticism of participation in the being of ideas.

Thinking became an exercise in successful life, able to climb up above a hierarchy of concepts on a divine ladder of abstractions. Where was it headed? To the point from which being as a whole is revealed as the well-regulated good. Plato depicted an inspired universe, a spheric harmony with which thinking accords. Platonic cognition meant discovering the good in the world and becoming good in the process.

One could hardly imagine a sharper contrast to the empty space of atoms and the senseless and unintentional motion of Democritus. For Democritus, nature was sublimely indifferent, beyond good and evil. For Plato, on the other hand, the whole was good. Evil betrays deficient understanding, which would inhibit the individual from adapting to this whole. Plato's ontology of the good was his response to the neutralized universe of Democritus. It was a matter of energetic remoralization and remythification of the essence of the world. Why this whole idealistic reaction on the part of Platonism? Nietzsche's answer: "Fear about one-self becomes the soul of philosophy" (8,106). A person who has awakened to consciousness simply cannot tolerate existence in a cold, atomistic universe, but instead longs for the feeling of being at home. Philosophy is nothing but a longing to get home. In this sense, Nietzsche noted in his comparison between Democritus and Plato, Plato's philosophy was an "attempt to think everything through to the end and be the redeemer" (8,106). Nietzsche knew the history of the polis well enough to understand that Platonic idealism was a response to political anxiety. The Democritean disenchantment of being and the triumph of an objectifying enlightenment could unravel the moral foundations of the polis. Plato fought against the specter of moral nihilism and a material-ist devaluation of values.

In his notebooks, Nietzsche first committed to paper what he would come to express frequently in later writings, namely his astonishment at the success of Platonism in the Christian West. Plato was aiming to pro-tect the small circle of the polis intellectually, and in the process created an intellectual framework for an entire cultural domain over the course of many centuries. The Platonic-Christian view prevailed in myriad forms, contending that good and evil are not conventional value judgments devoid of actual truth value, but "true" aspects of the objective world. Nietzsche now regarded the world viewed in scientific terms as a "senseless" universe. Socrates (and Plato) could not endure cold knowledge, and they proceeded to moralize and idealize the world once again. Nietzsche noted down under the heading "The Consequence of Socrates" this perplexing phrase: "obliterated science" (8,108). This wording is perplexing because Nietzsche, as we have already seen, had in *The Birth of Tragedy* presented Socrates as *the* representative of the scientific and theoretical spirit.

In defending the will to knowledge against intentional self-enchantment, reintroduction of myth, and religious pathos in the mid-1870s, Nietzsche modified his critique of Socrates (and Plato). Socrates warranted criticism not because he wanted to comprehend but because he did not want to comprehend in a radical and "cold" manner. He lacked the courage of comprehension; there was too much romanticism and idealistic sentimentality involved. As Democritus demonstrated, a terrifying universe had been revealed to the truly knowledgeable individual even in that era. Blaise Pascal, who became one of Nietzsche's favorite authors, described this universe as follows: "Swallowed up in the infinite immensity of spaces of which I know nothing and which know nothing of me, I take fright" (Pascal 19).

Enduring such a fright without seeking refuge in religion (as Pascal had) or resorting to neoreligious artificial myth or art as a "protection and remedy" (1,101; *BT* § 15) became Nietzsche's ideal for a time, in the course of which he put the cold gaze to the test. In his preface to the second volume of *Human, All Too Human,* written a decade later, Nietzsche looked back on this period of upheaval: "At that time I waged a lengthy and patient campaign with myself against the unscientific basic tendency of all romantic pessimism to interpret and magnify individual personal experiences into universal assessments, even universal condemnations" (2,374f.; *HH* II Preface § 5).

The fact that knowledge can triumph even if it looks a monster in the eye—therein lies the optimism inherent in cognition. The man of knowledge proudly declares: I will endure my knowledge even if it kills me. Nietzsche prescribed himself this optimism as a remedy for a consciousness that craved tragedy and was so eager to indulge in postsirenian dejection when the music stopped. "Optimism for the sake of restitution in order to regain the right to be a pessimist at some point—do you understand that?" (2,375; *HH* II Preface § 5).

Human, All Too Human

THE WORLD, life, and the self might well have vast or even tragic proportions, but Nietzsche chose to experiment with the nontragic side of knowledge and optimism. He hoped to ascertain how far it could be taken, and what would happen if he sketched out several possible lines of development. In all likelihood, thrill of the chase would not be satisfied. Nietzsche—a fan of puzzles who could appreciate the "enigmatic character" (12,142) of the world—committed himself to a regimen of fortifying his will to clarity and sobriety against the allure of the twilight, and hardening his gaze against pathos and emotion. "The higher stage of culture, which places itself under the rule of knowledge, requires a great sobriety of feeling and a strong concentration of all words" (2,165; *HH* I § 195).

The "strong concentration of all words" that Nietzsche sought meant that he would have to choose a fresh discursive style. "Sobriety" cannot be long-winded, rhapsodic, elegiac, or luxuriant, but this is how

Nietzsche viewed much of his previous writing. Sobrieties are not intended to be written "for a singing voice," as *The Birth of Tragedy* had been: they must be pointed and striking, full of startling insights. The "strong concentration of all words" that he hoped to achieve lent itself to the aphoristic form. Nevertheless, Nietzsche was not yet thinking in terms of a book of aphorisms. In the crucial period between 1875 and 1876, he was still planning a series of *Untimely Meditations*. He drew up lists of titles and thematic groupings and wrote to Malwida von Meysenbug on October 25, 1874, that he had amassed enough material for fifty meditations, which he planned to develop into lengthy essays over the course of the next few years. Nietzsche was working on this plan at the same time that he intended to undergo a self-styled detoxification program. "How will I feel once I have gotten all of this negativity and rebelliousness out of me?" (*B* 4,268). His goal was to grasp "the whole highly complex system of antagonisms that make up the 'modern world'" (*B* 4,269) in order to achieve his own creative goals.

It is unclear what kind of creative activity Nietzsche had in mind. Did he want to compose music, write literary texts, or develop a philosophy of life, or was he already dreaming of a revaluation of values and new "Tables of the Law"? He did not reveal his creative aspirations, and it is likely that he had not formulated them clearly in his own mind. He knew for a certainty, however, that he needed to evolve from the kind of secondary author who writes about others into a primary author about whom others write.

While compiling in 1875 his material for the fifth *Untimely Meditation*, on the topic "We Philologists," Nietzsche remarked in his notebooks: "I prefer to write something that deserves to be read in the way philologists read their writers rather than analyze an author. And anyway—even the most minuscule creation ranks higher than simply talking about the creations of others" (8,123). Still, he was well aware that he lacked stratagems to reach the maturity required to produce his own works: "If I were already free, I would have no need for the whole struggle and could turn to a book or project that would allow me to put to the test all of my strength. Now I can only hope to become free little by little; and I have sensed so far that I am becoming freer. So my day of actual work is most likely on its way" (8,94). This entry dates from the summer of 1875. At that time, he was in a transitional phase, as we have seen. The will to sober knowledge was gaining the upper hand. During this summer, therefore, while still dreaming of creativity, he declared his intention "to bring to light lack of reason in human affairs with no holds barred . . . to move human knowledge forward!" (8,45). Where should this knowledge be heading, and what ought to be its purpose?

Nietzsche's astonishingly pragmatic answer indicated how much distance he had gained from Wagner's pessimism and aesthetic mysticism of redemption. Nietzsche explained that his investigations served to differentiate which evils in human affairs are "fundamental and incorrigible" and which can be "improved" (8,45). In this way, the original plan for a personal detoxification evolved into a universal program of enlightenment. Just as Nietzsche aspired to contribute to the project of moving "human knowledge forward," he also recognized that this type of work could be achieved only by means of individual inquiries and initiatives. How might he be capable of systematically and exhaustively exploring this enormous continent that has suddenly been revealed to him! He was too impatient and, as he admitted, too "cruel." He wanted to attack; "in every attack there is fife and drum," as he said later. However, he did not merely wish to attack contemporaries such as David Friedrich Strauss and Eduard von Hartmann, but rather to clear out the underbrush of opinions that had choked off the growth of human facts. Myths, the meaning and significance of which he had just finished defending—notably, the Wagnerian mythology of art—now struck him as mystifications that would need to be combatted.

However, Nietzsche observed himself closely enough to recognize the origin of this cruel desire to attack. In September 1876, after his return from Bayreuth, he wrote: "Benefit of a depressed mood: People who live under an internal pressure tend to excess—even of thought. Cruelty is often a sign of a troubled inner disposition that yearns for repose, as well as a certain cruel relentlessness of thought" (8,315). His relentless program for enlightenment in the summer of 1876 comprised thirteen planned treatises. Nietzsche planned to write on the topics "Property and Work," "Religion," "Women and Children," "Social Life," "State," "Liberation," "Free Spirit," "Teacher," and "Easygoing People." He envisioned a series of extended essays rather than a collection of aphorisms, but aphorisms would round out each selection as a "supplement" (8,290).

Since Nietzsche's physical discomfort, neurological disorders, vision problems, and migraines had now worsened, he applied for and was granted a year's leave of absence. He intended to spend this year in the company of friends, especially his new friend Paul Rée, at the home of Malwida von Meysenbug in Sorrento. In the few weeks between the Bayreuth Festival and his departure for southern Italy, he compiled his notes for an expository essay called "The Free Spirit," which he had first collected in his notebook under the title "The Plowshare." While working on this project, Nietzsche must have realized that the material would not form a cohesive whole, but would instead retain an aphoristic character. From this point on, Nietzsche had to grapple with a nagging suspicion that the aphoristic form might be an admission of failure. Did he lack sufficient stamina for a sustained treatise? Could this vast continent of the human and all-too-human, as well as the superhuman *Übermensch* that came later, be presented in any kind of self-contained or even systematic form? Nietzsche, in any case, had a new problem. Later, in *The Twilight of the Idols,* he claimed: "I distrust all systematizers and stay out of their way. The will to a system is a deficiency in integrity" (6,63; *TI* "Maxims and Arrows" § 26). The reality of the situation was not as clear-cut. When Nietzsche was working on *The Will to Power* in the mid-1880s, he wrote to his publisher: "I now need profound tranquillity, for many, many years to come, because I am facing the elaboration of my entire system of thought" (*B* 7,297). So it *was* a system of thought after all? Certainly a closed system in the manner of Hegel repelled him, but Nietzsche did aim at articulating the links between his diverse ideas. He was interested in an implicit rather than an explicit system. "Do you think it has to be piecework because it is (and must be) given to you in pieces?" (2,432; *HH* II AOS § 128). The aphorisms, he insisted, must not be misunderstood as "piecework," but they would have to show that the time, or at least his time, was not yet ripe for a closed systematic work. Nietzsche demanded this avowal from himself and discerned how difficult it was for him. He longed for a work expansive enough for one to stretch out in; his aesthetic sense demanded it. Had he not felt this temptation so strongly in himself, he would not have been impelled to warn so passionately about "the systematizers" who "want to fill out a system and round off the horizon surrounding it . . . —they want to impersonate complete and uniformly strong natures" (3,228; *D* § 318). For the time being, Nietzsche was still resisting the temptation to pose as a "strong nature."

Before traveling to Sorrento in the fall of 1876, Nietzsche completed his set of notes in the form of aphorisms ("The Plowshare"), which correspond roughly to part 1 of *Human, All Too Human.* Over the next year and a half, additional chapters followed. Their titles indicate that topics from the planned series of "Meditations" had found their way in. The first book of *Human, All Too Human,* entitled "Of the First and Last Things," was the clearest reflection of Nietzsche's crisis-ridden radical change of 1875—the triumph of the will to knowledge over the will to art and to myth. The problem of truth was a primary focus, treated in a highly imaginative manner, from varied points of view. In this chapter, Nietzsche created a stage from which his thoughts would have no need to exit. He would use this stage to try out various postures and perspectives.

Let us recall once again the memorable image that Nietzsche had introduced in his essay "On Truth and Falsehood in an Extramoral Sense" for the precarious situation of a consciousness that is exposed to the truth of being: "hanging on the back of a tiger in dreams" (1,877; TF). Our curiosity will pay the price if we look down from the "chamber of consciousness" and discover "that man rests on the merciless, the

greedy, the insatiable, the murderous, in the indifference of his ignorance" (1,877). A radical, uninhibited will to truth confronts us with
something intolerable. How can this intolerable truth be grasped if it
paradoxically reveals itself only to a consciousness that has left its
"chamber of consciousness"? How is consciousness supposed to go
beyond itself and grasp unvarnished, nonperspectivist reality?

Nietzsche recognized that the concept of consciousness confronting
transcendence would have to be described in more precise detail than he
had achieved in *The Birth of Tragedy* or in his essay "On Truth and
Falsehood in the Extramoral Sense." As we saw in chapter 3, Nietzsche
had called transcending consciousness "Dionysian wisdom," but had
not yet delved into the complex logical and theoretical questions of epis-
temology. It is the old problem of the Kantian "thing in itself": no
reflection on the boundaries of knowledge can take place without a
crossing of these boundaries. Transcendental analysis must work with
the implicit assumption of an absolute reality, a reality that exists even if
it is only grasped as that uncertain something to which the processes of
consciousness and perception refer. The concept of absolute reality can
be introduced soberly as an additional theoretical remnant and a residual category. When Nietzsche was writing *The Birth of Tragedy,* this was
not his intended goal. At that time, he was concerned with establishing
the presence of the absolute in ecstasy, in feelings of horror and rapture,
in presentiment and vision. This presence was held to be stronger than
a mere concept—it would not only penetrate into consciousness but
find its way into being. The desirable outcome should be not merely
mimetic but participatory. We should bear in mind that Nietzsche's
Dionysian philosophy centered on participation in an all-encompassing
colossal reality, which featured ecstatic union and an "orgiastic celebration of music." His theme was an ontology of a vast domain that was
not just theoretical but experienced, as both agony and ecstasy.

For the moment, however, Nietzsche wished to ensure the necessary
distance. He put himself on a spartan diet. No more overindulgence in
aesthetics or metaphysics! Thus, in *Human, All Too Human,* absolute real-

ity was designated coolly as the logically "disclosed essence of the world" (2,30; *HH* I § 10). With this concept, Nietzsche sought to hold himself aloof from "religion, art, and morality," all of whose presentiments, feelings, and states of ecstasy somehow drew him to the mystery of the world. These are illusions, he explained, and with them "we are not touching the 'essence of the world in itself'" (2,30). We remain in the realm of the imagination, and no amount of presentiment will carry us further. And yet we cannot do without this concept of the "disclosed essence of the world." It is necessary as a logical postulate to understand the relativity and perspectivism of various accesses to reality. We cannot know anything about this disclosed essence of reality; it only serves to liberate us from the prison of our concepts of the world. The "disclosed essence of the world" is an empty point, a vanishing point, a way out into indeterminacy. Since, however, any determination can be relativized from a point of indeterminacy, this vanishing point of indeterminacy becomes an Archimedean point that can shake the foundations of our world by contesting its truth value. Nietzsche later contended that there are only interpretations, with no archetypal text to which we can trace them back. The logical postulate of every interpretation is that an archetypal text does exist, but no one knows it. The same situation applies to the "disclosed essence of the world." Nietzsche was obviously determined to leave aside something that had stimulated and enchanted him in his Dionysian phase, namely ecstatic participation in absolute reality. He called this phase "icing up" (2,16; *HH* I Preface § 3).

In the mid-1870s, Nietzsche studied a treatise called *Denken und Wirklichkeit* (Thought and Reality, 1877), by the philosopher Afrikan Spir. This work had long been consigned to oblivion, but it had a lasting impact on Nietzsche. Section 18 of *Human, All Too Human* cited Spir, not by name, but by presenting a "proposition by an outstanding logician" (2,38; *HH* I §18). Spir's philosophy was based on the notion that the concept of substance has no reality whatever, since in reality there is only a continual becoming. The identity theorem of A = A applies only in the sphere of logic; there is nothing that is truly identical with itself, because there is nothing that remains identical, even for the moment of comparison. For Spir, therefore, the disclosed essence of the world—concealed by the space of logic and language—is the world of absolute becoming.

Nietzsche, who wanted to accept the "disclosed essence of the world" for the time being only as a cooled-off logical postulate after his Dionysian excesses, was, of course, delighted with a logician who portrayed the world of becoming as absolute reality, because this severe man evoked visions of a Heraclitean world. At the same time, Nietzsche wished not to revel in imagery and visions but to conduct an experiment in radical nominalism. His interest in nominalism was already apparent in his essay "On Truth and Falsehood," in which he called truth a "mobile army of metaphors" (1,880; TF). Now, with the encouragement of Spir, he was developing this nominalist critique. What is language? It is our house of being, but this house is situated within a vast hushed expanse. By introducing nominalism, Nietzsche was taking leave of the fantastic claim to invincibility of a philosophy that failed to differentiate sufficiently between being and its expression in language. "To the extent that human beings have believed in the concepts and names of things as in external truths over long periods of time, they have acquired a pride they have used to elevate themselves above the animals, in the firm belief that in language they had knowledge of the world" (2,30; *HH* I § 11). Humans base their actions on the proud awareness that they are also capable of using their world of knowledge to "shake the very foundations of the world as a whole" (2,30).

Does the opposite then apply once they have taken a nominalist approach and seen through the world of knowledge they took to be sound? Does everything now become fragile and uncertain? Does ontological seasickness threaten a person who awakens from his dream of knowledge and finds himself out on the ocean of enormous uncertainties? How would reality appear if one were to attempt to undo the "monstrous error" (2,31; *HH* I § 11)? One would then have to admit—even if it were impossible to imagine—that there are no subjects, objects, substances, or characteristics that are affixed to "a something." All of those categories are fictions of grammar. The statement "I think" is also an inducement on the part of grammar. The predicate "think" demands a subject, as does every predicate. We therefore declare the "I" to be the subject and suddenly render it the agent. In reality, however, it is the act of thinking that gives rise to the awareness of an "I." In the process of thought, the act comes first, and only then does the actor follow. We have been so thoroughly deluded by language and grammar that we take this delusion to be our reality.

Nietzsche undertook his experiment with nontragic thought in the first book of *Human, All Too Human*. He adopted the view that it is "fortunately" too late "to revoke the development of reason, which is based on that belief [in language]" (2,31; *HH* I § 11). Why "fortunately"? Because these errors constitute all that we have; they weave the world in which we exist as well as the veil that humanely shields us from them. "Whoever revealed to us the essence of the world would disappoint us all most unpleasantly. It is not the world as a thing in itself, but the world as idea (as error) that is so rich in meaning, profound, marvelous, pregnant with happiness and unhappiness" (2,50; *HH* I § 29). What are the consequences of this idea? Should we surrender to the will to truth to its logical limit, which would spell crushing "disappointment"? Should we propel knowledge to the point that our whole familiar world explodes into thin air and the certainties and orientations are lost in the unforeseeable?

For Nietzsche, there was no doubt that the radical will to truth leads to a "logical denial of the world" (2,50; *HH* I § 29). Nietzsche did not mean a Schopenhauerian denial of the world that renounces the will, but rather insight gained through the self-reflection of knowledge, which reveals that the world as we know it is not the real one, but only a world pieced together by us. Logical denial of the world denies the truth value of the world as it is commonly known to us. This "logical denial of the world," in contrast to the Dionysian world, which is experienced with horror and delight, has nothing dramatic or tragic about it.

The "logical denial of the world" is somewhat analogous to the Kantian "thing in itself." We can rest easy with it. It simply reminds us that every act of cognition is always just "for us," but never can comprehend the "in itself" of things. It is a cool form of transcendence that is neither more nor less than the ever obscure flip side of our imagination. Kant's curiosity about a world beyond our imagination was piqued from time to time as well, but he muted it with an astute analysis of the antinomies of our reason by indicating that reason is troubled by metaphysical questions that it cannot dismiss but also cannot answer. Our reason, which must inquire into the absolute without being able to comprehend it, is faced with a contradiction that we have to endure, but we are able to do so because we get along quite well with our transcendentally delimited knowledge in a world that is "in itself" unknown. Although we do not possess any absolute knowledge, our reasonably effective insights allow for a gradual mastery of nature.

This Kantian "thing in itself" evolved in a peculiar way. It acted on Kant's successors like a hole in the closed world of knowledge through which disturbingly drafty air was seeping. Hegel, Fichte, and Schelling did not want to leave this "thing in itself" alone; they wanted to seize it at any price and penetrate into what they presumed to be the heart of things, which Fichte called "ego," Schelling "nature," and Hegel "spirit." They sought to peer behind the veil of maya, and if there was no magic word to be found, they wanted to invent one, which is precisely what they did.

Just as "Dionysus" had been Nietzsche's magic word to shake the world out of its slumber, now he was trying out Kantian composure. He repeatedly stressed that this logical and nominalist denial of the world (which disputes the absolute truth value of the world of experience) was altogether compatible with a "practical affirmation of the world" (2,50; *HH* I § 29).

Aphorism § 16 carries the heading "Appearance and Thing in Itself" (2,36; *HH* I § 16). Here Nietzsche analyzes several possible ways of reacting to the difference between the world of experience and the thing

in itself. We can feel pressured in a "ghastly and mysterious way to surrender our intellect" (2,37; *HH* I § 16) and to identify with the unknowable essence. We attempt to live out what cannot be known, "to arrive at
an essence by becoming imbued with essence" (2,37). Clearly, Nietzsche
had his Dionysian passion in mind.

Another option would be to indict the essence of the world "rather
than accusing intellect," because the essence of the world is concealed
and leads intellect astray. We want to get away from it all; we yearn for
"deliverance from being" (2,37; *HH* I § 16), which is how Nietzsche
characterized the Schopenhauerian method.

Then he noted a third option, the one he was currently exploring: to
leave aside the difference between the world as we experience it and the
essence of the world and to turn to an empirical "ontogeny of thought"
(2,37; *HH* I § 16). In the long course of history, humans have looked out
onto the world through countless eyes and acted with passion, imagination, morality, and knowledge. This is the way we have appropriated the
world, "marvelously vivid, frightful, profound, soulful. It has taken on colors," and obviously we ourselves are the colorists. "That which we now
call the world is the result of a number of errors and fantasies that arose
gradually along with the development of organic beings as a whole. They
have coalesced and are now handed down to us as a collected treasure of
our entire past—as a treasure, because the value of our humanity rests on
it" (2,37). We can consider this history of experience a "treasure" only if
we are prepared to relinquish the absolute point of reference. We should
stop brooding about the "First and Last Things" and move beyond a vertical orientation in order to achieve a horizontal perspective. Of course,
horizontal science will not be able to liberate us altogether from the
"power of ancient habits" of feeling, which would not even be desirable.
It would be sufficient if feelings were ennobled and knowledge enhanced
within the framework of their basic limitations. What matters is distance
rather than transcendence. Using a scientific approach, we can "elucidate"
our own history, customs, knowledge, and feelings, and "lift ourselves
above the whole process, at least for a moment or two" (2,37f.; *HH* I

§ 16). Nietzsche concluded this aphorism with the following observation: "Perhaps we will then realize that the thing in itself is worthy of Homeric laughter, since it seemed to be so much, virtually everything, but it is actually empty, that is, devoid of meaning" (2,38).

In *Human, All Too Human,* Nietzsche attempted to shore up our appreciation for practical truths against the siren song of disastrous and tragic sentiments. He sang the praises of practical science, which "can no longer even be conceived apart from the natural sciences" (2,23; *HH* I § 1). He also hoped that his inquiries would prove useful in expanding our knowledge of people. Still, Nietzsche was treading on thin ice with this pragmatism. Wherever he turned, the ice threatened to break. He actually welcomed this sense of jeopardy and thrilled at the pleasure of descent into a perilous realm. As we will see, he continued to be attracted to the sphere "in which you die and rise from the dead" (Benn, *Gesammelte Werke* 3,345). He was lured by mystery and the "orgiastic celebration of music," because he sought a state of ecstasy and preferred the abyss to terra firma. He was a canny and uncanny Romantic who prescribed himself a healthy dose of practical science from time to time.

For the moment, Nietzsche chose to leave aside the mystery of being, though the more limited mystery of the social sphere continued to preoccupy him. He was highly susceptible to it and, for this very reason, sought to be "lifted above" it to a safe distance.

Nietzsche's susceptibility to the lure of the social sphere was the direct result of a compassionate bent in himself of which he was not especially proud. He later inveighed against his own compassion. A sensitive capacity for empathy intuitively grasps the long causal chains of interpersonal suffering. If a link in the chain of cause and effect between a particular deed and its deleterious effect is short, we call it guilt; if it is somewhat longer, we call it tragedy. Guilt and tragedy can become diluted to mere discontentment when the chains grow very long. A person with a highly developed sense of justice will uncover scandal even in this diffuse discontentment: one's own survival is predicated on the suffering of others. Nietzsche, with his passion for tragedy and his penchant for sympathy, called this linking of individual destinies a universal bond of guilt that comprises all of human life.

This compassionate disposition caused Nietzsche to suffer. The philosopher who later assailed the morality of compassion displayed an almost osmotic sympathy. Nietzsche himself could not be nearly as cruel, callous, and ruthless as he later demanded from the *Übermensch*. His exquisite sensitivity to changes in people as well as fluctuations in the climate had unfortunate consequences. Although his mother and sister often humiliated and belittled him, simply because they could not understand him, he was compelled to feel compassion for them and suffered from an excess of forgiveness. It was quite difficult for him to stick to his resolve. Just when he had sworn not to write any more letters to his mother, packages of socks and sausages would arrive from Naumburg, and "Fritz" proceeded to write a polite note of thanks and obey his mother's demand to make up with his sister. Although he sought a very different outlook, he was a genius of the heart, and a need to sympathize was obviously an integral part of his "first nature" and his instincts. Compassion was not, as he tried to convince both himself and others, just a dogma adopted from Schopenhauer. In July 1883, he wrote to Malwida von Meysenbug: "Schopenhauer's 'pity' has always been the major source of problems in my life. . . . This is not only a soft spot that would have made any magnanimous Greek burst into laughter but also a serious practical hazard. We should persevere in realizing our idea of man; we ought to be adamant about enforcing it on others as well as on ourselves, and thus exert a creative impact! However, this also entails holding one's own pity in check and treating everything that goes against our ideal . . . as enemies. You notice how I am 'reading a moral lesson' to myself, but attaining this 'wisdom' has almost cost me my life" (*B* 6,404).

Clearly his "first nature" lacked a penchant for making enemies. He had to invent and instill his "second nature" in himself. At that point, however, he would expand the concept of the enemy into grand dimensions. At times, Nietzsche was still too fully attuned to his "first nature" and remained enough of a Schopenhauerian not only to see the monstrous, murderous process of life but also to acknowledge compassion as the passion that is exposed to this monstrosity.

The theme of two very revealing aphorisms from the first book of *Human, All Too Human* is the monstrosity of the social sphere and cruel totality of the human network. Nietzsche stressed that life carries injustice with it and everyone is the prisoner of a desire for self-preservation. Only because the individual considers himself more important than the rest of the world can he endure it. A person looks out onto the world as though able to see only through tiny slits. The resultant "great lack of imagination" allows him the necessary stalwart quality for the struggle. A person must not empathize with universal suffering. "However, anyone who could truly take part in it would have to despair about the value of life" (2,53; *HH* I § 33). Perspectivism of the individual consciousness proves to be a social immunization.

In contrast to German idealists, and to Hegel in particular, Nietzsche felt that an "overarching consciousness of mankind" would be more destructive than ennobling. Nietzsche accused Schiller of not knowing what he was saying when he proudly proclaimed "Be embraced, O millions. . . ." This "overarching consciousness" would not only have to suffer the untold anguish that people inflict on one another but moreover be unable to ignore the fact that humanity "as a whole [has] no goals" (2,53; *HH* I § 33). The individual may set goals for himself, shielded by his perspectivist reductions, but the whole is already at its goal precisely because it is already the whole. As a result, however, the "solace and support" (2,53) one might find in an idea of progress would collapse. Whoever looks beyond the fence of mere self-preservation cannot help discovering the "character of squandering" in the social arena. Nietzsche concluded this reflection with the following comment: "To feel squandered as mankind (and not merely as an individual) just as we see every single blossom squandered by nature is a feeling above all feelings" (2,53). His notebook entry, which was the basis for this passage, closed on this despairing note: "That is where everything ceases" (8,179). In *Human, All Too Human,* Nietzsche played out this thought as follows:

Who is in the position, he asked, of enduring this "feeling above all feelings? Surely only a poet; and poets always know how to seek solace" (2,53; *HH* I § 33). Nietzsche, however, was not satisfied with this remark about the solace of poets. After all, he was obsessed with truth, and sought to have the will to truth triumph over illusion. He hoped to dispense with aesthetic and mythic blinders in confronting the unendurable. Hence, the very next aphorism begins with the question of "whether we are capable of consciously remaining in untruth" (2,53f., *HH* I § 34). In this context, "untruth" consists not only of abandonment to the beautiful illusions of poets; just as false is a very real practical access that links the sphere of knowledge to the interests of preserving individual lives. Are there only two options—aesthetic and epistemic self-assertion, on the one hand, and the despair of compassion, on the other?

Nietzsche attempted to explore a third possibility against the background of these options: calm, almost cheery naturalism. An essential precondition is the willingness to shed the "emphasis" inherent in the idea that we are "more than nature" (2,54; *HH* I § 34). This development would represent a "cathartic insight" (2,54), which should not be equated with Schopenhauer's denial of the will. Nietzsche now regarded Schopenhauer's denial of the will as metaphysical violence. Nietzsche's "cathartic insight" was not aimed at embodied being; it was a natural instinct that ennobled man's nature. It did not involve metaphysical transcendence of the world, dying of pity, or (at least for now) Dionysianorgiastic feelings of unity, nor did it entail blind self-assertion. All of this was to be avoided. The third path of cheerful naturalism that hovered over him was *hovering* in the true sense. The "old motives of more fierce desire" had to be subdued, with the result that the soul, muted by the will to self-assertion, lost some of its gravity and gained distance from the tumult, "feasting one's eyes as in a spectacle, which in the past had evoked only fear" (2,54). Nietzsche described the condition of a soul that has been relieved in this manner as "that free, fearless hovering over people, customs, laws, and traditional assessments of things" (2,55; *HH* I § 34).

We might say that in *Human, All Too Human* Nietzsche embarked on his experiment of observing "people, customs, laws" as they appear to those who approach them with this "fearless hovering." Of course, we must recognize that this hovering can sometimes turn into circling and then into aggressive swooping down to prey. Once the one who is hovering, circling, and then swooping over human affairs has seized his prey, he turns it over with an "evil laugh" and seeks to discover "how these things appear *if* they are turned over" (2,17; *HH* Preface § 3). The "evil laugh" requires an element of surprise; it might turn out that there is little or nothing behind the veneer, which might be masking an awful reverse side. There may be less to it than meets the eye. Still, the element of surprise wears off. Nietzsche feared that the "important truths of science invariably become ordinary and commonplace" (2,208f.; *HH* I § 251). Even if, however, the others are too callous to be taken aback, it remains possible to hurt the part of one's own person that has remained reverent, romantic, and longing for metaphysics.

Human, All Too Human begins with a critique of the metaphysical way of thinking, to which Nietzsche himself was also subject. He strove to liberate himself from the so-called "first and last things."

He began with the metaphysical principle that the beginning, origin, or original cause holds the truth and that true being, integrity, purity, and abundance can be found there. If the origin contains the truth, as metaphysical thought assumes, it is a matter of rediscovering the original model and the true structure in the bevy of time and embodied forms. Nietzsche called for a "chemistry of concepts and feelings" (2,23; *HH* I § 1) that could conclude its investigation of origins with the finding that the "most splendid colors are extracted from base and even despised substances" (2,24; *HH* I § 1) and take the place of the metaphysical fiction of integrity and truth of beginnings. Nietzsche was proceeding according to the principle of this "chemistry" when he explained that the origin of morality was anything but moral, and that knowledge developed from obfuscation and deception. His psychology of suspicion was also indebted to this kind of "chemistry." Behavior, speech, feelings, and thoughts all appear to be more than they really are. If one delves into their origins, one winds up quite a long way off from the dignity and truth of their pretensions.

For Nietzsche, therefore, the antimetaphysical, "scientific" principle is based in a refusal to regard the originary, primary, and fundamental as higher, more valuable, and richer. A person's stance on origins determines whether that person will proceed in a metaphysical or a scientific manner. Metaphysics places a high value on lofty origins, whereas science proceeds in the opposite fashion and works from the assumption that the originary is nothing but a contingency and inertness from which more subtle, complex, meaningful structures can be developed. "All things that live for a long time gradually become so saturated with reason that their origin in nonreason thereby comes to seem improbable" (3,19; *D* § 1). Science should not be misled by the metaphysical illusion of lofty origins. Platonism sought pure forms in origins. This Platonism, as Nietzsche pointed out, is still evident in a philosophy that claims to know what something is if it knows or can derive its origin. This type of thinking values information about provenance over the essence of the matter. "Glorifying the genesis—that is the metaphysical aftershoot that . . . makes us imagine that in the beginning of all things lies everything that is most valuable and essential" (2,540; *HH* II WS § 3). Once we have transcended this "metaphysical aftershoot," a history is revealed that neither originates in an estimable commencement nor attains the fullness of a goal. There is only a swarming mass with occasional pinnacles, decline that spawns still other things, and so forth. Meaning, significance, and truth do not lie at the beginning or the end. Reality is everything that is in flux. And we ourselves are also in flux. We recognize change and eventually realize that not only the objects of knowledge, but the process of knowing is itself subject to change. All philosophers share a "hereditary defect": they cannot grasp the fact "that the faculty of knowledge has also evolved, while some of them even envision the entire world spun out of this faculty of knowledge" (2,24; *HH* I § 2). They are clearly conceding that the human faculty of knowledge has a long biological prehistory. If man spins out an entire world with "this faculty of knowledge," he also discovers that this world has spun him out along with his faculty of knowledge. He perceives the nature that allows him to perceive. Man is a historical and scientific event of the self-perception of nature. Nature sets the stage within man to make its appearance. For a brief moment, nature within man, this "clever animal," sees itself. "It was the most haughty and inauthentic minute of 'world history,'" Nietzsche wrote in his essay "On Truth and Falsehood," "but only a minute. After nature had taken a few breaths, the star froze, and the clever animals had to die" (1,875; TF). Knowledge is born together with the human race, and knowledge dies along with it.

What kind of a world is not yet or no longer mirrored in knowledge? We apprehend animate and inanimate nature, which is itself devoid of apprehension. A stone does not know that it is there, nor do plants or, most likely, animals. Primitive forms of perception develop, means of reaction and reception. But the knowledge to which we have access enables us to know that we are perceiving and to perceive that we know. One aspect of this doubling and reflexivity of the human faculty of knowledge is our insight into the historicity of the faculty of knowledge. Knowledge attempts to penetrate into the night from which it emerged. How could we picture a condition completely devoid of knowledge other than as night? The hypothesis of a biological evolution of knowledge leads us into the murkiness of a world devoid of knowledge, which we are entirely incapable of imagining. We cannot imagine a situation that is without imagining. We cannot perceive nonperception. If the "clever animals invented knowledge" (1,875; TF) in a remote corner of the solar system on a star, and if after a few short breaths by nature the humans died and the star froze, how does nature live on without being recognized? And in what sense was nature extant before a knowing gaze registered it?

It is a common belief that the mere presence of something is the simplest thing in the world, but actually it is the most puzzling thing of all. It is easier and more natural to imagine a God and an entire animated nature, because in doing so we project onto the external world what we ourselves are—namely spirit, consciousness, and soul. The greatest challenge is to posit a blind, opaque, merely existing being. If a stone does not know that it is there, how is it there? Is it there? Where is it situated in time and space if there is no perspectivist consciousness that draws up the coordinates of classification in time and space? How does a stone "live"? Can we endure knowing that it is nothing but a stone? Novalis once said that stones are solidified tears and that some mountains look as though they had grown petrified from sheer horror at the sight of human beings. Michelangelo was certain that the idea of plastic form is inherent in the stone; it is only a matter of chiseling off the superfluous elements to allow it to emerge.

By immersing himself in the attributes of knowledge, Nietzsche touched on the enigma of being devoid of consciousness. He contended that it is the spontaneous tendency of knowledge to encounter its own principle in all of nature precisely because being devoid of consciousness is actually inconceivable and unfamiliar to it. "In the great prehistorical era of mankind, spirit was presumed to be everywhere and it did not occur to people to revere it as a privilege of man" (3,41; *D* § 31). Because man had made the spiritual dimension a common property of nature, man was not ashamed of being descended from animals, trees, or even stones. The notion of animated nature and omnipresence of the spirit was not an overextension of human consciousness, but an expression of modesty. In *Daybreak,* Nietzsche wrote that people saw "in the spirit that which joins us with nature, not that which separates us from it. Thus, people were educated in *modesty*" (3,41; *D* § 3). It is not immodest to look upon nature as though nature might look back. Anyone who receives this look back from nature experiences an encounter of the originated with its origin. Anyone who seeks out origins, supposing that he might find truth there, hopes to discern what can discern him. The origin is nothing but the experience that signifies knowing: being known. The big eye of nature that sees me, its meaning that shoulders me, this living world to which I give back and mirror back what it entrusted and displayed to me—that is the origin from which I emanate and yet cannot escape.

This intuitive recognition that nature is infused with spirit and soul has yet to turn back in on itself. It is a recognition that readily steps outside of itself and discovers its counterpart in nature. Man invented the gods as a knowledgeable thinking creature. He saw the gods by sensing that they were looking at him. The gods are the internalized image of a nature that looks back if one looks at it. That circumstance may be oppressive and make us feel persecuted and observed, but it also nourishes our pride. Man looks into space and imagines "the eyes of the universe telescopically trained from all sides on his action and thought" (1,875f.; TF), which makes even the most modest of men "instantly swell up like a tube" (1,875; TF).

If, however, knowledge is no longer as readily directed outward and mirrored in external nature, but is instead turned back in on itself, it may regard itself as a lone principle within a nature devoid of consciousness. Knowledge becomes self-referential and registers its own particular autism. The bond between the knowledgeable animal and the rest of nature is severed. Nature becomes the alien Other with which it is impossible to communicate, but which must be explained. We get along quite well with this kind of knowledge and even learn to master nature better than before, but we also experience ourselves as altogether separate from it. Nature no longer responds the way it did for religious and mystical sentiments. There is no nature left to protect us and provide us with a meaningful origin. The idea of an ultimate cosmic teleology comes to an end as well, and the idea of a being overarching everything forfeits its validity. There is no being before becoming, behind becoming, and after becoming.

Metaphysical tradition, smitten with the "world behind" being, seeks to read the world "pneumatically" like a text, with a "double meaning" (2,28f.; *HH* I § 8) in mind. However, the world stands nonmetaphysically before the knowing gaze as a becoming without meaningful beginning and significant end. Although nature develops dynamically, the causalities that drive it onward are "blind," because they do not have any objectives. They are not intentional, but if we know them, we can employ them for our purposes. The meaning of religious and mystical cults had been to influence nature in the medium of a spiritual context. This connection is sundered once we introduce a scientific explanation of nature. However, we are now in a position to use nature for our own benefit by exploiting its laws.

Scientific civilization has greatly facilitated our lives on a practical level, as Nietzsche acknowledged. It can also ease our minds in matters of morality. To whatever degree the knowledge of natural causality waxes, the sphere of causalities associated with fantasy and morality wanes accordingly. If, for example, lightning can be traced to meteorological conditions, it no longer weighs on our conscience as divine punishment. With every discovery of natural causalities in matters of morality, "a piece of anxiety and constraint [vanishes] from the world" (3,24; *D* § 16).

The grand disenchantment of nature by means of scientific knowledge does away with the intentionality of a world that has a meaningful genesis and culmination and a goal-oriented process in the middle and reduces it to a universe of chains of causality that clash and become entangled and produce new causalities time and again. Yet another sanctuary of religious and metaphysical thought disappears as well, namely the idea of human freedom. When causality is discovered in external nature and handled more and more successfully, it is inevitable that this principle of causality ultimately also reaches the knowledgeable authority itself. Mind and body once constituted a whole that was infused with spirit. Now the other extreme has been reached, and the whole is infused with nature. In the past, nature was an embodied spirit, but now the spirit is nothing but a sublime form of nature. On the path from spiritualization to naturalization, the idea of freedom falls by the wayside, and, along with it, the accountability for actions and responsibility we associate with freedom.

Under the heading "The Fable of Intelligible Freedom," Nietzsche provided a brief outline of the decline of responsibility. "So we make people responsible first for the impact of their actions, then for their actions, then for their motives, and finally for their nature. Ultimately, we learn that this nature is also not responsible, since it is an absolutely inevitable result and a concretion of the elements and influences of past and present things: hence, people cannot be held responsible for any-thing, including their nature, their motives, their actions, and the impact of their actions. We therefore realize that the history of moral feelings is the history of an error, the error of responsibility" (2,63; *HH* I § 39). Nietzsche was well aware of the significance of this outlook: "Man's utter lack of responsibility for his actions and his nature is the bitterest pill for the knowledgeable person to swallow" (2,103; *HH* I § 107). Especially bitter for Nietzsche was the circumstance that our lack of responsibility makes praising and blaming human conduct just as sense-less as "praising and blaming nature and necessity" (2,103).

Nietzsche would nonetheless keep right on judging human affairs as though people did have a choice and could make decisions. He would thus delve into the problem Kant referred to as the antinomy of free-dom. Nietzsche denied the existence of freedom and laid claim to it at the same time—even in this very act of denial. He was free to explain away freedom. The antinomy of freedom implies that it is experienced from a dual perspective. As a creature who acts spontaneously, I experi-ence the freedom of action on my inner stage. My intellect, however, drawing on the laws of causality, teaches me that culture does not make leaps and neither do I; everything is causally determined. We act now, and we will always be able to find a necessity and causality for our actions in retrospect. In the moment of action and choice, causality does not help us, yet we must decide nonetheless. The experience of freedom is like a revolving stage: we live from freedom, but when we try to analyze it, it cannot be grasped. This antinomy was the secret center of gravity underlying all of Kantian philosophy. Kant himself conceded it when he confessed in a letter that the problem of freedom had awakened him from his "dogmatic slumber" and brought him to the critique of reason:

"Man is free and yet there is no freedom; everything is necessity bound by the laws of nature" (Gulyga 143).

Nietzsche also dealt with this antinomy of freedom explicitly and momentously in the context of his doctrine of recurrence, entreating us to love our destiny—*amor fati*. Loving necessity means adding something to it, which alters it. When we embrace our fate, it evolves from something that was merely endured. We can therefore rest assured that the free spirit, which makes freedom vanish with its "evil laughter," is bound to conjure it up again in due course.

CHAPTER 8

The Bicameral
System of Culture

*Leaving academia • Thinking, the body, language • Paul
Rée • From* Human, All Too Human *to* Daybreak *• The
immoral bases of morality • Desecrations • Religion and
art demystified • The bicameral system of culture*

*I*N EARLY JANUARY 1880, Nietzsche wrote to his doctor
Otto Eiser: "My existence is an *awful burden*—I would have dispensed
with it long ago, were it not for the most illuminating tests and experiments I have been conducting in matters of mind and morality even in
my state of suffering and almost absolute renunciation—the pleasure I
take in my thirst for knowledge brings me to heights from which I triumph over all torment and despondency. On the whole, I am happier
than I have ever been in my life" (*B* 6,3). This is only one of the numerous letters in which Nietzsche linked physical suffering and mental triumph. Between 1877 and 1880, his health was quite precarious. There
were regular bouts of terrible headaches, vomiting, dizziness, and
painful eye pressure. A combination of severe visual impairments
brought on almost total blindness. Nietzsche's previous winter in
Sorrento (1876–77) had offered some relief, but when he took up his
teaching duties in Basel again, in the spring of 1877, his suffering
returned.

Nietzsche struggled through the following semesters by holding lectures and seminars on topics that did not require undue creative effort, and he was excused from his supplementary teaching at the *Pädagogium* (a public school loosely affiliated with the university). His friends were quite concerned. Ida Overbeck's diary contains an account of a conversation she had with Nietzsche's sister, which lists a few of the reasons "that would probably land her brother in a mental institution" (15,76; *Chronik*). Nietzsche himself was worried now that he was approaching the age at which his father died of brain disease. He feared that a similar fate was awaiting him. In Bayreuth, where people were horrified by the changes in Nietzsche, Dr. Eiser's diagnosis was the talk of the town. In his view, Nietzsche's most recent publication indicated "the onset of softening of the brain" (15,86; *Chronik*).

Nietzsche made every effort to meet his professional obligations until early 1879, but managed at the same time to forge ahead on supplementary volumes of *Human, All Too Human*. On March 1, 1879, after completing work on the page proofs of the second part, he wrote to Peter Gast: "Good heavens! Perhaps this is my last production. It strikes me as having an audacious tranquillity" (*B* 5,389). In the collection of aphorisms in the second part of *Human, All Too Human*, Nietzsche was clearly attempting to create a mental counterbalance to his oppressive physical woes. "All good things, even every good book that is written against life, are strong stimulants to life" (2,386; *HH* II AOS § 16).

This remark is an indication of what Nietzsche expected from the thought process. Thinking had to go beyond merely propositional truths. Another criterion of truth stemming from his battle against physical ailments was what we might call existential and pragmatic. An idea has truth value if it demonstrates a sufficiently imaginative and stimulating power to posit something in opposition to the tyranny of pain, which would otherwise claim all of one's attention. This autosuggestive aspect of Nietzsche's philosophy later assumed great significance in his doctrine of eternal recurrence. The idea of eternal recurrence cannot be grasped fully if it is shrugged off as cosmological

or metaphysical speculation. Nietzsche certainly believed in its propositional truth, but regarded the existentially transformational power that
emanated from this idea as still more significant. He understood it as a
challenge to live every moment in such a way that it could return without causing horror. This idea could make the moment shine and confer
dignity on life. We will go into further detail on this point later.

For Nietzsche, an idea can attain this degree of transformational
power over the body only if it is couched in a linguistic form of great
beauty and pithiness. Style had an almost corporeal sensitivity for him.
He reacted to linguistic forms with physical symptoms ranging from elation and physical well-being to lethargy and vomiting. He aspired to set
himself and others in motion with his remarks, which is probably why
he usually took walks while formulating them and setting them to
rhythm. In the following passage, Nietzsche let his readers in on several
trade secrets of his workshop of thoughts and words: "Let us pay careful attention and listen to ourselves at the moments in which we hear or
discover a proposition that is new to us. Perhaps it will displease us
because it is so defiant and so autocratic. Unconsciously we ask ourselves whether we cannot juxtapose an opposition to it as an adversary,
whether we can fasten a 'perhaps,' an 'occasionally' onto it; even the little word 'likely' gives us a sense of satisfaction because it breaks the personally oppressive tyranny of the unconditional. If, on the other hand,
that new proposition enters in a more gentle form, nicely patient and
humble and, as it were, sinking into the arms of the contradiction, we
put our autocracy to yet another test. How can we not come to the aid
of this weak creature, stroke it and feed it, give it strength and generosity, even truth and unconditionality?" (2,389; *HH* II AOS § 26).

The beauty and strength of propositions become virtually synony-
mous with their truth value. The will to know must come to terms with
a sense of style and rhythm. There needs to be a subtle, enthralling, awe-
inspiring, and seductive performance on the stage of propositions. It is
essential for ideas to be quite vigorous, "as though they were individuals
with whom one had to fight and whom one must join, protect, care for,

and nourish" (2,389; *HH* II AOS § 26). Ideas move about like people and wage their battles on their inner stage. Nietzsche's pronouncement about Greek tragedy applies equally to this theater of ideas: "It is the magic of these battles that those who watch them must also battle them out!" (1,102; *BT* § 15).

For Nietzsche, thinking was an act of extreme emotional intensity. He thought the way others feel. The passion and excitement that pulsated through his ideas never allowed their presentation to degenerate into mere reflex or professional routine: "I am still alive, I can still think; I have to keep on living because I have to keep thinking" (3,521; *GS* § 276). Nietzsche was not presenting his ideas simply to fulfill a moral obligation. For him, thinking was an unparalleled pleasure. He was loath to renounce it and was grateful to life for bestowing this pleasure on him. He wanted to live so that he could think and, by doing so, endure the assaults on his body that would otherwise make life miserable for him. He honed his words and thoughts so as to create something that "defies everything" and is even "immortal" (2,391; *HH* II AOS § 26), moving along with the flow of time. Nietzsche dreamed of this glimpse of eternity and noted that he would do honor to himself with any finely crafted thought, even if it was quite shocking. We must treat our own thoughts like "independent forces, as an equal among equals" (2,391). A passionate love story was being played out between Nietzsche and his thoughts, with all of the intrigues we expect from love stories; misunderstandings, discord, jealousy, desire, revulsion, fury, anxieties, and rapture were all in evidence. Passion for thought inspired him to structure his life so as to yield food for thought. He was seeking not merely to produce a series of quotable phrases but rather to render his life a quotable basis for his thought. Life was a testing ground for thought.

In January 1880, when Nietzsche wrote the letter cited earlier about the link between the pleasures of work and physical well-being, *Human, All Too Human* was complete. In his notebooks, material was already piling up for *Daybreak,* which was published a year and a half later. For Nietzsche, these two works fell into the same creative period because they both nurtured his "thirst for knowledge" while he was in great physical distress. In *Ecce Homo,* he wrote: "Never have I felt happier with myself than in the sickest and most painful periods of my life: one need look no further than *Daybreak* or possibly *The Wanderer and His Shadow*" (6,326; *EH* "Human, All Too Human" § 4).

Human, All Too Human and *Daybreak* belong together for the additional reason that Nietzsche was undertaking an experiment to "turn over" morality, art, and religion in both of these works, which meant he would observe them as phenomena that do not have a privileged access to truth, as is alleged by history. He found an auspicious and inspiring formulation of the principle of his analyses in a statement by Paul Rée, who was his friend at that time. On the subject of morality, Rée contended that "the moral person does not stand nearer to the intelligible (metaphysical) world than does the physical person, because there *is* no intelligible world." Nietzsche quoted part of this proposition in *Human, All Too Human* (2,61; *HH* I § 37) and continued to return to it, even much later in *Ecce Homo* (6,328; *EH* "Human, All Too Human" § 6). However, he went beyond Rée by wrenching religion and art as well as moral feelings from their basis in metaphysical truth. Rée, whose *Ursprung der moralischen Empfindungen* (Origin of Moral Feelings) had been published in 1877, admired Nietzsche's greater boldness. "I see my own self projected outward on a magnified scale" (15,82; *Chronik*), he wrote to Nietzsche after receiving the first volume of *Human, All Too Human.*

Nietzsche had met Rée in 1873. The son of a Jewish landowner in Pomerania, Rée took up philosophy after studying law and came to Basel in order to hear lectures by Nietzsche, who was only a few years his senior. In the winter of 1876–77 in Sorrento, at the home of Malwida von Meysenbug, the friendship between the two grew quite close. The result was an intensive collaborative effort. They read their manuscripts aloud to each other, provided advice, criticized, and revised. Five years later, in the late fall of 1882, this friendship collapsed under the strain of their romantic involvement with Lou Salomé. After Rée and Nietzsche had gone their separate ways, Rée published several additional books on moral philosophy, then studied medicine and became a practicing doctor back in his father's neighborhood. He led the life of a Tolstoyan; he helped farmers and was considered an eccentric and a virtual saint. When Nietzsche died, Rée moved to the vicinity of Sils-Maria and provided medical care for the residents of the mountain region. One year after Nietzsche's death, while hiking in the Alps, Rée fell to his own death from a slippery cliff. It is unclear whether it was an accident or suicide. Shortly before his death, Rée declared: "I have to philosophize. When I run out of material about which to philosophize, it is best for me to die" (Janz 1,644).

Even after the rift between them, Rée wanted to dedicate his book *Die Entstehung des Gewissens* (The Origin of Conscience, 1885), to his former friend. Nietzsche, however, refused this gesture. Although he never denied having been influenced by Rée, he later adamantly emphasized his divergences from Rée's theoretical positions, going so far as to claim in his preface to *On the Genealogy of Morals* that he had rarely read something to which he felt so compelled to say no, "proposition by proposition, conclusion by conclusion" (5,250; *GM* Preface § 4). He concurred with Rée's critique of the metaphysical basis of morality, but disputed his opinion that morality arises from the altruistic nature of man. In *Human, All Too Human,* and even more in *Daybreak,* Nietzsche followed the trail of morality back to its nonmoral basis. The history of morality is not moral. Moral feelings do not originate in virtue, but result from a very long history of cultural habits and ingrained attitudes that come to the surface. The physiological dimension is also important. People who act morally may consider themselves moral, but in reality, Nietzsche explained, it is this history of the body and culture that is "acting" within us. How does it "act"? First and foremost by splitting people apart. As Nietzsche wrote in *Human, All Too Human,* morality presupposes a capability for "self-splitting" (2,76; *HH* I § 57). Something within us gives orders to another something within us. Conscience, incessant self-commentary, and self-evaluation come into play. Although a powerful tradition focused on the "individual," the indivisible core of man, Nietzsche pondered the nuclear fission of the individual, declaring that, "in matters of morality, people treat themselves not as *'individuum'* but as *'dividuum'*" (2,76). Because the individual is not a discrete entity, it can also become the setting for an interior world history, and anyone who studies it may well become the "adventurer and circumnavigator of the inner world known as 'human'" (2,21; *HH* I Preface § 7). Just like Nietzsche.

Morality was a lifelong obsession for Nietzsche. As he pondered this topic, he began to realize that the basic human condition was actually a person's relationship to himself. Man—the *dividuum*—can and must relate to himself. He is not a harmonious being, but a discordant one, both condemned and privileged to conduct experiments on himself. Individual life as well as the life of cultures as a whole is therefore a series of self-experimentations. Man is the "undetermined animal" (5,81; *BGE* § 62). If we cannot be determined, how we deal with ourselves is crucial. Nietzsche's philosophy provided a response to the tremendous demands posed by freedom, which he then proceeded to minimize. Nietzsche was well versed in the medley of voices within us, which offer people a choice as to which of the voices they will grant the power of determination. We tend to regard the medley as profusion. But could we be wrong? Perhaps in the beginning there were only the weak and the strong, who differed according to the unanimity and hence the strength of their wills. A strong will was able to subjugate and command a weaker one. Although the weaker one obeyed, the sting of these commands remained behind as a foreign body. The commands were "incorporated," and evolved into our conscience. Perhaps this is how the *dividuum* originated, as a creature wounded and torn apart by the sting of commands who painstakingly learns to transform the passion of obedience into the obsession of domination, but who is plagued by a bad conscience. We have learned to obey and now need to learn how to command, particularly to command ourselves. In order to do so, however, we must gain a strong sense of self-esteem and discover the master within ourselves. Anyone who has learned how to obey too well will search in vain for an authority bold enough to give commands. Internalized commands have not only fractured the individual but awakened self-doubt. This complicated history eventually gave rise to something that later centuries would call the depth of soul, this whole inner labyrinth of veiled meaning, profundity, and nonsense.

Nietzsche knew that the "dividual" way of life was now inevitable. The path back to prehistoric harmony within individuals—if it ever existed at all—had been closed off. A basic breach and inner disjunctions have become part of the *conditio humana*.

Nonetheless, Nietzsche would continue to insist that we "make a whole person of ourselves" (2,92; *HH* I § 95). This quest for wholeness would not entail overcoming the dividual mode of existence, which would be impossible, but effective self-configuration and self-instrumentation. We need to take charge of our impulses, learn to smooth over our disjunctions, and become the conductor of our medley of voices. The ominous "will to power"—which, as we will see later, builds up to a cosmic explanation and directive of grand-scale politics in Nietzsche's later years—is always tuned to a concert pitch, and signifies a quest for self-empowerment. Nietzsche's works as a whole are an extended chronicle of the complex events in an experiment to attain power over oneself. Let us here recall Nietzsche's moral imperative: "You should become the master of yourself and also the master of your own virtues. Previously, they were your masters, but they must be nothing more than your tools, just some tools among others. You should achieve power over your pros and cons and learn how to put them forth and hang them back in accordance with your higher aim. You should learn to recognize the perspectivism inherent in every appraisal" (2,20; *HH* I Preface § 6). The relationship to oneself that is here envisaged is one of sovereignty in which "bourgeois morality no longer has a say," because it demands reliability, steadiness, and predictability. Nietzsche felt that making "a whole person of ourselves" was the loftiest task that any individual could achieve in a lifetime. This type of issue does not ensue from the history of morality, in which nothing matters less than the goal of ensuring that each individual become "a whole person." On the contrary: the history of morality is a bloodstained lunacy that has devoured people. Anyone who has been successful in making "a whole person" of himself accomplished it despite history.

The first contours of this sort of disillusioning history of morality are presented in *Human, All Too Human* and are developed further in *Daybreak*. *On the Genealogy of Morals* brings the analysis of the nonmoral history of morality to a conclusion.

As far back as *Human, All Too Human,* Nietzsche was testing a hypothesis that would continue to define his writings, namely that behind the moral distinction between good and evil lurks the older distinction between "noble" and "base" (2,67; *HH* I § 45). Who is noble? Nietzsche's answer was those who are sufficiently strong, determined, and fearless to "engage in retaliation" (2,67; *HH* I § 45) when attacked. Those who can stand up for themselves and know how to protect and avenge themselves are noble. The actions of a noble person are good because the person is fundamentally good. The "base" individual is bad because his lack of self-regard prevents him from defending himself with whatever limited means he has at his disposal. Hence, "noble" and "base" are designations for differing measures of self-regard. From the perspective of the noble person, a bad person is an insignificant person from whom nothing needs to be feared, because he does not even have regard for himself.

Insignificant people can pose a danger to noble people if they compensate for their frailty by banding together and taking the offensive, either in the physical sense of an actual slave revolt or mentally by overturning the hierarchy of values and replacing imperious virtues with a morality of tolerance and humility. In *Human, All Too Human,* Nietzsche began to develop his critique of ressentiment in morality and to pick apart Schopenhauer's morality of pity by shifting the accent from the sensation of pity to the arousal of pity and interpreting the use of pity as a weapon of the weak. The weak discover the vulnerable aspect of the strong, namely their ability to experience pity, and the weak exploit this vulnerability by arousing pity. In this way, sufferers have found a means of "inflicting pain" (2,71; *HH* I § 50) on others.

Nietzsche sought to strip the dialectics of pity—in which the sufferer inflicts pain on others by arousing pity—of its sentimental coating, thereby revealing the power struggle beneath the surface. In his view, the dialectics of pity impelled the battle between master and servant. When a person arouses pity, his "conceit rises up; he is still important enough to cause pain to the world" (2,71; *HH* I § 50). At the same time, the person experiencing pity feels wronged and trapped, although he may otherwise be the master.

Gratitude presents another example of the insignificance of morals and reveals how much underlying struggle is involved. Nietzsche contended that gratitude is a mild form of revenge. A person on the receiving end of an act of generosity is made aware of the power of his benefactor. Although this power may be benevolent, it still makes one individual beholden to another. The indebted individual expresses his appreciation and repays his debt, perhaps even beyond the measure of what was received. He then seeks to be free once more by inverting the debtor relationship. Nietzsche recalled Swift's remark "that people are grateful to the same extent that they harbor revenge" (2,67; *HH* I § 44).

Nietzsche's analysis of morality is positively obsessed with revealing the primal cruelty that is masked in morality. Consequently, for him, open cruelty is the moment of truth. The primeval history of hostility comes to light, and elemental forces break through the crust of civilization. "We need to consider the people who are now cruel as stages of *earlier cultures* that have been left over: the mountains of humanity are openly revealing the deeper formations here that otherwise remain concealed" (2,66; *HH* I § 43).

In *Daybreak,* Nietzsche further advanced his analysis of the cruelty that constitutes the basis of human interaction. He described the ways in which "refined cruelty" (3,40; *D* § 30) could become an acknowledged virtue. When someone is intent on excelling in an otherwise laudable manner, does he not desire to "inflict pain" on others by means of his exalted status and enjoy the envy he arouses? Is there not an "anticipated delight" (3,40) in an artist's ability to defeat his artistic rivals, which heightens his euphoria in creation? Perhaps the agonistic character of culture as a whole is really a sublimation of cruel readiness for battle. What clandestine pleasures lurk behind the chastity of a nun? "With what reproving eyes she looks into the face of women who live otherwise! How much lust for revenge there is in these eyes!" (3,40; D § 30).

Nietzsche found ample evidence in religion to support his hypothesis that cruelty was a creative force in civilization. In many cultures, the gods were held to be cruel, and required mollification in the form of sacrifices. People obviously pictured the gods as creatures who took pleasure in witnessing torture and carnage. Even the Christian God had to be placated by the sacrifice of his son. Gratifying the gods entails providing them a festival of cruelty. Their pleasure is a magnified version of the pleasure of humans; hence "cruelty is one of the oldest festive joys of mankind" (3,30; *D* § 18).

When Nietzsche called the history of moral feelings the "history of an error" (2,63; *HH* I § 39), he was not denying that this error had shaped culture. Moral feelings are certainly in error if they purport to be an organ of truth and a guide to the true destiny of man, but errors of this sort are necessary illusions that make possible man's cultural self-definition. However oppressive moral laws may be, they do yield extraordinary self-esteem. Let us consider, for example, the taboo against incest. There is no natural reason, in terms of either instinct or physiology, not to violate this taboo. The boundary that precludes incestuous relations is not physical but moral. Obedience ultimately evolves into self-control, which signals our initiation into culture. Only those who exercise self-control can learn self-regard.

Cultural commandments and proscriptions serve practical ends that are eugenic, economic, health-related, and political. Nietzsche, however, warned us against projecting a utilitarian purpose back onto origins, since a purpose often emerges only much later. The same applies to self-control, which was not designed as a pedagogical program but was instead a subjective consequence of the precepts governing objective morality. Customs were meant not to provide advantages to particular individuals but to preserve and develop an entire human cultural network. Who is targeted in this process? Not the individual, not even the ruling individual, but the subjectless "subject" of the cultural process. This subjectless subject is embodied in the system of customs and taboos. This system merits our attention regardless of any utilitarian purpose. It provides the explanation for puzzling prohibitions that appear to be altogether senseless and impractical. Prohibitions of this sort inspired Nietzsche's observation that "among primitive peoples there exists a species of customs whose purpose seems to be customs in general" (3,29; *D* § 16). Nietzsche cited the example of a Mongolian tribe, the Kamshadales, who are allegedly forbidden to scrape the snow from their shoes with a knife, to skewer coal on a knife, or to put iron into a fire. Any one of these transgressions is punishable by death. Taboos of this sort evidently have the sole function of "maintaining a perpetual proximity of custom, the constant compulsion to adhere to custom: to reinforce the mighty proposition with which civilization commences. Any custom is better than no custom" (3,29).

Customs function as a system of directing our drives. One and the same drive can be experienced under the pressure of particular customs as a painful feeling of cowardice or as a "pleasurable feeling of humility" (3,45; *D* § 38)—if, for example, it is dictated by Christian morality. Drives do not have a moral character in and of themselves. This character develops only gradually as a "second nature" (3,45). An agonistic culture such as that of ancient Greece did not consider envy offensive, in contrast to cultures that placed a high value on equality. In ancient Israel, wrath was considered proof of the greatest vitality, and for this reason divine wrath was a prominent attribute of the Jewish God.

Across the various cultures, morality is regarded as a system that goes beyond differentiating between good and evil and also extends to distinctions between truth and untruth. According to Nietzsche, moral systems are linked to an overt or implied metaphysics of self-legitimacy. In a comparison of cultures, though, no one specific metaphysical claim to truth can be maintained. The grand truths become fragmented into the myriad forms that culture can assume. Nietzsche reminds us that this inclination to analyze foreign cultures in relative terms provided the foundations of enlightenment as far back as Greek antiquity. The comparative historiography of Herodotus contributed to breaking open mythically sealed Greek culture. In the modern era, Montaigne in particular used cultural comparisons to dismantle claims to truth. Nietzsche situated himself in this tradition. He had no intention of relinquishing the principle of morality just because its implicit metaphysics had become untenable. Morality remained essential. Nietzsche placed a high value on the power of morality to direct our drives and create a second nature. He therefore felt confident in his contention that "without the errors that underlie the assumptions of morality, man would have remained an animal" (2,64; *HH* I § 40).

Nietzsche's critique of the metaphysical and religious self-legitimacy of morality was not aimed at changing the concept of directing drives and the achievements of the "second nature." He simply wanted to ensure that it be managed in a more enlightened manner in the future and be subject to more deliberate control. The system of morality should evolve from a hot, murky project to a cold, clear one. Certainly, some will feel "far too wintry in the breath of this manner of seeing things" (2,61; *HH* I § 38). Still, we need to move forward in our quest to enlighten culture about itself without any inhibitions about probing its innermost secrets. In a culture that is insulated against self-enlightenment, the internal temperature rises, which we might think of as warmth from the nest. If the fear of freedom and of metaphysical homelessness evokes feelings of panic, the warm nest can become a boiling kettle, which is Nietzsche's reason for appealing to "the more spiritual beings of an era that is clearly going up in flames more and more" to use the sciences as a means of "dousing and cooling" and to employ them as "mirrors and self-reflection" (2,62; *HH* I § 38) of the prevailing spirit.

In *Human, All Too Human,* Nietzsche placed great faith in this kind of "self-reflection," which could reach well beyond the level of the individual. He considered the possibility that an entire civilization, by gaining a clear understanding of itself and taking leave of the old religious belief in fate, might be capable of setting for itself "ecumenical goals spanning the whole earth" (2,46; *HH* I § 25). If mankind is not to be destroyed by such deliberate total regulation, "a knowledge of the conditions of culture exceeding all previous degrees of such knowledge would have to be found as a scientific measure for ecumenical goals" (2,46).

Nietzsche was approaching Max Weber's subsequent distinction between value judgments and factual research of the means of their realization. Science cannot make value judgments; by elucidating the cultural network, however, it provides actions with criteria to assess the expediency of its means. Nietzsche also expected science to provide insight into the "conditions of culture," which could be used to determine whether the "ecumenical goals" can even be realized. As for the goals themselves, Nietzsche had not departed from his visions in *The Birth of Tragedy*. His basic principle of anthropodicy, according to which mankind and history are justified only by the birth of genius, continued to inform his work, as did his insistence that history attains the "peak of rapture" in great individuals and great works.

When scientific observation undermines the metaphysical basis of truth, morality, religion, and, ultimately, art are all affected. As for religion, *Human, All Too Human* and *Daybreak* portray it initially as metaphysics for the people, altogether in keeping with enlightened critiques of religion in Nietzsche's era. He experimented with the simple idea that religion serves the function of "narcoticizing" (2,107; *HH* I § 108) people when misfortunes cannot be mitigated in any other way. If our knowledge of nature advances and the true causalities are discovered to take the place of "imaginary causality" (3,24; *D* § 10), it will no longer be necessary to view illness, for example, as a divine punishment. In lieu of prayer and sacrifice, the correct medicine can be administered. The authority of fate—the source of all sorts of religious fantasies—will not be gone altogether, but restricted, limiting the authority of "priests" and "tragic poets" (2,107; *HH* I § 108). Suffering that can be cured relinquishes its dark, momentous pathos.

If religion were merely compensation for the inevitability of evil and a means of casting spells on nature, it would have been an easy target of criticism. Instead, several further aspects of religious sentiments gave Nietzsche pause. Before delving into these additional aspects, he began, as a strict and uncompromising follower of the existing enlightened critique of religion, to establish firm ground. "Never yet has a religion, directly or indirectly or as dogma or as allegory, held any truth" (2,110; *HH* I § 110). We should not be taken in by the "theologian's trick" of mingling scientific knowledge and edifying speculation. By the same token, science warrants criticism if it "allows a religious comet's tail to gleam out into the darkness of its ultimate vistas" (2,111; *HH* I § 110). Religion should not pass itself off as science, and science should not start sounding religious when its arguments are muddled. Nietzsche made a case for clarity, recognizing, however, that the lure of religious sentiments is not fully explained by disclosing their errors.

What is left to discover in religious sentiments? For one thing, there is a penchant for feeling sinful, particularly in Christianity. Where does this feeling originate, and what does it entail? It is surely astonishing that man "considers himself even blacker and more evil than is actually the case" (2,121; *HH* I § 124). Ancient Greek religion had not posited such a dark view of man. On the contrary, since the gods shared their virtues and vices with human beings, everyone could feel relieved. Human beings even allowed the dark sides of their natures to be reflected in their gods. *Human, All Too Human* provides an answer to the question of how feelings of sin originated—an answer that appears in several variations throughout Nietzsche's later works. Christianity, it runs, was originally the religion of people who lived in a state of oppression and misery. They were not noblemen and hence did not harbor noble thoughts about themselves. It was a religion of low self-esteem. Christianity sank mankind all the way down into the "deep sludge" (2,118; *HH* I § 114) in which it already found itself.

This explanation was unsatisfactory, even to Nietzsche himself. Pointing out a connection between social misery and low self-esteem was really quite trivial. Consequently, Nietzsche entertained the idea that the waning of late Roman culture responded to the feeling of sin as to a stimulant or a drug. The "glow of a divine mercy could shine in" (2,118; *HH* I § 114) on a dispirited populace. Was it pleasure in peripeteia, the drama of unexpected reversals, or was it an "excess of feeling" (2,118) that they wanted to enjoy? The Roman Empire had expanded immeasurably and comprised a huge expanse in which circumstances and people grew more and more similar. The historical dramas had shifted to the far reaches, and perhaps the inner drama of conversion offered a more exciting and invaluable option. Was the extremism of early Christianity a solution to a monumental degree of boredom? When a culture grows old, and the "circle of all natural feelings" has been run through countless times, it is crucial to find a "new order of stimuli for life" (2,137; *HH* I § 141). Perhaps Christianity was the requisite stimulus. It offered to the converted the psychological drama of sin and redemption. And the others took pleasure when martyrs, ascetics, and stylites took the stage, once they had become "impassive to the sight of animal and human contests" (2,137).

Even with this explanation, we remain stuck in the historical genealogy of Christianity. Its role in human emotions all the way into the current era is still mystifying. In order to make any headway in this matter, Nietzsche immersed himself in the psychology of saints, martyrs, and ascetics, whose religious sentiments were most palpable. These virtuosos of religion showed what immense power of self-elevation and what ecstatic energy accompanied religious sentiment. The mood was neither downtrodden nor oppressed, nor was there evidence of humility or modesty. These saints and ascetics were combatting something within themselves that they considered base and sordid. However, they were fighting on both sides: they were at once wretched and triumphant over wretchedness, base and sublime, feeble and powerful.

An individual with a rich inner life moves through a house of mirrors.

By looking into the "bright mirror" of his image of God, his own nature strikes him as "so dismal, so unusually contorted" (2,126; *HH* I § 132). In his most secluded moments, however, he knows that this "bright mirror" is nothing but a magnification of himself and that he is catching sight of his own better potential, which both exalts and humbles him. These reflections are one aspect of his "self-splitting" (2,76; *HH* I § 57), leading man to become a religious as well as a moral being. Religious "self-splitting" can take the radical form of self-sacrifice when "man loves some aspect of himself, a thought, a desire, a creation more than some other aspect of himself, causing him to split his being and sacrifice one part of himself to the other" (2,76). Ascetics, saints, and martyrs revel in humbling themselves, and they burst with pride in their humility. "This shattering of oneself, this mockery of one's own nature . . . that religions have made so much of is actually a very high degree of vanity. The entire morality of the Sermon on the Mount should be seen in this context: man takes positive pleasure in violating himself with excessive demands and afterward idolizing this tyrannically demanding something in his soul. In every ascetic morality, man worships one part of himself as a god and in doing so demonizes the other part" (2,131; *HH* I § 137).

In his finest moments, the religious man wants what every artist seeks: "powerful emotion." Both are intrepid enough to strain toward "enormity" (2,132; *HH* I § 138), even if they feel devastated by it. The resultant destruction is their "peak of rapture of the world" (7,200). Because surrender to enormity is a shared obsession of religion and art, Nietzsche placed the chapter "From the Soul of Artists and Writers" right after the chapter "Religious Life" in *Human, All Too Human*.

In religious sentiment and in art, "powerful emotion" attains extraordinary dimensions. It signals intensity and effort and at the same time relaxation and the unleashing of creative powers. There is a euphoria of success, strength streaming in and out. In a word, it is a heightened state of being, but—and this is Nietzsche's chilling antithesis—there is no higher truth inherent in it. We must not interpret a heightened religious and artistic state of being as a medium of hidden grand truths, even if religious and artistic ecstatics view themselves in those terms.

Up to the time of his essay on Wagner, Nietzsche himself had regarded art as a loftier form of knowledge. In his thoughts on art in *Human, All Too Human,* it becomes quite evident what he meant when his preface described his experiment with enlightenment as a "desecrating clutching and glancing backward" (2,16; *HH* I Preface § 3). Until the mid-1870s, he had called art "the truly metaphysical activity" (1,17; *BT* "Attempt at Self-criticism" § 5), and now he was entering its temple with a strained will to sobriety and dissent. He scrutinized his enthusiasm and harbored the suspicion that it might mask imprecise thinking, vague feelings, weakness, and mystifications of all sorts. Why this enforced sobriety? In his preface to *Human, All Too Human,* Nietzsche provided an answer. He hoped to avoid the danger "that the spirit might somehow lose itself on its own paths and fall in love and stay put, intoxicated, in some corner" (2,18; *HH* I Preface § 4).

How can art manifest itself to an initiate who is wary of his own enthusiasm and who, like a former alcoholic, defends his unstable sobriety against potential temptations?

The "problem of science," Nietzsche wrote in *The Birth of Tragedy,* "cannot be recognized in the context of science" (1,13; *BT* "Attempt at Self-Criticism" § 2). He wished to see "science from the perspective of the artist, but art from the perspective of life" (1,14; *BT* "Attempt at Self-Criticism" § 2). Now focusing on art, he found that his hypothesis about science applied equally to art. The problem of art cannot be recognized in the context of art. In the case of art, as in that of science, it is crucial to select another vantage point. Only by getting out from under the influence of art will it be possible to avoid becoming a victim of its self-mystifications.

Artists shape, create, and produce a new reality. Scientists observe reality. The artist provides forms, and the scientist supplies truth. From the perspective of the artist, Nietzsche discovered in science a fictionality that tended to remain suppressed and unacknowledged. Science seeks the truth, but the imagination is also engaged in the process—more than scientists care to admit. Science aims at finding truths, but it invents them as well. Art readily acknowledges its basis in the imagination; it creates a world of illusions and weaves a beautiful cloak to lay over reality. Whereas science demands that truth be unveiled, art loves veils. Since art is well versed in invention, it is no secret to art how much invention and drive for refined education is involved in science, much as science is loath to acknowledge that. Nietzsche called this disparity the "problem of science" as seen from the perspective of art.

When Nietzsche ventured to contemplate art from the perspective of science, he found that its central quandary was its claim to truth. This claim to truth is generally just as unacknowledged in art as is fictionality in science. Art wraps its implicit claim to truth in illusions, and science conceals its implicit fictionality in its claim to truth. Nietzsche attacked art for feigning truth that it cannot provide. He stated baldly that, when it comes to art, "we do not make contact with the 'essence of the world in itself'" (2,30; *HH* I § 10). Even though artistic intuition may be inspiring, stimulating, and profound, ultimately it is nothing but "representations." They give shape to feelings, but are not necessarily felt.

Nietzsche knew his obsessions well enough to gauge the extent of his disillusionment. A long habit of metaphysics resisted it. The metaphysical need that loves a mystery wished to fathom what holds the world together. After this metaphysical drive had been pushed beyond the boundaries of strictly regulated science, it found refuge in art. Nietzsche cited the effect of Beethoven's music to illustrate how strong it remains in the enlightened "free spirit." Beethoven's music, he wrote, produces "a reverberation of a metaphysical string that was long silenced or even split apart," for example, when a person feels himself "floating above the earth in a starry vault with the dream of immortality in his heart" (2,145; *HH* I § 153) while listening to Beethoven's Ninth Symphony. Nietzsche's words allude to Wagner's essay on Beethoven, but he was also criticizing his own definition of art as "truly metaphysical activity," and now claimed that anyone seeking to satisfy his metaphysical needs in art had failed the "test" of his "intellectual character" (2,145). Metaphysics in art is the devious legacy of religion. Art that is misinterpreted when approached through metaphysics lays a "gauze of impure thinking" (2,144; *HH* I § 151) over life. Precise thinking and precise knowledge are nowhere to be found in art. Artistic impulses are more likely to stand in the way of the hard and harsh project of knowledge and impede the "maturation of mankind" (2,142; *HH* I § 147). Seen in a positive light, art is leisurely regression, a temporary respite from efficiency and the principle of reality. Art enables us to be children again; "the old feeling comes alive again, at least for a brief time, and the heart beats to an otherwise forgotten rhythm" (2,142). But caution is indicated. If regression goes too far, mankind faces the threat of "infantilization" (2,143; *HH* I § 147). If we too often take advantage of the temporary "alleviation of life," we are hampering our ability "to work at a genuine improvement of our circumstances" (2,143; *HH* I § 148).

This is Nietzsche's most direct condemnation of the "tragic perspective," which he had otherwise valued so highly, and his most explicit endorsement of utility and practical efficiency. Nietzsche paints a vicious picture of the sociology of contemporary artistic exigencies. Who demands art and what is being demanded of it? There are the educated people, who no longer consider incense a pleasant smell but are not quite prepared to give up the "consolations of religion" (2,447; *HH* II AOS § 169) altogether. They appreciate art because they perceive in it a faded echo of religion. Then there are the indecisive people, who would really like to live a different life but lack the strength to turn their lives around and look to art to fulfill them; there are the conceited people, who shy away from "self-sacrificing labor" and enjoy art as a locus of leisure; there are the clever idle ladies from upper-class families, who need art because they have no defined duties; and there are doctors, merchants, and civil officials, who conscientiously do their work but steal a glance upward with a "worm in their hearts" (2,447; *HH* II AOS § 169).

What does art mean to these people? According to Nietzsche, "It is intended to ward off discomfort, boredom, the half-clear conscience for hours or moments and, if possible, transform the mistakes of their lives and characters into mistakes of the world's destiny" (2,447; *HH* II AOS § 169). It is not an overabundance of well-being and health but rather privation that makes us crave art. Art lovers of this sort are people who abhor themselves. In Nietzsche's view, it is not "delight in themselves" but "disgust in themselves" (2,447) that now draws people to art.

Self-disgust on the part of spectators is a fitting counterpart to the ruthless smugness of many artists. At times, the latter are so passionate about their artworks that they long for an "overthrow of all circumstances" (2,149; *HH* I § 159) just so that they can heighten the resonance of their works. Nietzsche was not naming names, but he clearly had Richard Wagner in mind. Wagner did indeed beome a political revolutionary—for the sake of his art.

The rumors and legends that spring up around great artists, and are often nourished by them, make a lot of fuss about inspiration and the anguish of mankind. For Nietzsche, that is one of the mystifications of art. In fact, there is less inspiration involved than is generally believed. "All of the great people were great workers" (2,147; HH I § 155). As for the alleged "suffering of genius," caution is advised. Some artists feign interest not only in people but also in the destiny of mankind, and they want not merely to create a work but to revitalize an entire culture. They claim to be met by incomprehension and narrow-mindedness on all sides, which occasions their great suffering. Nietzsche recommended that we treat these megalomaniacal self-assessments with a healthy dose of skepticism. Great artists, he explained, feel rebuffed when they sound their "pipes" (2,147; *HH* I § 157) and no one wants to dance. Even if this sense of rejection is exasperating to an artist, can we really call it "tragic"? Perhaps we can, Nietzsche cynically remarked, because the sufferings of the artist who considers himself misunderstood are "really very great, but only because his ambition and his envy are so great" (2,147).

Nietzsche passed harsh judgment on art and his own passion for it. Music continued to be the language of the tremendous Dionysian mystery of the world and was sacred to him; for this very reason, however, his "desecrating clutching" could not shrink back from it. He wrote with a forced courage that came close to invalidating his own love of music: "No music is profound and meaningful in itself; it does not speak of the 'will' or the 'thing in itself'" (2,175; *HH* I § 215). Only a philosophically cultivated and perhaps miseducated intellect reads a so-called deeper significance into it. We only "fancy" that a colossal power speaks through music. In fact, though, it is the history of symbols, habits of listening, techniques, projections, feelings, and misunderstandings that we are hearing. Music is "empty noise" (2,176; *HH* I § 216) upon which meaning is gradually superimposed by way of childhood memories, associations of images, and physical responses. It is not a "direct language of feeling" (2,176).

These remarks are decidedly mean-spirited. Nietzsche targeted everything that looked and sounded like more than it was. We can well imagine the fury of Richard Wagner when he read these words. Cosima Wagner remarked tersely: "I know that evil has won out here" (15,84; *Chronik*).

Nietzsche prescribed himself a regimen of sobriety in order to prevent the "profoundly aroused feelings" of poets, musicians, philosophers, and religious enthusiasts from "overpowering" him (2,204; *HH* I § 244). These feelings needed exposure to the spirit of science, "which renders us somewhat colder and more skeptical in general and in particular cools down the scorching current of belief in ultimate truths" (2,204). Nietzsche called the era of grand redemptive feelings in metaphysics, religion, and art a "tropical" epoch and predicted the imminent approach of a "tempered" cultural climate (2,198; *HH* I § 236). He sought to bring about and accelerate this change of climate, although it unsettled him as well. He knew that the cooling process also held dangers inherent in the "shallowness and externalization" (2,199; *HH* I § 237) of life.

In *Human, All Too Human,* Nietzsche forged ahead with his cooling-down experiment, but just as a play's protagonist sometimes adds an

aside to reveal his thoughts beyond what he articulates to the other characters, Nietzsche divulged the transitional nature of his reflections. His
anxiety as to how far we can go along with the spirit of science without
winding up in a desert comes through on several occasions. Scientific
curiosity is initially refreshing, enlivening, and liberating, but truths turn
gloomy once we have become accustomed to them. If, however, science
affords us less and less pleasure and at the same time takes our pleasure
away "by casting suspicion on the solace offered by metaphysics, religion, and art, then the greatest source of pleasure to which mankind
owes almost all of its humanity is impoverished" (2,209; *HH* I § 251).

Nietzsche was already starting to revolve the stage here once again.
The metaphysical magic of art and a Dionysian and tragic sensibility
were almost poised to reappear—but only almost. Nietzsche did not
complete the revolution; instead, he stopped short with an astonishing
suggestion for compromise that one would hardly expect of him given
his detachment from a technological approach to culture (which would
explain why so few readers have picked up on it). He argued for a bicameral system of culture. A higher culture must give people "two chambers
of the brain, as it were, one to experience science and the other nonscience: lying juxtaposed, without confusion, divisible, able to be sealed
off; this is necessary to preserve health. The source of power is located
in the one region; the regulator, in the other. Illusions, partialities, and
passions must provide the heat, while the deleterious and dangerous
consequences of overheating must be averted with the aid of scientific
knowledge" (2,209; *HH* I § 251).

The idea of a bicameral system flashes up again and again in
Nietzsche's work and then vanishes, much to the detriment of his philosophy. If he had held to it, he might well have spared himself some of
his mad visions of grand politics and the will to power.

Daybreak and Grand Inspiration

"*ILLUSIONS, PARTIALITIES,* and passions must provide the heat" (2,209; *HH* I § 251), Nietzsche wrote in *Human, All Too Human,* but he added that these alone would not suffice. In the interest of self-preservation and culture, science would need to be added to the mix to cool things down, otherwise artistic idiosyncrasies would be in peril of becoming "deleterious and dangerous consequences of over-heating" (2,209).

In this scheme of things, science functions as a force of equilibrium. Individual lives are perspectivist, enveloped in an atmosphere of delusion and ignorance. However, this very limitation is indispensable for the creative process. Artists are well aware that manias and obsessions are their driving forces. At the same time, they have found that cold calculation, a reflective will to form, and constructive intellect solidify the hot materials of enthusiasm into an auspicious shape, in art and in culture as a whole. The course of life infused with vitality and passionate haughtiness must be cooled off in the medium of science. "Scientific methods," Nietzsche wrote in a fragment of 1877, "relieve the world of a great pathos; they show how pointless it was for man to have worked his way into this height of feeling" (8,428). Although the sciences are also constrained by perspectives, they can be elevated above them. They broaden our outlook and enable us to see our own position in relation to the whole, not because science more closely approximates absolute truth, but for precisely the opposite reason—namely that passion, owing to its vigorous focus, posits itself as absolute and admits of no alternative beyond that focus. Science, however, by dint of its methodical distance, keeps us aware of the relativity of knowledge. Passions aim for totality, whereas science, as Nietzsche understood it, teaches reserve. We can grasp particulars, but never the sum total. Nonetheless, our passionate hunger for integrated knowledge remains intact, and it is difficult to renounce the "pathos" of the grand truths. "The interest in truth will cease, the less it provides pleasure" (2,209; *HH* I § 251).

Even though science is to be commended for cooling down our passions, it should not take this process too far. Society is threatened not only by unbridled passions but also by the prospect of paralysis once science has tempered them. Nietzsche depicted his bicameral system as a guard against the twin perils of unleashed vitalism in the one direction and nihilistic paralysis in the other. When new insights begin to bore us and the magic of stripping away illusions wears off through force of habit, this nihilism begins to loom as a threat. It is not enough for passions to be subdued by science; we must also remain vigilant so as to defend the obstinacy of life against knowledge. Nietzsche expected "higher culture" to provide people with "two chambers of the brain, as it were, one to experience science and the other nonscience" (2,209; *HH* I § 251). He advocated an art of living that takes into account the fact that life can no longer be a single entity and that our world consists of several worlds. The two worlds of science and nonscience are further subdivided into various scientific disciplines as well as diverse cultural spheres such as religion, politics, art, and morality. Categorizing philosophy is an elusive task: Is it a science or more of a creative and artistic form of expression?

During the period in which Nietzsche wrote *Human, All Too Human* and *Daybreak,* he tended to regard conventional philosophy as an edifying product of the imagination rather than a rigorous form of knowledge. His view of the discipline was about to change, however. He envisioned his own endeavors as a paragon of precision, certainly not in the positivistic sense, but rather as a reflection of the relation between the parameters of ideas and life. He looked beyond the field of knowledge proper and embraced life's dogged pursuit of its own purpose and direction, however trivial the twists and turns of everyday life might appear. These are philosophical considerations, designed to keep the will to knowledge from an ill-advised bid for power. Nietzsche's philosophical thinking evolved into a science of self-reflection not only on methods but also on the link between knowledge and real life. This type of thinking is at once moderate and immoderate. It is moderate because it bears in mind the basic limitations and relativity of knowledge, and immoderate because it brings into play the unbridled singular logic of scientific reason. Knowledge has its own dynamics: although intended to cool down passions, it can itself evolve into a new "passion that considers no sacrifice too great and essentially fears nothing but its own extinction" (3,264; *D* § 429). This passion born of insight can inflict suffering, by destroying friendships and a familiar sphere of life, for instance. The ethos of knowledge demands sacrifices. Are we prepared to make them? Are the sacrifices worth it? What do we gain by them?

These were the questions running through Nietzsche's mind as he worked on *Daybreak* while recuperating in Marienbad in the summer of 1880 and painfully recalling his severed friendship with Wagner. Nietzsche had admired and loved Wagner and felt confident that his admiration and love were requited. This familiarity and friendship had lent him a creative edge. Why did their friendship have to crumble? Nietzsche wrote to Peter Gast on August 20, 1880, from Carlsbad, after spending several nights in a row dreaming about Wagner: "Now it is a thing of the past. What good is it for me to be right in many respects? As though that could wipe this lost affection from my memory!" (*B* 6,36). Prevailing against Wagner meant, as we know, feeling justified in his criticism of Wagner's metaphysics of art, his claim to superiority, and his pathos of redemption. But did prevailing compensate for the loss of love?

In the course of this summer in Marienbad, Nietzsche struck up an acquaintance with an engaging devotee of Wagner, and their conversation forced him to continue recollecting the past period of his friendship with the composer. He was consumed by doubts concerning the practical value of his philosophy. Did it make up for his loss of an intimate bond of friendship? Should we renounce love for the sake of truth? Is it defensible to offend someone we value so highly in other respects just because of a few ideas we hold near and dear? Must we stick to our guns? Is it necessarily treacherous to be flexible or to allow for differences? Does belief itself require that we close ourselves off from other people? Does self-affirmation demand purity? Nietzsche struggled with all of these questions. The same letter to Gast continued in this vein: "Even now my entire philosophy wavers after just an hour of friendly conversation with complete strangers. It strikes me as so foolish to insist on being right at the expense of love" (B 6,37).

In the weeks following his summer sojourn in Marienbad, Nietzsche suspended his work on *Daybreak* and confessed to Gast on October 20: "Since I sent you that letter in August . . . I have not dipped my pen into the inkwell: my condition was and still is so dreadful and demands so much patience" (*B* 6,40). During the winter in Genoa, he regained his strength and motivation to forge ahead with his project, and in *Daybreak* he described the "defectiveness of the machine" in people of a "highly intellectual nature: As long as genius dwells within us, we are spirited, indeed virtually insane, and pay no heed to life, health, and honor; we fly through the day more freely than an eagle. . . . But all of a sudden it leaves us, and just as suddenly a deep sense of fearfulness descends on us: we no longer understand ourselves, we suffer from every experience and everything we do not experience . . . like pathetic souls of children scared off by a rustling sound and a shadow" (3,307; *D* § 538). The souls of children require protection; they are vulnerable and need to be loved. They have yet to experience the heroism of the truth. This aphorism in *Daybreak* depicts the distress of an eagle with injured wings in Nietzsche's disheartening summer of 1880.

Nietzsche tried to pull himself together, declaring that only the pathetic soul of a child had caused him to question the value of truth. It is crucial, he asserted, to ward off doubts that set in at a moment of weakness when we crave love. When truth grows weak in confronting the power of love, one must simply transform the will to truth into passion. Nietzsche wrote in this vein in *Daybreak*: "*Truth requires power.* Truth is not power in and of itself. . . . Rather, it has to draw power over to its side" (3,306; *D* § 535). He did not mean political or social power, but rather the power of life. It is a question of whether the driving force behind knowledge is sufficiently "powerful" to stand up to other motives, and whether it is possible, at least after the fact, to equip knowledge and "truths" with a driving force and thereby make them fit for life. Nietzsche's thoughts had been circling in on this connection since the summer of 1880, and he used the term "incorporation" to describe it. His first recorded reference to this term is a notebook entry of August 1881, after a flash of inspiration on the Surlej boulder of Sils-Maria, when the idea of eternal recurrence came to him. He was determined to "support instincts as a basis of all knowledge, but recognize where they become adversaries of knowledge; in summa, find out to what extent knowledge and truth can be incorporated" (9,495).

By about 1875, Nietzsche had grasped the fact that we cannot deliberately cling to illusions that are useful for life. Once he had projected himself into the role of the free spirit "who wants nothing more than to lose some comforting belief on a daily basis" (*B* 5,185; Sept. 22, 1876), there were no more "forbidden" truths that had to remain unspoken for the sake of life. It was not merely this more recent fearless attitude toward knowledge that made him reject a regimen of truth; it was also a clearer realization that we are unknown to ourselves and do not reach down deep enough inside of ourselves. Since we lack this knowledge, how could we possibly assess our sources of life and what we can demand from life? The argument for a pragmatic approach to life feigns insight as to what life needs and enjoys, but this is not so. "We have tried very hard to learn that external things are not as they appear to us—well, then! The same applies to the inner world! (3,109; *D* § 116).

Genoa, where Nietzsche completed his work on *Daybreak* in the winter of 1880–81, was the birthplace of Columbus. He compared his own inquiries into the terra incognita of the human interior to Columbus's voyages of discovery. Columbus had his ships and his art of navigation, and Nietzsche had his nimble language, but it was not nimble enough for this vast interior continent. The boundaries of language function as the boundaries of reality. We have words only for the "superlative degrees" and the "extreme circumstances" of physical and mental processes. Since, however, we no longer clearly register when words fail us, the "realm of existence" stops where the "realm of words" ends. Anger, hatred, love, pity, desire, knowledge, joy, and pain are the "superlative degrees" of internal conditions that can be formulated in words and hence possess visibility and acceptability in the cultural sphere. "The milder middle and even lower degrees, which are continually in play, elude us, and yet they are the very states that weave the web of our character and destiny" (3,107; *D* § 115).

Nietzsche was not thinking along the lines of Freud's later architecture of the unconscious, which placed the unconscious at the basement level. The sphere of what is unnamed and unformulated (and perhaps even inconceivable) that Nietzsche had in mind is more musical in nature, like tones that resonate without being heard individually but impart an unmistakable nuance to the audible sound. He knew that his reference to the infinite number of unconscious stimuli, of which only an infinitely small number enters our consciousness, was just the first step of an immense project. Although he did not call it a phenomenological program, that is precisely what it was. Nietzsche was setting out to render visible the jumble of the collaborative resonating stimuli and ideas as if under a magnifying glass, by means of heightened attentiveness and the aid of nimble language. He was aiming not at clarifications and constructions but at visualization and contemplation. The precondition of his reflections was, of course, the assumption that the unconscious is potentially capable of being rendered conscious.

For Nietzsche, physiology, perception, and consciousness form a continuum. Focusing in on one particular thing functions like a mobile beam of light that illuminates varying facets of life and moves through the zone of what is visible and imaginable. The beam of light sweeps back and forth and illuminates one thing while letting another sink into the obscurity of the unconscious. Obscurity does not signify an absence, but the presence of the matter that has receded once more into the unnoticeable and unnoticed.

This program is phenomenological; its fundamental principle states that the only things that can be known are those that are subject to observation. It is therefore crucial for us to focus our attention as well as our language to maximize what we can observe. Everything accessible to our consciousness is a "phenomenon," and the research of consciousness scrutinizes the internal order of the phenomena of consciousness in a process of exacting introspection. It neither interprets nor explains, but attempts to describe what the phenomena are and what they indicate of their own accord. Attentiveness to the activities of consciousness eliminates the dualism of being and appearance in one fell swoop. To put it more precisely, we discover that one of the operations of that consciousness is to make this very distinction. Consciousness is oddly aware of what escapes it in perception. And since everything that enters our consciousness is a phenomenon, this invisibility is itself also a phenomenon of consciousness. Essence is not something hidden behind a phenomenon, but is itself a phenomenon to the extent that we think it or the extent that we think that it eludes us.

Even the Kantian "thing in itself," which Nietzsche had subjected to such ridicule as a nonconcept for the nonapparent, is still a phenomenon since it is something that is thought.

Nietzsche had no intention of reviving artificial solipsistic doubts about the reality of the external world. On the contrary, he regarded the inner world as an internalized outer world that is only revealed to us as a phenomenon. As a result, the monstrous forces outside of us reside within us as well. Consciousness itself, however, is neither inside nor outside, but somewhere in-between. It is always alongside of what it is conscious of. If it is consciousness of that tree out there, it is "out there." If it is consciousness of pain, or desire, it is inside where the pain and desire originate. Nietzsche hoped to heighten our awareness and attention, guided by the insight "that all our so-called consciousness is a more or less fanciful commentary on an unknown, perhaps unknowable, but felt, text" (3,113; *D* § 119).

What is consciousness? It is not an empty mirror, nor is it an empty container in need of replenishment. Consciousness is filled with the being that is itself consciousness. Consciousness is the being that is conscious of itself. It is therefore not the sum total of being, but by the same token it does not amount to less than being. Consciousness is not a discrete entity, but each time we fall asleep it experiences the mystery of the transition from existence that is conscious to existence devoid of consciousness. Consciousness is aware of these vast boundaries. It fills its void not with "objects" but always in reference to something. It is this referentiality itself and the "self" of this referentiality. Consciousness has no "within," but rather is the "outside" of itself. If we dig down deeply enough into our consciousness, we suddenly find ourselves back at the things outside; we are actually flung back to them. Nietzsche depicts acts of consciousness as arising from a "hunger" (3,112; *D* § 119). Phenomenologists, for whom Nietzsche paved the way with his analyses of consciousness, use the terms "intention" or "the intentional structure of consciousness" in this context.

A series of types of intentions corresponds to the various types of processes of consciousness. The desire to grasp something in distancing intention is only one of the possible forms of intentional consciousness. In addition to this intention, which is often mistakenly equated with the phenomenon of consciousness as such, there are many other intentions that are forms of directedness toward something. It is not the case that an object is registered in, as it were, "neutral" terms and only "wanted," "loved," "desired," or "assessed" in an auxiliary act. Wanting, assessing, and loving each has its own reference to an object, and the "object" in these acts is quite distinct. The same "object" differs for consciousness according to whether it is grasped in a context of curiosity, hope, or fear, or with a practical or theoretical aim. Nietzsche was a master of shading the particular tinge, color, and mood of experience, and since he used his own suffering as a springboard to construct his philosophy, we find in his writings exquisite depictions of experiencing the world while racked with pain. Phenomenologically speaking, these are model analyses of an intentional design of the world. Nietzsche was not content with mere expression and self-expression. He used the example of his own experience to probe the question: What kind of world would create a consciousness that suffers? "People who are in a state of profound suffering look out at things from their condition with a frightful coldness: all those little lying charms with which things are normally surrounded when the eye of a healthy person gazes at them are lost on them; indeed, they themselves lie before themselves without any vestige of plumage and color. Assuming that they have been living in some dangerous fantasy up to that point: this extreme sobriety effected by pain is the means of tearing them away from it: and perhaps the only way. . . . The enormous tension of the intellect, which attempts to counter pain, ensures that everything they now see appears in a new light: and the inexpressible appeal that all new illuminations impart is often strong enough to defy all enticements to suicide. . . . They now hold in contempt the cozy warm world of mist in which healthy people saunter without thinking" (3,105; *D* § 114).

It was certainly a great accomplishment on Nietzsche's part to have depicted the subtle and varied manners in which our consciousness functions and the primitiveness and coarseness of the concepts that consciousness employs to understand its workings. Usually this process is accomplished by juxtaposing a subjective interior and an objective exterior and then asking how to fuse back together what was artificially split by ascertaining how the world comes into the subject and the subject into the world. Nietzsche demonstrated that our perceptions and thought processes function differently from how we generally imagine them to do; they form a series of discontinuous clarifications in a stream of acts not focused on the individual. Only secondary reflection, namely the consciousness of consciousness, splits the world into a world of ego and a world of objects. Still, the continuous process of life, which goes virtually unnoticed by consciousness, serves to mask this boundary. Nietzsche's philosophy attempts to expand consciousness for the more sublime and broadening experiences in which we are already caught up with our bodies and lives. His descriptions opened up a door and, just as he had suspected, opened out to a boundless expanse—the world of consciousness and conscious existence. This world is so diverse and spontaneous that any ingenious description inevitably comes into conflict with a scientific concept that is oriented to systematization and rules. Thus, Nietzsche's work—if we count the enormous *Nachlass*—has ultimately itself become an expression of the stream of consciousness that he set out to describe. Nietzsche wished to approach the system from a particular vantage point. Nevertheless, he was a passionate singularist. For him, the world consisted of nothing but details. He considered even himself a detail composed entirely of further details. And so, by the same token, he contended that there was no actual history, but only moments and events. Therefore, an alert consciousness can never reach a point of termination. Every synthesis resolves into details. There are only details, and although they are everything, they do not constitute a whole. No whole could encompass the plethora of details. Nietzsche began to recognize more and more clearly, once he had delved deeply into the basis of the drive for knowledge, that the will to wholeness and to synthesis is not merely a quirk of the philosophical will to construct.

Nietzsche kept returning to the brilliant insights of his early essay "On Truth and Falsehood in an Extramoral Sense." There, he had shown the practical necessity of reduction and simplification in knowledge. Knowledge that fully grasps itself discovers that it is above all creative and productive, and should not be taken to signify mere imitation. Knowledge is more *poiesis* than *mimesis*. Nietzsche now followed up on this idea with more determination and subtlety than in the earlier essay. He applied it not only to the phenomenality of the outer world but to the inner world as well. He clung to this approach for the rest of his life. Even in the winter of 1888, one year before his breakdown, he noted: "I am affirming the phenomenality of the inner world as well: everything that becomes conscious to us is first thoroughly organized, simplified, schematized, interpreted" (13,53; *WP* § 477). "Phenomenality" means that we do not "have" even the inner world in the sense of a unity of consciousness and being. A phenomenon that enters our consciousness is always a phenomenon of something. But this something is not identical with the phenomenon, even if it concerns the phenomena of "inner" experiences. The self that appears on the interior stage of self-perception is a character in the great drama of being oneself. It can never appear, but it makes all appearance possible.

Nietzsche's reflections are directed at what philosophical tradition calls *individuum est ineffabile*. The individual is ineffable not because individuals are profoundly mysterious or overflowing with inner riches that should not be squandered. There are certainly mysteries and riches of this sort, but at issue here is the structural problem that a consciousness of one's own being remains mere consciousness and does not blend with being. There is absolutely no point of convergence between being and consciousness. Nonetheless, a consciousness of self that is aware of itself comes so close to the point that this consciousness can picture and potentially even aspire to a convergence of this sort. Speculative explanations of God draw on this awareness by envisaging the point where the ineffable abundance of totality comes to rest, where being fully merges with consciousness.

Of course, these are "excesses" of the head and heart, but they are defensible. Shouldn't the head and heart try to attain the point of convergence on their own, this "in and of itself," even if consciousness keeps turning on its own axis in the process? The "free spirit" is surely not there to prohibit "excesses." Nietzsche did not wish to be thought of as advocating a prohibition of this sort. He had nothing against excesses, festivals, and orgiastic mischief, even if thinking celebrated beyond its scope. He clung resolutely to the difference between being and consciousness not for the sake of sober enlightenment, but in order to preserve the mysterious nature of being. To Nietzsche, the principle of *individuum est ineffabile* meant discovering a vastness within the individual as well, even though people might be thrown by it and feel more comfortable escaping into what is familiar and customary. The "majority" of people have nothing more pressing to attend to than seeking out a "phantom of their ego" that provides protection from the overwhelming vastness of themselves. This phantom can be found in other people. The ways in which others judge me or what I imagine their judgments might be, and what I myself do to generate a particular image to the world and to myself—these impressions and actions engender a situation in which "one person is always in the head of the other, and this head in turn in still other heads" (3,93; *D* § 105).

How real is this reality? In this "wondrous world of phantasms" (3,93; *D* § 105), everything is real, but it is the reality of the unleashed power of collective self-evasion. Nietzsche was not undertaking cultural criticism. The theater of self-evasion is an outgrowth primarily of anthropology and only secondarily of cultural history. Martin Heidegger later explored the implications of the inexpressibility of the individual and formulated the idea of structural self-evasion: "Everyone is the other, and no one is himself" (Heidegger, *Being and Time* 165). One's own individuality is like a hot plate that turns every drop into steam on impact. Every concept used to describe "man" and "mankind," from the ordinary to the sublime, is reduced to nothing but hot air in the process. All of these concepts are fictions; yet they are powerful enough to assume their places on the stage of social life. Everyone is implicated in everyday reality, and yet we have no language for our reality. We act and do not recognize what acts within us. We talk, but silence reigns within. The correlations of the human network are rationally accessible. We can comprehend the connections between the points, but not a given individual point. Envisioning how each point relates to the others is within our grasp, but what something really is remains unfathomable. We use relations between things or people as guides to infer their essence. *Individuum est ineffabile* focuses attention on the unfathomable nature of what is fundamentally unique. The true mystery lies in the individual, who cannot be explained in reference to anything else. Since the time of Plato, every type of mysticism has sought to apply this notion of the irrationality of the unique individual to other domains. These other domains are abstract universal concepts: the soul of a people, nations, class, the objective mind, the law of history, God, and other grand images of truth and delusion in which man, even Heideggerian man, engaged in flight from his own ineffability, seeks to disappear in order to dispense with himself.

Daybreak explores this terra incognita of man from a series of premises and opens up a vast field of phenomenological research. This book follows the tortuous, labyrinthine paths from the ego to the self and to the Other. Nietzsche's *Gay Science,* which was planned as a sequel to *Daybreak,* contributed significant perspectives on the ineffability of individuality and on self-evasion. Aphorism § 354 developed a line of thought of such extraordinary pithiness that it managed to encapsulate ideas that could fill volumes. The problem of consciousness, Nietzsche explained, begins to concern us only when we fathom the extent to which most of life's processes dispense with consciousness. We take this absence of consciousness for granted when considering vegetative, animalistic, and physiological activities. But the more "cerebral" acts of volition, memory, and even thinking could also take place without any accompanying mirroring and self-reference. They have no absolute need to enter into consciousness to realize their full meaning. Even consciousness need not enter into consciousness; its self-doubling is not structurally imperative. In short: "All of life would be possible without, as it were, seeing itself in a mirror; as in actuality even now the major part of our life unfolds without this kind of mirroring" (3,590; *GS* § 354).

Why have a consciousness, then, if it is by and large "superfluous"? Nietzsche contended that consciousness is the sphere of the in-between. The human network is a system of communication, and consciousness is a means of surmounting the individual by means of integration into this structure of communication. "Consciousness is actually only a network to connect one person to another" (3,591; *GS* § 354). Within this network, language functions as a set of "communicative signs." There are, of course, additional communicative signs, such as facial expressions, gestures, the use of objects, and an entire symbolic universe in which communication takes place. Nietzsche concluded "that consciousness does not really belong to individual human existence, but rather to aspects of man's social and herd nature" (3,592; *GS* § 354). The individual is hardly in a position to "understand" his unique qualities with the aid of this communalized consciousness. Consciousness does not serve that end. It promotes circulation rather than self-comprehension; if it is used toward the latter end anyway, we should not be surprised if man ends up eluding his own grasp. The inexpressible that we ourselves are is not addressed by this network of language and consciousness of socialization. Nietzsche reminds us that we have all had the experience of attempting to know ourselves and finding that we bring "only the specifically nonindividual into our consciousness" (3,592).

Here again, Nietzsche revealed himself as a nominalist by applying the inexpressible absolute singularity of God to the individual. The individual is just as inexhaustible and inexpressible as God once was. The realm of the numinous, formerly reserved for God, is now the concrete reality of the individual. And just as our consciousness inevitably fails to grasp God, the individual also eludes it. Whatever is right in front of our eyes—as well as everything that is quite remote—must remain lofty, unfathomable, and mysterious. There is transcendence in both directions. The only firm ground is in the middle zones of socialized consciousness. For this reason, we need to understand what Nietzsche calls his "actual phenomenalism and perspectivism," namely that the world of consciousness is "only a world of surfaces and signs, a generalized and debased world, and that everything that becomes conscious in that very process becomes shallow, thin, relative and dumb, general, a sign and a distinguishing feature of the herd" (3,593; *GS* § 354).

We should not, however, conclude that Nietzsche wished to retreat into a preverbal *unio mystica* with his "phenomenalism" and his references to the communicative nature of consciousness. He would have considered a retreat of that sort nothing but Romantic evasion. We cannot step outside of our world of language and consciousness, nor is the unspeakable a silhouette of the spoken and bespoken world. We perceive what eludes the grasp of language as a phantom pain of language. Language, which is aware of its limitations, becomes expansive. It expands outward, seeking to compensate for its lack of being, and gets enriched in the process. Nietzsche noted that the capacity for the "power and art of communication" has accumulated to the point that the "late born" might now squander it (3,591; *GS* § 354). They may not always hit upon the essence of the matter, because the essence can never be captured perfectly in language and consciousness. This "second" communicated world, however, is also rich in its way. The games we play with language and consciousness are inexhaustible, and even if they are not "true," they still have the power to render themselves "true" in a secondary act. The world of language and consciousness of the in-between is, after all, a world in which we live, act, and exist.

Nietzsche was obviously grappling with a well-known quandary. If we wish to describe the rich world of consciousness, we are, even on methodological grounds, prone to the temptation to have it originate in an actual zone or to attach it to a fixed point. If, like Nietzsche, we hope to steer away from naturalistic and psychological reduction, and also stay away from a divine perspective, we must find a way to elucidate the rich life of the consciousness without destroying it, develop a language that expresses more than the usual commonplaces, and move away from the middle zones of socialized discourse. People who have this skill become poets. Since the time of Plato, poetry has been the comforting or discomfiting predilection and temptation of philosophers.

This affinity with poetry is especially salient in view of Nietzsche's talent. As a phenomenologist, Nietzsche wondered how we really feel when we think. As a poet, he was determined to articulate these overtones, nuances, niceties, and imponderables. The result is a series of exquisite passages, such as the following excerpt from *Daybreak:* "Where is this whole philosophy headed with all of its meandering? Does it do anything more than translate a constant strong drive into reason, a drive for gentle sunlight, bright and breezy air, southern vegetation, a breath of the sea, fleeting nourishment with meat, eggs, and fruits, hot water to drink, silent walks that last for days, sparse discussion, infrequent and cautious reading, solitary living, clean, simple, and almost military habits—in short, for all things that taste best to me specifically and are healthiest for me specifically? A philosophy that is essentially the instinct for a personal diet? An instinct that seeks my air, my height, my climate, and my personal health by taking a detour through my head? There are many other, and surely also many higher, sublimities of philosophy, and not only those that are gloomier and more demanding than mine. Perhaps all of them are also nothing but intellectual detours of these sorts of personal drives?" (3,323f.; *D* § 553).

The expression "drives" is subject to misinterpretation because it automatically brings to mind a system of primitive, basic biological urges, which was precisely Nietzsche's intention. He depicted a highly differentiated network of subtle motions. The sensual and the mental blend into a swarm of abstruse events in which even a "deep" thought is merely superficial. This is not a reductive process, but rather a demonstration of how all senses are engaged in the philosophical progression of thought. It is easy to contend that thoughts are a collaborative effort of body and life, but Nietzsche attempted to track down these processes and elevate them wherever possible into the sphere of language and consciousness. This attempt can succeed only if language is able to stretch its wings, becoming free, mobile, and elastic in the process, flying over the broad landscape of humanity, constantly vigilant, but not in search of prey. In *Human, All Too Human,* Nietzsche had called this form of knowledge "free, fearless hovering" (2,55; *HH* I).

The meticulousness of love also comes into play. Love does not seek to destroy what it has grasped by the very process of having grasped it, but prefers to let it be. Of course, Nietzsche also saw love from the opposite point of view and pronounced it a poor guide to knowledge. In *The Gay Science,* he wrote: " 'The person under the skin' is an abomination and a horrifying thought for all lovers, a blasphemy against God and love" (3,423; *GS* § 59).

Love sometimes shuts its eyes, preferring not to dissect things and people, but to leave them alone and grasp them in their living state. To the will to knowledge that is in love with life, natural and mechanical laws as well as anatomy and physiology present a potentially "horrifying" assault on the living. Nietzsche claimed that we must go through this sort of loveless knowledge as well. Radical thinking must also come to terms with death because the knowledge that originates from uplifting feelings cannot remain our sole source of knowledge. It is also imperative to cool off and shed illusions, not in order to linger in the zones of ice and lifelessness, but in order to pass beyond them and be readied for new rebirths. We endure the winter so as to earn the spring. We should not fear the night, because if we bear with it, it will reward us with a new morning and an incomparable early morning light. Nietzsche had concluded the first part of *Human, All Too Human* with a rhapsody on the philosophical "wanderer" and his relationship to the night and the coming morning. "Of course, a person like this," he wrote in aphorism § 638, "will have bad nights when he is tired and finds that the gates of the city, which should offer him rest, are closed" (2,363; *HH* I § 638). This situation is dire because "the desert extends up to the gate" and the night sinks "like a second desert upon the desert." Still, once he has survived this, there is a prospect of a rapturous morning "in which he already sees, as the light begins to dawn, the bevies of muses dancing by him in the mist of the mountains. Later, when he quietly takes a walk under trees with the peace of mind of his morning soul, many good and bright things are thrown to him from the treetops and leafy recesses, the gifts of all those free spirits who make their home in mountains, forests, and solitude and who, like him, are wanderers and philosophers in their sometimes joyful and sometimes reflective way." (2,363). This peripatetic philosopher, "born from the mysteries of dawn" (2,363), is the phenomenologist Nietzsche. His phenomenology is the philosophy of the early light and the morning.

Phenomenological attentiveness to the world of consciousness requires an attitude that clashes with the demands and complexities of everyday life. We become so caught up in our daily routines and ensnared in our many obligations and habits that anxiety and opportunism gain the upper hand. As a result, we are not sufficiently composed to let the world work its magic. We fail to provide it with a stage on which to appear as an epiphany, rich and enigmatic, and give ourselves the opportunity to warm up to it. For this to be possible, we must not have become too established as creatures of habit. Leeway is required to allow consciousness to observe itself, not in an autistic sense, but in such a way that receptivity for the world can be experienced on an individual level. This degree of attention to the way in which the world is "given" to us entails a decided departure from our customary attitude toward the world. We need to undergo a genuine transition in attitude, the kind we experience every morning when we awaken.

This moment of transition affords us the opportunity to see the world anew. The temporary worldlessness of the night enables us to come to the world afresh. This fresh outlook is requisite for both everyday experiences and the sphere of philosophy. The image of morning awakening is perhaps too cheerful, since it fails to take into account that a rupture in consciousness and a temporary deprivation of the world can be distressing. According to Nietzsche, however, we are compensated for this distress when we discover a highly diverse inner ontology, a richly diverse realm of what is stimulating and real. The objects of memory, fear, longing, hope, and thought represent just as many "realities," which inundate the neat divisions of subject and object. Nietzsche reveled in the images of great currents, oceanic expanses, and departures to new shores. Envisioning himself as the second Columbus, he stood poised at the shores of Genoa, brimming with the desire to put out to sea. "We aeronauts of the spirit!" was his heading for the final aphorism of *Daybreak* (3,331; *D* § 575).

In the winter of 1880–81 in Genoa, Nietzsche finished his work on *Daybreak* and spent the first few months of 1881 revising the galleys. He then suggested to his old friend Gersdorff, with whom he had had a strained relationship after he voiced objections to Gersdorff's marriage plans, that they spend a year or two in Tunis. Nietzsche was attracted to the sun, the bright desert, and the dry climate as well as the promise of a new beginning. The phenomenologist in him longed to see his old Europe in a new light from the vantage point of distance. "I want to live among Muslims for a good long time, especially where their faith is most devout: in this way I expect to hone my appraisement and my eye for all that is European" (*B* 6,68; March 13, 1881).

Gersdorff was hesitant about embarking on this journey, and Nietzsche decided against Tunisia when war broke out there. Then his thoughts turned to Mexican mesas. Why remain in Europe, he reasoned, if his works would ensure his lasting reputation anyway? Nietzsche knew that his time would come. Despite recurrent bouts of illness, Nietzsche's spirits were buoyed by his latest book, slated for publication in the early summer of 1881. He remarked to his publisher Ernst Schmeitzner when submitting the manuscript: "This book is what is known as a 'decisive step'—more a destiny than a book" (*B* 6,66; Feb.

23, 1881). Nietzsche declared to his friend Franz Overbeck in Basel: "This is the book with which people are likely to associate my name" (*B* 6,71; March 18, 1881). He laid it on even thicker to his mother and sister, although his words were tinged with irony. He sent them a copy of his new book with the following comment: "This is how the object looks that will make our none-too-beautiful name *immortal*" (*B* 6,91; June 11, 1881). Their reactions led him to conclude that they had a poor grasp of the situation. For his mother, Nietzsche was nothing but a failed professor who traveled restlessly from place to place in poor health and had yet to find a wife. She still had to send him socks and sausages. Well aware of her attitude, Nietzsche addressed an earnest letter to his mother and sister: "If you take into account the enormous amount of work my nervous system has to accomplish, it is in splendid shape. . . . Thanks to it, I have produced one of the boldest and most sublime and most thought-provoking books ever born of the human brain and heart" (*B* 6,102f.; July 9, 1881).

A scant two months later, his assessment of *Daybreak* had changed dramatically. He wrote to Paul Rée: "And this same year that has seen the publication of this work is now to see publication of another work as well, in which I may be permitted to forget my poor piecemeal philosophy in the larger context" (*B* 6,124; late Aug. 1881). *Daybreak,* which he was so recently calling an "immortal" work, was now a "poor piecemeal philosophy"? Something must have happened in the interim that had so drastically altered his view of his own work.

Nietzsche began the first of a series of extended stays in Sils-Maria, in the Upper Engadine mountains of Switzerland, in July 1881. During one of his walks around the lake in Silvaplana, he experienced a vision concerning the nature of inspiration, which he later described in the "Zarathustra" chapter of *Ecce Homo* in terms that suggested a momentous event in European history: "Does anyone at the end of the nineteenth century have a clear idea of what poets of strong eras called *inspiration?* If not, I would like to describe it. With the slightest remnant of superstition remaining in ourselves, we would scarcely be capable of rejecting outright the thought of being no more than a mere incarnation, a mere mouthpiece, a mere medium of overpowering forces. The concept of revelation in the sense that suddenly, with indescribable certainty and subtlety, something becomes visible and audible, something that shakes us to the core and knocks us over—all of that simply describes the state of affairs. We hear, and we do not seek; we take, we do not ask who is giving; a thought flashes up like lightning, with inevitability, without hesitation as to the form—I never had a choice. A rapture, the immense tension of which at times is released in a stream of tears, and in the course of which your pace sometimes quickens involuntarily, and then slows down; being outside of yourself with the most distinct consciousness of a host of subtle shudders and shivers running all the way down to your toes.... All of this is involuntary in the extreme but as in a storm of a feeling of freedom, absoluteness, power, divinity. ... Everything presents itself as the nearest, most correct, simplest expression. It really seems ... as though the things themselves were approaching and offering themselves as metaphors.... This is *my* experience of inspiration; I have no doubt that we would need to go back entire millennia to find someone who could say to me 'it is mine too'" (6,339f.; *EH* "Thus Spoke Zarathustra" § 3).

The idea that it would be necessary to go back "millennia" to find a similar inspiration came to Nietzsche well after the event, but this incident of August 6, 1881, near the Surlej boulder had an instantaneous impact on him. It was immediately apparent that his life was now divided into two halves: before and after the inspiration. He wrote in his notebooks: "6,000 feet above the ocean and far higher still above all things human!" (9,494). He was also spun upward above his own daily concerns. How was he faring up there? Peter Gast was the first to hear about the event from him: "On my horizon, thoughts have arisen unlike any I have ever seen before. I will not speak of them and will retain my unshakable tranquillity. I will presumably have to stay alive for a few more years! Oh, my friend, sometimes the notion passes through my head that I am actually living quite a dangerous life, since I am one of those machines that can explode! The intensities of my feelings make me shudder and laugh. Several times I could not leave my room for the ridiculous reason that my eyes were inflamed—and why? Each time I had wept too much during my walks of the preceding day. My tears were not sentimental, but tears of joy. I sang and said nonsensical things, filled with a new vision that puts me ahead of everyone else" (*B* 6,112; Aug. 14, 1881).

Nietzsche was in a skeptical frame of mind at the time this inspiration came to him. He had, after all, written in *Human, All Too Human* that inspiration, like many other things that appear to be sublime, looks better than it is in reality. In the fall of 1877, he had entered the following remark in his notebook: "Our vanity promotes the cult of genius and inspiration" (8,475).

Nietzsche's letter to Peter Gast is evidence of his effort to remain calm. Before drawing any definitive conclusions, he hoped to summon up all the presence of mind needed to weigh and examine the colossal idea that had overtaken him. He already recognized, however, that these conclusions would be unfathomable, and from now on his life would be devoted to this inspiration at the Surlej boulder. Prior to this day in August, Nietzsche had had a presentiment of his calling, and now he had found it. His mood fluctuated between euphoria and alarm. It was not so simple to become the "mouthpiece" of a great message. Five months after the event he wrote to Gast: "In regard to my 'thoughts'—it is no problem for me to *have* them; but *getting rid of them* when I want to do so is always infernally hard for me!" (*B* 6,161; Jan. 29, 1882).

Nietzsche proceeded slowly and cautiously in proclaiming his grand new scheme. He provided gentle hints at the conclusion of the fourth book of *The Gay Science,* written in the summer of 1882. Another full year would pass before he had Zarathustra take the stage, tentatively and almost gingerly confiding to him the thought that "takes 'millennia' to evolve into something" (*B* 6,159; Jan. 25, 1882). When broaching his idea to friends, and in particular to Lou Salomé, his lover during the summer of 1882, he spoke only in hushed tones.

CHAPTER 10

Eternal Recurrence
and *The Gay Science*

*Thinking cosmically in Sils-Maria • Dehumanized nature
• Lofty reckonings • The doctrine of eternal recurrence •
The holy January in Genoa • Happy days, gay science •
Messina*

*W*HAT WAS GOING through Nietzsche's head as he was hatching his theory of the "recurrence of the same," the theory that would utterly transform him? Did it hit him all of a sudden, without warning? We have no reason to doubt the details of his description of the moment of inspiration. Still, it is very difficult to imagine that this insight came to him so abruptly, since there is evidence to indicate that the idea was already quite familiar to him. The notion of time circling within itself, playing through its limited repertoire over and over, is part of a well-established philosophical and religious tradition found in Indic myths, in the philosophy of the pre-Socratics and the Pythagoreans, and in heretical undercurrents in the West. Nietzsche learned about them as a schoolboy. His 1862 essay "Fate and History" contained allusions to perpetual circles of time presented in the image of a cosmic clock: "Does the eternal becoming never reach an end? . . . Hour by hour, the hand of the clock moves along, only to begin its passage all over again after twelve; a new cosmic era dawns" (*J* 2,56). However, the cosmic era is not in fact new, because "the events are the dial," and hence any "new" phase will repeat each event number by number.

Nietzsche found ample support for the worldview he espoused in "Fate and History" in the writings of Schopenhauer. Although Schopenhauer did not think in terms of physical reincarnation, he did affirm the immortality of the essence of the will, which is embodied in the world of phenomena in diverse and manifold forms and which returns in that capacity. In *The Birth of Tragedy,* Nietzsche linked to this his concept of the "eternal life of the core of existence, with the perpetual destruction of phenomena" (1,59; *BT* § 8). Schopenhauer had also invoked the image of time as an "endlessly revolving sphere" (Schopenhauer 1,279), which deeply impressed Nietzsche, as did Schopenhauer's characterization of the present as a Now that cannot be lost in awareness. Schopenhauer saw the present as the vertically streaming sun of an "eternal noon": "The earth moves on from day to night; the individual dies, but the sun itself burns without intermission, an eternal noon" (Schopenhauer 1,281). For him, the fact that the present cannot be lost meant that in the course of time everything can change, except the form of existence in the present, which persists. The landscape is modified, but the window through which we look out at it remains. And why should the stability of this window onto the present be imperceptible to us? Schopenhauer meditated on this question. The present, he explained, is the tangent that has one point of contact with the circle of time. This point does not turn with the circle, but stays in place, yielding an eternal present or eternal noon. Our problem is that we look at the turning circle and not at the persistent point of contact with the tangent, even though we can perceive this turning only in contrast with the persistent point. We are the turning wheel as creatures in time, but as presence of mind and attention we are ourselves the sun and the eternal noon. That Nietzsche would use the image of eternal noon in *Zarathustra* specifically in connection with the doctrine of eternal recurrence shows how deeply he was affected by these ideas. The terms "great" noon, and "noon and eternity" all appear in *Zarathustra.*

The doctrine of the recurrence of the same is also found in the Dionysian myth of the god who dies and is perpetually reborn. Since Nietzsche had embarked on his philosophical path with Dionysus, it seems logical that he did not originate his doctrine of eternal recurrence in his later writings but simply *re*-originated it after it had eluded him temporarily. If, therefore, the doctrine of eternal recurrence was already familiar to him as an intellectual construct, this renewed encounter with things he had known for so long must have sparked something altogether different in him. Otherwise, the sheer level of excitement he was experiencing would be incomprehensible. Why would a long-familiar idea be so rousing, and why now? What was the intellectual environment that lent it such explosive force? What was going through his head and his heart? An examination of Nietzsche's notes in the weeks immediately preceding and following this major event would be a logical source of information.

In the early summer of 1881, under the heading "Main Idea!" (9,442), Nietzsche jotted down a thought that was scarcely new to him, namely that people puzzle out the existence of nature and themselves "with false standards" and are consequently incapable of achieving authentic knowledge. "Everything that takes place within us is per se something else, which we do not know" (9,443). He then proceeded to give this familiar thought a new twist. He almost exploded with anger when considering the medium of refraction, which impedes any straightforward encounter with reality; he called this medium "a fantasy of the 'ego' and all 'non-ego.'" In *Daybreak* he was singing the praises of perspectivist vision and knowledge. At that point, he appeared to have made his peace with perspectivism, having discovered its phenomenological value. Now he was saying: The devil with perspective! I want to step out of the cage of my perspectivist perceptions! He emphatically underlined his admonition to *"Stop feeling like such a fantastic ego! Learn to cast off* bit by bit *your alleged individuality!"* But how is this to work? Should we adopt an altruistic point of view about knowledge, which would entail trying to see out of many eyes? If so, should we take our place among the community of researchers and join their endless debates about the authenticity of reality, hoping that somewhat tenable compromises and consensus might ensue? No, said Nietzsche; recognizing "egoism as an error" does not mean opting for epistemological "altruism." There must be an alternative. Two emphatically underlined sentences follow: "Go beyond 'me' and 'you'! *Experience on a cosmic level!*" (9,443).

Now, we might expect that Nietzsche would seek a fusion of the microcosmic individual with the macrocosmic organism, as well as a communion with the universal soul in the manner of Giordano Bruno. But this is exactly what he did not want. Although experience on a cosmic level does mean establishing contact with the colossal vastness of which we are a part, it does not mean turning this vastness into a living organism, which would render it too pleasant, anthropomorphic, and reverent. A few weeks later, Nietzsche noted down: "The modern scientific counterpart to belief in God is belief in the universe as an organism: I find that revolting" (9,522). He wanted nothing to do with this sticky, mushy, proliferating whole. He ruled out any desire to return to the womb. Nietzsche had not gone to all the effort of liberating himself from a sheltering God just to crawl back into the godlike womb of the universe. "We must picture it [the All] as a whole as far removed from the organic as possible!" (9,522).

The truth of the organic *is* the inorganic. The stone is the ultimate end of wisdom. When Nietzsche wrote that we should "let ourselves be possessed by things (not by people)" (9,451), he really meant *things,* as cold and dead as possible. He attempted to empathize with the inanimate realm. His longing for the world of minerals began to take precedence over his former attraction to oceans. Sentient life is an enormous error, an excrescence, a huge detour. Back to the peace and silence of stones. "Absolutely false assessment of the sentient world versus the dead world," he wrote, and went on to say: "The 'dead' world! Always in motion and without error, power versus power! And in the sentient world everything false, vainglorious! It is a festivity to pass from this world into the 'dead world.'" (9,468).

Nietzsche tried out different formulations. He underlined, crossed out, inserted several exclamation points and question marks in the middle of sentences, stopped and started up again, deleted some words and abbreviated others. There were abrupt switches between distractedness and decisiveness. He passionately railed at passion for its obfuscation. He carried on an emotional tirade against emotions for their misinterpretation of reality.

With strong feeling, he went into raptures describing lack of feeling as a condition that brings us closer to being. Feelings are worthless; they are nothing but an "oversight of existence" (9,468). Surely it ought to be possible to correct this oversight? What had happened to the phenomenologist of *Daybreak,* who wanted to direct attention to things and the world and initiate an altogether different type of festivity that would engage all of our senses and contribute to the epiphany of a world that triumphs over the deadening force of reduction? How is this cold "festivity" of the transition "from this world into the 'dead world' " to proceed? Perhaps the answer lies in man's venture into the dimension in which everything is "countable and measurable" (9,468). The only things that would count are things that could be counted. The measure of all things is measurement. "Once," Nietzsche wrote, "the incalculable world (of the spirits and of the spirit) had dignity; it inspired more fear. We, however, see eternal power elsewhere altogether" (9,468f.).

Nietzsche embarked on several physiological excurses in which intellectual movements and emotional stimuli are portrayed as symptoms of fundamental bodily processes. All of this is merely hinted at, since at this point he was evidently concerned only with conveying the living and sentient as close as possible to the zone of the dead and mechanical, those devoid of spirit. Nietzsche happily engaged in expunging the mind from the field of being. He ultimately derived a formula for this procedure: "My task is the dehumanization of nature and then the naturalization of humanity once it has attained the pure concept of 'nature' " (9,525).

This sentence was penned after Nietzsche's great moment of inspiration. It demonstrates that the idea of recurrence not only does not thwart and undermine experimentation with a stagnant metaphysics but is obviously part and parcel of it. Astonishing as it may seem to us, it was the allegedly arithmetic and physical evidence of this doctrine that over-whelmed him. The key calculation established that the quantum of force of the universe as matter or energy is limited, but time is infinite. Therefore, in this infinite period of time, all possible constellations of matter and energy, and consequently all possible events pertaining to both the animate and the inanimate realms, have already taken place, and they will recur ad infinitum. In addition to many brief reflections on the notion of recurrence that we find in the notebooks, there is only a sin-gle sustained passage on this theme, which contains the statements on recurrence that Nietzsche frequently iterated in subsequent writings, statements in which the lava of inspiration had indeed gone cold and solidified into theory: "The world of forces is not subject to any stand-still; because otherwise it would have been reached, and the clock of existence would stand still. The world of forces therefore never reaches a state of equilibrium. It never has a moment of respite; its force and its movement are equally great at any given moment. Whatever condition this world may reach, it must have reached it already; not once, but innu-merable times. This moment, for instance: it has already been here once, and many times, and will return, all of the forces distributed exactly as they are now: and so it is with the moment that gave birth to this one and the moment that is the child of this one. Humanity! Your whole life becomes like an hourglass, always being inverted and always running out again—one vast minute of time in-between until all conditions under which you arose converge once more in the revolution of the world" (9,498).

"Gratification" is the word that springs to mind to express this amaz-ing feeling of having solved something akin to a difficult math problem; everything has been thought out completely and brought to a state of flawlessness. The fact that astute observers such as Georg Simmel later pointed out that the philosopher had miscalculated is beside the point.

For Nietzsche, it was a problem solved, and his delight soared into ecstatic rapture. He shed "tears of joy," as he wrote to Peter Gast on August 14, 1881 (*B* 6,112).

Eternal recurrence is supposed to be the cold mechanical and mathematical law of the universe, but for this very reason it leaves us cold. How can it find its way into experience? It may well have happened to Nietzsche in roughly the following way: an idea that was already familiar to him as a religious fantasy and intellectual intuition now carried the authority of exacting science. In early 1881, he read Julius Robert Mayer's *Beiträge zur Dynamik des Himmels* (Celestial Dynamics, 1848) and sent an enthusiastic letter to Peter Gast, who had brought this work to Nietzsche's attention: "In splendid straightforward and joyous books like this book by Mayer, you can hear the harmony of the spheres: a music that is accessible only to a man of science" (*B* 6,84; April 16, 1881).

Julius Robert Mayer, a doctor who died in 1878, was also a distinguished natural scientist whose research focused on materialism. He refined the principle of the conservation of material substance by employing the hypothesis of the conservation of energy. The elemental force in the universe, he taught, could be altered only in quality; the quantity would remain constant. Change was nothing but a transfer of energy: energy into matter, heat into motion, and so forth. Between these conversions, constant proportions in the sum total could be calculated.

Nietzsche later dissociated himself from Mayer, accusing him of introducing an ominous element of divine omnipotence into the material harmony of the spheres. For the time being, however, he was enthusiastic, and we can assume that reading Mayer contributed to his vision at the Surlej boulder. Mayer had not linked his law of the conservation of energy to a doctrine of returning constellations and conditions. That was Nietzsche's contribution, deduced from his conjecture of a perpetual continuum of time, which was amply documented in the scientific and materialist literature that he studied during the course of these months, despite excruciating pain in his eyes and head.

Nietzsche's notebooks reveal that he was not only delighted by these insights but also shocked and terrified. He pondered the difficulty of "incorporating" them (9,504). Later he came to regard the ability to incorporate this knowledge as the very hallmark of the *Übermensch*. But both his agony and his ecstasy raised a question: How should this numerical theory be transformed into experience? Infinite recurrence could terrify us only if consciousness were to recall the infinite repetitions—in other words, if it not only remained the same but were also aware of being the same. If, however, our consciousness believes that it is beginning anew every time, and if it continually reenacts this illusion of a new beginning, consciousness does experience a new onset again and again rather than any repetition, even if a calculation is presented to it that would appear to prove eternal recurrence. The very fact that repetition is predicted for us means that we have yet to experience it. Both dismay and rapture can result only from experience.

In the notebooks written in the summer of 1881, there are no traces of true horror, but we do encounter soberly argued tentative remarks as to the circumstances under which the doctrine of eternal recurrence could evoke horror. When Nietzsche wrote that "even the idea of a prospect [of recurrence] can devastate and reconfigure us, not just feelings or specific expectations! What an effect the *prospect* of eternal damnation has had!" (9,523f.) he was speaking not of actual horror but of his vision of horror.

Evidently Nietzsche, thoroughly delighted with his theory of eternal recurrence, was equally tickled at the prospect of intimidating others with it. He indulged in fantasies of how there would one day be a dividing line between those who could bear this insight and those who would be driven to despair and destruction by it. "The finest representatives, who are established and dedicated to preserving the status quo, are the last to be exposed to a new doctrine. . . . The weaker, emptier, sicker, and more needy are the ones who catch the new infection" (9,497f.)—and are destroyed in the process. Emotionally, Nietzsche was captivated by the idea of disseminating dread and horror and then himself being one

of the heroes who even put the doctrine of eternal recurrence to practical use. As early as his notebooks from the summer of 1881, we find
reflections on this notion.

Nietzsche certainly understood the idea of eternal recurrence as a
propositional truth, but he also applied it as a pragmatic, autosuggestive
aid in structuring our lives. In this way, he succeeded in putting an existential flame under "cold" knowledge. The fact that every moment
recurs should lend the here and now the dignity of the eternal. We
should always be asking ourselves while engaged in any activity: "Is this
something I want to be doing countless times?" (9,496). Nietzsche, who
had wished to transcend the strictures of "Thou shalt" was now preaching a new "Thou shalt," namely that one should live each moment in
such a way that it can recur without occasioning horror. Ever the music
enthusiast, he called for a da capo of life. "Let us etch the image of eternity onto our own lives! This thought embodies more than all religions,
which taught us to disdain life as something ephemeral and to look
toward an unspecified *other* life" (9,503). Just as Kant wished to reinforce
moral imperatives by rendering them unconditional, "as if" a God had
imposed them, Nietzsche also braced his imperative of an ecstatic and
intensive here and now with the argument that we should live "as if"
every moment were eternal because it recurs eternally.

All the ecstasy, all the bliss, all the ascensions of feeling, all the hunger
for intensity previously projected into the beyond would now be concentrated in the immediate life of the here and now. The doctrine of
eternal recurrence was designed to function by preserving the powers of
transcendence for immanence or, as Zarathustra proclaimed, remaining
"faithful to the earth" (4,15; *Z* First Part, Prologue § 3). In *The Gay Science,*
written a few months after the inspiration, Nietzsche used rich imagery
to conjure up this bliss in the here and now, which opened up the perspective of eternal recurrence to him. He would remove any oppressive
or deadening aspects from the image of the circling course of time by
coupling it with the great Heraclitean cosmic game. This game is, of
course, based on repetition, but Nietzsche gave it a playful twist. For

him, the death of God revealed the precarious and playful nature of human existence—an *Übermensch* would have the strength and facility to penetrate through to the invariable cosmic game. Nietzsche's transcendence goes in the direction of regarding play as a basis of being. His Zarathustra dances when he has reached this basis; he dances like the Hindu god Shiva. Nietzsche would himself dance naked in his room shortly before his mental collapse during his final days in Turin. His landlady, watching him through a keyhole, caught him in the act.

So much for the existential and pragmatic aspect of this idea of eternal recurrence, which becomes true by asserting itself as truth. Let us not forget that he considered this doctrine true in a propositional sense, as a description of the world as it is. With this firm claim to truth, he got tangled up in contradictions, since he ultimately considered knowledge a series of "fabrications." He did not exempt even the "figures of mathematics," which he used to determine the idea of eternal recurrence (9,499). Thus, he was not really in a position to feel confident about asserting the propositional truth value of his doctrine. Nonetheless, he sought to go even further by infusing his theory with metaphysical dignity. In order to render this truth more impressive, Nietzsche the anti-metaphysician let it take the metaphysical stage. He laid claim to insights into the natural sciences, but tried to avoid the pure immanence of the natural sciences, because that immanence obstructs every metaphysical quest from the outset. Nietzsche hoped to lead thinking to the point at which traditional metaphysics veers off into transcendental speculation in pondering the question of what lies behind the world of appearances. He posed this question as well. He mounted the stage that was otherwise reserved for God, the absolute, and the spirit. However, in lieu of these illustrious figures of meaning, he introduced "quanta of force," in the form of multifaceted constellations and cyclical repetition, to enact a metaphysical (rather than positivistic) drama on this stage of pathos. It is metaphysical curiosity that sets the stage for the whole play. Isolated from this drama of ultimate metaphysics, his doctrine of eternal recurrence might conceivably come across as trivial.

Nietzsche himself sensed this and was therefore quite hesitant about presenting it. He recognized that this doctrine was ultimately fit only for a prophet or a clown.

The summer of inspiration in Sils-Maria brought Nietzsche giddy elation, but also unbearable headaches, stomach cramps, and nausea. During the day, he sometimes spent as many as eight hours on his feet, and in the evenings he sat in his tiny room, with a view out onto a sodden wall of rock. It was so cold in August that he had to wear gloves even in his room. His tears were not just tears of joy. In a letter to Franz Overbeck, which he wrote in Latin so that Overbeck's wife would not be able to read it, he described his dire situation as follows: "Pain is vanquishing my life and will. Oh, what months I have had, and what a summer! I have experienced as much torment to my body as I have seen changes in the sky. Every cloud conceals some form of lightning that can hit me with surprising force and altogether destroy my hapless self. I have already summoned death as a doctor and hoped yesterday would be my final day—but I hoped in vain. Where on earth is there a sky that is eternally cheerful, *my* sky? Farewell, my friend!" (*B* 6,128; Sept. 18, 1881). A few days later, he registered the same complaint in a letter to Peter Gast with the comment "that a sky that stays clear for months at a time has become an *essential condition of life* for me, as I now realize" (*B* 6,131; Sept. 22, 1881).

Then came a period of recuperation, a great climatic turning point. Nietzsche had the good fortune of spending an uncharacteristically bright, mild, and sunny winter in Genoa. After completing the first three books of *The Gay Science,* he wrote to Gast on January 29, 1882: "Oh, what a time we are having! Oh, the wonder of this beautiful January!" (*B* 6,161). To commemorate this winter, "the most beautiful of my life," he called the fourth book of *The Gay Science* "Sanctus Januarius."

This book, completed in early 1882 and originally conceived as a sequel to *Daybreak,* set out to depict the landscape of life and knowledge by incorporating his insights of the summer. He composed it in a state of bliss. Weeks would pass that were free of physical pain and oppression. Sunny strolls took him to the outlying areas of Genoa. The book is replete with references to the varied coastal landscape, the cliffs, the villas and summer houses that dotted the hills, and the vistas of the sea. This scenery, in which success in life was revealed to Nietzsche, crops up time and again in *The Gay Science,* as in the following passage: "This area is studded with the images of bold and high-handed people. They have *lived* and have wanted to live on—they tell me this with their houses, which are built and decorated for centuries to come and not for the fleeting hour; they were positively disposed to life, however angry they often may have been at themselves" (3,531; *GS* § 291).

Apart from its lighter tone, does this book offer a central focus? Nietzsche often cautioned readers who perused the potpourri of his thoughts not to overlook the "fundamental productive ideas," and he pointed out the inner unity of his aphoristic production to his friends. He claimed that his writings dealt "with the long logic of a very specific philosophical sensibility" and not "with a hodgepodge of a hundred random paradoxes and heterodoxies" (Löwith 120). However, there is something forced about any attempt to grasp this "logic," which holds everything together even while spreading it out. Nietzsche was well aware of why he did not present it in a pure and simple form, but instead, as a master of circuitousness, dropped hints and clues—usually from the sidelines. He organized his gardens of theory in such a way that anyone on the lookout for their central arguments would almost inevitably fall flat on his face. Nietzsche hid out in his labyrinth, hoping to be discovered by means of long, winding paths. And why should we not lose our way on the search for him? Perhaps it would even be the best thing that could happen to us. Later Nietzsche had his Zarathustra tell his disciples: if you have yet to find yourselves, you have found me too soon. Hence he arranged his books in such a way that the ideal outcome of a reader's search for ideas would culminate in an encounter with the reader's own ideas. Discovering Nietzsche in the process was almost beside the point; the crucial question is whether one has discovered thinking per se. One's own thinking is the Ariadne to which one should return.

Nonetheless, the doctrine of recurrence is not the explicit central idea of the book. In the first three books, only aphorism § 109 is devoted to recurrence. That aphorism, which followed directly from notes jotted down during the summer of 1881, declares that "the whole musical mechanism eternally repeats its tune" (3,468; *GS* § 109). It is not until the famous final two aphorisms of book 4 that eternal recurrence is mentioned as such, and Zarathustra takes the stage for the first time under the title "Incipit tragoedia" (3,571; *GS* § 342). Even though the idea of recurrence is not placed squarely in the foreground, it is still omnipresent behind the scenes.

The doctrine of eternal recurrence imagines the universe as a self-contained entity directed by merciless necessity. It is necessity that turns the cosmic event into the "musical mechanism" in which we play and yet are only played with in the process. *The Gay Science* develops this idea right from the first aphorism. Subsequent aphorisms can be read as a commentary on this first one, which imparts a jaunty and even mocking tone to the text as a whole. How could we not laugh at a cosmic event, which, unbeknownst to us, is in actuality a marionette play? Although it is still "the age of tragedy, the age of moralities and religions," it is really the "comedy of existence" (3,370; *GS* § 1) that is being performed. Behind the scenes, the "instinct to preserve the species" is at work, while in the foreground we are busily setting goals and purposes; in our own eyes, all of this activity makes us remarkable, lofty, heroic, and insightful. "In order for necessary and constant things to function by themselves, devoid of any purpose, they should appear to be purposeful from now on and to make sense to us in rational terms as a final commandment— the ethical teacher comes into play as the teacher of the purpose of existence" (3,371; *GS* § 1).

Thus, although the world of nature is dominated by an imaginary teleology, the original "instinct to preserve the species" is still very much intact, and continues becoming more refined, subtle, roundabout, indirect, and imaginative. Human life increases in sophistication and invents ways and means to render itself interesting. It would be foolish to long for a return to primitive nature. Man is an inventive animal that promises something *to* life in order to get something *from* life in return. Man is also an "imaginative animal" whose unique sense of pride originates in the human penchant for fantasy. Humans have one more "condition of existence" to fulfill than any other animal: "the human being needs to believe, to know, from time to time, *why* he exists; his species cannot thrive without periodic confidence in life! Without faith in the existence of reason in life!" (3,372; *GS* § 1).

There is less to "reason in life" than meets the eye. It considers itself absolute, but is actually only one thing among many. In the great "musical mechanism," it is a mere cog or bolt. It feels free, but remains tied to the apron strings of nature. It regards itself as an achiever and yet is merely an effect. Isn't that a laugh! But reason, for the sake of its self-esteem, does not wish itself or its creativity to be laughed at. When Nietzsche chimed in with his own laughter, he did not wish to mock reason. The laughter in *The Gay Science* is not denunciatory. It recognizes and even celebrates the human imagination, but keeps in mind that the products of the imagination are in part pure invention. Nietzsche was not out to attack, but to seek comic relief.

In *The Gay Science,* Nietzsche discussed the "instinct to preserve the species" (3,371; *GS* § 1), but he dodged the larger issues, implicit throughout the book, of whether knowledge and the will to truth are really subordinate to the "instinct to preserve the species," or whether this will to truth might break free from life and even take aim against it. Might the will to truth aspire to become the master of life instead of its servant, even if the result is the destruction of life? Might there be a dualism between the will to live and the preservation of the species, on the one hand, and will to truth, on the other?

Nietzsche weighed the possibility of this sort of dualism in aphorism § 11. Consciousness, he concluded after examining pertinent studies of physiology and evolutionary biology, is the consummate and ultimate development of the organic, but it is still incomplete and fragile. Humans should absolutely not rely on consciousness; otherwise they

would even more frequently go astray and commit "errors" (3,382; *GS* §
11) than is now the case if the much older "group of instincts" failed to
act as a "regulator." We should not overestimate the power of consciousness and overlook the fact that it is still in the process of development and growth. For the time being, consciousness is not fully
prepared to "incorporate" the enormous reality and its cyclical flow,
which is devoid of any purpose, substance, or meaning. Nietzsche was
taking up the notion of incorporation once again here, as he had in 1881
in a series of extended notebook entries. What does "incorporation"
mean? We know, for example, that we live on a planet that races through
outer space around the sun. We also know that we owe all of life to the
sun. It will one day burn out, and mankind as a whole will come to an
end even if a recurring cosmic age performs the entire theater of life
once again. All of this is knowledge in our heads, but it is not incorporated. We see the sun go up as we always have and fail to notice that we
are living on a shifting foundation. We do not absorb the end and the
new beginnings into our sense of life. We construct an imaginary horizon of time around ourselves, which is not the actual one, but it allows
us to remain convinced of our own importance. Although we may have
a Copernican worldview—and in our era an Einsteinian one—when it
comes to incorporation, we are still Ptolemaists. Nietzsche wrote that
we need to understand "that as of now only our errors have been incorporated into us and that all of our consciousness is based on errors!"
(3,383; *GS* § 11).

Assuming that the dynamics of the growth of consciousness entail
both organic and cultural development, Nietzsche imagined what would
happen if expanding cerebral knowledge actually took over and transformed one's entire body and soul and full range of emotions—in other
words, if this ominous incorporation really took place. Might it not signal the destruction of the life of the mind and the demise of man under
the burden of consciousness? What if the creature of consciousness
turned out to be the drifter of evolution? And what if consciousness
were an excrescence that never should have been?

Nietzsche presented these ideas not as assertions but as deliberations to be set off against other considerations. Although science proves to be the "great bestower of pain," it can also bring into play its "counter-force, its tremendous capacity to make new galaxies of joy light up!" (3,384; *GS* § 12). What sort of joy that might be is not specified here, but we have already come to know Nietzsche's phenomenological pleasure in vigilance and attentiveness, and we have seen how much joy they occasioned. We also recall that Nietzsche cried for joy at the Surlej boulder as he contemplated the idea of eternal recurrence. His was not just the joy of discovery but an existential and pragmatic conviction that even individual life, because it recurs, carries enormous weight. Consequently, the idea that expands way out into the distance—he called it "cosmic"—culminates quite nearby, and thereby confers the dignity of eternity on the most intimate and individual sense of life. In this case, there is simply nothing ephemeral. No galaxy is expansive enough to destroy the significance of the little specks of dust we call "individuals."

"I cannot lose myself" could be construed as a statement conveying pleasure, but to reveal its appalling potential, one need only reformulate it ever so slightly: "I will never be rid of myself!" In *The Gay Science,* however, Nietzsche did not wish to grant depression any power over him, and fought it off with euphoria evoked by sheer force of will. This feeling of euphoria did not simply lift him up; he needed to summon up the courage to achieve it. When the book was published in the summer of 1882, he wrote to Lou Salomé: "What torments of every kind, what solitudes and surfeit of life! And against all of that, as it were against death and life, I brewed this medicine of mine, these thoughts of mine with their little stripes of *unclouded sky* overhead" (*B* 6,217; July 3, 1882). In a later preface to the second edition of *The Gay Science,* Nietzsche remarked: "Gratitude keeps on pouring out" (3,345; *GS* Preface § 1).

Where did this "gratitude" stem from? Did the will to truth actually reveal a conciliatory image of reality that gave Nietzsche a feeling of comfort? Had his sensations of fear, desertion, and senselessness simply vanished? Did the will to knowledge manage at the last moment to break free of the "dehumanization of nature" (9,525)? If that were the case, the dualism between life and knowledge would be surmounted, and the life-affirming impulse for knowledge would have triumphed over the life-denying affects that obviously exist and that can also accompany the will to knowledge. Even in his state of euphoria, Nietzsche remained clearheaded. He explained that even when we are experiencing happiness and ecstasy, we ought to remain conscientious "interpreters" of ourselves. The "founders of religions" might be lacking in "honesty," but he was determined to be a "person who thirsts for reason" and hence to "scrutinize as scrupulously as in a scientific experiment" (3,551; *GS* § 319). And what emerged from this sort of analysis?

Nietzsche recognized the essential fortuity of feelings. Knowledge, for example, is dependent on coincidental circumstances of the weather and its influence on physiological and other dispositions. In a letter of January 20, 1883, when Nietzsche reflected back on *The Gay Science,* he declared that this work was "only an effusive way of celebrating the fact that there had been a *clear* sky above for an entire month" (*B* 6,318). It may have been dictated in part by the weather, but other sorts of physiological circumstances were also potentially significant, since an instinctual basis is always involved. There is an infinite variety of instinctual bases that provide our insights with motives, energy, direction, and atmospheric tone. They give rise to both fundamental and secondary feelings and facilitate, inhibit, or prevent incorporation.

If the instinctual basis of the will remains at hand in knowledge in this way, will and truth can never be separated. And thus the potential conflict between life and knowledge would be a mere drama on the level of instinctual behavior itself. In the notebooks of 1881, Nietzsche wrote: "Here too we discover a night and a day as a condition of life for us: The desire for knowledge and the desire for desultory wandering are the ebb and flow. If one of them assumes complete control, it spells man's demise" (9,504).

This remark does not state unequivocally whether the urge to know corresponds to the ebb or to the flow. The desire for knowledge could be regarded as ebb to the extent that it is a retreat from the temptation to inundate reality with our own projections. Seen in this light, the flow would then be an image analogous to the desire for desultory wandering. An alternative interpretation is also possible, however, according to which the desire for knowledge would represent the flow in contact with reality, and the desire for desultory wandering would be the ebb, viewed as a retreat into our own imaginary world (in lieu of the knowledge of reality). The flow—like knowledge—sprays out and attacks, but the ebb, the desire for desultory wandering, pulls back in a positively fearful manner. Nietzsche took up this image of ebb and flow once again in a remarkable aphorism of *The Gay Science* called "Will and Wave" (§ 310). Here the metaphorical vacillation between the desire for knowledge and the desire for desultory wandering is intensified and presented as an unresolvable "mystery." "The wave creeps greedily into the innermost recesses of the rocky cleft" and comes "back, somewhat more slowly, still quite white with excitement—is it disappointed?" And the next wave is already beginning the game all over again. Although the waves are curious and have something to discover, they also have something to hide. When they foam up in their eager curiosity, they form "a wall between me and the sun . . . already nothing remains from the world aside from green twilight and green lightning" (3,546; *GS* § 310).

Nietzsche did not get beyond this metaphor, in which the desire for knowledge and the desire for desultory wandering are interpreted as contrary, and yet ultimately consistent, instinctual behavior. Consequently, when we judge things to be "true" or "false," there cannot be a standpoint outside of this instinctual behavior; only varying degrees of overwhelming strength, feelings of pleasure and displeasure, sufficiency and force of habit can be differentiated. "The strength of knowledge lies not in its degree of verity but rather in its age, the extent of its incorporation, its character as a condition of life" (3,469; *GS* § 110).

Nietzsche reviewed the complex history of truth once again from this perspective. When new knowledge enters the picture, a "vortex" throws the usual and accustomed truths into question. This situation remains relatively benign as long as it stays on the level of purely intellectual uncertainty and innovations. But when it becomes the kind of knowledge that intrudes on the life and customs of a culture, and when people have the incorporated aspects of previous knowledge to contend with, a struggle arises for a new incorporation. In the process, the new insights can be regarded as "madness" (3,431; *GS* § 76) and face adamant opposition because they blatantly challenge the conditions of life of an entire culture without offering an appealing alternative or being strong enough to accomplish incorporation on their own. Thus, incorporation implies that the truth of truth is its strength to render itself true. Truth is confirmed in the process of incorporation.

Nietzsche was thus disputing an idea he had advanced elsewhere concerning the dualism of knowledge and life, namely that knowledge stems from an instinctual basis and turns powerful when combined with instinctual bases. He explained "that it is certainly wrong to deny the power of instincts in knowledge and" to believe "that reason is an altogether free activity that is generated from within" (3,470; *GS* § 110).

The instinctual basis of knowledge is undeniable, which does not change the fact that this proposition concerning the power of instincts lays claim to a validity that is independent of instincts. If the proposition were only an expression of an instinct, it would not be true; but if it were not true, it would not be the expression of an instinct, which is what the proposition is claiming. This proposition, just like any other proposition that lays claim to a validity of truth, would fall into an abyss and be meaningless. There must therefore be a criterion for truth that involves something other than instinctual bases.

Nietzsche would wander despairingly through this labyrinth of self-referentialities, sometimes laughing and ironic, teetering between prophet and clown. In the end, it was perhaps his breakdown that offered him a way out of the house of mirrors of his theories. But let us keep in mind that, in this whole confusion about the question of truth,

Nietzsche always maintained an indisputable standard of judgment. For him, the formation of ideas was a matter not just of creating images but of forging paths to (self-)knowledge. An idea struck him as "true" if it brought together meaning and style to constitute a unit that was sufficiently strong and lively to endure his often unbearable pain and provide a vital counterbalance to it.

Nietzsche, who had pondered the agonistic character of life in other contexts, introduced this agonistic element as a key component of his argument. The interplay and counterplay of mind and body was the primary agonistic locus. Yet another struggle for truth was taking place here beyond the truth value of propositional statements. We will never understand Nietzsche if we do not realize that for him ideas possessed actual spiritual and physical reality on a par with passions. He might have said: How could his thoughts not be "true" if they engaged him, as he wrote in *The Gay Science,* in an extraordinary activity, a "perpetual stair climbing–like motion and at the same time feeling as though resting on clouds"? (3,529; *GS* § 288).

During that January of 1882, Nietzsche experienced the pleasurable side of knowledge as never before. Although knowledge is always associated with feelings and emotions, which are instinctual in nature, he now focused on the accompanying or supporting affects of knowledge, and was elated by the perspective that knowledge serves not to diminish or reduce the fullness of existence but rather to enhance it. The pursuit of knowledge is even an enhancement when it reveals horrifying realities. If, for example, the doctrine of eternal recurrence should prove to be true, we need to confront the fact that there is no possible refuge from time.

Nietzsche's elation could not be dampened by his awareness "that the human and animal past, indeed the whole primeval age and the past of all sentient being keeps on writing, loving, hating, and reaching conclusions within me" (3,416f.; *GS* § 54). He felt as though he had awakened from a dream but was aware that he "must continue dreaming so as not to perish: like a sleepwalker who must continue dreaming so as not to fall down" (3,416f). Life was so full of "self-mockery" as to give him the feeling "that it is all appearance and will-o'-the-wisp and a dance of ghosts and nothing more" (3,417; *GS* § 54), and yet he was enamored of knowledge in this light-hearted January. Aphorism § 324, a virtually programmatic explication of the title *The Gay Science,* declares: "No! Life has not disappointed me! Quite the contrary; with each passing year I find it truer, more desirable, and more mysterious—ever since the day when the great liberator came to me, the idea that life could be an experiment for the seeker of knowledge—and not a duty, not a disaster, not a deception!—As for knowledge itself: for others it may well be something different, for instance, a bed or the way to a bed, or a form of entertainment, or leisure—for me it is a world of dangers and victories in which heroic feelings also have their dance floors and playgrounds.— '*Life as a means to knowledge*'—with this principle in our hearts, we can not only live boldly, but even *live joyously and laugh joyously*" (3,552f.; *GS* § 324).

Nietzsche remained in Genoa until the end of March 1882. Spring had begun, and the weather was balmy. Normally, he would have returned to more northerly climes at this point, but instead he made the odd choice of traveling to Messina, Sicily, on a moment's notice. He was the only passenger on a freighter. This trip gave rise to a great deal of speculation. Was he hoping for an unexpected encounter with Wagner, who had moved into his vacation lodgings nearby? Was it the homoerotic colony on the outskirts of Messina that attracted him, in particular the photographer Wilhelm von Gloeden, who was then famous for his pictures of naked young men cavorting in poses that recalled Greek antiquity? Interpreters of Nietzsche who focus on his latent homosexuality suspect that this was the case. Certainly, he associated the south with emancipated sensuality and relaxation. He was happy to keep dreaming the dream of the "blissful islands." In *Zarathustra* he sent "sweeping-winged longing" out into "hotter souths than sculptors ever dreamed of: to places where gods in their dances are ashamed of all clothes" (4,247; *Z* Third Part, "On Old and New Tablets" § 2). The enchanting experience of hearing Bizet's opera *Carmen* for the first time in Genoa in late November 1881 had given flight to Nietzsche's fantasies of the south. When he later wrote about *Carmen* in his preliminary notes for *The Case of Wagner,* this lascivious south as he imagined it, and perhaps even experienced it, was once again apparent: "The African gaiety, the fatalistic cheerfulness, with an eye that gazes seductively, profoundly, and awfully; the lascivious melancholy of the dance of the Moors; blinking passion, sharp and sudden as a sword; and aromas wafting out of the yellow afternoon of the sea that seize the heart with fear as though recalling forgotten islands where it once tarried and where it should have tarried forever" (13,24).

A few days after his arrival on the island, Nietzsche wrote to Peter Gast: "So, I have arrived at my 'corner of the earth,' where, according to Homer, happiness is said to dwell. Truly, I have never been in such good spirits as in the past week, and my new fellow citizens are pampering and spoiling me in the most charming way" (*B* 6,189; April 8, 1882).

He indulged in this pampering for four weeks; then the sirocco drove him on to Rome, where he met Lou Salomé. This chapter of his life, Nietzsche later claimed, after he had ridden out the storm, was more excruciating than any sirocco could ever be (*B* 6,323; Feb. 1, 1883).

CHAPTER 11

Lou Salomé and the Quest for Intimacy

Homoeroticism • The sexual Dionysus • The Lou Salomé
story • Zarathustra as bulwark • Human and superhuman
• The Darwinist misconception • Fantasies of annihilation
• "I am so sick of tragic gestures and words!"

*N*IETZSCHE ENTITLED the fourth book of *The Gay Science*
"Sanctus Januarius" in order to commemorate the exhilarating
month of January (1882) he had spent in Genoa. The title also paid
homage to the martyred Sanctus Januarius. In Naples, this saint is
honored with many paintings and statues, which Nietzsche had first
admired in 1876. This martyr, who is known in Naples as San
Gennaro, was a man with striking feminine characteristics. He had a
soft beauty and experienced periodic bleeding. Legend associated his
martyr's blood with menstrual blood. Considered both man and
woman, he became the saint of androgyny. In the subterranean
chapel of the central church in Naples, which bears his name, the
head of the decapitated martyr was preserved along with two vials of
his blood, which was considered miracle-working. The poem that
opens book 4 of *The Gay Science* is addressed to this *femminiello*, as he
was also known in Naples:

With a flaming spear you crushed
All its ice until my soul
Roaring toward the ocean rushed
Of its highest hope and goal.
Ever healthier it swells,
Lovingly compelled but free:
Thus it lauds your miracles,
Fairest month of January!
$\qquad$ (3,521; *GS* Book 4)[1]

When Nietzsche asked his friend Gersdorff to read book 4, which was dedicated to the androgynous martyr, he declared that his books revealed "so much about me, which a hundred letters of friendship would not be able to match. Read the Sanctus Januarius in particular with this idea in mind" (*B* 6,248; late Aug. 1882). Some interpreters have viewed this statement as an indirect confession of Nietzsche's homoerotic tendencies, and assert that it provides a key to his life and works.

Speculations abound. The boy grew up without a father, surrounded by women. There are alleged indications of sibling incest in the early years. Did little "Fritz" perhaps even pull Elisabeth into his bed and wind up plagued by a bad conscience? Some researchers have traced Nietzsche's sexual secrets all the way back to his years in boarding school, citing the story of the decadent vagabond poet Ernst Ortlepp, who was famous and infamous around Naumburg. The students idolized Ortlepp, a shabbily clad genius who roved through the forests, nearly always inebriated, and on summer days recited and sang his poems under classroom windows. This unnerving man was notorious for his attacks on Christianity. He disturbed church services with loud interjections. His poem "The Lord's Prayer of the Nineteenth Century," which closes with the lines "Old time religion / Despised by the new

---

[1] Translation by Walter Kaufmann, in Friedrich Nietzsche, *The Gay Science* (New York: Vintage Books, 1974), p. 221.

era's son, / And comes the call throughout the earth: / 'Your name will have no holy worth'" (Schulte 33), was widely discussed. Nietzsche's poetry album from his years in Pforta featured several poems by the ostracized Ortlepp, who was suspected of pederasty. In early July 1864, Ortlepp was discovered dead in a ditch, and Nietzsche and his friends collected money for a tombstone.

In a poem called "Before the Crucifix," the eighteen-year-old Nietzsche portrayed this bizarre man as an intoxicated blasphemer who calls out to the man on the cross: "Come down! Are you just deaf? / You can have my bottle! (*J* 2,187). According to a biographical reconstruction by H. J. Schmidt, Ortlepp may have been the first Dionysian seducer in Nietzsche's life, engaging not only his imagination but also his sexuality. Nietzsche, who was both traumatized and exhilarated by this experience, as some surmise, never, in their estimation, got over this first molestation by Dionysus incarnate. They claim that this incident set the stage for his Dionysian experience, which he later alluded to, covertly and guilt-ridden, in *Ecce Homo:* "the absolute certainty as to what I *am* was projected onto some coincidental reality or other—the truth about me spoke out of a dreadful depth" (6,314f.; *EH* "Birth of Tragedy" § 4).

If we are prepared to relate Nietzsche's alleged sexual seduction (perhaps even rape) by Ortlepp and the homosexual inclinations that were awakened (or intensified) in the process to these "dreadful depths," we will uncover further references to this experience throughout his works—masked by encoded images and recollections. But if we were to do so, we would be reducing the immense range of life that inspired Nietzsche's thought to the secret history of his sexuality and making it the privileged focal point of truth. These days, sexuality is equated with the truth of the individual, which is arguably our era's most prominent fiction regarding the nature of truth. This fiction, however, was already being circulated back in the nineteenth century.

Nietzsche suffered from the brutality and veiled aggression of the sort of will to truth that judges people on the basis of their sexual history. Although he himself devoted considerable research to the subject of instinctual behavior, he considered it infinitely diverse. He approached instinctual behavior from a polytheistic perspective and did not subscribe to the unimaginative monotheism of the sexual determinists. It was none other than Richard Wagner who first offended and then "mortally" wounded him with this sort of psychology of sexualist suspicion.

In the early 1870s, Wagner gently counseled Nietzsche not to cultivate overly intimate friendships with men at the expense of women if he wanted to overcome his melancholy and dark moods. Wagner wrote to him on April 6, 1874: "Among other things, I found that I have never in my life had the kind of contact with men that you have in Basel in the evening hours. . . . What young men seem to be lacking is women: . . . it is a question of knowing where to find them without stealing them. Of course, you could always steal one if necessary. I think you ought to marry" (*N/W* 241).

The Wagners were not the only ones on the hunt for a bride for Nietzsche. His mother and Malwida von Meysenbug went to great lengths to get him married off, and he did not always resent their interference. Sometimes he even sought help in finding a wife. Behind the scenes, though, Wagner often spread rumors and gossip, as Nietzsche probably learned much later, just following Wagner's death in early 1883. Even before then, the rumor was circulating that Nietzsche was an effeminate man and chronic masturbator, and it is quite possible that he had already caught wind of these rumors during the bittersweet summer he spent with Lou Salomé in Tautenburg.

On March 13, 1882, Paul Rée traveled from Genoa, where he was visiting Nietzsche, to Rome. It was in Rome that Rée met a twenty-year-old Russian woman named Lou Salomé at the house of Malwida von Meysenbug. This highly gifted daughter of a Russian general of Huguenot descent had left Russia with her mother after the death of her father in 1880 in order to study in Zurich. The young woman suffered from a severe lung disease, and doctors gave her only a few years to live.

This prognosis caused her to dedicate herself even more intensively to her study of philosophy and the history of religion and culture. Her precocious intellectual passion as well as her curiosity and zest for life were impressive. In the fall of 1881, Salomé wrote a poem called "Prayer for Life" while in Zurich. Enraptured by this poem, Nietzsche set it to music with the new title "Hymn to Life." In 1887, long after they had broken off all contact, he had his musical rendition arranged for choir and orchestra by Peter Gast. It was the only one of his compositions he wanted to have printed. The lines he cherished were the following: "Surely this is how a friend loves a friend, / I love you, quixotic life. /... to be and to meditate and live for thousands of years; / Embrace me with both of your arms / If you have no more happiness to give me, / Well then, give me your anguish (Andreas-Salomé 301).

Salomé broke off her studies in the fall of 1881 because she could no longer endure the climate. Her doctors recommended an extended convalescence in the south, and she traveled to Rome with her mother. There, in the Meysenbug home, she quickly became the center of the local social scene. When Paul Rée arrived, he fell in love with the young Russian woman on the spot. The two of them strolled through the streets of Rome night after night, engrossed in conversation as Rée explained his ideas for his forthcoming treatise on moral philosophy. He wrote to Nietzsche that he had never encountered such a good conversationalist; she grasped his thoughts before he had even finished formulating them. Rée was ecstatic, and wanted Nietzsche to share in his happiness. He was hoping, however, that the bond they had formed would not be compromised. He invited his friend to Rome, and Malwida von Meysenbug also issued an invitation. She was equally impressed by the young Russian woman and felt that Nietzsche absolutely had to meet her: "A very unusual girl . . . she strikes me as someone who has reached much the same philosophical conclusions as you. . . . Rée and I concur in our wish to see you together sometime with this extraordinary creature" (Janz 2,121).

The invitation to Rome and the stories about Salomé aroused

Nietzsche's curiosity and provided a fresh impetus to his plan to seek a partner in marriage. He wanted a mate who would run his household and take over his secretarial work, as his sister had often done for him, and, if at all possible, be his intellectual equal, as his sister had never been. Nietzsche sometimes acted impulsively in situations like this, as was evident in April 1876 when he made a highly aggressive impromptu proposal of marriage to Mathilde Trampedach after they had met on only three occasions. The woman was quite startled and rejected him outright, whereupon Nietzsche retreated as if nothing had happened. Not a trace of love or passion. Just as precipitate was his renewed idea of marriage in March 1882 when he heard the news from Rome.

In a letter to Overbeck of March 17, 1882, after complaining about his defective typewriter and his failing eyesight, and adding the comment that he would be well served by a "reading machine," he went on to say: "I need a young person around me who is intelligent and educated enough to be able to work with me. I would even agree to two years of marriage for this purpose—in which case, of course, a few additional considerations would apply" (*B* 6,180). In a letter to Paul Rée dated March 21, Nietzsche expressed the same wishes, but this time in an ironic, flirtatious tone tinged with hesitancy: "Give that Russian girl my regards if that makes any sense: I lust after this kind of soul. Indeed, I plan to go on the prowl for one quite soon; considering what I wish to accomplish in the next ten years, I need one. Marriage is an altogether different story—I could agree only to a maximum of two years of marriage" (*B* 6,185f.). Nonetheless, Nietzsche stopped in Messina before going on to Rome. He learned from Rée that this side trip had raised him in the estimation of the Russian woman, almost as though his trip had been well orchestrated. Rée wrote to Nietzsche that this sojourn "astonished and worried the young Russian. . . . She has grown so eager to see you and to speak to you" (15,120; *Chronik*).

Such was the beginning of this relationship before it really began. Their first face-to-face meeting took place at the end of April at Saint Peter's Basilica in Rome. Nietzsche's first words were these: "From which stars did we fall to meet each other here?" (Janz 2,123). Just as suddenly as he had proposed marriage to Mathilde Trampedach six years earlier, Nietzsche asked Salomé to marry him in a matter of days. The story is quite complicated because he brought in his friend Rée to help court her, although Rée was himself taken with her. Salomé turned Nietzsche down on the pretext of economic constraints, but she passionately embraced the plan to form a kind of work-study group *à trois* and to share an apartment, perhaps in Vienna or Paris. For reasons of propriety, they could include Salomé's or Rée's mother, or Nietzsche's sister. Nietzsche warmed up to this plan after the rejection of his marriage proposal, and he clung to it for the whole year to follow. This intellectual ménage à trois suited Salomé's fantasies perfectly. As she wrote in her memoirs, she dreamed of a "pleasant study full of books and flowers, flanked by two bedrooms, and work companions going in and out, bound together in a jovial and solemn circle" (Janz 2,125). Nietzsche could well imagine the advantages of a tightly knit work commune; since the time of his Surlej inspiration, he had been determined to substantiate his doctrine of eternal recurrence with a thorough study of the natural sciences.

On their way back to Germany, they met at Lake Orta, in northern Italy. At long last, Nietzsche found the opportunity to take a walk alone with Salomé. The path led up to Monte Sacro. Nietzsche later recalled this walk as a virtually holy event, full of promises that never materialized, but we do not know what happened on Monte Sacro. Nietzsche did not express himself on the subject, and Salomé said very little. She later confided to a friend: "I don't really know whether I kissed Nietzsche on Monte Sacro" (Peters, *Lou Andreas-Salomé* 106). Whatever the case, Nietzsche gathered his courage and proposed marriage once again the next time they met in Lucerne, this time without the aid of an intermediary. Again Salomé said no. She was both attracted to and repelled by Nietzsche. She was allured by the cerebral adventures he offered her, but put off by his pathos, rigid manner, and formality, which alternated with an unbecoming free-spirited attitude and jaunty flirtatiousness.

Nietzsche's awkward attempt at seduction nonetheless aroused the jealousy of Rée, who was very eager to learn from Salomé exactly what had taken place on Monte Sacro. In a bantering but wary tone, he advised Salomé that Nietzsche's next proposal would soon follow.

After being rejected for the second time, Nietzsche pinned all of his hopes on their plans for a threesome. By this point, it could not have escaped Nietzsche's attention that, the bond between them notwithstanding, he was competing with his friend for Salomé. He recognized that the time had come to give explicit reinforcement to their friendship: "It would be impossible to be friends in a more wonderful way than we are now," he wrote to Rée on May 24, 1882. On the same day, he declared to Salomé: "Rée is in every way a better friend than I am and am capable of being: pay attention to this difference!" (*B* 6,194f.). Up until then, Nietzsche and Salomé had been together for only a few days or hours at a time, and he hoped to engineer a more sustained encounter alone with her. Perhaps he would then be able to win her over for himself. But did he even know what he wanted? He made a point of informing Peter Gast that the "concept of a love affair" (*B* 6,222; July 13, 1882) did not apply in this case. In a draft of a letter to Malwida von Meysenbug, he defined the relationship as a "fast friendship." He called Salomé a "truly heroic soul," and expressed the wish "to gain a disciple in her, and if I should not live too much longer, an heir and successor" (*B* 6,223f.; July 13, 1882). He also expressed this desire to Salomé herself. He had to dispel her misgivings; she was not to think that he wanted her merely as a secretary. He wrote to her: "It never occurred to me for a single moment that you should 'recite and write' for me; but I would greatly wish to be allowed to be your *teacher*. In the end, to be quite frank: I am looking for people who could be my heirs; some of the things that preoccupy me are not be to found in my books—and I am looking for the finest, most fertile ground for them" (*B* 6,211; June 26, 1882). Salomé did not necessarily understand this letter to be a declaration of love—Nietzsche's letters to her do not exactly brim over with eroticism. But they do contain sentences here and there that must have made it clear to her that he was smoldering under the surface: "I had to be silent," he wrote to her on June 27, 1882, "because I would have keeled over at the mere mention of you" (*B* 6,213).

Then came the summer in Tautenburg, in Thuringia. Salomé accepted Nietzsche's invitation to join him there. Prior to her departure, she attended the Bayreuth Festival, frequented the home of the Wagners, and got acquainted with Nietzsche's sister, Elisabeth. The latter found herself in the uncomfortable role of envious witness to Lou Salomé's social status in the salons and at the receptions. The conversations Elisabeth overheard about her renegade brother were unkind to him, and she felt that this young Russian woman ought to have unfailingly defended her brother. Instead, Salomé turned against him and cast aspersions along with the others. This is how Elisabeth saw the situation, or at least this is how she later reported it to her brother.

During their trip to Tautenburg, Elisabeth Nietzsche and Lou Salomé engaged in a series of nasty altercations. From then on, Nietzsche's sister became Salomé's vindictive antagonist. She later alleged that Salomé responded to her moral censure by declaring that Nietzsche himself was a hypocrite who had feigned hospitality to try to manipulate her into living "in sin" with him. Nietzsche, she claimed, was an egotist, and his writings were testimony to his madness. We have no record of what Salomé really said, but this is how Nietzsche's sister recounted the exchange to him. Nietzsche later wrote that the very thought of this incident brought him to the brink of "insanity" (*B* 6,435; Aug. 26, 1883).

These feelings of animosity notwithstanding, Elisabeth Nietzsche spent the following weeks together with her brother and Lou Salomé in Tautenburg, although the latter barely noticed her and failed to include her in their intense discussions. Since Rée was now jealously observing the relationship between the two, Salomé kept a journal of these weeks in the form of her letters to Rée and provided very specific information about the idyll in Tautenburg. Just a few hours after they arrived, she reported, they were able to get past their "small talk" and return to their former familiarity. They were housed in separate apartments, and

Nietzsche came to her front door every morning so that they could take long walks and converse for hours on end. Salomé wrote: "We have been talking ourselves absolutely to death. . . . Strange how in the course of our conversations we manage inadvertently to descend into abysses and those dizzying places people go all alone to gaze down into the depths. We have always chosen the mountain goat paths. If somebody had listened in on our conversations, he would have thought that two devils were talking" (15,125; *Chronik*).

What were they talking about? Surely not about their feelings for each other. On only one occasion did Nietzsche whisper to Salomé: "Monte Sacro—I have you to thank for the most delightful dream of my life" (Peters, *Lou Andreas-Salomé* 133). The death of God and religious longing were their major topics of conversation. Salomé wrote: "We share a religious streak in our natures. Perhaps it has become so prominent in us precisely because we are free spirits in the extreme. In a free spirit, religious feeling cannot appeal to any divine power or heaven and culminate in frailty, fear, and avarice, which are the cornerstones of religion. In the free spirit the religious need that originates in religion can . . . be reflected back onto itself and become the heroic strength of one's being, the desire to dedicate oneself to a illustrious goal." She claimed that Nietzsche's character exhibited a high degree of this heroic trait. For this reason, we should expect "that he will appear to us as the promulgator of a new religion, and it will be the sort that recruits heroes as its disciples" (Peters, *Lou Andreas-Salomé* 136). Salomé, a keen observer of human nature, wrote this statement several months before Nietzsche actually undertook the attempt to expound a kind of religion in *Zarathustra*.

These weeks in Tautenburg were happy and intense, but there were also moments in which Salomé sensed Nietzsche's alien, uncanny quality: "In some deep dark corner of our beings," she wrote, "we are worlds apart. Nietzsche's nature is like an old castle that conceals within it many a dark dungeon and hidden basement room, not apparent at first glance and yet likely to contain all the essentials. It is strange, but recently the idea suddenly struck me that we could wind up facing each other as enemies someday" (Peters, *Lou Andreas-Salomé* 134). This is exactly how things turned out. Nietzsche did not want to acknowledge that Salomé did not love him as he perhaps wished. The intensity between them and the special delight Salomé took in her conversations with him, he had mistaken for love, which she did not feel. He could not hold anything against her, because love cannot be produced on demand, and his self-deception in this matter did not result from conscious deception on her part. Salomé never deluded him. In *Im Kampf um Gott* (A Struggle for God, 1885), the autobiographical novel she wrote three years later, Salomé shed light on the dramatically misguided relationship they had shared: "There is no avenue from sensual passion to an intellectual meeting of minds—but many avenues from the latter to the former" (Peters, *Lou Andreas-Salomé* 157).

Clearly, on Nietzsche's side, their "meeting of minds" had evolved into a passion with sensual overtones, which Salomé could not reciprocate. Even for Nietzsche, the sensual aspect was only ambivalent at best. After their breakup, all of the physical revulsion he appears to have harbored toward Salomé rose to the surface. He described her in a letter to Paul Rée's brother in these terms: "This scrawny dirty smelly monkey with her fake breasts—a disaster!" (*B* 6,402; mid-July, 1883). The letter remained unsent.

When Nietzsche looked back on the whole story, it seemed to him like a "hallucination" (*B* 6,374; May 10, 1883). He interpreted the circumstances as follows: a recluse in the extreme and unaccustomed to contact with people, he no longer understood them. He was at the mercy of others: "my soul was missing its skin, so to speak, and all natural protections" (*B* 6,423; Aug. 14, 1883). Consequently, he did not figure out the game that was being played with him. He had been lured to Rome to meet Salomé. Could it be that Malwida von Meysenbug and Rée had actually had the best of intentions and only wanted to provide him with an interesting conversational partner? His friend Rée had deceived him by not revealing his own feelings for Salomé. Nietzsche also chided himself for having been oblivious to all of these circumstances and for having had such a poor grasp of human nature. He had gone along with the idea of a threesome and failed to notice, as he later realized, that this plan was just a scheme to put him off. After Tautenburg, Salomé and Rée carried on with this plan for a while so as to phase him out gradually. While he was still clinging to the idea of the threesome, Salomé and Rée had already put their plan for communal living into practice in Berlin. To make matters still worse, there were the awful denigrations communicated to him by his sister, which he believed more fully once he felt excluded by Salomé and Rée. Allegations that he was an egotist, that he was pursuing sexual objectives under the guise of idealism, and that his writings were those of a semideranged man (*B* 6,399; mid-July 1883) etched themselves into him, and were extremely difficult to ignore.

Nietzsche had put his finger on the problem when he claimed to lack immunity and "natural protections," such as the diversion of regular contact with other people. The recluse was tortured by his fantasies. Later, when he read Flaubert's *Temptation of Saint Anthony,* he found literary confirmation of what it meant to be a victim of one's own tortured fantasies. But Nietzsche struggled for a will to power over himself. He became wary of his own suspicions and was suddenly able to see all of this tumult in another light. As he wrote on August 14, 1883, Salomé once again seemed to him "a creature of the first rank; it is such a pity about her. . . . I miss her, warts and all" (*B* 6,424).

He never clearly stated what these alleged "warts" actually were; we can only conjecture what he meant. He had bared the innermost workings of his mind to her as never before to another human being, sensing an unparalleled depth of understanding between them. Salomé touched the core of his "talents and objectives" (*B* 6,254; Sept. 9, 1882), and Nietzsche felt that she understood him completely: "Several major directions of the spiritual and moral horizon are my *most powerful* source of life. I am glad that our friendship has struck its roots and hopes in *this very soil*" (*B* 6,204; June 12, 1882). In fact, he considered the two of them *"all too similar,* 'blood relatives'" (*B* 6,237; Aug. 14, 1882). Nietzsche employed this logic to defend Salomé to his sister, claiming that "any disparagement of her is a disparagement of me first and foremost" (*B* 6,254; Sept. 9, 1882). When Nietzsche decried Salomé after their separation, he was indeed hurting himself. To return to our earlier question: What did he hold against her? The fact that she understood him so well? Surely that could not be turned to her disadvantage. No, the truly unbearable realization for Nietzsche was the fact that she understood him completely and then, with her boundless curiosity for people, simply moved on to others and did not remain under his spell. To make matters worse, she left him behind as a mere stage in her educational career. It was impossible for him to tell Salomé: You have been invited to the table of another king. Nietzsche did not display the imperturbable sovereignty of Zarathustra, who requires his disciples to let go of him and leave once they have found him.

It deeply wounded Nietzsche that Salomé had broken free of him and gone her way without him. He felt exploited and abused because his disciple had made it clear that she understood him, but also understood how to find other teachers for herself. Nietzsche was greatly offended. He had abandoned himself to her and then found himself abandoned by her. Now, in the winter of 1882–83, he felt that he had to rely on himself as never before. In December 1882, he wrote to Franz Overbeck: "Now I am facing my task all alone. . . . I need a bulwark against the unendurable" (*B* 6,306). Two weeks later came the period of ten days in which he wrote the first part of *Zarathustra* as though in a trance. Without a doubt, this work was his ominous "bulwark against the unendurable."

The work on *Zarathustra* did not really feel like work; it was more like an ecstatic game that transformed Nietzsche, lifting him above the tumult of everyday existence into the serene atmosphere of dignified messages. He wrote to Franz Overbeck on February 10, 1883: "I feel as though lightning has struck—for a brief period, I was completely in my element and in my light. And now it is over" (*B* 6,325).

The first scenes of *Zarathustra* betray obvious traces of the pain and suffering of these weeks. The opening pages depict Zarathustra's departure from the bliss of solitude and his venture out among people, initially as an object of derision. The preface states that Zarathustra has left his home and retreated to the mountains for a period of ten years: "Here he enjoyed his spirit" (4,11; *Z* First Part, Prologue § 1) to the point of excess: "This cup wants to become empty again, and Zarathustra wants to become a man again" by telling poeple about his wealth. "Thus Zarathustra began to go down!" (4,12; *Z* First Part, Prologue § 1). Nietzsche soon learned that this pathos could also have an unintended comic effect. When he hurriedly left town in the late summer of 1882, after an argument with his mother and sister about Salomé, his sister noted sardonically: "Thus Zarathustra began to go down!" (*B* 6,256). She knew this sentence from his 1882 book *The Gay Science,* in which Zarathustra makes his first appearance, at the end of the fourth book.

Going down to the people spells Zarathustra's demise, which is how Nietzsche himself experienced his own complicated situation in 1882. After finishing the first part of *Zarathustra,* he thought back to this summer in a letter to Overbeck: "Because of my exclusive contact with idealist images and processes, I have become so sensitive that I suffer incredibly from contact with actual people and forgo it" (*B* 6,337; Feb. 22, 1883).

The first message that Nietzsche's Zarathustra announces is the doctrine of the *Übermensch,* but he chooses the wrong time and the wrong place to disseminate his message. The people are gathered in the marketplace to admire the artistry of a tightrope walker. They want to enjoy themselves and relish the thrill of danger to which the tightrope walker exposes himself. Zarathustra speaks to this sensation-seeking crowd as though it were a community of metaphysics enthusiasts in need of being talked into savoring earthly pleasures. "Remain faithful to the earth," he calls to the onlookers, "and do not believe those who speak to you of supernatural hopes!" (4,15; *Z* First Part, Prologue § 3). How could Zarathustra ever get the idea that these were people who needed dissuasion from "supernatural hopes"! Nothing would appear to be further from the truth. Zarathustra comes with a message, but he does not know the people and consequently his pathos rings hollow. Nietzsche purposely set up this discrepancy because Zarathustra needed to learn at the end (of the prologues) that he had to go about his missionary work in a different manner: "It became clear to me: let Zarathustra speak not to the people but to companions!" (4,25; *Z* First Part, Prologue § 9).

Since Zarathustra subsequently steers clear of the open market and preaches only to "companions," he has no need to modify the tone of his sermon. He avoids not pathos but only the situations in which it would come across as embarrassing. He speaks to "all and none," to "brothers" and "friends," and yet confesses to himself that his speaking is a monologue that invents the existence of a third party—be it friends, disciples, or mankind as a whole—so that the conversation between "I and me" does not remain inward directed. "The third is the cork that stops the conversation of the two [I and me] from sinking into the depths" (4,71; *Z* First Part, "On the Friend"). But after the prologue, in which a commonplace audience provides the opposing "third," Nietzsche refrains from matching a real disputant to his Zarathustra, at which point Zarathustra's speeches take a turn for the monotonous as non-oppositional monologues. Once Zarathustra has retreated from the open market—the locus of his possible disgrace—he speaks into the void. Nietzsche should have left the "last people" on the stage so that Zarathustra would have had to contend with them. Only in this way would the doctrine of the *Übermensch* have emerged in sharper contours.

But what is the *Übermensch,* and how are we to picture him? First of all, this term is just a new expression for a theme Nietzsche had already broached in the period of the *Untimely Meditations,* namely that of self-configuration and self-enhancement. In the essay "Schopenhauer as Educator," he showed, using the example of his own experience with Schopenhauer, how a young soul finds the "fundamental law" of a person's "real self" (1,340; SE § 1) by examining the series of exemplary models that have molded the person. A soul that is determined and encouraged will discover a positive direction. Each model functions as an encouragement to itself. Guided by these models, we need to reach beyond ourselves to realize our full potential. We can find our true selves not within ourselves, Nietzsche wrote at that time, but above ourselves: "Your true being does not lie buried deep within you, but rather immeasurably high above you or at least above what you normally take to be your ego" (1,340f.; SE § 1). We should therefore not betray our better selves (which we are by becoming better selves). We can and should expect something from ourselves, not just from life in general. We should be able to maintain high personal expectations and keep to these expectations, of which we are the unrealized embodiment. The will to the *Übermensch* is already at work in any attempt at self-configuration that seeks enhancement.

This meaning of the *Übermensch* has not addressed the issue of biology, but it does take into account the autoplastic powers of the human mind and man's capability for ascending self-control and self-configuration. Nietzsche had already formulated a conceptual model of the *Übermensch* in *Human, All Too Human:* "You should become the master of yourself and also the master of your own virtues. Previously they were your masters, but they must be nothing more than your tools, just some tools among others. You should achieve power over your pros and cons and learn how to put them forth and hang them back in accordance with your higher aim" (2,20; *HH* I Preface § 6). Zarathustra has this *Übermensch* in mind when he proclaims: "I love the one who has a free spirit and a free heart" (4,18; *Z* First Part, Prologue § 4).

The *Übermensch*'s mastery of self-configuration is not the only issue here. There are also biologistic overtones in Zarathustra's speeches, especially when he explains that man in his current form evolved from the ape, but that there is still too much of the ape in him and too much laziness, which wants to revert to the animal kingdom. Man is a creature in transition. He is still in flux between the ape from which he originated and the *Übermensch* into which he may evolve. "What is the ape to man? A laughing stock or a painful embarrassment. And this is exactly what man should be for the *Übermensch*: a laughing stock or a painful embarrassment" (4,14; *Z* First Part, Prologue § 3).

The metaphoric style of presentation in *Zarathustra* only hints at its biologistic contents. In his notebooks from the period of *Zarathustra*, Nietzsche was more forthright. He wrote that the "goal" was the "evolution of the entire body and not just of the brain" (10,506). Overt references to the specifics of the physical evolution of man would have been ill-suited to the pathos of Zarathustra's speeches. Ought Zarathustra to have said something about, for instance, the quantity of hair, musculature, arm length, or head size of the *Übermensch*? This would have been unintentionally comical. In matters concerning the physical appearance of the *Übermensch*, Zarathustra confines himself to this advice for those contemplating marriage: "Do not *re*produce yourself, but rather produce *upward*! May the garden of marriage help you do this" (4,90; *Z* First Part, "On Child and Marriage").

Nietzsche was thoroughly familiar with his contemporaries' ideas on biological breeding and evolution. While in Sils-Maria in the summer of 1881, he had sent for literature on this subject. He would have had to be completely ignorant of the widespread trend of biological evolutionary thought spurred by Darwinism to have escaped its influence. Despite all of his criticism of the specifics of Darwinism, Nietzsche was unable to extricate himself entirely from the powerful implications of this theory. Two basic ideas were considered common knowledge in the intellectual culture of those years, and they had become unquestioned assumptions on his part as well.

The notion of development was one of them. It is not a new idea, at least not in reference to the cultural sphere. All of Hegelianism and the subsequent historical school introduced it as a law of development of intellectual metamorphoses. Darwin's new contribution, the second of these basic ideas, was the application of the thesis of development to biological substance.

The implications of a biological history of man's evolution from the animal kingdom could be viewed as a drastic debasement of man. It makes the ape an early relative of man, which led Nietzsche to have his Zarathustra explain: "Once you were apes, and even now man is more ape than any ape" (4,14; *Z* First Part, Prologue § 3). The definition of man as a product of biological development implied that even the so-called mind was regarded as a bodily function of the head, spinal cord, nerves, and so forth.

It is in this sense that Nietzsche also turned his attention to the physiological side of mental faculties and in *Zarathustra* wrote about the "great rationality of the body: the creative body created the mind for itself as a hand of its will" (4,40; *Z* First Part, "On the Despisers of the Body"). But this naturalization of the mind and the consequent relativization of the special status of man, which was in effect a disparagement of man, is only one of the two major aspects of the effects of Darwinism.

The other aspect, in stark contrast to the first, is marked by positively euphoric visions of human evolution, because it was now possible to extend the idea of progress to biological development. If evolution has led to man, why should it stop with man? Why might there not be an even higher form of life, an *Übermensch* as a higher biological type? Darwin did not use the term *Übermensch,* but the application of biological futurism to man was not unfamiliar to him. The logic of the idea of development was bound to lead to fantasies of this sort. Darwin wrote: "Man may be excused for feeling some pride at having risen, though not of his own exertions, to the very summit of the organic scale; and the fact of his having thus risen, instead of having been aboriginally placed there, may give him hope for a still higher destiny in the distant future" (Darwin, *Descent* 644).

Darwin maintained a certain degree of skepticism. He was well aware that this envisioned future was a product of the human mind, which was subject to wishful thinking and inflated self-assessment. "Can the mind of man, which has, as I fully believe, been developed from a mind as low as that possessed by the lowest animal, be trusted when it draws such grand conclusions?" (Darwin, *Autobiography* 93).

Many Darwinians were less hesitant. David Friedrich Strauss, for example, who was roundly criticized by Nietzsche, wholeheartedly endorsed the idea of biological elevation. Nietzsche found fault not with this Darwinist idea of development but only with Strauss's prosaic notions of a higher type of man who was still domesticated. Eugen Dühring in particular, whom Nietzsche had quoted extensively and from whom he had learned a great deal (although he later spoke of Dühring only in mocking tones), developed an elaborate argument to show that evolution condemns most species to degeneration and extinction, but that an incredible success was imminent for man. He wrote that all indications pointed to a development "that would someday not lead man to death, but instead transform man into a refined, substantially different species" (Benz 102).

The *Übermensch* viewed as a biological type certainly came across as a voguish figure of Darwinism, which was quite discomfiting for Nietzsche. He was wary of the trendiness of his visions. He wanted in particular to keep his distance from vulgar Darwinism, especially the arena of pamphleteering, and ensure that his *Übermensch* was something original and unique.

Nietzsche sought to shed another potential affinity with Thomas Carlyle and Ralph Waldo Emerson as well, although he had made complimentary statements about the latter in the past. Carlyle and Emerson had also expressed the idea that mankind could and would culminate in a series of *Übermenschen:* heroes, geniuses, saints, and other figures in whom creative humanity is displayed impressively and rousingly in the areas of art, politics, science, and warfare. Here, too, the idea of development was crucial, because Carlyle and Emerson recalled figures like Luther, Shakespeare, and Napoleon not only as isolated instances but as heralds of a far-reaching qualitative transformation of the human race.

Nietzsche vehemently denied any tie to Darwinist or idealist conceptions of the *Übermensch.* In *Ecce Homo,* he complained that his idea of the *Übermensch* had been completely misunderstood: "The word *Übermensch* to designate a type of supreme achievement, as opposed to 'modern' men, 'good' men, Christians, and other nihilists (a word that in the mouth of a Zarathustra, the *demolisher* of morality, turns into a very contemplative word) has almost universally, in complete innocence, been taken to mean the very values that are the exact opposite of what Zarathustra was intended to represent, namely the 'idealistic' type of a higher kind of man, half 'saint,' half 'genius.' . . . Other academic blockheads have suspected me of Darwinism on that account. Even the 'hero worship' of that major unwitting and unwilling counterfeiter Carlyle I have so roundly rejected has been read into it. When I whispered into the ears of some people that they were better off looking for a Cesare Borgia than a Parsifal, they did not believe their ears" (6,300; *EH* "Why I Write Such Good Books" § 1).

Nietzsche had clearly forgotten his own beginnings when he complained that his *Übermensch* had been mistakenly interpreted as an " 'idealistic' type of a higher kind of man." In *The Birth of Tragedy*, and particularly in "Schopenhauer as Educator," he had developed the concept of a genius that strongly resembled the type of "half 'saint,' half 'genius' " he was now criticizing. In a draft of a preface to *The Birth of Tragedy*, he had written: "Who would dare to claim that the saint in the desert has failed to achieve the highest purpose of the cosmic will?" (7,354). For Nietzsche, the genius and the saint were the "peak of rapture" of the world. There were ascetics, ecstatics, and intelligent and creative people, but they were not Cesare Borgia types. They were not heroes of vitality or bastions of strength, nor were they athletes of amorality. In the period of *Zarathustra* and beyond, Nietzsche deleted several idealistic and quasi-religious traits from his image of the *Übermensch*. It was not until the fifth book of *The Gay Science* (written after *Zarathustra*) that the *Übermensch* appeared as a dastardly grand player, a bogeyman of the middle class and amoral bastion of strength. There Nietzsche depicted the "ideal of a spirit who plays naively—that is, unintentionally and from a position of overabundance and power—with everything that has always been called holy, good, untouchable, divine . . . ; the ideal of a human-superhuman well-being and well-wishing that will quite often appear *inhuman*" (3,637; *GS* § 382).

In *On the Genealogy of Morals,* written one and a half years before his breakdown, Nietzsche introduced that notorious "blond beast" who, "with the innocent consciousness of a beast of prey . . . might come away from a revolting succession of murder, arson, rape, torture with a sense of exhilaration and emotional equilibrium, as if it were nothing but a student prank" (5,275; *GM* First Essay § 11). In this context, it is not altogether clear whether these exemplars of the "noble race" (5,275), which Nietzsche located primarily in the Italian Renaissance, truly embodied the desirable type of the prospective *Übermensch*. He picked examples of this sort to indicate the vital forces dormant in man. However, he was not merely advocating that we shed our inhibitions. For Nietzsche, the principle of active creation was always decisive. Great force must be given a form by a strong will. Zarathustra advises his listeners to exercise caution: "You want to soar up to the free heights, your soul thirsts for stars. But your wicked instincts also thirst for freedom" (4,53; *Z* First Part, "On the Tree on the Mountainside"). Even after he had moved away from the image of the idealistic *Übermensch* and Schopenhauer's genius of the denial of life, Nietzsche was still not prepared to exorcise the intellect from the arena of strength.

In Nietzsche's view, the Schopenhauerian "genius" who denies the world because he considers it a moral scandal, and is nonetheless such a powerful nature that he transcends it within himself, suffers from an excess of Christian morality. Nietzsche did subscribe to the Schopenhauerian ideal of self-transcendence, but he wanted no part of Schopenhauer's renunciation of the world. For Nietzsche, self-transcendence was now an aspect of the will to power, namely power over oneself. The *Übermensch* himself furnishes the law of action, which is therefore an individual law beyond traditional morality. Traditional morality serves to keep the ordinary person in check, but can only stand in the way of an *Übermensch*.

Hence the *Übermensch* also becomes a great player who abides only by the rules he has set for himself. He will not, however, keep on playing to the point of exhaustion or boredom. One feature of the sovereignty of an *Übermensch* is the strength to break off a game. Those who decide when to break off the game are the ones who wield the power. The *Übermensch* is this sort of powerful player. Although he may join in the game we call morality for a specified period of time, he does so with loose restrictions. For him there are no categorical imperatives, which strike a weak subject's conscience like lightning, but only rules that serve the art of life. An *Übermensch* is also able powerfully to play out the urges and goals that are normally called "evil." But they cannot be crude; they must be refined. The *Übermensch* should appropriate the entire spectrum of human vitality in a formative way. In his notes for the *Will to Power*, Nietzsche states: "In great men, the specific characteristics of life—injustice, lies, and exploitation—are at their greatest" (12,202; *WP* § 968).

The *Übermensch* should therefore not be burdened by idealism. So much for Nietzsche's setting the record straight on the "idealistic" misconception. And how does it relate to the Darwinian misconception, which Nietzsche opposed in *Ecce Homo*? The statements that introduce the *Übermensch* in *Zarathustra* are inconceivable without Darwin: "You have made your way from worm to man, and much in you is still worm" (4,14; *Z* First Part, Prologue § 3). Nietzsche retained two basic Darwinian ideas: the theory of development in the specific arena of the theory of evolution, and the idea of the struggle for existence as a driving force in evolutionary development. Of course, he interpreted the struggle for existence not as a fight to survive but as a fight to overpower. This shift of focus continued in his philosophy of the "will to power."

Why did Nietzsche resist the Darwinian misconception if his affinity to Darwin was so obvious? He claimed that "Darwin forgot the spirit (that is English!)" (6,121; *TI* "Skirmishes of an Untimely Man" § 14). He accused Darwin of having applied the logic of development in the animal kingdom, which is unreflective, to man. In man, however, all developmental processes are refracted through the medium of consciousness, which means that the higher development of man cannot be conceived of according to the model of the insensible development of nature, but must be regarded instead as a product of free will and creativity. It is therefore impossible to rely on any natural process in regard to the *Übermensch* of the future; human intervention is called for. But what kind?

Nietzsche had at any rate absorbed enough biologism from the theory of evolution and genetics to consider the idea of breeding to regulate reproduction. His recommendation—"Do not *re*produce yourself, but rather produce *upward*!" (4,90; *Z* First Part, "On Child and Marriage")—was cited earlier. What this "upward" means for biology remains vague, but Zarathustra leaves no doubt that the "far too many" should not be allowed to reproduce indiscriminately. "Far too many live, and far too long they hang on their branches. If only a storm would come to shake all of this rot and worm-eaten decay from the tree!" (4,94; *Z* First Part, "On Free Death"). Rampant reproduction must be stopped. Chance and the power of the great masses must not continue to have the upper hand: "We are still fighting step by step with the giant that is accident, and so far only nonsense, senselessness, has governed over the whole of humanity" (4,100; *Z* First Part, "On the Gift-Giving Virtue" § 2). To prevent the "madness" (4,100) of past generations from erupting in current and future generations and landing all of history in an awful state of "degeneration" (4,98; *Z* First Part, "On the Gift-Giving Virtue" § 1), specific measures must be undertaken. Which ones?

As long as Zarathustra was singing arias full of pathos, Nietzsche had no need to turn specific: "Pay careful attention, my brothers, to every hour in which your spirit wants to speak in parables: that is the origin of your virtue" (4,99; *Z* First Part, "On the Gift-Giving Virtue" § 1). The virtue of parables affords Zarathustra the luxury of speaking in veiled hints: "All names of good and evil are parables: they do not declare, they only beckon" (4,98; *Z* First Part, "On the Gift-Giving Virtue" § 1). Dropping only vague hints subject to a variety of interpretations allows one to dodge responsibility. One merely has to declare that one has been misunderstood. Zarathustra's speeches are carefully orchestrated, however, to ensure that the prophet encounters no opposition, demands, or pressure to be precise. He speaks into an echoless space. No one can pin Zarathustra down to any particular meaning; he is far too elusive. He says in reference to the "far too many: If only preachers of quick death would come" (4,94; *Z* First Part, "On Free Death"). This declaration could be seen as an incitement to kill the weak and infirm before they could reproduce. Nevertheless, Zarathustra does not actually say this. Nietzsche did sometimes harbor thoughts of this kind in fits of fury and rage about what he considered a stifling air of banality. In early 1884, he wrote in his notebook that in the future it would be crucial "to gain that immense energy of greatness in order to shape the man of the future by means of breeding and also by destroying millions of failures, and not perish from the suffering that one creates; nothing of this sort has ever existed!" (11,98; *WP* § 964).

In his final writings, Nietzsche would shed his inhibitions, break out of the parable form, and draw conclusions on an open stage that did not bode well for the concept of the *Übermensch*. "Mankind sacrificed en masse so that one single *stronger* species of man might thrive—that *would* be progress" (5,315; *GM* Second Essay § 12), he wrote in *On the Genealogy of Morals,* and in *Ecce Homo* we find some notorious pronouncements on the tasks of the future "party of life." He wrote that mankind is entering into a "tragic era." Why "tragic"? The affirmation of life will have to arm itself with an awful naysaying of everything that diminishes and domesticates life. "Let us glance ahead to one century in the future and suppose that my assassination of two millennia of perversion and human disgrace were to succeed. The new party of life, which takes charge of the greatest of all tasks, raising up humanity, including the relentless destruction of all that is degenerate and parasitical, will again make possible the *excess of life* on earth from which the Dionysian state must reawaken" (6,313; *EH* "Birth of Tragedy" § 4).

Creating this "excess of life" can succeed only if the "far too many" can be prevented from reproducing or even be eliminated. For Nietzsche, these truly murderous thoughts were an outgrowth of the "Dionysian state." Why did he bring the Dionysian into the context of his visions of large-scale human annihilation? His response was as follows: if we experience the Dionysian tragic sensibility profoundly enough, we will find, as far back as Greek tragedy, "the eternal pleasure of evolving *to be oneself,* the pleasure that even embraces pleasure in destruction" (6,312; *EH* "Birth of Tragedy" § 3).

Nietzsche gave a voice and shape to this pleasure in destruction with his Zarathustra. At times, the process made him queasy. After completing the second book of *Zarathustra* in late August 1883, he wrote a letter to Peter Gast in which he spoke of the "most awful antagonism I carry around with me in my heart against the whole Zarathustra configuration" (*B* 6,443). And after he finished the fourth book of *Zarathustra,* he wrote to his friend Overbeck: "My life now revolves around the wish that all things proceed in a manner *different* from the way I comprehend them, and that someone will render my 'truths' implausible" (*B* 7,63; July 2, 1885).

The fantasies of annihilation that are associated with his image of the *Übermensch* have two bases: the internal logic of his thoughts and a constellation of existential issues.

The internal logic of his thoughts built on a notion Nietzsche had already developed in *The Birth of Tragedy,* which held that culture is justified by great works and great individuals. If mankind does not exist "for its own sake, if, rather, the goal lies in its peaks, in the great 'individuals,' the saints and the artists (7,354), it is also permissible to use mankind as material for the production of genius, masterpieces, or even the *Übermensch.* And if the masses are more of a hindrance, space has to be created—by getting rid of the "degenerates," if necessary. Even in his fantasies of annihilation, however, Nietzsche was still a highly sensitive soul and hence more amenable to the option that the "misfits" could offer to "sacrifice" themselves willingly (11,98).

As for the existential constellation, all of Nietzsche's past humiliations fed into his destructive fantasies. Nietzsche had wanted to use the power of thought to create a "second nature" that would be greater, freer, and more sovereign than his first nature, which he described in these terms: "I am a plant, born near the churchyard." He considered his power of thought a tool to craft his past, a posteriori, "from which we would prefer to be descended as opposed to the past from which we did descend" (1,270; HL § 3). Nietzsche, who had stretched upward so mightily to reach his "second nature," clearly had to exert himself increasingly to prevent any return to his "first nature. " He had sought refuge in self-discovery and self-invention and now felt open to attack from all sides. He was always friendly, but vulnerable to any indications of chumminess on the part of others. He was offended when people saw him as one of them. Hatred festered in him toward everything that had dragged him down: the milieu of Naumburg, his family, his sister, his mother, ultimately his friends as well—and, of course, Wagner. All of them failed to understand him, but felt they had a right to his friend-liness and compassion. No one treated him in a matter befitting his sta-tion in life. During his Zarathustra period, he was exquisitely sensitive to remarks he considered insulting. He wrote to Ida Overbeck on August 14, 1883: "I feel as though I am condemned to silence or tactful hypocrisy in my dealings with everybody" (*B* 6,424).

He sensed the "affect of distance" (*B* 6,418) that separates "higher man" from the others, but his own exterior failed to convey his special inner qualities. People did not see him as he saw himself. He was "con-vinced that no living person could do something in the way this Zarathustra is" (*B* 6,386; late June 1883). Nietzsche could endure this incognito if need be. People could ignore him, but they could not drag him down; he considered the very notion unbearable. Every time he completed some writing that struck him as inspired, he became acutely aware of the oppressive atmosphere surrounding him. Shortly after fin-ishing the first book of *Zarathustra,* he wrote to Peter Gast: "The past year has given me so many indications that people (including my 'friends' and relatives) are ridiculing me, my *actual* life and activities" (*B* 6,360; April 17, 1883).

In his view, all of these insults, affronts, and disdain stemmed from the tedious world of mediocrity. Nietzsche, the critic of ressentiment, was himself sometimes full of vengeance toward the common man of ressentiment, wishing to make room for his *Übermensch* in *Zarathustra* by attacking the "far too many." He felt surrounded by those "last people" who have their "little pleasures" for the day and the night and who "blinkingly" contrive the joy of work. To such people, the lofty and sublime are just plain boring: "What is love? What is creation? What is longing? What is a star? Thus asks the last man and blinks" (4,19; *Z* First Part, Prologue § 5). This is a burden that prevents man from soaring upward. Nietzsche responded with fantasies of annihilation. He, the *Übermensch*, with whom they will all come face to face. Woe unto them . . .

Nietzsche's image of the *Übermensch* betrays his own ambivalence while unfolding an entire existential drama. The *Übermensch* represents a higher biological type and could be the product of deliberate breeding. However, he can also function as an ideal for anyone who wishes to gain power over himself and cultivate his "virtues," anyone who is creative and knows the whole spectrum of the human capacity for thought, fantasy, and imagination. Nietzsche's *Übermensch* is the consummate realization of human potential and, in this sense, is also a response to the "death of God."

Let us recall the famous scene in *The Gay Science* in which the "madman" runs about in the bright morning hours yelling "I am seeking God! I am seeking God! . . . We killed him! . . . Is the magnitude of this deed not too great for us? Must we not ourselves become gods just to seem worthy of it?" (3,481; *GS* § 125). The murderer of God must himself become God—that is, an *Übermensch*—otherwise he will sink into banality, as Nietzsche attempted to illustrate in this scene. The issue is whether man can retain the ingenuity he employed in inventing an entire heaven of gods, or whether he will be left empty after attacking them. If God is dead because people have realized that they invented him, it is crucial that their powers to posit divinity remain intact. The *Übermensch* embodies the sanctification of this world as a response to the "death of God." The *Übermensch* is free of religion. He has not lost it, but reclaimed it for himself. The typical nihilist, by contrast, the "last man," has merely forfeited religion and retained life in all its profane wretchedness. Nietzsche aspired to salvage sanctifying powers for the here and now from the nihilistic tendency of vulgarization by means of his *Übermensch*.

Nietzsche invoked this idea with powerful imagery, and without sounding preachy, in *The Gay Science:* "There is a lake that forwent flowing off one day and formed a dam where it had been flowing off before: since then, this lake has been rising higher and higher. Perhaps this very privation will also grant us the strength to endure privation ourselves; perhaps from that point on, man will continue to rise up by not *flowing out* into a god" (3,528; *GS* § 285). The *Übermensch* is the Promethean man who has discovered his theogonic talents. The God outside of him is dead, but the God who is known to live through man and in him is alive. God is a name for the creative power of man. This creative power enables man to partake of the vast dimensions of existence. The first book of *Zarathustra* closes with these words: "All the gods are dead; now we want the *Übermensch* to live" (4,102; *Z* First Part, "On the Gift-Giving Virtue" § 3). The section called "On the Blissful Islands," in the second book of *Zarathustra*, expands this idea: "Once you said God when you looked out onto distant seas; now, however, I have taught you to say: *Übermensch*. God is a conjecture, but I do not want your conjectures to reach beyond your creative will. Could you *create* a god? Then do not talk to me about any gods. But you could certainly create the *Übermensch*" (4,109). At the very instant that man discovers and affirms his theogonic power and in the process learns to revere himself, he stops disparaging his own achievements. When this stage is reached, *Zarathustra* exclaims: "Only now is the mountain of man's future in labor" (4,357; *Z* Fourth Part, "On the Higher Man" § 2). The *Übermensch* who develops after the death of God is the person who no longer requires a detour via God to find faith in himself.

We have yet to reach, however, the aspect of the *Übermensch* that was of critical importance to Nietzsche. We approach it by recalling that it was actually the doctrine of the eternal recurrence of the same that Nietzsche wanted to have his Zarathustra preach. Not until the third book of *Zarathustra* does he almost hesitantly broach this theme, in the section called "On the Vision and the Riddle." The actual significance of the *Übermensch* becomes clear at this point: the *Übermensch* is the person who is capable of comprehending and enduring the vastness of this doctrine. He is not undone by the doctrine of eternal recurrence and can, to use Nietzsche's term, "incorporate" it. This is shown to gruesome effect in the scene in which a black serpent is hanging out of the mouth of a young shepherd who is writhing in agony, his face horribly contorted. Zarathustra commands him to transcend his fear and loathing and to bite off the head of the serpent that has crept into his mouth. The shepherd does so, and thus commences his development into an *Übermensch:* "No longer shepherd, no longer man—he was transformed and radiant, and he was laughing" (4,202; *Z* Third Part, "On the Vision and the Riddle" § 2).

The serpent is the symbol of revolving time. Biting off its head signifies the conquest of fear. The *Übermensch* is strong enough to recognize that there is no flight from time and no beyond. We do not escape from the sphere of being, and there will be no liberation by nonbeing, because we will, according to the doctrine of recurrence, awaken to a new consciousness. The period of time that has elapsed "between" our absences is nonexistent, since this time exists only for consciousness.

But even in *Zarathustra* Nietzsche was dogged by the problem that the doctrine of recurrence comes across as peculiarly banal and trivial if it is expressed directly as an idea. During the summer of 1882, with Salomé in Tautenburg, he noted down: "The more abstract the truth that one wishes to teach, the more one must seduce the senses into it" (10,23). With the gothic setting of the scene at the gateway, the dwarf, the shepherd, and the serpent, Nietzsche offered rich illustrations for his doctrine. He also demonstrated what would happen if the doctrine were to be trivialized and misperceived. The dwarf heaps "scornful" commentary on Zarathustra's sermon, as though he were listening to old truisms: "Everything that is straight lies. . . . All truth is crooked; time itself is a circle. Zarathustra responds somewhat helplessly: "You spirit of gravity! . . . do not make it easy on yourself!" (4,200; *Z* Third Part, "On the Vision and the Riddle" § 2). Zarathustra is baffled and disappointed by his obvious inability to communicate the colossal dimensions of his doctrine. He begins to speak in more muted tones "because I was afraid of my own thoughts and ulterior motives" (4,200f.; *Z* Third Part, "On the Vision and the Riddle" § 2). This is the same whispered tone Nietzsche had adopted when describing his doctrine of eternal recurrence to Salomé. Her reaction mirrored that of other friends to whom he outlined this doctrine: she was moved by his method of presentation, but disappointed by the message itself. He sensed this reaction during their summer in Tautenburg. It prompted him to record this underlined entry in his notes for the doctrine of the eternal recurrence: "Oh, I am so sick of *tragic gestures and words!*" (10,33). This phase did not last long, however. The four books of *Zarathustra* he wrote between 1883 and 1885 are laden with the very "tragic gestures and words" he was so "sick of" in the summer of 1882.

When Nietzsche had completed the third book, he wrote to Peter Gast on February 1, 1884: "My *Zarathustra* was finished fourteen days ago, altogether finished" (*B* 6,473). He considered the work complete. Recurrence had been proclaimed, the song of the "Seven Seals," with its refrain "Because I love you, O eternity!" (4,287f.; *Z* Third Part), had been sung, and he could have turned to other matters. But in the winter of 1884–85, Nietzsche decided to publish a fourth volume of *Zarathustra*. He appears to have modeled it on Goethe's *Faust, Part II*. Just as Faust awakens to a second life after restorative sleep, we reencounter Zarathustra at the commencement of the fourth book as a very cheerful old man.

Nietzsche's hints to his friends while writing this fourth volume indicate that he intended to tone down its tragic and lofty pathos. He described the book in terms of "Dionysian dances, books for fools," and "devils' tools" (*B* 6,487; March 22, 1884). He later claimed to have written this last part in the "mood of a clown." The fourth book offers a virtual masked parade of types of spirits, featuring as it does the "soothsayer," the "conscientious man of the spirit," the "magician," and the "voluntary beggar." These masks appear to have been inspired by specific models: Jacob Burckhardt, Richard Wagner, Franz Overbeck, Otto von Bismarck, and others. These figures come into Zarathustra's cave, where he is holding court. Since they convert to the doctrine of eternal recurrence, they are well on their way to becoming *Übermenschen*. Although they still suffer from irresolution and faintheartedness, and do not succeed, they do earn the honorary title "higher men." Nietzsche was clearly attempting to strike a frivolous, light, and at times operetta-like tone for the book as a whole, but he did not manage to do so. The exalted tone of the first three volumes prevailed here as well.

Still, this fourth book features passages of a self-critical clarity that approaches the threshold of pain. Nietzsche detected a sham existence lurking behind his pathos: "I have figured out your secret: you became everyone's enchanter, but you have no lies or wiles left to use against yourself—you are disenchanted to yourself!" (4,318; *Z* Fourth Part, "Magician" § 2).

Setting the Stage
for *The Will to Power*

ZARATHUSTRA IS NOT just preaching to others; he must also
convince himself. Nietzsche stated unequivocally in his notebooks that
a teacher can "incorporate" his own doctrine only by teaching it.
Zarathustra's conversation with the dwarf, however, conveys the impression that Zarathustra does not succeed in clarifying his doctrine of eternal recurrence. His ideas remain abstract, inciting the dwarf's "scornful"
rejoinders.

Did Nietzsche write a fourth *Zarathustra* book in early 1885 because
he found that he had not really expressed the crux of the matter in the
earlier sections, even though he was convinced after writing the third book
that his work on *Zarathustra* was complete? After the fourth book, he did
not feel that he could put Zarathustra behind him. He may have disen-
gaged himself from the character, but not from the doctrines for which
Zarathustra served as the "mouthpiece." Nietzsche continued to work on

these ideas, particularly the association of his three doctrines of eternal recurrence, the *Übermensch,* and the will to power, painfully aware that he had yet to locate and articulate everything that needed to be considered.

During the summer of 1881, the period of his inspiration at the Surlej boulder, Nietzsche noted down the following organizational principle he would use to frame his doctrine of the recurrence of the same: "The doctrine of the repetition of everything prior will be presented only at the end, after the general idea has taken root to create something that can flourish a hundred times more powerfully under the sunshine of this doctrine!" (9,505). His original organizational plan for *Zarathustra* was to outline the contours of an art of living and highlight everything that makes life worth living and loving. His Zarathustra wishes to be like the sun, radiating light and pleasure. He comes across as a benevolent man. A doctrine of joie de vivre might sound effortless in the abstract, but it is difficult, if not impossible, to achieve in reality. It would entail restoring childlike spontaneity or, to put it in philosophical terms, mediated immediacy. Zarathustra uses graphic imagery to convey this idea in the speech "On the Three Metamorphoses" (4,29; *Z* First Part). The initial stage of this process takes the form of a "camel," burdened with a plethora of "Thou shalts." The camel turns into a "lion," who fights the whole world of "Thou shalts" once he has discovered his "I want," but, because he fights, he is bound to the "Thou shalt" in a negative sense. His ability to exist is consumed in an urgent need to rebel. There is too much spite and tension in this "I want," and the true leisure of creative volition is still lacking. A sense of self and the fullness of life have yet to be achieved. These attributes are possible only when one becomes a child again and regains one's initial childlike spontaneity toward life on a new level: "The child is innocence and forgetting, a new beginning, a game, a wheel that moves on its own, a first movement, a holy pronouncement of 'yes' " (4,31; *Z* First Part, "On the Three Metamorphoses").

The themes of the "game of creation" (4,31; *Z* First Part, "On the Three Metamorphoses") and the "holy pronouncement of 'yes' " recur quite frequently. Zarathustra tries to designate concrete aspects of restored health and spontaneity as principles to live by. One should heed the "great reason" (4,39; *Z* First Part, "On the Despisers of the Body") of one's body and eat properly, reduce contact with people to a wholesome level, and limit communication of feelings, experiences, and thoughts so as to avoid becoming entangled in misunderstandings. Misunderstandings arise when our own thoughts are distorted and deformed by idle chatter with others and come back in some unrecognizable form to distract us from ourselves. Hence one should not yield to the market of opinions, or "bury one's head in the sand of heavenly things" (4,37; *Z* First Part, "On the Afterworldly"), which would also signify alienation from the core of life. That core is found in love, Zarathustra explains in paradoxical terms: "We love life not because we are used to life but because we are used to loving" (4,49; *Z* First Part, "On Reading and Writing"). It is not life that justifies love; on the contrary, love is the creative force that keeps life alive. Once we have familiarized ourselves with love, we take the rest of life into the bargain. Only the will to love can enable man to discover the potentially lovable sides of life; otherwise man is likely to focus on its repulsive, ugly, and torturous aspects. We ought to use our will to love to enchant the world around us as well as ourselves. We need to fall in love with love.

Inversion and self-referentiality are characteristic for both Nietzsche and Zarathustra. Our attention is shifted from the object of an intention to the intentional act. The "will to . . ." is brought into focus. Knowledge works in this same way. It is not knowing the "object" that justifies delight in knowledge, but rather the will to knowledge that warrants our delight. The will to knowledge can be a pleasure that bears and endures even the unbearable nature of what is known. Nietzsche had already stated in *Daybreak* that we always seem to forget "that knowledge of even the ugliest reality is beautiful" (3,320; *D* § 550). Why? Because knowledge itself is something beautiful. Consequently, the "happiness of the man of knowledge" may serve to augment the "beauty of the world" (3,320). Still, we should not forget where this beauty originates.

Its source is pleasure in knowledge and not the attributes of what is known. Since, however, it is so easy to confuse matters in the excitement and pleasure of knowledge, it is difficult to maintain one's "honesty" and not wind up a "eulogist of things" (3,321; *D* § 550). These circumstances apply equally to love. Only if one maintains a bond with the living power of love does life assume a lovable form. Where does the will to love find sustenance? Solely in itself, not in the world. The will to love is simply one particular form of the will to power. Is there any power greater than the magical transformation that renders something lovable?

The *"Übermensch,"* "eternal recurrence," and the "will to power" form a triad of doctrines in *Zarathustra*. The "will to power" is first mentioned in Zarathustra's speech on self-transcendence. The ideas developed in this speech are introduced by three songs immediately preceding it: "The Night Song," "The Dancing Song," and "The Tomb Song." These songs explore the relationship between life and love, and point up the dire aspects of self-referentiality in loving. "The Night Song" includes a graphic illustration: "But I live in my own light; I drink the flames back into me as they break out of me" (4,136; *Z* Second Part). In "The Dancing Song," Zarathustra comes across a bevy of dancing girls. He wants to dance with them, even though the "spirit of gravity" (4,200; *Z* Third Part, "On the Vision and the Riddle" § 2) holds him back, but the "little god" stirs within him as well. This "little god" is a satyr, a Pan who wants to move and is on the hunt for "butterflies." Zarathustra does want to dance, but in his self-referentiality he muses about dancing instead of simply dancing. To make matters worse, he speaks to a dancer and thereby prevents her from dancing. At the same time, however, he transforms her as a symbol of dancing life. Her raillery is full of contempt: "Even if you men call me 'the profound one' or 'the fateful one,' 'the eternal one,' 'the mysterious one'—you men still always bestow your own virtues on us—O you virtuous men!" (4,140; *Z* Second Part, "Dancing Song").

"Life" makes Zarathustra aware that projections render it profound and mysterious. Those who stand apart from life and do not participate in the dancing are the ones who register its inherent profundity. Keeping a distance preserves the mystery. Anyone who wants to dance should not meditate on it. Life is to be lived, not to be deliberated. But Zarathustra stays remote from the circle of dancers and is alone in his "wisdom." He considers wisdom an advocate of life; it "reminds me of life so very much" (4,140; *Z* Second Part, "Dancing Song"), but wisdom is not the same thing as life. And what is worse, his "wisdom" was meant to lure him into life, yet it drove the dancing girls away from him, since they want to dance and not to be analyzed. Zarathustra, left alone with his wisdom, lapses back into the "unfathomable" realm of his own design. Only in dance do the questions that preoccupy him become superfluous. As soon as the dance floor clears, they come back to haunt him once again: "What! You are still alive, Zarathustra? What for? How so? Where to? Where? How? Is it not folly to stay alive?" (4,141; *Z* Second Part, "Dancing Song"). Wisdom, which seeks to apprehend life, also insists on distance. Is this still "Dionysian wisdom" if it drives away pleasure? In any case, when he is with the dancing girls, Zarathustra does not achieve his desire of becoming Dionysus. He has scarcely achieved anything: "one looks through veils, one snatches through nets" (4,141).

"The Tomb Song" is presented just after "The Dancing Song." Zarathustra goes to the grave of the unfulfilled dreams and hopes of his youth. He speaks to them as though they were ghosts who have betrayed him, and reproaches them bitterly. They struck up a dance and then spoiled the music for him. Why? Had the past made him so weighty? Did his unlived life impede him or confine him to a past that did not seem to pass? Zarathustra uses the image of a "monstrous owl" (4,144; *Z* Second Part, "Tomb Song")—a perverted figure of the philosopher's bird, the owl of Minerva—to describe what is holding him back. Zarathustra quarrels with his wisdom, which ruined the dance for him. "Only in dance do I know how to speak in parables of the loftiest things—and now my highest parable stayed unspoken in my limbs!" (4,144). Zarathustra is exhausted and hurt, but not for long. He soon recovers from his injuries and, as he proudly explains, arises once again from the tomb of his life. "Something invaluable, unburiable is in me, something to explode rocks, namely *my will*" (4,145; *Z* Second Part, "Tomb Song").

The path from the power of life leads through the dance of life and the obstacles posed by knowledge, past injury and fatal lethargy to the philosophy of the will to power, which is finally thematized in the presentation "On Self-Transcendence," the section immediately following "The Tomb Song." In this section, Zarathustra declares: "Wherever I found living beings, I found will to power" (4,147; *Z* Second Part, "On Self-Transcendence"). The tone changes here. Lyricisms of the night, dancing, and tomb songs are replaced by harsh strokes of fate. These are fragments of a philosophical doctrine that had been suggested in earlier writings, in which Nietzsche had probed the driving forces of life and knowledge, but he did not begin to regard them as a task for systematic elaboration until he wrote *Zarathustra*.

The doctrine of the "will to power," as delineated in *Zarathustra*, consists of the following principles. Its crux is the principle of self-transcendence. The will to power is first and foremost the will to power over oneself. As the progression from night song to dancing song to tomb song demonstrates, there is a rebirth from the grave of suffocating depression, induced by the memory of a creative power that is inherent in us but manages to slip away and must therefore be seized deliberately and boldly. There is obviously no endeavor that could or should be activated without the "will to . . ." Even creativity requires the will to creativity. If there is such a thing as a Münchhausen effect, this is it: a life that wills itself can yank itself out of its muck and mire. Zarathustra asks what the will to power is, and supplies this answer: "You still want to create the world before which you can kneel: this is your final hope and intoxication" (4,146; *Z* Second Part, "On Self-Transcendence").

Self-transcendence as the creation of an entire imaginary world of ideas, images, and scenes, which is what we find in the Zarathustra project, goes beyond self-preservation and becomes self-enhancement, the second aspect of the will to power. We underestimate life if we take note only of its instinct for self-preservation. The self is an expansive force. A proclivity for enhancement and accumulation is peculiar to man. Mere preservation leads to demise; only enhancement ensures preservation. Nietzsche's critique of self-preservation is, of course, somewhat facile. Zarathustra explains that the "will to existence," as described by the theoreticians of self-preservation such as Darwin, does not exist. "What does not exist cannot will; but what *is* in existence, how could that still want existence!" (4,149; *Z* Second Part, "On Self-Transcendence").

One could argue that, if life is reflected in the medium of consciousness, explicit self-affirmation is both feasible and essential. It is therefore altogether possible to embrace or reject the fact that we find ourselves in existence. We can opt to flee from existence by our own hand, but we can also be gripped by the will to existence and remain. We already exist, but we require the will to existence in order to stay in existence. Nietzsche would concede this point, but retort that there is more to explicit self-affirmation than the will to existence. Anyone who does not yield to self-destructive powers, but instead chooses to resist them, anyone who counters "no" with a categorical "yes" has the will to power, the spirit of taking the offensive. A person of this sort wants not merely to endure but to triumph over the powers of denial. Nietzsche's notebooks illustrate this idea with examples from the world of physics and mechanics. A quantum of force is at work when one object does not yield to another. If the quantum of force is smaller, the object yields; if it is greater, it overpowers other objects. Staying within a form and its boundaries is a consequence of balanced proportions of force.

During the period in which Nietzsche wrote *Zarathustra,* he began to use the "will to power" not only as a psychological formula for self-transcendence and self-enhancement but also as a universal key to interpret all life processes, as indicated in the aforementioned statement "Wherever I found living beings, I found will to power" (4,147; *Z* Second Part, "On Self-Transcendence"). The will to power inheres not only in the inorganic and organic world but also in the process of knowledge itself. Knowledge is an expression of the will to power. "You want to bring all being to the point of being thinkable: because you doubt, with good reason for your doubts, whether it is already thinkable" (4,146; *Z* Second Part, "On Self-Transcendence"). Hence there is a hermeneutical circle of the knowledge of power: the will to power in knowledge discovers the will to power in the world as we know it.

Nietzsche had attempted an ontological interpretation of the world from the perspective of the "will to power" in his earlier writings. In 1885 and 1886, after completing *Zarathustra,* he made explicit reference to these antecedents by composing new prefaces for his earlier works. The external rationale for these prefaces was his desire to switch publishers. His current publisher, Ernst Schmeitzner, was facing bankruptcy, and Nietzsche had long since wanted to get out of what he called Schmeitzner's "anti-Semitic dump" (*B* 7,117; Dec. 1885) because it printed pamphlets from the Bayreuth group. He found a new publisher in his former publisher E. W. Fritzsch, who had brought out his *Birth of Tragedy* and the first two *Untimely Meditations.*

Fritzsch, who had resolved his economic difficulties, now wanted to have the "complete" Nietzsche in his publishing program. In the course of his negotiations to switch publishers, Nietzsche learned that more than two-thirds of his books were lying unsold in Schmeitzner's warehouse. He became aware that although he had attained a certain status in Germany—some still considered him a Wagnerian, and others a dangerous, morally disreputable fellow—he intrigued the public as an object of gossip, but was barely read. Only about five hundred copies of his works all told had been sold to date. As Nietzsche was now just learning, Schmeitzner had barely continued supplying bookstores with his publications over the course of the last decade. His books were sold only at the urgent and sustained demands of customers. Aside from review copies and complimentary copies, *Human, All Too Human* had not been shipped out for sale at all. Nietzsche had been writing books for fifteen years and now had to acknowledge that they had no market and no readership. He anticipated enjoying a better beginning with his new (and old) publisher. For this reason, he hoped that his earlier books, supplemented by new prefaces, would finally find their way to an audience. Nietzsche considered the five new prefaces to the books from *The Birth of Tragedy* through *The Gay Science,* which had been expanded with a fifth book, "perhaps the best prose I have ever written" (*B* 7,282; Nov. 14, 1886). He also felt that they provided "a sort of developmental history" (*B* 8,151; Sept. 14, 1887) and would allow him to make a "clean break" with his "previous existence" (*B* 8,213; Dec. 20, 1887).

In this year full of prefaces and clean breaks, Nietzsche decided to undertake a major work with the title "The Will to Power / Attempt / at a new Interpretation / of Everything That Happens." From August 1885, when he coined this title, until his final autumn in Turin in 1888, he would develop classifications, indexes, and tentative titles. He scribbled down countless notations on this theme. Later his sister and Peter Gast took his outline of March 17, 1887, as a basis for their compilation of materials from the immense *Nachlass* and call it *The Will to Power.* Nietzsche had been developing the will to a major work, the will to *The Will to Power,* since 1885–86, and he tried to organize the events of his life around this project. In early September 1886, he wrote to his sister and brother-in-law in Paraguay: "I have announced that for the next four years I will be preparing a major four-volume work. The title alone can scare you off: The Will to Power: Attempt at a Revaluation of All Values. I have *everything* required for this project: fine health, solitude, a good frame of mind, and perhaps a wife" (*B* 7,241; Sept. 2, 1886).

Nietzsche, whose books of the preceding few years had been collections of aphorisms and compilations of brief essays on sweeping topics, felt a "compulsion," which pressed down on him "with the force of a hundredweight, to build up a coherent structure of thought over the next few years" (*B* 8,49; March 24, 1887). In moments of depression, and when he felt especially lonely, the thought of this magnum opus sustained him. On November 12, 1887, he wrote to Franz Overbeck that he was facing "a task that does not allow me to think of myself very much. . . . This task has made me ill, and will make me healthy once again—not only healthy, but also more humanitarian and everything that entails" (*B* 8,196).

Nietzsche held fast to his plan for a magnum opus until the summer of 1888. "The Revaluation of All Values," which was his original subtitle, evolved into the book's main title. However, the basic idea of the plan remained unchanged. The will to power as a basic principle of life was to lay the groundwork for a revision of all moral ideas. All values would be revalued. In his rough drafts composed in the last year before his mental collapse, the central theme of revaluation grew in significance. In a great rush, as though foreseeing his impending breakdown, he hastened to his work and threw himself into the painstaking ontological, scientific, and cosmological interpretations he had plotted out. Revaluation would be the outcome of a universal interpretation, with the will to power as a guide. However, Nietzsche ultimately settled for this outcome without systematic argumentation. He was facing time pressure. In the fall of 1888, he completed the manuscript of *The Antichrist,* which was initially intended as the first book of the "Revaluation," but wound up becoming the entirety of that text.

Thus, the title "The Will to Power" was soon abandoned, followed by the second main title, "The Revaluation of all Values." Only *The Antichrist* remained. "My revaluation of all values, which has 'The Antichrist' as its main title, is finished," Nietzsche wrote to Paul Deussen on November 26, 1888 (*B* 8,492). However, the original project of "The Will to Power" was not altogether exhausted in *The Antichrist.* In fact, the preliminary sketches for "The Will to Power" found their way, directly or indirectly, into several other works. Although Nietzsche did not even come close to using all of the material from the preliminary work in these books, he did express what he considered the most significant ideas in *Beyond Good and Evil,* the fifth book of *The Gay Science* (1886), the new prefaces, *On the Genealogy of Morals, Twilight of the Idols,* and *The*

Antichrist. It is therefore reasonable to infer that shortly before his break-down, he recognized that he was actually finished with his project "The Will to Power." He had said everything of importance.

When Nietzsche wrote in 1883: "Wherever I found living beings, I found will to power" (4,147; *Z* Second Part, "On Self-Transcendence"), he was recapitulating an entire past history that had set him on the path of this will to power. If we track this past history, we find that it commenced with the power of art and artists. When Nietzsche was analyzing the interaction of the Dionysian and Apollonian forces in Greek culture, he was referring to precisely these artistic life forces. What is the power of art? Art creates a magic circle of images, visions, tones, and ideas that hold us spellbound and transform anyone who enters the circle. The power of art is a life force to the extent that it provides insight into the dark tragic web of life, but creates a clearing of livability. Since human life is challenged by consciousness and carries within it the potential for creating hostility with itself, artistic power is also a counterforce that protects life from any possible self-destruction.

In addition, the power of art involves opening the door to representations, thereby sublimating the cruel battle of forces into a contest and a game. Nietzsche had broached the idea of the basic agonistic structure of life as early as *The Birth of Tragedy,* and he developed it in his essay "Homer's Contest." He sought to make sense of the basic model of archaic Greek culture, hoping to form an ontological principle in the process. The study of Darwin and his disciples acquainted him with the concept of the "struggle for existence." But these doctrines were not sufficiently dynamic for him. For Nietzsche, as we have seen, it was a question not of defensive self-preservation but of offensive self-enhancement. Life is a process of expansion. Safeguarding one's existence might be of import to the anxious petty bourgeois, but life as a whole cannot be envisioned as a world of philistines. Zarathustra provides a pithy formulation of life's proclivity for self-enhancement: "Only where there is life is there also will, but not will to life . . . rather will to power" (4,149; *Z* Second Part, "On Self-Transcendence"). What is the "sense" of all of this fuss about power? Nietzsche ranked the question of sense with notorious attempts to "humanize" nature, and he rejected it, but not for long, because he needed to apply his theory of the will to power to these projections of meaning for the sake of consistency. Questions of meaning and projections of meaning are ultimately also forms of expressing the will to power. Under the rubric of "sense," a transformation of an otherwise senseless reality takes place in the human sphere. "You want to make all being thinkable. . . . It should yield and bend for you!" (4,146; *Z* Second Part, "On Self-Transcendence"). By imparting sense to the course of life, man overpowers it and brings it into a form that accords with himself. The world becomes a "reflection" to the spirit. Man recognizes himself in it, but also recognizes the Other confronting him. Cognition is a power play of creative forces, a process that culminates in successful, powerful, and vital forms and ideas. Whatever holds its own in this way is called truth. Truth is a power that renders itself true by prevailing. This truth applies not only to knowledge in the narrower, more scholarly sense but to the creation of entire mental constructs that are held to be valid.

The attention of the young Nietzsche had already begun to focus on the power plays that establish their validity. The construct that prevailed in agonistic intellectual contests proved its mettle not only in victory but by justifying life as a whole as the culmination of human capability. This was Nietzsche's early idea that life is justified by means of the birth of a genius. He illustrated this idea by citing the examples of Sophocles, Wagner, and Schopenhauer. These intellectual heroes vindicate the life of an entire culture. Their works create a magic circle within which human potential is realized and transformed. The "peak of rapture" is the point of culture, and it is the challenge of life forces that conveys man to this peak. "Mankind," Nietzsche wrote in a draft to a preface for *The Birth of Tragedy,* does not exist for its own sake, "but rather the goal lies in its peaks, in the great 'individuals,' the saints and the artists" (7,354). The young Nietzsche's assertion in this early text that "there is no higher cultural proclivity than the preparation and production of genius" (7,355) was a prelude to the idea of the will to power. Genius is the highest embodiment of power on the foundation of the cultural power struggle.

On this foundation—be it human, all-too-human, or superhuman—Nietzsche had a certain degree of success in portraying the drama of the will to power. Here the power struggles became overt, not only in culture in the narrow sense, but in the organism of society as a whole. Power was right at home in society.

In his *Human, All Too Human,* Nietzsche had developed a morphological theory of social forces. He contended that while cold societies represent an equilibrium of forces, hot societies are set in motion as a result of a shift in the equilibrium and struggle to establish a new balance. He further asserted that an "equilibrium" of forces "is the basis of justice" (2,556; *HH* II WS § 22). The sense of justice originates not in a morality high above the embattled parties but in a state of equilibrium. If the forces that make up this equilibrium shift, morality shifts in response. A ruler who has been considered just suddenly appears to be a criminal and vice versa. In revolutions, which reflect a dramatic shift of equilibriums, the truth of morality becomes blatant. It is a morality of classes and parties. On this point, Nietzsche was furnishing the same information as his somewhat older contemporary Karl Marx.

Nietzsche realized at an early stage that power is not just agonistic but also imaginative, not substantive but relational. It exists only in relation to how it is regarded, which means that we need to move away from a mechanistic model with a material basis. Power exists if it is considered powerful. The power of one person becomes concrete in the imagination of another. A powerful individual is powerful only to the extent that "the one person appears valuable, essential, indispensable, unconquerable, and things of that sort to the other" (2,90f.; *HH* I § 93). If power relations are inextricably linked to the powers of imagination of all parties involved, the imagination is part of the process of the "magical outpouring of innermost power from one living thing to another" (1,349; SE § 2).

As we now know, Nietzsche's will to power was aimed at every aspect of life. He regarded not only human beings as spheres of power but nature as well. We should keep in mind that in the summer of 1881, during the period of his inspiration at the Surlej boulder, Nietzsche had grown wary of the seductive power of "imagery" (9,487). He had set himself a task of clear, cold thinking: "the dehumanization of nature and then the naturalization of humanity" (9,525). Nature is certainly humanized if the power principle derived from the agonistic world of humans is inserted into it. Nietzsche, though, felt justified in taking this approach, in part because cognition itself is a will to power and a form of overpowering, and in part because he did not read an ideal wish list into nature and "humanize" it accordingly. On the contrary, he allowed nature to reveal to him the cruel and inhuman innermost secrets of its power struggles. The "dehumanization of nature" Nietzsche called for was not meant as a quest for objectivity or the establishment of a morally neutral field of knowledge. In fact, he summoned up its jarring aspects, inviting the world to rear its monstrous head and reject the human yearning for meaning, security, and refuge.

Nietzsche saw a Gorgon's head lurking at the outermost edge of the horizon. Because he did not want to conceal the monstrous and uncanny aspects of being, he vehemently assailed the metaphysical principle that a unified substance forms the basis of the world. He suspected that the metaphysical quest for a unified substance was intended as a path to serenity, the way Augustine had found serenity in God. Now, however, Nietzsche was presenting his will to power in the very way that metaphysicians approached their basic principle. Although he was unable to escape this ultimately metaphysical reliance on principles, he insisted that the principle not become a point of repose, but rather a locus of trepidation, perhaps even a heart of darkness. If we envision the will to power as a driving force, we will be stirred and driven all the more forcefully by it. Moreover, the will to power occurs not in the singular but only in the plural, which also works against the metaphysical obsession with unity. The philosophy of the will to power is a vision of an agonistic, dynamic plurality at the basis of Being. As Nietzsche pointed out, there are only "will points, which perpetually gain and lose their power" (13,36f.; *WP* § 715).

Even if the metaphysical quest for tranquillity and longing for unity failed to satisfy Nietzsche, he was still unable to dodge the humanizing implication of metaphysical "imagery." The monster he had described took on a face, and still worse a "*causa prima*" (prime cause), which is precisely what he had sought to avoid. His vision of a "truly great liberation" would be realized when "the mode of Being cannot be traced back to a *causa prima* [and] the world does not constitute a unity, either as a sensorium or as 'spirit'" (6,97; *TI* "Four Great Errors" § 8).

When Nietzsche began to fight tooth and nail for his systematic magnum opus in the mid-1880s, he ran the risk of forfeiting his "great liberation." He wanted his theory to be a unified whole that would explain and clarify everything. He sought to grab the brass ring that would yield the secret of the universe and tackle monstrous forces with a monstrous theory. The will to power, which had started out as a principle of free self-configuration and self-enhancement, a magical transformational power of art, and an inner dynamics of social life, was now becoming a biologistic and naturalistic principle as well. Despite his best efforts, Nietzsche was succumbing to the power of a "*causa prima.*"

Nietzsche had resisted moral, metaphysical, and historical "reason" for the sake of life, but he was unable to guard himself against that other "reason," which was arguably far more dangerous for life, namely the reason associated with biologism and naturalism. In a fateful way, he remained a child of his era's belief in science. As early as *Human, All Too Human,* he had come under the sway of a scientific illumination of life. In that book he wrote: "All that we need and what can be given to us only now that the various sciences have achieved their current high level is a *chemistry* of moral, religious, aesthetic ideas and feelings, as well as all of those stimuli that we experience in ourselves in the course of major and minor interactions of culture and society and even in solitude: what if this chemistry were to conclude that even in this field the most fabulous colors have been extracted from base and even despised substances?" (2,24; *HH* I § 1).

This outlook propelled depreciation of life to its limit. Whatever the effects of a belief in historical laws, hypostatization of metaphysical essences, and a religious outlook on life and the morality it spawned— all of that is probably harmless compared with naturalistic disenchant- ment of living things, which get lost in the shuffle of chemical, instinctual, and physical processes. After all, Nietzsche did not call any of his *Untimely Meditations* "On the Benefits and Drawbacks of Natural Science for Life." The critic of the metaphysical "world behind" was being seduced by scientific worlds behind. He dabbled in perspectives that objectify human beings, using the phrase "man is nothing but . . . ." Man was now considered a locus of mental and physiological processes, erotic tensions, and chemical activities. This is where "thinking from without" (Foucault) triumphs—an outside view of the human condition that accepts inner self-awareness as nothing more than an epiphenome- non. Of course, Nietzsche did not abandon inner awareness, but he suc- cumbed to outside pressures and sometimes identified with his adversaries. He went over, tentatively and playfully, to the other side and sang the praises of physics in a tortured and provocative manner: "We must become the best learners and discoverers of everything in the world that is lawful and essential. We must be *physicists* to be able to be *creators* in that sense, although in the past all valuations and ideals were based on *ignorance* of physics or *dissension* from it. Therefore: Long live physics! And even longer live that which *compels* us to seek out physics— our honesty" (3,563f.; *GS* § 335).

On the one hand, Nietzsche subsumed mankind into nature com- pletely, naturalized and depersonalized human beings, and treated man as "one thing among others." On the other, he claimed that we could be "creators" who would enact the laws over which we would have no con- trol. But what might this creative aspect consist in if we are determined by the laws of nature? Nietzsche's response is astonishing and, quite apart from its pathos, fairly inadequate. We are creative when we can accept and even embrace the notion of an existence entirely determined by the laws of nature without breaking down, and when the senselessness of absolute determinism no longer shocks us and we succeed in recognizing determinism without needing to turn fatalistic. Nietzsche had to wage battle against his own theories and his passion for free play. He was captivated by the very idea he had mocked in the past, namely the quest to elucidate the world from one specific point. In *Beyond Good and Evil,* a book written in the winter of 1885–86 and containing material planned for inclusion in his *Will to Power,* Nietzsche wrote: "Assuming, finally, that we were able to explain the whole of our instinctual life as the development and ramification of one basic form of the will—namely the will to power, as is my proposition—assuming that all organic functions could be traced back to this will to power . . . we would have earned the right to designate *all* effective force unequivocally as: *will to power.* The world viewed from within . . . would simply be the 'will to power' and that alone" (5,55; *BGE* § 36).

Nietzsche had assailed monocausal concepts according to which a given x is actually a y and "nothing else." This view was widely held in the sciences of his day. Explanations of this sort struck him as bad mythology. However, when Nietzsche synthesized several axioms taken from biological Darwinism and the physics of his era into a key that would explain the world as a whole and contrive a metaphysical philosophy of the "will to power," he was indulging in some mythologizing of his own. Luckily, he did not elaborate this mythology beyond a handful of axioms, notably that individual life is force and energy. Life as a whole is a force field in which the quantities of energy are unevenly apportioned. Of primary importance is the proposition of the conservation of energy. There are no "empty" gaps. Wherever one thing advances, something else recedes. An increase in force in one place means a decrease in another. One force overpowers the other, absorbs it, disintegrates, is swallowed up by yet another force, and so forth. It is a meaningless, but dynamic, play of growth, enhancement, overpowering, and struggle.

So far he was being consistent. Still, we have come to expect "consistent" systems to yield the very premises that have been inserted into them, and the "systematizer" Nietzsche was no exception. Following the materialistic spirit of his age, he discovered brutalities in nature after positing them there.

Events in nature can be regarded not just as a murderous "struggle" but also as a play of forces. It all depends, as we know quite well from Nietzsche, on the evaluative perspective. No single perspective is absolute, but it is significant that one and the same threshold at times makes life seem like a battleground ruled by power, and at other times like a game. It is a threshold of a comprehensive vision of life. Nietzsche lived in the wrenching tension between two such visions—one of the great cosmic game and the other of power as "*causa prima.*" These two visions differed in one important respect: the grand game encouraged ironic self-relativizing. The will to power as a "theorem of *causa prima*" enabled Nietzsche to exact imaginary revenge for the humiliations and insults he had suffered. He was succumbing to the phantasms of power suggested in the chilling sentences from *Ecce Homo* that hail "the new party of life, which takes charge of the greatest of all tasks, namely raising up humanity, including the relentless destruction of all that was degenerate and parasitical" (6,313; *EH* "Birth of Tragedy" § 4).

Nietzsche's vision of the cosmic game set a very different tone. Elisabeth Förster-Nietzsche and Peter Gast placed a wonderful and celebrated passage that Nietzsche had written in the summer of 1885 at the conclusion of their compilation of Nietzsche's writings (which they published as *The Will to Power*). It is an attempt to capture in a few all-encompassing sentences what could be the essence of the will to power when seen as a great cosmic game: "And do you really know what 'the world' is to me? Should I show it to you in my mirror? This world: a monster of force, with no beginning and no end, a firm, iron magnitude of force that grows neither larger nor smaller, that does not get expended but only transformed, as an entity invariably large, a household without expenses or losses, but also without a growth or income, surrounded by 'nothingness' as by its borders, not something blurry, wasted, or infinitely extended, but set into a specific space as a specific force, not into a room that might be 'empty' somewhere, but rather as a force everywhere, as a play of forces and waves of forces, both one and 'many,' increasing here while decreasing there, a sea of forces storming and flowing into one another, eternally changing, eternally flooding back with immense years of recurrence, with an ebb and flow of its forms, striving outward from the simplest to the most complex, from the stillest, most rigid, coldest outward to the glowing-hot, wildest, most self-contradictory and then returning home once again from this abundance to the simple, from the play of contradictions back to the pleasure of harmony, continuing to affirm itself in this uniformity of its courses and years, blessing itself as what must return eternally, as a becoming that knows of no satiety or disgust or fatigue: this, my *Dionysian* world of eternal self-creation, eternal self-destruction, this mystery world of the double voluptuous delights, this, my beyond good and evil, lacking any goal unless there is a goal in the happiness of the circle, lacking any will, unless a ring has good will toward itself—would you like a *name* for this world? A solution for all of its riddles? A light for you as well, you most concealed, strangest, bravest, and midnightly?—*This world is the will to power—and nothing besides that!* And you yourselves are also this will to power—and nothing besides that!" (11,610f.; *WP* § 1067).

This statement, which resounds with the great music of the spheres, also establishes a connection to Nietzsche's doctrine of the recurrence of the same. The principle of a finite quantity of force in infinite time suggests the recurrence of all possible constellations and uses the image of the "ebb and flow" of forms as a metaphor. Of course, this is metaphysical "imagery," as Nietzsche was well aware. He realized that he was attempting to know the unknowable and think the unthinkable. During his summer of inspiration in 1881, he noted down: "Only after an imaginary counterworld had arisen in opposition to the absolute flow could something be discerned on this basis" (9,503f.). The "absolute flow" is the image representing the unknowable. All thinking and knowledge exist in an "imaginary counterworld"; but "because it is possible to draw conclusions from an imaginary counterworld," the unthinkable enormity of life is revealed. It is equally true, however, that "the ultimate truth of the flow of things does not tolerate *incorporation*; our vital *organs* are equipped for error" (9,504).

This imagery of approaching the enormity of life sketches a dramatic course. In another fragment from the period in which he wrote *Zarathustra,* Nietzsche added a suspenseful twist to his description: "Suddenly the dreadful chamber of truth opens up. There is an unconscious self-preservation, caution, concealment, shielding from the weightiest knowledge. . . . Now I roll away the last stone: the most dreadful truth *stands before me . . . —conjuring up truth from the grave.* We created it, we awakened it: the highest expression of courage and feeling of power. . . . We created the weightiest thoughts—*now let us create the creature who can cope with it!* To be capable of creation, we must grant ourselves greater freedom than was ever granted us; in addition to that, liberation from morality and relief in celebrations (Intimations of the future! Commemorate the future, not the past! Write the myth of the future! Live in hope!). Joyous moments! And then draw the curtain once again and turn our *thoughts to concrete specific goals!*" (10,602).

This "truth from the grave" is a virtual horror story. The "dreadful" aspect of it seems to be that everything man instinctively desires— namely unity, stability, meaning, and goals—is lacking in the world. Not everyone is capable of enduring this reality. Most people require blinders. In Nietzsche's view, one must "write the myth of the future" and seek "relief" in "celebrations."

But is this prospect of the Heraclitean flow really so dreadful? It certainly arouses feelings of the sublime, hence the poetic luster of the imagery. The real horror and foundations of terror come up elsewhere, namely in Nietzsche's sketch called "European Nihilism," dated June 10, 1887, which provided essential groundwork for his planned *Will to Power,* "European Nihilism" depicts true horror in the face of nature, pointing up the overwhelming injustice and ruthlessness inherent in it. Nature produces the weak and the strong, the advantaged and disadvantaged. There is no benevolent providence and no equitable distribution of chances to get ahead in life. Before this backdrop, morality can be defined as an attempt to even out the "injustice" of nature and create counterbalances. The power of natural destinies needs to be broken.

In Nietzsche's view, Christianity represented an absolutely brilliant attempt to accomplish this aim. It offered the "underprivileged" three advantages. First, it granted man an "absolute value, in contrast to man's smallness and coincidental status in the flux of becoming and passing on" (12,211; *WP* § 4). Second, suffering and evil were rendered tolerable once they had "meaning." Finally, the belief in creation made people regard the world as infused with spirit and therefore recognizable and valuable. Christianity thereby prevented people who were disadvantaged by nature from "hating themselves as people and taking sides against life" (12,211). The Christian doctrine subdued the cruelty of nature, roused people to life, and kept those who might otherwise have despaired clinging to hope. In a word, it sheltered "the underprivileged from nihilism" (12,215; *WP* § 55).

If we consider it a commandment of humanity not just simply to let nature take its course but to establish a livable order for as many as possible, we ought to be grateful to Christianity for introducing its "theory of morality" to the world. Nietzsche greatly admired the power of Christianity to set values, but he was not grateful to it, because its consideration for the weak and the morality of evening things out impeded the progress and development of a higher stage of mankind.

Nietzsche could envision this higher stage of mankind, as we now know, only as a culmination of culture in its "peaks of rapture," which is to say in successful individuals and achievements. The will to power unleashes the dynamics of culmination, but it is also the will to power that forms a moral alliance on the side of the weak. This alliance works at cross-purposes with the goal of culmination and ultimately, in Nietzsche's view, leads to widespread equalization and degeneration. As a modern version of the "Christian theory of morality," this alliance forms the backbone of democracy and socialism. Nietzsche therefore adamantly opposed all such movements. For him, the meaning of world history was not the happiness and prosperity of the greatest possible number but individual manifestations of success in life. The culture of political and social democracy was a concern of the "last people," whom he disparaged. He threw overboard the state-sponsored ethics of the common welfare because he regarded such ethics as an impediment to the self-configuration of great individuals. If, however, the great personalities were to vanish, the only remaining significance of history would be lost in the process. By defending the residual significance of history, Nietzsche assailed democracy and declared that what mattered was "delaying the complete appeasement of the democratic herd animal" (11,587; *WP* § 125).

The problem may be formulated as follows: Nietzsche was incapable of reconciling the ideas of self-enhancement and solidarity, or at least allowing them to coexist. Strongly as he opposed Christianity, he might have taken a lesson from this religion on one crucial issue. The genius of Christianity was its time-honored achievement of linking solidarity and self-enhancement. Bringing God into the debate in a context that transcended the merely moralistic point of view signified an immense expansion of the spiritual dimension. Spiritual refinement might lead to self-enhancement, which could be equally valid on a social level. These enhancements and advancements were viewed not as personal achievements but as mercy, which diminished the pride of individual accomplishment. Moreover, self-enhancement could take place in the context of both the religious and the secular spheres: *civitas dei* and *civitas civilis*. In the one sphere, an individual could loom large and, in the other, remain small. Those able to exist in both worlds would have few difficulties reconciling the principles of self-enhancement and solidarity.

Nietzsche had similarly conceived of a "bicameral system" of culture in *Human, All Too Human*. In that earlier work, he described the system as one chamber being heated up by the passions of genius while the other was cooled off with principles of common sense and balanced out with collective pragmatism. Thus, Nietzsche ultimately envisioned one single world and rejected the elaborate two-world theory of Augustine and Luther. In doing so, he opted against democratic life organized according to the principle of welfare. For him, a world of that sort would signal the triumph of the human herd animal. Above all, he sought to preserve the difference between himself and the many others. His writing is one long avowal of this effort. It documents his lifelong attempt to mold himself into a great individual.

If we are content to regard this highly personal philosophy and these maneuvers of self-configuration with fascination and perhaps even admiration, but are not willing to abandon the idea of democracy and justice, it is likely that Nietzsche would have accused us of feeble compromise, indecisiveness, and epitomizing the ominous "blinking" of the "last men."

Perhaps, however, he ought to have realized that he himself was calling for ironic reserve on the part of his readers. "It is absolutely unnecessary, and not even *desirable,* for you to argue in my favor; on the contrary, a dose of curiosity, as if you were looking at an alien plant with ironic distance, would strike me as an incomparably more *intelligent* attitude toward me" (*B* 8,375f.; July 29, 1888).

While he was working through his ideas for *The Will to Power,* Nietzsche wrote *Beyond Good and Evil* (1885–86), the fifth book of *The Gay Science* (October 1886), and *On the Genealogy of Morals* (summer 1887). Each of these books was completed in a matter of weeks. All three sum up, highlight, and develop ideas discussed in earlier works, and all incorporate materials he had been considering for *The Will to Power.* We need to keep in mind that Nietzsche, who spent much of his time traveling from place to place, had boxes of books shipped to him, but did not always have his own earlier works on hand and often found that his memory of what he had written had faded. On February 13, 1887, for example, when the second edition of *The Gay Science* was in production, he asked Peter Gast to edit the galleys and added this comment: "I am actually rather curious about what I might have written back then. It is completely gone from my memory" (*B* 8,23). Sometimes Nietzsche even shied away from reading his own writings. In 1886, the year in which he added a series of prefaces to his earlier books, he still resisted rereading the books themselves. On October 31, 1886, he wrote to Gast: "It seems lucky in retrospect that I had neither *Human, All Too Human* nor *The Birth of Tragedy* on hand when I wrote those prefaces. Just between us, I can no longer stand all of that stuff" (*B* 7,274). This remark was written in a fit of depression. Two years later, during his final autumn in Turin, when he was brimming with euphoria after reading his earlier works, he wrote to Gast: "For the past four weeks, I have finally understood my own writings; not only that, I admire them. In all seriousness, I really never knew what they signify. I would be lying if I claimed that they (apart from *Zarathustra*) had impressed me" (*B* 8,545; Dec. 22, 1888). During the summer of that year, he asked Meta von Salis for a copy of *On the Genealogy of Morals,* which had been published the preceding year. Rereading this book, which was barely one year old, induced him to remark: "I was astonished when I first looked at it. . . . Essentially, I remembered only the titles of the three treatises; the rest, which is to say the contents, had gone right out of my head" (*B* 8,396; Aug. 22, 1888). The frequent repetitions in Nietzsche's works are partly attributable to the fact that he simply forgot what he had already written.

In 1888, Nietzsche remarked that his *Twilight of the Idols* contained his "essential philosophical heterodoxies" (*B* 8,417; Sept. 12, 1888). The same could be said of *Beyond Good and Evil*. He scrutinized the series of metaphysical fictions the Western mind had conjured up for the imaginary world of durability, unity, and permanence as a bulwark against the Heraclitean "absolute flow" (9,503) of becoming and fading. There are no "dialectic" antitheses, he concluded, but only fluid transitions, and most assuredly no historical laws. (Kantian) ideas of the a priori nature of our reason are nothing but religious holdovers. They are cherished notions of the little eternities within finite human understanding. The "ego" is a fiction altogether. There are only events and actions, even for people, and because we cannot endure the dynamics of anonymous actions, we append an invented agent to the acts. The "ego" is an invention of this sort. In the course of a few sentences, the Cartesian *cogito ergo sum* (I think, therefore I am) is swept from the stage. The thought process, in particular, reveals that it is the act of thought that gives rise to the actor. It is not the I that is thinking, but rather the thinking that has me say "I." Nietzsche's subtle analysis of will demonstrates that it has been treated far too simplistically. The will is not, as Schopenhauer would have it, a dynamic unity, but rather a swarm of diverse ambitions, an arena of energies battling for power.

In one inspired chapter, Nietzsche explored the power of religion. Especially important to him was the idea that although the Christian religion's "theory of morality" protects the "misfits" from the cruelty of the unjustice of nature and thereby from "nihilism," for this very reason it is also an expression of the will to power. Christianity is living proof that the revaluation of values is possible. With this perspective in mind, he spoke admiringly of religious geniuses, notably Paul, Augustine, and Ignatius of Loyola. They managed to impose their obsessions on a substantial part of the world. They revolved the stage of history and created a milieu in which people lived and breathed spirituality. In comparison with these religious athletes, the ordinary man in the age of deconstructed modernity and nihilism is a pitiful workhorse: "it seems as though they have absolutely no time left for religion, especially since it remains unclear to them whether it involves a new business or a new pleasure" (5,76; *BGE* § 58). Nihilistic cultures recognize only business and pleasure. Nietzsche even found himself defending earlier religious cultures against this modern nihilistic impoverishment of life. The incredible vigor with which earlier religions were able to create and impose values encouraged him to regard a future revaluation of values, which he considered his task, as both possible and auspicious.

On the Genealogy of Morals, written one year later, consolidated the analysis and critique of morality developed in earlier works into a unified whole that was both pithy and ambitious. Nietzsche had a point when he remarked in a letter to Meta von Salis: "I must have been in a state of nearly uninterrupted inspiration to have made this book flow like the most natural thing in the world. You cannot even notice any trials and tribulations in it" (*B* 8,397; Aug. 22, 1888).

On the Genealogy of Morals was Nietzsche's first book since *The Birth of Tragedy* and *Untimely Meditations* to be structured as a self-contained major treatise. It is divided into three sections, which treat the subjects of "'Good and Evil,' 'Good and Bad'" (first essay), "'Guilt,' 'Bad Conscience,' and the Like" (second essay), and "What Is the Meaning of Ascetic Ideals?" (third essay). Following the principle that the foundations of morality are themselves not moral, but instead mirror existing strengths and positions, Nietzsche in the first section presented a set of ideas he had already broached in *Daybreak*. He now undertook the synthesis of these ideas into a unified theory that would explain the birth of morality from the spirit of ressentiment. He contended that behind the moral distinction between good and evil lurked the older distinction between "noble and base." The weak and those in need of protection accused those who were dangerously strong of being "evil." The weak, in turn, were considered "bad" in the eyes of the strong, in the sense of being ordinary and menial. The entire moral universe originated in these perspectivist attributions and assessments. Those who have been disadvantaged in life can protect themselves against the predominance of the strong only by banding together and revaluating values in such a way as to redefine the virtues of the strong—relentlessness, pride, boldness, extravagance, idleness, and so forth—as vices. By the same token, they can declare that the typical consequences of their weaknesses—humility, pity, diligence, and obedience—are actually virtues: "The slave revolt in morality begins when ressentiment itself becomes creative and gives rise to values: the ressentiment of beings who, once they are denied the real reaction of taking action, compensate for it only in the form of imaginary revenge" (5,270; *GM* First Essay § 10). Establishing their morality is the "imaginary revenge," which succeeds when the strong have no choice but to judge themselves from the perspective of the weak. The strong face defeat when they allow themselves to be enveloped by the imaginary world of the morality of ressentiment. The battle in morality boils down to the power of definition. It is ultimately a question of who allows himself to be judged by whom.

The battle for definitional power leads straight into a house of mirrors of self-assessments. How should one define oneself? Who is the "ego" of assessment, and who is the "self"? The second essay refers to the immense arena of the "prehistoric labor" by which the human race created itself. It is difficult to determine how certain facets of our habits and customs came into being over the course of millennia: how we constrained ourselves to seek constancy and even predictability, how we checked and patterned our emotions, formed a network of rituals and behaviors, imbued instinct with conscience, and willingly surrendered to conformity. All of these developments have been obscured in the mist of prehistory. Nietzsche speculated on how it was possible "to breed an animal that can make promises" (5,291; *GM* Second Essay § 1). He examined the long history in which man became an *individuum* by experiencing himself as a *dividuum,* both a divided being and living self-counterpart. How did it happen that man became an aching wound? One thing lives within him, and something else thinks within him. Man finds that he has leanings in one direction, but a conscience that sets up resistance. Something within him issues commands, and something obeys. Christianity is, of course, only a short episode in this long history, albeit the most recent episode.

In Nietzsche's view, the Christian morality of charity, humility, and obedience signified a victory for "slave morality." As a result, strong individuals, who naturally continued to exist, were forced into all sorts of compromises, clandestine behavior, and circuitousness in asserting their strength. The third chapter, which describes the genesis and embodiments of ascetic ideals, provides an example of how priestly ascetics mask their strength in a religious culture of humility. A priestly ascetic is a man who secretly strives for power. An inversion of power has taken place inside him. The ascetic priest, as is characteristic of asceticism in general, manifests his controlling nature by establishing rigorous control over his own body and its array of sensual needs. The ascetic is a virtuoso of saying no and a powerful anti-Dionysus. Ascetics embody life as a spirit that engages with life. Nietzsche admitted to a certain admiration for this stance because he was aware that he himself had ascetic leanings despite his Dionysian affirmation. The dynamics of the final chapter center on this very issue. Nietzsche realized that he himself was a part of the problem he was attempting to address with the "pathos of distance" (5,259; *GM* First Essay § 2). He had devoted his life to knowledge, and the will to truth was his most powerful impetus. But isn't the will to truth that turns against spontaneity, beneficial illusions, and pragmatic restrictions itself an ascetic spirit that engages with life? If ultimately this will to truth relegates human beings and their world to the background, if the sciences work toward the "self-belittlement of man" (5,404; *GM* Third Essay § 25) in the cosmos, and if the will to truth ushers in honest atheism, it will be "the awe-inspiring catastrophe of spending two millennia to breed truth, which ultimately forbids itself the lie of *belief in God*" (5,409; *GM* Third Essay § 27). This breeding of truth, however, is Christian asceticism. Nietzsche was well aware that he was a belated heir of this breeding. Thus, toward the close of the *On the Genealogy of Morals,* Nietzsche turned introspective: "What meaning would our whole being have if it were not that in us that will to truth has become conscious of itself *as a problem* within us?" (5,410; *GM* Third Essay § 27).

Nietzsche wrote *On the Genealogy of Morals* in great haste during the summer of 1887 in Sils-Maria. In August, it was already beginning to snow. Everything around him turned white and silent, and the hotel guests began to depart. Only Nietzsche remained behind, proving himself an ascetic of the will to truth. On August 30, he wrote to Peter Gast: "Nevertheless, I have found a kind of contentment and progress in every regard; above all, a good will to experience *nothing more that is new,* to avoid the 'outside' somewhat more strenuously, and to do what one is there for" (*B* 8,137).

But what *is* one there for?

CHAPTER 13

The Finale
in Turin

The last year • Thinking about his life; thinking for his life
• The smile of the augurs • Adversity and cheerfulness •
The silence of the ocean • The finale in Turin

IN THE FINAL year preceding his breakdown, Nietzsche continued his work on *The Will to Power*. He gathered ideas on this topic incessantly, constructing rubrics and subdivisions with a growing sense of impatience. He was hastening toward his goal of completing his "revaluation of values," and drawing the requisite moral conclusions. Nietzsche sensed that his time was running out; his moment of ultimate reckoning had arrived. As a young man, he had empathized with the great philosophers of antiquity and elucidated their will to rule. For him, a great philosopher was more than a member of a community of discourse; his words bespoke authority. The stage of history revolves when a great philosopher enters onto it. A great philosopher reduces the Gordian knot to shreds, as Alexander had in the political arena. In this final year, Nietzsche blended with his ideals of historical grandeur. Ultimately, he vanished in them, or perhaps we should say that he plunged into them and thought of himself as one of those great philosophers. He emerged from the depths of time and rose up to a summit from which he could survey everything and prepare to mark a new epoch. The mountain had gone into labor and given birth to a message, which now had to be announced to the people. Nietzsche descended from his Sinai with new Tables of the Law. It was now time to speak unequivocally, perhaps even too plainly. The intellectual preconditions for the coming era would now be proclaimed resolutely, not muted by reflections any longer. Philosophizing with a "hammer," as heralded in the *Twilight of the Idols,* written during the summer of 1888, would entail not simply tapping off previously valid notions and principles—in the manner of a doctor tapping a patient's chest to locate a hollow spot—but shattering idols. Two levels were at work here: a little hammer and a big one, probing and smashing, diagnosis and massive therapy.

Nietzsche's final works, *The Case of Wagner, Twilight of the Idols, The Antichrist,* and *Ecce Homo,* which appeared in rapid succession, no longer developed new ideas, but generalized or particularized familiar concepts. Nuances, objections, and contradictions fell away. In the process, the directorial and theatrical lavishness of the presentation expanded. *Ecce Homo* keeps circling in on this question: How did I come to be privileged enough to think the way I do, and what kind of person does that make me?

The central concerns of Nietzsche's last works are, as we might expect, the will to power in its dual version as politics on a grand scale and the individual art of living, a critique of morality based on ressentiment, and praise of Dionysian life as a means of transcending nihilist superficiality and depression. There are few surprises here, but it is quite fascinating to observe how Nietzsche, the creator of his "second nature," gradually united with his creation. As he continually pointed out, he had burrowed inside and probed himself, looked out onto the world from "many eyes," and observed himself in the process, peering at his many eyes with even more eyes. He had plumbed the depths of his soul to the point of exhaustion and exhilaration. This "self" had become a whole uncharted continent, which he sought to explore. All of his investigations kept leading him to the creative force that forms the basis of practical living, art, morality, and science. Even science figured here, because for him it was still another expression of our productive imagination in the face of incomprehensibility. Ultimately, however, the creative principle saps all resistant reality. The character that Nietzsche had fashioned out of himself claimed the stage, and everything else yielded to the sensation of this imaginative self-production.

In the struggle with his "first nature," Nietzsche also invented a past and a descent of his own choosing. In *Ecce Homo,* he claimed to be a "pure-blooded Polish nobleman" (6,268; *EH* "Why I Am So Wise" § 3). In December 1888, he added the following remarks, which were suppressed first by his publisher and Peter Gast and later by Nietzsche's sister: "When I look for the most profound contrast to myself, the unfathomable vulgarity of instincts, I always find my mother and sister— the very thought of being related to either scoundrel would be blasphemous to my divine nature" (6,268). The combination of his mother and sister yielded a "consummate machine of hell" (6,268), and it filled him with pride to have emerged from this background unscathed. His success at having done so stemmed from his creative ability to produce his "second nature." He could not feel altogether secure, however, because the "recurrence of the same" could bring back the old unhappy circumstances once again. "But I confess that the most profound objection to 'eternal recurrence,' my truly *devastating* idea, is that of my mother and sister" (6,268). He would be able to close off the possibility of encountering them in this frightening context only once his breakdown had enabled him to escape from himself. As long as he retained his alertness, he had to escape the machine of hell at home by becoming "dynamite: I know my destiny. Someday my name will be associated with the memory of something tremendous, a crisis like no other on earth, the profoundest collision of conscience, a decision conjured up against everything that had been believed, required, and held sacred up to that time. I am not a man; I am dynamite" (6,365; *EH* "Why I Am a Destiny" § 1).

During his final, euphoric autumn in Turin in 1888, he considered it "tremendous" to have explored every possible repercussion of his discovery that God is dead.

"Dionysus versus the Crucified" (6,374; *EH* "Why I Am a Destiny" § 9) was his signature closing for his final letters. However, it was not only these "crazy notes," as they were later called, that concluded with this phrase. *Ecce Homo,* his ultimate grandiose self-interpretation, which was certainly intended for public scrutiny, ended with these words: "Have I been understood?—Dionysus versus the Crucified!" (6,374).

As we know, Nietzsche's announcement that God is dead was no longer a unique revelation in the late nineteenth century. Particularly among the intellectuals who were his intended audience, religion had generally been cast aside, and the natural sciences were on the advance. The world was explained in terms of "laws" of mechanics and energy. Man's quest was no longer for significance and meaning, but to discover how everything functioned and how it would be possible to intervene in this process of functioning so as to utilize it to best advantage. The triumphant advance of Darwin had familiarized the public with the notion of biological evolution. People had learned that there was no purposeful development of life. The happenstance of mutation and the law of the jungle that determined selection steered the process of natural history. Man continued to speculate beyond issues specific to human beings, but instead of looking up to the divine, man was gazing down to the animal kingdom. The ape had replaced God as an object of inquiry. God had lost his jurisdiction over nature as well as over society, history, and the individual. In the second half of the nineteenth century, society and history were also viewed as something that could be understood and explained on their own terms. Any theological hypothesis had become superfluous.

Nietzsche was hardly alone in declaring that God was far too overwhelming a hypothesis. Faith in God had become nothing more than a hazy background assumption. The workers' movement had helped popularize the natural and social sciences. Modern atheism as a style of thought and life was not restricted to the educated class, but had filtered to the "wretched of the earth" (Frantz Fanon) as well. The "wretched" ought to have been highly receptive to the consolations of religion, but under the influence of Marxism they dared to hope that the course of history would bring them a better future. The vertical hypothesis of God had been shifted horizontally. Nietzsche had certainly taken note of the widespread erosion of belief, so how could he now announce that his discovery of the death of God was something "tremendous"? Could his message have come too late? Was he breaking down barriers that no longer existed?

There are several possible responses, the first of which is biographical. Nietzsche, who was known as "the little pastor" at the age of twelve, "a plant, born near the churchyard," in his own estimation, had a great deal of difficulty shedding his God, even though he misled readers on this score in *Ecce Homo*: "When I wage war against Christianity, it is appropriate that I do so because I have not experienced any misfortunes or frustrations in this area" (6,275; *EH* "Why I Am So Wise" § 7). That is not true. A few pages later, he even admitted as much when he interpreted his attack on Christian morality as an essential step in overcoming his propensity for pity. To this extent, the Christian God of pity was a thorn in his flesh. God may have been dead for quite a while in the public consciousness, but Nietzsche continued to detect his influence in the morality of pity. Moreover, Nietzsche had retained a certain submissive tendency. He was still suffering the effects of the devaluation of life, for which he also held Christian belief responsible. He accused Christianity of having sapped the will to live. Christianity, he asserted, was itself only a symptom of this debilitation, a monumental revolt of the weak against the strong.

Nietzsche was unable to shed this submissive tendency. He had to force himself to be life-affirming, at times with a decisiveness bordering on hysteria. There was too much intentional play and not enough playful intention. Nietzsche's declaration in *Ecce Homo* "I do not know any way to tackle great tasks other than with play" (6,297; *EH* "Why I Am So Clever" § 10) was intriguing, but somewhat misleading. These words were more wish than reality for Nietzsche. Infused with his vision of the will to power, he regarded play as a foundation of existence: his

Zarathustra dances like the Hindu god Shiva when he has reached this foundation. Shortly before his breakdown, Nietzsche was observed by his landlady, the wife of the kiosk owner in Turin, behaving in this very way. She reported hearing the professor singing in his room. Alarmed by a series of odd sounds, she peered through the keyhole, where she found him "dancing naked" (Verecchia 265).

There is no doubt that, at his best moments, Nietzsche achieved a playful facility of language and ideas and an agility suitable for dancing even amid suffering and a heavy burden of thought. His cheerfulness "in spite of it all" was a mixture of ecstasy and composure. He located viewpoints from which life really did seem one big game. During his final weeks in Turin, however, he shed the inhibitions that are necessary even for games, and he began to let himself be pulled along by the drift of his language and his unencumbered thoughts without offering any resistance. This lack of restraint could no longer be considered a "game," because the player had forfeited his sovereignty.

In addition to the morality of pity and a submissive tendency, which self-encouragement to embrace life necessitates, so-called decadence was also a Christian burden for Nietzsche. His *Case of Wagner,* a polemic against the composer written in early 1888, made the theme of decadence its focal point. Nietzsche owned up to his brush with decadence, but asserted that he had surmounted it, in contrast to Wagner, whose art continued to be shaped by decadence through and through. "Just as much as Wagner, I am a child of these times, which means a *decadent:* the difference being that I understood this and resisted it. The philosopher in me resisted it" (6,11; *CW* Preface).

What is decadence? For Nietzsche, it is a major cultural force, like the Dionysian and Apollonian, shaping not only the artistic sphere but all areas of life. Decadence can be summed up as the attempt to draw subtle pleasures from the phantom pain of a vanished God. "Everything that has ever grown on the soil of *impoverished* life, all the counterfeiting of transcendence and of the beyond, has its most sublime advocate in Wagner's art" (6,43; *CW* Postscript). In the epoch of decadence, the "problems of hysterics" (6,22; *CW* § 5) take a creative turn. Faith may no longer be in evidence, but there is a will to faith. When instincts grow flabby, there is a will to a healthy instinct. Because things in life no longer really work out, because the flow of what is self-evident grinds to a halt, and because light things have become so weighty, the ominous "will to . . ." becomes the prefix for all kinds of things. The wonderful self-concealment of earlier epochs, when thinking, belief, and feeling had different polarities, is no longer there. Thinking disappears into thoughts, feeling into things that are felt, will into what is wanted, and belief into what is believed. A fury of disappearing bewitches and captures the actor in his act. Now the stage is revolving, the actor is emerging from his creation, placing himself in front of it, and declaring: Look, I did this, this is where I felt and believed, and this is where my "will to . . ." did its job. Decadence is more the pleasure in pleasure than pleasure itself, and more suffering about suffering than actual suffering. Decadence is religion and metaphysics that blinks. If this is how decadence works, and its characteristic formula is "will to . . . ," what should we conclude about Nietzsche's formula of the "will to power"? Is it perhaps also just a "problem of hysterics"?

The "monstrous aspect" that Nietzsche associated with his philosophy is therefore the revolution in morality triggered by the "death of God" and the "revaluation of values," for which he employed extremely caustic language in his last writings. At the end of *Ecce Homo,* for example, he bundled all of his objections to Christian morality into one big reproach, "that we seek the evil principle . . . in our deepest requirement to flourish, in *strict* selfishness and, conversely, we deem the *higher* value—what am I saying?—*value* per se to reside in the typical insignia of decline and conflict of instincts, in 'selflessness,' in the loss of gravity, in 'depersonalization' and 'charity.' . . . The morality that would remove man from himself is the morality of decline par excellence" (6,372; *EH* "Why I Am a Destiny" § 7). Hence a "revaluation" would give out moral bonuses for the "proud and successful," and particularly for the "person who says yes" (6,374; *EH* "Why I Am a

Destiny" § 8). The "selection" should proceed in a way that allows this type of person to prevail against the "support of all that is weak, sick, deficient, suffering from itself" (6,374).

In both *Twilight of the Idols* and *The Antichrist,* Nietzsche evaluated a book he had discovered in Turin, namely the *Laws of Manu,* edited and translated from the ancient Sanskrit by Louis Jacolliot. This book was alleged to be a moral code of the caste system based on the Vedas. Nietzsche was captivated by the chilling consistency with which this corpus of laws divided society into mutually exclusive social milieus according to an ominous requirement of purity. He regarded the fact that members of the various castes could not interact with one another as a clever biopolitics of breeding that would prevent degeneration. He concluded his discussion of the *Laws of Manu* in the *Twilight of the Idols* with the following comment: "we may declare it as the highest principle that in order to make morality, we need to have the unconditional will to its opposite. This is the great, uncanny problem, which I have been pursuing for the longest time" (6,102; *TI* " 'Improvers' of Mankind" § 5).

Nietzsche's role-playing and masques are here enhanced by a further variant: he tries to adopt the smile of the augurs, who create morality in lieu of embodying it, who instill beliefs but do not believe. The augurs, these priests of cunning, are clever enough to manage without convictions. They smile to one another in the secret accord of those who deceive without being deceived themselves. Nietzsche may well have pictured the *Übermenschen* recognizing one another by their augurlike smiles.

His letters from Nice, where he was spending the winter before moving to Turin, were testimony to his fluctuations between depression and euphoria. On January 6, 1888, he wrote to Peter Gast: "And finally, I should not fail to mention that this recent period has been rich in sweeping insights and inspirations for me, and that I have summoned up my courage to undertake the 'unimaginable' and commit to writing the philosophical sensibility that distinguishes me right down to its last conclusion" (*B* 8,226). One week later, on January 15, he wrote to Gast again: "There are nights in which I can no longer endure myself; it is thoroughly humiliating" (*B* 8,231).

Several years earlier, he had asserted that "nothing is true, and everything is allowed," but added the encouraging remark that we would be able to let our creative power have free rein to invent practical and life-enhancing truths. Now, he declared, we can establish principles that will advance the finest exemplars of the human race; we can move ahead in free territory and embark on a voyage to unknown shores of the creative spirit. Horizons will recede and the unknown penetrate into us. Nietzsche had written all of this and worked it through in his mind. Having done so, he sensed that the boundless horizon was no longer just a conceivable notion. It began to suffuse his basic disposition and his entire attitude toward life. He was being taken over by something oddly lacking in resistance, as though his thinking were breaking free of its supports and drifting away. Nothing could hold him back.

It is quite easy to locate the very moment of Nietzsche's transition from breaking free to letting go. In a letter to Franz Overbeck on February 3, 1888, he depicted the "black despair" that was clutching at him, and lamented the "perpetual lack of a truly refreshing and *healing human love,* the absurd isolation it involves and the fact that any remaining connection to people only causes afflictions" (*B* 8,242). Because he considered himself a monster in the captivity of people to whom he meant nothing, and because he was surrounded by people who were not there (to state it paradoxically), he had to fight, struggle, and rant. In a condition like this, "any emotion does a person good, provided it is a violent emotion. People should no longer expect 'beautiful things' of me" (*B* 8,242). So much for "breaking free."

Three months later in Turin came the moment of "letting go." On May 17, 1888, Nietzsche wrote to Peter Gast: "Dear Friend, forgive me this letter, which is perhaps overly cheerful, but after I have been 'revaluating values' day after day and had reason to be very serious, there is a certain disastrous inevitability to cheerfulness" (*B* 8,317). Cheerfulness became a disaster, causing him to drift away. The intoxicated current pulled him along and ultimately removed his inner world from our gaze while we remained behind at the shore. The final image became "Shipwreck with Spectator." The strange thing was that Nietzsche, adrift, was simultaneously standing at the shore as a spectator regarding himself. His mind was still full of its old acuity and vigor. He was driven and at the same time capable of observing his drivenness.

Full of plans and ideas, Nietzsche indulged in the small pleasures of life as well. He relished the fine cuisine in Turin, explored the trattorias in the neighborhood, began to pay closer attention to his wardrobe, and sipped cups of coffee in public squares. He wanted to be noticed and was tickled to observe people observing him. He wanted to catch them in the act of looking at him. The women at the marketplace selected the finest fruit for him, passersby turned around to watch him, and complete strangers said hello. Children interrupted their play and regarded him with awe. His landlady entered his room on tiptoe. "The most remarkable thing here in Turin is the complete fascination I radiate—to all classes of people. I am treated like a prince with every glance. There is an extreme air of distinction in the way people open the door for me or serve me my meals. Every face is transformed when I enter a large shop" (*B* 8,561; Dec. 29, 1888). He wrote this letter to Meta von Salis shortly before his collapse, but letters of this sort date back to the early part of his summer in Turin.

Nietzsche loved gazing at his hands. He chuckled at the idea that the fate of mankind lay in his hands. He had the power to break mankind in two. Is this what a revaluer of values looks like? Then he recalled a passage in *Zarathustra*: "The stillest words are what bring on the storm. Thoughts that come on doves' feet guide the world" (4,189; *Z* Second Part, "Stillest Hour"). He looked in the mirror: "Never have I looked so well" (*B* 8,460; Oct. 30, 1888). He read the books he had written: "For the past four weeks, I have finally understood my own writings; not only that, I admire them" (*B* 8,545; Dec. 22, 1888). He had enjoyed a tremendous sense of well-being in the fall, basking in the autumnal "great harvest season. Everything comes to me easily, everything succeeds," he wrote to Franz Overbeck in high spirits, but these cheery sentiments were punctuated by sentences like the following: "I am afraid that I am shooting the history of mankind into two halves" (*B* 8,453; Oct. 18, 1888). How are we to interpret this statement? Nietzsche sent Peter Gast instructions to take him as an "inspiration for an 'operetta.'" He did not want to be regarded as a tragic figure. "I indulge in so many silly jokes with myself and entertain so many clownish private notions that now and then I stand *grinning* for half an hour right on the street. . . . I believe that when a person has achieved such a state, he is ready to be a 'savior of the world'" (*B* 8,489; Nov. 25, 1888).

For all of its exuberance, this statement was meant in earnest. In a letter to Ferdinand Avenarius on December 10, 1888, he indicated as much: "It is almost a formula for my philosophy that the deepest mind must also be the most frivolous" (*B* 8,516f.). As long as he was feeling extraordinarily well, he had little incentive to expedite publication of his final works, in particular *Ecco Homo:* "Sometimes I see no reason why I should unduly hasten along the *tragic* catastrophe of my life, which begins with 'Ecce'" (*B* 8,528; Dec. 16, 1888). Why not linger a while at the beautiful plazas, drinking coffee, meandering from tavern to tavern, greeting women at the market, and enjoying the afternoon light and the colors of Turin, which he compared favorably to the landscape paintings of Claude Lorrain: "a Claude Lorrain such as I never dreamed" (*B* 8,461; Oct. 30, 1888). Why not stay a "satyr" (*B* 8,516; Dec. 10, 1888) instead? A famous and enigmatic aphorism in *Beyond Good and Evil* wonders: "All around the hero everything becomes a tragedy, all around the demigod, a satyr play, and all around God everything becomes—what? Perhaps a 'world'?" (5,99; *BGE* § 150) If Nietzsche had advanced all the way to a satyr and satyr play, he was already halfway down the road to deification and rebirth.

But even in the final weeks, Nietzsche was assailed by doubts. Friends let him down. If even the market women showed him respect, why not his friends? Surely they ought to discern the demigod in this clown! Only Peter Gast was able to do so. No matter how friendly and cordial the others were, they did not convey the impression of treating him in a manner befitting his station in life. Nietzsche had already broken off all contact with Rohde in the preceding year, because Rohde had made disparaging remarks about the distinguished French historian and philosopher Hippolyte Taine. "I will not allow anyone to speak about Monsieur Taine with such a lack of respect" (*B* 8,76; May 19, 1888), he noted tersely. When Malwida von Meysenbug reacted to *The Case of Wagner* by remarking that one ought not to treat one's "old flame" so badly, even if the spark is gone, he answered her: "I have gradually broken off almost all contact with other people, out of *disgust* that they take me to be something other than what I am. Now it is your turn" (*B* 8,457; Oct. 20, 1888). He went on to call her an "idealist," the sort of person who does not and cannot comprehend anything, especially not Nietzsche or his *Übermensch*. An idealist does not understand the nature or necessity of cruelty. He accused her of having too innocuous an image of him. He was decidedly not good-natured, well-behaved, or idealistic, and did not wish to be so. Malwida had never grasped and was incapable of grasping "that the type of person who would not be repellent to me would be precisely the antithesis of the revered idols of the past, a hundred times more like the type of Cesare Borgia than like a Christ" (*B* 8,458; Oct. 20, 1888).

Nietzsche found the ultimate barbs to direct at his sister in return for the constant stream of insults he had endured from his family. However, the only extant versions of most of his malevolent letters to Elisabeth are drafts. It cannot be determined to what extent they reflect the contents of the letters that were actually sent, since, as we now know, Nietzsche's sister suppressed certain materials. In a draft of a letter dated mid-November 1888, he wrote: "You do not have the foggiest notion of being next of kin to a man and destiny in which the questions of millennia have been resolved" (*B* 8,473).

Nietzsche felt as though he were floating on air when he gazed at the vast landscape of things and people. Nothing could aspire to drag him down; any sensations of this sort could only infuriate him. When he was left in peace or had retreated to his lofty position, he could compose passages of exquisite tranquillity and composure: "At this moment, I still look out toward my future—an *extensive* future!—as though I am looking at a calm sea: no desire is rippling on it. I do not in the least want anything to become different from the way it is now; I myself do not want to become different" (6,296; *EH* "Why I Am So Clever" § 9).

Earlier writings of Nietzsche resonate in these words. In *Daybreak,* he had described the "great silence" of the ocean: "This enormous muteness that suddenly comes over us is beautiful and dreadful, the heart swells at it . . . it is startled by a new truth, *it cannot speak either.* . . . Speaking and even thinking become hateful to me: do I not hear laughing behind every word the error, the imagination, the spirit of delusion? Must I not mock my compassion? Mock my mockery?—O ocean! O evening! You are bad instructors! You teach man to *cease* being man! Should he surrender to you? Should he become the way you are now, pale, shining, mute, vast, resting above himself? Exalted above himself?" (3,259; *D* § 423).

On January 3, 1889, just after Nietzsche left his apartment, he caught sight of a carriage driver beating his horse on the Piazza Carlo Alberto. Nietzsche, weeping, threw himself around the horse's neck to protect it. He collapsed in compassion with the horse. A few days later, Franz Overbeck came to collect his mentally deranged friend. Nietzsche lived on for one more decade.

Nietzsche's philosophical history ended in January 1889. Then commenced the other history, the history of his influence and resonance.

Epilogue: Europe Discovers Nietzsche

Lebensphilosophie *catches on* • *Thomas Mann's experience of Nietzsche* • *Bergson, Max Scheler, Georg Simmel* • Zarathustra *in the war* • *Ernst Bertram and knight, death, and devil* • *Alfred Baeumler and the Heraclitean Nietzsche* • *Anti-anti-Semitism* • *On the trail of Nietzsche: Jaspers, Heidegger, Adorno/Horkheimer, and Foucault* • *Dionysus and power* • *A story without an end*

"*WHILE EUROPE'S* top putrescence savoured / Bayreuth and Epsom, Pau and Rome, / with hugs two hackney nags he favoured, / until his landlord dragged him home."[1]

Within months of Nietzsche's breakdown, the news had spread well beyond Bayreuth, Epsom, Pau, and Rome. From high society to the intellectual elite, everyone was discovering Nietzsche. In retrospect, his grand finale of insanity lent his work an eerie ring of truth: evidently, he had penetrated so deeply into the secret of existence that he lost his mind in the process. In a famous passage in *The Gay Science,* Nietzsche

---

[1] Translation of Gottfried Benn's poem "Turin" by Michael Hamburger, in *Gottfried Benn: Prose, Essays, Poems*, ed. Volkmar Sander (New York: Continuum, 1987), p. 217.   —Translator

had called anyone who denied God a "madman" (3,481; *GS* § 125)—
now he was himself mad. Since these circumstances were certain to fire
up readers' imaginations, his last publisher, C. G. Naumann, sensed the
potential for big profits, and by 1890 he had published new editions of
Nietzsche's works. Finally, the books flew off the shelves. When
Nietzsche's sister returned from Paraguay in 1893, she deftly and
unscrupulously took all further marketing of her brother's writings into
her own hands. Even before his death, she set up archives in Weimar and
arranged for the first complete editions of his works, amply demonstrating her own will to power by attempting to establish a particular
public image of her brother, even when it involved forgeries. All of this
is now common knowledge. She hoped to mold Nietzsche into a
German chauvinist, racist, and militarist, and was successful in conveying this image to a substantial cross section of the public.

She knew how to respond to the more sophisticated needs of the era
as well. In the Villa Silberblick, in Weimar, which housed the Nietzsche
archives after 1897, Nietzsche's sister set up a podium for the semicon-
scious Nietzsche to be presented to the public as a martyr of the mind.
A good Wagnerian, Elisabeth was able to turn her brother's condition to
sublime and chilling advantage. A metaphysical endgame was being
enacted before "Europe's top putrescence" in the Villa Silberblick. Half
a century earlier, Thomas Carlyle, who was esteemed in these circles
(although Nietzsche did not think very highly of him), had described
what was at stake in endgames of this sort: "[Man] enlarges somewhat,
by fresh discovery, his view of the Universe, and consequently his
Theorem of the Universe,—which is an *infinite* Universe, and can never
be embraced wholly or finally by any view or Theorem, in any conceivable enlargement" (Carlyle 101f.). Carlyle warned against attempting to
embrace the universe. Any individual who employed the powers of logic
in this quest would be devoured in the process. Nietzsche dared to con-
ceive of the inconceivable, and was ultimately undone by his efforts to
do so. He fell victim to the colossal dimensions of life.

Nietzsche, more than virtually any other philosopher of his era, gave the word "life" a new ring that was both mysterious and seductive. The academic community was initially wary of this approach. Heinrich Rickert, a leader in the neo-Kantian school, explained: "As researchers, we need to master and consolidate life conceptually, and therefore we must advance beyond fidgeting our way through life to achieve a systematic world order" (Rickert 155). Beyond the confines of academic philosophy, however, in daily intellectual life during the period 1890–1914, *Lebensphilosophie* (life philosophy) began its triumphant advance, impelled by the reception of Nietzsche. "Life" became a pivotal concept, as had the terms "being," "nature," "God," and "ego" in earlier eras. It also became a battle cry on two fronts. On the one hand, it posed a challenge to the halfhearted idealism of German neo-Kantian professors and bourgeois moral conventions. "Life" countered the system of eternal values that had been laboriously deduced or mindlessly parroted. On the other hand, the watchword "life" was directed against soulless materialism, the legacy of the late nineteenth century. Neo-Kantianism had already offered a response to this materialism and positivism, but the proponents of *Lebensphilosophie* judged that response ineffectual. They contended that it does the mind a disservice to separate it dualistically from material life, and surely fails to accomplish the goal of defending the mind. Instead, the mind must be integrated into material life itself.

The adherents of *Lebensphilosophie* rendered the term "life" so all-inclusive and elastic that it subsumed everything: soul, mind, nature, being, dynamism, and creativity. *Lebensphilosophie* revitalized the eighteenth-century Storm and Stress protest against rationalism, the battle cry of which was "nature." The term "life" now assumed this same function. "Life" signaled a plethora of forms, a wealth of invention, and an ocean of possibilities so incalculable and adventurous that no "beyond" would be required, since it would be amply represented in the here and now. Life was a departure to far-off shores, yet remained, at the same time, quite close at hand. It incorporated an individual's own vitality in a process of self-configuration. "Life" became the motto of the youth movement, art nouveau, neo-Romanticism, and pedagogical reform. Zarathustra's call to "remain faithful to the earth" (4,15; *Z* First Part, Prologue § 3) was now fervently heeded. Even sun worshipers and nudists could fancy themselves the disciples of Zarathustra.

In Nietzsche's day, young people were determined to look old. Youth was considered a barrier to success. Products that claimed to accelerate the growth of facial hair were being hawked to teenage boys, and eyeglasses became a status symbol. Young men donned their fathers' stiff stand-up collars, and adolescents were paraded around in frock coats and taught a formal style of walking. Formerly, "life" had been considered something sobering, and young people were encouraged to use it to sow their wild oats. Now "life" had taken on an impetuous and dynamic quality, like youth itself. "Youth" was no longer a blemish that had to be hidden from view; instead, older people now had to justify and defend themselves against the suspicion that they were deadwood. The entire Wilhelminian culture was summoned before what the philosopher Wilhelm Dilthey called the "judicial bench of life" and was confronted with the question "Is this life still alive?"

Lebensphilosophie viewed itself as a philosophy of life in the sense of a subjective genitive. Rather than its philosophizing *about* life, life itself was doing the philosophizing. As a philosophy, it aspired to be an organ of life, improving its quality, developing new forms, and conferring new shape. It did not stop at specifying which values were to apply, but dared to aspire to create new values. *Lebensphilosophie* was the vitalist variant of pragmatism. It evaluated the quality of an insight not by its potential for practical application but by its creative capability. For *Lebensphilosophie,* life was richer than any theory, and thus it abhorred biological reductionism. It preferred a life of the alert mind.

These attitudes were decisively influenced by Nietzsche. Even those who had never read him were affected by him, and his name became a badge of recognition. People who valued youth and vitality, considered themselves high-minded, and were not fastidious about moral obligations could call themselves Nietzscheans. Nietzscheanism became so popular that the first parodies, satires, and lampoons appeared as early as the 1890s. Max Nordau, for example, spoke on behalf of the obdurate sector of the bourgeoisie when he called Nietzscheanism a "practical emancipation from traditional discipline" and warned about "the unchaining of the beast in man" (Aschheim 28). To these critics, Nietzsche was a philosopher who made consciousness degenerate into intoxication and blind instincts. Quite a few Nietzscheans also understood his philosophy as such and believed that their indulgence in wine, women, and song was their direct path to Dionysus.

Adherents of this sort debased Nietzsche's philosophy. It is important to bear in mind that Nietzsche had equated "life" with creative potential and called it the "will to power" on those terms. Life aspires to itself and strives to configure itself, but consciousness maintains an ambivalent relationship with this principle of the self-configuration of living things. It can act as an inhibiting or an enhancing force. It can elicit anxieties, moral scruples, and resignation, and can cause the élan vital to snap, but consciousness can also place itself in the service of life by pronouncing valuations that encourage life to engage in free activity, refinement, and sublimation. However consciousness functions, it remains an organ of life, and hence its effects, whether auspicious or disastrous, shape the destinies that life makes for itself. At times, life is enhanced by consciousness; at other times, it is destroyed—again, by consciousness. It is not, however, an unconscious process of life that decides whether consciousness goes in one direction or the other; it is the conscious will, the element of freedom in one's life, that determines this.

Nietzsche's *Lebensphilosophie* liberated "life" from the deterministic straitjacket of the late nineteenth century and restored its characteristic freedom, namely the freedom of artistic creation. Nietzsche had declared that he wanted to be the poet of his life, and we have already seen the consequences of this outlook for the concept of truth. There is no truth in an objective sense. Nietzsche's pragmatism held that truth is the kind of illusion that proves useful for life. Unlike its Anglo-Saxon counterpart, his pragmatism drew on a Dionysian vision of life. In

American pragmatism, "life" is a matter of common sense. Nietzsche, however, was an extremist—particularly as a philosopher of life—and he detested Anglo-Saxon banality as much as the Darwinist dogma of "adaptation" and "selection" in the evolution of life. For him, those concepts were projections of a utilitarian morality, which holds that adaptation is rewarded even in nature. Nietzsche considered "nature" the playful Heraclitean world child. Nature builds up forms and then breaks them down, in an ongoing process of creation in which a powerful vitality triumphs over adaptation. Survival is not in itself a triumph. Life becomes triumphant when a state of abundance has been achieved, when life is squandered and lived to the fullest. Those who knew how to enjoy life interpreted Nietzsche's philosophy as a philosophy of magnanimity and extravagance. His philosophy of a "will to power" was initially taken to be an aesthetic rather than a political vision. His famous statement in *Zarathustra* concerning the power of creativity was widely quoted: "*no one knows yet* what is good and evil unless it is the one who creates!—He, however, is the one who creates man's goal and gives the earth its meaning and future. He is the one responsible for something's being good or evil" (4,246f.; *Z* Third Part, "On Old and New Tablets" § 2). Creativity, not imitation, is the goal. Morality has to follow the creative impulse.

Nietzsche held that if art and reality did not mesh, so much the worse for reality. He gave readers an incentive to unlock their own creative potential by descending into the unconscious. Freud acknowledged that Nietzsche had ably paved the way for him. In his *On the History of the Psycho-Analytic Movement,* Freud wrote of having denied himself "the very great pleasure of reading the works of Nietzsche" in order not to be hampered "in working out the impressions received in psycho-analysis by any sort of anticipatory ideas. . . . [There are] many instances in which laborious psycho-analytic investigation can merely confirm the truths which the philosopher recognized by intuition" (Freud 15–16). Because pyschoanalysis aspired to establish itself as a scholarly discipline and even take its place among the natural sciences, its practitioners attempted to play down its Nietzschean, aesthetic essence. There was a reluctance to admit that theories of the soul were based more in fantasy than in fact. But Nietzsche never entertained the slightest doubts on this score. The will to knowledge—whether the object of inquiry was the soul or anything else—was always linked to the imagination.

The psychoanalytic establishment, already inspired by Nietzsche, kept a wary distance from him in its initial phases, putting this new field at a tremendous disadvantage. Nietzsche had the intuition, and particularly the vocabulary, for the highly nuanced instinctive drives at the boundary of the unconscious. Psychoanalytic theories of instincts, by contrast, tended to the simplistic, being ultimately reduced to sexuality and death. The result was a disastrous advance of a metaphoric use of steam boilers, hydraulic machinery, and swamp drainage. Even the architecture of Viennese residences around 1900 was indicative of how people imagined the "structure" of the soul. All of this was a far cry from Nietzsche. Although he also employed imagery, and even commandeered a whole "mobile army of metaphors" (1,880; TF § 1), he rarely conveyed the impression of reducing and objectifying. Even when his subtle analyses probed specific issues, the vastness of the horizons stretching beyond them remained in view and gave his analyses their unmistakable profound irony: he left a track in the sand and gave us to understand that the next wave would once again wash it away.

All of the significant artistic currents in the early twentieth century, from symbolism to art nouveau and expressionism, were inspired by Nietzsche. Every self-respecting member of these circles had a "Nietzsche experience." Harry Graf Kessler gave eloquent expression to the manner in which his generation "experienced" Nietzsche: "He did not merely speak to reason and fantasy. His impact was more encompassing, deeper, and more mysterious. His ever-growing echo signified the eruption of *Mystik* into a rationalized and mechanized time. He bridged the abyss (*Abgrund*) between us and reality with the veil of heroism. Through him we were transported out of this ice age, reenchanted and enraptured (*entrückt*)" (Aschheim 23).

Numerous composers concurred that Nietzsche had triggered an eruption of myticism. In 1896, Richard Strauss composed a symphonic work called *Thus Spoke Zarathustra,* and Gustav Mahler originally intended to name his Third Symphony *Gay Science.* Architects such as Peter Behrens and Bruno Taut were inspired by Nietzsche and constructed spaces for free spirits. It is hardly surprising that Nietzsche's writing was also set to dance: as he had written in *Zarathustra,* "we should consider a day lost if we have not danced at least once" (4,264; *Z* Part 3, "On Old and New Tablets" § 23). In the 1920s and 1930s, Mary Wigman developed a so-called Dionysian style of dance, complete with drumbeats and recitations from *Zarathustra.*

The "Nietzsche experience" could take myriad forms. For some, it was just a passing phase; for others, it lasted a lifetime. Thomas Mann belonged in the latter group. He declared in 1910: "We have from him our psychological sensitivity, our lyrical criticism, the experience of Wagner, the experience of Christianity, the experience of modernity" (Aschheim 37). Mann was spurred on by reading Nietzsche to seek a will to art that would proudly reject any social, political, or other practical application and preserve dignity as an end in itself, as well as the mystery of human existence for art, love, and death. While working on his *Betrachtungen eines Unpolitischen* (Reflections of a Non-political Man, 1918), Mann studied Nietzsche's *Untimely Meditations* and picked apart nearly every sentence together with his friend Ernst Bertram, who was writing a major study of Nietzsche at the same time. For Mann, Nietzsche's idea that art originated in a Dionysian impulse and was ironically refracted into an Apollonian form became an essential and indispensable insight for his own writing. In his lengthy essay on Nietzsche, "Nietzsches Philosophie im Lichte unserer Erfahrung" (Nietzsche's Philosophy in the Light of Recent History, 1947), a companion piece to his novel *Doctor Faustus,* Mann called him the "most uncompromisingly perfect aesthete" of intellectual history. He justified this view as follows: "that life can be justified only as an aesthetic phenomenon applies exactly to himself, to his life, his thinking, and his writing . . . down to his self-mythologizing in his last moment, down to madness, this life was an artistic production . . . a lyric, tragic spectacle, and one of utmost fascination" (Mann 172). Still, Mann warned against unbounded aestheticism: "we are no longer such aesthetes that we need to be ashamed of subscribing to the good, nor need to snub such trivial ideas and guides as truth, freedom, justice" (Mann 176). That these political concepts were alleged to be aesthetically trivial and that no art could be made with them did not have the slightest effect even on this lecturer on democracy and antifascism.

Particularly in view of his experience with Nietzsche, Thomas Mann knew that the logic of art differed from the logic of morality and politics, but he was equally aware of the importance of keeping art and politics separate. Politicizing art would be just as deleterious as aestheticizing politics.

"Rebels in the name of beauty" (Mann 172) have frequently overlooked the reality that politics needs to defend the commonplace and the spirit of compromise, and that politics should serve life in the most practical way. Art, however, works with extremes. It is radical and, in the case of Thomas Mann, fascinated by death. For the true artist, the desire for intensity is stronger than the will for self-preservation, which is what politics is intended to serve. If politics loses this orientation, it becomes a public danger, which is why Mann warned about the "ill-omened proximity" of "aestheticism and barbarism" (Mann 173).

Mann remained faithful to his Nietzsche experience throughout his life, but in his later years he guarded against letting his aesthetic obsessions extend too far into other spheres of life. Mann heeded Max Weber, who had declared all the way back in 1918 that democracy thrives on debating and balancing spheres of values. Mann held to the view that the Dionysian would need to sober up before treading on political ground. Aesthetically Mann drank wine, but politically he preached water. This attitude was altogether in keeping with the idea Nietzsche proposed in his early writings that a bicameral system of culture enabled one chamber to heat up with the passions of genius while pragmatic reason cooled down the other.

The coolness of Thomas Mann's later writings almost makes us forget the heat of his enthusiasm for Nietzsche in the early years of the twentieth century. The Dadaists were also fired up by Nietzsche. Adamantly opposed to any separation of the aesthetic and political spheres, they called for a "rebirth of society by unifying all artistic means and powers" (Hugo Ball). The followers of Stefan George, known as the "George circle," and the symbolists also believed in political and societal "rebirth" from the sovereign spirit of art. Franz Werfel proclaimed the "enthronement of the heart." Fantasies of the omnipotence of art and artists reigned supreme. The spirit of Nietzschean *Lebensphilosophie* had liberated the arts from subjugation to the reality principle. Artists regained confidence in the visions with which they registered their protest against the wretchedness of reality. Vision, protest, and transformation constituted the holy trinity of expressionism.

The fact that Nietzschean *Lebensphilosophie* paved the way for the powerful influence of Henri Bergson's philosophy before World War I in Germany, and that in turn France became receptive to Nietzsche by way of Bergson, must be considered an aspect of Nietzsche's resonance. Bergson's major work, *L'Evolution créatrice* (Creative Evolution, 1907), was published in German translation in 1912. Bergson, like Nietzsche, developed a philosophy of the creative will, although he, of course, stopped short of naming it "will to power." Nonetheless, the manner in which the two philosophers linked the individual to the universal was similar. Everything that acts in the world and in nature as a whole simultaneously acts as creative energy for the individual. According to Bergson, we feel the forces that operate in all things within ourselves as well. His enthusiastic description of the creative universe included the same wave metaphor that Nietzsche had employed. In contrast to Nietzsche, though, Bergson made the enigma of freedom the central concern of the universe. Cosmic events unfolded in a circular fashion for both men, but Bergson thought more along the lines of an upward spiral. Nietzsche also sought to link the cosmic recurrence of the same with a dynamics of enhancement, but never altogether succeeded in this attempt, because he could not get beyond the traditional notion of time as "space" in which life processes take place. Bergson was better able to picture time as a creative, dynamic force. He regarded it not as a medium in which something is "contained" but as a productive power. For Bergson, time was not a mere stage on which a drama unfolds; time takes on the role of actor. Man does not just experience time, but produces time by means of his actions. The inner organ of time is initiative and spontaneity. Man is a beginner creature. According to Bergson, the innermost reaches of man's experience of time contain within them the experience of creative freedom. The creative cosmos attains its self-awareness in human freedom.

In this respect, Bergson's line of thought was ultimately more closely allied to Schelling than to Nietzsche, but Max Scheler's *Vom Umsturz der Werte* (Attempt at a Philosophy of Life, 1915) paired Bergson and Nietzsche as like-minded *Lebensphilosophen*. According to Scheler, both philosophers sought to liberate people from the "prison" of the "purely mechanical and mechanized" and lead them "into a blossoming garden" (Scheler, *Umsturz* 339). In the philosophy of Nietzsche (and of Bergson), the lava of life eventually breaks through any encrustations and petrifactions. "We exist, revolve, and live in the absolute" (Scheler, *Umsturz* 339).

Georg Simmel also interpreted Nietzsche as a philosopher of creative life in his famous lecture series of 1907. He put his finger on the exact set of questions that had perplexed Nietzsche and on the panorama of meaning that Nietzsche had sketched out. In the past, Simmel explained, life came equipped with a supreme goal and value, but modernity no longer has these foci. The complex and immense mechanism of society has now become a universe of means no longer applied to a central sense of purpose. Modern consciousness is "bound up with the means" (Simmel 3), entangled in long chains of events that have no link to an ultimate purpose. Consciousness has relinquished sublime infinity and gained in its stead the pointless infinity of a being that runs like a hamster on a treadmill. The result is "the anxious question of the meaning and purpose of it all" (Simmel 3). Schopenhauer had responded to this situation by interpreting senseless activity as a metaphysical characteristic of the will. According to Simmel, Nietzsche, in turn, linked Schopenhauer's metaphysics of the will to the concept of development and the idea of enhancement. However, both Schopenhauer and Nietzsche rejected the notion of a final purpose and a goal of development. Nietzsche was therefore required to think in terms of an open rather than a teleological enhancement, a self-referential dynamics of enhancement where life is its own purpose, designed to investigate and elicit the possibilities inherent in it. Man, awakened to consciousness, is the privileged locus of this kind of self-scrutiny of life. Life undertook a very risky experiment with itself by using man. The result is passed along to the drama of human freedom. As Ernst Bloch later said, an *"experimentum mundi"* takes place within man.

Philosophy prior to 1914 intoned the theme of "life" in this lofty, enchanting, and enchanted manner, full of levity and promise. Nietzsche became the source of and the medium for this theme.

The outbreak of war in 1914 gave major new impetus to philosophical vitalism. A bellicose form of Nietzscheanism made its presence felt. There were many powerful oppositions: vigorous (German) culture versus superficial (French) civilization; Dionysian community versus mechanistic society; heroes versus merchants; tragic consciousness versus utilitarianism; musical spirit versus calculating attitude. Nietzsche's interpretation of Heraclitus was cited in declarations that war was the great analyst that would separate the wheat from the chaff and reveal the true substance. To the agitated academics, the war seemed like the final examination of a state needing to prove whether there was any life still in it. Either way, war was the hour of truth: "The image of the whole, great, extensive Man, of whom peace had revealed only a small grayish middle zone . . . this image now stands right before us. Only war measures the circumference and the scope of human nature. Man becomes aware of his absolute grandeur and his absolute insignificance" (Scheler, *Genius* 136).

What spiritual substance did the war bring to light? Some claimed it was a victory of idealism. For a long time, idealism had been stifled by materialism and utilitarianism. Now it was breaking through, and people were once again prepared to sacrifice themselves for nonmaterial values—for nation, fatherland, and honor. Ernst Troeltsch called this hawkish attitude a return to "faith in the spirit," which was triumphing over the "worship of money," "hesitant skepticism," "pleasure-seeking," and "dull resignation to the laws of nature" (Troeltsch 39). Others, namely the Nietzschean adherents of *Lebensphilosophie,* regarded war as the release of vital forces that had been in danger of growing numb during the long period of peace. They celebrated the natural power of war, claiming that culture would finally reestablish contact with the elemental. Otto von Gierke defined war as "the most powerful of all destroyers of culture and at the same time the most powerful of all conveyers of culture" (Glaser 187).

At the beginning of the war, Nietzsche was already so popular that 150,000 copies of his *Zarathustra* were printed in a special edition and handed out to the soldiers at the front along with Goethe's *Faust* and the New Testament. The distribution of Nietzsche's book to these fighters conveyed the impression to the British, Americans, and French that Nietzsche was a warmonger. A letter by the great novelist Thomas Hardy typified the British reaction to Nietzsche: "I should think there is no instance since history began of a country being so demoralized by a single writer." (Aschheim 130). A London bookseller dubbed the war the "Euro-Nietzschean War" (Aschheim 128). Nietzsche's American popularizer, H. L. Mencken, was even arrested and charged with being a war agent of "the German monster, Nietzsky [*sic*]" (Aschheim 131).

There are certainly numerous passages in Nietzsche that commend martial prowess. A famous excerpt from *Twilight of the Idols,* often quoted at the time, can serve as one example among many: "The human being who has become free, and all the more the *spirit* who has become free, tramples on the despicable type of well-being dreamed of by shopkeepers, Christians, cows, females, Englishmen, and other democrats.

The free man is a *warrior*" (6,139f.; *TI* "Skirmishes of an Untimely Man" § 38).

Nietzsche was hardly a standard-bearer for jingoist attitudes, but during the period of the conservative revolution, military adventurers with a literary bent found enticing ideas in his writings. They were especially taken with his conviction that the meaning of battle, and of life in general, was not any goal and purpose it might achieve but a heightened intensity of life. Anyone seeking or envisioning nihilistic ecstasy in battle could find guidance in Nietzsche's *Zarathustra:* "You say it is the good cause that hallows even war? I say to you: it is the good war that hallows any cause" (4,59; *Z* First Part, "On War and Warriors"). Ernst Jünger and Oswald Spengler were both nihilistic ecstatics who felt a strong affinity with Zarathustra's conviction that "courage is the best slayer— courage that *attacks:* because in every attack there is fife and drum" (4,199; *Z* Third Part, "On the Vision and the Riddle" § 1).

Hermann Hesse's "Zarathustras Wiederkehr" (Zarathustra's Return, 1919), demonstrates that Nietzsche's Zarathustra lent itself to a very different interpretation. Hesse emphasized the outrageous abuse to which Nietzsche, and in particular his Zarathustra, had been subjected. After all, Nietzsche was a foe of "herd mentality," was he not? In pondering this question, Hesse had Zarathustra return once again to address the men coming home from war. The lesson of Zarathustra's reappearance is a variation on Nietzsche's call "Become who you are!" The will to be true to oneself was now mobilized against any form of obsequiousness, even in a military or heroic guise, and Nietzsche was cited as an authority. Hesse defended him against the songs of rancor of his militant admirers: "Haven't you noticed," Hesse has his Zarathustra say, "that wherever this song is struck up men reach for their pockets; it is a song of self-interest and self-seeking—alas, not the noble self-seeking that elevates and steels the self, but the self-seeking that hinges on money and money-bags, vanities and delusions" (Hesse 384).

Ernst Bertram's *Nietzsche* was published just after World War I. This work was unquestionably the most influential interpretation of

Nietzsche to come out of the period between the two world wars. Thomas Mann was a close friend of Bertram's during the time in which the latter was writing his book on Nietzsche. Mann admired the book, and his views on Nietzsche were shaped by it. Bertram belonged to the "George circle," which propagated the idea of leadership by the intellectual elite. The book's subtitle was *Attempt at a Mythology,* which is precisely what it was.

Bertram was carrying on a tradition ushered in by the Romantics and expanded by Richard Wagner and the young Nietzsche: the creation of a myth suited to uniting a nation under a common banner now that religion had faded. Nietzsche's life and works would be recast as a "legend of a man" (Bertram 2). Bertram explained that there is no such thing as objectivity when it comes to describing and analyzing a human life and its accomplishments; there are only interpretations, which is just how Nietzsche would have seen it. Bertram proposed to set forth an interpretation that would make Nietzsche a mirror of the German soul, its suffering, its upsurges, its creative power, and its destiny. Nietzsche had wanted to be a "poet of his life," and Bertram carried forth this project by becoming the poet of Nietzsche's life and works. Bertram claimed that the "image" that emerges from this process "slowly rises on the starry horizon of human memory" (Bertram 2). Nietzsche was not an exemplar in the pedagogical sense but a prototype: studying him would provide insight into the tensions, impulses, and contradictions of German culture and its contribution to the grand history of the mind. This is an image of a culture facing a crisis, which, according to Bertram, would guide people to an awareness of its prospects and dangers. Bertram cited Hölderlin's question "When will you appear in your entirety, soul of the fatherland?" (Bertram 72) and provided the response: it *has* appeared, in Nietzsche, with its full array of inner discord.

Passion for music is at the very center of this discord. Music sounds the Dionysian driving force of life; it aligns itself with both the monstrous and the tragic dimensions of life. Bertram featured this passion for music in drawing his distinctions between (German) culture and

(French) civilization. Culture, he explained, is infused with the tragic Dionysian spirit of music; civilization, as necessary as it may be, is an outgrowth of the bright, optimistic arena of practicality. Civilization is rational, whereas culture transcends rationality and becomes musical, mystical, visual, and heroic. Bertram cited Nietzsche's contention that "civilization aims at something different from the aims of culture: perhaps something opposite" (Bertram 108). What would this "opposite" be? Civilization is self-preservation and facilitation of life; culture maintains a bond with the profound problematic issues of life. In the words of Nietzsche in his first letter to Richard Wagner, on May 22, 1869: "I have you and Schopenhauer to thank for having managed to hold fast to Germanic seriousness, to a deepened reflection on this highly enigmatic and questionable existence" (*B* 3,9).

Bertram devotedly explicated two emblematic passages in Nietzsche. One stems from a letter to Rohde dated October 8, 1869, declaring that Nietzsche cherished the "ethical air, the Faustian odor, cross, death, and grave" (*B* 2,322) in both Wagner and Schopenhauer. The other comes from *The Birth of Tragedy,* in which Nietzsche chose the symbol of "the knight with death and devil, as Dürer has drawn him for us, the armored knight with the stern, cold gaze who can pursue his dreadful path undaunted by his ghastly companion, yet hopeless, alone with horse and hound" (1,131; *BT* § 20) to characterize Schopenhauer's heroic pessimism. Thomas Mann also invoked this image to play off a spirit of German culture, which was heroic, obsessed with death, romantic, and at the same time disillusioned, against what he regarded as insipid Western optimism and its naive ideology of reforming the world. This emblem of knight, death, and devil would go on to make its mark in an appalling fashion. The knight would become the racially pure Aryan, and ultimately Adolf Hitler himself. Poems, plays, and paintings on this subject were commissioned and subsidized by the Nietzsche archives, which were thoroughly infused with Nazism, but they have little in common with the tragic poeticism of Nietzsche, Mann, and Bertram.

To Bertram, Nietzsche was himself a knight with death and devil. He was armored and masked to guard against not only the dangers from without but also the perils hatched within himself. Bertram asserted that because Nietzsche embodied creative chaos, he was representative of German culture, which, like Nietzsche, required restraint from within and protection from without, and quite possibly a mask as well. Bertram cited Nietzsche's claim that "everything profound loves a mask" (Bertram 171) to lead in his discussion of the distinction between culture and civilization. Culture seeks out the spectacle of masks as a means of protection in the face of its excess of elemental forces. Donning a mask is a response to the experience of the elemental. Civilization, by contrast, has severed all ties to the elemental and is now focused on the hollow center of the play of masks itself. No longer is there any profundity in need of concealment. Civilization seeks secure terrain, while culture is drawn to the edge of the abyss. Culture craves tragedy and death, and senses more than it knows. Sacrifice is more important than gain. Culture is extravagant and loves abundance and superfluity. Using its subject as a case in point, Bertram's book on Nietzsche is one long meditation on the question "Why aspire to culture if civilization enables us to lead a perfectly good life?" When civilization does succeed, everything becomes clear and bright, as both Nietzsche and Bertram were well aware. The end of Bertram's book highlights a passage from a letter by Nietzsche: "How often I have experienced this very thing under all kinds of circumstances: Everything is clear, yet everything is also over" (Bertram 353).

Nietzsche and Bertram were loath to conjecture that the end would be marked by disappointing clarity. Nietzsche often declared that it was the enigmatic character of things he found attractive. This longing for enchantment and mystique was also the ongoing theme of Bertram's book. Nietzsche was portrayed as a figure who seductively and knowingly pointed the way to creative chaos, courting demise in the process. Bertram heard the siren song in Nietzsche and supplied his own melodies. His myth of Nietzsche did not point toward a martial or Teutonic world. Instead, everything culminates in a hymn to the

Eleusinian bond of friendship, and everyone assembles around the cult of Dionysus, this "future God" who sanctifies Goethe's principle of "expire and expand," pleasure and passion, agony and ecstasy. Bertram blended Nietzsche's and Stefan George's religion of art in the following statement: "The existence of the pinnacle of human achievement and the eternal efficacy of the forces that have shaped man into man from the outset depend on an inexplicable force somewhere in the world, an intellectually productive and soul-uniting force existing and being practiced and passed along. If this force occurs two or three times in the name of God somewhere in the world, and again and again—that alone is what *preserves* the world" (Bertram 343). This God is Dionysus, who was conjured up by Nietzsche and who returns with him. By 1938, Bertram was no longer striking these delicate, elegiac tones and no longer favoring the thoughts that "come on doves' feet" (4,189; *Z* Second Part, "Stillest Hour"). Instead, he depicted the knight with death and devil in the Nazi newspaper *Der völkische Beobachter* as a homegrown self-assured peasant figure, a combination of Faustian man, lansquenet, and mystic. This metamorphosis did not, however, necessarily follow from Bertram's earlier ambitious book on Nietzsche, which was dedicated not to the ancient Norse berserker who fought with frenzied rage in battle but to the German Dionysus.

The second influential study of Nietzsche that was published in Germany between the two world wars was Alfred Baeumler's *Nietzsche: Der Philosoph und Politiker* (Nietzsche: The Philosopher and Politician, 1931). *The Will to Power,* which was compiled from Nietzsche's *Nachlass* by his sister and the staff of the Nietzsche archives in Weimar and published in 1906, had barely figured in Bertram's book, because Bertram focused on Nietzsche as a Dionysian. Baeumler, however, who was to compete with Alfred Rosenberg for the top ideological spot in the National Socialist Party after 1933, gave particular emphasis to a very different side of Nietzsche, namely the philosopher of power. In Baeumler's view, it would be more fitting to ascribe Nietzsche's doctrines to a Greek philosopher who really existed than to a god the philosopher had resorted to inventing. "Let us call the image of the world that Nietzsche envisioned *Heraclitean* rather than Dionysian. This is a world that is never at rest; it keeps on evolving. However, evolving entails struggle and conquest" (Baeumler 15).

Even though Baeumler became an important ideologue of National Socialism, it must be acknowledged that his study of Nietzsche reconstructed a series of compelling links between the philosopher's ideas in a precise and philosophically astute manner. His distortion lay in the one-sidedness of his approach.

The basis of Baeumler's argument was Nietzsche's contention that truth no longer exists; it is the will to power that molds the material of experience into what we then call truth. Hence Baeumler built his argument on the underlying assumption that issues of truth are actually issues of power. Since conflicts and battles of antipodes, also known as the Heraclitean "war," determine evolution on a grand scale, questions of truth are resolved when life forces are pitted against one another. Baeumler attempted to establish the path by which a given truth becomes powerful and triumphant, and found the key to his inquiry in Nietzsche's reference to the "great reason" of the body (4,39; *Z* First Part, "On the Despisers of the Body"). Only thought that arises in the forces of the body and the senses is truly powerful. Baeumler cited Nietzsche's words of advice: "Start from the body and use it as a guide. It is the far richer phenomenon and allows for more distinct observation. Belief in the body is better established than belief in the spirit" (Baeumler 31; 11,635; *WP* § 532).

There are many bodies and, consequently, many sources of power. Power structures require no justification; only when reason is intent on preserving balance do justifications enter the picture. Since, however, reason itself is based in the body as one of its organs, its claim to universality becomes transparent. There is no realm of the spirit as a court of appeal presiding over the power centers engaged in conflict. Contingency is everything. There is no overarching meaning, but only a dynamics of struggle, self-assertion, and self-enhancement, both individually and collectively. Baeumler's Heraclitean universe has no place for counterfactual normativity. People come into contact with one another, collide, disengage, and part ways in corporeal reality. Hostility culminating in war is truly the father of all things. Life exists only within its boundaries. It needs to be confined, and can expand only within particular limits. The reality-based dialectics of mutually hostile antitheses derives from a vital need for boundaries. We underestimate these antitheses if we reduce them to dialectics. A battle of life and death is being waged, and there is no possibility of synthesis. Anything resembling synthesis is actually the victory of one side. In the course of the conquests, the conqueror might well have adopted something from the conquered.

If there is no synthesis to bridge the battle of the antitheses, world history is a history of contradictions that cannot be resolved, but must be fought out until there are winners and losers. A totality, while conceivable, cannot be realized as such, but only by fighting through contradictions and by acknowledging the history of hostilities. Everyone is steeped in wrenching hostile antitheses. The contingency of existence dictates that we be born into one particular side of the dispute. We cannot choose our bodies, nor can we select the corporate body, known as a "nation," to which we would like to belong. We cannot pick our locality, but only accept what we get. The question of whether it is the "good" side is moot. The opposite logic applies: the side I have is good *because* I belong to it and my people are here. Us and Them—that is a clear-cut distinction. It is only a matter of clarifying the boundaries of the "us," which continually shift because there are always people who forfeit their affiliation. Even if the collective memory of myths and the project of conceptualization undertaken by philosophers is traced all the way back to the beginnings to capture the moment of unity, it turns out that the horizon keeps receding. There is no way out of the history of hostilities.

Baeumler concurred with Nietzsche in criticizing peacemaking approaches and considered them pure self-delusion. Any project to bring peace to conflicting parties would wind up becoming a party to these conflicts itself. After all, he noted, even the Jewish God had waged jealous battle against the other gods. He, too, distinguished only friends and foes among both men and deities. In the Gospel of Saint Matthew, Jesus declares that he has not come to bring peace, but a sword. Only after swords have done their work can they become plowshares, according to the wisdom of Heraclitus.

Baeumler, like Michel Foucault several decades later, regarded Nietzsche as a philosopher who radically pursued the contingency of the battling bodies and the contending forces that underlie existence. Baeumler asserted that we can learn from Nietzsche that there is no "mankind," but only concrete, defined entities in a state of conflict with one another. These entities are "a race, a people, a class" (Baeumler 179).

Nietzsche would not have used these terms. Although he would have concurred that the individual is a concrete entity, he would have been quick to point out that this individual is a relatively recent product of history. Since the individual has existed, the complex of power relations has become still more complicated and confusing. Baeumler's exclusive application of Nietzsche's will to power to "race," "people," and "class" set the stage for his own racial and nationalist ideology; he threw in Nietzsche for good measure. The result is ideological assessment and falsification. Baeumler wrote that "anyone whose thought is guided by the body cannot be an individualist" (Baeumler 179). Nietzsche, however, had already proven that one can, and Michel Foucault would go on to prove it once again.

Other authors of the "new right" of that period went even further in linking Nietzsche's philosophy of the will to power and biologism, typically with the backing of his sister and the Nietzsche archives in Weimar. Nietzsche's call to put a stop to reproduction by the weak and infirm was iterated in very crude terms. A widely circulated tract by Karl Bindung and Alfred Hoch, which argued for the "Release of Unworthy Life in Order That It Might Be Destroyed" (Aschheim 163), made specific reference to Nietzsche.

Anti-Semitism also looked to Nietzsche for confirmation; a great deal has already been written on this topic. It is indisputable that Nietzsche was an "anti-anti-Semite," for the simple reason that when he pictured anti-Semitism, he saw the hated figures of his brother-in-law Bernhard Förster and his sister. Furthermore, he abhorred German chauvinism. He regarded the anti-Semitic movement of the 1880s as a mutiny of the mediocre, who unjustifiably played themselves up as the master race just because they considered themselves Aryans. Nietzsche was even prepared to assert and defend the racial superiority of the Jews to anti-Semites of this ilk. He contended that because the Jews had had to defend themselves against centuries of attacks, they had become resolute and clever and introduced an invaluable richness into European history. The Jews, he wrote, had the "most sorrowful history of all peoples," and for this very reason we have the Jews to thank for "the noblest human being (Christ), the purest sage (Spinoza), the mightiest book, and the most effective moral code in the world" (2,310; *HH* I § 475). He decried the misguided notions of the nationalists, who led "the Jews to the slaughterhouse as scapegoats for every possible public and private misfortune" (2,310; *HH* I § 475).

Nietzsche's hatred of anti-Semites grew in intensity in the final two years before his breakdown. He broke off with his anti-Semitic publisher Schmeitzner and called his publishing house an "anti-Semitic dump" (*B* 7,117; Dec. 1885). In a draft of a letter to his sister in late December 1887, Nietzsche wrote: "Now that I have even seen the name Zarathustra in the *Anti-Semitic Correspondence Newsletter*, my patience has run out. I am against your husband's party as a matter of self-defense. These cursed anti-Semitic nincompoops should not take hold of my ideal" (*B* 8,218). In the fall of 1888, Nietzsche assembled his thoughts on the psychology of anti-Semitism. He described anti-Semites as people who, seized with panic when they realize they are too weak to give their lives meaning, join whatever party satisfies their "tyrannical quest for meaning." For example, they become anti-Semites "simply because the anti-Semites have an extraordinarily handy target: Jewish money."

Nietzsche then added his psychograph of the typical anti-Semite: "Envy, ressentiment, blind fury as a leitmotif of instinct: the claim of the 'chosen'; complete moralistic hypocrisy—they perpetually rattle off virtuous and grand words. Here is the typical sign: they do not even notice whom they are the spitting image of! An anti-Semite is an envious, i.e., extremely stupid Jew" (13,581).

Nietzsche was an "anti-anti-Semite" to the point of writing in one of his last letters, which were all tinged with madness: "I will simply have all anti-Semites shot" (*B* 8,575; ca. Jan. 4, 1889). Yet he also developed a theory in *On the Genealogy of Morals, Twilight of the Idols,* and *The Antichrist* according to which Judaism had played a major role in ushering in and guiding the "slave revolt in morality" (5,268; *GM* First Essay § 7). In *On the Genealogy of Morals,* Nietzsche even managed to express a grudging admiration for the incomparably creative ressentiment that had imposed a "revaluation of all values" on the world, first when Jewish law was introduced and later when the Jewish apostate Paul transcended this law. Nietzsche regarded this revaluation as an essential component of a "secret black art of a *truly grand-scale politics* of revenge" (5,269; *GM* First Essay § 8). A renaissance of "noble" values would now need to be enacted against the Jewish revaluation, but the Jewish success story still merited our respect as an example of an unconditional will to power that understood how to win over the allegiance of the weak. The Christian commandment to love thy neighbor impressed Nietzsche as an extraordinarily clever and sublime strategy of the will to power. In his last writings, notably in *Twilight of the Idols,* he employed even more adamant moral and philosophical arguments to advocate anti-Judaism, and introduced an occasional hint of racial biology: "Christianity, with its roots in Judaism and comprehensible only as a growth from this soil, represents the *countermovement* to any morality of breeding, of race, of privilege: it is the *anti-Aryan* religion par excellence" (6,101; *TI* "Improvers of Mankind" § 4).

Hence the anti-Semites, whom Nietzsche despised, had no trouble using some of his ideas as ammunition, even though their image of the

Aryan master race was miles apart from the image of nobility that had guided him. This disparity did not escape the attention of many National Socialists, who continued to use Nietzsche while warning against his free-spiritedness. Ernst Krieck, an influential National Socialist philosopher, remarked ironically: "All in all, Nietzsche was an opponent of socialism, an opponent of nationalism, and an opponent of racial thinking. Apart from these three bents of mind, he might have made an outstanding Nazi" (Riedel 131).

During the National Socialist era, Karl Jaspers and Martin Heidegger used the regime's official recognition of Nietzsche to bring a different, non-ideological Nietzsche into play and to develop in his wake ideas that could go beyond the scope of ideology, or at least not be limited by it. Theirs was a subversive reading.

Jaspers' 1936 book portrayed Nietzsche as a philosopher whose passion for knowledge drove him away from any ideological school. His Nietzsche was essentially an experimental philosopher drawn to the "magic of the extreme" (Jaspers 425). Jaspers admired Nietzsche for relinquishing transcendence but not transcending, and for exploring the possibilities of boundless thinking. Nietzsche favored the process of thinking over its products. In Jaspers' view, Nietzsche had crossed the desert of nihilism and in the process created a new receptivity to the miracle of existence. Jaspers expressed his assessment in somewhat vague and tentative terms: "In this case, Nietzsche's greatness consists in an awareness of nothingness which enables him to speak more clearly and passionately of the other—of being—and to know it better than those who perhaps share in it without even being sure of it and consequently remain inarticulate" (Jaspers 427). Jaspers sensitively portrayed the drama of this immoderate thinking and proceeded to the point at which "the fullness of being is lacking" and the "buffoon" (Jaspers 428) is manifest. Evidently he considered Nietzsche's unconstrained philosophy of power "buffoonery." He hinted at this view but did not express it directly. Had he done so, he would have clashed too obviously with the official version. This caution notwithstanding, Jaspers was barely tolerated by the ruling authorities, and at the end of the 1930s he was relieved of his teaching post and prohibited from teaching elsewhere.

At the same time that Jaspers was writing this book, Heidegger was holding a series of lectures on Nietzsche. The resulting book, published after the war, was one of the key works in Nietzsche's academic reception. Some especially narrow-minded philosophers considered Nietzsche worthy of study only after they had read Heidegger's book.

After resigning from his rectorship, Heidegger had to endure allegations of "nihilism" from Nazi ideologues. Krieck wrote in 1934: "The meaning of this philosophy is categorical atheism and metaphysical nihilism of the kind that has generally been represented in our country by Jewish literati; in other words, an enzyme of decomposition and dissolution for the German people" (Schneeberger 225). In the lectures on Nietzsche that Heidegger held between 1936 and 1940, he turned the tables and attempted to demonstrate that, unbeknownst to the followers of Nietzsche, the will to power to which the Nazi ideologues referred was not the transcendence but the consummation of nihilism. These lectures came to represent a frontal attack on what Heidegger considered the nihilistic metaphysics of racism and biologism. He conceded that Nietzsche was somewhat suited to the reigning ideology, but at the same time distanced himself from it. Heidegger sought to align himself with Nietzsche while presenting his own thinking as a transcendence of Nietzsche in Nietzsche's footsteps.

Heidegger explicated Nietzsche's concept of the will, underscoring the significance of growth, the desire to be stronger, enhancement, and transcendence. He concurred with Nietzsche's critique of idealism and applauded his call to "remain faithful to the earth" (4,15; *Z* First Part, Prologue § 3). However, it was on this very point that he also criticized Nietzsche, accusing him of not having remained faithful to the earth with his philosophy of the will to power. To Heidegger, "remaining faithful to the earth" entailed not privileging the products of existence over existence itself. He argued that Nietzsche, proceeding from the principle of the will to power, drew everything into the sphere of the man who is engrossed in value assessment. Existence, in which man engages and which man embodies, was being appraised as nothing but a "value." Nietzsche wanted man to be emboldened and to stand up for himself. Heidegger contended that the process of rising up had escalated into uprising, an uprising of technology and the masses, whose mastery of technology was now turning them into what Nietzsche had called the "last men." These "last men" were "blinkingly" settling into their little dwellings and their mundane pleasures and defending themselves with utter brutality against any threat to their safety and possessions. "Man enters into insurrection," Heidegger claimed, with an eye to the current situation in Germany. "The world changes into object. . . . The earth itself can show itself only as the object of assault, an assault that, in human willing, establishes itself as unconditional objectification. Nature appears everywhere—because willed from out of the essence of Being—as the object of technology" (Heidegger, "Word of Nietzsche" 100). According to Heidegger, Nietzsche had set the stage for these developments because his philosophy portrayed Being solely from the perspective of aesthetic, theoretical, ethical, and practical assessment, and therefore missed the mark. For the will to power, the world winds up as nothing more than the quintessence of "conditions of preservation and enhancement."

Heidegger wondered, however: "Can Being possibly be more highly esteemed than through being expressly raised to a value?" His answer was as follows: "In that Being is accorded worth as a value, it is already degraded to a condition posited by the will to power itself. . . . When the Being of whatever is, is stamped as a value and its essence is thereby sealed off, then within this metaphysics—and that means continually within the truth of what is as such during this age—every way to the experience of Being itself is obliterated" (Heidegger, "Word of Nietzsche" 103).

Heidegger was not speaking of a higher world when using the expression "experience of Being." He was referring to man's experience of the inexhaustibility of reality and astonishment at finding a clearing in which human nature opens its eyes and realizes that it is there. Man discovers that he has a bit of latitude. He is not caught or trapped in what exists. Amid all of the things, he has "play" in the way that a wheel needs to have "play" at its hub in order to be able to move. The problem of Being, according to Heidegger, is ultimately a problem of freedom.

In Heidegger's view, the thinking of Being was precisely that "playful" movement of holding open for the immense horizon of Being in which all that exists can appear. In his essay "The Word of Nietzsche: 'God is Dead,'" Heidegger used the following statement to avoid answering the question of Being: "Being has nothing to it" (Heidegger, "Word of Nietzsche" 104).[2] He meant that Being is nothing to cling to. In contrast to the ways of seeing the world that are fixed and grant security, it is the ultimate dissolution. Inquiry into Being is designed to prevent the world from becoming a worldview. For Heidegger, Nietzsche was still a philosopher of the worldview.

Nietzsche's thinking certainly came across with exceptional pictorial plasticity in his doctrine of the eternal recurrence of the same. The idea of recurrence effaced the dimension of time by rounding it into a circle, although Nietzsche, taking up the "becoming" of Heraclitus, had actually hoped to think out into time. The heart of the contrast between Nietzsche and Heidegger is most likely right here. Nietzsche thought of time in his dynamic of the will to power and rounded it back into Being with his doctrine of eternal recurrence, whereas Heidegger tried to stay with the idea that the meaning of Being is time. Nietzsche turned time into Being; Heidegger turned Being into time.

However, as Karl Löwith pointed out in a critique of Heidegger's lectures on Nietzsche, it is debatable which of the two, Heidegger or Nietzsche, pushed his thought out into the open more radically and

---

[2] William Lovitt renders the German phrase "Mit dem Sein ist es nichts" as "Nothing is happening to Being." The context makes it clear, however, that the elusive essence of Being is at issue.   —Translator

which of them nonetheless ultimately sought support in something expansive. To Nietzsche, certainly, the all-embracing "Dionysian" life was not a supporting basis but an abyss, posing a threat to our "Apollonian" attempts at self-reinforcement. He might well have accused Heidegger of a lack of radicalism in transcending the need for security. Perhaps he would have considered Heidegger's "Being" nothing more than a Platonic world behind that can offer protection and security.

Heidegger interpreted Nietzsche's philosophy as a final stage of metaphysics. This metaphysics cannot grasp Being in a practical, evaluative manner. The obscurity of the forgetfulness of Being, which Heidegger traced back to Plato, was still evident in Nietzsche. Heidegger felt drawn to Nietzsche because he saw clear parallels between them. Nietzsche had also set the beginnings of the Western affliction of alienation from the Dionysian sources of culture at Plato and Socrates. To the one, this was forgetfulness of Being; to the other, a betrayal of Dionysus. Both maintained that the calamity of the present had begun long ago in the deep recesses of history.

A few years after Heidegger's Nietzsche lectures, Theodor W. Adorno and Max Horkheimer published *Dialektik der Aufklärung* (Dialectic of Enlightenment, 1944). An analysis of Nietzsche was the basis of this work as well, which has since become a classic of contemporary critical philosophy. Adorno and Horkheimer moved away from the ideological focus of their earlier years, when they had pitted the values of bourgeois enlightenment against capitalist reality and had sought and found subversive potential in the disparities of late capitalism. That was still enlightenment. Now, in the aftermath of war, National Socialist and Stalinist rule, the American culture industry, and the triumphant advance of noncontemplative applied science, they felt that the time had come to enlighten enlightenment about itself, specifically its involvement in spinning a web of delusions. "The fully enlightened earth radiates disaster triumphant" (Adorno/Horkheimer 3).

Nietzsche and Heidegger had dated the moment of the Fall back to Plato and Socrates. Adorno and Horkheimer looked back still farther, to the moment at which Odysseus had himself bound to the mast in order to resist the song of the sirens. The self that was attempting to assert itself in this instance had to brace and shackle itself and inflict violence on itself. Above all, it could not give in to music. "Without music, life would be an error" (6,64; *TI* "Maxims and Arrows" § 33), Nietzsche had said, and Adorno and Horkheimer were now demonstrating how life succumbed to error by opting for self-affirmation against the music of the world.

Nietzsche inspired the authors of *Dialectic of Enlightenment* by laying out the track of Dionysus, which they proceeded to follow. When things are Dionysian, life is where it ought to be, in the heart of its creative, consuming commotion. The life that Adorno and Horkheimer saw disappearing before their very eyes under the force of socialization, which they called "nature in the subject," was Dionysian and siren seeking. To become a subject, one must be bound to the mast of rational self-affirmation. Anyone wishing to be the master of his own fate must not follow the voices of the sirens, whose beauty signals demise. Becoming a subject means applying force to one's outer and inner nature. "Nature," however, was for Adorno and Horkheimer, as it had been for their philosophical forebear Nietzsche, "that which transcends the confines of experience; whatever in things is more than their previously known reality" (Adorno/Horkheimer 15). Nietzsche's "Dionysus," Heidegger's "Being," and Adorno and Horkheimer's "nature" are all designations for the colossal dimensions of existence.

Adorno and Horkheimer expanded Nietzsche's analysis of power. Since Nietzsche interpreted the will to truth as a form of the will to power, power games appeared to reign supreme. No matter how deeply absorbed in the truth a person might be, no matter how pure and selfless, ultimately the will to power would rear its head. The authors of *Dialectic of Enlightenment,* who felt let down by Western reason, saw the situation in much the same way. The magic of the humanistic ideas of the Enlightenment had vanished, and the cold heart of power—or, one might say, the dynamic structure of an anonymous exercise of power— was everywhere manifest.

The basic outline of *Dialectic of Enlightenment* is thus Nietzschean, because the book centers on the wrenching tension that was found in Nietzsche. In Adorno and Horkheimer's study, the focus is power; in Nietzsche, it was music. The twentieth-century text featured Odysseus in chains; Nietzsche looked to Dionysus, the future god. In his way, Adorno would become a disciple of this Dionysus, perceiving what was once real life only as a remote echo from works of art.

Dionysus and power were the two themes that drew Michel Foucault to Nietzsche as well. In 1961, Foucault published his first major work, *Madness and Civilization,* which analyzed the modern universe of reason from its peripheries, from the perspective of the disenfranchised and marginalized confines of madness. When he described "other" reason as a negation of the civilization of the classical age and thus provided it with an identity, it was not hard to recognize the face of Dionysus lurking behind this "other." Of course, it was Georges Bataille who had brought the Dionysian Nietzsche to Foucault's attention as the voice of "other" reason. Bataille also introduced the ecstatic and mystic Nietzsche into French philosophy as early as the 1930s. Foucault built on this philosophical foundation with his research into the birth of modern reason. He contended that we need to retrace the history of dispersions and divergences and locate the moment at which Western reason prevailed against the experience of tragedy, domesticated the "blithe world of pleasure," and was no longer prepared to attend to the voice of madness. Foucault considered his investigations a project of "great Nietzschean research" that "seeks to confront the dialectics of history with the fixed structures of tragedy" (Foucault, *Wahnsinn* 11).[3]

When Foucault expanded on his project by making disenfranchised forces his theme and conducting an analysis of power, he remained

[3] This prefatory remark by Foucault appeared in an introduction to the German edition of *Madness and Civilization.*   —Translator

solidly in Nietzschean territory. By describing modern practices of the production of truth in hospitals, psychiatry, and prisons, he showed how right Nietzsche had been to interpret the will to truth as an epistemic form of the will to power. In his essay "Nietzsche, la généalogie, l'histoire" (Nietzsche, Genealogy, History, 1971), which reprised themes from his inaugural address at the Collège de France, Foucault explicated Nietzsche's genealogical principle and clarified what he was adopting from it for his own research.

A genealogist investigates the true origin of historical events and ways of thinking without making absolute or teleological assumptions; he is not taken in by the metaphysical notion that the origin bears the truth and that meaning radiates out from it into practices, institutions, and ideas. Foucault intended to destroy such originary myths, as had Nietzsche before him. "The genealogist needs history to dispel the chimeras of the origin" (Foucault, "Nietzsche" 80). Nietzsche had demonstrated in *On the Genealogy of Morals* that a specific practice at some point in the past had led to the imposition of punishment for those who deviated from it, and myriad justifications for these disciplinary procedures were supplied in the process. In other words, there was some initial way of reining in our instincts, which was then transformed in the course of time into a whole spectrum of human introspection, and eventually emerged as our conscience. Like Nietzsche, Foucault poked fun at the notion of "solemnities of the origin" (Foucault, "Nietzsche" 79) and demonstrated that there was in fact no plan, intention, or grand design at the beginning, but only a contingent constellation of "barbarous and shameful confusion" (Foucault, "Nietzsche" 89).

Foucault applied Nietzsche's genealogical principle to concrete historical research, maintaining that the bases of reason are not rational. History regained its opaque factuality and no longer came across as a realm full of meaning. Foucault drew on Nietzsche to develop his ontology of contingency: "The forces operating in history are not controlled by destiny or regulative mechanisms, but respond to haphazard con-

flicts. They do not manifest the successive forms of a primordial intention, and their attraction is not that of a conclusion, for they always
appear through the singular randomness of events" (Foucault,
"Nietzsche" 88). This idea was quite liberating for Foucault. It was no
longer necessary to be led astray by the phantasm of a great order to
which we feel compelled to conform because the order of things is
expressed through it. Who is doing the expressing, and who is doing the
ordering? Posing these questions, Foucault separated the doer from the
deed, the author from his work, and the contingent swarm of power in
all of its manifestations from so-called history.

In *Daybreak*, Nietzsche had written that mankind's passion for knowledge might lead man to perish under the strain of too much self-illumi-
nation. Instead of going down in "fire and light," we might prefer to sink
"in the sand" (3,265; *D* § 429). Foucault returned to this image in the
famous closing passage of *The Order of Things*. He explained that, at one
point in the past, a particular type of the will to truth focused on man.
For some time now, this quest for knowledge about man had been fruitful, but it might be nearing an end. Quite possibly a new turn of events
was imminent, in which case it would be likely "that man would be
erased like a face drawn in sand at the edge of the sea" (Foucault, *Order
of Things* 387).

In his final creative phase, Foucault turned to what we might call
"strategies of power on one's own body." This, too, is a Nietzschean
project, centered on regaining the art of living. In lieu of analyzing the
conditions under which the subject would be dissolved, Foucault probed
the arena of sovereignty in the last volumes of *The History of Sexuality*.
He cited the wisdom of antiquity, but also took another look at
Nietzsche, who had written: "You should become the master of yourself and also the master of your own virtues. Previously, they were your
masters, but they must be nothing more than your tools, just some tools
among others. You should achieve power over your pros and cons"
(2,20; *HH* I Preface § 6). There were many twists and turns in the life of

Foucault, but at no point did he seek to break free of Nietzsche, most likely because he did not regard this attachment as a constraint.

Nietzsche's philosophical biography is a story without an end and will need to continue being written. It remains to be described how American pragmatism discovered the side of Nietzsche that had declared truth the illusion that helps us cope with life. Nietzsche was divested of his Old World pathos by these pragmatists, who thought that it is really not so bad to get by without absolute truth. Nietzsche's dramatic "God is dead!" was laid to rest. To William James, for example, it was clear that if there is a will to power, there might as well be a will to faith if it renders individual life richer and society more stable. When analyzing Nietzsche, the pragmatists drew a sharp distinction between the momentous and the utilitarian. They disregarded Nietzsche's grand-scale political pronouncements about breeding and selection, and focused instead on his philosophical art of self-configuration and self-enhancement. Richard Rorty and other philosophers who have approached Nietzsche in this way have demonstrated its effectiveness as a means of revealing traces of benevolence in Nietzsche's sometimes cruel philosophy.

Nietzsche was a laboratory of thinking, and he never stopped interpreting himself. A powerhouse of interpretive production, he enacted the drama of what can be envisioned and effected. In doing so, he investigated the scope of what was humanly possible. All of us who regard thinking as a central concern of life will keep coming back to Nietzsche, and may well find that it is the colossal grand music of life that is actually haunting us.

As I wrote this book, I kept picturing a painting by Caspar David Friedrich: *The Monk at the Sea*. An individual is standing all alone at the shore in front of an immense horizon of sky and sea. Can this immensity be fathomed? Does every thought simply dissolve in the face of experiencing immensity? Nietzsche was the monk at the sea. He always had immensity in view and was always prepared to let thinking be submerged in the indeterminable and to reemerge with new attempts at configuration. Kant had asked whether we ought to leave the terra firma of reason and venture out into the open sea of the unknown. Kant had advocated remaining here. Nietzsche, however, ventured out.

There is no point of arrival in Nietzsche's philosophy, no outcome, and no end result. There is only the will to an unceasing adventure in thinking. Sometimes, however, the feeling creeps over us that perhaps this soul should have sung after all.

Chronicle of
Nietzsche's Life

1844

October 15: Friedrich Wilhelm Nietzsche is born as the first of three children to the pastor Karl Ludwig Nietzsche and his wife, Franziska, née Oehler, in Röcken, a small village near Lützen. "Born on the battle-field of Lützen. The first name I ever heard was Gustav Adolf" (1858).

On his father: "The perfect picture of a country parson! Endowed with a good spirit and heart, adorned with all the virtues of a Christian, he led a quiet and simple but happy life" (1858).

On his childhood in Röcken: "Various characteristics developed very early in me—for example, a certain penchant for tranquillity and a taci-turn nature, which I used to keep other children at arm's length, although my passionate nature erupted from time to time. Sequestered from the outside world, I lived in a happy family. The village and its vicinity were my world; anything beyond that was a magical realm alto-gether alien to me" (1858).

1849

July 30: Death of his father. Diagnosis: softening of the brain. "Although I was still very young and inexperienced, I did have some idea of death; the thought of being separated forever from my beloved father seized me, and I wept bitterly" (1858). In *Ecce Homo* (1888), N. writes about his father: "I consider it a great privilege to have had a father like this: it even seems to me that this explains any other privileges I might have—even apart from life, the great Yes to life."

1850

January 9: Shortly before his second birthday, N.'s brother, Ludwig Joseph, dies. "At that time I once had a dream of hearing organ music in the church of the sort that is played at funerals. When I saw what was making these sounds, a grave suddenly opened and my father emerged from it, wrapped in a shroud. He hurried into the church and soon returned with a small child in his arms. The tomb opened up, he entered it, and the cover closed over the opening. Just then, the deafening organ sounds fell silent, and I awoke. On the day following this night, little Joseph suddenly fell ill with cramps and died in a matter of hours. Our grief was overwhelming. My dream had come utterly true" (1858).

Early April: A new parson comes to Röcken. The family—two unmarried aunts, his mother, and the two children, Friedrich and Elisabeth—relocates to Naumburg. The family has some savings, and his mother receives a widow's subsidy and a small pension from the court of Altenburg, where his father had worked as an educator for several years.

Attends the local boys' public school (until February 1851). His sister gave the following account of this period in his life: his fellow pupils called him "the little pastor" because he could recite "biblical verses and spiritual songs" with such feeling that "you almost had to cry." His sister told this anecdote: "One day, just as school was letting out, there was a heavy downpour of rain, and we looked along Priester Lane for our Fritz. All of the boys were running like mad to get home—at last, little Fritz also appeared, walking along slowly, his cap covered by his slate and his little handkerchief spread on top. . . . When our mother scolded him for coming home soaked to the skin, he replied in a serious tone: 'But Mamma, the school rules state that the boys are forbidden to jump and run when they leave school, but must walk home quietly with proper manners.'"

N.'s mother gives him a piano. N. takes lessons with an elderly choir-master.

1853

January: N. contracts scarlet fever. The family expects N. to follow in his father's footsteps and become a pastor. Friendship with Gustav Krug and Wilhelm Pinder.

1856

People talk about N. in school. His sister recounts a schoolmate's story about N.: "He often noticed my brother, who had big wistful eyes, and he was surprised at how much influence he wielded on his fellow students. They never dared to say a nasty word or indecent remark in his presence. . . . 'What does he do to you?' he asked them. 'Well, he looks at you in a way that makes the words stick in your throat.' . . . Fritz always reminded him of the twelve-year-old Jesus in the temple."

N. writes his first philosophical essay, "On the Origin of Evil." He fills notebooks with poems.

1858

Summer: N. prepares for the Pforta school entrance examination, and begins to write his first autobiography. N. sums up his experience as follows: "By and large, I am in charge of my own upbringing . . . I have had to do without the strict and senior guidance of a male intellect." Over the next ten years, N. produces eight additional autobiographical essays.

October: Acceptance into the Pforta school, an elite boarding school in the Saale valley. "It was a Tuesday morning when I rode out of the gates of the city of Naumburg. The ground was still heavy with the morning dew. . . . This gloomy daybreak lay within me as well: the real brightness of the day had yet to dawn in my heart."

1859

N. discovers Jean Paul: "The fragments of his works that I have read appeal to me uncommonly with their blooming, effusive descriptions, their subtle ideas, and their satirical wit." N. is first in his class for several years. On his fifteenth birthday, he notes down: "I have been seized by an inordinate desire for knowledge and universal enlightenment."

1860

Paul Deussen: "We formed a bond of friendship by getting together . . . in a solemn hour and agreeing to use the familiar form of address the way close friends do, even though the polite form is customary among the pupils at Pforta. We toasted our friendship not with a drink but by taking snuff together."

1861

N. discovers Hölderlin, who was almost forgotten at the time. He calls him his "favorite poet" and writes an essay on him. The teacher's comment: "I would like to give the author the friendly advice to stick to poets who are healthier, more lucid, and more German."

1862

Together with a few friends, N. founds the literary club Germania. According to its statutes: "Anyone is free to submit a musical composition, a poem, or an essay. However, each member is obliged to complete at least six essays a year, of which two must deal with contemporary history or issues of the day."

N. is in the infirmary. "Congestion in my head (headache keeps traveling to different spots)." N. writes the essay "Fate and History" and the draft of a drama, "Ermanarich." Numerous compositions.

1863

From Paul Deussen's memoirs of their time together at the Pforta school: "His indifference to the everyday interests of his schoolmates and his lack of esprit de corps were regarded as a lack of character, and I recall how one day a certain M., who was taking a leisurely stroll through the school garden, discreetly and to the great amusement of a group of bystanders, produced a jumping jack that was cut out and assembled from a photograph of Nietzsche. Luckily my friend never learned of this."

N. drinks four pints of beer on an outing with friends in the bar of the Kösen train station and returns to Pforta drunk. As a result, he is demoted from first in his class, and forfeits his position as monitor of the younger fellow students. He writes to his mother, overwhelmed with remorse: "Write me as soon as you can and be strict with me, because I deserve it."

Associates with Ernst Ortlepp, a vagrant poet. N. records several of Ortlepp's poems on love and anguish in his diary: "Now that I no longer have you, / I will soon be in my grave." Shortly thereafter Ortlepp is found dead in a ditch.

An excerpt of N.'s letter to his mother on September 6: "The autumn and its chilly air drove away the nightingales. . . . But the air is so crystalline and you can get such a clear view of the heavens that the world lies naked before your eyes. If I think for a moment about what I want, I look for words to a melody I have and a melody to words I have, and the two simply do not match up, although they both came from my soul. But that is my destiny!"

1864

While still at Pforta, N. writes his first major essay on classical philology. The topic is Theognis. Effusive praise from his teachers. N. thinks otherwise: "Am I satisfied with it? No, no." August: Takes his university entrance examination. October: Begins studying theological and classical philology in Bonn. N. rents a piano and joins the "Franconia" fraternity. Attends lectures by Friedrich Ritschl.

1865

February: "I have definitely settled on philology." Involuntary visit to a brothel. Letter to his mother: "My recent experiences have been limited to enjoying the arts." N.'s fraternity brothers call him "loony" because "whenever he was not on campus, he could usually be found at home studying and playing music." N. avoids the carnival in Cologne.

Semester break in Naumburg. Quarrel with his mother because N. refuses to take communion. Return to Bonn. Submits to a duel as a rite of passage. A witness reports: "The two adversaries bumbled around directing blows to their bandaged arms for the course of eleven minutes. Nietzsche got a superficial cut on the bridge of his nose that was about two centimeters long." Close friendship with Carl von Gersdorff and Erwin Rohde. N. is disgusted with the "beer materialism" of the Franconia. Leaves Bonn. "I fled from Bonn like a refugee." Switch to Leipzig, where his favorite teacher, Ritschl, had accepted a professorship.

October: The Schopenhauer experience. "A need for self-knowledge and even self-doubt took hold of me with great force. My troubled, melancholy diary entries of that time with their pointless self-accusations and their desperate search for sanctity and transformation of the entire core of mankind are testimony to this change of outlook." Founding of the "Philological Club." N. gives up tobacco and alcohol, but becomes a regular at the pastry shop, where he consumes large quantities of cakes and pies.

1866

Lengthy hikes in the vicinity of Leipzig. Describes a storm as follows: "How different the lightning, the storm, the hail, free powers, without ethics! How happy, how powerful they are, pure will, untarnished by intellect!" (April). Admires Bismarck and declares his solidarity as an "enraged Prussian" (July). Writes about Bismarck's military policy: "Ultimately this Prussian manner of getting rid of princes is as easy as can be" (July). N. describes his reaction to Prussia's "national program" to Gersdorff: "If it fails, let us hope that we both have the honor of falling on the battlefield, struck by a French bullet."

Reads Emerson and Friedrich Albert Lange.

1867

Works on "De fontibus Diognis Laertii." Writes to Deussen: "You cannot imagine how personally beholden I am to Ritschl; I cannot and may not tear myself away" (April 4). His will to style awakens: "The scales have fallen from my eyes. I have been living in stylistic innocence for far too long. The categorical imperative 'Thou shalt and must write' has roused me" (April 6). Works on a study of Democritus. October 31: His study of Diogenes Laertius is awarded a prize by Leipzig University.

October 9, 1867, to October 15, 1868: One-year military service in the Naumburg artillery. N. learns to ride and to fire cannons.

1868

March: Serious riding accident. Injury to his sternum. Intense pain. Takes morphium. Drug-induced dreams: "What I fear is not the dreadful figure behind my chair, but its voice: not so much its words as the terrifyingly unarticulated and inhuman tone of that figure. Yes, if it only spoke the way people speak!"

June through August: Convalescence in Wittekind, near Halle. N. makes plans; he would like to loosen his ties to philology: "But I have an unfortunate weakness for Parisian culture . . . and would rather eat ragout than roast beef. . . . But perhaps I will find philological material that can be treated musically" (July 2). October: Continues his studies in Leipzig.

November 8: Makes the personal acquaintance of Richard Wagner at the Brockhaus residence. N. is invited to Tribschen. Feelings of euphoria.

1869

February 12: Although N. has not finished his dissertation or postgraduate thesis, he is appointed to the University of Basel at the urging of

Ritschl. He writes to his mother and sister: "You can do me the favor of looking for a servant I can take along" (February). Relinquishes his Prussian citizenship. Finishes his university studies without examination or defense. Takes leave of student life: "the golden days of free unconstrained activity, the sovereign present, enjoyment of art and the world . . . are gone forever. . . . Yes, yes! Now I have to be a philistine myself!" (April 11).

April 19: Arrival in Basel.

May 17: First visit to Richard Wagner and Cosima von Bülow in Tribschen, outside of Lucerne. On the occasion of Wagner's birthday (May 22), N. writes: "I owe it to you and Schopenhauer that I have so far held fast to a Germanic seriousness of purpose and a deepened sense of this very enigmatic and precarious existence."

May 28: Inaugural lecture: "On Homer's Personality." Numerous invitations to Basel's high society. Acquaintance with Jacob Burckhardt. "Intelligent eccentric."

Cosima on N.: "a cultured and pleasant individual." Frequent weekend visits to Tribschen. Wagner persuades N. to give up his strict vegetarian diet. Christmas and New Year's in Tribschen.

1870

January 18: Lecture entitled "Greek Music Drama." February: Lecture called "Socrates and Tragedy." Wagner comments: "I am worried about you and hope from the bottom of my heart that you don't break your neck." He advises N. to present his "incredible views" in a "large comprehensive treatise." Wagner is concerned that "Schopenhauer's philosophy ultimately has a bad influence on such young people because they apply pessimism, which is a form of thinking and attitude, to life, and develop a practical despondency" (Cosima Wagner).

N. is enterprising: "Scholarship, art, and philosophy are now growing together in me so fully that someday I am sure to give birth to a centaur" (February 15). Strikes up a friendship with Franz Overbeck (April). Rohde joins N. in Tribschen (June 11). "As far as Bayreuth is concerned, I have considered that it would be best for me to relinquish my professorial duties for a few years and join the pilgrimage to the Fichtelgebirge" (June 19).

When the Franco-Prussian War begins (July 19), N. is at work on his essay "Dionysian Worldview." N. asks to be granted a leave of absence to participate in the war "as a soldier or medical orderly."

August 9 to October 21: Military service as a medic. Gathers corpses and wounded soldiers on a battlefield. During a transport of the wounded, N. falls ill with dysentery and diphtheria. Upon his return to Basel, N. writes: "Right now I consider Prussia a highly dangerous power for art" (November 7).

Christmas and New Year's in Tribschen. Quite harmonious. Presents Cosima with a copy of his "Dionysian Worldview."

1871

N. suffers from insomnia. "It is difficult to get down to my real work, and I am throwing away the best years of my life by teaching too much" (January 21). N. applies for a philosophy professorship in Basel, but is turned down (February). "I have absolutely no compass to point me toward my destiny" (March 29). Conflagration of the Tuileries by the communards stuns N.: "What does it mean to be a scholar in the face of such earthquakes of culture! . . . It is the worst day of my life" (May 27). Work on *The Birth of Tragedy.* Frequent visits to Tribschen, but this year he does not go at Christmastime. Wagner is disappointed.

1872

January: The Birth of Tragedy from the Spirit of Music is published. Wagner is enthusiastic. Writes to Rohde: "I have formed an alliance with Wagner.

You cannot imagine how close we are now and how fully our plans mesh" (January 28). The experts in his field reject the book. Ritschl calls it "witty carousing."

January to March: Lectures "On the Future of Our Educational Institutions." Jacob Burckhardt to Arnold von Salis: "You should have heard the things he said! Parts of it were quite captivating, but you could discern a deep sadness" (April 21). N. wants to resign from his professorship and work as a publicist for Bayreuth. Wagner dissuades him. Wagner moves to Bayreuth (April). May 22: In attendance at the ceremonial laying of the foundation stone in Bayreuth together with his friends Gersdorff and Rohde. Wagner to N.: "Strictly speaking, you are the only benefit apart from my wife that life has brought my way." Wagner does publicity work for N.

N. composes his "Manfred Meditations." Hans von Bülow pronounces them "awful." Lecture: "Homer's Contest." Christmas and New Year's in Naumburg.

1873

N. is frequently ill. Rohde publishes an essay to defend *The Birth of Tragedy* (March). N. studies Afrikan Spir's *Denken und Wirklichkeit* (Thought and Reality). Works on "Philosophy in the Tragic Age of the Greeks." Eye disease. N. dictates "On Truth and Falsehood in an Extramoral Sense" to his friend Gersdorff (June). N. works on the first *Untimely Meditation.* After rereading *The Birth of Tragedy,* Wagner writes to N. that he anticipates a time "when I will have to defend your book against you" (September 21). N. is despondent. "Only when I produce something am I truly healthy and do I feel well. Everything else is a bad musical interlude" (September 27). N. writes "Exhortation to the Germans" for the Wagner Society of Patrons (to finance Bayreuth) in October. The society rejects the text ("too bold"). Works on the second *Untimely Meditation.* Christmas and New Year's in Naumburg.

1874

January: The second *Untimely Meditation* is published. Wagner to N.: "I have only one comment for you: I feel a wonderful sense of pride that I no longer need to provide commentary and can leave everything to you." February: David Friedrich Strauss dies. N.: "I really hope that I did not make the end of his life more difficult, and I hope he died without knowing anything about me.—It does rather concern me."

Rohde criticizes N.'s style when asked to do so by N.: "You do not deduce nearly enough. . . . It seems to me that you use images that are not well chosen, and often downright clumsy."

Wagner reacts to N.'s laments about his bad health and matters of that sort: "He needs to get married or write an opera. Of course, the latter would be the kind that would never be performed, and that does not lead to life either." N. to Gersdorff: "If you only knew how disheartened and melancholy I feel about myself as a productive individual! I am looking only for a little freedom and a little of the real air of life, and I am fighting off and rebelling against the many, unspeakably many constraints that I cannot shed" (April). N. on the function of his *Untimely Meditations:* "I now have to pull everything polemical negative hateful agonizing out of myself" (May 10).

July: Work on the third *Untimely Meditation.* N.'s excommunication by his academic field sets in: in the spring semester and the following fall, N. has only three, "incompetent" students. Studies Max Stirner. N. votes for the admission of female students into the doctoral program (July). His sister temporarily runs his household in Basel. He discusses plans for marriage with his friends and his sister. Visit to Bayreuth (August). Rouses displeasure because he raves about Brahms. October: The third *Untimely Meditation* is published. Christmas and New Year's in Naumburg.

1875

N.'s reaction to a Dürer engraving he receives as a gift: "I rarely enjoy pictorial representations, but I feel a real affinity with *Knight with Death and Devil.* I can hardly express how powerful this affinity is" (March).

April: N.'s sister comes to Basel to live with him. Franz Overbeck vacates the neighboring apartment (known as Baumann's Cave). N. plans fifty essays in the style of the *Untimely Meditations,* but his work on the essays on Wagner and philology does not progress. "Horror of publishing" (September 26). To Rohde: "If the time should come that we are together for an extended period and find that our lives become entwined, I should wish to tell you that everything is a real part of our lives and therefore difficult for me to shake off" (October 7). Makes the acquaintance of Köselitz (October 25). Christmas and New Year's in Basel. Quite ill.

1876

To Gersdorff: "My father died of an inflammation of the brain at age thirty-six. It is possible that it will happen to me even faster" (January 18). Strikes up a friendship with Paul Rée (February). Precipitate and unsuccessful proposal of marriage to Mathilde Trampedach (April). N. draws strength from reading the memoirs of Malwida von Meysenbug. To Heinrich Romundt: "Now that I am back to my old self, I respect . . . moral liberation and insubordination and hate everything that makes us worn down and skeptical" (April). Peter Gast (= Köselitz) encourages him to finish his essay on Wagner. N. applies for a leave of absence (May). It is granted as of the fall 1876 semester.

July 23: N. in Bayreuth for the first festival. Ill. Leaves for Klingenbrunn during the rehearsals. Returns for the performances. Disappointment with the audience and Wagner's lack of attention to him. Makes his mind up to break with Wagner, who is enthusiastic about the fourth *Untimely Meditation.*

October to May 1877: Spends time with Paul Rée in Sorrento at the home of Malwida von Meysenbug. Writes notes that are later integrated into *Human, All Too Human*. N. becomes aware of his "divergence from Schopenhauer's philosophy" (December).

1877

N. explains to Malwida von Meysenbug that he is aiming at "absolute concentration on one single idea that would become like a mighty flame to scorch the individual" (April). Cosima writes to Malwida: "I think that there is a dark, productive foundation in Nietzsche of which he is himself unaware" (April). N. considers resigning from his professorship. His friends try to dissuade him.

September: Return to Basel. New apartment with his sister. Illness. Extension of his leave from the *Pädagogium*. Lectures at the university. Works on *Human, All Too Human*. Thorough medical examination by Dr. Eiser (October): "It has been determined that my eyes are almost certainly the source of my sufferings, specifically of my awful headaches." His doctor forbids him to read and write for several years. Richard Wagner learns of Eiser's diagnosis and writes the doctor that in his view the cause of N.'s disease is "masturbation," and N.'s "altered way of thinking" is a result of "a series of unnatural dissipations with indications of pederasty." When N. later learns of this (probably not until 1883), he categorizes Wagner's statement as a "mortal insult."

1878

January: Wagner's *Parsifal* arrives. N.: "It is all too Christian . . . nothing but fanciful psychology . . . no flesh and much too much blood . . . and I do not like hysterical women" (January 3). Negotiations for a pseudonymous publication of *Human, All Too Human* fall apart when the publisher refuses to go along with this idea. The book is published in April. Wagner is horrified. Cosima: "I know that evil has triumphed here." Rohde also rejects the book: "Can a person really discard his soul in this way and don a different one in its place?"

June: Moves out of his apartment with his sister and relocates alone to an apartment at the outskirts of the city. N. is harsh on himself: he wants to put an end to "metaphysical obfuscation of everything that is true and simple" and the "battle of reason against reason." Quite ill. Spends the Christmas holidays in Basel. A visitor reports: "His whole appearance cut me to the quick."

1879

March: N. has to cancel his lectures because of illness. "Assorted Opinions and Sayings" (part 1 of volume 2 of *Human, All Too Human*) published (March). Submits a letter of resignation to the University of Basel. N.'s resignaton is granted with an annual pension of 3,000 Swiss francs. N. begins his nomadic period. Spends the summer in St. Moritz. From September to February 1880 in Naumburg. N. gives up his plan to relocate to a tower along the Naumburg town wall and to plant vegetables. Physical breakdown, but continues work on "The Wanderer and His Shadow." The volume appears in December.

1880

"My existence is an *awful burden*—I would have dispensed with it long ago, were it not for the most illuminating tests and experiments I have been conducting in matters of mind and morality . . . the pleasure I take in my thirst for knowledge brings me to heights from which I triumph over all torment and despondency" (January).

March to June: In Venice with Peter Gast. His state of health improves. After stops in Naumburg and Stresa, N. spends his first winter in Genoa (January to April 1881). Works on *Daybreak*. Intensive study of books on natural science. Resolves to remain on his own for the sake of his writing.

1881

Summer: First visit to Sils-Maria. *Daybreak* is published (July). Early August: the concept of eternal recurrence. N. has his great inspiration.

Writes to Peter Gast: "I am one of those machines that can shatter!" (August 14). To Overbeck: "It is a commencement of my commencements—what still lies before me! On me! At some point, I will have no choice but to vanish from the world formally for a couple of years, in order to delete everything from my memory of the past and all of my interpersonal relationships and the present, including friends, relatives, everything, everything" (August 20). N. discovers his intellectual affinity to Spinoza. Euphoria is followed by deep depression. Rohde and Gersdorff fade out of his life.

Genoa from October to March 1882: N. attends a performance of Bizet's *Carmen*. Works on a sequel to *Daybreak,* which becomes *The Gay Science*. "We have had the most beautiful weather lately, and all in all I have never had it better. Every afternoon I sit at the ocean. Because there are no clouds, my head is free and I am full of good thoughts" (November 18).

1882

The beautiful clear weather lasts throughout the month of January. Works on *The Gay Science:* "Oh, what a time! Oh, these miracles of the beautiful Januarius!" (January 29). Paul Rée comes. They visit a casino in Monaco. Rée loses a large sum of money. Because of problems with his vision, N. has a typewriter sent to him. It breaks after a few weeks. "The typewriter is at first more intimidating than any process of writing" (February). In Rome, Rée meets the "Russian woman" (Lou Salomé) and is charmed by her. He suggests that N. join them.

N. travels to Messina as the only passenger on a freighter (April). On the way back, he meets Lou Salomé in Rome. They travel together back to Orta, Basel, Lucerne, and Zurich. N. proposes marriage to Salomé twice, but she turns him down both times, first in Rome and then in Zurich. Plan for a ménage à trois of N., Rée, and Salomé. May and June in Naumburg. August in Tautenburg, first alone and then with Salomé and N.'s sister. Intense discussions: Salomé: "We have always chosen the mountain goat paths. If somebody had listened in on our conversations, he would have thought that two devils were talking" (15,125; *Chronik*). Animosity between Salomé and N.'s sister as well as between N. and his sister. In Leipzig, N. competes with Rée for Salomé. Beginning of their estrangement. N.'s sister schemes against Salomé. N. is at a complete loss. He does not know what to think of Salomé. Winter in Santa Margherita and Rapallo. N. feels desperate.

1883

N. writes part 1 of *Thus Spoke Zarathustra* as though in a trance, encouraged by a "whole series of absolutely clear days" (late January).

February 13: Death of Wagner. "Wagner's death affected me terribly" (late February). N. temporarily breaks away from from his family. "I do not like my mother, and hearing my sister's voice annoys me. I always fell ill when I was with them" (March 24). Reconciliation with his sister in Rome (May).

Writes part 2 of *Zarathustra* in Sils-Maria (July). Part 1 is published in late August. Disputes flare when N. visits his family in September. Spends the winter in La Spezia, Genoa, and Nice. Works on part 3 of *Zarathustra*.

Quite ill: "I don't know what to do with myself anymore" (November). To Overbeck: "Whenever it occurs to me that I have no one with whom I can discuss the future of man, I always get furious—by going without the companionship of like-minded people for such a long time, I have become very ill and wounded" (November).

1884

In Nice. Part 2 of *Zarathustra* is published (January). After some initial doubts, N. becomes convinced that his *Zarathustra* is an epochal work. After finishing part 3, he writes to Overbeck: "It is possible that for the first time the idea has come to me that will split mankind in two" (March

10). New conflicts with his sister: "This cursed anti-Semitic business . . . is the cause of a radical break" (April 2). Part 3 of *Zarathustra* is published in April. April to May in Venice. Concerning his visit to Jacob Burckhardt in Basel: "The height of my enjoyment was Burckhardt's embarrassment in having to tell me something about *Zarathustra:* he could only manage to say that I might try writing a drama sometime" (July 25).

July to September in Sils-Maria. Works on part 4 of *Zarathustra:* "my doctrine that the world of good and evil is only an apparent and perspectivist world is such an innovation that sometimes I lose my ability to hear or see" (July 25). Reconciliation with his mother and sister in Zurich (late September). Visits Gottfried Keller, who says about N.: "I think that fellow is crazy." N.'s publisher Schmeitzner wants to sell the publishing rights to N.'s works for 20,000 marks, but fails to find a buyer. N. spends the winter in Nice.

1885

N. completes part 4 of *Zarathustra,* which is printed as a private edition for friends and acquaintances. N.'s sister marries Bernhard Förster (May). May and June in Venice. N. is ill. "I can stand life in the morning, but by the afternoon and evening I can hardly endure it, and it even seems to me that I have achieved enough, under difficult circumstances, to be able to leave with honor" (May). Summer in Sils-Maria. The publisher Schmeitzner is on the verge of bankruptcy. N. looks for a new publisher, hoping to get out of Schmeitzner's "anti-Semitic dump." Winter in Nice.

1886

N.'s sister and Förster move to Paraguay to found a German colony. N. writes *Beyond Good and Evil.* He still has no publisher for it "because it is a terrible book that flowed from my soul this time" (April 21). In June, he sees Rohde for the first time in years. Rohde writes to Overbeck: "An indescribable atmosphere of peculiarity emanated from him, something that deeply unsettled me. . . . As though he were from a country in which no one else lives." Summer in Sils-Maria. Plan for a major work in four volumes, to be called "The Will to Power: Attempt at a Revaluation of Values." *Beyond Good and Evil* is published. J. V. Widmann comments on it: "The supplies of dynamite that were used in building the Gotthard railway line displayed a black warning flag that signaled danger. Only in this sense can we speak of the philosopher Nietzsche's new book as a dangerous book." Rohde comments: "The actual philosophical part is pathetic and almost childish." N. returns to his first publisher, Fritzsch. Composes new prefaces for the books he has already published. The result is an intellectual autobiography. Winter in Nice.

1887

Works on the fifth book of *The Gay Science* (for the new edition). N. reads Dostoevsky. Works on *The Will to Power*. Numerous organizational drafts and compilations of appropriate aphorisms. "I am now delighting and refreshing myself with the coldest critique of reason, which turns your fingers blue without your realizing it. . . . A sweeping attack on all of the 'causality' of previous philosophy" (January 21).

Earthquake in Nice: "The house in which two of my books were written has become so thoroughly damaged and shaky that it has to be torn down. This has the advantage for posterity that people will be required to make one pilgrimage fewer" (March 4). Quarrel with Rohde (May). Summer in Sils-Maria. Compiles notes about European nihilism. N. writes *On the Genealogy of Morals* (published in November).

Winter in Nice. First letter from Georg Brandes (November 26). N. becomes quite ill. "I now have forty-three years behind me and am just as alone as when I was a child" (November 11).

1888

Works on *The Will to Power*. "The idea of 'publicity' is entirely out of the question" (February 26). Correspondence with Carl Spitteler. "I have decided to tackle the psychological problem of Kierkegaard during my trip to Germany" (February 19).

Turin from April 5 to June 5. "I like this city in a way that defies description" (April 10). Works on *The Case of Wagner* while continuing work on *The Will to Power*. "After I have been 'revaluating values' day after day and having had reason to be very serious, there is a certain disastrous inevitability to cheerfulness" (May 17). Reads the *Laws of Manu*.

Last summer in Sils-Maria. "I am not speaking to anyone, although I would like to, because I am less and less willing to let anyone see the problems of my existence. It has really gotten quite empty around me" (late July). Intense work on *The Will to Power*. On August 29, N. opts to divide up his material for *The Will to Power* into *Twilight of the Idols* and *The Antichrist*. September 9: *Twilight of the Idols* goes to the printer.

Final stay in Turin, from September 21 to January 9, 1889. *The Case of Wagner* is published in late September. The Wagner community is furious. Vitriolic reviews. August Strindberg reads *The Case of Wagner* and sends an enthusiastic letter to N. N. begins work on *Ecce Homo* (late October). N. wants to introduce himself as an individual to his readership "before undertaking the unnervingly solitary act of revaluation. . . . I have no desire to present myself to people as a prophet, a savage beast, or a moral monstrosity" (October 30). Malwida von Meysenbug criticizes *The Case of Wagner:* "I believe that you cannot treat an old flame as badly as you have treated Wagner, even if the spark is gone." N. breaks off his friendship with Malwida "because you are an 'idealist' . . . every page of my writings reveals my contempt for idealism" (October 22). N. feels that people on the street, in cafés, in theaters, and everywhere else are treating him with great respect. "I would be absolutely incapable of reporting anything bad about myself, my old friend Overbeck. Things are progressing on and on in a *tempo fortissimo* of work and good spirits" (November 13).

Draft of a letter to N.'s sister, reporting his desire to break off all contact with her: "You do not have the foggiest notion of what it means to be next of kin to a man and destiny in which the questions of millennia have been resolved" (mid-November). Negotiates with his publisher to buy back his works: "It would be possible to become a millionaire from my *Zarathustra* alone; it is the most decisive work there is" (November 22). First list of the "Dionysus Dithyrambs" (end of November). Draft of a letter to Kaiser Wilhelm II: "I am hereby granting the German Kaiser the highest honor that can befall him; an honor that is all the more significant because I have to surmount my deep loathing of everything that is German. I am placing the first copy of my book into his hand, which signals the arrival of something colossal" (early December). N. revises the *Ecce Homo* manuscript, inserting the condemnations of his mother and sister. Fantasies about a grand political design. To Peter Gast: "Did you know that I will need the backing of all the Jewish financiers for my international movement?" (December 9).

N. rereads his own books: "I did everything very well, but never had a clue about it—quite the contrary" (December 9). N. calls himself a "satyr" and a "clown" (December 10). N. attends operettas and open-air concerts. Beautiful sunny weather. Good climate. N. feels healthier than ever. "Sometimes these days I see no reason to accelerate the tragic catastrophe of my life that began with *Ecce*" (December 16). *Ecce Homo* is ready for printing (late December). "I consider the question of who I am settled once and for all now that *Ecce Homo* is in press. From now on, no one should be concerned about me, but only about the reasons that I exist" (December 27). N.'s landlady sees him dancing naked.

1889

N. embraces a horse to protect it from the blows of a carriage driver (early January). Letter to Jacob Burckhardt: "Ultimately, I would much rather be a Basel professor than God, but I have not dared to carry my private egotism to the point that I would forgo creating the world. You see, we must make sacrifices no matter how and where we live" (January 6). When Burckhardt receives this letter in Basel, he goes to Overbeck and asks him to watch over his friend. Overbeck immediately travels to Turin and reports: "I see N. huddled up reading in the corner of a sofa . . . the incomparable master of expression is incapable of conveying even the delights of his merriment in anything but the most trivial expressions or by dancing and jumping about in a comical manner." Overbeck brings N. to Basel, where he is admitted to a clinic. N.'s mother comes to Basel and takes him to Jena's psychiatric clinic, where he remains for one year. In May 1890, his mother takes N. home to Naumburg. After his mother's death in 1897, N. is brought to Villa Silberblick, in Weimar, by his sister.

August Horneffer visits N. in the final months of his life, and describes him as follows: "Of course, we did not know him back in his healthy days, but only saw him as an invalid in the final stage of paralysis. Nonetheless, the minutes we spent in his presence were some of the most valuable memories of our lives. . . . Although his eyes were vacant and his features slack, and although the poor man lay there with crooked limbs, more helpless than a child, a sense of magic radiated from his personality, and his appearance revealed a majesty that I would never experience again with any human being."

N. dies on August 25, 1900.

Selected List of
English Translations
of Nietzsche's Works

Unless otherwise noted, all quotations from Nietzsche's writings were newly translated for this edition. The following selection is intended as a guide to the available Nietzsche translations.

Collections of Works by Nietzsche

The Complete Works of Friedrich Nietzsche. Edited by Oscar Levy. 18 vols. New York: Macmillan, 1909–11. Reprint, New York: Russell & Russell, 1964. Although quite comprehensive, this compilation by several translators is considered unreliable. *The Philosophy of Nietzsche,* edited by Geoffrey Clive and published as a Meridian paperback in 1965, contains selections from this edition.

The Portable Nietzsche. Translated and edited by Walter Kaufmann. New York: Viking Press, 1954. Contains the full texts of *Thus Spoke Zarathustra, Twilight of the Idols, The Antichrist,* and *Nietzsche contra Wagner,* as well as excerpts from additional texts and selected notebook entries and fragments.

Basic Writings of Nietzsche. Translated and edited by Walter Kaufmann. New York: Modern Library, 1968.

Philosophy and Truth: Selections from Nietzsche's Notebooks of the Early 1870s. Translated and edited by Daniel Breazeale. Atlantic Highlands, N.J.: Humanities Press, 1979.

Nietzsche Selections. Edited by Richard Schacht. New York: Macmillan, 1993.

Unpublished Writings from the Period of Unfashionable Observations. Translated by Richard T. Gray. Stanford: Stanford Univ. Press, 1999.

Editions of Nietzsche's Letters

Selected Letters of Friedrich Nietzsche. Translated and edited by Christopher Middleton. Indianapolis: Hackett, 1996.

Nietzsche: A Self-portrait from His Letters. Translated and edited by Peter Fuss and Henry Shapiro. Cambridge: Harvard Univ. Press, 1971.

Translations of Individual Works

Alternative titles are listed in brackets following entries.

The Birth of Tragedy
Translated by Frances Golffing, with *The Genealogy of Morals.* Garden City, N.Y.: Doubleday, 1956.
Translated by Walter Kaufmann, with *The Case of Wagner.* New York: Vintage Books, 1966.
Translated by Ronald Speirs. Cambridge: Cambridge Univ. Press, 1999.
Translated by Douglas Smith. New York: Oxford Univ. Press, 2000.

Untimely Meditations
Translated by R. J. Hollingdale. Cambridge: Cambridge Univ. Press, 1983.
Translated by Herbert Golder, Gary Brown, and William Arrowsmith. New Haven: Yale Univ. Press, 1990. [*Unmodern Observations*]
Translated by Richard T. Gray. Stanford: Stanford Univ. Press, 1995. [*Unfashionable Observations*]

Human, All Too Human I
Translated by Marion Faber, with Stephen Lehmann. Lincoln: Univ. of Nebraska Press, 1984.
Translated by R. J. Hollingdale. Cambridge: Cambridge Univ. Press, 1986. [Also includes *Human, All Too Human* II]
Translated by Gary Handwerk. Stanford: Stanford Univ. Press, 1997.

Daybreak
Translated by R. J. Hollingdale. Cambridge: Cambridge Univ. Press, 1997.

The Gay Science
Translated by Walter Kaufmann. New York: Vintage Books, 1974.

Beyond Good and Evil
Translated by Walter Kaufmann. New York: Vintage Books, 1966.
Translated by Marion Faber, with an introduction by Robert C. Holub. Oxford Univ. Press, 1999.

On the Genealogy of Morals
Translated by Carol Diethe. Cambridge: Cambridge Univ. Press, 1994. [*On the Genealogy of Morality*]
Translated by Douglas Smith. Oxford Univ. Press, 1996.

The Case of Wagner
Translated by Walter Kaufmann. New York: Vintage Books, 1967. [*The Birth of Tragedy* and *The Case of Wagner*]

Twilight of the Idols
Translated by Duncan Large. New York: Oxford Univ. Press, 1998.

Ecce Homo
Translated by Walter Kaufmann and R. J. Hollingdale. New York: Vintage Books, 1989. [*On the Genealogy of Morals* and *Ecce Homo*]

The Will to Power
Translated by Walter Kaufmann and R. J. Hollingdale. New York: Vintage Books, 1968.

Bibliography

Abel, Günter. *Nietzsche*. Berlin and New York: Walter de Gruyter, 1998.

Adorno, Theodor W., and Max Horkheimer. *Dialectic of Enlightenment*. Translated by John Cumming. New York: Continuum, 1993.

Aschheim, Steven E. *The Nietzsche Legacy in Germany, 1890–1990*. Berkeley: Univ. of California Press, 1992.

Baeumler, Alfred. *Nietzsche der Philosoph und Politiker*. Leipzig: Reclam, 1931.

Bataille, Georges. *On Nietzsche*. Translated by Bruce Boone. With an introduction by Sylvère Lotringer. New York: Paragon House, 1992.

Benders, Raymond J., and Stephan Oettermann. *Friedrich Nietzsche: Chronik in Bildern und Texten*. Munich: Hanser, 2000.

Benn, Gottfried. *Gesammelte Werke*. Edited by Dieter Wellershoff. 4 vols. Wiesbaden and Munich: Limes, 1978.

——. "Turin," in *Gottfried Benn: Prose, Essays, Poems*. Edited by Volkmar Sander. New York: Continuum, 1987.

Benz, Ernst. "Das Bild des Übermenschen in der europäischen Geistesgeschichte." In *Der Übermensch: Eine Diskussion*. Edited by Ernst Benz, 19–161. Zurich and Stuttgart: Rhein, 1961.

Bernoulli, Carl Albrecht. *Franz Overbeck und Friedrich Nietzsche: Eine Freundschaft*. Jena: E. Diederichs, 1908.

Bertram, Ernst. *Nietzsche: Versuch einer Mythologie*. Berlin: G. Bondi, 1922.

Cancik, Hubert. *Nietzsches Antike: Vorlesung*. Stuttgart and Weimar: Metzler, 1995.

Carlyle, Thomas. *On Heroes, Hero-Worship, and the Heroic in History*. Introduction by Michael K. Goldberg. Berkeley: Univ. of California Press, 1993.

Colli, Giorgio. *Nach Nietzsche*. Frankfurt: Europäische Verlagsanstalt, 1980.

Danto, Arthur C. *Nietzsche as Philosopher*. New York: Columbia Univ. Press, 1965.

Darwin, Charles. *The Autobiography of Charles Darwin, 1809–1882*. Edited by Nora Barlow. New York: Norton, 1993.

———. *The Descent of Man, and Selection in Relation to Sex*. Part 2. Edited by Paul H. Barrett and R. B. Freeman. Vol. 22 of *The Works of Charles Darwin*. New York: New York Univ. Press, 1989.

Deleuze, Gilles. *Nietzsche and Philosophy*. Translated by Hugh Tomlinson. London: Athlone, 1983.

Emerson, Ralph Waldo. *Representative Men, Nature, Addresses and Lectures*. Boston and New York, 1876.

Figal, Günter. *Nietzsche: Eine philosophische Einführung*. Stuttgart: Reclam, 1999.

Fink, Eugen. *Nietzsches Philosophie*. Stuttgart: W. Kohlhammer, 1960.

Fleischer, Margot. *Der "Sinn der Erde" und die Entzauberung des Übermenschen: Eine Auseinandersetzung mit Nietzsche*. Darmstadt: Wissenschaftliche Buchgesellschaft, 1993.

Foucault, Michel. *The History of Sexuality*. Vol. 1. Translated by Robert Hurley. New York: Vintage 1978.

———. *Madness and Civilization: A History of Insantiy in the Age of Reason*. Translated by Richard Howard. New York: Pantheon, 1965.

———. "Nietzsche, Genealogy, History." In *The Foucault Reader*. Edited by Paul Rabinow, 76–100. New York: Pantheon, 1984. This essay translated by Donald F. Bouchard and Sherry Simon.

————. *The Order of Things.* New York: Vintage, 1973.

————. *Wahnsinn und Gesellschaft.* Frankfurt, Suhrkamp, 1973. German translation of *Madness and Civilization;* citation is from Foucault's introduction to the German edition.

Frank, Manfred. *Gott im Exil: Vorlesungen über die Neue Mythologie.* Frankfurt: Suhrkamp, 1988.

————. *Der kommende Gott: Vorlesungen über die Neue Mythologie.* Frankfurt: Suhrkamp, 1988.

Frenzel, Ivo. *Friedrich Nietzsche: An Illustrated Biography.* Translated by Joachim Neugroschel. New York: Pegasus, 1967.

Freud, Sigmund. *On the History of the Psycho-Analytic Movement.* In *The Standard Edition of the Complete Psychological Works of Sigmund Freud.* Translated by James Strachey. Volume 14. London: Hogarth, 1957.

Gabel, Gernot U., and Carl Helmuth Jagenberg, eds. *Der entmündigte Philosoph: Briefe von Franziska Nietzsche an Adelbert Oehler aus den Jahren 1889–1897.* Hürth: Gabel, 1994.

Gamm, Hans Jochen. *Standhalten im Dasein: Nietzsches Botschaft für die Gegenwart.* Munich and Leipzig: P. List, 1993.

Gerhardt, Volker. *Friedrich Nietzsche.* Munich: C. H. Beck, 1995.

————. *Pathos und Distanz: Studien zur Philosophie Friedrich Nietzsches.* Stuttgart: Reclam, 1988.

————. *Vom Willen zur Macht: Anthropologie und Metaphysik der Macht am exemplarischen Fall Friedrich Nietzsches.* Berlin and New York: Walter de Gruyter, 1996.

Gilman, Sander L. *Begegnungen mit Nietzsche.* Bonn: Bouvier, 1981. An abridged English version of the book was published as *Conversations with Nietzsche: A Life in the Words of His Contemporaries.* Translated by David J. Parent. New York: Oxford Univ. Press, 1987.

Glaser, Hermann. *Sigmund Freuds Zwanzigstes Jahrhundert: Seelenbilder einer Epoche.* Munich: Hanser, 1976.

Goch, Klaus. *Franziska Nietzsche: Eine Biographie.* Frankfurt: Insel, 1994.

Gödde, Günter. *Traditionslinien des "Unbewußten": Schopenhauer—Nietzsche—Freud.* Tübingen: Edition Diskord, 1999.

Gregor-Dellin, Martin. *Richard Wagner: His Life, His Work, His Century.* Translated by J. Maxwell Brownjohn. San Diego: Harcourt Brace Jovanovich, 1983.

Gulyga, Arsenij. *Immanuel Kant.* Frankfurt: Insel, 1985.

Heftrich, Eckhard. *Nietzsches Philosophie: Identität von Welt und Nichts.* Frankfurt: V. Klostermann, 1962.

Hegel, Georg Wilhelm Friedrich. *Phenomenology of Mind.* Translated by J. B. Baillie. New York: Harper & Row, 1967.

Heidegger, Martin. *Being and Time.* Translated by John Macquarrie and Edward Robinson. New York: Harper & Row, 1962.

———. *Nietzsche.* Translated by David Farrell Krell. 4 vols. San Francisco: Harper & Row, 1979–87.

———. "The Word of Nietzsche: 'God Is Dead.' " In *The Question concerning Technology and Other Essays*, 53–114. Translated by William Lovitt. New York: Harper & Row, 1977.

Heine, Heinrich. *Sämtliche Schriften.* Edited by Klaus Briegleb. Munich: Hanser, 1968–76.

Heller, Edmund. *Nietzsches Scheitern am Werk.* Freiburg and Munich: Alber, 1989.

Hesse, Hermann. "Zarathustra's Return." In *Nietzsche: A Collection of Critical Essays.* Edited by Robert C. Solomon, 375–85. Translated by Ralph Manheim. Garden City, N.Y.: Anchor, 1973.

Hillebrand, Bruno. *Nietzsche und die deutsche Literatur.* 2 vols. Tübingen: Niemeyer, 1978.

Hölderlin, Friedrich. *Sämtliche Werke.* Edited by D. E. Sattler. Frankfurt: Verlag Roter Stern, 1975ff.

Hoffmann, David Marc. *Zur Geschichte des Nietzsche-Archivs.* Berlin and New York: Walter de Gruyter, 1991.

Hofmannsthal, Hugo von. *Poems and Verse Plays*. Edited and with an introduction by Michael Hamburger. Preface by T. S. Eliot. New York: Bollingen Foundation, 1961. The translation of the poem cited in the text, "Many truly ...," is by Vernon Watkins.

James, William. *Pragmatism: A New Name for Some Old Ways of Thinking: Popular Lectures on Philosophy*. New York: Longmans, Green, 1907.

Janz, Curt Paul. *Friedrich Nietzsche: Biographie*. 3 vols. Munich: Hanser, 1978–79.

Jaspers, Karl. *Nietzsche: An Introduction to the Understanding of His Philosophical Activity*. Translated by Charles F. Wallraff and Frederick J. Schmitz. Tucson: Univ. of Arizona Press, 1965.

Jünger, Friedrich Georg. *Nietzsche*. Frankfurt: V. Klostermann, 2000.

Kant, Immanuel. *Werke*. Edited by Wilhelm Weischedel. 12 vols. Frankfurt: Suhrkamp, 1964.

Kaufmann, Walter. *Nietzsche: Philosopher, Psychologist, Antichrist*. Princeton: Princeton Univ. Press, 1974.

Kaulbach, Friedrich. *Nietzsches Idee einer Experimentalphilosophie*. Cologne and Vienna: Böhlau, 1980.

Klossowski, Pierre. *Nietzsche and the Vicious Circle*. Translated by Daniel W. Smith. Chicago: Univ. of Chicago Press, 1997.

Köhler, Joachim. *Nietzsche and Wagner*. Translated by Ronald Taylor. New Haven: Yale Univ. Press, 1998.

———. *Zarathustras Geheimnis: Friedrich Nietzsche und seine verschlüsselte Botschaft*. Nördlingen: Greno, 1989.

Kuhn, Elisabeth. *Friedrich Nietzsches Philosophie des europäischen Nihilismus*. Berlin and New York: Walter de Gruyter, 1992.

Lange, Friedrich Albert. *Geschichte des Materialismus*. 2 vols. Leipzig: Reclam, 1905.

Laska, Bernd A. "Dissident geblieben: Wie Marx und Nietzsche ihren Kollegen Max Stirner verdrängten und warum er sie geistig überlebt hat." *Die Zeit*, Jan. 27, 2000.

Latacz, Joachim. "Fruchtbares Ärgernis: Nietzsches 'Geburt der Tragödie' und die gräzistische Tragödienforschung." In *Nietzsche und die Schweiz*. Edited by David Marc Hoffmann. Zurich: Offizin/Strauhof, 1994.

Lessing, Theodor. *Nietzsche*. Berlin: Ullstein, 1925.

Löwith, Karl. *Nietzsche*. Stuttgart: W. Kohlhammer, 1987.

Lütkehaus, Ludger. *Nichts*. Zurich: Haffmans, 1999.

Mann, Thomas. "Nietzsche's Philosophy in the Light of Recent History." In *Last Essays*, 141–77. Translated by Richard and Clara Winston. New York: Knopf, 1959.

Marti, Urs. *"Der große Pöbel- und Sklavenaufstand": Nietzsches Auseinandersetzung mit Revolution und Demokratie*. Stuttgart and Weimar: Metzler, 1993.

Meyer, Theo. *Nietzsche und die Kunst*. Tübingen: Francke, 1993.

Meysenbug, Malwida von. *Memoiren einer Idealisten*. Berlin and Leipzig: Schuster & Loeffler, 1903.

Montinari, Mazzino. *Friedrich Nietzsche: Eine Einführung*. Berlin and New York: Walter de Gruyter, 1991.

Müller, Ulrich, and Peter Wapnewski, eds. *Richard Wagner-Handbuch*. Stuttgart: A. Kröner, 1986.

Müller-Lauter, Wolfgang. *Nietzsche: His Philosophy of Contradictions and the Contradictions of His Philosophy*. Translated by David J. Parent. Foreword by Richard Schacht. Urbana and Chicago: Univ. of Illinois Press, 1999.

Nehamas, Alexander. *Nietzsche: Life as Literature*. Cambridge: Harvard Univ. Press, 1985.

Niemeyer, Christian. *Nietzsches andere Vernunft: Psychologische Aspekte in Biographie und Werk*. Darmstadt: Wissenschaftliche Buchgesellschaft, 1988.

Nigg, Walter. *Friedrich Nietzsche*. Zurich: Diogenes, 1994.

Nolte, Ernst. *Nietzsche und der Nietzscheanismus*. Frankfurt: Propyläen, 1990.

Oehler, Dolf. *Pariser Bilder*. Frankfurt: Suhrkamp, 1979.

Okochi, Ryogi. *Wie man wird, was man ist: Gedanken zu Nietzsche aus östlicher Sicht.* Darmstadt: Wissenschaftliche Buchgesellschaft, 1995.

Osho. *Zarathustra: Ein Gott der tanzen kann.* Cologne: Osho, 1994.

Ottmann, Hennig. *Philosophie und Politik bei Nietzsche.* Berlin and New York: Walter de Gruyter, 1987.

Pascal, Blaise. *Pensées.* Translated by A. J. Krailsheimer. New York: Penguin, 1995.

Penzo, Giorgio. *Nietzsche e il nazismo: Il Tramonto de Mito del Super-Uomo.* Milan: Rusconi, 1987.

Peters, Heinz Frederick. *Lou Andreas-Salomé: Femme fatale und Dichtermuse.* Munich: Kindler, 1995.

———. *Zarathustra's Sister: The Case of Elisabeth and Friedrich Nietzsche.* New York: Markus Wiener Publishers, 1985.

Picht, Georg. *Nietzsche.* Stuttgart: Klett-Cotta, 1988.

Pieper, Annemarie. *"Ein Seil geknüpft zwischen Tier und Übermensch": Philosophische Erläuterungen zu Nietzsches erstem "Zarathustra."* Stuttgart: Klett-Cotta, 1990.

Plato. *The Collected Dialogues.* Edited by Edith Hamilton and Huntington Cairns. Translated by Lane Cooper et al. Princeton: Princeton Univ. Press, 1961.

Prossliner, Johann. *Licht wird alles, was ich fasse: Lexikon der Nietzsche-Zitate.* Munich: Kastell, 1999.

Rahden, Wolfgang von. "Eduard von Hartmann und Nietzsche: Zur Strategie der verzögerten Konterkritik Hartmanns an Nietzsche." *Nietzsche-Studien: Internationales Jahrbuch für die Nietzsche-Forschung* 13 (1984): 481–502.

Reichel, Norbert. *Der Traum vom höheren Leben: Nietzsches Übermensch und die conditio humana europäischer Intellektueller von 1890 bis 1945.* Darmstadt: Wissenschaftliche Buchgesellschaft, 1994.

Rickert, Heinrich. *Die Philosophie des Lebens.* Tübingen: Mohr, 1922.

Manfred Riedel. *Nietzsche in Weimar: Ein deutsches Drama.* Leipzig: Reclam, 1997.

Rorty, Richard. *Contingency, Irony, and Solidarity*. Cambridge and New York: Cambridge Univ. Press, 1989.

Ross, Werner. *Der ängstliche Adler: Friedrich Nietzsches Leben*. Stuttgart: Deutsche Verlagsanstalt, 1984.

Safranski, Rüdiger. *Wieviel Wahrheit braucht der Mensch: Über das Denkbare und Lebbare*. Munich: Hanser, 1990.

Salaquarda, Jörg, ed. *Nietzsche*. Darmstadt: Wissenschaftliche Buchgesellschaft, 1996.

Salomé, Lou. *Nietzsche*. Edited, translated, and with an introduction by Siegfried Mandel. Redding Ridge, Conn.: Black Swan Books, 1988.

Scheler, Max. *Vom Umsturz der Werte: Abhandlungen und Aufsätze*. Bern and Munich: Francke, 1972.

Schelling, Friedrich Wilhelm Joseph. *Ausgewählte Schriften in*. Edited by M. Frank. 6 vols. Frankfurt: Suhrkamp, 1985.

Schipperges, Heinrich. *Am Leitfaden des Leibes: Zur Anthropologik und Therapeutik Friedrich Nietzsches*. Stuttgart: Klett, 1975.

Schlegel, Friedrich. *Schriften zur Literatur*. Munich: Deutscher Taschenbuch Verlag, 1985.

Schmidt, Hermann Josef. *Nietzsche Absconditus, oder Spurenlese bei Nietzsche*. Parts 1–3. Berlin and Aschaffenburg: IBDK, 1991.

Schneeberger, Guido. *Nachlese zu Heidegger: Dokumente zu seinem Leben und Denken*. Bern: n.p., 1962.

Schopenhauer, Arthur. *The World as Will and Representation*. Translated by E. F. J. Payne. 2 vols. New York: Dover, 1958.

Schulte, Günter. *Ecce Nietzsche: Eine Werkinterpretation*. Frankfurt and New York: Campus, 1995.

Simmel, Georg. *Schopenhauer and Nietzsche*. Translated by Helmut Loiskandl, Deena Weinstein, and Michael Weinstein. Amherst: Univ. of Massachusetts Press, 1986.

Sloterdijk, Peter. *Thinker on Stage: Nietzsche's Materialism.* Translated by Jamie Owen Daniel. Foreword by Jochen Schulte-Sasse. Minneapolis: Univ. of Minnesota Press, 1989.

Steiner, Rudolf. *Friedrich Nietzsche: Fighter for Freedom.* Translated by Margaret Ingram deRis. Englewood, N.J.: Rudolf Steiner, 1960.

Stirner, Max. *The Ego and His Own.* Translated by Steven T. Byington. New York: Libertarian Book Club, 1963.

Strauss, David Friedrich. *Der alte und der neue Glaube: Ein Bekenntnis.* Stuttgart: Kröner, 1938.

Taureck, Bernhard H. F. *Nietzsches Alternativen zum Nihilismus.* Hamburg: Junius, 1991.

———. *Nietzsche und der Faschismus.* Hamburg: Junius, 1989.

Troeltsch, Ernst. *Deutscher Geist und Westeuropa.* Tübingen: Mohr, 1925.

Türcke, Christoph. *Der tolle Mensch: Nietzsche und der Wahnsinn der Vernunft.* Frankfurt: Fischer Taschenbuch Verlag, 1989.

Vattimo, Gianni. *Introduzione a Nietzsche.* Rome: Laterza, 1991.

Verrecchia, Anacleto. *Zarathustras Ende: Die Katastrophe Nietzsches in Turin.* Vienna, Cologne, and Graz: Böhlau, 1986.

Volkmann-Schluck, Karl-Heinz. *Die Philosophie Nietzsches: Der Untergang der abendländischen Metaphysik.* Würzburg: Königshausen & Neumann, 1991.

Wagner, Cosima. *Die Tagebücher.* 2 vols. Munich and Zurich: Piper, 1976.

Wagner, Richard. *Mein Denken.* Munich and Zurich: Piper, 1982.

———. *Der Ring des Nibelungen: Vollständiger Text.* Munich and Zurich: Piper, 1991.

Wolff, Hans M. *Friedrich Nietzsche: Der Weg zum Nichts.* Bern: Francke, 1956.

Additional English Language
Studies of Nietzsche

Ackermann, Robert John. *Nietzsche: A Frenzied Look*. Amherst: Univ. of Massachusetts Press, 1990.

Allison, David B. *The New Nietzsche: Contemporary Styles of Interpretation*. Cambridge: MIT Press, 1977.

————. *Reading the New Nietzsche:* The Birth of Tragedy, The Gay Science, Thus Spoke Zarathustra, *and* On the Genealogy of Morals. Lanham, Md.: Rowman & Littlefield, 2001.

Ansell-Pearson, Keith. *Nietzsche Contra Rousseau: A Study of Nietzsche's Moral and Political Thought*. Cambridge: Cambridge Univ. Press, 1991.

Babich, Babette E. *Nietzsche's Philosophy of Science*. Albany: SUNY Press, 1994.

Babich, Babette E., and Robert S. Cohen, eds. *Nietzsche, Theories of Knowledge, and Critical Theory*. Dordrecht and Boston: Kluwer Academic Publishers, 1999.

Bauer, Karin. *Adorno's Nietzschean Narratives: Critiques of Ideology, Readings of Wagner*. Albany: SUNY Press, 1999.

Behler, Ernst. *Confrontations: Derrida, Heidegger, Nietzsche*. Stanford: Stanford Univ. Press, 1991.

Bergmann, Peter. *Nietzsche: "The Last Antipolitical German."* Bloomington: Univ. of Indiana Press, 1987.

Berkowitz, Peter. *Nietzsche: The Ethics of an Immoralist.* Cambridge: Harvard Univ. Press, 1995.

Blondel, Eric, ed. *Nietzsche: The Body and Culture: Philosophy as a Philological Genealogy.* Translated by Séan Hand. Stanford: Stanford Univ. Press, 1991.

Burgard, Peter J., ed. *Nietzsche and the Feminine.* Charlottesville, Va.: Univ. of Virginia Press, 1994.

Chamberlain, Lesley. *Nietzsche in Turin: An Intimate Biography.* New York: St. Martin's Press, 1999.

Clark, Maudemarie. *Nietzsche on Truth and Philosophy.* Cambridge: Cambridge Univ. Press, 1990.

Conway, Daniel W. *Nietzsche and the Political.* New York: Routledge, 1996.

Cox, Christoph. *Nietzsche: Naturalism and Interpretation.* Berkeley: Univ. of California, 1999.

Del Caro, Adrian. *Nietzsche Contra Nietzsche: Creativity and the Anti-Romantic.* Baton Rouge: Louisiana State Univ. Press, 1989.

Derrida, Jacques. *Spurs: Nietzsche's Styles.* Translated by Barbara Harlow. Chicago: Univ. of Chicago Press, 1978.

Detwiler, Bruce. *Nietzsche and the Politics of Aristocratic Radicalism.* Chicago: Univ. of Chicago Press, 1990.

Diethe, Carol. *Nietzsche's Women: Beyond the Whip.* Berlin and New York: Walter de Gruyter, 1996.

Frey-Rohn, Liliane. *Friedrich Nietzsche: A Psychological Approach to His Life and Work.* Zurich: Daimon, 1989.

Gillespie, Michael Allen. *Nihilism Before Nietzsche.* Chicago: Univ. of Chicago Press, 1995.

Gillespie, Michael Allen, and Tracy B. Strong, eds. *Nietzsche's New Seas: Explorations in Philosophy, Aesthetics, and Politics.* Chicago: Univ. of Chicago Press, 1988.

Golomb, Jacob, ed. *Nietzsche and Jewish Culture.* New York: Routledge, 1997.

Hales, Steven D., and Rex Welshon. *Nietzsche's Perspectivism.* Urbana: Univ. of Illinois Press, 2000.

Hayman, Ronald. *Nietzsche.* New York: Oxford Univ. Press, 1980.

Heller, Erich. *The Importance of Nietzsche: Ten Essays.* Chicago: Univ. of Chicago Press, 1988.

Higgins, Kathleen Marie. *Comic Relief: Nietzsche's* Gay Science. Oxford: Oxford Univ. Press, 2000.

———. *Nietzsche's* Zarathustra. Philadelphia: Temple Univ. Press, 1987.

Hollingdale, R. J. *Nietzsche: The Man and His Philosophy,* London: Routledge, 1965.

Irigaray, Luce. *Marine Lover of Friedrich Nietzsche.* Translated by Gillian C. Gill. New York: Columbia Univ. Press, 1991.

Klein, Wayne. *Nietzsche and the Promise of Philosophy.* Albany: SUNY Press, 1997.

Koelb, Clayton, ed. *Nietzsche as Postmodernist: Essays Pro and Con.* Albany: SUNY Press, 1990.

Kofman, Sarah. *Nietzsche and Metaphor.* Translated by Duncan Large. Stanford: Stanford Univ. Press, 1993.

Krell, David Farrell. *Infectious Nietzsche.* Bloomington: Univ. of Indiana Press, 1996.

———. *Nietzsche: A Novel.* From the SUNY Series in Contemporary Continental Philosophy. Albany: SUNY Press, 1996.

———. *Postponements: Women, Sensuality, and Death in Nietzsche.* Bloomington: Univ. of Indiana Press, 1986.

Krell, David Farrell, and Donald L. Bates. *The Good European: Nietzsche's Work Sites in Word and Image.* Chicago: Univ. of Chicago Press, 1997.

Krell, David Farrell, and David Wood, eds. *Exceedingly Nietzsche: Aspects of Contemporary Nietzsche Interpretation.* New York: Routledge, 1988.

Lampert, Laurence. *Leo Strauss and Nietzsche.* Chicago: Univ. of Chicago Press, 1998.

————. *Nietzsche and Modern Times: A Study of Bacon, Descartes and Nietzsche*. New Haven: Yale Univ. Press, 1995.

————. *Nietzsche's Task: An Interpretation of* Beyond Good and Evil. New Haven: Yale Univ. Press, 2001.

————. *Nietzsche's Teaching: An Interpretation of* Thus Spake Zarathustra. New Haven: Yale Univ. Press, 1986.

Love, Nancy. *Marx, Nietzsche, and Modernity*. New York: Columbia Univ. Press, 1986.

Magnus, Bernd. *Nietzsche's Existential Imperative*. Bloomington: Univ. of Indiana Press, 1978.

Magnus, Bernd, and Kathleen M. Higgins, eds. *A Cambridge Companion to Nietzsche*. Cambridge: Cambridge Univ. Press, 1996.

Magnus, Bernd, Stanley Stewart, and Jean-Pierre Mileur. *Nietzsche's Case: Philosophy as/and Literature*. New York: Routledge, 1993.

Oliver, Kelly, and Marilyn Pearsall, eds. *Feminist Interpretations of Friedrich Nietzsche*. University Park, Pa.: Pennsylvania State Univ. Press, 1998.

Owen, David. *Nietzsche, Politics, and Modernity: A Critique of Liberal Reason*. London and Thousand Oaks, Calif.: Sage, 2000.

Patton, Paul, ed. *Nietzsche, Feminism, and Political Theory*. New York: Routledge, 1993.

Pavur, Claude Nicholas. *Nietzsche Humanist*. Milwaukee: Marquette Univ. Press, 1998.

Pletsch, Carl. *Young Nietzsche: Becoming a Genius*. New York: Free Press, 1993.

Porter, James I. *Nietzsche and the Philology of the Future*. Stanford: Stanford Univ. Press, 2000.

Richardson, John. *Nietzsche's System*. Oxford: Oxford Univ. Press, 1996.

Rickels, Laurence A., ed. *Looking after Nietzsche*. Albany: SUNY Press, 1990.

Ridley, Aaron. *Nietzsche's Conscience: Six Character Studies from the Genealogy*. Ithaca, N.Y.: Cornell Univ. Press, 1998.

Roberts, Tyler T. *Contesting Spirit: Nietzsche, Affirmation, Religion*. Princeton: Princeton Univ. Press, 1998.

Rosen, Stanley. *The Mask of Enlightenment: Nietzsche's* Zarathustra. Cambridge: Cambridge Univ. Press, 1995.

Sadler, Ted. *Nietzsche: Truth and Redemption: Critique of the Postmodernist Nietzsche*. London: Athlone, 1995.

Sallis, John. *Crossings: Nietzsche and the Space of Tragedy*. Chicago: Univ. of Chicago Press, 1991.

Schacht, Richard. *Making Sense of Nietzsche: Reflections Timely and Untimely*. Urbana: Univ. of Illinois Press, 1995.

———. *Nietzsche*. London and Boston: Routledge & K. Paul, 1983.

———, ed. *Nietzsche, Genealogy, Morality: Essays on Nietzsche's* Genealogy of Morals. Berkeley: Univ. of California, 1994.

———, ed. *Nietzsche's Postmoralism: Essays on Nietzsche's* Prelude to Philosophy's Future. Cambridge: Cambridge Univ. Press, 2000.

Schrift, Alan D. *Nietzsche and the Question of Interpretation: Between Hermeneutics and Deconstruction*. New York: Routledge, 1990.

———. *Nietzsche's French Legacy: A Genealogy of Poststructuralism*. New York: Routledge, 1995.

———, ed. *Why Nietzsche Still? Reflections on Drama, Culture, and Politics*. Berkeley: Univ. of California, 2000.

Schutte, Ofelia. *Beyond Nihilism: Nietzsche Without Masks*. Chicago: Univ. of Chicago Press, 1984.

Sedgwick, Peter R., ed. *Nietzsche: A Critical Reader*. Cambridge, Mass.: Blackwell, 1995.

Shapiro, Gary. *Nietzschean Narratives*. Bloomington: Univ. of Indiana Press, 1989.

Silk, M. S., and J. P. Stern. *Nietzsche on Tragedy*. Cambridge: Cambridge Univ. Press, 1981.

Sleinis, E. E. *Nietzsche's Revaluation of Values*. Urbana: Univ. of Illinois Press, 1994.

Solomon, Robert C., and Kathleen Marie Higgins. *What Nietzsche Really Said*. New York: Schocken, 2000.

———, eds. *Reading Nietzsche*. Oxford: Oxford Univ. Press, 1988.

Stack, George J. *Nietzsche and Emerson: An Elective Affinity*. Athens, Ohio: Ohio Univ. Press, 1993.

Stambaugh, Joan. *The Other Nietzsche*. Albany: SUNY Press, 1994.

Staten, Henry. *Nietzsche's Voice*. Ithaca, N.Y.: Cornell Univ. Press, 1990.

Stauth, Georg, and Bryan S. Turner. *Nietzsche's Dance: Resentment, Reciprocity and Resistance in Social Life*. Oxford and New York: Basil Blackwell, 1988.

Strong, Tracy B. *Friedrich Nietzsche and the Politics of Transfiguration*. Expanded Edition. Urbana: Univ. of Illinois Press, 2000.

Tanner, Michael. *Nietzsche*. Oxford: Oxford Univ. Press, 1994.

Thiele, Leslie Paul, ed. *Friedrich Nietzsche and the Politics of the Soul: A Study of Heroic Individualism*. Princeton: Princeton Univ. Press, 1990.

Thomas, Douglas. *Reading Nietzsche Rhetorically*. New York: The Guilford Press, 1999.

Van Tongeren, Paul J. *Reinterpreting Modern Culture: An Introduction to Friedrich Nietzsche's Philosophy*. West Lafayette, Ind.: Purdue Univ. Press, 2000.

Waite, Geoff. *Nietzsche's Corps/E: Aesthetics, Politics, Prophecy, or, the Spectacular Technoculture of Everyday Life*. Durham, N.C.: Duke Univ. Press, 1996.

Warren, Mark. *Nietzsche and Political Thought*. Cambridge: MIT Press, 1988.

White, Alan. *Within Nietzsche's Labyrinth*. New York: Routledge, 1990.

White, Richard J. *Nietzsche and the Problem of Sovereignty*. Urbana: Univ. of Illinois Press, 1997.

Winchester, James. *Nietzsche's Aesthetic Turn: Reading Nietzsche after Heidegger, Deleuze, and Derrida*. Albany: SUNY Press 1994.

Young, Julian. *Nietzsche's Philosophy of Art*. Cambridge: Cambridge Univ. Press, 1992.

Index

About the Author

Rüdiger Safranksi, born in Rottweil, Germany, in 1945, is a renowned scholar of philosophy. As a young man, he worked in a home for troubled youths before entering the university, where he studied German literature, philosophy, history, and art history, and taught at the Free University of Berlin before beginning a distinguished career as a writer and critic in 1985. His previous books, all published in Germany by Carl Hanser Verlag, include *Schopenhauer and the Wild Years of Philosophy* (1991) and *Martin Heidegger: Between Good and Evil* (1998), both of which are available in English, a biography of E. T. A. Hoffmann, and other philosophical works. Praising the Heidegger biography, Richard Rorty commented in the *New York Times Book Review,* "It is the first comprehensive biography of the man, and supersedes both Victor Farías's *Heidegger and Nazism* and Hugo Ott's *Martin Heidegger: A Political Life.*" Over the course of the last decade, Safranski has been awarded the Friedrich Merker Prize for Essays (1995), the Wilhelm Heine Medal of the Mainz Academy (1996), the Ernst Robert Curtius Prize (1998), and the Friedrich Nietzsche Prize (2000). He lives in Berlin.

About the Translator

Shelley Frisch was born and educated in New York City. She received a doctorate in Germanic languages and literatures from Princeton University and has taught German literature, film studies, and humanities at Columbia University, Haverford College, and Rutgers University. Her scholarship on exile literature has been supported by the American Council of Learned Societies, the National Endowment for the Humanities, the DAAD, and other granting institutions. She has served as executive editor of the *Germanic Review* and has won a prestigious journalism award. Her translations from German into English include several books and numerous essays for leading newspapers and journals. She lives in Princeton, New Jersey, with her husband and their two sons.

FRANTZ FANON
A Life

David Macey

Frantz Fanon was one of the great figures of the Third World revolutions of the 1950s and 1960s. The author of such classic books as *The Wretched of the Earth* and *Black Skin, White Masks*, his angry and eloquent writings on race, racism, psychiatry and anti-colonialism made him a notorious figure in his lifetime. After his early death he was transformed into a prophet of the cleansing and liberating effect of violent revolution.

Based on extensive and original research this is the first complete biography of Fanon.

'A biographical tour de force' *New Statesman*

'An excellent addition to the library of books concerned with anti-colonialism. It is not just a lucid and well-researched account of the man and his works. It is one of the best books about contemporary history to have been published in recent years, a wonderful evocation of an entire era' *Literary Review*

THE LANGHORNE SISTERS

James Fox

'Compare the plots of *Gone With the Wind* and *The Remains of the Day*, add a dash of Henry James and F. Scott Fitzgerald, and you come close to the remarkable mix of family history, political intrigue and high society *hauteur* that is James Fox's *The Langhorne Sisters*' *Independent*

'*The Langhorne Sisters* is not just a study of a family, or of an age, it is a living, breathing recreation of a singular way of life . . . Fox has done more than create a monument to his family – he has captured a fading impression and made it glow. The Langhornes are alive again' *Observer*

'In *The Langhorne Sisters* Fox displays all the qualities that made *White Mischief* a bestseller' *Literary Review*

'I read it with huge enjoyment and continuous fascination, utterly enmeshed in these extraordinary lives' William Boyd

DOROTHY HODGKIN
A Life

Georgina Ferry

Shortlisted for the Duff Cooper Memorial Prize.

This is the first biography of the only British female scientist to receive the Nobel Prize.

Ferry's biography is far more than a clear exposition of Hodgkin's scientific work. She reveals the inner life of a strong and passionate woman who set out against unimaginable odds in the Oxford of the 1920s. This is a wonderful book about love of science and love for humanity.

'For me, the science book of the year' John Gribbin, *Independent*

'This life of Hodgkin is in the top rank of scientific biographies, hooking the reader from the first page and keeping you absorbed to the end' *Sunday Times*